Pocahontas's People

The Civilization of the American Indian Series

POCAHONTAS'S PEOPLE
The Powhatan Indians
of Virginia
Through Four Centuries

By

Helen C. Rountree

University of Oklahoma Press : Norman

By Helen C. Rountree

The Powhatan Indians of Virginia: Their Traditional Culture (Norman, 1989)
Pocahontas's People: The Powhatan Indians of Virginia Through Four Centuries (Norman, 1990)

In memory of
Mildred Ellen Clark Rountree
and
Henning Ainsworth Rountree, Jr.

Library of Congress Cataloging-in-Publication Data

Rountree, Helen C., 1944–
  Pocahontas's people : the Powhatan Indians of Virginia through four centuries / by Helen C. Rountree. — 1st ed.
    p. cm. — (The Civilization of the American Indian series ; no. 196)
  Includes bibliographical references.
  ISBN 0-8061-2280-3 (cloth)
  ISBN 0-8061-2849-6 (paper)
  1. Powhatan Indians — History.   I. Title.   II. Series
E99.P85R67 1990
975.5'004973 — dc20

90-33598
CIP

The paper in this book meets the guidelines for permanence and durability of the Committee on Production Guidelines for Book Longevity of the Council on Library Resources, Inc.∞

5 6 7 8 9 10 11 12

Contents

Illustrations

Maps

Preface

THIS HISTORY OF the Powhatan Indians of eastern Virginia is the second volume of what I consider to be a single work: the reconstruction of Powhatan culture and history, along with an explanation of the people's survival, over a four-century period. The first volume, *The Powhatan Indians of Virginia: Their Traditional Culture*, was published in 1989 and gives a detailed account of the Indians' traditional culture, summarized briefly here in the Prologue. (My original prologue, titled "On The Nature of Ethnicity," was deemed "too interdisciplinary for a history book.")

The present volume, recounting over four hundred years of Powhatan history, is a rather "undaring" one, since I was aiming at reliability rather than excitement. I knew that my writing would affect the reputations of living people. I would serve them best, and myself as well, if I trod carefully and stated clearly what was and was not recorded about Indians in eastern Virginia. Once a trustworthy set of data is published—and I believe both these volumes are fully that—then we scholars can play cross-cultural, interdisciplinary "theory games" with it. I plan to join some of the games myself. But establishing the basic data comes first.

I became interested in the modern Powhatan Indians in the fall of 1969, one year after joining the faculty of Old Dominion University and about two years after I had done linguistic and historical fieldwork among Shoshone Indian people on the Duck Valley Reservation in Nevada. There I had worked with full-bloods who spoke their language fluently and remembered much of the traditional culture; my primary contact also practiced the traditional religion. Back in Virginia, I went, reluctantly at first, to the Mattaponi Reservation, where I saw people who still had an "Indian look" and whose conversations with me—in eastern Virginia English—reminded me in subtle ways of the people I had known in Nevada. "There's something still here," I thought to myself. When the chief's wife suggested that I write the tribe's history, I readily agreed and prepared as well to do a modern community study such as I had done at Duck Valley. It would be the work of only a year or so, I thought, for there wasn't *that* much any more to be found. Two decades later I know better.

I have always done most of my research in the summers, with occasional

weekends and vacations added during the school year. I found out early
that there was not much funding available for studying a history that is
never supposed to have been recorded (eastern Indian history is only buried, instead) or a modern people who are supposed to be gone. Also, there
were not many publishers willing to "take a chance" on such a subject until
recently. My work was helped by two small grants in 1974 and 1983 from
the School of Arts and Letters of Old Dominion University and by a larger
grant for the summer of 1976 from the Faculty Senate of the same school.
Otherwise, I have saved madly all winter in order to do my work in the
summers; my parents were always generous with their camping gear. After
a very few years, I concluded that I preferred to finance my own work anyway: I rarely knew from week to week who was going to be willing to talk
to me or what document collection was going to prove rich in "finds."
Grant-giving agencies usually want to know ahead of time about such
things, and I am not good at building castles in the air. It felt better to be on
my own. On the whole, I do not recommend a long-term project such as
mine, for someone as fiercely independent as I am, to anyone who does not
already have a secure wintertime job, preferably with academic tenure.

In the first summer that I worked with Virginia reservation Indians, I discovered rapidly that they were desperately sensitive and taciturn about
their history; at the same time, they felt strongly that I could never understand them without knowing their background. I began trying to resolve
this "catch 22" by talking to non-Indian old-timers who knew the Indians
and by beginning what has become an obsessive collecting of documents.
The latter activity also proved a good way to kill time when the Indians
weren't talking.

Within two years I had enough data to undertake a doctoral dissertation
on Virginia's land policy toward Indians, so I went back to school and acquired a doctorate in 1973 under Nancy Oestreich Lurie (the one anthropologist in the country at the time who welcomed a project that supposedly
couldn't be done on historical coastal Algonquian Indians). After that, I
went back to teaching in the winters and researching in the summers, making occasional daytime visits to modern Indian folk. After I received tenure
at Old Dominion in 1975, I took the plunge and began writing my mam-
moth cultural history, of which these two volumes are a product. The writing was slow and the publishing was slower, and I fell behind my cohort in
salaries and promotions, but it has been well worth it.

In 1980–81, I became involved in a grant-supported project on our cam-
pus to educate faculty about the Third World. I used the opportunity to
spend two years (while still teaching, of course) studying the nature of ethnic groups around the world. I hoped to compare them to what I had seen
among the modern and historical Powhatans and thus make sense of the
latter. The effort paid off. Ethnicity theory explained the Powhatan history

that I had collected. At last I had a theme with which to organize the Powhatans' history and explain their survival over so many years.

I could have written most of the Powhatan Indians' history without consulting the modern Indians, but I did not dream of trying. What I write about their history affects their reputation too deeply. Although their memories of their history before 1900 are often fuzzy, I still wanted their input. Therefore, once I had a contract for this volume, I finished a second draft of the history chapters more than four months before the contract deadline, made copies at my own expense, and sent them out to Indian leaders, who had already agreed to read and comment on them. I am thus greatly indebted to the following Indian people for their assistance: Chief and Mrs. William Miles and Assistant Chief Warren Cooke (Pamunkey); former Chief and Mrs. Curtis L. Custalow, Sr. (Mattaponi); former Chief (and Dr.) Linwood Custalow, Mrs. Eunice Adams, Mr. Malcolm Tupponce, and Mr. Ronald Adams (Upper Mattaponi); the late Chief Oliver Adkins, Assistant Chief Stephen R. Adkins, and Mr. Ronald Jefferson (Chickahominy); Chief Marvin D. Bradby and his tribal council (Eastern Chickahominy); former Assistant Chief Oliver Fortune (Rappahannock); and Chief Emeritus (formerly Assistant Chief) Oliver L. Perry (Nansemond). The late James R. Coates, Dr. Nancy O. Lurie, and Dr. Christian F. Feest also gave me comments on the entire manuscript, while my good and perfectionist friend Martha McCartney, formerly of the Virginia Historic Landmarks Division, went over chapters 4 through 7 with a rake. And my mother, bless her, has always willingly gone over my manuscripts with the pages in one hand and Fowler's *Dictionary of Modern English Usage* in the other, throwing what she deemed unacceptable on the floor. No pages of this volume reached the floor, so I must be improving.

Several people have helped me over the years with the indexing and proofreading of the chronological document index from which I wrote the present volume. I appreciate the help of Mrs. Jean Mathias, Mr. William G. Shea, Mr. Steven A. Ellis, Ms. W. Jean Homza, and Mrs. Jerry P. Walker. The first is a member of the Archeological Society of Virginia, whose members have always been enthusiastic about what I was trying to do; the rest are both former students and friends. The Old Dominion University Publications and Graphics Office made the photomagnetic transfers of my maps. Michael G. Ditto was a superb proofreader of the page proofs.

I have always been grateful for the helpfulness I have met at the libraries and courthouses where I have worked. I could have done the courthouse work through duplicates at the state library, but I preferred to camp in the country, work at the county seats themselves, and meet the courthouse characters. Some of the people in the clerks' offices became my friends, notably Miss Virginia Williams and Mrs. Catherine Belote in Northampton County and Miss Augusta Wilkerson in Essex County. The staff of the Library of Congress, the National Archives, Colonial Williamsburg, the Virginia Historical Society, the Virginia Baptist Historical Society, and the Virginia State Library have been a great help over the years. At the last-named, I especially appreciate the friendliness of Mr. Donald Morecock, Mr. William Lange, and Mr. Gwynne Tayloe. Gwynne provided outstanding moral support: on several occasions he gleefully brought me more documents than I could keep up with, and he invited himself to my publication party before I was even sure there would be one.

Last but not least, I am deeply grateful to all the amateur historians—actually semi-professionals, many of them—whose work made much of mine possible. Some of them, such as Mrs. Jean Mihalyka, fed me references that I had missed. Others, like Mrs. Elizabeth Wingo, compiled and published large numbers of less accessible materials, at their own expense if necessary, thus saving me a great deal of time. Finally, there are the organizations such as the Daughters of the American Revolution and the Daughters of the American Colonists which see to it that fragile, worm-eaten original documents are laminated or microfilmed or both. I have become acutely aware of the low survival rate of old papers in Virginia and elsewhere because of my dependence upon such documents, so I cannot begin to praise these ladies enough for their work. Without them, more would have been lost and Virginia would have been much the poorer for it.

HELEN C. ROUNTREE

Hampton, Virginia

Pocahontas's People

The Powhatan Indian Way of Life in 1607

BEFORE WE EMBARK upon a comprehensive history of the Algonquian-speaking Indians in Virginia (hereinafter collectively called "Powhatan Indians"[1]), we need to describe their way of life so that their actions through history will make better sense. The English colonists at Jamestown left a few moderately comprehensive descriptions of this way of life, though not nearly so comprehensive as an anthropologist would wish.[2] The English writers lived in an era before the advent of any of the social sciences. Full and objective descriptions of alien cultures were not even conceived of back then. The colonists were also male, with all that that meant in early Jacobean England, and they came to Virginia not to observe Indians but to explore the territory and to make their fortunes. Their descriptions of Indian lifeways are therefore spotty and essentially incidental to the records they left about their colonizing enterprise. Nonetheless, we can reconstruct the skeleton of Powhatan culture, and I have done so at length in another book.[3] For our purposes here, I will summarize the culture briefly, laying emphasis upon the parts of it that are most relevant to Powhatan-English relations. As we shall see, the Powhatans were closely involved with and limited by their territory; they had a sophisticated government (though it was *not* a confederacy, as the older history books call it); and they viewed ownership of land and the relations between men and women very differently from the way the English did.

The Powhatans occupied a region that corresponds handily to the coastal plain of modern Virginia, extending about one hundred miles from east to west (including both shores of the Chesapeake Bay) and one hundred miles from north to south. The six thousand square miles of land available were occupied by at least fourteen thousand Algonquian speakers in 1607–1608.[4] There had probably been many more people than that a century earlier, before European contact brought new diseases to North America.[5]

The Powhatans' eastern boundary was the Atlantic Ocean. Their western boundary, which they contested with the Siouan-speaking Monacans and Mannahoacs, was approximately at the "fall line," where the rivers cease to be navigable. Their southern boundary, which they usually shared peacefully with the Algonquian-speaking Pamlicos and Chowanocs, was roughly where the Virginia–North Carolina border is,[6] though the Iroquoian-speaking Nottoways and Meherrins peacefully inhabited the inner coastal plain south of the James River.[7] And their northern boundary was approximately the Virginia-Maryland line on the Eastern Shore and, on the western shore, the Potomac River,[8] down which marauding Iroquoians called Massawomecks came from time to time. The man Powhatan, father of Pocahontas, claimed to dominate all of this region,[9] though the claim was exaggerated.

The territory that was—and still is—home to the Powhatans is a coastal plain that tilts gently eastward into the Atlantic.[10] It is a well-watered plain (average annual rainfall: forty-six inches) crossed by more water in the form of rivers and partially covered by still more water from the Atlantic. The Chesapeake Bay, which is in fact the drowned lower valley of the Susquehanna River, has the Potomac, the Rappahannock, and the York as major tributaries from the northwest; the James, parallel to them, now flows into the bay but in Ice Age times had its own separate path between the Virginia Capes.[11] All four of these southeastward-flowing rivers are genuine rivers, carrying massive amounts of fresh water annually to the Chesapeake from the piedmont (Rappahannock and York) and the Appalachian Mountains (Potomac and James). But because the coastline is drowned by the ocean, the rivers gradually become estuaries to the eastward, first brackish and then salty.[12]

Eastern Virginia is riddled with navigable waters, a fact that was lost on neither the Indians nor the English. Large boats can (and still do) penetrate more than one hundred miles inland. The Chesapeake varies between twelve and twenty-two miles wide in its Virginia reaches, and its parent stream, the Susquehanna, is navigable far up into Pennsylvania. All of the four major rivers of the Powhatan region are wide: at least half a mile wide in their middle reaches as they cross the coastal plain, and anywhere from two miles (the York) to seven miles (the Potomac) wide at their junction with the bay. All of them have sizable tributaries, some of the tributaries have sizable tributaries of their own, and most of these again have branches or swamps at their heads. (The same is true of the western edge of the Delmarva Peninsula, whose "creeks" are tributaries to the bay.) It is therefore possible, in a canoe, to get almost anywhere in the region by water. And it is not surprising that the Powhatans—and the English, until the advent of paved roads for motorcars[13]—chose most often to travel by water. (There were also footpaths on land, allowing rapid communication with some neighbors.[14]) The variety in size, salinity, and tidal impulse in all these watercourses is phenomenal, with a corresponding variety in the plants and animals that live in or near them.

The climate of eastern Virginia is a mild one. Real winter lasts only three months at most, and berries and fruits and nuts are available fresh for some seven months of the year.[15] Most of the land supports a cover of deciduous trees mixed with pines and cedars.[16] Many of the deciduous trees are nut bearers (hickory, walnut, chestnut, chinquapin, beech), while a wide variety of berry bushes grows in the forest's understory along with native fruit trees such as the persimmon. All of these, in addition to the marine foods available year-round, support raccoons, opossums, muskrats, beavers, wild turkeys, and (now making a comeback) brown bears. In the freshwater marshes there are plants such as arrow arum, with a root (tuckahoe) that human ingenuity can make edible, as well as reeds for mat making. Meadows, manmade or natural, provide a number of wild greens. And the grasses there and the tender leaves of the understory feed the Indians' favorite prey, the Virginia white-tailed deer, which was hunted by individual men year-round and by whole tribes in communal hunts in the late fall.[17] The only domesticated—or domesticable—animal the Powhatans had was the dog.[18]

Given these conditions, Indians in Virginia after the end of the last Ice Age lived very well by hunting, gathering, and fishing, in spite of the extinctions that carried off the mammoths and mastodons. The Powhatans of the early seventeenth century kept up all these ancient skills. The English colonists called it "living from hand to mouth," but it was precisely these skills that were needed in the spring and early summer, when the previous year's supplies ran out and the crops were not yet ripe,[19] or when a summer drought—no uncommon occurrence in Virginia—blighted the (nonnative) crops.

The Powhatans kept up their foraging skills, but they were by no means nomadic. They were a farming people, accustomed to a settled life with an orderly government. Unfortunately, their farming was done in a manner that the English observers were hardly able to appreciate. All of the farming work except the clearing of fields was done by the women, assisted by children.[20] That was a standard Woodland Indian practice, and being food producers as well as food preparers seems to have given Powhatan women a higher status in their society than English women had in theirs. For their part, Powhatan men had their hands full being hunters and fishers; yet the English persisted for centuries in viewing them as lazy because they did not do the farming.

Powhatan fields also looked less smooth and, because of their smallness, produced less food than expected by the English, with their intensive plow agriculture. Indian fields were cleared by the slash-and-burn method, which left tree stumps behind.[21] Lacking draft animals as well as plows, the Powhatans had no need for meticulously smoothed fields, and their digging-stick horticulture was time consuming enough that most women did not plant really big fields.[22] The crops planted—maize, beans and squash—grew handsomely and were nourishing. But the women planted them amongst one another (a practice called intercropping), so that by midsummer Indian fields looked overgrown with vegetation.[23] In years with normal rainfall, fresh garden vegetables were available from July (early August for corn) through October.[24]

The Powhatans, like other coastal Algonquians, used no fertilizer on their fields,[25] and after a few years they would leave some fallow and move on to others. Land was "owned" strictly by usufruct; deserted fields could be cleared again later by anyone who wanted to use them. Ultimate ownership remained with the tribe or, once he had established supremacy, with the *mamanatowick*, or paramount chief.[26] Most Powhatan towns had a dispersed settlement pattern in which the houses were scattered randomly among the gardens.[27] Since dwellings were made of perishable materials (see below), women found it expedient to build new houses near their new fields. Thus a whole town would gradually move, amoeba-like, to another location after a couple of decades.[28] The new town would be called by the name of its new location, although the residents remained the same.[29] The English eventually used this Indian practice of "abandonment" to their own advantage, while the Powhatans remained woefully uncomprehending of fallowings and land sales that became "for ever." Even after the Powhatans had learned the English system of land tenure, white neighbors sometimes forced them to leave (see chapter 5).

The Powhatans divided up their territory in a way different from the English or modern American one. Like their fellow Algonquians up and down the Atlantic Coast, they saw watercourses as centers of districts, not boundaries. Waterways were major sources of food and avenues of transportation, and if a waterway was narrow enough (a mile or less), the people in a tribe would build their towns on both sides of it in much the same way that we build on both sides of our major highways. Werowocomoco, the capital of the paramount chiefdom, comprised houses built on two points between three small intersecting creeks.[30] Many subject tribes (e.g., Nansemond and Pamunkey) lived on both sides of the rivers that were named after them,[31] and the Rappahannocks and the Weyanocks claimed territory on both sides of the big rivers they lived on (the Rappahannock and the James, respectively).[32] The English would choose to ignore this custom in a law of 1705, to gain more Indian land (see chapter 5).

Waterways, which provided fish, shellfish, migratory birds, and marshes, where reeds and edible plants grew and muskrats lived, made up the center of tribal territories and even, at times, of major Indian towns. The houses of towns and satellite villages alike were always located fairly close to the shore, usually on or near a point[33] commanding a view of the water and the people (including enemies) traveling upon it.[34] With the dispersed pattern that was used, a small village might stretch along a mile of waterfront.[35] "Town center" was wherever the *weroance*'s (chief's) house stood. All houses were barrel-vaulted frameworks of saplings, with coverings of mats (doubled in winter) or, for those of higher status, bark slabs.[36] *Weroances*' houses and the temples, which were usually built outside the towns, differed from other buildings only in their greater length and in their multiple rooms.[37]

Beyond the villages lay a zone of forest cleared of underbrush, used both for sanitation and for firewood gathering.[38] Beyond that lay the forest proper, where men went hunting and warring, and women and children went foraging for nuts, berries, greens, and fiber for cordage. Landward boundaries among the Powhatans appear to have been inexact, one tribe's hunting territory shading gradually into the next tribe's.[39] A man who merely wounded a deer expected to be able to chase it down, no matter where the chase took him—a fact lost upon the boundary-conscious English settlers of a later date.

The English found much to deprecate in the simplicity of Indian field clearing and house building, but in fact the Powhatans' ability to elaborate their material culture was severely limited by the nature of their cutting tools. Before European iron became available in the late sixteenth century,[40] the Powhatans were a Stone Age people faced, in many areas, with a shortage of stone. On the coastal plain, where the bedrock is covered with up to 2,300 feet of sediment,[41] stones are available only in occasional exposures along shorelines and river cliffs, unless the plow brings them up. These cobbles are rarely the kind of fine-grained stone needed for elaborate knapping into razor-sharp edges. Smooth stone axes with reasonable cutting edges were made by chipping and then laborious grinding.[42] Well-crafted stone knives and arrowheads were made, but sometimes hunters had to substitute mussel shells or sharpened reeds for the knives and shaped oyster shells or wild-turkey spurs for the arrowheads. Scraping of wooden surfaces was usually done with beaver incisors for small jobs and with clamshells (after burning the surface) for big jobs such as canoe making.[43] It is no wonder, then, that the Indians were reluctant, in the early days of the Virginia colony, to see their canoes burned by threatening Englishmen. It is even less wonder that in 1607 the Powhatans were already fiercely eager to obtain English iron tools: the men wanted hatchets[44] and the women wanted knives and "paring irons" (digging sticks).[45] The men's desire for firearms came soon afterward.[46] However, Indian house-building methods remained the same for more than 150 years after iron tools came into use. Flimsy as Powhatan houses may have seemed to the English, they were better adapted than English ones to the hot Virginia summers, when a smoky but partially ventilated house meant sleeping cooly and mosquito free, and to the cold winters, when the extra mats or bark and the roaring central fires made them as "warme as stooves."[47]

Wealth among the Powhatans consisted mainly in things, many of them perishable, that were available to all people if they made the effort. People could work extra hard to get large quantities of foodstuffs, especially high-status venison for generous feasts, and maize for making cornbread at all seasons of the year. They could also aspire to wear many deer hides, nicely tanned and made into long, fringed, and decorated mantles[48]; or strings of pearls from freshwater mussels[49]; or strings of smooth-edged tubular beads called *peak,* the white variety made from the inner column of the whelk's shell, the more rare purple ("blue") kind made from the small purple area on the quahog clam's shell.[50] (*Roanoke,* made from disk-shaped pieces of various shells[51] strung on thread, was mentioned only later in the century.) There was also a glittering antimony ore, used mixed with body paint, which was excavated in Patawomeck territory and traded widely.[52] A highly prized face and body paint was made from puccoon.[53] The *mamanatowick* Powhatan exacted tribute comprised of all these things,[54] but some were retained by ordinary folk.

The only item of high value found outside the Powhatan area was nearly pure copper ore, which was cold-hammered into "long linckes" or other forms.[55] Powhatan held a monopoly on it and used it as gifts and as payment to *weroances* of his subject tribes for military services.[56] The English rapidly discovered that copper rings, bracelets, and bells were excellent trade goods to bring; glass beads, especially blue ones (analogous to the more valuable "blue" *peak*), were also in high demand.

On most days, the Powhatans did not appear to pay attention to social status, as the English did. All men, even ruling ones,[57] could and did go hunting, fishing, and warring,[58] often taking their sons along in the first two activities. For these they wore the basic men's garb: buckskin breechclout, leggings, moccasins.[59] They also wore a hairstyle they believed had been given them by one of their gods:[60] long hair in a knot on the left, a roach along the crown, with head shaved on the right to avoid the tangling of hair in bowstrings.[61] All women and girls spent most of their time producing food, preparing food, making pottery, making and repairing houses and mats and baskets, and caring for the younger children.[62] (The English practice of "fostering out" their own children and rearing other people's seems to have appalled the Indians.) For this work they wore the basic women's garb: buckskin apron and, in the forest, leggings and moccasins.[63] Their hair was worn loose, or in a single long braid with bangs in front, or cut short all around the head. Prepubescent girls went naked[64] and wore their heads shaved except for a long braid at the back.[65] Both sexes wore buckskin mantles ("matchcoats"[66]) for warmth in winter.[67] Because the men's world and the women's world did not meet often, and because the women did a great deal of outdoor work, the patriarchal English assumed that women had a very inferior status.[68]

But appearances were deceiving. Women did, in fact, control their family's food supply and their own bodies, both before and after marriage.[69] They were choosy about husbands and insisted that the men provide economic and military security.[70] A man who was a good provider could therefore have more than one wife, and the women appear to have been willing to join such polygynous households. Romance could be found, usually with a husband's permission, in the arms of a lover.[71] Inheritance among the ruling families was matrilineal (see below); it may have been matrilineal or bilateral among the common folk.

Social differences between families became apparent on dress-up occasions, such as feasts for visiting dignitaries. Chiefs and the "better sort" in general[72] had long, fringed buckskin mantles[73] to wear for such events, along with multiple necklaces of pearls and copper and shell beads. They also had immense quantities of high-status food such as venison and cornmeal to dispense at all seasons of the year. The Powhatan status system was even more evident in the people's behavior toward one another. Ruling families, men and women alike, were paid great deference. They expected to give orders at home,[74] for they had servitors to cook and serve their food[75] and help them dress.[76] High-ranking women, such as Pocahontas, were expected to travel with an escort, although not necessarily with a relative.

Chiefs, called *weroances*, "commanders," could be male or female (*weroansqua*) and were creatures set apart. They kept and traveled with large retinues.[77] They received elaborate welcomes when they reached their destinations, the welcomes including feasting,[78] dancing, oratory, and, for the men, young female bedmates for the night.[79] Chiefs had the power to punish disobedience with a quick death by knocking out the brains.[80] They presided at the execution of thieves and murderers, who were bound and thrown into a fire to burn to death.[81] ("Theft" referred only to stealing from one's own people; Europeans were fair game.[82]) *Weroances* knew how to procure their own food, but they normally had huntsmen to bring in game[83] and whole towns to plant fields of crops specially for them.[84] They also collected "tribute," which consisted of tanned deerskins, pearls and *peak,* and maize.[85] (Apparently, wild plant foods were not "taxable," which may have been another incentive for people to keep up their foraging skills.) Only *weroances*, along with the priests, were allowed inside the holiest temples on a regular basis.[86] When they died, they received special burials,[87] and they and the priests were believed to be the only people who had an afterlife.[88] Male *weroances*, with their greater incomes, were able to pay the bridewealth to acquire more wives than ordinary men; more wives working in the fields meant still more income, which could be used to acquire yet more wives. The *mamanatowick* Powhatan had more than one hundred wives in his lifetime and kept more than a dozen at any one time.[89] He had only one child by each wife,[90] so that his children were all half-siblings to one another.

Weroances acquired their positions most often by matrilineal inheritance.[91] Thus it was rare that any of the children by all those wives became *weroances* themselves, though Powhatan did appoint several of his sons to govern subject tribes.[92] A ruling position passed from a female ancestor to her sons in order of age, thence to the daughters in order of age, and thence to the sons and then daughters of the eldest daughter. Powhatan's successor was therefore his next brother, Opitchapam, a lame and unimpressive man [93] who was overshadowed in his lifetime by his more able and charismatic brother and successor, Opechancanough. There were also two sisters who would have become paramount chiefs had they lived long enough.

It was the sensible practice of Virginia *weroance*s to make their successors viceroys while they lived. Thus, Opitchapam, Opechancanough, and a third brother, Kekataugh, jointly ruled the powerful Pamunkey tribe for their brother.[94] The doughty Opussunoquonuske acted as *weroansqua* of a satellite town for her brother, the *weroance* of the Appamattuck tribe and a subject in turn of Powhatan,[95] while Iopassus (Japazaws), the Indian collaborator in the capture of Pocahontas in 1613, ruled the satellite town of Passapatanzy for his brother, the *weroance* of Patawomeck.[96]

Most of the Indians of eastern Virginia were organized into chiefdoms [97] in the late protohistoric period,[98] judging by what William Strachey heard about the Kecoughtan "chief" who was conquered by Powhatan in the 1590s.[99] The only exception was the Chickahominies, who deliberately remained on a tribal level.[100] It was not until very late in the protohistoric period that a paramount chief (Powhatan) emerged (see chapter 1). The reason for the development of chiefdoms and, later, a paramount chiefdom may have been a "natural" movement toward more complex political organizations in an ecologically rich area,[101] although nearly all of the riches of the Virginia coastal plain are so widely available that the economic specialization which Elman Service sees as a major factor in the rise of many chiefdoms [102] was not in operation there.[103] I feel, instead, that though the chiefdoms may have been a "natural" development, a major factor in the rise of a paramount chiefdom in eastern Virginia was the increased military threat the people of the region felt from Europeans and other Indians alike, possibly coupled with social disruption caused by epidemics. Internal pressures with external causes have been known to open the door to political takeovers elsewhere.

Powhatan claimed to rule nearly all of eastern Virginia.[104] He had inherited six chiefdoms (Powhatan, Arrohateck, Appamattuck, Pamunkey, Mattaponi, and Chiskiack) and had then gathered more tribes into his fold, either by warfare or by intimidation.[105] He had added the Kecoughtans to his collection in 1597 or 1598; he had exterminated the Chesapeakes, who would not join him, by the summer of 1608 (see chapter 1). By 1608, then, Powhatan had received at least a nominal submission, if not full subjection, from all the surviving Algonquian-speaking chiefdoms of the coastal plain. The Chickahominies were an exception. This populous tribe persisted in governing itself by a council of elders, while holding Powhatan at bay with a large population of warriors and by making judicious payments to him.[106]

The Algonquian-speaking ethnic groups of the James, the York, and probably the Rappahannock river basins were chiefdoms fully integrated into Powhatan's "empire"—which was *not* a "confederacy." [107] The chiefdoms of the southern shore of the Potomac and of the Eastern Shore were, according to Powhatan's accounts and occasionally to their own, officially part of the "empire," [108] but in fact they were a "fringe" on the new ethnic group that the paramount chief was trying to create (see below). That fringe was the first part of Powhatan's empire to be detached through English influence.

Powhatan's organization was in three levels, with his viceroys being the tribes' *weroances*, and their viceroys in turn being the petty *weroances* of satellite towns. [109] The proper term to apply to Powhatan's organization is "paramount chiefdom" rather than "empire," since Powhatan himself did not exert enough coercive force for his organization to be called a monarchical "state." [110] He either could not or did not control his subject tribes rigidly. Tribes occasionally fought among themselves, as did the Weyanocks and Paspaheghs on the James and the Rappahannocks and Moraughtacunds on the Rappahannock in 1607–1608 (see chapter 2). They also negotiated on their own with the English, until Powhatan decided that the newcomers were important enough to deal with himself, and even then the tribes were allowed great latitude in their behavior. But Powhatan expected obedience to his wishes and he was prepared to punish disobedience with annihilation, which he inflicted upon the Piankatanks in an ambush in 1608. [111] Peripheral peoples, such as the Accomacs and Occohannocks on the Eastern Shore and the Patawomecks and Onawmanients on the Potomac, paid him lip service as often as real obedience.

There was no "state" religion among the Powhatans. Varying beliefs about the creation of the world and life after death were recorded by the English colonists. [112] All accounts agree, however, that the Powhatans believed in multiple gods, with an anthropomorphic male tutelary deity ("okeus," or *kwiokos*) in each town to whom the temples were dedicated. [113] The latter god was served by full-time (or nearly so) priests, who wore special garb [114] but were allowed to marry; one priest, Uttamatomakkin, married a daughter of Powhatan. [115]

Priests had functions other than sacerdotal ones. They communicated with gods, so they could make rain and cure disease. [116] They could foretell the future, so they became extremely influential in councils of war. They were able to determine secret things and were therefore called upon to identify criminals [117] and intuit the motives of foreigners, as they tried to do with John Smith. [118] The priests' powers made them highly sought after both by *weroances* and by the *mamanatowick*. Although these rulers were free to make final decisions for themselves, the priests were said to have "the final voice" in council meetings, [119] where everyone's opinion was consulted. [120] Given their connection with the source of temporal power, it is not surprising that Powhatan priests became as unalterably opposed to English settlement, once that intention was revealed to them, as were the hereditary chiefs.

Warfare was endemic to eastern Virginia when the English arrived. There were genuinely lethal Indian enemies to the west and northwest[121] and—before long—in the English colony in the Indians' midst. War against such outsiders probably helped Powhatan to impose his "empire" upon Woodland Indian people, who had not previously had such a polity, by directing their resentment outward. And war still gave an ambitious man not born into a ruling family a chance to earn prestige. The Powhatans knew how to fight in massed formations,[122] but most of their warfare took the form of small-scale raids and ambushes,[123] in which feats of individual bravery were easy to observe.

All men, except possibly the priests, were trained from infancy to be hunters of animals or of people. Babies were washed daily in cold water to make them hardy, a practice that both sexes followed throughout life.[124] Boys were not fed their breakfast by their mothers until they had hit targets their mothers tossed for them.[125] Boys were expected to increase their hunting exploits over time, receiving new personal names denoting their achievements; grown men, even brothers of Powhatan, did the same thing in war and politics throughout their lives (see chapter 4).[126] Boys heard about and occasionally saw the fate of male war captives (women, children, and "royals" were adopted[127]), who were slowly tortured to death by townspeople of both sexes.[128] Some time before puberty, boys were expected to go through a harrowing ordeal of several months' duration called the *huskanaw*, in which they were ceremonially "killed," isolated, and fed a "decoction" that sent them mad and gave them amnesia, and then were "reborn" and retrained by men, away from women's influence. Some boys did not survive. The effects on those who did were incalculably deep.[129]

Powhatan men were "real he-men," ever ready for war and councils of war, ever ready to gain honor in going against foreigners and in taking revenge for perceived slights, ever prepared to meet stoically a death by torture, and in the meantime ever ready to prove themselves as great deer hunters in order to acquire wives. Men and women alike expected this role of men; the women's role (which included farming) was complementary and separate. Indian men literally hated to be shamed, to be "made a derision of,"[130] and public shame could come easily in a culture in which a man's very name told what he had or had not done lately. The women would not marry any man who did not measure up. The men had no respect for other men who did not measure up—including most of the Englishmen they met, except for John Smith.

Such men and women did not suffer gladly the English attitude of cultural superiority—not when those Englishmen proved repeatedly that they could not even feed themselves. And as we shall see, such men and women did not change their roles willingly, even after a century of defeat and decline.[131]

As Powhatan built up his paramount chiefdom, he was, in fact, attempting to build a new ethnic group out of chiefdoms that spoke closely related languages and possessed closely similar cultures.[132] Many ethnic groups are known to have formed originally because of a commonality of interest—especially a political interest[133]—in opposition to some other people's interest. A forceful personality may or may not be present to hurry the process. The United States is a case in point, the opposition having been to the mother country. The interest that bound Powhatan's organization together was defense against enemies—Siouan, Iroquoian, and European (see chapter 1). By 1607 the territory occupied by the coalescing ethnic group had a name: Tsenacomoco.[134] If its inhabitants had a collective name for themselves, the English did not record it. (Modern scholars' use of the term "Powhatan" for these Virginia Algonquians is primarily for our own convenience.) If the paramount chiefdom had remained untampered with by Europeans, it would have become a full-fledged ethnic group in a few more decades.

Powhatan's new polity was not a monolithic affair. Tribal identities such as "Pamunkey" and "Appamattuck" remained very strong, even in the loyal core of the organization.[135] That is nothing unusual. The same was true for at least a century in counties like Burgundy and Gascony after their incorporation into the French state, and many developing countries today are forging "national" identities in the attempt to dominate all the tribal identities within their (European-drawn) boundaries.[136] Powhatan's organization did not complete the process. When it came to a premature end in 1646, the older tribal identities remained, but by that time the people had long since come to see themselves as "Indians" (a supratribal ethnicity that did not presuppose a single polity) as a collective way of distinguishing themselves from the English.[137]

Even if Powhatan's new ethnic group had lasted, it still would not have been monolithic, with neatly defined boundaries. Even modern nation-state ethnic groups (e.g., Portugal), with their lists of citizens to be taxed, do not have conveniently demarcated boundaries except on paper. All ethnic groups actually have an easily recognized core surrounded by a fringe that contains people who are less recognizable and less intensely involved.[138] Fringe status embraces a great variety of relationships to the core. In modern nation-states, with their carefully recorded censuses, it can include expatriate, formerly core people; in-married foreigners; tax-paying expatriates from other countries, nationalized or not; persons with dual citizenship; members of separatist movements; and some of the more disaffected and non-tax-paying poor. This list shows another characteristic of many fringe people: they belong to two or more ethnic groups and feel some loyalty to both.

Fringes change as cultures change over time. This book describes not only the history and the changing culture of the Powhatan core people but also what the Powhatan fringe people were like. In Powhatan's paramount chiefdom in 1607, the fringe consisted of the more distant and less loyal groups such as the Patawomecks, as well as the autonomous but peaceful

Chickahominies in the chiefdom's midst. In the same chiefdom of Ope-chancanough's time, some of the geographical fringe groups had been wooed away by the English and a new fringe of partially Anglicized Indians was forming. That fringe remained a major source of culture change on Virginia Indian reservations until the core Indian people were almost entirely Anglicized. After that, the tribes' fringes consisted of people who were simply not as actively involved or as fully accepted (e.g., white spouses) as core people were.

Ethnic groups are always complicated entities, and the Powhatans have always been no exception. People are capable of a wide variety of responses to the world around them. All but the most repressively conformist ethnic group (e.g., Old Order Amish) will show a considerable spectrum of such responses at any one time. As the centuries pass, the groups that survive use the parts of the spectrum that work for them in dealing with outsiders, and thus they retain or change the customs they consider to be "normal" and uniquely "theirs." After making many adaptive changes, they may scarcely resemble their ancestors, but their group identity will still exist.[139] The following chapters document and explain the ethnic survival process for the Powhatan Indians of eastern Virginia.

CHAPTER 1

Before the English Came

HUMAN OCCUPATION in Virginia goes back at least ten thousand years.[1] However, the Algonquian-speaking Indians collectively called "Powhatans" in this book had a tradition of arriving in the Tidewater only "300. years" earlier,[2] a tradition that has yet to be borne out by archaeology.[3] As far as the excavations tell us, the Powhatans were the *in situ* result of at least fifteen hundred years of Woodland Indian adaptation to life in the Chesapeake Bay region. As such, they were the end-product of a long process of development, not the pitiable practitioners of a static and unproductive society that the English and Spanish thought them to be.

Europeans made sporadic visits to the eastern coast of North America for six centuries before they began serious attempts at settlement. However, it appears that the earliest visitor to the Chesapeake was Giovanni da Verrazzano, who in 1524 probably sailed past the Virginia Capes.[4] In 1546 a storm forced an English ship into a "very good bay" in "the land of La Florida in 37°," according to the cabin boy's account made to the Spanish in 1559.[5] While that ship rode at anchor, "over thirty canoes in each of which were fifteen to twenty persons" came alongside to trade. The bay may well have been the Chesapeake; the thirty-seventh parallel runs through its entrance.

The first documented contact of Europeans with a Powhatan Indian occurred between 1559 and 1561, when a Spanish exploratory party picked up an Indian who was visiting to the south of his homeland. This man, who was later baptized with the name of his sponsor, Don Luis de Velasco, was probably a youth at the time.[6] European explorers made a practice of kidnapping adolescents, who could learn a new language quickly while retaining their own and thus become useful as interpreters. The Indian youth was taken to Mexico, where he was baptized and educated by Dominicans. He was then taken to Spain, where the Jesuits who met him described him as the "son of a petty chief" and a "self-styled 'big chief' and a 'big talker.'"[7] He remained in Spain for two years, during which time he met King Philip II and "received many favors" from him.[8] Lastly, he went to Havana with some Dominicans, whom he eventually persuaded to found a mission to the "heathen" in his homeland, which he called *Ajacán*.

In 1566 the governor in Havana sent Don Luis with two friars and thirty soldiers to carry out that mission, but the expedition aborted when Don Luis failed to find the Virginia Capes.[9] Meanwhile, the Jesuits in Cuba had become discouraged with their conversion rate and were ready to try a mission farther north. Thus, in August 1570 a second expedition, consisting of Don Luis, eight Jesuits, and one young novice named Alonso de Lara, set out for Chesapeake Bay.[10] One historian has suggested that Don Luis may have pretended to fail to find the Chesapeake in 1566 because of the expedition's preponderance of soldiers over priests; the 1570 roster was entirely religious and Don Luis had no trouble finding his homeland.[11]

The Jesuit mission arrived in Tidewater Virginia on September 10, 1570, and sailed up the river later called the James. Judging from the testimony of the ship's captain, they landed at College Creek, five miles east of Jamestown Island. Then, for reasons unknown, they crossed the Peninsula by way of creeks until they reached the mouth of either Kings or Queens Creek on the York River.[12] There they settled, in a spot that was on another river entirely from their intended debarkation place.

The timing of the mission was poor: the region was enduring a famine,[13] so that the Indians they wanted to convert had already dispersed to go foraging for the winter. The location of the mission was also unfortunate. The people at the debarkation place, possibly those later known to the English as Paspaheghs (or perhaps Chickahominies; see below), had welcomed Don Luis back as a relative. But the missionaries settled, perhaps inadvertently, among people of another group, later known as the Chiskiacks. No Spanish writer mentions the nature of relations, peaceful or hostile, between the two groups. Nevertheless, it is not surprising that Don Luis "lived with the Fathers but two nights and not over five nights in the village"[14] before going off to live among his own people. It is also understandable that at a distance from the mission his eagerness to help the Jesuits faded, especially when his younger brother, now the ruler of his people, offered his own position to Don Luis. Don Luis declined the offer[15] and decided to live with an uncle who ruled another (unidentified) group, also some distance away from the mission. As a privileged member of a ranking family, Don Luis soon succumbed to the temptation to live well in the Indian fashion, which, to the Jesuits' horror, included taking several wives.

The Jesuits, left behind at their camp, were soon in dire straits. They had brought few supplies from Cuba because they counted on the services of an interpreter and expected to be supported by new converts, a standard practice in Jesuit missionary work at the time. When their supplies ran out, they had to sell many of their tools to Indian neighbors and eke out an existence by foraging. Their messages to Don Luis, imploring him to return, went unanswered. Finally, in early February 1571, three missionaries sought out the "apostate" in his uncle's household and put direct pressure on him. That was their final mistake. Don Luis seems already to have felt caught between loyalty to his own people and loyalty to the missionaries who had brought him home; whatever he did, he would be publicly criticized and shamed by somebody, a terrible fate for one brought up in the Powhatan world. But the Jesuits were more ready than his own people to blame him for disloyalty just then, and the missionaries were few in number. Therefore, the solution Don Luis chose was to eliminate the Jesuits.[16]

The three men from the mission were killed in the woods as soon as they started back.[17] Later, on the morning of February 9, Don Luis and a party of warriors arrived at the mission, offering to work with the mission's axes. As soon as they had the axes, however, the Indian party used them to kill the remaining five missionaries, after which they looted the camp. Only young Alonso was spared, in keeping with Powhatan warfare practices. Don Luis, knowing his Europeans, advised his people to kill the boy before he could talk to the Spanish punitive force that was sure to come later, but two tribal rulers in succession insisted on keeping him alive.

A Spanish relief ship did indeed come looking for the missionaries later that year. The ship's master became suspicious when he saw none of the prearranged signals for guiding him to the Jesuits' camp. Instead he saw Indians walking on the beach wearing Jesuit cassocks and beckoning him ashore, and when he approached the shore, his men were ready for the canoes of attacking warriors. In the fray that followed, three Indians were captured, one of whom was successfully carried to Cuba. There the man told his captors what had happened and that Alonso was still alive.

Thus, in August 1572, after several delays, the punitive force that Don Luis feared arrived in the Chesapeake and anchored in Hampton Roads. Its commander was the governor of Cuba himself. A boat bearing the Indian captive was sent up College Creek to the Jesuits' debarkation place, where, after some deliberately friendly trading, the Spanish suddenly took more captives. That at least some of the captured Indians had played a part in murdering the Jesuits was apparent because one of them had met the Spanish wearing a silver paten from the mission.[18] Carrying the captives, the boat then returned to the creek's mouth. There the people agreed to fetch Alonso from the place where he was being kept, two day's journey away, in what was later known as Kecoughtan territory. However, when no Alonso was forthcoming, the frustrated Indians tried to ambush the boat's occupants before the Spanish reacted violently to the delay. The boatmen beat off the attempt and waited one more day for Alonso. When the boy was not delivered, they approached the shore and fired arquebuses into the midst of the warriors gathered there, killing many of them. Ironically, Alonso's host had sent him directly to the Spanish ship in Hampton Roads, where the boat's occupants found him on their return from the shore.

The Spanish commander, Menendez, now sent one of the Indian captives upriver with orders to bring back Don Luis within five days or he would punish the other captives in Don Luis' place. Meanwhile, he held an inquest, with Alonso serving as interpreter.[19] Five Indian captives were declared innocent and released, but when Don Luis was not brought in the time allotted, the others were hanged from the ship's rigging. The Spanish then went home. Alonso lived to be interviewed by Jesuit writers.[20] In later decades, Indians and English colonists alike still dreaded a return of the vengeful Spanish.

The Powhatans learned from the Spanish Jesuit mission and its aftermath that Europeans expected to have their own way and were willing to wreak vengeance on people who thwarted them.[21] It is unlikely that the Powhatans recognized either the same qualities in themselves or that their own violence was a contributing cause to Spanish violence. Instead, the people who had lost warriors merely hated the Spanish. One group, the Chickahominy, was particularly outspoken about it to the English in later years,[22] which may indicate that the occupants of the debarkation place in 1570 were not the Paspaheghs but the Chickahominies. However, the Indians' understanding of Europeans' true intentions for New World people, as well as for their land, depended upon how much they heard from Don Luis (who probably told them plenty) and how much of his talk they believed. Judging from Indian behavior in the first years of the English colony (see chapter 2), they believed little.

No European ever seems to have learned what Don Luis' eventual fate was among his own people. However, rumors about alleged non-Virginian origins of Powhatan rulers circulated for more than a century in the English colony (their Indian sources were not recorded), making some scholars wonder whether one of these rulers was the returned Don Luis living under an Algonquian name. One rumor from the early seventeenth century stated that the Chickahominies hated the Spanish because the Indian emperor "*Powhatans* father was driuen by them from the *West-Indies* into" Virginia;[23] but Powhatan and Don Luis were probably contemporaries, not father and son.[24] The other rumor, from the early eighteenth century, based itself on a foreign origin to account for the undying hostility of Opechancanough, Powhatan's brother, to Europeans: Robert Beverley claimed that the Powhatan Indians of his time denied the brotherhood of Opechancanough and the more pacific Powhatan ("They say he was a Prince of a Foreign nation, and came to them a great way from the South-West; And by their Accounts, we suppose him to have come from the Spanish Indians, somewhere near Mexico.").[25] Yet Thomas Rolfe, Pocahontas's son and a grandson of Powhatan, specifically claimed Opechancanough as a relative whom he wanted to visit in 1641.[26] And all the early English accounts agree that Opechancanough was indeed a brother of Powhatan. The late-seventeenth-century Powhatans may only have been trying to disassociate themselves from a leader the English still detested.

Some modern historians, notably Carl Bridenbaugh, have speculated that Opechancanough and Don Luis were the same person. Indeed, Briden-baugh has written a composite life history of them as though they were one, saying only parenthetically that the idea cannot actually be proved.[27] I think there is little likelihood of their being the same, as do some of the authorities on the Spanish Jesuit mission.[28] My reasons are both historical and cultural. Don Luis and Opechancanough were approximately contem-poraries, since Don Luis and Powhatan were contemporaries. But Don Luis had only a younger full brother, as far as the Spanish accounts show, while Opechancanough had two older full brothers who became *mamanatowick* ahead of him. That means there were different sets of people in their imme-diate families. Additionally, Don Luis came from a territory somewhere around the mouth of the Chickahominy River in 1559–1561. Powhatan and, by extension, Opechancanough came from a territory that included tribes up near the fall line of the James and York rivers (see below). In 1559–1561, when Powhatan was at best only newly installed as a ruler, it is possible, yet unlikely, that his dominion already extended down to the Chickahominy's mouth; his immediate family and Don Luis's would there-fore have been different, though perhaps related.

Bridenbaugh notes that in 1621 Opechancanough disclosed some knowl-edge of astronomy (i.e., that the Big Dipper revolved around the North Star and was called the "Great Bear"[29]); this he takes as persuasive evidence of a European-bred sophistication.[30] Yet astronomical knowledge of that basic sort (revolving heavens, naming of constellations) is easily arrived at after only a few years of casual observation, and anthropologists have found that most peoples in the world have at least that much knowledge. The Great Bear's Powhatan name, *Manguahaian,*[31] is Algonquian (though it is possi-bly Opechancanough's impromptu translation of the European name), and the correspondence of Powhatan and European names for the constellation is probably coincidental, since bears are among the animals native to both continents. On the other hand, there is Opechancanough's recorded deep fascination with English gadgets, such as the lock on the door of his English house in 1621 (which he is said to have spent hours playing with).[32] That fact seems to argue a lack of experience with European technology, though it could have been a show for the English missionary who had the house built for him. Had he been Don Luis, he would not really have felt such a fascination, because the gadgets would have been familiar to him already.

But most convincingly, Opechancanough showed himself to be non-Europeanized in a truly essential matter and at a time when Don Luis would not have pretended for *anyone's* benefit: when Opechancanough tried to drive the English out of Virginia in 1622 and again in 1644, he did not follow up on his initial victory, a failure that gave the English time to regroup.[33] In Indian-style warfare, vicious "hints" such as that were enough to make the survivors withdraw, at least for a time, until they could bear (or adopt) and rear more warriors. Opechancanough was confident that one strike was enough, as he told the Potomac River tribes.[34] But Europeans in colonies the size of Jamestown did not take "hints" of that sort: they usually stayed in their well-established forts and sent home to their densely populated mother countries for reinforcements. A follow-up was definitely needed in 1622 to make the English even think about abandoning their colony; Don Luis would have known that, after spending a decade among the Spanish. He had been Europeanized enough to want to kill the boy Alonso and complete the job in 1571. Had he led the attack of 1622, he would almost certainly have come back to finish that job, too. Opechancanough was deadly serious in his aim of routing the English from Virginia, but his methods show him to be woefully unacquainted with the nature of Europeans. We must therefore conclude that Opechancanough was not Don Luis. No one knows what became of the Jesuits' erstwhile convert.

The 1570s and 1580s saw several European expeditions visit the mid-Atlantic Coast; the Powhatans met some of their members firsthand. One of the Roanoke Colony's ships may have entered Chesapeake Bay and encountered a hostile reception in 1584, though the Englishman who described that trip was vague about it.[35] The Spanish sailed along the coast a number of times, and in 1588 they sailed up the bay as far as the mouth of the Potomac River. There they seized an Indian youth and carried him away, along with another boy from the Eastern Shore. The former soon died of grief, while the latter lived to reach Santo Domingo, where he converted to Christianity and subsequently died of smallpox.[36]

One pre-Jamestown English expedition is known beyond question to have spent time with the Chesapeake Indians, who occupied what are now the cities of Norfolk, Portsmouth, Chesapeake, and Virginia Beach. It is a pity that the Chesapeakes did not survive to tell the Jamestown colonists about their visitors and that the English records of the trip were subsequently made classified information and then lost.[37] That expedition, which included the scientist Thomas Hariot and the artist John White, came from the first "Virginia" colony on Roanoke Island and spent some months, probably the early and middle winter of 1585–1586,[38] with the "Chesepieans."[39] The location of that group's capital town, where Lane's party presumably stayed, is uncertain. John White's map[40] shows it as "Skicoak," rumored to be Virginia's "greatest citie,"[41] on what is now the south branch of the Elizabeth River; two other villages, one named Apasus, are shown between two branches of Lynnhaven Bay. John Smith's map[42] shows a "king's house" called "Chesapeake" at approximately the location of White's "Skicoake." Given the difference in time of compilation, both maps may give the name of the capital correctly. The Chesapeakes may have concentrated all their population on the more protected Elizabeth River after Europeans began visiting the region frequently.

That winter Hariot and White collected information about the lower Chesapeake Bay. Their superior, Ralph Lane, also heard later from the

Chowanocs[43] about a rich ruler to their north whose main stronghold, an island, answered to the description of Old Point Comfort,[44] in Kecoughtan territory. While based with the Chesapeakes, the English party was visited by members of several other tribal groups, most of which cannot be identified (one, the Mangoags, may have been the Nottoways or Meherrins). Significantly, no visitors from the James River tribes came; in 1607 they told the Jamestown colonists that they were enemies of the Chesapeakes.[45] The richness of the bay region and the cordiality with which the Roanoke party was received caused the English to decide to move their colonial enterprise northward.[46] It was only the stubbornness of a ship's pilot bent on privateering that placed the third (and later "lost") colony back on Roanoke Island.

It is likely that some of the "lost colonists" went northward as refugees in 1587 and stayed among the Chesapeakes, while others moved (or were abducted) westward to the Carolina mainland. David B. Quinn believes strongly in the idea[47] and has constructed a scenario of the northern refugees' gradual assimilation with the Indians.[48] I agree that this is likely. As Quinn notes, the Chesapeakes had been friendly two years earlier and the colonists knew that any later English attempts at settlement would be directed north of the Carolina Sounds. In addition, I would point out that the Indians who assaulted the English at Cape Henry in April 1607 showed a suspicious lack of panic when faced with English firearms (see chapter 2), as though they were familiar with those firearms' limitations. However, the fate of any English people among the Chesapeakes can only be guessed at, for as we shall see, the Chesapeakes were exterminated by Powhatan before the Jamestown colonists could interview them. Archaeological excavations have yet to turn up solid evidence of an English presence in Chesapeake territory before the 1630s.

Quinn further suggests that some Roanoke refugees survived until sometime just before the Jamestown colonists' arrival, at which time Powhatan's forces exterminated the Chesapeake Indians as well as the English and half-English people living among them. After that, Quinn says that Powhatan and his people systematically kept their "crime" a secret by attacking the English at the first landing at Cape Henry and then by deflecting the English explorations away from that area.[49] Quinn's evidence is William Strachey's statement that King James had been told by 1609 that although the Roanoke colonists had lived for "20. and od yeares" outside his dominions, Powhatan had killed them.[50] In fact, "the slaughter at [of] *Roanoak*" had happened "at what tyme this our Colony, (vnder the conduct of Capt. *Newport*) landed within the *Chesapeack* Bay."[51] King James may have heard this news from John Smith, for according to Samuel Purchas, who talked with Smith, Powhatan admitted to Smith during his captivity that he had killed "those at [from] Roanoke."[52]

I find the evidence for this part of the story circumstantial, not to say dubious. The refugees may have been killed at the time Quinn suggests, just before the English arrived at Chesapeake Bay in April 1607, but I think that if any such attack occurred, it was on the Carolina mainland. John Smith himself never wrote that Powhatan had killed any Roanoke colonists; only Purchas did, and he wrote it in 1625 as part of an anti-Indian polemic titled "Virginia's Verger." William Strachey accused Powhatan directly, but he did so in a passage exhorting Englishmen to settle in Virginia and convert the "heathen." The context of both charges is biased, so the charges themselves are flimsy.[53] The Virginia Company's instructions to Sir Thomas Gates in 1609[54] speak of "the slaughter of [by] Powhaton of Roanocke [colonists], vppon the first arrivall of our colonie" (i.e., in 1607; the partial copying here by Strachey is plain), but there is no mention of where it was thought to have happened. In addition, Strachey wrote of the "Roanoke" murder (*Historie of Travell*, pp. 34, 91) and of the extermination of the Chesapeakes by Powhatan (*Historie of Travell*, pp. 104–105) in entirely different places; at no point in his book does he indicate any connection between the Roanoke colonists and the obliterated Chesapeakes. It seems that Strachey expected most, if not all, Roanoke survivors to have taken refuge among the Carolina tribes, and that is where the leaders at Jamestown did, in fact, send emissaries to look for them (see below).

As for the Jamestown colonists' being systematically kept away from the Chesapeakes' old territory, that is questionable. The attack they experienced at Cape Henry did not deter them from an initial exploration of the Lynhaven area, which they found apparently deserted. (A reason for that desertion has already been advanced.) Instead, the colonists do not seem to have been interested in the Chesapeakes' territory—for any reason—until the summer of 1608, and then merely as a matter of curiosity. Before John Smith's captivity of December 1607–January 1608, they were far too eager to find a "Northwest Passage" up the major rivers of the region, and at other times their hunger drove them to concentrate on trading for corn with tribes nearer to Jamestown. If Smith learned of any "guilt" of Powhatan's during his captivity, a subsequent confirmatory expedition of some sort would have been logical, considering that the English already distrusted Powhatan and were unaware that word of their other explorations had reached him. But the Jamestown colonists made no such move. They did not sail up the Elizabeth River until several months later, and then only at the end of an expedition that had traveled freely (though not unmolested) over the entire Chesapeake Bay region. It seems doubtful that Smith heard anything about any English being among the Chesapeake Indians or about the Jamestown colonists being discouraged by anyone from going there.

I suspect that the extermination of the Chesapeakes took place shortly after Jamestown was founded (see below) but that few, if any, of the English refugees among them survived long enough to be killed by Powhatan's men. Adult male English refugees probably did not live very long among the

Chesapeakes. Englishmen had already demonstrated their ability to antagonize most of their Indian neighbors in the Roanoke region: the English and the Indians of that time were both apt to be arrogant and touchy. Even Englishmen from a peaceful, non-military colony were ethnocentric enough to be perceived by Indians as abrasive, given long enough contact; sixteenth-century Europeans were quick to give advice to "barbarians," by whose standards such advice was probably insufferably rude and aggressive.[55] If they offended the Chesapeakes, the men would have been eliminated by their Indian hosts, who might later have attacked the newly arriving English at Cape Henry before the English, as the Indians expected, attacked them in reprisal. The female and young male Roanoke refugees would have been spared, adopted, and resocialized.[56] But mortality was high, by modern standards, for both sexes and all ages among both the Indians and the English of that era. It is entirely possible that only half-blood children would have remained by 1607; those children would have been considered Indians, not English, by Powhatan's raiders, and therefore not worthy of notice.[57]

One person, possibly half-English, was actually observed by the Jamestown colonists. He was "a Saluage Boy about the age of ten yeeres [in 1607], which had a head of haire of a perfect yellow and a reasonable white skinne . . ."[58] This boy, who would have been born around 1597, was observed living in Arrohateck territory, near the falls of the James, in the core of Powhatan's territory; there is no mention in the account of his being a captive from another tribe, Chesapeake or Carolina Algonquian. No English account mentions any questions being asked about him, either, although the Indians there were exceedingly friendly. But he may well have been the child of a "lost colonist."

Neither the Jamestown settlers nor any other English ever went searching to Croatoan (now Hatteras Island), where the "lost colonists'" message found by John White in 1590 had indicated they were going.[59] Instead, the Jamestown English made inquiries among the Powhatan groups, who invariably suggested the North Carolina mainland. In December 1607, Opechancanough told the captive John Smith about Europeans in "Ocanahonan,"[60] which may have been the town of Ohanoak on the lower Chowan River that was visited by a party from the first Roanoke colony.[61] In the spring of 1608 the ruler of Paspahegh offered to take an English party to "Panawicke beyond Roonok," but the offer proved to be fraudulent.[62] Both towns were described to William Strachey in 1610–1611 as having two-story houses of stone and people who bred tame turkeys and hunted "apes" in the mountains. Strachey also heard about a place called Ritanoe, where the king of "Eyanoco" (possibly Eno, a Siouan-speaking group) kept four English men, two boys, and a young girl as servants.[63] However, the only expeditions to search so far afield for "lost colonists" were the ones sent to the Chowanocs and to the Nottoways; both took place in the spring of 1609 and both failed to hear news.[64] Thus, the ultimate fate of the "lost colonists" remains a mystery only archaeology may solve.

On July 26, 1603, an English ship captained by Bartholomew Gilbert was driven into what may have been Chesapeake Bay (Quinn believes the bay was Delaware Bay) by foul weather.[65] Already low on food, water, and firewood, the ship was in desperate straits by July 29, so a landing party was sent ashore.[66] Without warning the party was attacked and five men were killed, including Captain Gilbert. The ship thereupon weighed anchor and sailed to England, still short of supplies. The reason for the Indians' hostility was never discovered, but it may have had something to do with earlier Spanish movements in the area.

Another European ship visited the Chesapeake either "the yeare before"[67] or "some twoe or three yeeres before"[68] the settling of the James-town colony in 1607. The nationality of the crew was unknown to the Indians who told the story of its visit, but Quinn has suggested[69] that it may have been an English ship captained by Samuel Mace, a companion ship to Gilbert's which had become separated. It may, in turn, have been Mace's ship that brought to England the Indians who are documented in 1603 as giving a canoe-handling demonstration on the Thames River.[70] All these connections are tenuous, given the scanty surviving records. Whatever its nationality, the ship visited Powhatan himself first and got a cordial reception, after which it went exploring in the Rappahannock River area. There the Rappahannock ruler made the crew welcome, but suddenly the Europeans turned on the Indians, killed their ruler, kidnapped some of the people, and sailed away. That, of course, is the Indian view, which acknowledged no culpability in creating a misunderstanding. The Powhatans appear not to have held that stealing from Europeans was "theft," since unpleasant incidents arising from thefts were common in the early days of the Jamestown colony; so it is likely that Rappahannock behavior played some part in causing the Europeans' violence. Nevertheless, the Rappahan-nocks still felt deeply offended in 1607, and for that reason John Smith was taken to them during his captivity in the winter of 1607–1608. He was exonerated because he was too short to have been the "great man" who captained the European ship.[71]

In the decades before 1607, then, the Algonquian-speaking Indians of Vir-ginia met a number of Europeans and heard about more. They must have had mixed impressions, for both their firsthand experiences and those re-lated by neighbors were with Europeans who could be either friendly or violently angry. Spanish and English visits to the Chesapeake Bay area must have caused unease. Stories of the repeated attempts to settle Roanoke Is-land may have been downright alarming, though the Powhatans would naturally not confess such a thing to the Jamestown settlers whose records we must use. There is also evidence that Iroquoian-speakers expanded their territory in the protohistoric period, and that their ritual torture of male captives was a means of further terrorizing other Woodland groups.[72] The Massawomecks who so frightened some Powhatan groups[73] may have been the Eries, moving down the Potomac valley in the late sixteenth and early seventeenth centuries.[74] The probability is high, therefore, that the Indians of eastern Virginia felt more threatened militarily at the end of the sixteenth century than they had ever felt before.

There may also have been serious epidemics of European diseases in eastern Virginia. Epidemics devastated other regions where the native people had no immunity,[75] and in the Pamlico region the Roanoke colonists noted that dreadful diseases causing high mortality afflicted any Indian groups who offended the English (i.e., most Indian groups) a few days after the English left.[76] That the Indians in Virginia experienced epidemics is indicated by Powhatan's statement to John Smith that he had "seene the death of all [his] people thrice"[77] and by John Smith's hearing of mass deaths after the exhumation of two children's bodies at Accomac.[78] Archaeological proof has yet to surface in the form of mass graves for the victims,[79] but the likelihood of epidemics having occurred is still high. Severe epidemics can cause great social disruption, as Europeans had found out in their experiences with the Black Death.[80] If such had been the case in late-sixteenth-century Virginia, an ambitious chief who wanted to become a paramount chief would have found circumstances aiding him.[81]

Powhatan began his career as a paramount chief on a small scale sometime between the 1550s and the 1580s. From one or both of his parents, about whom nothing else is known,[82] he inherited the chiefdoms of Powhatan, Arrohateck, and Appamattuck near the falls of the James River and the chiefdoms of Pamunkey, Mattaponi, and Youghtanund in the upper York River drainage.[83] He then expanded his holdings, either by intimidation or by outright military conquest,[84] until by 1607 he claimed all the peoples of the coastal plain except the Chickahominies as his.[85] (See map 1.)

Powhatan added Kecoughtan to his collection in 1596 or 1597, conquering it after its chief died.[86] Until that time the Kecoughtans had been strong enough to refuse to join the growing paramount chiefdom, and enmity had existed between the two peoples; only when a new and weaker chief reigned could Powhatan move in. His warriors killed the new chief and "most of" the people, according to Strachey, and the survivors were borne away in captivity, their territory being occupied by loyalists under one of Powhatan's sons.

The Chesapeake chiefdom also held out against Powhatan's expansionist aims. Apparently, a massive effort was required to conquer the Chesapeakes, and Powhatan made that effort after hearing a prophecy from his priests to the effect that his empire would be eclipsed by a nation coming "from the *Chesapeack* Bay."[87] Powhatan took this to mean his enemies the Chesapeakes, and accordingly he completely obliterated that people with a

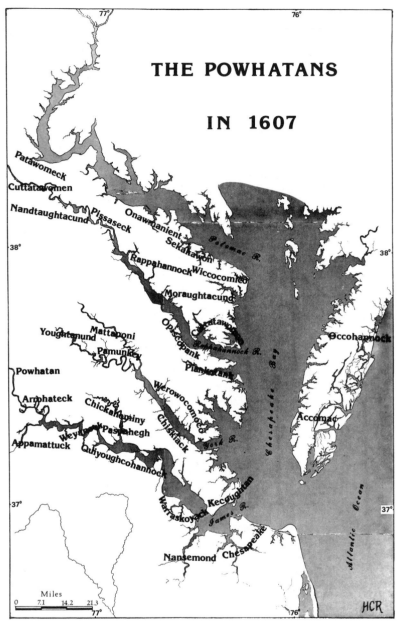

THE POWHATANS

IN 1607

Patawomeck
Cuttatawomen
Nandtaughtacund
Pissaseck
Onawmanient
Sekakawon
Rappahannock
Wiccocomico
Moraughtacund
Opiscopank
Matawom
Rappahannock R.
Occohannock
Youghtanund
Mattaponi
Pamunkey
Piankatank
Powhatan
Arrohateck
Werowocomoco
Chickahominy
Chiskiack
York R.
Accomac
Weyanock
Paspahegh
Appamattuck
Quiyoughcohannock
Waraskoyack
Kecoughtan
James R.
Nansemond
Chesapeake
Potomac R.
Chesapeake Bay
Atlantic Ocean

Miles
0   7.1   14.2   21.3

38°   38°

37°   37°

77°   76°

HCR

Map 1. The Powhatans in 1607. Base map adapted from *Bathymetry of Chesapeake Bay* (Virginia Institute of Marine Science, 1977).

thoroughness unusual in Virginia Algonquian warfare. Their territory was then resettled, probably by the neighboring Nansemonds.

The date at which the Chesapeakes were bludgeoned into extinction is unknown and therefore open to speculation. Quinn, as mentioned above, believes it to have been just before the English arrived. There is evidence for his view in Smith's statement, written in the spring of 1608, that the Indians who attacked the English at Cape Henry, in Chesapeake territory, in April 1607 were Nansemonds: "the riuer of Nausamd, [Nansemond], a proud warlike Nation, as well as may testifie, [by what happened] at our first arriuall at Chesiapiack . . . ," an "iniury" which the English avenged in the spring of 1608.[88]

However, the timing may have been different. Smith's later accounts[89] do not repeat his assertion of 1608. William Strachey, the sole source for our knowledge of the Chesapeakes' demise, interviewed Indian informants far more carefully than Smith did, and his statements leave the timing uncertain. Strachey never mentions an attack on the English at Cape Henry, and he is deliberately vague about the identity of the people who occupied the area after the Chesapeakes, calling them "such new Inhabitants that now people *Chessapeak*."[90] Strachey said the extermination occurred "not long synce," i.e., not long before 1612. The extermination was carried out also as part of a general assault on "all such who" might be meant in the prophecy, a movement that could include the otherwise unexplained attack on the small, apparently inoffensive Piankatank group in the fall of 1608.[91] (That would mean that repercussions from the prophecy continued for a year and a half beyond the time of the English arrival.) Strachey's use of a prophecy to explain the massacre of the Chesapeakes does not prove that the event happened before Jamestown was founded. True, when the prophecy was made, with its seemingly obvious reference to people in the east, the English may not yet have been on the scene. Yet after the English did sail in from the east, Powhatan did not immediately apply the prophecy to them; instead he waited a long time, hoping to make them into allies, before he decided they were enemies. What is obvious to us (and was to William Strachey) was not obvious to him. On the other hand, if the English came before the prophecy was made, then Powhatan, upon hearing it, may have feared that the unpredictable strangers would make common cause with the Chesapeakes, who were definitely his enemies, thus creating a powerful bloc to the east. Elimination of those he knew to be enemies would now be a necessity, regardless of whether any Roanoke colonists survived among them.[92] Thus, the Chesapeakes could have been obliterated after the English arrived.

And there is still that nagging point about the English firearms, which the attackers at Cape Henry "little respected,"[93] unlike Indian people upriver (see chapter 2). The Chesapeakes were much more likely, given their geographical location, to know the limitations of European firearms than

were the Nansemonds, with or without refugee colonists from Roanoke Island. Therefore, Smith may have been wrong about Nansemonds having
assaulted the English at Cape Henry in 1607. I suspect, instead, that the
attackers were men from a Chesapeake chiefdom that was not exterminated until after Jamestown was founded. However, neither Quinn's belief
nor mine can be proved from the scanty evidence presently available.

CHAPTER 2

Watching a Struggling Colony

IN THE EARLY ill-organized and even worse-supplied years of the James-town colony,[1] the Powhatans played a waiting game, watching for signs that the English would make useful allies against Indian enemies. Some-times they offered the colonists the foodstuffs they needed, and sometimes they attempted to put the English "in their place" as interlopers. But always the paramount chief tried to retain the foreigners as allies.

Unlike the English, the Powhatans did not see the situation as "Indians versus Europeans" in those first years. They realized immediately that they were dealing with a second, non-Spanish kind of European. So they thought in terms of "some Indians versus other Indians" (i.e., Powhatan's para-mount chiefdom versus the Monacans) and "English versus Spanish," with coalitions possible where interests ran parallel (i.e., Powhatans and English versus Monacans and Spanish). In other words, the English might prove useful in local military maneuvers. At the very beginning, Powhatan even allowed his chiefdoms to act as they pleased toward the English, as a means of testing the newcomers.

It took the Indians several years even to begin to realize that the English saw the land and its people in terms of European politics (competition with the Spanish for colonies), religion (spreading their own version of Christian-ity, and by extension, their own way of life), and an ideology of "savagism" with its unrealistic stereotypes of native people, who were either innocents in paradise or demonic near-animals.[2] When they did realize these things, the Powhatans appear to have been incredulous, for they were slow to take action against the arrogant intruders and then that action was on a small scale (see below and chapter 3). They had good reason to be incredulous. It was difficult for the Indians, who knew their world thoroughly, to believe that these blustering foreigners who could not even feed themselves actu-ally intended to make Virginia into an outpost of English culture. In the early years, when the English periodically starved in their fort, it probably seemed to the Powhatans that adopting English culture would mean they would *all* starve. Ridiculous, they thought. In fact, in the first year of the colony, it was all too apparent that the English were novices in the region, both in their selection of a place to settle permanently in May 1607 and, in

February 1608, in their inability to deal with shallow, tidal waters and the stake-and-pole bridges across them. Their firearms and metal tools were desirable, but little else about them was.[3]

The first three shiploads of the English arrived on April 16, 1607, at Cape Henry, where they were attacked by Indian warriors, who charged them "within Pistoll shot" and showed little fear when men on one of the ships fired larger guns at them.[4] The English explored ashore during the next two days and found a few signs of life, but no Indians showed themselves.[5] It was not until April 30 that contact was made with the Powhatans, when the English were hospitably entertained at Kecoughtan.[6] They apparently carried a list of words and phrases with which to communicate with the Indians.[7]

The English then sailed up the James River, and on May 4 they were feasted at Paspahegh,[8] where the name of the *weroance* was Wowinchopunck.[9] Word of their arrival had spread rapidly after April 26, and while they were at Paspahegh, the *weroance* of Rappahannock moved temporarily down to Quiyoughcohannock[10] across the James. He undoubtedly wanted to discover, in a cautious way, whether the strangers were the people who had done his subjects violence shortly before. He called on the Paspaheghs and insisted[11] that their English guests visit him in his temporary home, which they did.[12] He showed them the utmost respect by meeting them at the shore himself, and the hospitality at his house was lavish. It is safe to say, however, that if any of his attendants had identified members of the landing party as their assailants of a few years before, the feast would have turned into an ambush.

The English then proceeded upriver, scouting for a place to settle and making further contact with the native people. On May 8 they went ashore near the mouth of the Appomattox River and were met by several armed men, one of whom stood forth holding a tobacco pipe and a bow, symbolizing a choice of peace or war. The English chose peace and were allowed to remain.[13] They then went back down the river, still scouting, until on May 13 they found the place they wanted: an island in Paspahegh territory, without Indian habitations, easily defended, and with deep water so near the shore that their ships could be "moored to the Trees in six fathom water."[14] At the time, they took no notice of the mosquito-infested swamp nearby. The James River, from which they would often have to get their water, was deceptively fresh at that time of year; it would turn brackish in the summer and stay that way.[15] Jamestown Island was an excellent choice for a temporary visit but a poor one for long-term settlement. Archaeology shows that over the centuries the Indians merely camped there occasionally; they knew what they were doing.

The English assumed that Wowinchopunck's lavish welcome of nine days before, as well as their choice of uninhabited "waste" land, made formal negotiation for the island unnecessary.[16] They were mistaken. They went on to make other mistakes which showed arrogance toward "savages" and a lack of self-awareness of how they might appear to the natives.[17]

The English started the next day to build a triangular, palisaded fort,[18] and the Paspaheghs immediately became suspicious of "visitors" who did not merely pitch camp. Building a fort was sensible, given English intentions of staying, with or without Indian acquiescence, but it was not a tactful move. This was only the third European attempt at a permanent colony in the region between Nova Scotia and Florida (the first two were Ajacán and Roanoke; for the names of longer-lasting colonies, see map 2); but the Powhatans could see that a fort meant intentions of both permanence and defensiveness on the part of the builders. That defensiveness became immediately apparent. The first Paspaheghs to investigate the fort were some men who paddled in quietly by canoe around midnight that first night, only to flee when the English guard sounded an alarm.[19]

The English heard no more from the Indians for three days, during which Wowinchopunck may have been consulting with Powhatan. Then two well-dressed and highly decorated messengers informed the English that their *weroance* was coming, and on May 18, Wowinchopunck paid a formal call on the English,[20] bringing with him a deer for a feast and "a hundred" armed men. There seemed now to be nearly as many Paspaheghs as English in the fort,[21] which made the English uneasy. They therefore refused Wowinchopunck's request that they be the first to disarm, and shortly afterward all parley ceased when a "theft" occurred. A Paspahegh took an Englishman's hatchet, either to examine it or to keep it. The Englishman grabbed back his tool, striking the Indian on the arm; another Indian took umbrage and went for the Englishman with his warclub, at which point all the English cocked their guns. Seeing this, Wowinchopunck angrily called his men together and left.

When some Englishmen casually visited a Paspahegh town the next day,[22] they were received in a friendly fashion while an armed man went plunging into the woods, presumably to notify Wowinchopunck. The next day, May 20, forty Paspahegh warriors arrived at the still uncompleted English fort, intending to feast with the deer they brought along and then stay the night. That many men in a body is suspicious; an ambush may have been planned. However, the Paspaheghs soon left because of what was for them another uncomfortable incident. An Englishman invited a Paspahegh to shoot at his wooden shield propped against a tree, thinking no arrow could pierce it. The warrior promptly shot the shield "a foote thorow, or better," which was more than an English pistol could do. Alarmed that the Indians might think their defenses weak, other Englishmen had the man shoot again, this time at a shield made of steel. The arrow shattered, which so infuriated the bowman that he pulled out another arrow and "bit it in his teeth." The Paspahegh party then departed, once more in anger.[23]

From May 21 to May 27, part of the English colony under Captain

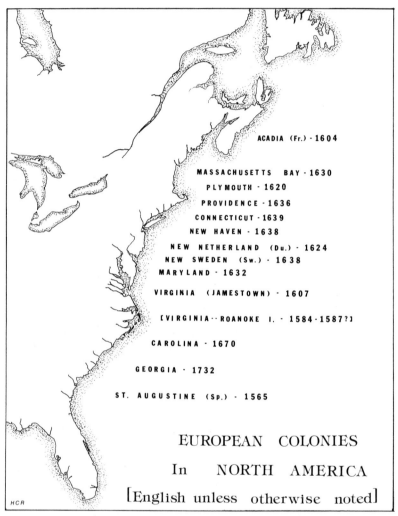

ACADIA (Fr.) · 1604

MASSACHUSETTS BAY · 1630
PLYMOUTH · 1620
PROVIDENCE · 1636
CONNECTICUT · 1639
NEW HAVEN · 1638
NEW NETHERLAND (Du.) · 1624
NEW SWEDEN (Sw.) · 1638
MARYLAND · 1632

VIRGINIA (JAMESTOWN) · 1607

[VIRGINIA··ROANOKE I. · 1584-1587?]

CAROLINA · 1670

GEORGIA · 1732

ST. AUGUSTINE (Sp.) · 1565

EUROPEAN   COLONIES

In   NORTH   AMERICA

[English unless otherwise noted]

HCR

Map 2. European Colonies in North America. Plymouth was not the first permanent English settlement in North America. In fact, the colonists originally intended to go to Jamestown.

Christopher Newport explored upriver.[24] This expedition was the first of several that made the Powhatans wonder whether the English were really the "visitors" they claimed to be, for wherever they went, the English asked bluntly what the region was like and what lay to the west of it. The first thing the English did on their way upriver was try to make friends with the Weyanocks, whom they found to be at odds with the Paspaheghs. Judging by the written record, it did not cross English minds that a friendship with the Weyanocks might make the "savages" who were their nearest neighbors angrier yet. The explorers were also hospitably received by the Arrohatecks, and while they were being feasted, Parahunt, the *weroance* of Powhatan town, came to inspect them. Because he was called by the name of his chiefdom, the English erroneously took him for the paramount chief about whom they had heard.

When the English moved upriver to Powhatan town, they were cordially received and Parahunt proposed a formal alliance, which Newport sealed by giving the *weroance* his "gowne" or mantle. Parahunt then let the English go further upriver and be disappointed in finding falls blocking navigation. When the explorers returned and asked him probing questions about the enemy territory that lay to the west, he reluctantly agreed to meet them back at the falls, and once there he managed to dissuade them from going further. After he left again, the English party set up a cross, claimed all the region for King James, and then lied to their Arrohateck guide about the meaning of their actions.[25]

On the way downriver, the English stopped at Powhatan and Arrohateck for more gestures of friendship, the ones at Arrohateck being particularly drawn out. It was there that the English demonstrated their firearms for the first time on the trip; the noise caused considerable fright among the Indians.[26] When the English reached the mouth of the Appomattox River, they got a sour reception from Opossunoquonuske, the "fatt, lustie, manly" woman who was a sister of the Appamattuck *weroance* and under him the *weroansqua* of the Appamattuck satellite town. She did not like the "visitors," and she let them know it immediately by refusing even to let them stand, much less sit, near her. She also requested a demonstration of firearms, showing "not neere the like feare as Arahatec."

Farther downriver, on the north side, the English met one of the three *weroance*s of Pamunkey, who, like others before him, had come to inspect them. Here, unknown to the English at the time, was one of the brothers of the paramount chief, possibly Kekataugh.[27] The English soon made him wary by refusing to let Newport walk alone with him, apart from everyone else. He promptly had them escorted politely to the river and sent on their way.

The next stop was Weyanock, on May 27. There, their Arrohateck guide suddenly left them, and the veneer of friendship in the town was so thin that the English decided to go directly to the fort on Jamestown Island.

They arrived back the same day, to find that on the day before a very large force of Indians had attacked; later it was learned that the Paspaheghs, Quiyoughcohannocks, Weyanocks, Appamattucks, and Chiskiacks were involved.[28] Thus, within thirteen days of settling on Jamestown Island, the English had inadvertently healed a breach between two James River chiefdoms and made most of their Indian neighbors into wary friends, if not enemies.

Raids and sniping on the part of the Indians continued for some time thereafter, while the English hastened to finish their fort, shooting at any armed warriors who came near them.[29] Only two Arrohatecks were allowed to parley. These told the English who their enemies were and then rendered the sensible advice that the English ought to cut down the "long weedes" around their fort.

Newport, who had been hired merely to bring the colonists to Virginia, departed for England on June 22, leaving behind 105 men and enough provisions to last until late September.[30] In fact, the supplies soon ran low, and long before Newport returned in January 1608, the colonists became panicky. They were factionalized, vulnerable to typhoid and dysentery from drinking James River water in summertime,[31] prone to sicken from local microbes for which they lacked immunity,[32] ignorant about the wild foods available in Virginia, and hampered by having too many gentlemen and would-be gentlemen averse to manual labor. The neighboring Indians had contributed to English fears by using Englishmen for target practice that spring when opportunity afforded, presumably to gain possession of English weapons.[33] About half the colony would die during the summer, while the survivors attempted to keep their true condition a secret from the Indians.

On June 15, 1607, Powhatan himself took action at last by issuing an order that raiding of the English was to cease.[34] By sending word of the order to the English, he enlightened them about the real identity of the paramount chief of the region, though they remained uncertain of the location of his capital town until John Smith was taken there as a captive months later.[35] After June 15, peace reigned and Powhatan and his brothers sent occasional presents of venison to Jamestown. The bearers of one deer asked where Captain Newport and his ship had gone. The colonists defensively replied "Croatoon."[36] an answer which probably did little to allay Indian suspicions. On July 7 the *weroance* of Quiyoughcohannock[37] grudgingly summoned the colony's leader to a tête-à-tête in which he agreed to sell some corn when his crop came in; the next day, when the English returned a canoe, he swore firm friendship with them.[38] However, other chiefdoms remained aloof.

July and August were the worst months of the summer for the English. The Indians' corn crop was late coming in, and English supplies ran low. They exhausted their wine supply; not having dug wells, they drank from the James, which was at its most polluted, and so they contracted typhoid, dysentery, and salt poisoning. They refused to ask their Powhatan "allies" for help, but their Indian neighbors knew that they were enduring a "starving time" because some Englishmen ran away to the Indian towns. These runaways were dutifully returned, apparently unaccompanied by presents of food.[39] Finally, in September, the summer's first corn became ripe enough to eat,[40] and then some neighboring chiefdoms contributed to the colony's supplies, as promised. It was typical of the English attitude toward "savages" that they attributed the gifts of corn not to a Powhatan sense of honor about promises made but to the grace of God.[41]

No relief ships came that fall from England. The colonists realized that they would have to buy winter supplies from the Indians. That would prove difficult, for after a mediocre crop year, the Powhatans had little corn to spare, especially for people they were learning to dislike.

The Englishman who set about buying Indian corn was John Smith, whose star in the colony was now in the ascendant. Smith was a yeoman with ambitions to become a gentleman.[42] He already had considerable foreign experience, having sought his fortune as a mercenary soldier in eastern Europe and beyond. His genuine organizational ability made him a natural leader, and his military credentials had earned him a place on the colony's council from the beginning. Now his ability was desperately needed to keep the colony from perishing. Though he subscribed to the stereotypes of the "savage" held by his English contemporaries, he had seen enough of the world to realize that native people are not all uniform personalities. He was able to deal differently with various Indians (e.g., Powhatan, Wowinchopunck, and Pocahontas) under varying circumstances (e.g., as captive, guest, and enforcer of agreements). However, he was abrasive to his own countrymen, eventually wearing out his welcome with most of them, and in spite of all his experience abroad he was still insensitive and occasionally bullying in his dealings with native people. One historian has described him as "a talented, experienced culture-broker who intimidated *selectively* and more to avoid, than to provoke, wholesale slaughter."[43] That is true, given the trying conditions under which Smith had to work. He had to feed do-nothing colonists whom the mother country would not support, in a colonization project that was expected to bring territory, converted souls, wealth, and glory to that same mother country. John Smith was certainly the man for that job. But with his ambitions and his self-promoting tendencies, it is doubtful that he would have been an effective "culture broker" under more realistic and egalitarian conditions of contact with the Indians.

At Kecoughtan, Smith was initially "scorned . . . as a starved man,"[44] after which the people sold him some supplies. He then made friendly contact with the Warraskoyacks, who sold him corn in the same proportion to their population that the mistrustful Kecoughtans had;[45] neither chiefdom had much to sell. By this time it was early November, and Smith turned his attentions upriver.[46] He found the Quiyoughcohannock capital town deserted by the men and most of the women and children, who had all probably gone on the annual communal hunt. Unable to trade there, he proceeded to Paspahegh, where he found the men in residence. Unfortunately, during the trading session the Paspaheghs tried to take English weapons by stealth and became violent when they were caught.[47] Encouraged by being able to trade at all, the English visited Paspahegh twice more, buying small amounts of corn.

Smith then set out again to trade with still-friendly upriver chiefdoms, but his success on a side trip to the Chickahominy River[48] prevented him from reaching his original goal. The Chickahominy tribe had not previously been contacted by the English, and they were eager to trade for English trinkets. They were probably also eager to appear better friends to the English than Powhatan's subjects were. On November 20, Smith and his party went from one town to another on the lower Chickahominy, and within a short time he had bought so much corn that he had to go back to Jamestown to offload it. Two days later he returned to the middle reaches of that river and again filled the colony's "barge" (a large shallow-draft rowboat). The colony was still in danger of going hungry before spring, so around the first of December, Smith made a third trip covering the entire Chickahominy River. Not surprisingly, by that time the insatiability of the English for corn, coupled with the bad harvest, had made their welcome wear thin even among the Chickahominies, and less corn was forthcoming on this visit. Ignoring these signs, John Smith decided to make a fourth trip up the river, this time mainly for exploration.[49]

Leaving Jamestown on December 10, 1607,[50] he and his party went to Apocant, the Chickahominy town farthest upriver, where he engaged a canoe and two guides and left most of his men behind in the barge. Those men soon went ashore, against orders, and were attacked. One man, George Casson, was captured and tortured to death; the survivors watched in horror from their boat and then returned to Jamestown. Meanwhile, in the headwaters of the Chickahominy River, Smith's party blundered into a huge communal hunting party consisting, he learned later, of Paspaheghs, Chickahominies, Youghtanunds, Pamunkeys, Mattaponis, and Chiskiacks,[51] and led by Opechancanough, Powhatan's brother and eventual successor. Smith was captured and kept comfortably at the camp called Rasawrack[52] while the hunt continued.

Smith's account in his *Generall Historie* (1624) of being repeatedly threatened with death during his captivity is probably apocryphal. That account was written seventeen years after his capture, after the great attack of 1622 had occurred, and at a time when Englishmen looked for excuses to root out the "savages" from Virginia. In contrast, the account Smith wrote only a few months after his release is shorter and depicts Indians who were much less illogical, changeable, and "treacherous."[53]

In the first phase of his captivity, Smith remained at Rasawrack and made friends with Opechancanough.[54] He told him about English ships and "the earth & skies and of our God." Opechancanough described eastern Virginia, "Ocanahonan" where the people wore European clothing, and "a great turning of salt water" that was "4 or 5 daies iourney" west of the falls of the James. Smith was well fed, according to the custom of chiefly hospitality toward a guest: "each morning 3 . women presented me three great platters of fine bread, more venison then [sic] ten men could devour I had . . . Though 8 ordinarily guarded me." He was allowed to send a message to Jamestown, telling all he had seen and heard. The only untoward incident occurred when the father of a man he had slain during his capture tried to kill him, and his guard saved his life. The hospitable treatment indicates that Smith was considered a potentially powerful ally, not an enemy. "Three or foure dayes after [his] taking,"[55] priests were summoned to perform a divining ritual over him to determine his and his countrymen's intentions in Virginia.[56] The priests, who were tremendously influential in military matters, pronounced him harmless, and thereby assured his continued success in charming the Indians, as he later claimed he did.[57]

The next phase of Smith's captivity was a journey around the central region of Powhatan's empire.[58] Opechancanough took him first to Youghtanund, where he was feasted as a guest, and then to hunting camps on the upper Mattaponi River. They then returned to Rasawrack, where most of the men had remained on the communal hunt, and dismantled the camp, after which the hunting party presumably dispersed. Opechancanough next took Smith to his permanent headquarters on the Pamunkey River, a place called Menapacunt.[59] At the invitation of Kekataugh,[60] another brother of Powhatan, the party then moved downriver. There Smith was invited during the festivities to shoot his pistol at a target well beyond its range; he had to conceal the gun's limitations by covertly damaging the cock and telling his disappointed hosts that the pistol was broken. Opechancanough then took his captive northward for the Rappahannocks to see, thinking that Smith might be the European captain who had attacked them previously (see chapter 1). Finally Smith was taken to the paramount chief's capital, Werowocomoco, on the York River;[61] the third and last phase of Smith's captivity was passed there.[62]

Powhatan welcomed Smith with full chiefly ceremony. Assured of Smith's worth by Opechancanough and the priests, he allowed himself the full enjoyment of visiting with and impressing an exotic stranger. The two men talked as best they could, given Smith's very imperfect command of the Powhatan language.[63] Smith wrote later that they discussed the lands their people ruled and the lands beyond; Smith's explanation of the English presence in Virginia was that their ships had been damaged by the Spanish, making it necessary to take refuge from the Spanish and from bad weather. The English, he said, were repairing their pinnace (one of the ships) and would leave when Newport came back to escort them. When Powhatan asked the reason for the explorations and the blunt questions, Smith blandly replied that the people on the shore of the ocean to the west had killed an Englishman, and the English sought a route there to avenge the murder. With these half-truths and untruths, however well he understood them, Powhatan was apparently content. He then made what Smith understood as an offer: the English should "forsake Paspahegh" and move to his satellite town of Capahosic,[64] where he would feed and protect them, and in exchange they would make him metal tools. Smith glibly promised that the English would, in effect, become Powhatan's vassals. Finally, "hauing with all the kindnes hee could deuise, sought to content [Smith]: hee sent [him] home with 4 . men. . . ."[65]

Pocahontas is not mentioned in this early account by Smith. It is only in the account of 1624 that she appears; Smith writes that she saved his life after her father decided to have him killed by beating his brains out on an altar stone.[66] Many historians have accepted that account of a rescue as authentic,[67] while others have had their doubts.[68] Readers of Smith's later works will note that in his lifetime he was conveniently saved "by a fair lady at the moment of direst peril—not once but three times." And the women are not depicted as real people, but "were stage deities who intervened at the proper moments, and always women of high rank—an aid no doubt to Smith's pretensions to being a gentleman, coat of arms and all."[69]

Smith may have manufactured the peril from which Pocahontas supposedly saved him. The Indians throughout his 1624 account are prone to sudden and brutish violence.[70] Pocahontas, whom his readers knew from her visit to England in 1616–1617, is made to shine as an exception to the "savagery" around her and depicted as a heroine who "saved" the English colony in the months to follow. She is also pictured as an instigator of any friendly treatment the English received from other Indians.[71] Yet no contemporary of Smith's described her in that way or mentioned any saving of Smith's life; William Strachey and Samuel Purchas in his early editions would have been sure to mention the rescue incident had it happened, for it would have meant that the English had a useful friend in high favor with the Indian "emperor." (Purchas included the incident in his 1625 edition, quoting Smith verbatim without comment.)[72] Smith's "memory" is even more suspect because he added to his 1624 account two incidents that definitely did not happen in December 1607. One was his claim that Indians told him they planned to plant stolen English gunpowder the next spring, a story first recorded about Opechancanough in 1622."[73] The other was his claim that an undescribed "Queene of *Appomattoc*" waited upon him at Powhatan's house during his captivity. In fact, she waited upon him during a feast of February 1608, and she was a "comely yong Salvuage"[74]—probably a wife of the *weroance* of Appamattuck rather than his sister, the "fatt, lusty, manly," and above all hostile *weroansqua* Opossunoquonuske that knowledgeable readers in 1624 would remember. Smith's claim to have been rescued by Pocahontas is therefore doubtful for historical reasons, as is his claim (made in 1624) that in 1617 he had written to Queen Anne of England on Pocahontas's behalf, relating the rescue.[75] In 1617, Pocahontas had her own friends in high places in England (see chapter 3), and a letter from a would-be gentleman would have been superfluous to her social advancement there.

The rescue of John Smith by Pocahontas does not bear scrutiny from an anthropological viewpoint, either. We are expected to believe that Powhatan welcomed and feasted a powerful guest whom his astute brother and his most trusted priests had tested and approved, and then suddenly, after "a long consultation," he tried to have that guest's brains clubbed out on an altar stone—a quick death normally meted out to disobedient subjects, not to captured foreigners (see Prologue). This scenario simply does not ring true. Pocahontas probably did see John Smith for the first time in that January of 1608, but it is highly unlikely that his life needed saving at the time.

While he was still at Powhatan's capital, Smith was taken to a house "in the woods," probably a temple, where he was seated in an anteroom. Then, in a room next door, Powhatan and a large number of men, all painted black, made "the most dolefullest noyse" Smith had ever heard. Coming into the room where Smith was, Powhatan informed him that "now they were friends" and he should send to Werowocomoco "two great gunnes, and a gryndstone," in exchange for the York River town of Capahosic. Powhatan would henceforth treat Smith as a "son."[76] This incident, along with the "rescue," has been taken by some historians to be a formal adoption procedure.[77] The incident by itself (conference, decision, announcement) may have been something of the sort, since it approximates descriptions of adoption procedures in other Indian groups (e.g., Iroquois), and Powhatan is known to have placed his real sons in ruling positions and expected them to send him tribute. However, Smith did not write of the "rescue" itself as though it were part of a ritual, and no identical sequence of events is recorded as an adoption procedure for any other native American group.[78] We have no information at all about the nature of the Powhatan adoption procedure.

Smith and his escort left Werowocomoco on January 1, 1608, and reached Jamestown the next day. That night Newport arrived, bringing more Englishmen and some long-overdue supplies.[79] Those supplies and the corn remaining from the fall's trading were destroyed in a fire on January 7, leaving the English once more in desperate straits.

Now Powhatan stepped into the breach and fed the English colony, sending provisions to his allies and subordinates (as he thought them) at regular intervals. Contemporary accounts agree: the person who sent the food that saved the colony was Powhatan, not Pocahontas, as Smith claimed in 1624.[80] Indians and English alike lived in a world in which prepubescent girls had little real power. Captain Newport began sending presents to Powhatan in return, and after Powhatan repeatedly invited him and Smith to visit his territory (or to move there)[81] a diplomatic visit was arranged in late February 1608.[82]

One of the most uncomfortable aspects of doing fieldwork among native peoples is the realization that one looks foolish in native eyes. Dignity and self-confidence are hard to preserve under such conditions. The English now found this out firsthand.[83] Their visit to Powhatan got off to an awkward start when their landing party was guided to the wrong point on Purtan Bay, a wide, shallow bay with three tributary creeks.[84] Some of the men were sent around in the barge to the correct point, while Smith and the others tried to get there by way of an Indian-made bridge. The bridge, consisting of forked stakes connected by a few poles, defeated the heavily clothed and booted English, and their Indian hosts had to ferry them, a few at a time, across the creek. It was just as well for English pride that Newport had stayed aboard the ship in order to stage a late entrance the next day.

As a representative of his people, Smith was welcomed and feasted in great style after he gave Powhatan "a sute of red cloath, a white Greyhound, and a Hatte." He gave noncommittal explanations for Newport's failure to appear that day, as well as for his men's failure to bring along the demi-culverins (small cannon) that he had promised in December. Powhatan had Smith's companions brought in two by two and given "foure or fiue pound of bread" each, an extravagant gift at that season and after a bad crop year. Then Smith asked for the territory promised him two months before, and Powhatan demanded that all the English lay down their arms first, "as did his subiects." The nature of Powhatan's "gift" of land was now clear, and in Indian eyes, Smith must now have abrogated the agreement about Capahosic by continuing to refuse to have his men disarm. However, when he indicated that the English would "deliver to Powhatan as subjects the enemy countries of Monacan and Pocoughtaonack," the emperor expressed delight and declared the English to be "Powhatans"—and still subjects. Smith had to admit defeat for the time being. He and his men were given more bushels of bread as they left, and, to crown a day of discomforts, they failed to get back to their ship because the tide was out and their barge drew too much water. They had to be put up for the night in the town armory.[85] Smith was summoned back to Powhatan's presence for supper, where he was stuffed with more food.

The next morning, after Powhatan showed Smith the canoes in which his men collected tribute from all his dominions, Newport came ashore and Powhatan retired to his house for a formal reception of the supposed leader of all the English. At their meeting, Newport handed Thomas Savage over to Powhatan, ostensibly as his "son" for a goodwill token but in reality for young Savage to learn the Powhatan language and to serve later as an inter-

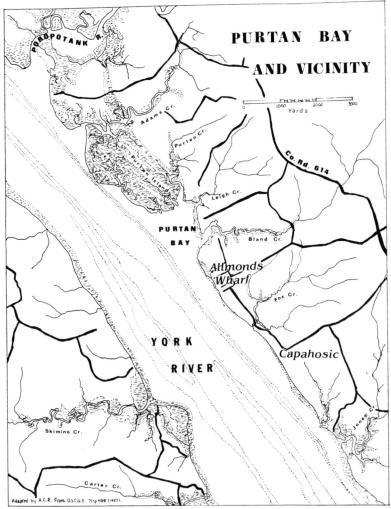

Map 3. Purtan Bay and Vicinity. It was on Purtan Bay that Powhatan had his capital of Werowocomoco until 1609. Adapted from U.S. Coast Guard Survey Map 495, 1957.

preter. Several days later,[86] an Indian youth named Namontack was handed over to the English for just the same reasons. The rest of Newport's first day ashore was passed in feasting and pleasant conversation.

The next day was less comfortable for everyone. The English not only refused to disarm but would not all come into the town at once and leave their barge unattended. These were sensible and possibly necessary precautions, but they heightened Indian suspicions nonetheless. Powhatan, Newport, and Smith then got down to the real business that the English, at least, had come for: bargaining for corn. Powhatan priced his corn high[87] and insisted on his price, and Newport was all for paying it, until Smith offered Powhatan blue beads. That turned the tables. Powhatan offered a large quantity of corn for the beads, probably because he thought them analogous to the more valuable kind of shell beads. The English were quick to follow up on this weakness[88] and bought "2 or 300 bushells of corne" for "a pound or two of blew beades."[89] The next day was again passed in trading considered successful by both sides, though once again the English refused Powhatan's requests that they disarm.

On that fourth day of their visit, the English once more had trouble getting back to their ship because the tide was out. This time the situation was just as embarrassing in its way as it had been the first time. The barge reached the river safely, but Smith and some of the men who had been left behind, for fear the barge would go aground if overburdened, tried to follow in a canoe which itself promptly ran aground. Helpful Indian men then threw off their clothes and waded out in the freezing mud, intending to carry the English ignominiously to shore "on their heads." Instead, Smith made them bring "some wood, fire, and mats, to couer me," while he and his men stolidly waited in the canoe until midnight for the tide to rise. The Englishmen ashore, meanwhile, had "passed the dreadful bridge" in their determination to leave, only to find the other creek no deeper. They were forced to spend the night in a hastily erected Indian house. In Powhatan eyes, the English cannot have looked like competent travelers.

The following day was spent in negotiations about a joint assault on the Monacans beyond the falls of the James.[90] Powhatan coyly asserted that the Monacans were not his enemies but that he would help his friends the English attack them. On the same day an invitation arrived for the English to visit Opechancanough; when Powhatan asked Newport to stay for more trading, a refusal was sent upriver. The same thing happened the next day: an invitation from Opechancanough was refused because the elder brother urged the English to stay. Some fraternal rivalry may have been involved. On the seventh day of the English visit, they finally accepted Opechancanough's "intreatie," moved upriver, and spent the day in feasting with Opechancanough and his brothers and the next two days in trading blue beads for corn. After that the English stopped at Werowocomoco on their way home to take formal leave of Powhatan and to receive the youth Namontack as a token of goodwill. When they visited Chiskiack a little later, they met with a hostile reception and left again, arriving back at Jamestown on March 9, 1608.[91] As a result of their voyage, they had procured a good supply of corn, made Powhatan suspicious in firsthand encounters, and contracted an alliance that neither he nor they fully trusted.

While Newport was still in Virginia, he explored the Nansemond River.[92] The English went prepared for hostility from the outset, and when people came to the shore and made signs of welcome, Newport sensed a trap[93] and fired into them, killing one and wounding two more. The *weroance* then tried to lure them ashore, in what by that time probably was indeed a trap. The English came ashore only after many messages and an exchange of hostages, after which supposedly friendly trade took place.

Captain Newport returned to England on April 10, 1608,[94] taking Namontack with him. In England the Virginia Company paraded the youth as a son of "the emperor of Virginia" and encouraged him to demand royal dignities, such as not having to remove his hat when he met King James.[95] The show convinced the Venetian ambassador of Namontack's importance.[96] Namontack remained in England as long as Newport did and apparently enjoyed his stay.

In the spring of 1608 the English at Jamestown began drilling their men outside their fort, preparatory to an exploration beyond the falls of the James. Neighboring Indians became alarmed, and Powhatan himself sent Thomas Savage to ask the English whether they were planning an assault upon him. The colonists replied blandly that they were merely planning to go to the town of Powhatan "to seeke stones to make Hatchets" (a palpable lie from people who had steel tools), and they asked that the *weroance* of the Weyanock chiefdom be sent to them as a guide. This brazen answer, which assumed utter naïveté in the *mamanatowick* and a lack of importance in one of his viceroys, put Powhatan out of patience. He sent Savage back, requested another boy in his place, held conferences with the Chickahominies, and allowed his subjects to begin harassing the English and filching tools at their fort, a behavior that soon reached epidemic proportions.[97] When at length the English took hostages to exchange for the stolen tools, the Paspaheghs retaliated by capturing two straggling Englishmen for their own hostages.[98] The English escalated the hostilities that night by raiding and burning some Paspahegh towns. Wowinchopunck thereupon released the two Englishmen; in return the English released one Indian prisoner but kept the rest, whom they interrogated to learn who their enemies really were. These hostages were not released until personal requests and a gift of corn[99] came from Opechancanough and Powhatan. The bearer of the latter request was Pocahontas.

John Smith gives us little personal information about Pocahontas; other writers do a bit better by her. She was a girl, not a young woman, in that May of 1608. Her age was about twelve[100] and she had the standard appearance for prepubescent girls among her people: she wore no clothing and her head was close cropped except for a long, braided lock at the back. On this first visit[101] she came on business, but her later visits were social ones that included playing with the English boys: she would "gett the boyes forth with her into the markett place and make them wheele, falling on their handes turning their heeles vpwardes, whome she would follow, and wheele so her self naked as she was all the Fort over."[102] Her nickname, Pocahontas, or "little wanton,"[103] did not mean then what it does in modern usage. "Wanton" then meant "mischievous," and as her powerful father's favorite child she probably earned it by being spoiled and willful. No contemporary record survives about her dealings with John Smith on any but that first official visit. However, when she was not playing with the boys she appears to have shown admiration for him,[104] which is understandable, because by Powhatan standards the swaggering but capable Smith was a "real man." She may even have fallen in love with him, as her legend insists; the violence of her anger with him in 1617 (see chapter 3) could indicate an unrequited love. But no real love affair blossomed between the two. Smith was impressed by the girl's "feature, countenance and proportion, [which] much exceedeth any of the rest of [Powhatan's] people" and also by her "wit, and spirit."[105] Yet, on the whole, he seems to have been too wrapped up in his own ambitions to consider her anything but a child,[106] albeit a child well placed to be of use.

Rawhunt, the man who accompanied Pocahontas to Jamestown, did most of the talking,[107] pointing out that the *mamanatowick* had sent his daughter into English hands and formally requesting that the Indian hostages be released. Pocahontas merely seconded him; she had the poise not to seem to notice the presence of the Indian prisoners until their "fathers, and friends" and a present-bearing messenger from Opechancanough came to the fort later that day to ask for their freedom. Finally, Smith released his captives to Pocahontas.[108]

Indian harassment of the English lessened but did not cease. The English continued to inflame Indian suspicions by remaining in Virginia and exploring further. In fact, they now began contacting groups who were in the fringe area of Powhatan's dominions, people of whose loyalty he felt less sure.

Smith led two expeditions to explore the upper Chesapeake Bay in the summer of 1608. On the first, which lasted from June 2 through July 21,[109] the English made friendly contact with the Accomacs, forced the people of the Pocomoke and Nanticoke rivers to become "friendly," and explored the Potomac River looking for a "glistering mettal, the Salvages told vs they had from Patawomeck."[110] Near the mouth of the Potomac they acquired a bearded, presumably half-European guide named Mosco, who was of great use to them on their second voyage.[111] Among the Potomac chiefdoms, the English met an initially hostile reception at Onawmanient, which they soon learned had been instigated by Powhatan.[112] They received the same treatment at Patawomeck and Sekakawon for perhaps the same reasons. Powhatan cannot have been at ease with the English explorations. He was probably still less happy later on if he heard that the Moyaons, Nacotchtanks, and Tauxenents farther upriver received the English with cordiality; the latter two, at least, were enemies of his "empire" throughout the early seventeenth century.

The Patawomecks had apparently evaded divulging the location of their "mine," so on the way back downriver[113] the English stopped there and inquired again. This time they persuaded the local people to show them the site, which was near Aquia Creek. The mine was small and the "mettal" was antimony. Disappointed, the English left the Potomac River chiefdoms, considering them "friends," which at that time meant merely "someone who can be helpful in advancing one's career or prospects."[114] Smith intended to go on to the Rappahannock River, but lack of supplies and illness from a stingray stab made him head back to Jamestown. He stopped at Kecoughtan on the way in, where the people saw him looking sickly, his boat full of gifts from the Potomac River chiefdoms. They concluded that he had been battling Massawomecks. Failing to convince them otherwise, Smith gave in and made up a tale that satisfied them.

The second expedition, which lasted from July 24 through September 7,[115] began with a friendly visit to Kecoughtan, where Smith deliberately told the people he was going up the bay to wreak revenge on the dreaded Massawomecks. The English party then went to the head of the bay and explored up the rivers as far as possible. In the process they encountered some Massawomecks in birchbark canoes.[116] The Massawomecks attacked but were repulsed by a bluffing maneuver, after which a meeting took place. The two sides traded peacefully and agreed to meet the next day, but the Indians did not appear; that one meeting was the only time Smith and his men ever encountered any Massawomecks.

The English then made contact with the people of Tockwogh (now Sassafras) River, who were impressed with the Massawomeck goods they saw in the English boat. They then helped Smith's party to summon Susquehannocks from farther north for a trading session. John Smith described the Susquehannocks as giantlike men, but archaeological excavations in their homeland have not borne this out.[117] From the Susquehannocks, Smith learned about people still farther north and heard that the Massawomecks obtained their metal tools from the French in Canada.[118] Then, after visiting the Patuxent River and being cordially received there, the English picked up Mosco at the mouth of the Potomac and began an exploration of the Rappahannock River.

Smith wanted to renew contact with the Rappahannock group, but his party had first to bypass the territory of the Moraughtacunds, who, according to Mosco, had incurred the Rappahannock *weroance*'s enmity by stealing three of his wives. However, their passing through that territory, together with their being Europeans, was enough to make the English objects of hostility to the Rappahannocks; bowmen even followed the explorers farther upriver, shooting at them. In contrast, the English found all the chiefdoms upriver to be friendly. They pushed on toward the fall line, but before they reached it they were given a hostile reception from some Siouan-speaking Mannahoac men who were fishing in the area.[119] Because they captured a wounded man during the skirmish and treated him kindly, the English finally made friends with the Mannahoacs and questioned them about lands to the west.

The English then returned downriver, bringing with them some of the Algonquian-speaking people from the towns of Matchopick, Wecuppom, Pissacack, Nandtaughtacund, and Cuttatawomen whom they had contacted earlier. These people were triumphant about the English "victory" over the Mannahoacs, and they wanted to get their new allies to help patch up matters between the Rappahannocks and the Moraughtacunds downriver. A meeting was therefore arranged, with the *weroance*s of Nandtanghtacund and Pissacack present. After parleying, a compromise was agreed upon: instead of giving up his son as a hostage, the Rappahannock *weroance* gave Smith his claim to the three women stolen from him. This technically ended the quarrel, and everyone concerned adjourned to Moraughtacund to inform the women's captor. The *weroance* of Moraughtacund, meeting the English for the first time and hearing that his neighbors' enmity was at an end, expressed delight and gladly gave up all three women to Smith. Smith then sealed the rapprochement by parceling out the women: the Rappahannock *weroance* chose the one "he loued best," the Moraughtacund *weroance* chose another, and Mosco got the third. A tremendous feast followed the next day, with "six or seauen hundred" people attending and everyone promising to plant corn specifically for the English the next year. When the English stopped to see the Piankatanks on the way down the bay, they also promised to plant corn to sell. Now it looked to John Smith—and perhaps also to Powhatan—as if the English had become allies of all the Potomac and Rappahannock river groups.

Smith and his men explored two more rivers before returning to Jamestown.[120] Sailing up "a narrow river vp the country of *Chisapeack*" (probably the Elizabeth River), they found practically no signs of habitation. From this, we may conclude that the Chesapeakes were definitely exterminated before September 1608.

On the Nansemond River, the English found people who tried to ambush them as they approached the chiefdom's principal town. A round of musket shot and the destruction of some of the people's laboriously made canoes brought the Indians around: in return for leaving intact the town and the remaining canoes, the English would accept "their Kings bowes and arrowes," a chain of pearls, and four hundred baskets of corn. These were delivered, and the English once more left the Nansemonds "good friends," as Smith put it (remember the seventeenth-century meaning of "friend"), and returned to their fort.

In the early fall of 1608, Smith was made president of the Jamestown colony, and Newport arrived in Virginia with the Second Relief Supply. Newport brought more colonists, including some Germans and Poles, along with limited supplies that threatened to be inadequate to see everyone through the winter.[121] Nothing is recorded of any harvest from crops that the English themselves planted; the Indians said they themselves had had a bad crop year.[122] Smith was still confident that corn could be bought from the Indians, but to his intense displeasure Newport overruled him about trading expeditions and, instead, had the colony engage in activities that netted it no corn and further antagonized the native people.

The first expedition under Newport's orders was a diplomatic one, designed to pacify Powhatan so that he would have his people trade willingly later. Another motive was to make Powhatan officially a vassal of King James. Powhatan guessed both motives, and his knowing the second made it impossible to accomplish the first. Powhatan saw even the invitation to come to his own "coronation" as demeaning. The English simply could not comprehend that this "savage" was not the naïve child they thought him.

Newport had brought presents, supposedly from King James, for Powhatan: a basin and ewer, a bed, clothing, and a fake crown. Smith was now sent to Werowocomoco to invite Powhatan to come to Jamestown to collect these presents.[123] Powhatan replied that since he was the ruler of Virginia, a mere ship's captain like Newport should come to him; he would wait eight days. Newport gave in and took the presents, the youth Namontack, and a party of Englishmen to Werowocomoco.

Powhatan was away from his capital when the English arrived. While they waited for him to be summoned, they were entertained by several young women who put on a warlike dance. When Powhatan appeared, Newport gave him the furniture and, with Namontack's help, got him to don the clothing, but the "coronation" itself went awry because Powhatan sensed what it meant. The paramount chief refused to kneel to receive a crown. Smith wrote that Powhatan could not know the meaning of "bending of the knee," but Smith was wrong. The Powhatans, like the people of many other complex societies in the world, had a sense that to keep one's head erect and at least as high as the heads of others was to retain superior status.[124] The English managed to put the crown on Powhatan's head only by having someone lean hard on his shoulders so that "he a little stooped," but that was enough for the English to claim afterward that Powhatan had acknowledged King James's dominion over Virginia.[125] Powhatan then reciprocated by presenting Newport with "his old shoes and his mantle."[126]

Not surprisingly, in the talks that followed, negotiations for the projected joint assault on the Monacans fell through, and the English succeeded in buying very little corn.

Soon afterward Newport and 120 of the colony's 200-odd men went on a military expedition up the James to Monacan territory, against Powhatan's specific wishes. However, Powhatan need not have worried. The English under Newport (Smith was not along) were so heavy-handed in dealing with the Monacans, taking one of their "petty kings" prisoner to use for a guide when the people gave them an indifferent reception,[127] that the Monacans were antagonized. By 1611 they were known to have buried their traditional enmity and become allies of the Powhatans against the English.[128] Newport got corn neither from the Monacans nor from Powhatan town, where he stopped on the way back. At the latter place the people had hidden their supplies in the woods before the English arrived, which means that they were expecting trouble. Newport had to return to Jamestown with no corn and some new enemies for the colony.

Newport set sail for England to get more supplies soon afterward. He left behind a colony that had food for only a few weeks and few friends left among the native people. The season for fishing and gathering wild plant foods was past, spent in futile diplomatic and military maneuvers. Conditions in the colony were already bad when Newport left, and yet the Virginia Company did not hurry about sending aid: the Third Relief Supply expedition was not to leave England until May 1609; thanks to a hurricane, none of its cargo arrived until May 1610. In the interim the English colony became desperate for food and acted in such a way as to alienate its few remaining Powhatan friends. In all likelihood, only the fact that the colony seemed to be starving to death by itself kept the *mamanatowick* from sending warriors to annihilate it altogether.

In the late fall of 1608 the English attempted to buy corn at Chickahominy, where they forced the Indians to sell; at Werowocomoco, where Namontack's persuasion was needed; at Nansemond, where the people traded only after the English shot off muskets and set fire to a house; at Appomattox, where the few people they found were forced to sell; and at other James River towns, which were found to be deserted.[129] As hunger in the colony increased, individual Englishmen sold the colony's tools to neighboring Indians in exchange for food until hardly any tools were left in the fort.[130] The English gradually realized that Powhatan intended to starve them out of Virginia.[131] All pretenses at being allies were at an end.

Finally Smith decided to go to Werowocomoco and capture "Powhatan and al his provision."[132] The rest of the account of that expedition (written by others and approved by Smith) makes the Indians sound like treacherous enemies attacking Englishmen who were on their lawful business, but Smith himself planned treachery from the outset. Like other Europeans, he believed that his people had a "right to trade" even with recalcitrant natives.[133] Some members of the colony's council opposed Smith's plan, but when Powhatan made the first move by inviting the English to Werowocomoco to trade, the opportunity could not be passed up.

Powhatan sent an offer of a shipload of corn in exchange for a grindstone, fifty swords, some guns, a cock and a hen, copper and beads, and some men to build him an English-style house.[134] His open demand for firearms shows that he was fully aware of the colony's desperation. Smith accepted the offer, sent some men to begin on the house, and himself set off for Werowocomoco on December 29, 1608. He stopped on the way at Warraskoyack,[135] where he bought provisions and received a warning that Powhatan planned to ambush him. In all probability the warning was perfectly accurate, but the tone in the account changes from that point onward to one of injured innocence. Proceeding on their way, the English took refuge during bad weather with the Kecoughtans, who acted friendly, and with the Chiskiacks, who did not. They finally arrived at Werowocomoco on January 12, 1609.[136]

The tide was out. Smith and his party got ashore by wading through freezing mud, after which they put up in a house near the shore and sent a request to Powhatan for food, for they had not brought any ashore with them. Imperial hospitality was laid on the next day, although it was marred by the prominent display in the town of the scalps of the recently ambushed Piankatank men. Long, wrangling discussions then took place, during which Powhatan raised his prices for corn and warned the English against trying to take over his dominions, which the Nansemonds had told him the English intended to do. A conquest like that was hardly feasible, Powhatan said, when the English could not even feed themselves without Indian help; the Indians could withdraw out of reach and leave them starving (which was true).[137] Smith denied that the English were so dependent upon Indian goodwill, and the wrangling over the price of corn continued.

Smith and Powhatan tried to ambush each other almost simultaneously. While Smith's men made their way ashore, Powhatan's women and children fled and his men assembled. The Indian forces were ready first, and shortly after Powhatan excused himself from Smith's presence and fled, Smith sensed the trap and fought his way to the Englishmen who had originally come ashore with him. The Indian force then tried to talk down Smith's suspicions but to no avail. Training their guns on Powhatan's warriors, Smith and his men made them carry the already purchased corn to the shore. The tide, needless to say, was out again, and the English party then had to stay in town, feasting as though they had forgotten the afternoon's unpleasantness,[138] until midnight when they could row out to their ship. They left behind some Germans to continue work on the house, as well as a message for Powhatan that they would "inioy his company" later. Either that message or the afternoon's proceedings made Powhatan decide to abandon his capital and move to Orapax, in the headwaters of the Chickahominy, where the English could not reach him so easily,[139] even across mudflats.

The English then went up the Pamunkey River and were received, at first hospitably, by Opechancanough. However, when serious trading began, the Pamunkeys balked, and on the next day they attempted to ambush the English. Smith seized Opechancanough by his bracer, put a pistol to his chest, and "led the trembling king (near dead with feare) amongst all his people"[140]—an unpardonable affront to a warrior of royal status[141] and an insult that Opechancanough probably never forgave. His people capitulated and grudgingly sold much of their remaining winter supplies of corn to the English. They showed some resistance, as when men tried to kill Smith as he slept in an Indian house; the entrance of the men through the low door of the sapling-and-mat house shook the house so much that Smith woke up in time.[142] There was also a near-skirmish when the Pamunkeys actually began bringing their corn to the shore. Later some of them tried unsuccessfully to poison the intruders.[143]

When the English sent a barge back to Jamestown, the Pamunkeys interpreted it as a call for reinforcements, so they appeased the English by having their people for ten or twelve miles around bring corn. However, the English were not yet satisfied. When they had finished with the Pamunkeys, they went up the Pamunkey and Mattaponi rivers, extracting corn from the people in spite of occasional resistance from the men. Eventually they were moved to desist by the "complaints and tears from women and children." John Smith's followers later wrote complacently that the English "maie be thought verie patient to indure all those iniuries. . . . The maine occasion of our temporizing with the Salvages was to part friends, (as we did)."[144] Even given the different meaning of "friend" in those days, we may wonder if those Indian people felt like advancing English interests as they looked at their depleted winter supplies.

The English then went back to Werowocomoco and were genuinely surprised to find Powhatan and his household permanently gone and the few remaining people very hostile. Blaming the Germans for having incited Powhatan to move, and noting that since no corn could be taken there it was "an vnfit time to revenge [the Indians'] abuses,"[145] the English returned to Jamestown. They assumed that the childlike "savages" had nevertheless been taught some sort of lesson and were now ready to be "friendly" and supportive, as it was "their place" to be. They did not realize that they had secured the survival of their colony that winter at the expense of personally alienating the paramount chief of the region, as well as his powerful younger brother.

Indian men (probably Paspahegh) continued to harass the English in the spring and summer of 1609, but in accordance with Powhatan preferences in warfare, no large-scale move was made. Far from taking the "hint," the English remained where they were and continued to place most of the blame for Indian ill-will on the Germans who had gone to live with Powhatan at his new capital. In one skirmish near the fort, the *weroance* Wowincho-punck was captured by Smith and some of the Polish colonists.[146] He was visited frequently in prison by his wives, children, and subjects, and at length he managed to escape. Smith retaliated by raiding several Paspahegh villages, killing six or seven people in the process. Ironically, the Paspaheghs did not direct their resentment at Smith because they thought Captain Winn did the raiding;[147] hostile though that chiefdom was, they still did not yet hate all Englishmen.

Later that spring, Smith revived a Chickahominy prisoner, incarcerated for stealing tools, who had been nearly asphyxiated by smoke in his cell. As a token of goodwill, Smith released the man and his brother, who had wit-nessed the "cure," with instructions to tell their people that the English could work miracles.[148] This phenomenon and "other such pretty acci-dents" made the Indians request a truce, in the English view; in reality, the planting season had come and the English had shown too much willingness to raid Indian habitations.[149] In 1623 the Powhatans would formally pro-pose a truce for the planting of corn;[150] their thinking in 1609 may not have been much different.

The English agreed to the truce (or subjection of "savages" as they saw it) and were soon glad that they had. In late spring the food taken from Werowocomoco, Pamunkey, Youghtanund, and Mattaponi in January ran low, and the water became bad in the James River. But now many English-men could be billeted in Indian towns, where they lived at the native people's expense and learned something of Powhatan foraging practices.[151] Some English soldiers were among the Indians without leave; these were returned to the fort.

The Quiyoughcohannocks became especially friendly that spring of 1609. One of their *weroances*[152] sent guides with an English expedition to Chowanoc to seek "lost colonists," and he also acted receptive to English evangelistic efforts. The summer was apparently a dry one; this *weroance* frequently sent presents to Smith, asking him to pray "for raine, or his corne would perish, for his Gods were angrie all the time."[153]

A poor harvest both in summer and in fall threatened the Powhatans and the English alike with hunger, though the Indians would suffer less. The Third Relief Supply from England was long overdue. On July 10, Samuel Argall arrived in the Chesapeake region to fish for sturgeon; before he de-parted for England, he gave the colonists what he could and told them of the fleet under Lord de la Warr that had left England in May.[154] In Septem-ber the colonists received word of the scattering of de la Warr's fleet by a hurricane; seven of the fleet's nine ships limped up the James, bringing a small part of the fleet's provisions and many people, including some con-tentious enemies of John Smith as captains.[155] This arrival only made the plight of the colony more desperate. Smith decided to establish English settlements outside Jamestown and disperse the people somewhat. In Indian eyes, these attempts ended the truce.

One band of Englishmen, under Captain John Martin, went to settle in Nansemond territory. No reason was recorded for the choice,[156] but the decision was a poor one on the whole. English past dealings with that chiefdom had been almost as heavy-handed as those with the Paspaheghs, in contrast to their recently friendly contacts with the Warraskoyacks and Quiyoughcohannocks. The Nansemond territory was also farther away than the two latter chiefdoms, which meant that although the settlers could buy corn from sources different from those of the Jamestown inhabitants (an advantage), military assistance from Jamestown was farther away in case of trouble (a serious liability).

Trouble appeared immediately.[157] Two English messengers sent to negotiate for an inhabited island disappeared, so Martin had half his men occupy the island by force. When the messengers were found to have been killed, Martin assumed that the murders had preceded the occupation and ordered the Indian habitations and the temple on the island destroyed. Meanwhile, some Nansemonds had visited Martin on his boat, quarreled with him, and been captured. One captive was the son of the primary weroance of the chiefdom. Another man was accidentally shot during his internment, after which he managed to escape. The Nansemonds then attacked the would-be settlers repeatedly, and when it was found that even reinforcements from Jamestown were of no use, Martin's men straggled home. Some of them did not get there: several were later found dead in Nansemond territory with their mouths stuffed full of bread—an obvious Indian gesture of contempt—while others went to Kecoughtan for refuge and were ambushed.

The other settlement attempt fared no better.[158] This time the choice of place was even worse: the Powhatan town's territory, always a touchy frontier area for the Indians and the *mamanatowick*'s home ground to boot. A large force of Englishmen under Francis West went to the falls of the James and built a fort there, three miles from Parahunt's capital town. Predictably, Parahunt's men began raiding the fort. Smith came up from Jamestown to investigate, and now English factionalism made things worse. Smith "bought" Powhatan town from Parahunt in exchange for copper, "protection" from the Monacans, and the boy Henry Spelman.[159] But the settlers did not want to move to the Indian town and did not stay in it for long. After Smith left again, Parahunt's people resumed their raiding. Even the Arrohatecks, so friendly to the colonists two years before, proved hostile, exterminating a boatful of visiting settlers. At length West's people gave up and returned to Jamestown.

On his way back from Powhatan town, Smith was seriously burned in a powder explosion, and on his return to Jamestown he was deposed as president by a coalition of his enemies. Suffering both pain and defeat, he sailed for England on October 4, 1609, never to return. He left no messages for Indian girls. When Pocahontas came to the fort again and asked after him, the colonists told her he was dead, either to soften the blow of her friend's leaving without a word or because they did not expect him to survive his burns. Seven years later, when she discovered that he was still alive, she was furious (see chapter 3). She may have continued visiting Jamestown for a time,[160] but the next year she was married to "a pryvate Captayne called *Kocoum*," about whom nothing else is known.[161]

The English had lost about one hundred men in their settlement attempts,[162] but there were still many more people in the colony than could be fed that winter of 1609–1610. They had few boats to go trading in, thanks to losing some in skirmishes and sending some to England for help. Most Indians would not trade with them in any case. When Captain Ratliffe was invited to Orapax to trade in November, he was ambushed, and he and most of his men were killed.[163] In late October the English had managed to establish a fort at Old Point Comfort, which they named Fort Algernon;[164] that move cannot have been palatable to the Kecoughtans, half a mile away, nor to Powhatan, so the ambush of Ratliffe may have been a form of retaliation.

Thomas Savage and Henry Spelman, living with Powhatan all this time, now sensed a new hostility in him toward themselves. Savage made an excuse to return to Jamestown,[165] while Spelman narrowly escaped the *mamanatowick*'s anger when he left Orapax to go and live with Iopassus, the *weroance* of Passapatanzy, a satellite town of Patawomeck.[166] Patawomeck friendship for Englishmen was soon endangered, however, because Francis West, fresh from his failure at the falls of the James, was sent there by the Jamestown leadership to buy corn. He managed to buy a small amount, but there was also a quarrel in which he bullied the Indians and beheaded two of them. West and his thirty-six men then compounded their disservice to the colony by absconding for England, leaving the colony with one less boat.[167]

It was hard to blame West for leaving while he could,[168] for as the winter continued many other colonists would have abandoned Virginia had they been able.[169] They had so few boats that trading expeditions were out of the question, even if they could have extorted corn from any of the natives. They sold all their tools to neighboring Indians, who then would not give them credit. Then when they tried to leave the fort to hunt or forage or even to seek refuge in the Indian towns, they were ambushed. After the food in Jamestown ran out, the colonists ate "doggs Catts Ratts and myce" and finally each other.[170] By May 1610 only 100 out of some 220[171] English people remained alive in Virginia, sixty of them in Jamestown. Powhatan had nearly succeeded in starving the English out, thus eliminating them without the trouble of organizing a mass attack.

On May 21, 1610, two English ships under Sir Thomas Gates and Sir

George Sommers arrived in Virginia with new colonists and provisions. It is ironic that the instructions given Gates stated plainly that the Indians of the region were to be Christianized and absorbed into the new colony.[172] Intercultural relations as they stood made it impossible to achieve that goal either quickly or peacefully. Seeing the state of the people at Jamestown, Gates decided to evacuate the colony altogether. The Jamestown colonists were jubilant; only with difficulty could Gates prevent them from burning down the fort on the day they left.[173] It looked as though Powhatan had won.

On the second day under sail, the evacuating colony met an advance ship of the missing remainder of Lord de la Warr's fleet. Three hundred people and provisions for all were on the way. So Jamestown was reoccupied the day after it was abandoned. On the following day Lord de la Warr arrived and took the whole enterprise in hand.

The tide had turned, though Powhatan did not realize it. Seeing the English still there and with reinforcements, Powhatan merely had his bowmen resume harrassing the fort and ambushing stray Englishmen.[174] That policy would work even less well against a tougher English governor.

De la Warr now took the offensive. On July 9 he sent Gates to revenge the Kecoughtan killing of the would-be Nansemond settlers the year before. Gates lured the Kecoughtans out of their town by having a tambourine player play and dance, after which he and his men attacked them. Those Kecoughtans still able to run fled the town, which now became English property.[175]

De la Warr then sent a message to Powhatan, on July 15, offering him either peace or war; the peace option required the return of English captives and stolen tools. De la Warr reminded Powhatan of his "coronation" two years earlier, saying that as a subject of King James his cooperation was expected.[176] Not surprisingly, the paramount chief hurled back "prowde and disdayneful Answers."[177] He said that the English should either confine their activities to their fort or get out of Virginia. And if de la Warr wanted to communicate with him again, he could send along a coach and three horses, which the Indians who had been to England had told him was the conveyance of great lords there.[178]

This answer outraged de la Warr,[179] himself one of those lords,[180] who thought of Powhatan as only a "savage." He therefore had the hand of a captured Paspahegh cut off and sent the mutilated man to Powhatan with an ultimatum; if English captives and arms were not returned, the English would burn all the neighboring Indian towns. The *mamanatowick* did not reply. If his people had already tortured to death the English captives they held, as was the norm in Powhatan warfare, then no reply would have been of use for long anyway.

De la Warr took the silence for the noncooperation it was and went into action on August 9, 1610. He sent George Percy and seventy men with a reluctant Indian guide[181] to the capital town of Paspahegh. There, in a chiefdom that had only forty fighting men, they put "some fifteen or six-tene to the Sworde" [182] and shot some "fiftie or threescore," [183] after which they fired the town and cut down all the growing corn they could find. A wife of Wowinchopunck and her children were captured and taken along when the English left. Back aboard their boat, the English decided to kill the children, which was done by throwing them overboard and shooting them in the water. Percy managed to keep the woman alive in spite of op-position, but back in Jamestown, de la Warr wanted her killed by burning. Percy managed to persuade the governor to give her the quicker death of being taken into the woods and put to the sword. [184]

The Paspaheghs never recovered from the raid. Wowinchopunck and the other survivors abandoned their own permanently, [185] and after Wowincho-punck's death in a skirmish the next February, [186] the remnants of his people appear to have merged with other chiefdoms.

The raid had its effect upon Powhatan and upon all his people as well. The killing of Paspahegh women and children, including "royal" ones, went directly against the rules of Indian warfare; Powhatan chiefdoms rarely did such a thing to others, and those who did it to them were consid-ered beyond the pale. Indian raids now occurred without letup. No more diplomatic messages were sent or received by either side. The English, in-tent upon a successful expansion of their territory, knew they were consis-tently opposed by all the Indians, but they only dimly realized [187] that the Powhatans now considered themselves to be fully at war. The First Anglo-Powhatan War had begun. [188]

CHAPTER 3

Powhatan's Last, Ineffectual Years

FROM THE SUMMER of 1610 until Powhatan's death in April 1618, the English colony not only held its own but expanded, regardless of Indian opposition. Some compensation may have been paid to the Arrohatecks, the Appamattucks (who were definitely hostile), the Quiyoughcohannocks, and the Weyanocks, in whose territories new settlements, called "hundreds," were made between 1610 and 1617. But no record of such payment was made, the transactions (if they existed) having been informal ones.[1]

Much of the English colony's success in these years was due to two factors: better support from the Virginia Company and, toward the end of the period, the first growing of tobacco as a cash crop. The first factor derived from the company's belated realization that it would have to feed its colonists if they were to survive, and that it had to recruit people with the farming skills needed to found a viable enterprise. However, the second factor, tobacco growing, negatively affected the carrying out of the first. Tobacco soon attracted Englishmen wanting to farm in Virginia, but nearly all were bent on making their fortunes and returning home rich. In 1619 the Virginia Company would formally begin allotting land to individual Englishmen, and then the "boom" was really on (see chapter 4).

Powhatan leadership remained traditionalist and unimaginative in dealing with the persistent English. The paramount chief had reached an old age, in which he was "delighted in security, and pleasure,"[2] a poor mental condition for a ruler with a new set of enemies. Therefore, his warriors merely continued to raid English settlements on a small scale. No massive strike was organized, although mass military movements were part of the Powhatan tradition. There is good evidence that the *mamanatowick* soon began to be politically superceded by his brother Opechancanough, although that informal change did not produce effective action against the English.

The tribes under Powhatan continued to be a core-and-fringe group, still primarily political rather than ethnic. The core and the fringe both expanded during these years in opposition to the English. The loyalist core tribes were joined in 1616 by the Chickahominies, who no longer wanted to oppose the English alone. It was Opechancanough who personally gathered them in (see below). The more distant fringe tribes on the Potomac River and the Eastern Shore remained neutral as long as possible.[3] By 1611 they were joined by a new western fringe group (a strictly military alliance): the formerly enemy Monacans,[4] who never played a major part in English-Indian politics.

In the fall of 1610, Samuel Argall went to trade with the Patawomecks and other neighboring tribes. The Patawomecks willingly sold him corn, but being neutral rather than "friendly," they released Henry Spelman to Argall only after he heard of the boy's presence from the Nacotchtanks upriver and specifically asked for him.[5] Meanwhile, Lord de la Warr established himself and a company of men at the falls of the James, where they stayed all winter in spite of attacks both military and magical[6] from their Indian neighbors. (The magical attack was a "spell" that completely disoriented the English soldiers for several minutes.) Shortly before, an English party had landed at Appamattuck and been ambushed during a feast; only one man escaped alive.[7]

The English did not grapple with starvation in the winter of 1610–1611, as they had in all the previous winters. Instead they survived comfortably under the firm hand of de la Warr and girded themselves for further expansion. On February 9, 1611, they scored a victory against Powhatan's forces when they managed to kill Wowinchopunck, ruler of Paspahegh and a great warrior, in a skirmish.[8] His followers revenged his death by killing several Englishmen, whom they enticed out of their blockhouse soon after Wowinchopunck's death,[9] but the loss to Powhatan's forces must have been keenly felt.

Lord de la Warr left Virginia because of ill health in March; in May his replacement, Sir Thomas Dale, brought colonists, cattle, and food and kept the colony tightly organized. Under Dale's leadership, the colonists managed for the first time to bring in "an indifferent crop of good Corne."[10] He set Indian men (presumably prisoners) to work[11] and ruled that no Englishman was to harm an Indian except on raids sanctioned by the colony.[12]

In the summer of 1611, Dale explored the Indian territories bordering the James, looking for places to found settlements. The people of Nansemond River attacked him,[13] but he succeeded in burning their houses and cutting down their growing corn. Finally Dale decided upon a place in Arrohateck territory, and when Sir Thomas Gates arrived in August with another fleet and replaced him as governor, Dale and 350 Englishmen went upriver and established their fort, called Henrico. They remained there in spite of factionalism among themselves and raids led by an outstanding warrior named Nemattanew, whose garish feathered battle dress led them to call him "Jack of the Feather."[14] Several malcontents deserted and joined the Indians; when they were recaptured, Dale executed them in various cruel ways as an object lesson to others.[15] Back at Jamestown, some Indian men came with food to trade and, suspecting them to be spies, Gates had them caught and executed.[16] One of the few Indians the English considered a friend died in the fort that year: Kemps had remained with the English on and off since 1608, and that summer or fall he died of scurvy,[17] a malady he would not have had if he had kept to the Indian diet.

Around Christmas of 1611 the English attacked and took Opossuno-quonuke's town in Appamattuck territory,[18] where Englishmen had been ambushed the year before. There, at the mouth of the Appomattox River, they established a settlement called Bermuda Hundred, which they fortified by building a two-mile palisade around the back of their fields,[19] while the Appamattucks withdrew upriver. In 1612 and the first part of 1613, the English consolidated their holdings and received more supplies and colonists, while Powhatan's people merely continued their raids. Only the Chiskiacks, two lesser rulers in Quiyoughcohannock,[20] and the more distant Patawomecks and Eastern Shore groups were perceived as friendly by the English at the time.[21]

Powhatan's inactivity in the face of English violence toward his James River chiefdoms led Opechancanough to become increasingly active in politicking: by the spring of 1614 the English heard that he had "already the commaund of all the people."[22] But then the raids by Powhatan's subjects were brought to an end with the capture of Pocahontas in April 1613, a capture accomplished with the grudging aid of the Patawomeck chiefdom in Powhatan's fringe area.

Argall had concluded a "peace" in December 1612 and bought a large amount of corn from Iopassus,[23] the lesser *weroance* of Patawomeck who had previously sheltered Henry Spelman. After taking the corn back to Jamestown, Argall returned to the Potomac region and explored far upriver.[24] Meanwhile, Pocahontas arrived at the capital town in Patawomeck "to exchange some of her fathers commodities for theirs" and to visit friends,[25] making a stay of about three months. Early in April Argall heard where she was and hastened to Patawomeck, intending to seize her as a hostage to exchange for English prisoners held by Powhatan.[26] He located Iopassus and propositioned him: if the Patawomecks assisted in the capture and incurred the wrath of Powhatan, the English would come to their aid; if, on the other hand, the Patawomecks did not lend their aid to the English in this matter, the "peace" between them was over. Being a lesser *weroance,* Iopassus had to take the matter to his brother, the "great King of Patowomeck," who after a long session with his council concluded that friendship with the English was worth preserving. Accordingly, Iopassus betrayed his brother's guest.[27]

Coached by her husband, a wife of Iopassus insisted on seeing Argall's ship, and Pocahontas was persuaded to bear her company in the absence of serving women. The party spent the night aboard, with Pocahontas in separate and privileged quarters in the gun room. The next morning she was informed that although the others would be permitted to leave, she would not. Since the alternative was to create an undignified scene,[28] such as leaping overboard and swimming ashore, she remained with the English, "exceeding pensiue, and discontented."[29]

Argall sent Powhatan a message from Patawomeck, relating his daughter's capture and stating the terms of ransom, which Powhatan promptly offered to meet.[30] Argall then took Pocahontas to Jamestown, whither Powhatan sent English men and tools in partial payment of the ransom.[31] With those items came a message that a large payment in corn would be made when the woman was returned and Powhatan would be a friend of the English ever after. The English retorted that they would return her when all their missing arms were returned, and in the meantime Powhatan could be a friend or an enemy, just as he liked. Negotiations stalled at that point, and Indian raiding of English settlements resumed. Some of the Englishmen who had been returned soon went back to Powhatan of their own volition, indicating that they found the Indian way of life congenial.[32] Pocahontas therefore remained at Jamestown for nearly a year. During her captivity she was instructed in English manners and religion by several men, one of whom was a twenty-eight-year-old widower named John Rolfe.

The English finally forced the issue in March 1614, when Dale took Pocahontas and a large force of Englishmen up the York and Pamunkey rivers to confront Powhatan.[33] The English found themselves taunted as they went by people on the river banks, until at what is now West Point[34] a shower of arrows exhausted their patience. The English went ashore and sacked the town. The next day, parleying out in Pamunkey River, the Indians agreed to return English arms the day after but did not keep their appointment. Finally, the English went directly to Powhatan's new capital town, Matchcot,[35] and landed. A large force of warriors threatened them but did no actual harm, and a message was dispatched to Powhatan, waiting in his town some distance from the shore. Meanwhile, "two of *Powhatans* sonnes" asked to see "their sister" (actually their half-sister; see Prologue). Delighted to find her looking healthy, they promised to persuade their father to make peace with the English. Two Englishmen, one of whom was Rolfe, were then sent to speak directly with Powhatan but managed only to see Opechancanough. The latter promised to work for peace and the men returned to their boat.

While Rolfe and his companion were ashore, Ralph Hamor gave Dale a letter[36] from Rolfe in which he confessed his love for Pocahontas and his desire to marry her. Knowing that Pocahontas returned his feelings and that such a marriage would seal a peace, Dale approved the match and agreed to return to Jamestown, it being time for the spring planting. Powhatan heard about the match from his two sons, in whom Pocahontas had confided, and he also gave his consent. (There is no record of his having been allowed to see his daughter before her marriage.) "Some ten daies" later he sent "an olde vncle of hirs, named Opachisco"[37] and "two of his sonnes"[38] to witness the Rolfe marriage, which took place at Jamestown "about the fift [sic] of Aprill"[39] of 1614. Before the wedding, Pocahontas was baptized into the Church of England,[40] taking the name Rebecca.[41] This marriage of 1614 was one of only three Powhatan-English recorded in Virginia in the sevententh century; all other such liaisons remained just that.[42]

The war was now officially over.[43] The peace between the English and Powhatan's paramount chiefdom left the Chickahominies at risk, and they hastened to make their own peace with the English before June 18.[44] They invited Dale, now governor of the colony, to meet with their eight councillors, an invitation that Dale accepted, although in the end he sent Argall ashore to do the negotiating.[45] The terms of the resulting formal treaty[46] were as follows: the Chickahominies would become subjects of King James, return any runaway men or livestock to the English colony, supply armed men to fight the Spanish if necessary, and pay the English two bushels of corn per bowman annually in exchange for iron hatchets. The eight councillors were to be given treaty presents annually, consisting of "a red coat, or liuery from our King" and "the picture of his Maiesty, ingrauen in Copper, with a chaine of Copper to hang it about [their] neck[s]." It is doubtful, however, that the fiercely independent Chickahominies meant to remain "subjects" of King James for long.

Having sealed an alliance with Powhatan through Pocahontas's marriage, the English sought to strengthen it further with a second marriage. Dale therefore sent Ralph Hamor to ask on his behalf for the hand of another favorite daughter of Powhatan.[47] That Dale was about forty and already married,[48] while the girl was only eleven and also married,[49] was considered immaterial by the English. Powhatan had the power to annul Indian marriages, which were civil unions anyway,[50] and Dale could give the young "wife" to one of his henchmen in the approved Indian fashion. But Powhatan would not cooperate. He was glad that the Rolfes were happy together, but it would be too much to lose a second favorite to the English, whose settlements he would not enter.[51] The English would have to be content with one daughter of his and his assurances that he would never commit more aggressions against them, "not though I should haue iust occasion offered, for I am now olde, and would gladly end my daies in peace, so as if the English offer me iniury, my country is large enough, I will remoue my selfe farther from you."

During the visit, Powhatan showed Hamor a beautiful "Table book" that had been given him, probably by Christopher Newport, and at one meal he served Hamor some sack from a bottle Newport had given him "sixe or seauen yeeres since."[52] But in spite of his assurances to Hamor that he was trustworthy, Powhatan objected loudly to having to return an

Englishman[53] who was now found to be living with him: he had told the colonists that the man was dead, but here the man was, eager to return to Jamestown. Relations between Powhatan and Hamor nearly broke down over the matter. Powhatan finally released the man, but asked now that Dale send him copper, a shaving knife, an iron wedge, a very large grinding stone, two bone combs, a hundred fishhooks or a fishing seine, and a dog and a cat.[54] After promising to relay the request, Hamor returned to Jamestown—not with a youthful bride but with a loincloth-clad Englishman.

This disconcerting meeting was the last recorded instance of Powhatan seeing an Englishman. There is no record of the Rolfes going to see him, though they probably did; to visit kinsmen was expected among the English, as among the Powhatans.

The years following Pocahontas's marriage were the golden age of Powhatan-English relations, in English eyes. Englishmen hired Indian men to hunt for them and trained them to use English firearms; the shooting practice went on not only at forts such as Jamestown and Kecoughtan but also at Indian towns on Pamunkey River.[55] One of the Indians so trained was the warrior captain Nemattanew, or Jack of the Feather. Some Indian men became very proficient shots.[56] Some Powhatan men acquired firearms by ambushing Englishmen who ventured away from the settlements;[57] the peace was imperfect, even in a "golden age." The English who stayed within their settlements were not molested. Ironically, it was in this period that the English stumbled onto tobacco as a cash crop when Rolfe introduced Orinoco tobacco to the colony. Tobacco farming would soon ruin any hopes of true coexistence between the two peoples.[58]

In 1615 the peace was probably aided by a poor harvest in Virginia, after which the English could receive supplies from home while the Powhatans actually had to buy food from the English. Rolfe wrote in 1616[59] that Indians even sold "their skins from their shoulders, which is their best garments, to buy corne—yea, some of their pettie kings have this last yeare borrowed four or five hundred bushells of wheate, for payment whereof, this harvest they have mortgaged their whole countries . . ." The debts were repaid to the English "at theyr haruest with graat [sic] aduantidge."[60] It may have been dissatisfaction over the prices they got from their "allies" that made the Chickahominies break the peace with the English the next year, when the English became hungry and applied to them for "tribute" in corn.[61]

Dale was in England with Pocahontas's party at the time (see below), so the colony's deputy governor, George Yeardley, sent to the Chickahominies to call in the corn they owed him according to the treaty of 1614. He got back an insolent negative. He then took a hundred armed men and Henry Spelman as interpreter up the Chickahominy River, where the people of one town after another told him that they owed him nothing because their agreement was with Dale. When Yeardley spurned this legalism, the people dared him to come ashore, which he did at Oraniock.[62] The English and the men of at least one town then marched upriver, each daring the other to start something, until they reached a newly harvested cornfield.[63] Yeardley wrangled further with the Chickahominies and then ordered his men to fire into them, which started a scuffle in which some Indians were killed, some were wounded, and some (including two tribal councillors) were taken prisoner. The English then started back downriver, assuming they had subdued the tribe. They were disillusioned, however, when at Oraniock they met Opechancanough and heard that he had "patched up" their difficulty for them. The people of Oraniock, at least, were now calling him "king" and paying him tribute, and he said that he would see that they remained peaceful. The English had to put on an agreeable face and return to Jamestown. Some of them wondered afterward whether Powhatan and Opechancanough had not started it all by encouraging the Chickahominies to balk.[64]

Thus, in the space of a few days the Chickahominies had, in their own view, broken their alliance with the English and joined Powhatan's organization to oppose the English. There is no record of their having either accepted a *weroance* or altered their political system, but after 1616 they appear to have become an integral part of Powhatan's paramount chiefdom.

Powhatan's reaction to his second-younger brother's coup was probably apprehension: rumors were already circulating about tension between the two. Before Dale left for England with Pocahontas and her retinue in the spring of 1616, the English had heard that "*Powhatan* was gone Southwards when our men came last thence; some thought for feare of Opochancanough [*sic*] his yonger brother, a man very gracious, both with the people and the English, jealous lest He and the English should conspire against him, thinking that hee will not retourne; but others thinke he will returne again."[65] Nevertheless, Powhatan appears to have remained in nominal control, with his next-younger brother, Opitchapam, his nominal successor.[66] Opechancanough still did not have the title—only the power.

Dale and his passengers arrived in England in June 1616. With Pocahontas were her husband, her son,[67] ten or twelve Indian people of various ages,[68] and Uttamatomakkin, a priestly advisor to her father.[69] This advisor had been instructed to find John Smith (whom Powhatan believed to be still alive), to see the English king, to see the English god, and to count the number of "both men and trees"[70] in England. Unfortunately for him, Powhatan record keeping consisted of notched sticks. Dale's ship landed in Plymouth and the party crossed southern England—the most heavily populated part of the country—to reach London; Uttamatomakkin soon had to give up his enumeration. In London, he found Smith but failed to see the English god, and he was completely unimpressed by the unstately James I,[71] who stingily gave him no present.[72] Uttamatomakkin also endured at least one long session with the Reverend Samuel Purchas and other clergymen, whose militant evangelism, coupled with the general self-righteousness he perceived in Londoners, eventually made him violently anti-English.[73]

Pocahontas was put on display by the Virginia Company of London and introduced into society, presumably by Lady Elizabeth Dale and others. Ninety years later Robert Beverley wrote that Lady de la Warr also took Pocahontas under her wing.[74] Moving in London society was expensive, and since the Rolfes were not a wealthy family, the Virginia Company had to help support Pocahontas.[75] She cannot have been unaware that she was being used as propaganda for the Virginia Company; the English then and later saw her as a "right-thinking savage" who had converted to the "right" religion and way of life. The evidence is that she enjoyed her time in London, regardless of how she was used by the Company. She was feted by the bishop of London "beyond what I have seene in his great hospitalitie afforded to other Ladies."[76] She was introduced to English royalty, and she made such a dignified impression that she and Uttamatomakkin were invited to the King's Twelfth Night masque and "well placed" (i.e., given a place of honor) at it.[77] Not all Londoners regarded Pocahontas highly, though: John Chamberlain, who gives us several of the rare surviving glimpses of Pocahontas's stay, usually referred to her as "the Virginian woman,"[78] and he made it plain to his friend Dudley Carleton that he thought her neither lovely nor a lady.[79] But Pocahontas so enjoyed the people she met that the critical Chamberlain recorded a rumor that "she is on her return [to Virginia] (though sore against her will) yf the wind wold come about to send them away."[80]

The Rolfes were delayed in leaving England, and Pocahontas spent the last part of her sojourn in the Middlesex village (now the London suburb) of Brentford. No contemporary writer mentioned why she was taken to the country. It was William Stith who wrote in 1747 that the city smoke (which at that time was mainly wood smoke) disagreed with her.[81] That is doubtful, since she had grown up in a longhouse full of wood smoke; it is more likely that she had contracted some pulmonary disease from contact with Englishmen. It was while she was in Brentford, delayed in quitting England, that John Smith finally "found time" to visit her.[82] Unfortunately, the only account we have of the meeting is Smith's own.

Pocahontas had undoubtedly heard of Smith's being alive and in London from friends in the Virginia Company and from Uttamatomakkin after his meeting with Smith. Her fury at having been "lied to" in Virginia and avoided by him in England burst out when Smith made his sudden, belated appearance: "without any word, she turned about, obscured her face, as not seeming well contented." Smith made an understatement there. Pocahontas was so upset that she had to be left alone for "two or three houres," rather a long time. Smith, who seldom comprehended other people's negative reactions to him, was chagrined. He wrote later that he had wondered at the time if Pocahontas could in fact speak English with him; when she was ready to face him again he was merely relieved that the interview could begin. The interview did not go well, however. Before long Pocahontas was taunting him with what she had been told about him in 1609 and telling him that "your Countriemen will lie much." Smith disingenuously ends his account there; she probably had him shown the door soon afterward.

In March 1617 the Rolfes finally left England, but when the ship reached Gravesend, Pocahontas had to be taken ashore because she was dying.[83] No writer of that time mentions the cause of her death; instead, her English contemporaries were impressed by the Christian way in which she met her end.[84] She was buried on March 21 in Gravesend Church, and her grave was later destroyed in a rebuilding of that church.[85] Her son was not able to leave England, either. Young Thomas was so sick[86] that by the time the ship reached Plymouth, he had to be left ashore in the care of an uncle.[87] He was reared entirely as an Englishman. Since he sailed to Virginia only in 1635,[88] thirteen years after John Rolfe's death,[89] he never saw his father again.

John Rolfe and Samuel Argall arrived back at Jamestown in May 1617, appalled by what they saw. The "golden age" had emptied the colonists' heads of all except greed: the palisade and buildings of Jamestown were in a ruinous state and the very streets were planted with tobacco. Indians moved freely about, owned firearms, and took part in English military maneuvers.[90] They supplied the colonists with food and even with drinking water, for the avid planters of Jamestown had allowed "the Well of fresh water [to become] spoiled."[91] Many colonists had died of the local microorganisms, to which they had no immunity, and fewer than half of the survivors were fit for agricultural work.[92]

Argall took charge of the fort, and the "golden age" of English-Powhatan relations, with its air of camaraderie, came abruptly to an end. Indian men were no longer to be traded with privately or taught to use firearms.[93] Simultaneously, Uttamatomakkin, who had returned from England with Rolfe and Argall, went straight to Opechancanough in Powhatan's absence[94] and made a report that was so vitriolic (no details survive) that the English exerted themselves to try to discredit him.[95]

As summer progressed, an epidemic hit Virginia. Argall wrote to England of "a great mortality among us, far greater among the Indians and a morrain [murrain, or plague] amongst the deer."[96] The disease among the people is impossible to identify, but because of the greater Indian mortality its origin would seem to be European. The summer was also a bad one for crops; the Indians were "so poor [they] cant [sic] pay their debts & tribute."[97] Everyone was in danger of going hungry that fall and winter. The next year was no better; English and Indian crops alike were parched with drought and battered by hail, and the relief ship from England was delayed by bad weather until August.[98]

   Powhatan did not live to see the second bad summer. He heard about his daughter's death, sorrowed over it, and took comfort that her son still survived. He and Opechancanough both expressed a wish to see young Thomas Rolfe some day,[99] but only Opechancanough lived long enough for the visit to take place.[100] Sometime in April 1618, Powhatan died, of unrecorded causes, and the paramount chiefdom he had built passed into the hands of others.

CHAPTER 4

Opechancanough's Regime

POWHATAN WAS officially succeeded as paramount chief by his next younger brother, Opitchapam. However, because Opitchapam was "decrepit and lame"[1] and lacked a magnetic personality, the real ruler was—or continued to be—Opechancanough. English records about Indian leadership for the next six years mention Opechancanough's name as often as Opitchapam's.

The ethnic groups over which Opechancanough ruled were much the same as those of Powhatan's heyday. The core, still more political than ethnic due to the newness of the paramount chief's organization, consisted of chiefdoms in the James, York, and possibly Rappahannock river drainages, plus the newly added Chickahominies. The fringe was made up of peoples on the Eastern Shore, the southern bank of the Potomac, and possibly still the Monacans west of the fall line. Before long the English would divest the "empire" of much of that geographically based fringe while simultaneously creating a new, culturally based and genuinely ethnic fringe consisting of Anglicized Indians.

When Opitchapam became paramount chief, Powhatan culture had changed very little; English culture still had few attractions for Indians. The traditional social organization and religion of the Powhatans seems to have been untouched by eleven years of contact with evangelistic aliens. What the Indian leadership seems to have felt instead was an economic and military threat.

The English now occupied large expanses of James River frontage from the fall line down, especially on the north bank. More land along the waterfront was taken in succeeding years. In 1619 alone more than a dozen new plantations, or "hundreds," were established. By 1622 all of the banks of the James were claimed by Englishmen, except for the south bank from the Nansemond River down.[2] All of the James River tribes except the Nansemonds had lost their riverfront property. The Accomacs had given up a few parcels on the Eastern Shore as well, though the giving up was voluntary and the English settlers few enough that relations remained genuinely peaceful.

This taking of James River waterfront land and the mouths of tributary creeks pushed the owner tribes back into the interior. The land taken was the Indians' prime farmland, as J. Frederick Fausz has pointed out.[3] It was also the link between two major elements of Powhatan subsistence: the hunting and foraging territories inland and the food- and reed-gathering areas on the rivers. In other words, the James River chiefdoms now found their two nonhorticultural subsistence areas separated not by their own villages but by settlements of foreigners, who did not always trust Indians passing back and forth. In times of unrest, the rivers were all but inaccessible to their former owners. Meanwhile, farming was carried out away from the rivers, but the soils were generally less fertile and the yields probably lower. Therefore, times were somewhat harder for the Powhatans of the James River basin; when the English leadership became more security conscious, in 1617, times became harder still. And every Indian adult could remember the time before 1607, when things were different.

Powhatan people had become partially dependent upon the English for trade goods, judging by English references to their "debts and tribute." (The tribute was probably nothing more than English expectations of surplus corn raised by the Indians.) This would have been particularly true of the groups living nearest the English settlements. The "debts" occurred even during a pair of bad years, 1617 and 1618, which does indicate some real dependence. The items the Indians bought were undoubtedly iron tools—hatchets, knives, hoes, shovels—which could be instantly incorporated into Indian culture with few social repercussions, at least until payment became difficult. The Powhatans were still far from dependent upon English firearms, as their marksmanship in 1622 would show, but they wanted guns whenever they could get them. They also still wanted glass beads and trade cloth, which the English took care to ration to prevent devaluation (see below). Some younger Indians, such as the youth erroneously called "Chanco," went to work for Englishmen, very likely to earn money for the tools they wanted. It was some of these people who began to become Anglicized, as a result of friendly firsthand experience with English families. And it was these somewhat Anglicized people who in 1622 were torn between the Powhatans and the English. Apparently, their numbers were not large, but "Chanco" was not alone (see below).

The English efforts to missionize the Powhatans after 1619 and the epidemics that killed many people in 1617 and 1619 must have sorely irritated Indians whose lives had been made poorer. Fausz has postulated that English settlement had badly beaten down the Powhatans and that the missionizing was the last straw. He further asserts that by the early 1620s a "nativist revitalization movement" had risen up to combat the evangelism, a movement culminating in the great attack of 1622.[4] He sees this Indian religious movement as more important in explaining the events of 1622 than any other factor, even the taking of Indian land.[5]

I disagree. First, there is no evidence in the surviving documents that a "revitalization movement" occurred among the Powhatans in the 1620s or at any other time. Such movements occur in societies "structurally riven by internal strain," usually after decades of foreign contact and military defeats have made large numbers of the people cease to believe in their old way of life.[6] Before the formation of such movements, there must first usually be massive social disorganization and/or economic breakdown, usually stemming from complete conquest by aliens. There must be a real crisis: "Anomie and disillusionment become widespread as the culture is perceived to be disorganized and inadequate; crime, illness, and individualistic asocial responses increase sharply in frequency."[7] There is no evidence of such a crisis in the Powhatan villages in the James and York river basins before 1622. They were a bit poorer and they were worried and angry, but that is all. The Sioux of 1890 were ripe for the Ghost Dance religion, for the buffalo that were the basis of their economy were gone. The Iroquois of 1799 were ripe for the Handsome Lake religion, for much of their land was taken away from them after the American Revolution. The Powhatans of 1620 were nowhere near ready for such a movement. One must look to the 1680s for evidence of readiness among them (see chapter 6), and there are no documents indicating that a religious movement occurred then, either.

On the other hand, land—literally living space—is basic to human societies, and people who live close to the land, as the Powhatans did, are acutely aware of events that alter their access to it. Add to this the fact that Englishmen who were successful farmers had little reason to tolerate Indians in their vicinity, except as laborers. As Francis Jennings has pointed out, "When the Indian was dispossessed of his land, he lost all hope of finding any niche in the society called civilized, except that of servant or slave."[8] Indians who produced useful foodstuffs or furs might remain independent of the burgeoning population of new landowners, but when their usefulness ended, their fate was the same as that of other Indians.[9] By 1620 the Virginia English no longer needed Indian corn; instead, they wanted more and more land for growing tobacco. Their evangelization efforts showed that they would not tolerate people of a different culture within their settlements. The handwriting was on the wall for the Powhatans, and they responded accordingly. They did so with the full approbation of their priests, as was traditional. But we may not conclude that preparations for the attack were a full-fledged "revitalization movement."

The cool period in Powhatan-English relations, which Argall had initiated on his return from England in 1617, continued into the early days of the new Indian regime.[10] In response to that coolness, or because of bitterness about old wrongs, or simply because living with invaders is not easy, some Powhatan bowmen began attacking English people again. One incident involved some renegade Chickahominies, who killed some English traders and an English settler's children and then robbed their own people's temple before going into hiding.[11] Opechancanough received complaints from both the robbed Chickahominies and the Jamestown English. He promised to have the culprits caught and even promised their town to the English, but he never delivered on the promise. The fugitive Chickahominies may have been the "Westerly Runnagados" who by 1621 had tried unsuccessfully to unseat the *weroance* of Accomac, retired to a place called "Rickahake betwixt Cissapeack and Nansamund," and become reincorporated in Opitchapam's ("Itoyatin's") empire.[12] Another raid in 1618 was led by two men, one of whom was Nemattanew, or Jack of the Feather. Opechancanough brazenly sent the English guns captured in that raid to Jamestown to be repaired by the next year; the English kept them.[13] At the same time, Opechancanough appears to have been deceiving the English in political matters: he led Argall to believe that he wanted to give the empire to Pocahontas's son, Thomas Rolfe, whenever the child might come to Virginia.[14] The Virginia Company of London rightly refused to give credence to this notion when Argall communicated it.[15]

Ironically, at the same time the paramount chiefdom came under new leadership less sympathetic to the English, the English prepared to embark upon a program whose implementation soon angered the Indian people even more. Philanthropic idealism about "civilizing" the "savages" was on the rise in England after 1617.[16] The Virginia Company therefore began urging colonists to take Indian children into their families to rear.[17] The English surmised correctly that young Indians would be more amenable than older ones to religious and cultural evangelism. They also knew how useful Indian children could be as hostages. However, they were so accustomed to their own practice of sending their children to be reared by others "for their own good"[18] that they never comprehended Indian parents' refusal to give up their children. Instead, throughout the first half of the seventeenth century, the English in Virginia continued and even increased their requests for Indian children to be reared "properly," in what must have seemed a series of deadly insults to Indian parents. By 1622 the English realized that Indian parents also feared "hard usage" for children sent to settlers' families;[19] from the accounts of Englishborn servants,[20] we know that their fears were justified.

As idealism increased, so did the English population; now there were more Englishmen in Virginia to pressure Indian parents. In 1619 the Virginia Company set up the "headright system," whereby people able to transport themselves (and, later, others as well) were granted land,[21] on which they grew the new cash crop, tobacco. The combination of "available" land for private ownership and a cash crop to grow on it drew many English people to come to the colony, scatter out along the rivers on "their" land, and try to make their fortunes. They did so even though Virginia continued to be unhealthy. In the summer of 1619 another epidemic afflicted both English and Powhatans, with high mortality.[22] The death rate continued to be high for many summers after that.[23] Nevertheless, where there had been 400 English people in Virginia in April 1618, a year later there were almost 1,000.[24] By 1622 there were about 1,240.[25]

Tobacco raising was the draw, and there was a tremendous demand for laborers. A "boom" developed, with all the usual "easy come easy go" vices.[26] A colonial legislature, the House of Burgesses, was formed in 1619. By one of its new laws, Indians were welcome on English plantations if they did menial work and lodged in a segregated house at night.[27] Some Indian people accepted these degrading conditions, though not as many as the English hoped. When Indian parents would not give up their children, the English began direct pressure on Opechancanough to send whole Indian families to English settlements, where they would be given houses and ground to plant and made part of a larger English household.[28] However, in the face of English territorial expansion and the unpleasant case of an English captain trading with Indians using strong-arm tactics,[29] Opechancanough understandably sent no families.

Tensions rose between the Powhatans and the English. Henry Spelman found himself caught in the middle, as interpreters usually did since they spoke both languages and knew both sides well.[30] On August 4, 1619, the English colony censured Spelman for giving too frankly to Opechancanough his opinion about the new English governor, George Yeardley.[31] Spelman showed no remorse for his act, which led the burgesses to feel that his time with the Indians had made him "more of the Savage then [sic] of the Christian."[32]

Another man who was caught in the middle was Iopassus, though the English seem never to have realized it. He and his brother, the primary ruler of Patawomeck, were *weroances* in a fringe group susceptible to annexation by either side. In early September of 1619, Iopassus visited Jamestown, and on behalf of his brother he asked that two ships be sent immediately to trade for corn, of which the people had plenty after a good season. He also wanted to return home by an overland route with an English companion. The colony obligingly sent the ships and the companion, and when the Patawomecks inexplicably held the ships up for several weeks until the English crews took the corn by force, Englishmen thought little of it.[33] "Savages" were as irrational and unpredictable as children, in the English view. Hindsight makes the case look different. Opechancanough must already have been organizing his forces for a major attack, and as a fringe group, the Patawomecks would have come under direct pressure to join the empire in the project. The Patawomecks neither refused Opechancanough nor took refuge in an alliance with the English.[34] Instead, they attempted to keep some autonomy by having the English "put in an appearance" at Patawomeck and by having an Englishman escort Iopassus home overland by a route that took them right through the Powhatan heartland.

Meanwhile, Opechancanough and the English governor began to test one another, or so the interpreter residing with the former made it seem.

Opechancanough offered to visit Jamestown, but when the English sent the requested two hostages beforehand into Indian country, the hostages were returned with a message that no such visit had ever been planned.[35] Yeardley then sent John Rolfe to Pamunkey to find out what was going on; he was worried, since the English colony had been weakened that summer by high mortality from fevers.[36] Spelman and another man went ashore and conferred with Opechancanough, at which time both sides agreed that the misunderstanding was the fault of Robert Poole, the interpreter, who had "turned heathen." Rolfe never went ashore, as it turned out, and his surprised and disappointed uncle-in-law had to be told that Rolfe was "syck of an ague."

Not long afterward Nemattanew was sent to an English settlement with an offer from Opechancanough: they would all join forces against the "Massituppamohtnock," a group beyond the fall line[37] which had killed "certaine weomen of his Contrary to ye law of Nations."[38] The English were enticed into the affair with an offer that they could keep any children captured.[39] However, nothing came of the proposal, as far as the surviving records indicate. Opechancanough was undoubtedly cynical in making it: the English had violated the same "law" at Paspahegh in 1610, and in one of the Powhatans' 1618 raids the children of an English family had been killed.

In late 1619 or early 1620 a lull set in when the contentious interpreter Robert Poole was sent back to the English settlements. The next year seems to have passed peacefully, during which Opechancanough quietly put the finishing touches on his great raid. His plan was that a tremendous concourse of Indians was to gather "at the takinge vpp of Powhatans bones at wch Ceremony great numbers of the Salvages were to be assembled to sett upon every Plantatione of the Colonie."[40] However, in the summer of 1621, Opechancanough made the tactical error of sending a message to the fringe area of Accomac asking for a poison herb[41] to use against the English. The ruler he applied to[42] promptly disclosed the scheme to the English,[43] who armed themselves immediately. Opechancanough had to deny his plan and allow another several months to pass while English fears died down. At least part of the Eastern Shore fringe was thus officially detached from the Powhatan core by the English in that summer.

Sometime before November 1621, when Francis Wyatt arrived in Virginia as the new governor, Nemattanew was killed,[44] and Yeardley had to deal with the wrath of Opechancanough.[45] Nemattanew had killed an Englishman named Morgan after persuading him to go into Indian country to trade. He returned to Morgan's settlement, wearing the victim's cap, according to one hearsay witness (John Smith). Morgan's friends deduced that he was the murderer and took him prisoner; in an ensuing scuffle, he was fatally shot.[46] Smith, writing at home in England, added that the dying man asked to be buried among the English, so that his death from English bullets—to which he was supposed by his people to be immune[47]—would never be known.

Nemattanew had been one of his people's greatest warriors, and his death must have been a severe blow to Opechancanough's plans. However, Opechancanough deliberately gave the impression that he was pleased:[48] Nemattanew had been "a man soe farr owt of the favor of Apochancono [sic] yᵗ he sent worde to Sr. George Yeardley being then Gou'nor by his interpreter, yᵗ for his parte he could be contented his throte were Cutt . . . and yᵗ the Skye should sooner falle then . . . Peace be broken."[49] The scare created by the incident died down after several weeks. When Francis Wyatt took over as governor in November 1621, the Powhatans' "natiue King" renewed the peace and asked that it be "stamped in Brasse, and fixed to one of his Oakes."[50]

After the new governor arrived, Opechancanough began entertaining his emissary, the English minister George Thorpe.[51] Thorpe genuinely believed that Indian people were "of a peaceable & vertuous disposition" and had been estranged by the wrongs done them by malicious colonists.[52] Of course the wrongs did not, in his view, include settling on land which the Powhatans considered theirs; the wrongs stemmed from a lack of Christian charity in trading and receiving Indian visitors in the English settlements. Thorpe, like all other English writers of his time, says nothing about Indian rights in the prime farmlands the English were taking over.[53]

Thorpe discussed religion with Opechancanough at length, and the latter encouraged him to believe that a conversion could be made.[54] Purchas later claimed that during these talks Opechancanough said that the English could settle anywhere they wanted;[55] no one living in Virginia reported any such thing. Thorpe had an English-style house built for Opechancanough. He also had some English mastiffs brought to Opechancanough and killed as a token of good faith, an action that outraged the dogs' owners.[56] Other Englishmen, such as the Reverend Jonah Stockham, persisted in believing Indian people to be greedy and perfidious devils.[57] Neither side saw Indians realistically as human beings.

Company policy was somewhere in between the two attitudes, as the stockholders tried by long-distance messages to get the colonists to raise less tobacco with which to get rich; the colonists were to begin supporting themselves and making the Indians dependent on them, not vice versa. One message to that effect also included instructions that the glass bead making that had recently started in Virginia should be kept secret from the Indians and limited enough in scope that beads did not become devalued in the Indian trade.[58] The Company remained adamant, however, about Indians having no right to the land; only the English Crown had such rights.[59] This belief was in direct conflict with the Powhatans' beliefs about their homeland.

One of the things that Thorpe learned in his talks with Opechancanough was that the imperial brothers had taken new names for themselves: Opechancanough was now Mangopeesomon, while Opitchapam, who had long had another "throne" name, Itoyatin, now became Sasawpen.[60] Neither the English nor subsequent Anglo-American historians (except Fausz) took notice of the name change. But Powhatan ethnography,[61] as well as the report of the Accomac ruler in 1621 and subsequent events in 1622, shows that the new names signified some important achievement, military or political, among the Indians, which boded ill for the English colony. I speculate that the achievement was the final readying of the Powhatan chiefdoms to attack the English en masse in the summer of 1621.[62] The new names for the Powhatan leadership were a danger signal which the English, still ignorant of Powhatan culture, did not recognize.

Opechancanough was now planning the mass attack for March 1622. Some historians have noted that most earlier Indian raids in Virginia did not occur at that relatively "hungry" season, which is true, and they have postulated that the unusual timing was a result of hurried preparations made after Nemattanew's death, which they accept as having occurred in early March.[63] As already discussed, I place Nemattanew's death five months earlier. It also seems to me that March was not an illogical time for the Powhatans to make their move. Early spring was a season of dispersal of families, which would take Indian noncombatants out of the immediate reach of angry English survivors. (That was probably also the reasoning behind the scheduling of the great attack of 1644 in mid-April, an attack not preceded by a great warrior's death.) More importantly, planting had not yet begun. If the English could be either annihilated or run out of Virginia, the lands they had taken could be planted soon thereafter by their original Indian owners.

In March of 1622 Indian people were welcome to come and go freely in the English settlements and to borrow tools and even boats from their inhabitants.[64] Some Englishmen followed Thorpe's example and treated Indian people kindly, a behavior that produced mixed feelings in the Indians so treated. When word came to these people that Opechancanough expected their aid in a general slaughter of the English, they found themselves in a delicate position. Several eventually gave warning to the English, for which the Virginia Company later expressed its gratitude,[65] though John Smith and most historians after him speak only of one faithful Indian among all the "treacherous savages." Real life, in contrast to propaganda, is complex. Several Indians were torn in their loyalty because they had become fringe people to both societies. Prime examples of such people are the two Indian men combined by Anglo-American history into the single legendary figure of "Chanco."

There was a young Indian man whose name was never recorded but who had been baptized—and was therefore given an English name. He worked for an Englishman, William Perry, and visited a neighbor, Richard Pace, who lived on a plantation across the James River from Jamestown.[66] This youth learned about the intended assault on the English from an Indian visitor to Pace's house the night before the attack, but even eyewitnesses to the attack differ about the time that elapsed before the youth decided to tell Pace to spread the news. One witness described Pace as having warned the people at Jamestown just before the first warriors arrived; the other said that Pace and others warned English settlements all through the night. The subsequent fate of the Indian youth was never recorded. He may have been the unnamed "boy" whom William Perry took to England early in 1624.[67]

Another Indian caught between his own people and the English was Chauco,[68] an adult male from the Pamunkey River region in the opposite direction from Pace's plantation, who had "spent much time" among the English.[69] He must have been an excellent actor, for he gave his warning to the English and was still trusted by Opechancanough himself. The sole English document in which his name appears is from 1623, when Opechancanough sent him with a message to the English; the English welcomed him as a friend who had warned them the year before. That Chauco remained with Opechancanough during those troubled times shows that although he sympathized with the English, his ultimate loyalty was with his own people.

The uprising occurred on the morning of March 22, 1622, at English settlements along both sides of the James River.[70] The morning's work was already well under way when the attack began. When the Indians found colonists who had been warned, they either began the attack or had it begun for them by the defending English. When they found unsuspecting people, they behaved in a normally friendly fashion until the appointed hour, when they suddenly attacked. Many of these English were assaulted with their own tools by Indians who had been working alongside them.[71] Both sexes and all ages of English were killed if possible, though a spirited defense such as Hamor's[72] could make the warriors withdraw rather than risk their own lives unnecessarily. The greatest mortality occurred at Martin's Hundred,[73] where the residents were already reported to be debilitated prior to the massacre.[74] In addition to the human casualties, livestock was killed and houses were burned, leaving the plantations useless to the survivors.[75]

The bodies of the dead were mutilated;[76] traditional trophy taking was probably augmented by the Indians' wish to show utter contempt for the people who had invaded their country, depended on them for food, and then tried either to push them off the land or to evangelize them into a "better" way of life. Thorpe went to his death, still incredulous at what was happening, and his body, like others, was mutilated.[77] Some prisoners were taken as well. The ones who did not escape[78] were dealt with in traditional Powhatan fashion: the men were killed,[79] probably tortured to death, while the women were put to work in the Indian towns until they were ransomed the next year. Governor Wyatt demanded their immediate return, but to no avail. Opechancanough returned an "insolent Answr" and let the English know that he had done "dishonor" to King James's picture as well.[80]

Opechancanough did not follow up his assault with more raids, although some sniping continued. In fact, he did not have any of his people raid the English again until September 9,[81] three months after English retaliatory attacks had begun. He assumed that the English would react in Indian fashion and withdraw their battered survivors to another territory, presumably England, and he told the Patawomeck ruler, who had not participated in the uprising with him, that "before the end of two Moones there should not be an Englishman in all their Countries."[82] Just in case the English dawdled, however, Opechancanough reportedly tried to provide ammunition for future "reminders" by having most of the captured gunpowder sown in his fields, in expectation of an increase in gunpowder at the next fall's harvest.[83]

The English did not react as Opechancanough expected. The loss of one-fourth of their colonists[84] did not make them want to withdraw; it made them want to send home for more people and eradicate "so cursed a nation, vngratefull to all benefitts,"[85] who opposed their spreading of the "right" way to live. The English believed so thoroughly in their religion and way of life that they genuinely could not comprehend any reason for Indian people not wanting to adopt it.[86] They therefore remained more or less blind to the fact that their expanding settlements would impoverish Indian people, who wanted to continue living by a traditional economy that required large tracts of land for each family. They also remained unaware that in those Indian people's eyes the English were a symbol of insulting, if well-meaning, pressure for culture change, and for ruthless determination to occupy Indian living space.[87] The English had continued to think that they and the Indians could live together only if the Indians adopted English ways, a conversion that, from their side of the cultural fence, looked easy. When the Powhatans did not make the effort in the 1620s, the English became angry; when the Powhatans used violence in 1622 to make the English leave, the English used violence to force the Powhatans to make room for them. And they did indeed send home for more people; by 1625, the colony's population was about 1,300, after which it grew rapidly.[88]

While the English regrouped, some of their people on the Potomac River dealt with the fringe of Opechancanough's "empire."[89] The Sekakawons and the Patawomecks remained neutral during the uprising, but hearing that the Wiccocomicos were sympathetic to the Indian side, Captain Henry Spelman visited them and elicited a show of friendship. Meanwhile, Captain Raleigh Croshaw visited Patawomeck and, hearing that their *weroance* had just refused Opechancanough's demand that he, Croshaw, be killed, he tried to pressure the *weroance* into declaring himself openly on the English side. After deliberating for two days, the Patawomeck ruler decided to remain neutral.[90] His neutrality was soon tested.

In May an English ship under Hamor arrived to trade for corn, and since the Patawomecks had run out of that commodity, their *weroance* and Hamor joined forces in a successful raid on the upriver enemy tribes who

still had corn.[91] Croshaw went on living at Patawomeck, but relations with
his hosts went sour. Soon afterward another English captain found Croshaw
and his men holed up in a fort to avoid Patawomeck hostility, the reason
for which was never recorded. In spite of this hostility, Croshaw remained
confident of his ability to buy corn for the colony in the summer,[92] so Captain Isaac Madison was dispatched in June to Patawomeck to join with
him and "defend them [the Patawomecks] and their Corn to his vttmost
power."[93]

Soon after Madison's arrival, Croshaw received a message from a Mrs.
Boyce, who with nineteen others was a captive among the Pamunkeys: she
wanted to be ransomed.[94] Croshaw therefore enlisted the Patawomecks
as allies in a future campaign to recover the captives[95] and departed for
Jamestown to make arrangements, leaving Madison behind.

Like Croshaw, Madison soon wore out his welcome among the Patawomecks.[96] He insisted upon living apart in Croshaw's fort, and he believed the tales of Patawomeck disloyalty to the English told to him by
other tribes and his own interpreter (the mischievous Robert Poole).[97] Finally, he killed some[98] of the Indian people he suspected of betraying him,
after which he took the *weroance* and his son and two others to Jamestown
as hostages. The Patawomecks were not mere innocent victims of Madison's
touchiness, however, as shown by subsequent events. The hostages were
returned to Patawomeck the next October by Hamor, who was not a no-
ticeably racist hard-liner in the colony. He had been authorized to use his
own discretion in choosing whether to release the hostages or take more
prisoners,[99] and now he "took Corne for their ransome."[100] The colonial
council wrote later to England that Madison had killed people who
"sought to Circumvent him by treachery."[101] Although the English regarded them as "friends" now detached from Opechancanough's organization,[102] the Patawomecks were apparently running true to form as a fringe
of the paramount chiefdom; they refused to be detached from it completely.

The English starved in the next year;[103] the James River basin Indians
may have done likewise. The English were likely to be shot while planting
crops,[104] supplies from England were slow in arriving,[105] and only a limited
amount of corn was available from fringe groups such as the Patawomecks
and new allies such as the Accomacs.[106] However, they managed to muster
the men and arms for retaliatory raids on Powhatan groups within reach.
The Chickahominies, Nansemonds, Warraskoyacks, and Weyanocks all
saw their houses, canoes, and growing corn attacked (and the latter carried
away),[107] but the chiefdoms of the York River drainage remained relatively
immune because of English weakness. The expedition to Pamunkey to re-
claim English prisoners was fobbed off with promises and then shot at with
captured English guns; the Pamunkeys escaped after hiding their corn and
burning their own houses.[108]

In the fall of 1622, after obtaining supplies from home and corn from the
Patawomecks (a pattern they would follow for the next several years),[109]

the English launched more attacks on their enemies: two on the Rappahan-nocks and one on the Powhatans at the falls of the James.[110] The food ac-quired during the summer and fall was not enough, however, and hunger decimated the English that winter. Opechancanough's people may not have been much better off, though the English knew nothing about it. However, in the spring of 1623 both peoples badly needed peace in order to plant and raise food for the next year. Opechancanough made the first move toward peace by sending Chauco to Jamestown with the message that his people were starving and a truce should be made. If the English would cease ha-rassing his people, he would return the surviving English prisoners, who by that time consisted of fifteen to twenty people, mostly women.[111] The En-glish agreed; they—and probably the Powhatans—planned to resume hos-tilities as soon as the Indians' corn was ripe.[112]

Opechancanough then returned precisely one English prisoner: Mrs. Boyce, "the Chiefe of the prisoners," dressed "like one of theire Queens, wch they desired wee should take notice of." He sent a message with her that the rest would be returned when interpreter Poole, once more among the Pamunkeys and making trouble, was recalled. The English obliged, using the truce period to scout the locations of Indian fields, which were being carefully hidden that spring.[113] English plans were given a blow, how-ever, when interpreter Spelman was killed on the upper Potomac River on March 27,[114] a death for which the Piscataways were blamed.[115]

In early May 1623, Opitchapam sent a message to the English offering to give back the English captives and also to "deliuer his Brother Opachan-kano [sic] . . . into the hands of the English either aliue or dead."[116] It was impossible then, as it is now, to determine whether or not Opitchapam really meant to rid himself of the brother who overshadowed him. On the other hand, Opechancanough was perfectly capable of masterminding a trap. He was the brother who actually held the prisoners,[117] and he was the most prominent member of the Indian side at the resulting meeting. What-ever the Indians' intentions, the English found it expedient to pretend to accept the offer.

On May 22, 1623, an English party under Captain William Tucker met with Opechancanough, the *weroance* of Chiskiack, and a large number of other Indian people.[118] The English women were handed over in exchange for a ransom,[119] a peace was made with many speeches, and finally a toast was drunk. Sleight-of-hand was employed; the Indians were given sack that had been poisoned by the colony's doctor, Dr. John Pott.[120] The poison sickened the Indians if it did not kill them (Opechancanough survived his drink). The English then took leave of their staggering "allies," but as they left, they suddenly turned and fired upon them, killing many outright.[121] Opechancanough and the *weroance* of Chiskiack were seen to fall. The En-glish then scalped some of their victims, so as to bring home souvenirs, and returned to Jamestown.

In July the English attacked several Powhatan chiefdoms: the Chickahominies, the Powhatans at the falls of the James, the Appamattucks, the Nansemonds, and the Weyanocks on both sides of the James. Later on the Nansemonds were revisited.[122] Thus, most of the surviving James River tribes lost their corn crop, their houses, and some of their people. Only a shortage of food for their soldiers kept the English from raiding chiefdoms on the other rivers.[123] In spite of their "success," however, English morale was low because Indians who so easily fled into the woods were hard to exterminate altogether, and soldiers grumbled about spending time away from their fields.[124] Another raiding party left Jamestown in search of Indians in November, but in that season of Indian dispersal they merely wasted two months in the wilderness.[125] The winter was a hungry one for everybody.

In the spring of 1624 the Powhatans harassed the English settlements,[126] whose people were given repeated orders to palisade them.[127] The English, for their part, prepared to go on summer raids.[128] They continued to buy supplies from neutral or friendly Indian people,[129] such as the distant Patuxents.[130] The major clash of the year occurred in July 1624.[131] The leader of the Indian side was "Itopatin" (or Otiotan, originally Opitchapam); Opechancanough is not mentioned in English records for several years after 1623, and in 1624 he may have been recovering his health. Both sides had prepared for a major battle, with the Pamunkeys going so far as to brag widely about what they would do; the Pamunkeys also planted extra corn in their territory for the James River groups, who had feared to plant in their homelands that spring. Word even reached the Patuxents far to the north, for they sent a man to the English "expressly to be an eye witnes of the evente."

The "evente" must have been worth watching. Contrary to normal Powhatan practice, the fighting went on for two days in open country and it involved an estimated eight hundred Indian bowmen, indicating that the fight was a major effort of the paramount chiefdom. The English had only about sixty men.[132] Their purpose was to provide cover for the two dozen or so of their number who were instructed to enter the nearby Pamunkey cornfields and cut the corn. Eventually they succeeded. When the Powhatans suddenly saw much of their corn already cut down, the fight went out of them: they "stood most ruthfully lookinge one while theire Corne was cut downe." The English did no more before they left. The devastated fields represented a major loss of prestige as well as the probability of another fairly hungry winter for the James and York river Indians.

The years after 1624 are more poorly documented for English and Indians alike.[133] Virginia became a royal colony and the copious records of the Virginia Company of London came to an end with the liquidation of the Company. As the colony grew in the 1620s and 1630s, the Indians occupied a smaller proportion of the records. The population of the colony has been estimated as 2,600 in 1629, 3,200 in 1632, 5,200 in 1634, and

8,100 in 1640.[134] The native population was never counted, but it was probably less than 5,000. The English colony was divided into "shires" in 1634, and local incidents involving the Indian people were usually dealt with on the county level. However, most of the key counties in Powhatan affairs of the 1630s and 1640s (namely, Nansemond, James City, and Charles City) lost their records in the nineteenth century, during the Civil War. Consequently, we can reconstruct local Indian history only on the Eastern Shore, and intercultural relations there were so peaceful that little was recorded about them.[135]

Losing the battle in July 1624 caused the hostile mainland Indians to lie low for a long time thereafter. The English remained uneasy, however, even questioning the loyalty of Thomas Savage,[136] who now lived on the Eastern Shore. He was the last in the chain of interpreters to be suspected of sympathizing with the "savages." It is hard to see deeply into two cultures and continue to think of them in simplistic terms.

The English wanted to attack their Powhatan enemies again in the summer of 1625, for they still wanted revenge for the great attack of three years before,[137] but they were too short of powder to make the attempt. In fact, there was so little powder left in the colony in the spring of 1625 that the Powhatans could have wiped out all of the colonists in one day,[138] had they been so minded. However, the chiefdoms seem to have been in no shape to attempt an assault; as far as the records show, not even raids were forthcoming. The hunger of the winter before and the disorganization following their defeat in 1624 made them as unfit for war as the English colony was. The year 1626 seems to have passed in much the same way,[139] and both sides got in another crop of corn. Hostility remained, however. An Englishman was detained on a trip to Pamunkey,[140] an Englishman's cow was killed by Indians in Charles City,[141] and a Weyanock man was captured and held,[142] probably for fear he would disclose the true weakness of the colony. At that time William Claiborn evolved a plan, the details of which were not recorded, for holding captured Indians in safekeeping so that they could be used on demand as guides. He got the governor's permission to try his plan with an Indian who had voluntarily come among the English,[143] but the outcome of the experiment is unknown.

On January 13, 1627, the English colonial council decided to occupy the site of Chiskiack town on York River, an idea previously considered in 1621 by the people of Martin's Hundred, directly across the Peninsula.[144] The motives in 1627 were to annoy the Indian leadership and to provide an overland refuge in case of a Spanish attack.[145] The Chiskiacks appear to have moved away already; they are last heard of planting their corn at the site in spring 1623,[146] and they next appear in the English records of the early 1650s living on the Piankatank River. Some English settled at the old town by 1629.[147] But the real incentive for moving there came in 1630, when the council offered free farmland for settlement.[148]

The summer of 1627 saw a renewal of raiding by the English.[149] The surviving James River groups (i.e., Chickahominies, Appamattucks, Powhatans, Warraskoyacks, Weyanocks, and Nansemonds)[150] were assaulted,
and a threatening gesture was made in the direction of the York River
groups. The attacks, which took place in August, where not wholly successful, for the English later had to "Ransom *Englishmen* prisoners to the
Nansemung Indians."[151] The Indians who were attacked also fought back.[152]
In the fall matters were further complicated when a ship's captain left on
the colony's hands some Carib Indians, who promptly escaped, with the
aim of joining the Powhatans. The colonial council ordered that their erstwhile unwanted guests be found and hanged, but there is no record of any
of them having been caught.[153]

An attack on the Pamunkeys was planned for October[154] and apparently
made, for a note "on a piece of barke" arrived next April from English prisoners at Pamunkey,[155] presumably informing the council that they were still
alive. That male prisoners were still alive among the Powhatans indicates
that the Indian leadership felt its position to be so weak that it was advan-
tageous to keep male hostages. Meanwhile, the English continued to distrust even their Accomac friends, as shown by an order, issued February 8,
1628, against selling them glass bottles.[156] In a period when the English
would not sell them firearms, the Accomacs were using bottle glass to make
arrowheads.

The Powhatans made so few offensive moves against the English after
1624 that the colonial council repeatedly issued proclamations to the colonists, warning them against becoming overconfident. English confidence
was probably increased by the small number of Indian people who moved
to their settlements to adopt their way of life.[157] However, in the summer of
1628 the English were still bent upon revenge. First, to get their countrymen back from the Pamunkeys they made a formal "peace," most of the
terms of which have been lost. The terms set out in surviving records are
military in nature: no Indian people were to visit English settlements or harm
English livestock, and messengers from "the greate king" (still Sasawpen,
originally called Opitchapam, according to a report of August 1629)[158]
were to deal directly with the governor or with local militia commanders.[159]

Neither side intended to abide by the treaty for long. The English planned
from the outset that the treaty should last only until "ye English see a fit
opportunity to break it,"[160] so in October 1628 they formally decided to
continue the peace[161] and the next January to end it.[162] The Powhatans
went on trying to visit English settlements for a variety of purposes and
killing English livestock that they found ranging in the woods, as though
no treaty had been made. The English took this behavior as evidence of the
"perfidy" of the Indian leadership and informed Sasawpen in March 1629
that the peace was over.[163] In reality, his influence over his people may still
have been at so low an ebb that many Indian men did not feel bound by any

treaty he made, particularly when their ancient rights of land use and hunting were involved.

Hostilities resumed after March 1629. An English party was killed by unidentified Indians and the English demanded satisfaction,[164] which was not forthcoming. The English then made war on the nearest Powhatan groups, as they had planned.[165] In these campaigns they did more damage to their enemies "than they had done since the great massacre."[166] One devastated Indian town was Cantauncack, on the north side of York River between Carter and Cedarbush creeks;[167] in 1640 the site was patented by William Claiborne, the man who led the English party that attacked it.[168] Limited warfare between the English and the Powhatans continued through 1630, 1631, and the first half of 1632, though records concerning it are few.[169]

By the spring of 1632 the Powhatans appear to have wanted to make another truce, for Englishmen were ordered not to "speake or parlie" with Indians "either in the woods or in any plantation, yf [they] can possibly avoyd it by any meanes."[170] The English persisted in regarding all Indian people except the Accomacs as "our irrecosileable [sic] enemies," who were to be attacked on any pretext,[171] until June, when their governor agreed to parley "with *Chickahominy* Indians."[172] Nothing came of the meeting initially, and after a drought-stricken summer[173] the English prepared to make more raids.[174] However, the raids never took place, because on September 30, 1632, a treaty was made "with *Pamunkeys* & *Chick^a* Indians"[175] and ten years' warfare finally came to an end.

Raiding ended, but enmity did not; clashes between individual Indians and Englishmen went on as before. The English severely limited the contact they allowed their people with Indians, and it is likely that Indian leaders tried to do the same. The Indian demand for English firearms and cloth was high,[176] indicating that technological change was taking hold among the Powhatans. As usual, the scanty documents that survived the Civil War tell the English side of the story. At some time during these years, Opitchapam died and the English found Opechancanough still alive and in control.

English settlements expanded further: on the Eastern Shore, if not elsewhere, the Indian ruler, Esmy Shichans, gave large tracts to Englishmen he liked.[177] The English, in all of their settlements, used their land to raise tobacco, and that fact kept tensions high between the two peoples. Tobacco, which quickly exhausts land, kept the English hungry for land. Because they were avid to get rich from their cash crop, they depended for foodstuffs upon the Dutch and upon the Indian people whose land they were simultaneously acquiring to raise more tobacco.[178] The Indians were thus caught in a double bind, being pressured to raise extra food on a shrinking land base, and they cannot have liked it. Tensions remained such that in 1638 the colony's secretary could still write of "the savages ever awake to do them injuries in the streightest time of peace."[179]

The Powhatans steadily lost territory in the late 1630s and early 1640s, and some chiefdoms ceased to function independently, merging with others that were still strong. In the lower York River drainage, only the Werowocomocos, represented by the town of Cantauncack, were left, and they appear to have dispersed during this time. Most of the Powhatans' land losses were along the James River and on the Eastern Shore. Much of the lower Eastern Shore was sold or given away to the English before 1650. Survival of records is poor for the English counties on the James River, but the land patent books show a steady passing of land into English hands during the period. The Warraskoyacks disappeared from history altogether as their land was "taken up" by English settlers. The Nansemonds, at least one of whom had an English spouse (see below), withdrew upriver on both the southern and northwestern branches in the late 1630s and early 1640s.[180] The Weyanocks abandoned their town south of the James by 1642[181] and retained "great Weyanoke Towne" north of the river.[182] The Appamattucks stayed in their old capital town near Swift Creek for the time being, though Englishmen came to settle near them.[183] The people of Powhatan town may also have moved beyond the falls of the James, though no record mentions them again until 1669. And the Chickahominies appear to have shrunk in population and territory until their one town appearing in the English records remained Oraniock on Diascund Creek; the English now called both town and creek "Warrany."[184]

The English began to claim lands north of the York River in 1640.[185] The legislative order of October 11, 1639,[186] which encouraged these claims, used the same incentive that the Stuart kings of England had used on a large scale for five decades in Scotland and Ireland as well as in the New World:[187] the government doled out "empty" lands that it "owned" (in reality, aborigines' lands which it claimed) to entrepreneurs, who were then expected to go out and make their claims good by establishing settlements at their own expense. If the settlements "took," the entrepreneurs could keep most of their profits from using the lands and the government collected quitrents; if the settlements failed (as when the aborigines did not cooperate), then the government lost no money and considered itself free to grant the "escheated" land anew.[188] The government could not lose, unless would-be entrepreneurs tried to buy land directly from the aborigines, a practice that was soon outlawed in Virginia. The government might or might not compensate the aborigines for the lands it took, depending upon its attitude of the moment toward "barbarians." In Virginia, it was only after two major Indian wars[189] that the colonial government became cognizant of the part that aboriginal land rights played in English-Powhatan conflict.

English would-be planters of tobacco began claiming land near Mobjack Bay in 1640, on the Rappahannock River in 1642,[190] and on the Potomac River in 1643.[191] Three years were allowed for actual settlement of the lands to get underway,[192] and references to salvaging property north of the York after the 1644–1646 war indicate that actual settlement of the Rappahannock and Potomac rivers had scarcely begun when the war started. However, the "taking up" of land by Englishmen around Mobjack Bay got well underway and undoubtedly helped Opechancanough's cause in reorganizing the Powhatans.

Powhatan-English relations remained outwardly peaceful in the early 1640s, as long as Englishmen behaved themselves. To that end, trade between Englishmen and Indians was limited to a few licensed Englishmen who could be trusted to be scrupulous.[193] On the Eastern Shore, the Accomacs were peaceful even when Englishmen misbehaved. When an English neighbor of the Accomacs tried to claim and work their land as well as his own, even though his patent stated clearly that the creek between them was the boundary of his land, the Indians took a complaint to the county court instead of resorting to violence.[194] After an investigation the court found for the Indians. In December 1640 the Accomac tribe had been assigned a tract of fifteen hundred acres, to be surveyed for them on the seaboard side of the Eastern Shore.[195] The tract was ancestral to the 650-acre Gingaskin reservation in the same area, which remained intact until 1813. However, the Indians' title to their land remained tenuous in 1643, when the county court ordered three English men to pay the "greate king of the Eastern Shoare" in roanoke for land they had already occupied.[196]

On the mainland, relations were more tense. Englishmen were more apt to treat Indians violently when they got in the way, while Opechancanough ostensibly swallowed his pride to keep the peace. A case in point is that of John Burton, who, angered by an Indian's theft of some of his property, killed the next Indian he met. A fellow Englishman had recently gotten permission to detain the next available Indian after a theft,[197] but Burton had gone much farther. An investigation by the English showed that Burton had killed an innocent man, putting English-Powhatan relations in serious jeopardy. The General Court at Jamestown therefore demanded from Burton a stiff fine and more money as security for his future good behavior; it also ordered him to move to another county.[198] The punishment fit the crime in the Powhatan view, for their culture included the institution of *wergild*,[199] or monetary payment for wrongs done, but Opechancanough hastened to make a compassionate gesture that would impress the English. When Burton petitioned for remission of the fine, the *mamanatowick* Opechancanough lent his weight to Burton's petition, sending some of his "great men" (councillors) with the message that the Powhatans understood that the killing had been a mistake.[200] Burton's fine was therefore remitted. The next year, in an attempt to prevent similar incidents, the General Assembly passed a law[201] that Englishmen with a grievance against Indian people should take it to the nearest militia commander, who would then detain "without violence" the next available Indian person from the same tribe as the one accused. The hostage would then guarantee the paying of compensation or the handing over of culprits, "as to the Com'ander shall seeme reasonable."

Some Englishmen and Indians got along peaceably, however. In 1638 a son of Captain Nathaniel Bass married a Christianized Nansemond woman, "y ͤ dafter of y ͤ King of y ͤ Nansemund Nation, by name Elizabeth"[202] (see fig. 1). John and Elizabeth Bass became ancestors of an Anglicized Nansemond group that may never have had a reservation or treaty status and which nonetheless survives today in Portsmouth and adjoining cities. Either the Nansemonds or the Weyanocks voluntarily lost a boy to English society, for in June 1641, George Menifye petitioned for funds from an educational philanthropy[203] to help him support a boy from the county of "Tappahannak" or Surry (old Quiyoughcohannock territory).[204] The boy, when examined, was found to be well grounded in Christianity and able to read and write, the result of living among the English for ten years.

Six months later Pocahontas's son, Thomas Rolfe, asked permission of the governor (required of all English subjects in those days) to go into Indian country to see "Opachankeno [sic] to whom he is allied and Cleopatra his mother's sister."[205] Thanks to the burning of all of the colonial council's records of this period in the Civil War, we know no more than that; "Cleopatra" may or may not have been the Matachanna who was wife to the priest Uttamatomakin.[206] Young Rolfe's passage to Virginia had been paid by his stepmother's father in 1635,[207] and he was an established planter by 1639.[208] The sparse records available to us say nothing more of this or any other visit to his Indian relatives, though visits probably occurred. Soon Rolfe would show that his sentiments were primarily English.

On April 18, 1644, Opechancanough staged the second major attack on the English. Because of the poor survival rate of Virginia records of the 1640s, we know little about the initial assault on the English or its aftermath.[209] By reconstruction, it seems that the Weyanocks, Nansemonds, Pamunkeys, and Chickahominies were involved; the participation of the Rappahannocks and other chiefdoms on the Northern Neck was questionable.[210] After killing about four hundred English people[211] and taking many prisoners,[212] Indian warriors melted away into the woods and attempted no follow-up attack,[213] once again giving the English time to regroup.

In the late summer of 1644, the English went on what they called the "Pomunkye and Cheychohominy march."[214] A force of men went on foot to the Chickahominy town of Oraniock, where they apparently won a skirmish and caused the Indians to abandon their town sometime afterward.[215] The English then met a fleet of their own boats on Pamunkey River across from Lee Marsh.[216] If the boats encountered resistance from Indian residents still living downriver, there are no surviving records of it. The boats then ferried the soldiers upriver to a landing place near Romancoke, later patented by William Claiborne,[217] on the north bank of the river. The as-

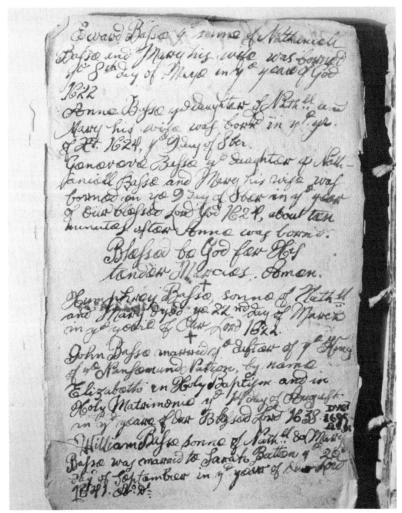

Fig. 1. Family record of an English-Nansemond marriage: page of a sermon book owned in 1987 by Mrs. Lucille Bass, wife of the Nansemond chief. (Photo by the author.)

sault on Opechancanough's capital town[218] was apparently made on foot. The English made assaults on other Indian groups as well that summer, losing some men in the process. The chiefdoms attacked were the Nansemonds, the Weyanocks, the Powhatans, and the Appamattucks.[219] Indian prisoners were sold, whether as servants or slaves is unclear.[220]

The Weyanocks fled far south of the James, probably after the English assaulted them that summer, and they left Opechancanough's organization altogether. Many years later their old men told an English interpreter that "Appatchancanough [*sic*] sent fourscore men to look [find] them & bring back, all which Indians the Eynokes [*sic*] killed and fled Lower down Roanoke [River].[221] Their defection seems to have remained a sore point with some of the Nansemonds, who treated them as enemies in the 1660s.[222]

In 1645 the English raided their enemies and built forts near enemy towns as bases for further harassment.[223] Details of the raids are few. Englishmen living in the counties south of the James were divided into two groups, probably to attack the Nansemonds and the Appamattucks, while one expedition went down near the Roanoke River,[224] presumably to attack the Weyanocks. One raid in July netted the English "many prisoners." On August 9, it was decided to send all these prisoners who were over the age of eleven to "the Western Island," to make their loss to "their respective tribes" permanent.[225] This tactic would be used again in 1705 against the Nanzaticos (see chapter 5).

The forts built were Fort Charles at the falls of the James, Fort Royal "at Pomunkey [*sic*]" opposite Tottopottomoy Creek in King William County,[226] and Fort James at "Ridge of Chiquohomine" west of Diascund Creek. The next year Fort Henry was built at the falls of the Appomattox River; as soon as the war was over, all the forts would be handed over, with adjacent acreage, to entrepreneurs who would maintain them and also turn a profit.[227] On October 6, 1646, Thomas Rolfe became the proprietor at Fort James; he later added 125 acres to his holding and patented the whole.[228] Perhaps he and the English colony—of which he was firmly a part—hoped that the presence of Pocahontas's son would be a healing influence (no documents say so).

By March 1646 the Powhatans had all but lost the war, while the English were considering "the great and vast expence" of fighting and "the almost impossibility of a further revenge vpon them, they being dispersed and driven from their townes and habitations, lurking vp & downe the woods in small number." The English therefore decided to seek an "honourable" peace with the Indians, if possible,[229] and resume expanding their settlements and raising tobacco. Accordingly, sixty men were levied and sent out, their leader being Governor Sir William Berkeley himself.[230] Peace was not come by easily, however: Opechancanough resisted Berkeley's proposal, and he was taken prisoner[231] and carried back to Jamestown. There "that bloody Monster[,] upon [i.e., nearly] 100 years old"[232] and so feeble that he was utterly dependent upon others, survived only a short time in prison before he was shot by an English soldier.[233]

At Opechancanough's death, his brother's empire had all but broken up. As far as the surviving records show, the English spent so much effort in attacking Opechancanough and the James River remnants, and so little effort in prosecuting a war with the Indian groups still living in considerable strength on the Rappahannock and Potomac rivers, that it is logical to conclude that the latter groups had already been detached from Opechancanough's organization by the English. The ethnic group that the man Powhatan tried to create was now, at best, a small political organization pared down to a few tribes in and near the old Powhatan heartland, an organization that the more numerous English were able to conquer in short order. Hereafter, the fringe of the Powhatan ethnic identity was Anglicized Indians, for after 1646 all the surviving Powhatan groups were inundated by English settlers and left on separate islands of tribal territory.

The English, however, preferred for convenience to retain and make a treaty with an "emperor" on the mainland, just as they welcomed a "loyal emperor" on the Eastern Shore. Then they would only have to deal with one paramount leader, who supposedly could control all his people. In practice, the system soon broke down and the English had to deal with rulers of many individual chiefdoms, but the treaty made in 1646 with the "emperor" of unknown (probably Pamunkey)[234] origin named Necotowance presumed that the old Powhatan "empire" still spanned all of the mainland of eastern Virginia. The makers of the treaty also presumed that the English were firmly in charge; only the English are referred to in it as "inhabitants."

The treaty of October 1646[235] stated from the outset that Necotowance held his dominions as a vassal of the king of England. As such, he had to pay an annual tribute of twenty beaver skins for those dominions, and he was not free to dispose of them as he wished or as Indian custom dictated: the English claimed the right to confirm or even to appoint his successors. The English were now the sole owners of the Lower Peninsula between the James and York rivers, and no Indian was to come there on pain of death unless he wore a striped coat, indicating that he brought a message from Necotowance. The only points of entry allowed into English territory even for messengers were Fort Henry and Fort Royal. Any Englishman harboring an Indian without authorization would be put to death. All English prisoners and "negroes and guns" were to be returned by the Indians, while Indian prisoners were not only to be kept by the English and made into servants but were also to be returned to their masters if they ran back to their people. Any Indian children aged twelve and under were welcome to live among the English.[236] And not the least in importance, the Indians were free to inhabit lands north of the York River, where the English were prohibited from going except to recover their property (before March 1, 1647) or to fell timber with the governor's permission. But there was an exception: if the governor and council permitted English settlement of the north bank of York River "from Poropotank [River] downwards" (i.e., where intensive English settlement had already begun), then "first Necotowance be acquainted therewith."

The treaty of 1646 did not open much new land for English settlement. The opening of the rest of coastal Virginia, which abrogated the treaty as ratified, resulted from another law made in the very same session of the General Assembly as the treaty.[237] The law's preamble states inaccurately that "by the articles of peace with the Indians that none of the inhabitants [English] shall seate or inhabitt on the north side of Yorke River vntil further order therein." Then the body of the law confirms all claims on northern lands, no geographical limitation being specified, and allows claimants three years in which to settle after the Assembly gives permission to move north at some future date. The burgesses cannot have forgotten the wording of the treaty so soon: the treaty is "Act 1" and the settlement law is "Act 6" of a fairly long legislative session. The two acts may even have been read and passed on the same day. We can conclude only that the settlement law was, in effect, an agreement among the English that they would move northward again when Indian rancor over the recent war had diminished, and that any protests made later by the nonliterate Powhatans would be pushed aside.

CHAPTER 5

A Declining Minority

THERE WAS NEVER any real chance of holding the English back after 1646, even had their government wanted to do so. There were simply too many of them, and they all were too determined to make their fortunes raising tobacco. They flooded Indian lands at a rate and on a scale that, as Edmund Morgan put it, "transforms crime into politics."[1] After 1622 the English were little interested in missionizing Indians or anyone else. They were Protestants who maintained a distance from "savages,"[2] and they were determined to acquire the land they wanted. Their relations with the Powhatans were therefore primarily military and economic in nature for much of the seventeenth century.

The Powhatans were soon isolated on ever-shrinking islands of tribal territory, their supratribal organization all but extinct. As each chiefdom's lands decreased, the core Indian people became poorer, yet they continued to resist the cultural changes that would have enabled them to survive better on the lands they retained. The Powhatan fringe, which now surrounded several separate tribal cores (see map 4), consisted of people who had adopted English ways, either while they worked temporarily for Englishmen or when they left their people altogether and tried to join English society. It is ironic that in the second half of the seventeenth century, while the fringe gradually increased in number, the poverty and shrinking population of the cores led the English to think so much less of Indian people in general that the fringe did itself little good by Anglicizing.

By the end of the century the Powhatans were as oppressed as free Afro-Virginians,[3] and the oppression appears to have made the remaining cores even more determined to survive. No Englishman foresaw, however, that they would survive; in the decades following the 1646 treaty, it looked to everyone as though the Powhatans were a vanishing people. That idea was a self-fulfilling prophecy as far as Anglo-Virginians were concerned. It led them to pay less attention to and make fewer records about the Indian groups that continued peacefully to survive in the late decades of the century. This near-disappearance from the English records has long given historians the erroneous impression that most of the Powhatan tribes "died out" by 1700. In reality, the second half of the seventeenth century was a

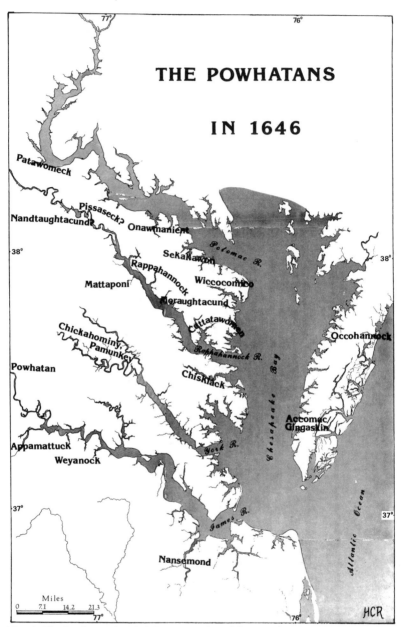

Map 4. The Powhatans in 1646. Base map adapted from *Bathymetry of Chesapeake Bay* (Virginia Institute of Marine Science, 1977).

time of culture change for a fringe that continually grew, while the core people stubbornly hung onto their old ways as long as possible.

The Powhatans of the second half of the seventeenth century were seldom a unified people. The Eastern Shore tribes had separated politically from Opechancanough's organization long before, and they were unaffected either by Bacon's Rebellion or by the Indian treaty that followed it. By contrast, the Powhatan groups on the mainland lived in constant danger of being implicated in raids by "foreign" Indians and punished by the English. The tribes downriver also had to contend with ambitious English neighbors who wanted ever bigger plantations. The records of both the colonial government and the county courts therefore show great diversity in Indian experiences with and responses to the English during the period. Thus, it is difficult to write accurately about the Powhatans in the aggregate except in the most general terms, and to do so would rob them of what little humanity is revealed in the English records about them.

Therefore, this chapter describes the Powhatans of the period on two levels. First there is a general history of Powhatan-English military affairs. Then each tribe is considered individually, with special attention to political leadership and lands owned. In the next chapter we explore the occupations and civil rights of individual Powhatans during the same period. Our cut-off point will be 1705, the year in which Virginia passed its "black code" and also legislated away part of each of the remaining Indian reservations.

Powhatan Military History

In the first three years after the treaty of 1646, the English remained within their agreed-upon boundaries and the new paramount chief, Necotowance, paid tribute to their governor. (In 1686, the tribute was formally ruled to be a perquisite of the governor,[4] which it is to this day.) The last appearance of Necotowance in the English records was in March 1648/49, when he and five of his "petty Kings" presented their twenty beaver skins to Sir William Berkeley.[5] Later that year the English informed him that they would begin settling north of the York River again, as allowed by the law their Assembly had passed the previous October.[6] Necotowance disappears from the records thereafter: he either died or fell from power. When the Indians petitioned the English for reservation lands, as they were now entitled to do, the petitioning was done by three different *weroances,* each of whom received five thousand acres: Tottopottomoy of Pamunkey, Ascomowett of Weyanock, and Ossakican, representing the "Northern Indians."[7] When no more Indian leaders came forward to ask for land, the General Assembly legislated in 1650 that all *weroances* were to have patents for lands, the amount to be calculated at fifty acres per bowman.[8] The law therefore established many separate Indian political units on reservations, usually in the groups' home territories. The lands allowed were adequate by English economic standards but grossly undersized for Powhatan use in hunting and foraging; the rapid increase of English settlers who cleared land and hunted for their own tables also decreased the game in the region. It is no wonder that by 1656 most Indians were facing starvation (see below).

As soon as the English began moving northward, the General Assembly passed several laws attempting to protect Powhatan rights. Indians were to be killed only if actually caught doing "mischief" (theft or damage to live-stock). Their children were not to be stolen and, if apprenticed voluntarily to Englishmen, were not to be transferred to other Englishmen or made into servants. Values were established for Indian shell beads (roanoke and peak),[9] which the English colonists were beginning to use as money in their dealings with Indians.

Not surprisingly, English and Powhatan people were far from being at ease with one another after 1649. Edward Bland and his companions found the Weyanocks, far to the southwest of English settlements, to be hostile.[10] John Mottram was summoned to Jamestown to give explanations after his Northern Neck neighbors complained that he allowed local Indian men to use his guns.[11] On the Eastern Shore there were repeated rumors of a joint war planned by local Indians and Indians to the north; some En-glishmen therefore attacked the Pocomokes, in what is now Maryland, in 1651.[12] The next year the English Assembly allowed settlers to confiscate Indian firearms and to execute runaway servants who carried arms to the Indians. In 1653 another law was passed forbidding Englishmen to lend firearms to Indians.[13] By 1656 the English realized that Powhatan lands were the cause of much of the strife. Anything less than inalienable title to their lands left Indians vulnerable to Englishmen who pressured them to sell or forced them to leave, so the Powhatans were forbidden by (English) law to sell any land to individual Englishmen.[14] This law applied every-where except the Eastern Shore, where the Indian chiefdoms had never risen against the English and intergroup relations were generally good. From 1654 onward it was legal there for *weroances* to sell land to individ-ual Englishmen.[15]

Meanwhile, unrest had reached a boiling point on the Northern Neck. On September 14, 1653, Lancaster County made a treaty of its own with the Rappahannock chiefdom, in which both sides agreed that wronged In-dians should take their complaints to the county court, that the *weroance* and his council would be tried in court for their people's stealing of English livestock, and that reparations would be accepted for killed livestock if the *weroance* reported the matter promptly.[16] Unfortunately, the treaty did no good: Englishmen continued to take up lands in the region and to shoot Indians who "trespassed" on "their" land, which the Indians naturally re-sented bitterly. Late in 1654 the militias of Lancaster, Westmoreland, and

Northumberland counties were combined and instructed to demand reparations from the Rappahannocks.[17] That meeting, or a subsequent one, became a brawl in which the tribe's *weroance*, Taweeren, was killed.[18]

Two years later, when tensions had still not eased, the English of Rappahannock County made treaties of their own with the Rappahannocks,[19] then living on the north bank of the river, and with the Mattaponis,[20] who lived in the headwaters of what is now Piscataway Creek. Both treaties provided that the county court would treat Indians as Englishmen, and that the *weroance* and his council were to appear with Indian defendants in trespass cases. Indians were to pay damages if they killed English livestock, and they were to be paid in roanoke for bringing in English fugitives. The Rappahannock treaty added assurances of good treatment for any Indian children sent to the English, while the Mattaponi treaty stated that Indians were also to be free to hunt outside the English fenced plantations, a proviso that was later written into colonial laws and treaties. The Mattaponi treaty did not remain in effect for long: they were forced to move from their lands within a decade. The Rappahannock treaty did little good, either, as we shall see.

The English had reason for alarm in 1656, when a large number of "Richahecrians" (apparently Siouan-speaking Mannahoacs and Nahyssans)[21] settled themselves near the falls of the James River. Six or seven hundred of them were reported.[22] The Weyanock *weroance* told the English that still other Indians, "Massahocks," had come south "to fight the Rickahockans."[23] An English force under Col. Edward Hill combined with a hundred Pamunkey men under Tottopottomoy and met some of the intruders far up the Pamunkey River, near the tip of the peninsula between the North and South Anna rivers. The meeting ended bloodily, with Tottopottomoy and most of his men slain.[24] Hill was censured for "crimes & weaknesses" in dealing with the Richahecrians, but since they obstinately remained within the colony, he was retained as the militia leader charged with facing them.[25] In April 1657 another complaint against the "Nessan" Indians resulted in another militia force being sent out;[26] this force apparently drove them from the colony.

In the next few years the Powhatans appear to have become resigned to the nearby presence of English people, although the English remained anxious about the possibility of an alliance between the Powhatans and hostile "foreign" Indians. Close scrutiny of the surviving documents shows that the Powhatans became violent toward Englishmen only when pushed beyond endurance; even then, only one chiefdom at a time was involved. The General Assembly recognized these facts more readily than did those settlers living near the Indians, and it did its feeble best to restrain the settlers. But making Indian lands inalienable (see above) and confirming existing tracts to them (in 1658)[27] did no good. The codification of Indian law and the

orders passed in the spring of 1662[28] illustrate the point well. The long pre-
ambles to the laws in that code, which give details on the conditions being
remedied, are extremely useful to historians.

Some Englishmen, aided by corrupt interpreters, had been buying land
when the Indian owners thought they were merely confirming their own
possession of it; therefore the Assembly passed once more the law against
purchase of Indian land by individuals and provided for annual inspections
by commissioners to detect encroachments. The English had been acquiring Indian "towns" (i.e., house sites and farmlands) by purchase or by
squatting, and when their livestock ate Indian crops and Indians protested,
they shot the Indians. Under the restated law, Englishmen were required to
help the natives fence their fields. Thieves posing as traders in order to rob
Indians were to be caught and fined. Powhatans who came to the English
settlements on business were to have safe conduct and were to be identified
by wearing silver or copper badges (see fig. 2) with the name of their tribe
engraved on them;[29] no other Indians were to be harbored in the settlements except by Englishmen licensed to employ them.

Several personalized orders were issued in that session of 1662. Wahanganoche, the Patawomeck *weroance,* had delivered a murderer to Col.
Gerard Fowke, who had let the miscreant escape; the *weroance* had then
been jailed, charged by Col. Giles Brent with treason and murder, possibly
in the culprit's place. The Assembly now ordered that Wahanganoche be
freed and paid reparations, while the militia colonels were fined. Two of
Wahanganoche's land sales to Englishmen were also confirmed. The Rappahannock *weroance* had also been jailed about that time after a dispute
over a land purchase by Col. Moore Fauntleroy; the Assembly deprived
Fauntleroy of his office and ordered him to pay what he owed. The cases of
the enslavement of a boy from Powhatan town and of the burning of the
Mattaponi *weroance's* English-style house were also dealt with (see below).

In the 1660s, English anxiety mounted because of increased frontier
raids by "foreign" Indians, lower tobacco prices, stiffer trade laws made by
the mother country, and the elimination of the Dutch as an alternate market for the colony's products. The colonists felt increasingly poor and more
vulnerable to Indian attack. Even the governor felt fearful, for in 1665 he
wrote to his king that the Indians were sure to realize before long that arms
and provisions arrived from England only once a year—and that they could
attack the settlements with impunity just before the next shipment arrived.[30] In their unhappiness, the English did not see that the Powhatans
were engrossed in troubles of their own.

The Weyanocks began feuding with a segment of the Nansemonds called
Pochicks[31] in 1663 and with the Tuscaroras in 1667; in both those years
they had to seek refuge among the English.[32] In 1666 the Assembly felt it
had to reiterate the Indian-English southern boundary and make it a capital
crime for an Indian to cross that boundary without official sanctions.[33]

Fig. 2. The Pamunkey Silver Badge. Collection of Anthony M. Phillips. (Courtesy Colonial Williamsburg.)

Meanwhile, several chiefdoms in the upper Rappahannock basin harassed English settlers in 1661 and in 1664.[34] The latter troubles could not be settled even with the mediation of Indian Ned, a Nanzatico man friendly with the English; in March of that year he had to be put under English protection.[35] In June 1666 the English governor ordered the Rappahannock County militia to attack and exterminate the Indians within reach, with permission to sell captive women and children into servitude. In July the county declared war specifically on the upriver towns of Doeg (formerly called the Tauxenents, who had moved south into the colony), Nanzemond (possibly a segment of the Powhatan Nansemonds), Portobacco (probably a combination of local Nandtanghtacunds and Maryland Portobaccos), and Patawomeck (possibly then living on the Rappahannock River; see below).[36] The outcome of the war is uncertain, but the Patawomecks disappear from the surviving English records thereafter.

On the Eastern Shore the major threat to the English came from Indian groups north of the colony and from the possibility of Occohannocks joining them. In 1661 an "Accomac" campaign involving Lancaster County Englishmen took place.[37] The move was apparently successful, for later that year the Nanticokes, Manokins, Wiccocomicos (of Maryland, not Virginia), Traskokins, and Anamessicks sent tribute to the Virginia governor through the Onancocks and Occohannocks.[38] In 1663 the Accomac County militia went north to investigate a dispute between the Anamessicks and the Quakers.[39] The Virginia government also issued a silver or copper medal and a writ of protection to the Pocomoke *weroance,* who needed the latter within a year: his people rose against him and the Virginia English sent troops to aid him in keeping power.[40] However, the alliance—and probably the puppet *weroance*—did not last long; by 1667 the Pocomokes had moved north of the river that bears their name and refused to submit to the Virginia English any longer.[41]

The English population in Virginia's coastal plain had grown to about 30,000 persons by the late 1660s.[42] The Powhatan population, on the other hand, had decreased drastically by 1669, the year in which the English took a census of Indian bowmen who could help exterminate wolves in the colony.[43] The list totals 725 bowmen, or about 2,900 people in all. The location and size of each group is discussed in the next section of this chapter, but a summary based on that section is useful here to show how Powhatan political groupings had changed in six decades under English pressure.

Among the tribes from the James River basin, there were Nansemonds, now split into two segments with one living west of its homeland, Weyanocks, living far to the south, Appamattucks, Powhatans (now called Powhites), and Chickahominies, now settled on Pamunkey Neck.

Among the tribes from the York River drainage, there were Pamunkeys, Mattaponis, and Chiskiacks, the last-named now living on the Piankatank River.

Among the tribes from the Rappahannock drainage, there were Rappahannocks and Totuskeys (including the Moraughtacunds), both of whom lived on the Mattaponi River; still living on the Rappahannock were Nanzaticos (perhaps formerly the Nandtaughtacunds), Portobaccos, and Mattehatiques, who were either migrants from Maryland or segments of old upriver Powhatan groups, or both.

Among the tribes from the Potomac River's south bank, there were Wiccocomicos and Machodocs (formerly Onawmanients); the latter were now called "Appomatux" or "Mattox"[44] and lived far upriver from their former territory.

All the other groups in Powhatan's and Opechancanough's paramount chiefdom had declined and merged with the surviving chiefdoms, losing their independent identities.

The late 1660s and early 1670s saw fewer alarums, except for a few scares at the falls of the James[45] and some minor troubles near the Rappahannock River in 1673 and 1674.[46] In 1671 the Assembly repealed the law legalizing the killing of Indians entering the frontier county of Henrico.[47] Yet the English colonists were increasingly oppressed in those years by their own economic and political unrest,[48] and by 1675 their frustrations were ready to erupt and pour out upon any available scapegoat. The tributary Indians were an obvious choice. Thus, when one more "Indian" incident occurred in July 1675, the English malcontents had their "cause" for rebellion.[49]

The Indians whose behavior sparked Bacon's Rebellion were not tributary Powhatans at all; they were the Doegs, who had had their differences

with neighboring Englishmen since at least 1658.[50] By 1670 they had moved
back north again to an island in the Potomac River.[51] After a dispute over
money with Thomas Mathew, they killed Mathew's herdsman, Robert
Hen, and fled to Maryland. A party of Virginia militiamen pursued and
succeeded in killing several of them, as well as several innocent Susquehannocks. The Maryland government protested about Virginians entering its
territory and killing innocent Indians. In August 1675, Governor William
Berkeley sent commissioners to investigate, one of whom had already been
instrumental in driving the Machodocs off their lands in Northumberland
County (see below). Not surprisingly, Berkeley's commissioners chose not
to investigate anything but to call out their local militia and demand help
from Maryland in a joint expedition that surrounded a Susquehannock
fort. Five Indian leaders who came out to parley were gratuitously killed.
The remaining Susquehannocks broke out of their fort and the next January took revenge on English settlers near the falls of the Rappahannock.
Honor satisfied, they offered peace to the Virginia English, who rejected it.
    The commissioners' prejudice and stupidity had created enmity with
northern Indian neighbors, but a sense of having been wronged and a paranoiac fear of all Indians seized the Virginia colony just the same. Berkeley
was powerless to make people see reason. While the Susquehannocks were
still prisoners in their fort, Nathaniel Bacon, Jr., had detained some peaceful Appamattucks in Henrico County on a charge of theft, and had been
censured by Berkeley for his rashness. At least one of those Appamattuck
captives was kept in servitude thereafter, for on January 22, 1676, an Englishman was confirmed in his ownership of a girl seized by Bacon's men.[52]
Berkeley attempted to reduce the "threat" from the tributary Powhatan
groups by having their arms and ammunition confiscated. This act, of
course, only made them more vulnerable.
    Few English people were actually killed after the Susquehannocks took
their revenge in January 1676, and as far as the surviving documents show,
the tributary Powhatans committed no hostile acts of any kind. But English
blood was up. Young Bacon fell into the position of leader of a vigilante
group that intended to combat the Indian "menace" and any Englishmen
who got in the way. Thus the lines were drawn between English colonists in
what was more of a civil conflict among themselves than a fight against
hostile Indians. In the following pages, however, we shall focus on the fate
of the Powhatan groups.
    First, Bacon intimidated the Pamunkeys so that they fled their town and
the English could occupy it.[53] Then, in May 1676, he and his forces marched
to the fort of the friendly Siouan-speaking Occoneechees and, after they
obliged him by killing a number of Susquehannocks camped nearby, he
turned on them and killed most of them. Bacon and his men deemed both
of these "campaigns" successes. The General Assembly that met in June re-
flected the feelings of the vigilante element in the colony: laws were passed

declaring all Indians who deserted their towns or harbored hostile Indians
to be enemies, and any Indians captured in "war" were to be slaves. All
trade with Indians was prohibited; "friendly" Indians were to hunt with
bows and arrows only; land deserted by any of them was to be sold to pay
the expenses of a general Indian war.[54] After more political wrestling between Berkeley and Bacon in Jamestown, Bacon emerged victorious and
prepared to embark upon his Indian "war."

In early June, before Bacon returned to Jamestown, some tributary Indians were called upon to join forces with the English, probably at Berkeley's behest. Tributary Indians in Northumberland County, for instance,
were summoned on June 4 for militia duty against unspecified Indians.[55] It
was probably at that time that the Pamunkey *weroansqua* was summoned
to meet with the governor's council.[56]

Cockacoeske, the *weroansqua,* had little to thank the English for, especially after Bacon's routing of her people three months before. She therefore
stood upon her dignity with the council and emphasized to the utmost the
ethnicity of her people. Although she owned European linen, broadcloth,
and other fabrics (see below), she dressed that day in traditionally regal
Powhatan style: a long deerskin mantle with a series of six-inch fringes extending from shoulder to heel, and a three-inch-wide coronet of black and
white *peak* on her head. Walking slowly into the chamber with an English
interpreter on one side and her twenty-year-old son on the other, she faced
the council and, after several invitations, graciously sat down. The council
chairman then asked her point-blank whom she would lend as guides on
expeditions against enemy Indians. Cockacoeske did not reply; instead, she
turned to the interpreter and asked him to translate the request for her.
This move was undoubtedly intended to put distance between herself and
her inquisitors, for Thomas Mathew, our witness of the meeting, believed
that she understood English well enough to dispense with an interpreter if
she wished. She also asked the interpreter to have her son, more fluent in
English than she, answer the council, but the youth declined to do so.

Receiving no answer, the council asked her again about guides. After a
moment she answered by breaking out in vehement protest in her native
language, saying repeatedly, among other things, "Tatapatamoi chepiack!"
(Tottopottomoy is dead!). Mathew's neighbor, Col. Edward Hill's son, explained to him that she meant, in effect, "The last time we helped you, we
lost our men because of your incompetence, and you never compensated us
for their loss," which he knew from his father to be the truth. However, the
chairman, according to Mathew, showed no interest in these past wrongs,
and simply asked her again how many men she would lend the English.
Cockacoeske turned away and refused to answer for some time, but eventually she was pressured into agreeing to send 12 men of the 150 she was
believed to govern. She then left the chamber with icy solemnity.

Even the indifference of the council's chairman was preferable to what
came next. In the last week of June, Bacon and his forces set out to attack
the Indian "enemies" within easiest reach, namely, the Pamunkeys, who
were still hiding out in a swamp. Cockacoeske's old "nurse" was captured
and forced to act as a guide; after she escaped and led the English on a wild
goose chase for the next two days, she was killed. Marching at random,
Bacon's forces happened upon the settlement of several Powhatan groups
and scattered them, killing several men and women and capturing a Nanzatico woman who was "half starved, and so not able to escape." [57]

Other vigilante campaigns were carried out as well, according to the limited evidence we have. On July 6, the Indian interpreter south of James
River sold an Indian woman, presumably a captive, into slavery.[58] And
eighteen years later a Mattaponi woman, captured during the "late rebellion" at a place probably far up the Mattaponi River, sued for her freedom
under a new law that forbade Indian slavery (see below). She lost her case
only because she lacked two years of being thirty,[59] the age at which non-
white servants got their freedom in those days. Her servitude was not considered by the court to have been wrong in the first place.

Bacon then returned to Jamestown and the impotent Berkeley fled to the
Eastern Shore. By late August, Bacon was ready to undertake another campaign against the Pamunkeys. This time his forces caught the people at
their town, taking forty-five prisoners and "looking for the Plunder of the
ffield which was Indian matts, Basketts, matchcotes, parcells of wampam-
peag and Roanoke (wch is their money) in Baggs, skins, ffurs, Pieces of Lyn-
nen, Broad cloth and divers sorts of English goods (wch the Queene [of
Pamunkey] had much value for." [60] Cockacoeske escaped into the woods in
terror and remained separated from her scattered people for the next two
weeks. When she did rejoin them, they were all frightened away from their
town again within a month, by the report of "Wilford, an interpreter" who
was later executed for thus aiding Bacon's cause.[61]

Still more vigilante campaigns were planned in the counties, judging by
the will that the Indian Ned Gunstocker made before his militia duty in
October 1676.[62] However, the rebellion was dying down after the death of
Bacon in that month. Governor Berkeley resumed control of the colony and
began contending with the three commissioners sent by King Charles to
investigate what had happened. Loyalists and rebels alike were eager to
claim damages suffered.

Out of the terribly confused situation existing in Virginia in 1677, the
commissioners found clear evidence on only one point: the tributary Indians had been gratuitously attacked and despoiled. They agreed with
Philip Ludwell, who wrote that the big landholders of the frontiers were the
main culprits first in robbing the Indians and then in claiming that they
were endangered by hostility from the natives:

Whilest the Indians had liberty to sell theire lands the english would ordi-
naryly either frighten or delude them into a bargaine and for a trifle get away
the grownd they should live on, then he comes and settles himselfe there and
with his cattle and hoggs destroyes all the corne of the other Indians of the
towne. This fills us with complaints and will if not prevented keep our peace
forever uncertaine. . . . This was a great cause of this last warr, and most of
those who had thus intruded and were consequently the principall cause of it
were notwithstanding amongst the forwardest in the rebellion and complained most of grievances.[63]

The commissioners therefore agreed that Indian captives should be returned to their people,[64] and that a formal treaty of peace should be made
with the tributaries. The return of prisoners was hindered by the Assembly's order in February 1677 that "loyal" soldiers could keep "prisoners
any of our Indian enemies,"[65] which left matters up to local opinion on the
matter; the keeping of a Mattaponi woman in slavery has already been
mentioned. The treaty, however, was duly made in May 1677, after Berkeley's departure for England. It is still in force today and is the reason that
Pamunkey and Mattaponi reservation people still pay a "tribute" of game
to the governor of Virginia every fall.

The Treaty of Middle Plantation exists in two versions, both of which
have been published.[66] The earlier version was signed on May 29, 1677, the
signatories being Cockacoeske and her son "Captain John West" from
Pamunkey, the *weroansqua* of Weyanock, and the *weroance* of Nansemond. The signing was done in a ceremony[67] in front of the guard house in
the locality that later became Williamsburg. The treaty was read aloud
paragraph by paragraph and translated by "severall Enterpreters." Cockacoeske was then "invited within the Barr of the Court to sign this Treaty
on behalf of herself and Severall Nations [presumably the Mattaponis,
Chickahominies, and Rappahannocks] now reunited under her Subjection
and Government as anciently," after which the other Indian leaders signed
as well. All the Indian signers then knelt and kissed the paper, after which
there were a volley of shots and some fireworks.

Peracuta, the *weroance* of Appamattuck, wished to sign the treaty as
well, but his wish was denied because of some recent trouble with his
people.[68] Some Nanzaticos also attended the ceremony, but left without
signing.[69] However, word traveled through Indian country that the treaty
was a fair one, so at the request of several other Indian leaders the treaty
was expanded to include them. The new version of the treaty, which was
signed between April and June 1680,[70] had as additional signatories the
leaders of the Iroquoian-speaking Meherrins and the Siouan-speaking Monacans and Saponis,[71] as well as Pattanochus, who signed for the Nanzaticos,
Nanzemonds (of Rappahannock River), and Portobaccos.

The terms of this "fair" treaty following a "war" which was no war were
as follows: the Indian leaders who signed it were to be subjects of the king

of England and were to hold their reservation lands by patent, paying only three arrows as an annual quitrent and twenty beaver skins as "rent" to the governor every March. The *weroansqua* of Pamunkey was to act as suzerain over the other signatories to the treaty. Indian rulers and their retinues were to be housed and fed at public charge when they came to the colony's capital on business. No English were to settle within three miles of any Indian town, to prevent incidents over marauding livestock. (This calm assumption, made by Englishmen living in nucleated settlements, that a ring three miles in diameter could be surveyed for a people who lived in dispersed, constantly changing settlements, was to cause difficulties later.) Indian people were to take any complaints of ill treatment to the governor and were to receive justice as though they were Englishmen. (That is not quite the same thing as having the status of Englishmen in the courts; Indians were later denied jury trials.) Indians were to be free to go "Oystering, fishing, and gathering Tuccahoe [arum root], Curtenemmons [arum berries], wild oats, rushes, Puckoone" or other plants not used by the English, so long as they gave notice beforehand to an English magistrate and went straight home afterward. The tributaries were to report the presence of foreign Indians, escort them to the English settlements if desired, and join English troops in marching against them if necessary. Indian servants were to serve for as long as English indentured servants did, and they were not to be enslaved by their employers, whose character was to be monitored by a system of licensing. Trade between the English and the tributary Indians was to be controlled by the governor, and the Indians were to nominate as interpreters people whom they trusted, since many of the earlier ones had proved dishonest.

The good will created by the treaty was to be reinforced by crowns for the Indian signatories of 1677. Originally the commissioners suggested purple robes of stout cloth and crowns made of silver plate, gilt, and false stones.[72] Additional expensive presents were to be sent to Cockacoeske and especially to her son,[73] indicating that the English sought "Captain John West's" favor as (they thought) the next ruler of Pamunkey. However, the crowns that were finally settled upon did not arrive in the colony until June 1680, when a new governor brought them, and then the General Assembly recommended that the gifts be withheld for fear that they might provoke jealousy on the part of the new signatories. The crowns were subsequently lost when Governor Culpeper's baggage was lost at sea on his return to England.[74] The engraved silver frontlet attributed to the *weroansqua* of Pamunkey (see fig. 3), now in the possession of the Association for the Preservation of Virginia Antiquities, may have been given to Cockacoeske at about that time, but no contemporary documents mention it specifically.[75]

The treaty article making Cockacoeske suzerain over the other tribes is interesting. This proud woman undoubtedly asked for the position, after the blows she had been dealt by the English, and in any case, the English

Fig. 3. The "Queen of Pamunkey's Frontlet." Collection of the Association for the Preservation of Virginia Antiquities. (Courtesy Katherine Wetzel.)

always preferred to deal with a few "powerful," complaisant Indian leaders, even when they had to create these leaders themselves. Cockacoeske had certainly presented her grievances early and loudly to the commissioners investigating the rebellion, and the Assembly ruled on her entitlements in February 1677.[76] Pamunkey goods were to be restored as far as possible, and the *weroansqua* would see that English goods taken from the English or "purchased of other Indians" were given back. No more than one-third of her men were to be required for English service at any time; those serving with the English were to have all the plunder acquired from other Indians except the horses and firearms. The Pamunkeys were given additional permission to gather bark for their houses on "any mans land" after securing the owner's permission. Since bark-covered houses had been a status symbol in traditional Powhatan culture, it is likely that Cockacoeske was trying to ensure that her nation could "keep up appearances" as a leading nation should. The Pamunkeys were given permission to hunt even on frontier lands (where hunting was better) as long as they left some people behind with a militia officer as hostages beforehand and did not wear paint while they hunted. Cockacoeske even had the temerity to ask permission to fish at the Powhite (Powhatan) town, whose inhabitants were probably not under her rule, but this request was denied; instead her people were allowed to fish anywhere in the colony after getting permission from landowners. Lastly, the Assembly halfheartedly allowed Cockacoeske to "Redeeme her Indians and goods" from English hands "(if shee can)." If the dispute was with an English "owner," the case was to go to the county court.

If the English and the ambitious Cockacoeske were trying to revive the old Powhatan paramount chiefdom, for whatever diverse reasons, the plan failed. By the middle of 1678 the Chickahominies and Rappahannocks had both refused to pay their dues to their "suzerain," and the resuscitated paramountcy, such as it was, expired soon afterward. Thomas Ludwell, for one, was not surprised. After all, he wrote, Sir William Berkeley had liberated the Powhatan chiefdoms in 1646 from the "house of Pamunkey" in order to keep them divided, "for they like to warr with each other and destroyed themselves more in a year than we can do it." [77]

Once the English had "subdued" the tributary Indians, they belatedly realized that those tributaries lived in as much fear of foreign Indians as they themselves did. And foreign Indians continued to harass the frontiers of the colony.[78] The name "Seneca" began to appear in English documents concerning Indian raids, and the Tuscaroras also began to give trouble, occasionally abetted by their Nottoway relatives. After 1691 the English sent out rangers, often with tributary men as guides,[79] but the raids continued. Sometimes the surviving Rappahannock River tribes were implicated in attacks, as in 1681, when the colony of Maryland asked Virginia for a Nanzatico Indian charged with murder.[80] In November 1683 the Senecas captured the Mattaponi Indian town and besieged the Chickahominy fort, both of which were then far up the Mattaponi River.[81] The English thereupon determined to merge the most vulnerable tributaries, the Nanzaticos and the Rappahannocks, into a well-defended town for the Indians' own good.[82] Accordingly, seventy Rappahannocks and their possessions were moved up to Portobacco, at county expense,[83] though they appear to have settled across the river with the Portobacco instead (see below).

The next year the Pamunkeys, Nanzaticos, Chickahominies, and Appamattucks participated in a peace conference with the Iroquois at Albany, New York, at the Virginia colony's expense,[84] but the outcome was not satisfactory for long. Tensions remained between foreign Indians and English and among the English themselves. For instance, in 1689 a wild rumor circulated in the northern part of the colony that the "papists" (of Maryland?) had hired ten thousand Senecas and nine thousand Nanticokes to kill all the Protestants in Virginia. The fact that there had never been that many people in either Indian nation made no difference.

Alien Indians were as likely to attack the Powhatans as the English: in 1692 an "Appamatuck" (probably Appamattuck rather than Machodoc) Indian had to be ransomed from captivity in Pennsylvania.[85] The Powhatans gradually became less useful as a military buffer as their population declined, by diseases (probably tuberculosis and malnutrition), or by migration, or by spin-off into English society. Only the Nanzaticos remained useful, because of their position on the northwestern frontier of the colony and their friendship with the Doeg nation. In 1691–1692 some Doegs were jailed in a livestock-killing case, and the Nanzaticos paid off the owners of the stock and had the Doegs released.[86] However, when the Piscataways of Maryland tried to move south to Virginia in 1697–1699,[87] the Virginia English used no intermediaries but, instead, cautioned all the tributaries against making a treaty with other Indians on their own. The tributaries asked permission in 1704 to go north to make a treaty with the Senecas. But the English allowed them only to go as far as the Potomac River, and then interpreters went with them to monitor the meetings and report back to the governor. That treaty effort also did no good, and real peace with the Senecas did not come until 1722.

By 1697, when another governor made a list of tributary Indian groups,[88] the Powhatan core population had declined further. There were four nations in the James River region, the two largest probably being the Iroquoian Nottoways and Meherrins; three nations in the York River drainage with a total of 50 bowmen; two nations on the Rappahannock with 40 bowmen; one nation (probably the Wiccocomicos) on the Potomac River with 12 bowmen; and nine small nations on the Eastern shore with fewer than 100 bowmen together. The total manpower of the tributaries, including the Nottoways and Meherrins was 362 bowmen, which indicates a coastal plain Indian population of less than 1,450 people. It is no wonder that in 1699 the tribute demanded of the Indians was reduced.[89] Five years later another list of tributaries was made,[90] with Powhatan manpower totaling only 120 plus the men on the Eastern Shore (no number recorded); the population left in the cores may have been around 600.

The diminished size of the cores and their eroded usefulness as military buffers led directly to a lowering of their status in Anglo-Virginian society. This is shown best by a law passed in 1705 that effectively reduced the size of most remaining Indian reservations by as much as half, the three-mile clause of the 1677 treaty having long been disregarded by English and Powhatans alike. The law provided that when an Indian town was located on a "navigable river"[91]—and all of them were—and when English people had seated on the opposite bank of the river within the three-mile limit, those English were to be confirmed in their ownership of the seated land. Some of those English, to be fair, had bought their land from the Indians (see below). However, the law encouraged more English to move in on the tribes. The Powhatans, whose traditional method of land use involved waterways in the center of territories, and whose settlements often spanned both sides of creeks and narrower reaches of rivers, now had to live on only one side of their former settlements. There may not have been much acreage lost in the process by that time for some groups, but the law subjugated all the Powhatans to English law rather than Powhatan law in an important area of their lives.

Powhatan Tribal Affairs

The history of the Powhatan chiefdoms in the second half of the seventeenth century is generally one of decline and merger into fewer and fewer groups (see maps 5 and 6). Details of the stresses involved in this decline and recombination are poorly recorded, though stress there must undoubtedly have been. James H. Merrell has reconstructed the stresses for piedmont Indian peoples, who experienced the poverty and loss of cultural knowledge that went with losing land to Englishmen and tribal members to malnutrition and disease.[92] The following pages tell only what has been recorded in Virginia. We will now examine the surviving Powhatan chiefdoms, one by one, working roughly from south to north.

In 1648 the Nansemonds still lived on the northwest and south branches of the river that bore their name, though the town on the latter branch was given up to be patented by an Englishman in 1653.[93] Some of the Nansemonds converted to Christianity and began intermarrying with the descendants of Nathaniel Bass as early as 1638 (see chapter 4); these people, whom I term the "Christianized Nansemonds," stayed near the Nansemond River until after the turn of the eighteenth century, when they moved to Norfolk County, near the Great Dismal Swamp. They appear never to have owned a reservation. Meanwhile, the other Nansemonds moved south-

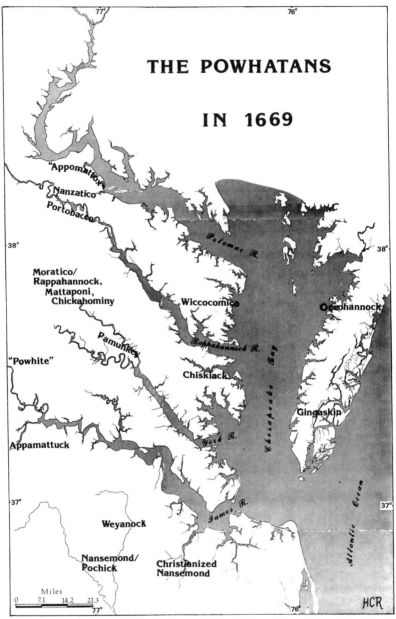

THE POWHATANS

IN 1669

"Appomattox"

Nanzatico

Portobacco

38°   38°

Moratico/
Rappahannock,
Mattaponi,
Chickahominy

Wiccocomico

Oceohannock

Potomac R.

Pamunkey

"Powhite"

Rappahannock R.

Chiskiack

Chesapeake Bay

Gingaskin

Appamattuck

York R.

37°   37°

Weyanock

James R.

Atlantic Ocean

Nansemond/
Pochick

Christianized
Nansemond

Miles
0   7.1   14.2   21.3

HCR

Map 5. The Powhatans in 1669. Based on the Assembly's Indian census of that year and other sources. Base map adapted from *Bathymetry of Chesapeake Bay* (Virginia Institute of Marine Science, 1977).

THE POWHATANS

IN 1705

NANZATICO

PORTOBACCO/
RAPPAHANNOCK

38°   38°

Potomac R.

CHICKAHOMINY   WICCOCOMICO   OCCOHANNOCK

PAMUNKEY

Rappahannock R.

Chesapeake Bay

APPAMATTUCK   *York R.*   GINGASKIN

37°   37°

James R.   *Atlantic Ocean*

WEYANOCK   CHRISTIANIZED
(OTHER)   NANSEMOND
Miles   NANSEMOND
0   7.1   14.2   21.3

HCR

Map 6. The Powhatans in 1705. Base map adapted from *Bathymetry of Chesapeake Bay* (Virginia Institute of Marine Science, 1977) and based on Robert Beverley's list of Indian tribes, 1705.

west to the Blackwater River region in the 1660s, and reservation land was surveyed for them there in 1664.[94] Thus, the Assembly's census of 1669 shows "[Christianized] Nansemonds" with forty-five bowmen living in Nansemond County and the other segment, called "Pochay-icks" or Pochicks, with thirty bowmen in Surry County, which then included the headwaters of the Blackwater River. A "King" of Nansemond signed both versions of the Treaty of Middle Plantation. The traditionalists may or may not have continued to intermarry with their Christianized relatives; however, toward the end of the century they became so embroiled in Nottoway affairs that they became speakers of Nottoway as well, and a single interpreter served the Nottoways, Meherrins, and Nansemonds.

The Weyanocks left the James River during the war of 1644–1646, after which they led a peripatetic life.[95] Their *weroance,* Ascomowett, got them a five-thousand-acre tract south of the James River in 1649,[96] but they appear to have sold or deserted it afterward.[97] The group then moved south of the Meherrin River for a few years, but in 1653 or 1655 they returned northward to the Nottoway Indians' territory, where they settled at a place called Wariecoke and paid tribute to their landlords for several years. Their relations with their fellow Powhatans were strained. On July 2, 1659, the *weroance* of Weyanock sold a boy from Powhatan town named Weetoppen (or Metappin) as a slave for life to Elizabeth Short of Surry County.[98] The sale was fraudulent, of course, and the boy was released by an Order of Assembly in March 1662.[99] By then he spoke English well and was said to desire baptism.

In September 1663 the Weyanocks requested asylum among the English after their *weroance* was killed, with six other people, by the Pochicks. Anglicization was underway in the group: the *weroance*'s name was Geoffrey, and the English who collected the survivors from the town defended by a "puncheon" fort (i.e., timber palisade) found an English-style house (presumably Geoffrey's) and an apple orchard.[100] Geoffrey's corpse, on the other hand, had been treated in the traditional manner: it had been taken outside the fort and "laid on a scaffold & covered with Skins & matts."

The new *weroansqua,* whose relationship to Geoffrey is unknown, and her people remained among the English for two years, by the end of which time their neighbors were becoming nervous about the Indians' practice of hunting anything that moved. The Weyanocks moved south of the Meherrin River and wandered for two years, managing during that time to kill the *weroance* and war captains of the Pochicks.[101] However, their fortunes changed in 1667, when they were living at a place called Unotee, for they ran afoul of the Tuscaroras and lost four people to them in a raid. Once again they asked for and got asylum from the English, who evacuated them from a half-moon–shaped puncheon fort.[102]

This time the Weyanocks stayed only a year before moving back to an old town of theirs called Musketank on the south side of Blackwater Swamp.

By then the Tuscaroras claimed the land and the Weyanocks had to buy it back.[103] The Assembly's census of 1669 shows them living in Surry County and having fifteen bowmen. They stayed at Musketank until 1675 or 1676, when they moved four miles downriver to a place variously called Towawink or Cotchawesco, where they were still living during the colonial boundary dispute of 1710. Their *weroansqua* was a signer of the Treaty of Middle Plantation, but her personal name was never recorded. Her brother was taken to England as a hostage in 1677 by Sir William Berkeley.[104] Relations with their Tuscarora landlords continued to be uneasy; they were attacked by that tribe and also by the Nottoways in 1682.[105] However, peace was restored by 1693, when the "queen" of a Tuscarora town visited the *weroansqua* of Weyanock with a gift, after which the Weyanocks formally bought the town.[106] However, peace proved as detrimental to the Weyanocks as war had been. In 1685 they were reported to have only ten to twelve people (bowmen?) left,[107] in 1702 they and the Nansemonds who lived near them had only ten men among them,[108] and in 1705 Robert Beverley reported them as "almost wasted, and now gone to live among other *Indians.*"[109] Those others were the Nottoways, judging by late-eighteenth-century Nottoway deeds signed by Indian men bearing the names of "Cockarous Tom" and "Wineoak Robin" (1730s and 1740s)[110] and Bob and Jim Wineoak (1790s to 1808).[111]

The Appamattucks moved upriver from their old town on Swift Creek during the war of 1644–1646, and the old town was patented in 1652.[112] In 1669 the group had fifty bowmen and in 1671 they were still living on their own land above the falls of the Appomattox River,[113] although tracts directly opposite the center of their southside lands were patented by Englishmen within the next two years.[114] John Lederer ended his second expedition at their town in 1670.[115] Although legal records are lacking, it appears that the Appamattucks continued to lose land in the last decades of the seventeenth century.[116] Their *weroance,* Peracuta, was a signatory to the 1680 version of the Treaty of Middle Plantation. On April 24, 1691, his successor, an unnamed *weroansqua,* asked permission for her people to live among the English,[117] and in 1705 Robert Beverley reported them as living "in Collonel *Byrd's* Pasture, not being above seven Families."[118] That is their last appearance in the English records, unless the surviving copper badge with their name on it (see above) dates from 1711.

The town of Powhatan near the falls of the James is very poorly recorded after 1646. One of its number was illegally enslaved through the machinations of the Weyanock *weroance* in 1659 and released in 1662 (see above). The group appears in a plat representing land owned by the Byrd family in 1662, with a village on the north side of the falls of the James River.[119] They were living in Henrico County in 1669 and had ten bowmen, according to the Assembly's census of that year, and the Augustin Herrman map of 1670[120] shows a "Powhite" settlement on the north side of the headwaters of the Chickahominy River. In 1677, as related above, Cockacoeske of Pamunkey asked the Assembly for permission for her people to fish at "Powhite," which must have been a site on the James River to be so desirable; her request was denied.[121] In 1689 the land "above the falls . . . just above the old Powhite fields . . . crossing branches falling into Chickahominy Swamp" was patented by an Englishman,[122] and a 1701 plat of land on Shoccoe Creek shows Powhite Indian cabins.[123] After 1701 nothing more was recorded about the group. However, a Pamunkey petition of 1708[124] lists a councilman named "Mister Powhite," which may indicate that the group finally merged with the Pamunkeys.

The Pamunkeys have remained in their homeland on Pamunkey Neck throughout recorded history, although they have moved around within their territory. During most of the seventeenth century they lived farther upriver than they do today, presumably for reasons of safety. Opechancanough's capital, Menmend, was on the large island situated in the mouth of Manquin Creek.[125] The whole of Pamunkey Neck remained unofficially "Indian country" until the 1690s, presumably because several Powhatan remnants had taken refuge there and it was in the colony's interest that they should not be pressured to sell out. However, patenting of the land was allowed to Englishmen, as long as the patentees did not attempt to seat their holdings before governmental permission was given. That, of course, did not mean that Indian occupation of Pamunkey Neck went unchallenged: impatient patentees and squatters were a continual problem. And repeated efforts were made by the Assembly to get the Indians onto limited tracts of land with safe titles in hand.

In 1649 the *weroance* Tottopottomoy applied for and was given five thousand acres for his nation.[126] The land was apparently on both sides of the upper Pamunkey River, for in 1650 an Englishman patented a tract southwest of it and upriver from modern Herrick Creek/Olson's Pond.[127] At the same time a contemporary map, probably made by Anthony Langston before 1662 (see fig. 4),[128] shows Tottopottomoy's town lying between Jacks and Harrison creeks, north of the river and only a little upriver from the modern reservation. In 1653 an Englishman patented land adjacent to a fort of Tottopottomoy's called "Asiskewincke,"[129] the location of which may or may not be the same as the town on the Langston map. In that same year Tottopottomoy was made to choose between a tract at Romancoke, downriver, and the tract of land upriver on which he then lived, and English people who were squatting on Indian land in Pamunkey Neck were ordered to be removed.[130] Tottopottomoy chose the upriver tract. After his death in 1656, his town continued to be occupied by his wife and successor, Cockacoeske, herself a descendant of Opechancanough.[131] By about 1660 she had remarried.[132]

In 1658 the Pamunkeys and other Powhatan groups received confirmation of their ownership of the land they then held, and once again squatters

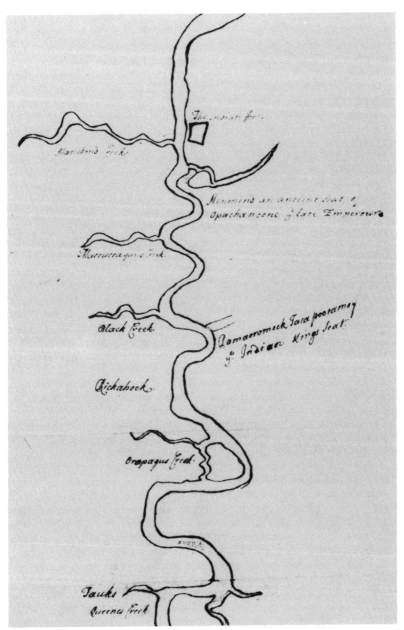

Fig. 4. Detail of the Anthony Langston map, showing Upper Pamunkey River circa 1662. (Courtesy Virginia Research Center for Archaeology, Richmond.)

were ordered to be removed from the lands of the Pamunkeys and Chick-ahominies in Pamunkey Neck.[133] In 1664 and 1665 the Pamunkeys complained again about squatters,[134] and their land was reconfirmed to them in 1668.[135] That did not prevent the Pamunkeys from occasionally selling land, apparently of their own volition (no records of coercion exist). Cockacoeske sold some land to an Englishman in September 1664; he got the governor's permission to keep his purchase and he patented it early the next year.[136]

In 1669 the Pamunkeys had fifty bowmen. The Herrman map of 1670 shows their town still upriver from Jacks Creek, as well as a "Manskins" town upriver that may also have been theirs.[137] In April 1674 the Pamunkeys and Chickahominies were indirectly reprimanded; they (or the Englishmen who pressured them) had leased to English settlers some of their land, which they were legally prevented from selling, and these leases were now banned. The county sheriffs were ordered to publish the order banning the leases,[138] but some sheriffs refused to cooperate and were ordered to be investigated the next September.[139]

The experiences of the Pamunkeys during Bacon's Rebellion have already been described. The twenty-year-old son that Cockacoeske brought with her to Jamestown in June 1676 was named "Captain John West" and had a reputation among the English of being the son of "an English colonel,"[140] presumably the Col. John West who owned a large plantation in Pamunkey Neck. A family tradition among some of Colonel West's descendants holds that West's English wife separated from him because of his relationship with the Pamunkey *weroansqua;*[141] the warmth of that relationship is indicated by the son's name and also by the fact that the "marks" of both mother and son on the 1677 treaty resemble a "W."

The Pamunkeys acted quickly after Bacon's Rebellion to get their lands restored, which was done by an Order of Assembly in February 1677.[142] Yet in October of that year they asked to have confirmation for sales of land that they had made; they had already received partial payment. The Pamunkeys themselves do not seem to have taken very seriously the three-mile limit specified in the treaty. These sales were immediately declared illegal by the Assembly and the "buyers" were summoned to answer for their behavior.[143] In 1678, Cockacoeske petitioned the Assembly about something,[144] possibly land, but thanks to the burning of many colonial documents during the Civil War, we do not know what the matter was.

In 1686, Cockacoeske died and was succeeded not by her son, who had disappeared from the records by then, but by her niece, whose name is uncertain (see below). In accordance with the Anglo-Virginians' treaty rights to confirm the succession of Indian leaders, she petitioned for and received confirmation of her new position as *weroansqua* of Pamunkey on July 1, 1686.[145] She continued the policies of her predecessor when, in 1688, she and some Indian leaders south of the James River asked that settlers be allowed to occupy lands that were still officially closed to them.[146] The Indian leaders probably understood that opening the lands to settlement would open a floodgate. However, they probably underestimated the amount of pressure they would be under to sell their remaining reservation land, seeing only a lucrative source of income from the sale of parts of their reservations that, with their small populations, their groups did not "need." They may also have feared that hostile foreign Indians would move in on them if the English did not. English colonists heartily approved of the Indians' petition and began exerting pressure on the government in their own behalf as well.[147]

In 1693 the English government gave in to the petition, but its ruling that the College of William and Mary should first have ten thousand acres surveyed for it in both Pamunkey Neck and "the Blackwater" caused a six-year delay in the actual opening up of the land.[148] Pamunkey Neck was finally opened in 1699, and the ensuing claims and patenting of land,[149] which required two more years to straighten out, show that the Pamunkeys had indeed let go much of the land that had been theirs under the Treaty of Middle Plantation. Whether or not they sold it all is open to question. The fact remains that at the Quarterly Court for the colony, held on October 22, 1701, they formally ceded their rights to some 5,287 acres[150] and left themselves with a reduced acreage (quantity uncertain) inadequate to support the forty[151] or fifty[152] bowmen and their families who then comprised the tribe. The *weroansqua* who signed the petition to that Quarterly Court[153] was one "Mrs. Betty," about whom nothing is known; she may or not have been Cockacoeske's niece. The *weroansqua* known to history as "Queen Ann" does not appear by name in any English document until 1706.[154]

The remaining reservation was insufficient from the outset to support the Pamunkeys, who clung to the traditional division of labor that made women horticulturalists and men hunters and fishers (see chapter 7). From the beginning the group had apparently counted on exercising their rights, given by the Assembly Order of 1677, to fish wherever they liked and hunt and forage on Englishmen's unfenced patented lands. However, their new neighbors resented those rights, and on April 23, 1705, the Pamunkeys had to petition the governor for aid in keeping them.[155] The governor noted as he acted on their behalf that their tribute, now down to ten beaver skins, was probably too much and should be reduced to one skin.[156] On April 28 the Assembly obligingly issued another order that the Pamunkeys—and also the Gingaskins on the Eastern Shore (see below)—had the right to hunt on patented lands within their own counties.[157] The history of the Pamunkeys after that is taken up in chapter 7.

The Mattaponis appear to have fled their homeland during the war of 1644–1646, for they turn up next in the records on the ridge between the Mattaponi and Rappahannock Rivers, living far up in the headwaters of Piscataway Creek.[158] The county of [Old] Rappahannock, in which they lived, made a treaty with them in 1656, as already described.[159] However, by 1660 their English neighbors were pressuring them to leave; the *weroance* and his council felt it necessary in that year to swear that their people had no designs upon the lands of neighbor Francis Brown.[160] It did no good. In 1662 some of the neighboring English burned the *weroance*'s English-style house, which he owned as a status symbol. When the *weroance* complained to the governor, militia Lt. Col. Thomas Goodrich was summoned for a conference,[161] the outcome of which was an agreement between the parties that three Englishmen (including Francis Brown) who wanted the group's land were to pay the *weroance* fifty matchcoats for it and the tribe would move.[162] The Mattaponis did not collect immediately; six years later, in March 1668, two of the three Englishmen sold their shares of the land to Lieutenant Colonel Goodrich, who agreed to finish paying the Indians what was still owed by Francis Brown.[163]

By 1667 the Mattaponis had moved back near the upper Mattaponi River, and within a year Englishmen were beginning to patent land around them and around the path that they had made between their town and the Indian towns on the upper Rappahannock River, variously called Portobacco and Nanzatico.[164] The Mattaponis had Indian neighbors as well. They lived either with the Chickahominies or very close to them; the "path to Potobacco" ran "from Mattapony Indian Towne, or Chickahominy."[165] Also nearby were refugee groups from the lower Rappahannock River, the Rappahannocks and the Moraughtacunds/Totuskeys (see below). All four groups are listed in 1669 as residing in New Kent County, which then included Pamunkey Neck; the Mattaponis had twenty bowmen at the time. The diversity of nations within that small an area may be the reason that Herrman's map of 1670 shows only one group of Indian houses on the Mattaponi River but no tribal name. All four groups were represented by Cockacoeske when she signed the Treaty of Middle Plantation.

The Mattaponis seem to have held their own until 1683, when the Senecas captured their town; survivors may have fled to the neighboring Chickahominy town, which was also besieged.[166] It is doubtful that the Mattaponis, already a small nation in 1669, recovered from the Seneca attack. They probably merged with the stronger Chickahominies, though some of them may have moved across Pamunkey Neck to join the Pamunkeys. In 1685 a land patent mentions land "whereon the Mattpony [*sic*] & Morratico Indians formerly lived,"[167] and beginning in 1686 the land patents for the area mention only one Indian town ("the Indian Town"), which must have indicated the still-flourishing Chickahominies.[168] No Mattaponi group is mentioned in any subsequent record until the early nineteenth century (see chapter 8).

The Chickahominies took refuge in Pamunkey Neck during the war of 1644–1646. They appear to have been politically a part of the Pamunkeys for some time afterward, and intermarriage occurred between the two peoples.[169] Squatters were ordered removed from their lands as well as from the Pamunkeys' land in 1653,[170] and the 1658 land confirmation law ordered more squatters removed from "the Pamunkies and The Chichominyes on the north side of Pamunkie river."[171] In 1661, however, they left the Pamunkeys and obtained land near the headwaters of the Mattaponi River, where there was immediate controversy over parcels that the Chickahominies had already sold.[172] One buyer was a neighbor named Philip Mallory, whose family would be intimately involved in the tribe's loss of its reservation (see chapter 7). The Chickahominies had continued to be governed entirely by councillors called *manguys* (or *mangois;* the word means "great men"); however, one of these was often dominant over the others in the English records, usually a man named Harquip (or Herquapinck) or, later, a man named Drammaco.

The Chickahominies appear as a separate nation with sixty bowmen in the census of 1669, the same year that John Lederer's first expedition left from their town.[173] However, their name is not found on the Herrman map of 1670, and Cockacoeske of Pamunkey claimed sovereignty over them in 1677. Yet the Chickahominies were not willing to remain under Pamunkey domination once the English vigilante threat was past. By 1678 they— especially their young men—were refusing to pay tribute to Cockacoeske or to do her bidding in domestic matters, and feelings were running hot on both sides.[174] The Pamunkey interpreter, Cornelius Dabney, noted in June 1678 that much of the trouble stemmed from the slanted views of the Chickahominy interpreter, Richard Yarborough.[175] Yarborough was a neighbor of the tribe and leased land from them;[176] his interests in acquiring their land probably led him to make them resist domination by another group. Eventually the matter went to an English court, since the treaty provided for English arbitration in such matters. The English were not eager to be caught between two angry Indian groups,[177] and the outcome of the case cannot be known, again thanks to the burning of the general court records during the Civil War. In any event, the Chickahominies subsequently went their own way.

The group tried repeatedly to sell or lease parts of their reservation land, and in 1674[178] and 1690[179] these efforts were thwarted by the governor. The English began patenting land around them in the 1680s,[180] and the Senecas besieged them in 1683. They took refuge for a time with the Pamunkeys after the Senecas drove them out of their town; but soon relations between the two peoples soured again and the Chickahominies asked the governor for lands at Rickahock on Mattaponi River. The request was made by the group's three *manguys*, Herquapinck, Paucough, and Hearseeqs.[181] In 1694 the tribe requested new lands at Quanohomock,[182] but the request was merely deferred.[183] On September 20, 1695, the Chickahominies deeded over 6,160 acres to Roger Mallory, whose heirs later sold the land.[184] The group sold more land as Pamunkey Neck was opened to English settlement, and the sales were confirmed. In September 1701 the Chickahominies were granted the land between the two Herring creeks, tributaries of the Mattaponi River,[185] although surveying the tract proved difficult because of the dispersed nature of Chickahominy towns: their town in 1677 (the base line for the survey) had been "a row [of houses] at least one mile in length."[186] Squatters were already moving in. In 1702, a year in which the Chickahominies had thirty bowmen,[187] their 14,910 acres[188] were declared too large a tract for them, and they and all English claimants were summoned to the general court to be held in Williamsburg.[189] It was probably during this time or in the 1694 request that Robert Beverley and some friends broke into the group's temple and recorded its contents.[190] Beverley was a neighbor, and only in 1694 or in 1702 would he have found a single Indian group in his vicinity on the upper Mattaponi River, with all that group's population conveniently called away to confer about tribal land.[191]

Pressure continued to be exerted on the Chickahominies to cede their land. In 1704 a violent dispute broke out within the group, during which Indian men named Coscohunk and James Mush burned the cabin of Tom Perry (a Chickahominy with an English name), split his canoe, and cut down his apple and peach trees.[192] A countercomplaint was lodged against Perry by Drammaco, then "one of the cheif [sic] Munguys" of the tribe. Perry had started it all, he said, by burning his (Drammaco's) cabin, beating his wife, and turning him out of his town;[193] he and most of his people had had to flee to the Pamunkeys, a statement which the Pamunkeys themselves confirmed.[194] Coscohunk and Mush were probably Pamunkeys themselves, or Chickahominy ancestors of later Pamunkeys, for the surname "Mush" persisted among the Pamunkeys until the 1830s (see chapter 8). The Assembly finally had the King William County court investigate the matter. The dispute between Perry and Drammaco was found to stem from the desire of part of the tribe to sell the reservation, a desire that the county court felt sure was fomented by some English neighbor.[195] The court was ordered to investigate further, but its findings no longer exist because of the burning of that courthouse in 1885. The Chickahominies had "about sixteen Bowmen, but lately increas'd" in 1705.[196] Their internal dissensions about land were not over.

The Chiskiacks left their old territory sometime in the 1620s and eventually settled on the Piankatank River. In 1649 their weroance, Ossakican (or Wassatickon[197]), got a patent for five thousand acres for them.[198] Already, in the previous year, an Englishman had obtained the rights to their land if they ever deserted it;[199] he would have a long time to wait. In 1651 the Chiskiacks exchanged their lands for a tract of equal size farther upriver,[200] although a formal survey was not ordered until two years later.[201] Ossakican gave some of these tribal lands to an Englishman before he died;

the gift was confirmed in 1655 by his son, acting through a "protector," or regent, named Pindavaco.[202]

In 1657 the Virginia General Court ruled that Chiskiack lands would be added to Gloucester County's church-owned lands if the tribe deserted them.[203] However, some English neighbors were eager to get some for themselves first: in 1661 the Assembly had to order all persons to desist molesting the Chiskiacks about their land or their guns,[204] and the following year one Mary Ludlow had to be ordered to cease encroaching on the tribe's reservation.[205] Sometime around 1660, John Gibbon met the group's "king."[206] In 1667 the original English patentee of 1648 was confirmed in his right to some land whenever the Indians deserted it;[207] he would have to wait longer yet.

The Assembly's census of 1669 showed fifteen Chiskiack bowmen living on their land in Gloucester County. Herrman's map also shows their village (called "Cheesecake") on the south side of the Piankatank River upriver from Cobb's Creek. The group is mentioned in a neighbor's land patent of 1672,[208] and a lease of theirs was declared invalid in 1675.[209] It is likely that during Bacon's Rebellion they took refuge with a stronger tribe, probably the Pamunkeys, whose hiding place during the strife was Dragon Run, just upstream from their reservation. The Chiskiacks appear in the records for the last time in 1677, when the Gloucester County court was ordered to set a time and place for them to trade regularly with the English.[210] By 1683, when part of their reservation was surveyed for an Englishman,[211] the Chiskiacks were apparently gone, most likely either to the Chickahominies on the Mattaponi River or upriver with the Rappahannocks in the wake of the Seneca raids (see below).

The Moraughtacunds moved early to the territory of their more powerful neighbors, the Rappahannocks. Their land surrounding modern Lancaster Creek began to be patented in 1652, though no records of Indian sales exist.[212] By that time they had already moved upriver to the drainage of Totuskey Creek and become neighbors of the Indians there (Rappahannocks or others), who were known as the Totuskey Indians.[213] The Moraughtacunds' exact relationship to the Totuskeys is uncertain. In 1658 their town is mentioned by itself as the eastern boundary between their group and the Rappahannocks.[214] "Rappahannock" and "Moratico" lands near Totuskey Creek began to be patented in 1653,[215] and *weroances* of both groups sold the remaining lands in 1662, though not without controversy over getting paid.[216] In 1667 the buyer of the separate Moraughtacund and Totuskey towns swore he had paid for them.[217] The same county court order dealing with the controversy in 1662 provided for Moraughtacund lands of two thousand acres on Totuskey Creek, which indicates that they had forty bowmen, or the same number the "Totas Chees" had in 1669 (see below); the two groups were combined in the eyes of some Englishmen.

The Moraughtacunds probably joined the Rappahannocks thereafter at their main town on Rappahannock (now Cat Point) Creek upriver. However, that site also became surrounded by the English, and both groups crossed the river and went to live in separate but neighboring settlements in the headwaters of the Mattaponi River, where they were recorded separately in the 1669 census. The Moraughtacunds appear there as "Totas Chees," with forty bowmen. They still lived there as "Moraticos" in 1671, adjacent to the former residence of the Chickahominy *manguy*.[218] That is their last appearance in the English records. They had gone to live with one or another of their neighbors by 1683, when the Rappahannocks were evacuated from the area (see below).

The Rappahannocks originally claimed the land on both sides of the Rappahannock River, but by the time the English began settling on the river they had withdrawn entirely to the north bank. Their principal town in 1652 was two miles up modern Cat Point Creek, according to a patent taken out for a neighboring tract.[219] Their land east of Totuskey Creek was deeded in April 1651 by *weroance* Accopatough to his "brother" Moore Fauntleroy.[220] Accopatough died before he could confirm the deed in Jamestown; confirmation was accordingly made in May 1651 by his successor, Taweeren, "the great King of Rappahannock and Moratoerin [Moraughtacund?]," and a man named Machamap, who was possibly the Moraughtacund *weroance*.[221]

The English were moving into the region in large enough numbers that in July 1653 the General Assembly ordered that land be allotted to all the Indians in the Rappahannock River drainage (then encompassed by Lancaster County).[222] According to the treaty that Lancaster County made with the Rappahannocks two months later, their *weroance* was also to have an English-style house.[223] However, any friendly feelings engendered by the treaty faded rapidly. By November 1654 the Rappahannocks had retaliated so often against encroaching English neighbors that the militias of Lancaster, Northumberland, and Westmoreland counties merged and met with the tribe to demand damages.[224] That meeting turned into a brawl in which Taweeren was killed.[225]

The English continued to move in so rapidly that tensions rose again to the boiling point. Therefore, in September 1656, Rappahannock County, newly budded from Lancaster County, made its own treaty with the group, as already described. This treaty did little good, and in March 1658 the Assembly had to assure the Rappahannocks of fifty acres for each bowman and order that their conflicts over land with Englishmen be settled.[226] The governor also gave Moore Fauntleroy permission to hunt unmarked hogs between "Moratico [i.e., Totuskey Creek] & great Rappahannock" [i.e., Cat Point Creek], which he claimed were his.[227] Two months later, Accopatough's deed to Fauntleroy was reconfirmed by Taweeren's successor, Wachicopa (Machamap?).[228] Fauntleroy was no longer "brotherly" to the

Rappahannock: this or another deed remained in question for some time. In March 1660, Fauntleroy was ordered to bring proof of a deed from the Indians to the next Assembly;[229] in March 1661, he was ordered to pay thirty matchcoats as the payment still outstanding on "his" land;[230] and a year later, when he had refused to pay and instead had jailed the Rappahannock *weroance*, he was ordered to pay fifteen of the thirty matchcoats forthwith, give up his militia office, and let commissioners investigate his dealings with the group.[231] The commissioners then set the boundaries for the tribe's land at Cat Point Creek to the west and Totuskey Creek to the east.[232]

The Rappahannocks finally gave up trying to resist the English settlers and moved away. The year 1669 found them living in the headwaters of the Mattaponi River, with thirty bowmen in their group; in 1677, Cockacoeske of Pamunkey signed the Treaty of Middle Plantation on their behalf. However, by 1678 they had reasserted their independence of the Pamunkeys.[233] When the Seneca troubles of 1683 erupted, they were living on the ridge between the Mattaponi and Rappahannock rivers. For their safety, the Assembly ordered that they either merge with the Nanzaticos or move to "their new fort" (location uncertain).[234] The Rappahannocks chose the former course, and in the winter of 1683–1684 they moved first across the river to their old territory and then upriver a month later, all at the expense of Rappahannock County. The attitude of the English toward the Indians' possessions is revealed in the reimbursement orders: seventy Indians and their "Corne and lumber" [obsolete meaning: old, seldom-used goods; junk] had been moved.[235] The Rappahannocks settled near the Indians established at Portobacco, then technically part of Nanzaticos (see below), where their identity seems to have become the dominant one. In 1690 the "king of Rappahannock" was summoned to the county court on business connected with concealing runaway servants.[236] Their reservation had been patented by English people since 1650 (see below), and eventually the Indians either deserted the land or were pushed off it (no records of the matter survive). On December 19, 1699, a neighboring Englishman got permission "to allow some Rappahannock Indians to live upon his land."[237] Thus it was that Robert Beverley reported in 1705 the presence in Essex County of Rappahannock Indians, who were "reduc'd to a few Families, and live scatter'd upon the English Seats."[238]

Portobacco town was located very near the site of Nandtaughtacund on John Smith's map (1608).[239] The place first appears by name in the English records in 1655, when land was patented across the river from it.[240] The site itself was patented by a man named Lunsford, without any mention of Indians, in 1650,[241] with the usual understanding that no seating would take place during Indian occupation. The Indians of Portobacco communicated by paths with the Mattaponis and Chickahominies,[242] but they were politically allied with the Indian towns of Nanzatico and Nanzemond across the river, and they may have been technically part of Nanzatico.[243] A *weroance* named Pattanochus signed the Treaty of Middle Plantation for the three towns jointly; Pattanochus' origins are unknown. The Portobaccos had sixty bowmen in 1669, but part of their reservation was declared "not used" the next year when Lunsford's daughter, the wife of Ralph Wormeley, got permission to build on it.[244]

In the winter of 1683–1684 the Rappahannocks became their neighbors[245] and may have absorbed most of them. Subsequent documents of the area mention only the Rappahannocks, except that the 1702 list[246] says that they and the Nanzaticos combined had thirty bowmen, and in 1705, Robert Beverley reported that the group lived north of the river and had five bowmen.[247]

The name "Nanzatico" may well have been an Anglicization of the old Powhatan name "Nandtanghtacund,"[248] which appears south of the river on John Smith's map of 1608. The precise relationship between the Nanzaticos and the Portobaccos is unclear, as is that between the Nanzaticos and the neighboring towns of Nanzemond, Warisquock, and Ausaticon, all of which appear in a patent of 1655.[249] All three may have been newly named towns from older groups like the Pissasecks and the upriver Cuttatawomens. On the other hand, Ausaticon may be the Nanzatico town proper, and Warisquock and Nanzemond may be segments of the same people. The combination of names of two neighboring chiefdoms in Powhatan's old paramount chiefdom is intriguing, but documentary proof of any connection between the old chiefdoms and the newer towns is lacking at present. There was also a "Mattehatique" town which appears only as a segment of Nanzatico in the 1669 census. The town of Nanzemond first appeared in patents of 1654[250] and survived long enough to be represented in the Treaty of Middle Plantation.

Most later references to the Nanzatico town place it on the north bank of the Rappahannock River, though two documents mention Nanzatico lands on both sides of the river.[251] Much of their land north of the river was patented by an Englishman in 1656 and regranted to another man, Ralph Wormeley, in 1680.[252] Wormeley married the Lunsford heir of the Portobacco tract; one of his daughters, Elizabeth, married John Lomax, and thus it happened that the Lomaxes "owned" Indian towns on both sides of the upper Rappahannock in the late seventeenth century.[253] The Nanzaticos lost ground steadily throughout the period. The only surviving deed made by the group is that signed by the *weroance* Attamahune in 1662.[254] Nanzemond was patented in 1667.[255] In the 1670s, the Nanzaticos deserted several outlying "habitations," which were thereupon patented and occupied by Englishmen.[256] In 1669 the Nanzaticos and "Mattehatiques" together had fifty bowmen, but in the same period they lost people like Edward Gunstocker (see chapter 6) to English society. In 1702 they and the Portobaccos combined had thirty bowmen.[259] By 1704 they were surrounded by English settlers, and hostile relations prevailed.

Nanzatico discontent with their English neighbors came to a head in 1704. In April of that year they complained to the governor that an English claimant to their land south of the river had broken down their fences and "turned them off their land," while the rest of their land on both sides of the river was claimed by the Lomaxes; they wanted new land.[258] The English deliberated on the matter, with no one seeming to want to act on it,[259] but justice was too slow for the Nanzaticos. On August 30 several of their men painted themselves for war and killed the John Rowley family, with whom they had had a long-standing dispute. The Richmond County militia thereupon rounded up all the Nanzaticos it could find (forty-nine people) and jailed them; in the process, all the Indians' possessions were either destroyed or plundered.[260] The five murderers confessed and were tried—in a court of oyer and terminer, without a jury—in the presence of witnesses from the other tributary tribes, and were convicted and hanged.[261] The other Nanzaticos were exonerated but were not set free.

The innocent Nanzaticos were sent to the jail in Williamsburg, partially for their own safety and partly because the English government contemplated making an example of them. Thus it was that after much deliberation in the Assembly;[262] the law of 1665[263] was invoked, whereby in case of murder, the nearest Indian town was to be held answerable until the culprits were found. This law was stretched, by common consent among the English, to include the Nanzaticos. The actual killers had been dealt with, but the tribesmen had made no effort to help the English find them in the first place. So the whole town remained guilty by association and was disposed of. Everyone of twelve years or older was sold into servitude in the West Indies for seven years and prohibited from returning to Virginia thereafter, while the children under twelve were bound out to Virginia Englishmen until the age of twenty-four (and any future children of the girls were to be servants likewise), after which they were prohibited from visiting any Indian town.[264] The Nanzaticos were thus eliminated as a tribal group.

The Patawomecks continued living in their homeland until the 1660s. Englishmen began taking up land near them in the 1650s, which rapidly caused conflicts. In August 1658 a dispute between the tribe and Giles Brent over payment for land had to be settled through the county court.[265] Brent and other prominent landowners continued to disagree with the Patawomecks, so that in 1662, after the *weroance* Wahanganoche was unjustly jailed (see above), the General Assembly had to intervene.[266] However, the offending militia officers remained in power, probably because of the continued fear of foreign Indian attack. Two years later the group's weroance gave a present to an Englishman.[267] In 1665 a tract of land near

Upper Machodoc Creek, "formerly in possession of the King of Potomack," was patented.[268] In that same year war was declared on them, along with other Rappahannock tribes (see above). No patent mentions the site of the Patawomeck town and no documents mention the Patawomecks at all after 1665. Presumably they merged with another group and lost their separate identity. Since they were warred upon with tribes near the falls of the Rappahannock, and since their silver badge of 1662 has been found near the site of Portobacco (see above), it is probable that they went to that town.

The Onawmanients became known by the name of Machodoc[269] in the mid-seventeenth century because the first English patents in their territory were taken up on a creek of that name. They appear to have included some Yeocomico people from Maryland, after those people sold their town to the English in 1634 and moved away.[270] The first English arrived in the early 1650s, patenting land on Lower Machodoc Creek and Yeocomico River, sometimes after a legal sale.[271] By 1657 the group was embroiled in a dispute with Isaac Allerton, who was said to be encroaching on their town on Lower Machodoc Creek. Commissioners for Northumberland County found the Indians willing to let Allerton stay if he desisted from further expansion onto their land, and a formal agreement to that effect was signed by the *weroance* Pertatoan.[272]

Feelings continued to run high, however, as the English continued to press in on the Machodocs. The outburst came in February 1659, when two Machodocs, one of whom was named George Casquesough, murdered an Englishman. Both culprits were delivered to the English by their people, tried by the county court, and executed by the governor's warrant.[273] But the Machodocs had deserted their town after handing over the culprits, and they had a hostile demeanor as they tried to return to the town in May 1660. The Northumberland County court therefore declared them to be accomplices in the murder and sent a force of men which drove them off, burned their cabins, and cut down their growing corn.[274]

The Machodocs withdrew into their upriver territory, which had a major town on Upper Machodoc Creek. This town, too, was surrounded by Englishmen beginning in 1654,[275] and the site of the town itself was patented by Gervase Dodson,[276] a surveyor of Indian lands and a major landowner who also "owned" the town of Cuttatawomen (see below). The Machodocs remained in their town through 1669, when they were listed as the "Appomatux," with ten bowmen living in Westmoreland County. The group disappeared after that. They may have taken refuge with the Nanzaticos, since one of the Nanzaticos transported to the West Indies was named "Mattox Will."[277]

The Cuttatawomens who lived on Corrotoman River remained there only until the early 1650s. By 1656 they had settled on the north bank of a tributary of Fleet's Bay then called Corrotoman Creek (now Dymer Creek); in that year their town was patented by Edwin Conaway and Gervase

Dodson.[278] They had some difficulty either with establishing their claim or with their neighbors early the following year.[279] Soon after that they seem to have moved north to join the Wiccocomicos,[280] in whose identity they quickly submerged their own.

The Sekakawons (Anglicized to Chickacones) were pressured by the English to merge with the Wiccocomicos almost as soon as Englishmen began taking up land in their territory. In 1655 the county court ordered a tract of land to be surveyed for the two groups combined [281] and the governor ordered that Machywap, the Sekakowon *weroance,*[282] govern both groups.[283] The political merger was not a happy one at first. A governor's order of January 20, 1657, stated that Machywap was in danger of his life from the Wiccocomicos and provided for six English bodyguards at the county's expense over a period of ten months.[284] John Gibbon met him and his son in 1659, by which time he had been deposed.[285] Nothing more was heard of either Machywap or the Sekakawons after 1659.

The Wiccocomicos left their homeland on Great Wicomico River in the mid-1650s. At the governor's instigation, the Northumberland County court ordered that land be surveyed for them and for the Sekakawons at Great Wiccocomico Town, where the two groups then lived. At the going rate of 50 acres per bowman, they were to receive 4,400 acres, which indicates that the groups had a total of eighty-eight bowmen. Gervase Dodson reported for his survey in February 1656 that the town was across what is now Dividing Creek from the Cuttatawomen town, a south bank tract that he himself was in the process of patenting.[286] Meanwhile, the Wiccocomicos ceded their title to their old lands on Great Wicomico River to incoming Governor Samuel Mathews, who formally claimed the tract in 1657 and secured Assembly confirmation of it.[287] The group's difficulties with the Sekakawon *weroance* appointed for them by the English has already been described.

The Wiccocomicos did not enjoy clear title to their Dividing Creek reservation for long. In April 1660 their councillors Pewem (or Pekwem, whom John Gibbon described as their "king") [288] and Owasewas (or Owasoway) complained to the county court that two Englishmen named Jones and Walle had encroached so badly on their land that their own people could not subsist.[289] Investigation showed that Walle was not encroaching,[290] but the case of Jones, an agent for the estate of Samuel Mathews, was less easily solved: the grant to Mathews was in doubt and the Assembly demanded proof, after which the county court ruled that Jones could remain.[291] Therefore, in November 1662 the councillors Owassewas, Chistecuttawance, and Tatamenoug sold Robert Jones the neck of land he had already occupied.[292]

That was not the end of the trouble. In April 1669, Jones complained of Wiccocomicos breaking into his house. The Wiccocomico councillor Oponomoy lodged a counter complaint against Jones.[293] At least part of the problem stemmed from the Indians' conviction that the 1656 survey had not been properly done. Accordingly, a new survey was made at the Indians' expense[294] and the boundaries between Jones and the Indians were then examined.[295] Meanwhile, the Assembly's census of 1669 showed seventy bowmen in the group.

By 1672 the Wiccocomicos and Jones were back in court, this time with Jones claiming that the Indians had "deserted" the land that he was taking up. Jones' claim was disproved.[296] However, the group continued to lose land to Englishmen, including one John Smyth of Gloucester County. Smyth already occupied a neck of Wiccocomico land in 1672,[297] and in 1683 he petitioned the governor for a survey, prior to patenting, of the "Yeocomico" Indians' lands, "after having paid the quit Rents and Beaver tribute due from the Indians."[298] Smyth's friendship appears not to have been disinterested. The Wiccocomicos complained against him and others again in 1693.[299] However, they lost ground steadily, with no sales or land cessions being recorded. By 1705 they were Smyth's tenants (see chapter 7) and were said to have only "three men living, which yet keep up their Kingdom, and retain their Fashion."[300]

The Algonquian speakers on Virginia's Eastern Shore were always more complex in their political organization than has usually been realized. Early English reports speak only of an Accomac and an Occohannock "king's howse." The reality seems to have been that the *weroance* of Accomac (Esmy Shichans, probably the same man as the "Laughing King" [see below]) was the paramount chief for the entire region, though nominally a subject *weroance* of Powhatan. The Accomac ruler's brother, Kiptopeke, acted as his viceroy in Occohannock, binding together the northern and southern halves of the paramount chiefdom. From the mid-seventeenth century onward, the English called the paramount chief "emperor" or "empress," which in a sense they were, once they left Powhatan's domination. The *weroances* under them were called "kings" and "queens." There were many district chiefdoms in both Accomac and Occohannock, though few from the former territory appear in the records.

The English began taking up land within Accomac territory before 1622,[301] and the easy-going Esmy Shichans gave away large tracts to people, such as Thomas Savage, whom he liked. By the time local English records were scrupulously kept there, only two Accomac towns survived: Esmy Shichans' seat near Cheriton, and a town called Mattoones near Hungars Creek. Mattoones was patented by an Englishman in 1637.[302] The Accomacs became known as "Gingaskins" in 1641,[303] when they accepted a patent for their remaining 1500 acres of land, located on the seaside.[304] Esmy Shichans had died by then and the leadership of the "empire" had moved northward (see below). At the same time, more Englishmen pressed in upon the Gingaskin lands. Relations soured between the two peoples, though they rarely became violent. However, in 1650 the governor had to write to the county court ordering that "the Laughinge Kings Indyans" had always been friendly and were not to be molested now.[305] This order was relatively easy for the English to obey because the Eastern Shore Indians were allowed to sell land to individual Englishmen;[306] Englishmen who wanted more land could easily go north and buy it from the Occohannock chiefdoms.

There was enough trouble over the Gingaskin boundaries, however, that in 1660 the Assembly ordered them to be surveyed by impartial people from the mainland. They were to be inalienable thereafter.[307] Seven years later the governor had to order an investigation of the rumor that John Savage (son of Thomas Savage, the interpreter who had lived with Powhatan as a boy) and others planned to take away the tribe's land.[308] A report came back the following spring that the lands claimed by the Gingaskins either lay within Savage's patent or had been sold to a man named Harmanson.[309] The tribe's patent of 1641 had come from the huge, ill-defined tract given to Thomas Savage by Esmy Shichans. The quarrel apparently dragged on: we know the Gingaskins were not run off because "ye Indian Towne" is mentioned in a document of 1671.[310] Finally, in 1673, the governor's council ordered that 650 acres be surveyed for the Gingaskins and that Harmanson be turned out if he was found encroaching.[311] The Gingaskins had apparently sued John Savage for good measure, for in April 1674 the governor's council ordered an inquiry into the patents, surveys, and claims of all involved.[312] The inquiry revealed that the titles of both Savage and the Gingaskins were doubtful and recommended that because the Indians had always been peaceful, they should have 650 acres of Savage's land, to be theirs as long as they occupied it and paid one ear of corn a year in acknowledgment. John Kendall, another neighbor who had often intimidated the Indians, was to give security for his good behavior.[313] The Gingaskins did not receive a patent for their new reservation until 1680.[314] Ironically, in that year they had more trouble with a neighbor.

In January 1680 the Gingaskins complained to the county court that a widow, Mrs. Kendall (mother of John?), was cutting their trees. The case was continued, and when the Indians complained again in March, two Englishmen went out to investigate. The case was finally settled in October, when the court accepted John Kendall's suggestion that the Indians keep the cut timber but also keep up their boundary fence better. A subsequent damage report showed that three hundred to four hundred fence logs had been cut.[315] The Gingaskins continued to live on their lands until the early nineteenth century. Their assignment of 650 acres means they had thirteen bowmen in 1673; no Eastern Shore groups appear in the Assembly's census of 1669. In 1705, Robert Beverley wrote that they were as numerous as all the Occohannock remnants put together, so their population may have grown somewhat.

When Esmy Shichans died (date uncertain), the position of paramount chief of the Eastern Shore went to someone in the Occohannock sector. The first holder of the title was Wackawamp, who appears in the records for the first time in 1643 as "the great Kinge of ye Eastern Shore"[316] and who sold off the lands of the Occohannock chiefdom in the early 1650s.[317] By 1656 he had to apply to the county court for protected land on which his people could live; the land (location uncertain) was duly assigned to him.[318] The next year he died, leaving a will recorded in the county courthouse that left his dominions to his daughter (no name given) and, after her decease, to his brother's sons, Akomepen and Quiemacketo.[319] None of these heirs appear in any subsequent records.

The next paramount chief was Tapatiaton (or "Debbedeavon"), who sold lands around Nandua, Nassawaddox, and Pungoteague creeks in the late 1640s and early 1650s.[320] He began as the *weroance* of Nandua in 1648, claimed to be the "great king" of Nandua in 1649, became *weroance* of Nassawaddox in 1651, claimed in 1660 to be *weroance* of Onancock (which had previously been governed by councillors),[321] and styled himself the "Great Emperor of the Eastern Shore" after 1662. It seems plain that he displaced the legal heirs of Wackawamp, or else he was an heir who had changed his name, which is possible. His district *weroances* were Norris, former councillor of Wackawamp, at Occohannock; Piney and Mr. Brooke at Machipongo; Ekeeks at Onancock; Nochetrawen at Chesconnessex; and others, such as Matahoquis, whose chiefdoms are uncertain. All of these men and Tapatiaton himself sold land continuously during the 1650s and 1660s[322] until their people were left on small islands of territory for which they never received patents. Most sales were straightforward. However, the Onancocks and the Curritucks ("Craddocks") occasionally had trouble getting paid for their lands and had to get assistance from the county courts.[323] Sometimes the fault lay with the Indians, who were not above chicanery: on one occasion the Onancocks also sold land to which they had no right, and on another occasion they prosecuted six English buyers for nonpayment, but their case was dismissed when they neglected to meet the Englishmen in court.

Except for occasional disturbances in their hunting because of rumors of war with Indians in Maryland, the Occohannock chiefdoms lived fairly peacefully on their dwindling lands in the late seventeenth century. Many of their young people indentured themselves to Englishmen to earn a living (see chapter 6). Tapatiaton died sometime between 1664 and 1672, leaving a daughter who appears in the records as Mary. Her position was usurped by a man called Johnson, who in 1672 complained to the governor that his "subjects" were mutinying against him. The case went to the Accomac county court, which found that Mary was the rightful *weroansqua*.[324] Declared "empress" by the governor in January 1674, she is probably the empress referred to by Beverley in 1705. Her people, under the name "Occahanock," presented claims to the English in 1699,[325] when the Pamunkey Neck opening forced a general clarification of conflicting land claims by Indian and English people.

In 1705, Robert Beverley listed the following groups, all small, as surviving within the Occohannock territory: Metomkin ("much decreased of late by the Small Pox"), Kegotank ("reduc'd to a very few Men"), Machipongo ("has a small number yet living"), Occohannock ("has a small number yet living"), Pungoteague ("Govern'd by a Queen, but a small Nation"), Onancock ("has but four or five Families"), Chesconnessex ("has very few, who just keep the name"), and Nandua where the "Empress" lived ("Not above 20 Families, but she hath all the Nations of this Shore under Tribute").[326] Many of these people migrated frequently between the Virginia and Maryland colonies. In 1697 the Maryland governor wrote of them: "The Eastern Shore Indians remove very often into Virginia and Pennsylvania, so that it is almost impossible to ascertain their numbers. But the Indians of these parts decrease very much, partly owing to smallpox, but the great cause of all is their being so devilishly given to drink."[327] The Occohannock groups seem eventually to have merged with groups to the north and to have given up their tiny reservations in Virginia altogether. The patents for taking their lands did not even mention their names, and since no deeds were involved, it is as though they vanished without a ripple.

Thus the seventeenth century saw the Powhatans not so much conquered militarily as inundated with settlers, in a period when their populations were decreasing. The reduction in manpower led directly to decreased military effectiveness, and to a decreased perception of that threat in English minds. Lesser military importance meant that the English could lower the legal status of individual Indians with impunity. And the Indians' inability to retain their lands, combined with smaller populations "needing" them, led to a vastly reduced landbase by the end of the century. That poverty in land and in civil rights, which gathered momentum in the seventeenth century, eventually became a crushing burden for the Powhatan people who survived.

CHAPTER 6

The Powhatans as Minority Persons

IT IS OBVIOUS that a people who continually lost their land to foreigners, by whatever means, and were forced to abandon their settlements would become impoverished and lose some of their members, as well, through spin-off. That is what happened to the Powhatans. In the late seventeenth century, an increasing number of Indian people had to begin working for the English in order to survive. Some of them "spun off" permanently, some only temporarily. The latter group became a culturally based ethnic fringe around their respective core groups.

The loss of people, however, did not occur with the rapidity usually assumed by historians, nor did it result in the complete disappearance of all the Powhatan groups by 1700—or 1800 or 1900. Several factors inhibited the complete impoverishment of the core groups and thereby limited their loss of people. The first and foremost factor was the Indians' genuine attachment to the way of life of their forefathers and their continued reluctance to give it up. With this attitude, core people admitted their poverty to themselves less readily than did fringe people or outsiders. Another factor was the English colony's permitting the people to hunt and forage within "English" territory. Still another was an English program of paying Indians to hunt the wolves that preyed on English livestock (see below). Neither of the latter two factors was very effective, given the times in which the Powhatans and the English lived.

The tributary Indians felt they had a right to hunt, fish, and forage on unpatented and unfenced patented lands, since the English were not obviously "using" them. It is doubtful that most Powhatan groups understood for many years that the sales they made to Englishmen were permanent. When Englishmen bought land but then either did not fence it in or farmed it and then let it go fallow, the Powhatans apparently felt that the land reverted back to their tribal ownership, as it did among themselves, so they proceeded to hunt and forage there. The repeated laws passed against killing Indians for "mischief" (see below) indicate such an attitude.

Other complications occurred as well. The livestock of the English—especially hogs, which are natural woods-dwellers—was often allowed to roam freely and therefore often grazed in the fields that the Powhatans were unaccustomed to fencing in.[1] The anger of the Indian owners was natural. At the same time, Powhatan men were accustomed to hunting animals that ran free in the woods, so they hunted English hogs along with the deer and incurred the wrath of the English owners.[2] The situation was further complicated by the fact that the first European farm animals the Powhatans themselves adopted were hogs, which they turned loose and hunted down as they wanted them. (Horses came later, and then sometimes only as status symbols; see chapter 7.) The practice of marking their hogs beforehand, as the English did, had to be forced upon some Indian groups. The first law to make Indians mark their hogs with cuts in the ears was passed in 1674,[3] but the Weyanocks and Nottoways had to be forced to cooperate in 1693.[4] Therefore, Indians' hogs were sometimes inadvertently killed by Englishmen.[5]

Not surprisingly, the English settlers' killing of Indians because they hunted English or unmarked Indian animals on English property reached such proportions after 1649 that the Assembly had to legislate about it. In 1655 a law was passed making it legal to kill Indians within English territory only if they were engaged in "mischief" (meaning premeditated theft or killing of livestock); the court oath of the English killer that "mischief" had been in progress was deemed sufficient proof.[6] A year later, after noting that a great deal of innocent Indian blood was still being shed, the Assembly made it legal to kill Indians on one's land only when they were engaged in a felony, and required two witnesses to testify to the fact in court.[7] At the very least, Indian men sometimes had their arms confiscated by hostile English neighbors who were moving in.[8] It was not until the Treaty of Middle Plantation in 1677 that the Powhatans' right to hunt and forage on unpatented and unfenced patented "English" lands was legally stated, and even then that right had to be legally reaffirmed at intervals.[9]

Even during "peaceful" periods, tributary Indians had difficulty going about their traditional occupations. However, any period of tension had an immediate economic effect upon the Powhatan core groups. It was much riskier for core people to go foraging on unfenced patented lands when the English were jumpy and apt to shoot Indians, painted or not. Those who did not shoot were likely to confiscate the Indians' weapons and make it harder for them to hunt. In addition, by 1646 the Powhatans were unquestionably dependent on the English for axes, firearms, and ammunition to use in their hunting and foraging, and in periods of tension the English would pass laws prohibiting the sale of these or any other commodities to any Indians whatsoever.[10]

The Powhatan core people developed a taste for English cloth (well documented) and liquor (poorly documented but highly probable), and they could easily be persuaded to exchange land for a few matchcoats.[11] The English frontiersmen, on the other hand, were all too willing to buy Indian furs and lands in exchange for cheap trade goods, so the colonial government had repeatedly to pass laws licensing traders.[12] As poverty and dependence on English goods made more Indian people willing to work for English settlers, laws also had to be made restricting the employment of Indians to those who would not exploit them.[13] And no laws for the protection of Indians could be thoroughly enforced in the scattered settlements of the English.

The Powhatans continued to follow their traditional way of life as long as they possibly could. This was not too difficult for the women, since their household, farming, and foraging work did not require huge tracts of land or bring them into much contact with Englishmen. The women also had an easier time, psychologically, when they sought work among the English, since many of their traditional tasks corresponded to the housework and light farm work their English employers wanted female employees to do. For the men it was another matter. Performance of their traditional tasks of hunting, fishing, and war was severely hampered as the English closed in on them. The men were the first Indian people to become unemployed, and they had the most changing to do (i.e., learning trades, learning to plow fields) if they were to become useful as employees to the English. Most of the late-seventeenth-century records of Indians hired by Englishmen concern male employees. The documents show that they either performed tasks conforming to their traditional definition of "manhood" or they tried English males' jobs with mixed success.

The first "occupation" the English proposed for Indian men was as killers of wolves. This program would benefit both sides, the English thought, since the Indians needed income and the English wanted the predators exterminated. Accordingly, bounties were offered on wolves' heads.[14] However, the English reckoned without the Indian men's strong feeling that hunting was an activity that provided food for the table. Wolf meat was never a Powhatan delicacy, so only a few Indian men ever shot wolves and claimed bounties on them.[15] On the other hand, some Englishmen began to collect bounties on wolves shot well beyond Virginia's frontiers, so the Assembly left the matter of wolf bounties entirely to the county courts.[16] Even assessing Indian towns a certain number of wolves' heads per year, with partial or entire remission of the towns' annual tribute as an inducement, did not work.[17] By the end of the century some counties were offering wolf bounties to Indians but not to Englishmen,[18] and in 1705, as Indian civil rights in general declined, the Assembly passed a law that counties paying wolf bounties had to pay a higher rate to Englishmen than to Indians.[19]

Powhatan men occasionally found temporary employment as guides on expeditions, such as those of Edward Bland in 1650, John Lederer in 1669–1670, and Batts, Wood, and Fallam in 1671.[20] They were also valued as trackers of fugitive servants[21] and, after the fears that surfaced during Bacon's Rebellion, of foreign Indians pursued by the English frontier rangers.[22] Some Indian men had served in a similar capacity during the Rebellion itself (see above).[23]

Powhatan men were also more proficient at fishing on a commercial scale than the colonists were. Weir building was an art—it is still learned by oral tradition in Virginia—and in the early days of the colony Indian men were sometimes hired to make the weirs the English wanted. In 1638, for example, an Indian (presumably a Nansemond) employed by an Englishman in Norfolk County was hired by another Englishman to build a weir. The customer, however, did not offer the craftsman enough, and in true Indian style the man put off building the weir until his customer confronted him. The price the man then asked for his weir was a steep one for those days: "a paire of breeches + a paire of shoes and stockings."[24] The outcome was not recorded.

Indians were also hired at times to make dugout canoes for English customers.[25] The Indian men of the Eastern Shore performed a variety of services for the English in 1667, "catching of fish being ye cheifest [sic]."[26] In 1682 an Indian is recorded as a co-owner, with an Englishman, of a weir.[27]

From the early days of the colony, Englishmen had hired Indian men to hunt for them. As English settlements closed around the islands of Indian territory, more Indian men hired themselves out as hunters until they became an arms-bearing group which had to be regulated by the colonial government. In 1654 the Assembly made it mandatory for Englishmen wanting to hire Indians as hunters to get permission first from their county court or from the governor himself.[28] Licensing was designed to ensure that the hiring was done by upright people who would treat their employees well and take proper responsibility for any damage the hunters might do to English livestock roaming in the woods. For instance, in 1685 the owner of a hog killed by an Indian employee sued the hunter's employer for damages.[29]

After 1654 many people duly applied for licenses "to employ Indians" who hunted and did other unspecified work,[30] but there were always people who did not bother with a license and who were caught.[31] Sometimes they were caught when their employees got into trouble, as the free Negro* Philip Mongram did in 1663.[32] But the number of unlicensed employers increased as the Powhatans grew poorer. In 1677 the governor ruled, at the Pamunkey *weroansqua* Cockacoeske's request, that no Pamunkey Indians

---

*For references to African-Americans, my policy throughout this book has been to use the terms that were current at any given time. Thus I use "Negro," "free Negro," and "mulatto" (all legal terms) for the period before the Civil War, "colored" until the civil rights era, and "black" thereafter. Although there is disagreement among scholars on this issue, many feel as I do that it is useless to "upstream" current terms like "black," which do not accurately describe the more complex situation existing before the Civil War (unless one refers to *all* non-whites).

were to be hired without licenses.[33] In 1691 the governor had to order the sheriffs of each county to report cases of Indians kept by Englishmen without licenses,[34] and eight years later all licenses were declared void and new ones were required to be obtained.[35]

Powhatan women and men produced some cash income by selling the goods they traditionally made. These items often turn up in the inventories of English estates and include mats,[36] baskets,[37] wooden trays,[38] tanned deer skins or clothing,[39] and pottery.[40] One Indian man turned his hand to an apparently "feminine" occupation, the making of pottery bowls. His other behavior was not "effeminate" by Powhatan standards: in 1671 one "John the Bowlemaker" beat up an English constable and got flogged for it.[41] Ceramic pipes continued to be made and sold to English smokers.[42] The coiled pottery made by Indian women was softer and less durable than European pottery; the main advantage of Indian pottery was its availability at all times. Durande de Dauphine recorded Portobacco Indian women selling pottery to him in 1687 (see chapter 7). The women now made it in styles that their customers would use, namely pots and bowls with handles and tripod legs for use in cooking on the hearth. Ivor Noel Hume believes that the actual users were probably the slaves of the English buyers.[43] Yet this Colono-Indian ware has been found at Varina Glebe "in association with relatively sophisticated ceramics,"[44] which indicates that English people also used it. The English did not consider Indian-made goods in general to be as valuable as European-made goods. One inventory lists some Indian pots amongst some "Old Lumber" (junk),[45] and the estates containing Indian goods usually belonged to middle- or lower-class Englishmen.

The currency commonly used to pay Indian people for their goods was shell beads, since English silver money was scarce in the colony. Shell "money" was rarely valued specifically in terms of English money, but a few cases exist. In 1649, when the English were resuming expansion into Indian territory, the Assembly set the rates for Indian money as follows: one yard of white peak[46] was worth two shillings sixpence, while a fathom (two yards) was worth five shillings; black peak was worth twice as much as the white. One yard of roanoke was worth only ten pence, and no Englishman should have to take more than five pounds sterling worth of it.[47] Shell money was devalued the next year: one fathom of white peak was now worth four shillings, with black worth double the white.[48] Devaluation seems to have continued thereafter, as Indian population and military power declined. In 1691 an Englishman who was apparently a trader died, leaving an estate containing 264 yards of roanoke valued at threepence a yard.[49] Roanoke was normally measured in arms' lengths, which only approximated yards, and it was the medium used in most cases of reparations. In 1661, for instance, the *weroance* Tapatiaton had to pay three hundred arms' lengths of roanoke to compensate for the English hogs his people had killed and the cattle his people's dogs had injured.[50] The Accomac County court ruled on the value of various Indian and English goods in 1667.[51] A "coat [matchcoat] of two yards of trading Cloath" was worth forty arms' lengths of roanoke, and each of these commodities was worth three hundred "well grown sheepsheads" (a kind of fish). Two sheepsheads were to be paid for "one large drum fish, [and] two small sheepsheads accounted for one large sheeps heads fish."

In 1676 the English Assembly considered that the Powhatans needed only a few trade goods, namely, "matchcoates, hoes and axes," in order to survive.[52] This stereotyped the Indians as the "savages" of former times. It is highly probable that the Powhatans themselves would have added guns and ammunition to the list. The full range of items sold to the Powhatans and other Indian peoples in the second half of the seventeenth century is revealed in the inventory of a trader who died in Henrico County in 1694: gun powder, shot, a "trading Gun," gun locks, duffel cloth,[53] "plaines" cloth, and blankets.[54] The presence of gun locks on the list indicates that some Indian men had learned how to repair guns by that time. On the Eastern Shore, if not elsewhere, such knowledge may have been a recent acquisition: an Indian took his gun to an Englishman for repair and had it confiscated during Bacon's Rebellion.[55]

One item for trade is conspicuously missing in the Virginia records until 1705: liquor, which certainly had no official sanction for the Indian trade. There are only two clear documentary references to Powhatan drinking before the late seventeenth century. In 1647 a drinking party took place at the house of a woman whose husband was away. All or part of a gallon of brandy was consumed by the woman, four Englishmen (one of whom committed adultery with her that night), and four Indians, who spent the remainder of the night sleeping "in yᵉ chimney corner."[56] John Lederer noted in 1672 that the hard bargaining practices of tributary Indians could be abated by giving them liquor.[57] By the late seventeenth century, English observers noted that liquor had become a major escape route for Indians whose world was falling to pieces (see chapter 7). Not until 1705 did the Assembly try (in vain) to prevent liquor sales by traders to Indians.[58]

The civil rights of individual Powhatans diminished along with their nations' population and military presence. As long as the tributaries had the power to threaten the English, they were assured by the colonial government of treatment in the courts reasonably equal to that accorded English plaintiffs and defendants. However, as the Powhatans decreased and the population of African slaves grew, the English became more concerned with maintaining their own superior position in Virginia society and more willing to place Indians in the inferior category of non-whites.[59] This downward trend for the Indians manifested itself in several areas of life, such as the right to bear arms, the right to be heard in court, the right not to be enslaved, and the right to marry freely.

The right of tributary Indians to bear arms was never completely abrogated except during Bacon's Rebellion, when a law was passed forbidding trade of any kind with Indians and stating that Indians could hunt on English lands only with bows and arrows.[60] At other times, however, individual Englishmen took Indian hunters' guns away and sometimes beat them as well; when the Indian took the case to a county court, he was usually vindicated.[61] It was legal after 1660 for Indians to use their own guns when hunting on their own lands.[62] The law of 1691 creating parties of rangers on the colony's frontiers allowed for the inclusion of two mounted Indians, and said nothing about whether they were to be armed.[63] However, the series of laws aimed at controlling non-whites in 1705 included an injunction against Indians' use of guns when they went hunting on English lands.[64] This was almost tantamount to prohibiting them from hunting at all, given the small reservations they had by then and their dependence upon guns in their hunting.[65]

In the county treaties of 1656 and 1657 and in the colony's treaties of 1646 and 1677, the tributary Indians were promised justice "as though they were Englishmen." Initially this meant that they had the same rights to sue and testify in court that English people did. Many Indian people did in fact go to court when they felt that they had been injured in some way,[66] and Englishmen sued Indians as individuals or as tribes for the same reasons.[67] Indians who resisted summonses to court were made to apologize or be punished,[68] just as Englishmen were. And Indians who sued and failed to appear lost their suits just as Englishmen usually did.[69]

In spite of the laws made to protect Indians from the actions of greedy and prejudiced English neighbors, Indians were occasionally beaten or killed by Englishmen[70] and, for their part, they sometimes assaulted and murdered Englishmen or their employees.[71] Cases of this sort, involving individual Indians, went to the county court for settlement, which usually involved the paying of reparations. One such case is that of Samuel Griffin, whose English servants had killed an Indian man in 1661. Griffin was held responsible for the actions of his servants and had to pay reparations to the victim's town (which is unnamed); the servants were punished by having their time of indenture extended.[72] In another case, an Indian named Misseteage and his wife had been beaten in 1677 by William Taylor for killing his hogs. The Accomac County court found fault on both sides and dismissed the case. Taylor, still feeling aggrieved, asked the court to pay the expenses of his two Indian employees, who came from Misseteage's town and had testified to his having killed Taylor's hogs. The court refused the request on the grounds that the two witnesses had appeared not on Taylor's behalf, but on that of the king of England, whose treaty assuring the tributary Indians of protection had been at stake.[73] And in 1670 the governor had to issue a proclamation that the Eastern Shore landowner Edmund Scarburgh was to be arrested for oppressing the neighboring Indians "by Murthering Whipping + burning them, By taking their children by force from them who are their parents. . . ."[74] Tried in a court case that required four interpreters for Indian testimony, Scarburgh was found guilty and deprived of his militia office.[75]

There were also cases of theft to be dealt with. Sometimes it was an Indian who was the thief, as in the case of one Pickpocket, who in 1667 was convicted of thievery over the course of several years, as well as of having recently stirred up his people against the English; he was transported from the colony.[76] Hog stealing by Indians became such a concern to the English that in 1674, when the Assembly legislated hog marks for Indian towns, it also stated specifically that "Indian proof" or testimony was acceptable in court cases against Indian thieves.[77] More often, however, the cases which appear in the court records involve Englishmen robbing Indians in order to drive them from their lands.[78]

Another kind of robbery committed against Indians involved unscrupulous traders who got Indian people deeply into debt and then imprisoned them. Few details are available in the surviving documents, because the Assembly moved to correct the abuse early. Their attention was drawn to the matter by the Weyanock *weroance,* the none-too-scrupulous man who sold a boy from Powhatan town into slavery in 1659 (see chapter 5). He was probably trying to raise money to pay his trading debts, for by March 1660 he was in custody and petitioning the Assembly for release. The Assembly freed him for a year and passed a law preventing traders from getting legal redress on bad Indian debts.[79] That law seems to have worked: there is only one other debt case in the records, and then the county court ordered the Indian to pay up; the Indian had an English first name and surname (Peter Mongram [see below]) and may have been detribalized.[80]

The English wished to detribalize all the Powhatans, and until late in the seventeenth century it was possible for detribalized Indian people to enter the middle- or lower-middle levels of English society. After 1691, when interracial marriage was prohibited to whites (see below), Indians were expected to join the lowest, non-white ranks. This change in status and civil rights can be traced in the documents relating to Edward Gunstocker, the detribalized Indian about whom the most information is available.

Gunstocker was probably the "Indian Ned" of Nanzatico who was rewarded by the colonial government in 1666 (see above). In 1665 he patented 150 acres on the north bank of the Rappahannock River, probably near Nanzatico town, after paying headrights for three Englishmen to come to Virginia; his patent was personally approved by the governor.[81] In October 1676 he planned to go to war with the English against "my countrymen, the Indians," so he made a will leaving all his possessions to his wife Mary, whose ethnic origin is unknown.[82] Gunstocker survived the rebellion, and in 1682 he leased his land to two English tenants,[83] who took him to court within three years for going back on his word and preventing them from using the land. The case was continued until after Gunstocker's death, which occurred between March 1685, when the suit began, and September 1686, when his wife and heir was ordered to answer the tenants' complaint.[84] The court finally ruled in early 1688 that the surviving tenant could use the land he had leased six years before.[85]

By 1697, Mary Gunstocker was dead and the land had been inherited by Gunstocker's sister's daughter. This woman was apparently not detribalized: her name was "Betty or Nonomisk,"[86] and, with her husband, Nump-skinner, and a female friend or relative named Pattiawiske, she sold the land.[87] The new English owner was promptly ousted by force by another Englishman, and in the subsequent court case various arguments were brought forward, the last being that the sale could not have been valid because Ned Gunstocker was an Indian and could never have owned the land in the first place. The court held that Gunstocker could indeed have patented land in his own right—and so, by implication, could other detribalized Indian people—and the buyer of the land was reinstated in 1699.[88] Though a small farmer's greed for land is plain here, so is the hardening of attitudes even toward detribalized Indians.

In the second half of the seventeenth century the English of Virginia showed considerably less interest in drawing Indians into their society as equals by religious means than had their predecessors. Governor Edmund Andros wrote in 1697 that "no endeavours to convert the Indians to Christianity have ever been heard of [in Virginia]."[89] Instead, the Virginia English tried to convert the Powhatans culturally, by other means which allowed for Indians to become part of the labor pool for English planters. An early attempt that failed was the 1656 law that provided for bounties on wolves: the bounty proposed in that early law was one live cow for every eight dead wolves. Receipt of the cow was specifically stated to be "a step to civilizing them and making them Christians."[90] The bounties soon changed to things the Powhatans appreciated more. Another, tacitly held, plan to "civilize" the Indians was the assigning to them of land at the rate of only fifty acres per bowman (see above). Intensive farming and animal husbandry were required to feed a family on a plot that size. The Powhatans got around that, too: they continued hunting and foraging on unpatented and unfenced patented lands until the colonial government was forced to legalize the practice to prevent another Indian war.

The primary method by which the English hoped to "civilize" the Powhatans was the only one that even came close to working: training of Indian laborers by English employers. The English preferred to start the training early. Throughout the second half of the seventeenth century, the colonial government exhorted Indian parents to part with their children, assuring them of the children's good treatment.[91] In particular, the English tried to convince the parents that their children would be "servants,"[92] not slaves, and would not be "assigned" (transferred) from one English family to another. In the late 1660s several Eastern Shore towns indentured some of their adolescent boys to English farmers, with mixed results (see below). However, few Indians on the mainland seem to have accepted the English offer until later in the century, when poverty had weakened their resolve. Then, after 1680, an occasional parent, such as the Rappahannock man named Tom,[93] left his or her children in the care of an English family. In 1691 Robert Boyle's estate created the Brafferton Fund, which paid for the setting up of a small school for Indians at the College of William and Mary; the school had few or no pupils until well into the eighteenth century (see chapter 7). Most of the Indian labor that the English got seems to have consisted either of adult tributary Indians or of the enslaved children of more distant tribes.

In the decades immediately after 1646, the English did not draw a clear line between "servants" (i.e., domestic employees) and slaves, either for Indians or for Africans.[94] Indian slaves there were, however: in 1651 an Englishman deeded an Indian slave to his sons "& their heyres as long as hee shall live."[95] In 1662, an Indian boy was passed from Englishman to Englishman to Englishman, being expected to serve these masters "for ye terme & time of . . . his life."[96] The Indian "slaves"—adults and a child—in the estate of Thomas Smallcombe in early 1646 were probably prisoners of war.[97] Two years later an Indian girl in the same county was ordered to serve until the age of eighteen,[98] and an Indian "servant" was sold the next year on the Eastern Shore for eight hundred pounds of tobacco.[99] What was sold was probably the time left to serve in the servant's indenture; that is true when Indians were included in other inventories of estates, such as the one in 1652 listing an Indian woman and her child with seven years left to serve.[100]

The General Assembly had to legislate again and again for the protection of people who were ideally to be treated as "Englishmen" but who were actually regarded by most colonists as a source of cheap labor. In 1649 the Assembly passed laws against stealing Indian children from their parents, inciting other Indians to do so, assigning the children to other English families, or keeping them beyond the age of twenty-five.[101] Six years later the Assembly renewed the law about freeing Indian children who were servants after the agreed-upon term, adding that they should also be educated as Christians.[102] In 1658 the law about keeping Indian servants until the age of twenty-five had to be repeated yet again. New laws were passed at that session as well, stating clearly that Indian children living with the English with their parents' permission were to be considered servants, not slaves, and that Indian children were not to be "bought" from Englishmen, for the Englishmen may have stolen them.[103] Some Indians were not above selling their countrymen, either: the case of the Weyanock *weroance* has already been described. An Indian named "Mister John" was hired by the Accomac County court in 1670 to procure "fatherless children" to be servants.[104] Indian youngsters continued to be held beyond their terms of indenture, unless they complained to the county court; in 1663, one Thomas got his free-dom three years late—plus damages.[105] Some Englishmen, on the other hand, were honorable in their treatment of their charges: in 1660 John Beauchamp got permission from the Assembly to take "his Indian boy" to England, after already getting the approval of the boy's parents.[106] And in 1668 the major landowner John Custis contracted with an Indian youth of sixteen to free him in eight years, give him clothes, a cow and calf, and a life interest in fifty acres of land.[107]

However, few employers were so generous, and the popular pressure in the colony for non-white servants to be held for life resulted in another clarification by the Assembly in 1670. Now free non-whites, Indian or Negro, could not buy indentured Christian (usually meaning white) ser-vants, and all non-white servants arriving in the colony by sea were to be slaves, while those arriving by land were to be servants for twelve years or until the age of thirty.[108] Runaway servants were a problem, whether they were English, Indian, or Negro. In 1672 the Assembly ruled specifically on slaves: Indians were to be paid twenty arms' lengths of roanoke for captur-ing runaways, and there would be no penalty for wounding or killing the Negro slaves. However, Negro slaves, at 4,500 pounds of tobacco, were more highly valued than Indian slaves, who were worth only 3,000 pounds.[109]

Powhatan Indians who became servants during this period reacted in di-verse ways. Many worked peacefully and disappeared from the English records after their initial indenture, at which time their ages were recorded for later reference and their English names were given them.[110] Some rose in their employment to become overseers, as "James Revell" did. James, whose Indian name was not recorded, was a Metomkin, bound out in 1667 at the age of eleven to Edward Revell until the age of twenty-four.[111] He died only a year after finishing his term; by that time he was the owner of hogs with English-style earmarks (he kept the hogs at his natal town) and was a debtor, presumably after buying English goods.[112] Before he left his employer, he became an overseer on one of Revell's farms. There he had problems with an English boy who worked under him and resented having to take orders from "an Indian Dogg"; on at least two occasions, James struck the boy for disobedience, and each time a fight ensued.[113]

Other Indian servants adjusted poorly to work on English farms and ran away, just as their English peers did. Sometimes their own people took them back and hid them, and at other times their people turned them in; Amongos, a councillor of Metomkin, did both. In 1667 a councillor of Metomkin, probably Amongos, bound out a boy of twelve named Wincewack (or Wincewough) to Robert Hutchinson, who gave him the name of James.[114] Either Wincewack or a fellow servant of his ran away to Nanticoke at Amongos's instigation in 1672, but after spending time in an English jail for the deed, Amongos brought the servant back to Hutchinson that July. Amongos also promised to bring in two Indian servants of Edmund Scarburgh's, but failed and was imprisoned again on suspicion of helping to hide them.[115] Wincewack ran away (again?) to Maryland in 1675, and Amongos was jailed yet again for abetting him.[116] Another Indian named Dick Shoes brought in the youth, who was ordered to serve extra time for the ninety-eight days he had been absent, while Shoes was rewarded.[117] Two years later Wincewack, who could still not adjust to life among the English,[118] got into a brawl with an Englishman who would not give him "some drink" on credit. After an exchange of insults—and James's English was more than adequate to the task, according to the deposition of a witness—the Englishman began to beat him. Wincewack defended himself only after a bystander yelled at him to do so; he probably expected to get into serious trouble for striking an Englishman.[119] Wincewack finished his term of service two years later and apparently went home; nothing more is heard of him.

During Bacon's Rebellion it became legal to enslave tributary Indians if they committed acts (such as flight) that could be construed by the English as hostile.[120] Although Bacon's anti-Indian faction lost, that law was nonetheless passed again after the rebellion, through an Order of Assembly in 1677 and an Act of Assembly in 1679.[121] It would remain on the books until 1691 and in practice for decades longer. In 1682 the Assembly repealed its law of 1670 about servants and slaves; instead it declared all servants who were not Christians at time of purchase, as well as all Indians sold by "neighboring Indians or any other" people, to be slaves.[122] This law was probably made in response to the increasing trade in Indian children brought into Virginia from the southwest—presumably Tuscaroras, Cherokees, and others. Immediately after the law was passed, a great number of Indian children from unnamed tribes were "adjudged for age," i.e., registered as servants or slaves, depending upon their time of arrival in the colony, and significantly, most of these registrations took place in frontier counties.[123] Some of these children were considered fairly valuable: in 1684 the estate of Thomas Shippy included an Indian "boy" worth 2,500 pounds of tobacco and a "girl" worth 2,000 pounds.[124] A "decrepit girl" in another estate was valued at 550 pounds, as was another Indian girl who was "a dwarf, and decrepid [sic]."[125]

Owners had to pay taxes on Indian slaves, including females over the age of sixteen (after 1682);[126] in 1685 the Henrico County clerk searched the records for Indian servants not "tithed" for by their masters, in order to make the owners pay.[127] Indian servants and slaves were not supposed to be transported out of Virginia: in February 1691 a Nansemond County man was prosecuted for selling two Indians to a ship's captain.[128] Sometimes the slaves' fate in Virginia was not entirely bleak, as, for instance, in the household of John Wells, who was accused by his neighbors of coarsely swearing with (not at) his wife and singing on the Sabbath with his servant girl and "his Indian boys." [129] However, considering the conditions under which most Indian people lived among the increasingly prejudiced English, it is little wonder that people in the Indian towns sometimes harbored fugitives of their own color, as the Rappahannocks were suspected of doing in 1690. [130]

Often the lives of Indian servants who finished their terms and decided to continue living among the English were not easy. Such people had acquired many of the skills needed for life among the English, but they rarely had the capital to begin farming on their own, as Edward Gunstocker tried to do. Women living without men had a harder time yet. A good example is that of "Indian Moll" and her daughter, Hagar Penny, who lived in Henrico County. Moll, or "Mary a free Indian Woman," petitioned the county court in 1688. She had finished her term of service for an English woman and now she wanted her daughter, whose father is unknown, to be freed also, on the grounds that Hagar was born in Virginia and an Act of Assembly (of 1670) made it illegal to hold natives of Virginia in servitude for life. The court ordered that Hagar be freed in six years, when she turned thirty. [131] In 1695 Hagar, free by now, petitioned the court unsuccessfully for exemption from county levies. [132] She did not give grounds for her request, but she was apparently destitute, a condition that was not much relieved when the next year she and her mother received small legacies from the estate of an Englishman. [133] In 1698, Hagar and her mother petitioned again to be exempted from county levies because Hagar was a "very Sickly person maintained by her mother"; this time the exemption was granted, [134] and the pair disappear from the records.

In April 1691 the Assembly allowed completely free trade with all Indians; according to William Waller Hening, this could be construed to mean that the enslaving of Indians was no longer legal. [135] The English of the time did not think that way, though, for they continued to bring Indian children into the colony, [136] some of whom were slaves. Many of these youngsters ran away when a chance offered itself, and they had to be pursued. [137] Some of them, on the other hand, stayed and became violent, like the slave Jamey, who was tried and executed for killing his master in Surry County. [138] On the other hand, mistreatment of Indian slaves was punished when it came to the attention of a county court, as in the case of the slave in Essex County who was denied treatment for a sore leg and given work to do instead. [139]

In most counties where there were Indians, they were considered to belong to a stratum below that of any Englishmen, along with free Negroes and African slaves. [140] Some association between Indians and Negroes did take place, though records about it are sparse. The only two bits of evidence are the indictment of three servants, an Indian and two Negroes, in a burglary case in Henrico County in 1695 [141] and the 1685 appearance of an Indian in Accomac County named "Peter Mongrame," [142] who may have been related to (or a servant of) the free Negro Philip Mongram who appears in records of 1663 in the neighboring county.[143]

On the whole, the records of Indian-English association, including liaisons and marriages, are more plentiful. English and Powhatan people had had liaisons since the English arrived in Virginia to find that the native people honored important overnight male guests by loaning them women. Very few of these liaisons resulted in marriage, as far as the surviving records show: there is only one other case (see below) besides those of Pocahontas and John Rolfe and the Nansemond Elizabeth and John Bass in 1614 and 1638, respectively. But liaisons continued to occur. Englishmen who visited Indian towns in times of peace may still have been given bedmates for the night; a few of them decided to remain with the Indians, as did William Clawson, whose English wife divorced him in 1655 for living among the Maryland Nanticokes and taking the "emperor's" daughter as a wife.[144]

Indians of both sexes who went to live among the English occasionally had affairs with members of the household or with neighbors. However, these affairs were recorded by the English only when an English male, a husband or an "owner" of an indentured servant, was "wronged." [145] Thus, in 1646 and 1647 there were rumors about two different English wives having had affairs with Indian men.[146] In 1684 an English servant named Margaret (last name unrecorded) had an illegitimate child by an Indian man; assuming that the man would not support the child, Margaret's employer got the county court to declare the child a servant until age twenty-one, so that this extra, unwanted member of his household would pay his or her way.[147] A similar case occurred in 1702, when an illegitimate daughter of an English servant woman and an Indian man was bound out until the age of twenty-four.[148] The same procedure was used in dealing with the children of Indian servant women and Englishmen. In 1681 the employer of an Indian woman took two of his countrymen to court, claiming they owed him damages (both of them, somehow) for making his servant produce a bastard the year before; he collected.[149]

The vast majority of the Indian-English liaisons within the English settlements did not result in marriage. An exception is the case of Sue, an Indian servant in Henrico County.[150] In 1688, Sue's master complained to the county court that she had recently had a bastard, which he had to support; Sue was ordered to remain in his service two extra years. The master then complained, a trifle belatedly, about a three-year-old child of Sue's by a neighboring Englishman, and asked that that child be bound out to him as a servant as well. But the child's reputed father appeared and agreed to pay damages, so the court ordered that he serve the master one year and pay a fine. In return, Sue's master gave her leave to marry her lover, and promised to release the couple punctually.

A happy ending to a story such as Sue's became impossible in 1691, when the Assembly passed a law forbidding white people to marry "Negroes, Mulattoes, and Indians" on pain of removal from the colony.[151] The law was aimed partially at putting all non-whites in "their place," and partially at preventing an increase in the mulatto population, which was termed an "abominable mixture and spurious issue" and which grew rapidly in the colony from the 1690s through the 1720s.[152] The problem was that people whose parentage was both European and African were difficult for English-men to place in a society that increasingly aimed at being biracial, i.e., whites and non-whites. The Assembly initially tried by law to prevent the creation of such people, and when that effort failed, it turned to defining "white" more strictly. A law of 1705[153] defined as "mulatto" anyone who had one-eighth or more African ancestry; interestingly, Indians were not defined at all, in genetic terms, until after the Civil War (see chapter 8). Meanwhile, the law against whites marrying non-whites was not univer-sally popular: in 1699 several Englishmen petitioned unsuccessfully that the law be repealed.[154]

In 1705 the Powhatans reached their low point in English estimation, ironically at the same time that another law for free trade with all Indians (especially those outside the colony) reinforced the idea that Indians should not be enslaved.[155] That was the year in which Virginia passed its "black code," and made Indians subject to it along with other nonwhites. Non-whites were no longer to be eligible to bear any office, "ecclesiastical, civill or military," in the colony.[156] "Popish recusants, convicts, negroes, mulattoes and Indian servants, and others, not being christians [sic]," were prohibited from being witnesses in court "in any cases whatsoever."[157] Now Indian servants could not sue for freedom from masters who kept them beyond their contracted time, and non-Christian groups (i.e., all the Powhatan ones) with reservations could not sue lessees who defaulted on payments. Neither non-Christians nor non-whites who were Christians could purchase a Christian servant except one "of their own complex-ion."[158] Women who were free, Christian, and white and who had a child by a non-white would be fined or made servants, and the children would also be servants.[159] Marriage with non-whites brought a fine and six months in prison, and ministers were forbidden to perform such marriages.[160] No non-white was to "lift his or her hand, in opposition against any christian [sic]" white person "at any time, on pain of getting thirty lashes on the bare back,"[161] an agonizing punishment that was forbidden to be used on white Christian servants.[162] Thus, the Powhatans were prevented legally from physically resisting white people who tried to keep them in servitude or to squat on their land. The only recourse open to Indians faced with ag-gressive Englishmen was to remain within their nations, which could still send complaints to the governor under the Treaty of Middle Plantation.

Like modern members of minorities, some Indians probably chose to merge as far as possible with their non-Indian neighbors, while others kept up their ties with their Indian relatives and remained an ethnic fringe of the Indian core groups. Those Indians who found reasonably comfortable places among the English stayed, but because of the legal powerlessness of individual Indians and other non-whites, the English records made about them after 1705, which are mainly legal records, tell us little. Those Indians who worked among the English but still felt most at home in traditional Indian society—also part of the Powhatan ethnic fringe group—probably went back home as often as they could. But the Powhatan core groups on the reservations would not be able to live in the traditional style much longer. Already their lifeways had changed in some ways, and as the eighteenth century wore on, even the core people became increasingly Anglicized.

CHAPTER 7

A Century of Culture Change

POWHATAN CULTURE remained more or less intact until well into the eighteenth century. Thus, the symbols of an "Indian" identity, namely a discrete language and way of life, remained the same as when the English arrived, despite massive if informal English efforts to "civilize" Indians. One writer has expressed surprise that an Algonquian group preserved its culture until 1700, even with English settlers keeping at a distance.[1] It is not really surprising at all. An examination of the Powhatans and of other coastal Algonquians in the eighteenth century shows that they were tenacious of their ancient way of life, even when surrounded at close range by Europeans. In this chapter I describe the relatively traditional Powhatan culture of circa 1700. Then I examine the historical processes that finally forced massive culture change in the Powhatan remnants, using ethnographic analogy with other eastern Indians where appropriate. The period covered is from 1705 to about 1830, when new pressures were brought to bear upon Indian people.

Several literate Englishmen visited Powhatan communities in the late seventeenth and early eighteenth centuries. Some of these were clergy, some were travelers, and others were neighboring landowners.[2] Their observations show that Powhatan core people still retained much of their traditional way of life,[3] in spite of having lost most of the land on which that way was based. However, Powhatan numbers were small enough (about six hundred)[4] that their dwindling landbase—as long as they had treaty rights enabling them to hunt and forage elsewhere—was still fairly sufficient. Nevertheless, a vicious circle was in action on the reservations. Traditional life there was difficult enough that people continued to "spin off" into English society, which caused Englishmen to pressure Indians to cede more land—"unused" land, by European standards. The new cessions then made traditional life continue to be difficult because the people-to-acreage ratio was once more about the same, so that still more people "spun off," and so on. Yet even total loss of land did not mean immediate change in the Indians' way of life: the Appamattucks kept up a reasonably traditional community with only seven or so families who lived without any reservation at all.[5]

Indian men throughout the eighteenth century were primarily hunters; only their weapons had changed. John Banister noticed that they thought "themselves undrest & not fit to walk abroad, unless they have their gun on their shoulder, & their shot-bag by their side."[6] They were still adept at camping in the woods, though they now made their fires either "out of the pans of their guns with a little powder & dry wood" or else "with a flint & steel,"[7] and they quelled the pangs of hunger on long marches by "girding up their Bellies" [i.e., tightening their belts].[8] The Indians of the Blackwater region, at least, had not yet learned how to repair their guns.[9] Powhatan males still used bows and arrows in the 1680s,[10] though by the 1720s it was boys who practiced archery, guns being reserved for men.[11] Men continued to hunt and fish not only for their families but also for "the neighbouring [English] gentry."[12] Deer drives were still practiced,[13] as was nighttime fishing, with a fire in the canoe to attract the fish,[14] and nighttime hunting of sora (or rail) birds in the marshes.[15]

Beverley wrote that Indian hunters—Powhatans and probably other tribes to the southwest[16]—were killing large numbers of deer for reasons other than food: "They make all this Slaughter only for the sake of the Skins, leaving the Carcases to perish in the Woods."[17] Instead of using the deerskins as tribute to a ruler, Powhatan or English, they traded them for the English goods that had become an integral part of their culture: guns, ammunition, cloth, and the iron hatchets long used for tree cutting and canoe making. Beaver skins also are mentioned as being traded by Indian hunters;[18] the animals were attracted to the traps by "medicine" known only "to some few of their old men, who keep it concealed as an arcanum of state, by which they awe the young ones, who did they not depend upon them, would hardly be ruled by them."[19]

Men and women alike produced tradeable items with which to buy English goods. The men produced the above-mentioned skins, plus "venison, Deer-suit [suet], & feathers," and women made "baskets, &c."[20] The women's ceramic pipes and pots, the latter made in styles modified for European methods of hearth cookery, brought in income throughout the eighteenth century and well into the nineteenth.[21] In 1687 the women at Nanzatico-Portobacco Bay charged as much Indian corn for a pot as was required to fill it up.[22]

Powhatan farming continued to be of the slash-and-burn variety, using iron hatchets for clearing[23] and, presumably, the iron hoes or dibble sticks that Indian women had preferred for nearly a century. Land was owned in common; Durand de Dauphine understood, perhaps incorrectly, that among the Rappahannocks/Portobaccos "the crop belongs to the community, each taking whatever he needs."[24] Planting, weeding, and harvesting were still work for women and children, as were the gathering of wild plants, making of household utensils, and cooking.[25]

The Indians' diet continued to be a mixture of domesticated and wild foods, but there were two notable additions: first Powhatan hogs running free in the woods were shot as game to eat;[26] second, some Powhatan groups, if not all, planted orchards and ate the fruit. John Banister wrote of peaches being gathered and dried,[27] the Weyanock *weroance* had an apple orchard at one of his group's stopping places circa 1662,[28] and a Chickahominy councillor, or *cockarouse,* had an orchard in 1704.[29] Indian people continued to eat heavily and irregularly during the day and night[30] whenever food was available. Hugh Jones, who was no admirer of traditional Indian cultures, wrote with some exaggeration, "They have no notion of providing for futurity; for they eat night and day whilst their provision lasts, falling to as soon as they awake, and falling asleep again as soon as they are well crammed."[31] The women retained strong feelings about serving "different sorts of Victuals" in separate dishes.[32]

In the late seventeenth century, many of the surviving Powhatans found it necessary to live in fortified, nucleated villages. The palisade was "two three or four thicknesses of timber, covered with earth, perhaps least they should be fired, they are very high."[33] Inside were a dance ground,[34] a water supply (undescribed), a temple, and the *weroance*'s house and "as many others as they judge sufficient to harbour all their People, when an Enemy comes against them."[35] Though the fortifications were strong and the living space somewhat crowded,[36] the Indians persisted in moving to new locations at (unrecorded) intervals "for fear of their enemies, or for the sake of game and provision."[37] The Chickahominy towns on Mattaponi River were an exception to the fortification rule: in 1677 their town had consisted of houses "in a row at least one mile in length." Thomas Story, who visited their town in a new location in 1699, makes no mention of a palisade in existence at that time.[38] Beverley broke into an Indian temple, probably the Chickahominy one (see chapter 5), sometime in the 1690s; his wording implies that it was placed in the woods away from any houses. All Powhatan towns were still located near rivers for easy access to transportation, fishing, and a cold plunge after steaming in sweathouses, which were still used.[39]

The Powhatans continued to live in near-traditional *yi·hakans* (now called "wigwams"[40] or, more commonly, "cabins").[41] There were only three changes in house building after a century of contact with Europeans. First, bark coverings became standard on most houses,[42] where before they had been status symbols available to few. The change may have been possible because everyone now possessed iron hatchets, tools that reduced the time needed to cut enough bark to cover a house. Second, houses usually had windows left between the slabs of bark: "Their windows are little holes left open for the passage of the Light, which in bad weather they stop with Shutters of the same Bark, opening the Leeward Windows for Air and Light."[43] And third, the Indian towns in early-eighteenth-century engravings had not only rectangular dwelling houses in them but also some smaller domed or conical dwelling houses,[44] which do not figure at all in early-seventeenth-century descriptions.[45] These may be sweathouses, moved into the town by the engravers' artistic license. On the other hand, if they are dwelling houses, their presence may indicate occupancy by nuclear families, which would be a response to a breakdown in a traditional social structure—the extended family unit—previously common in Powhatan society.[46] Each house still had a central hearth.

The core people among the Powhatans still favored traditional clothing styles, but they used English fabrics whenever they could, especially on formal occasions. Women's aprons and men's breechclouts were made, by preference, of blue or red cotton, with a matchcoat of "Duffields" (see fig. 5) added in cold weather.[47] Sometimes the matchcoat was "girt close in the middle with a Girdle."[48] The clothing of the women was "laced out with their money,"[49] which still consisted of shell beads (see below).

When an Indian man chose an English-style coat, he wanted it to be "of divers colours, like that Jacob made for his son Joseph, & therefore the traders have them cut partly from pale, gules, & azure."[50] Indians also wore clothing purchased from or cast off by Europeans. During a formal Indian visit to a neighboring planter, Durand de Dauphine saw Nanzatico or Portobacco men in English jerkins and women in "some kind of petticoats," while others had made tunics out of blankets by cutting a hole for their heads and belting in their waists with deerskin thongs.[51] The Powhatans kept these clothes, never washing them,[52] until they were completely worn out. Then they bought only as much new cloth, however cheap its price, as they needed to replace an old garment.[53] Leggings and moccasins continued to be worn, and were now made of "cotton or leather."[54]

Indian men now wore several hairstyles, which are poorly described and probably belonged to the several Indian groups the writers met. The styles used by men among the Powhatan remnants are impossible to determine, though Robert Beverley wrote that "the Great Men, or better sort, preserve a long Lock behind for distinction."[55] All Indian women, however, are usually described as wearing their hair long and either loose or bound up in a knot,[56] so it is likely that Powhatan women used these styles. Both sexes plucked facial and body hair,[57] and the plucking was still done with mussel shells.[58] Face painting was still practiced, though the colors were now bought from the English, the Indians, sadly enough, "being persuaded to despise their own, which are common and finer."[59] The women of the Nanzatico-Portobacco Bay area were still tattooed.[60]

Social distinctions still survived among the Powhatans. The wealthier people, who were also the higher-ranking people, dressed more elaborately than ordinary folk on special occasions. In 1676 deerskin matchcoats were still in vogue. Cockacoeske, *weroansqua* of Pamunkey, visited the governor's council wearing an elaborate one which had a series of six-inch fringes from shoulder to hem.[61] When Nathaniel Bacon's forces subsequently attacked

Fig. 5. Man in a matchcoat and crown. Detail of engraving, based upon and updated from a De Bry original, made for Robert Beverley's *History and Present State of Virginia* (1705). (From *The History and Present State of Virginia*, by Robert Beverley, edited by Louis B. Wright. Copyright 1947 The University of North Carolina Press. Published for the Institute of Early American History and Culture, Williamsburg.)

her town's temple, the tutelary god of the town lost "a very rich Deer match coat . . . painted with puccoon, & embroydered with peak & some fine pearls."[62] Cockacoeske also used European fabrics at that time; in the same attack she lost a stock of linen, broadcloth, and other English yard goods.[63]

Where common people went bareheaded or wore shiny feathers in their hair,[64] the wealthy wore jewelry made of their shell beads.[65] In her 1676 visit to Jamestown, Cockacoeske wore a coronet three inches high, and important men wore coronets of either *peak* or feathers.[66] Later there was a fashion for coronets four to six inches high (see fig. 5), made either of white *peak* or designs in white and black *peak*.[67] "Ladies of Distinction" also wore "deep [broad] Necklaces, Pendants and Bracelets" made of peak.[68] Other kinds of shell beads were worn as well: John Banister described a pendant consisting of "a round tablet of about 3 or 4 inches wrought out of a large Cunk [*sic*] shell," and "a bracelet of great bulging beads made of the same shell, which the Southern Indians call Rantees." Some people additionally wore the smoothed-down center of a conch shell, "about the bigness of the stem of a tobacco pipe," through their ears.[69] Sometimes important people wore "a Wreath of Dyed Furrs" around their necks.[70] However, even important people did not dress up every day. When Story visited the Chickahominy town without warning one day, the "Sagamor, or chief[71] . . . came out [of his house] with [only] a Piece of Cloth about his Middle.[72]

The Powhatan conception of a "real man" as being an invincible hunter and warrior still obtained, but it had been badly shaken by military defeats and loss of territory. Young men were still initiated into manhood by being put through the *huskanaw;* however, there were so few of them left among the core people that the *huskanaw* had ceased to be an annual affair and was now held "once every 14 or 16 years, as their young men grow up."[73] The last Pamunkey *huskanaw* before Beverley wrote his book was 1694, when the tribe lost two boys[74] whom it surely could not easily have spared. There was little for a "real man" to do on the reservations; he could not go to war except under the command of the English, and much of his hunting had to take place off the reservation. By the end of the seventeenth century the authority of the conservative rulers and older councilmen, who traditionally directed and rewarded "ideal" men, was either being undermined or had already collapsed due to circumstances beyond their control.

Traditional sources of authority seem still to have been reasonably strong among the Pamunkeys, who retained hereditary rulers well into the eighteenth century. Beverley also mentioned a "queen" at Pungoteague and the Eastern Shore "empress" at Nandua.[75] However, traditional power was fading among the other Powhatan remnants for whom we have records. Neither a ruler nor a council is recorded among the Gingaskins of the Eastern Shore from the 1660s on.[76] The Chickahominy dispute of 1704–1705, which concerned both land and political power, has already been described (see chapter 5). The Wiccocomicos still had a "kingdom" in 1705 but the "king" had only two elderly male subjects.[77] And the landless, rulerless Appamattuck elders were having difficulty keeping the respect of their young men.[78]

Those rulers who remained among the Indian communities kept up their positions as best they could.[79] They dressed richly and some, like the "King of Pomonkie,"[80] now kept saddle horses as a status symbol.[81] The titles of Powhatan rulers differed from those of a century earlier, at least according to Beverley.[82] *Weroance* was now strictly a military title, while "kings" and "queens" had different titles (unrecorded). Councillors were still *cockarouses*.

Where "royals" reigned, their power was still officially absolute and near-sacred,[83] and they were waited upon by servants,[84] some of whom were called "Black Boys."[85] They continued to entertain important visitors with lavish hospitality,[86] which they could presumably afford because of tribute in foodstuffs collected from their subjects. Commoners did the royal bidding voluntarily,[87] though the promise of participation in royal feasting may have been an inducement to obedience; they were otherwise free to take revenge for any personal wrongs they suffered, without interference from their leaders.[88] Councilmen remained important in society because of their consultations with strong rulers.[89] In some towns, at least, there were ordinarily seven such men, "because (according to their tradition) there were but seven saved in the great deluge."[90] Since the flood story was a recent addition to Powhatan mythology (see below), the number seven for councillors may have been also; the Chickahominies, who may have been the people being described, had eight councillors in 1607.

The status of women in Powhatan society probably remained high, since they continued to be major producers of income for their families. In the late seventeenth century, women were observed to "keep all their [the Indians'] money."[91] Their freedom to conduct themselves as they wished before marriage, coupled with their "Mirth and good Humour" and "excess of Life and Fire, which they never fail to have," had led many English to think that Indian maidens prostituted themselves[92] or simply slept with prospective husbands prior to marriage to test sexual compatibility.[93] Beverley countered this idea by asserting that bearing an illegitimate child prevented a Powhatan woman from ever marrying, and that he had never heard of such a case among the Indians.[94] However, he partially contradicted himself by writing later that two young women were normally offered as bedmates of an important male visitor, and their reputations were enhanced rather than destroyed by such experiences.[95] Beverley may have been writing in an early-seventeenth-century "ethnographic present" at that point. The continuation, if such was the case, of such practices among the Powhatans shows that they had not yet adopted English customs of patriliny.

Powhatan marriage customs appear to have remained constant up through the beginning of the eighteenth century. Prominent men who could afford them were allowed as many wives as they could support.[96] Marriage continued to be a secularly celebrated tie[97] which could be dissolved, leaving both partners free to remarry.[98] Hugh Jones heard that women who committed adultery were severely punished among "the Indians,"[99] but we know Jones' propensity for lumping Indian groups together, so those Indians may not have been the Powhatans. Severe punishment for female adulterers had not been the norm a century before.

Men and women in the Powhatan towns continued to use frequent dancing[100] both as recreation and as a social bonding mechanism. Some of the traditional games continued in use, including the gambling game with reeds,[101] the playing of which had taken on by 1689 an obsessive tone that argues indulgence in escapism.

> They sit sometimes whole dayes and nights at this game, and have an Indian by them to light their pipes, or to fetch them water to drink. They play away sometimes all they have; only what they lose in money, if it be payed in skins or matts or Inglish goods, the winner allows double the value more for it than if he were to buy it. Sometimes they play away their wives and children who become slaves to the winner, sometimes they play away themselves to be slaves, which they do thus: first they play away their feet, then their legs, and so forward till they come to their head: before they lose that, they may redeeme the other parts, with less than when they have wholly lost themselves, and can procure from their friends some more considerable summe for their ransom; they use to pawn their arms or legs etc. for some certain summe.[102]

Powhatan men and women alike smoked tobacco for recreation by the end of the seventeenth century,[103] but they used the mild tobacco of the English, not the native tobacco that had once had other associations. The mild tobacco was purchased from the English[104] and smoked in "short pipes of their own making"[105] or, more often, in English-made kaolin pipes.[106]

By the 1680s the Powhatans had acquired a new pastime—getting drunk on rum, which was in large part escapism. However, it was normally a carefully controlled escapism, a fine point that Europeans rarely appreciated.[107] The way in which Indian people—usually men, but sometimes women[108]—went about it resembles the drinking behavior of several modern Indian peoples: they did not bother to drink unless they had enough liquor to become fully drunk,[109] and then they went about their drinking "as solemnly . . . as if it were part of their Religion."[110] They also followed the pattern of drinking in groups of friends, one or two of whom would remain sober to watch over the others.[111] This was a good idea, since those who got drunk often became boisterous. The Indians who became drunk in the English settlements were usually observed to brag and to shout profanities at English passersby, who usually ignored them.[112] Drinking was therefore not only a sanctioned escape from a very difficult life, but also a safe outlet for releasing hostility toward whites.

Priests were still powerful men in Powhatan society, retaining most if not all of their traditional functions,[113] but their power was waning. In 1689 an English writer noted that the Indians "say that though their God can tell them when their neighbouring Indians have any design upon them, yet he cannot acquaint them with the designs of the Inglish [sic]."[114] Priests had not been able to stop the decline—and probably the increasing ill health due to malnutrition[115]—of their people. But Indian folk were still loath to abandon the traditional system for another that was still strange. Thus, John Clayton wrote variously that priests were the persons "in gravest veneration among them, next their King"[116] and persons "of the greatest honour & esteem among them, next to the King, or to their great War-Captain."[117]

The English heard a good deal about the powers of Indian priests in conjuring and making rain,[118] but they made light of what they heard and continued to pressure the Powhatans to convert to a "civilized" religion. A case in point was recorded by Beverley.[119] A drought was blighting the plantations of the upper James River, including that of William Byrd II. An Indian man, probably an Appamattuck priest, who lived in the neighborhood approached Byrd's overseer and offered to bring rain in exchange for "two Bottles of Rum." The overseer agreed, though he remained skeptical. The Indian man promptly began "*pauwawing*, as they call it,"[120] and within half an hour clouds formed and rain fell on Byrd's crops, "but none at all upon any of the Neighbours." The Indian did not ask the overseer for payment; instead he waited for some time until Byrd himself came to the plantation. The overseer, of course, had joyfully told Byrd immediately that his crops were saved. But when the Indian approached Byrd about his reward, Byrd toyed with him, pretending to know nothing about any rainmaking and replying to the Indian's assurances of having brought rain that he, the Indian, "was a Cheat, and had seen the Cloud a coming," and so forth. Byrd "made sport with him a little while, but in the end order'd him the two Bottles of Rum, letting him understand however, that it was a free Gift, and not the consequence of any Bargain with his Overseer." It was such treatment that made Powhatan people in general, and their priests in particular, a "sullen close people [who] will answer very few questions."[121]

English condescension must have made the Indians all the more bitter, because at times when English medicine failed, even aristocratic Englishmen would turn to Indian doctor-priests, as Nicholas Spencer once did to save the eyesight of a servant.[122] Indian cures for certain ailments were highly respected, even if the Indian physicians were not.[123] The Powhatan cures for wounds and fractures were said to be especially good,[124] but Indian medicine was most renowned for its ability to cure snakebites. The usual cure was an herbal powder carried by every Indian, which "in almost every Town . . . hath a different composition. . . ." All the powders were so effective that all the Indian victims recovered within a day, while English victims, presumably treated by English physicians, sometimes died.[125]

However, the only recorded eyewitness account of an Indian curing snakebite involves cauterization, not a powder. Once again, a practical joke—this time a vicious one—was involved.[126] An Indian was "charming" a rattlesnake at the behest of Col. William Claiborne, who in his old age liked to keep "these Snakes always in Barrells in the house." The performance was going well, and the Indian had discarded the wand he had been using and was working the snake with his bare hand. Suddenly Claiborne "hitt the Snake wth his crutch, & the Snake snapd the Indian by the hand, & bote him very sharply betwixt the fingers, wch put his charme to an end, & he roared out." But with great presence of mind, the man stretched his arm over his head, demanded a string, which he tied on for a tourniquet, and "clapd a hot burning cole" onto the bite, "whereby he was cured, but looked pale a long while after." John Clayton called this tale a "pleasant Story" he had heard, which indicates that he found Claiborne's joke funny. All life was cheap in the late seventeenth century, but Indian life was cheaper.

By the end of the seventeenth century the Powhatans had learned to hide their religious beliefs from Englishmen. When they responded to questions at all, they were likely to quell their interrogators by asserting that it was "reckon'd Sacrilege to divulge the Principles of their Religion."[127] Only if they were "surprised some way or other" would they say much.[128] And it seems that Robert Beverley was the only Englishman who "surprized" a knowledgeable Indian—by plying him with hard cider—and wrote about it afterward. Thus, Beverley recorded in detail contemporary Powhatan beliefs that other writers heard about only in outline.[129]

The Powhatans still believed in a distant, beneficent creator god and in lesser gods and tutelary deities for each town, variously called "Quioccos"[130] or similar names,[131] or "Tanto,"[132] who were active in demanding worship from humankind and in punishing offenses.[133] Temple-storehouses were still erected in the traditional manner, but the one that Beverley describes (probably the Chickahominies') was small by aboriginal standards,[134] perhaps reflecting the poverty of the Indians of his time. The reverence for the sun that some early colonists observed among the Powhatans had apparently been discontinued.[135] On the other hand, a new belief had appeared on the horizon: one Virginia Indian group, at least, now had "a tradition of the floud, [when] all the world was once drowned, except a few that were saved, to wit, about seven or eight in a great canoro."[136]

Powhatan ideas about the afterlife had also altered after a century of contact with the English. Where their ancestors had believed in a single pleasant world for all the dead, whence they returned to earth reincarnated again as Indians, the Powhatans now had their own, singularly Indian, concept of heaven and hell.[137] People who lived a good life went to a heaven of eternal springtime, "stor'd with the highest perfection of all their Earthly Pleasures; namely, with plenty of all sorts of Game, for Hunting, Fishing and Fowling; that it is blest with the most charming Women, which enjoy an eternal bloom, and have an Universal desire to please." Beverley's description is, of course, a man's view. Since it is doubtful that the Powhatan world was fully a man's world as yet, heavenly sexual partners may have included men for the Indian women. The wicked, however, went to "a filthy stinking Lake . . . that continually burns with Flames, that never extinguish; where they are persecuted and tormented day and night, with Furies in the Shape of Old Women." [138] If female Indians were also tormented by female furies, the furies' age is more significant than their sex: many cultures consider postmenopausal women to have great magical powers because they have survived their childbearing years, when delivering children was very risky, and their menses, which were ritually dangerous.

Intelligent, knowledgeable Indian people often still believed implicitly in their traditional religion, as Beverley discovered in the man he interrogated with the help of hard cider. The man had no idea that the god who appeared in the temple when the priests conjured him up was anything other than the supernatural being the priests said he was. When Beverley described the jointed wooden image he had found, the man was badly shaken; he muttered incoherently about priests making people believe, and then he refused to speak further. [139]

The Powhatans continued to practice several methods of disposal of the dead. High-ranking people were treated in the traditional way: exposure and bone-cleaning followed by wrapping the bones in the preserved skin and interment in the temple. [140] Commoners continued to receive secondary burial in ossuaries [141] or primary burial in the ground. [142] There is no mention of burning bodies, of criminals or of others, around 1700.

The first language of the Powhatan core communities continued to be the Indian one; however, by 1700 nearly everyone could speak at least some English. [143] The English of elderly people was either still poor or simply not used for official purposes; when Thomas Story conversed with an elderly Chickahominy leader in 1699, an interpreter was required. [144] At the same time, some younger people spoke mainly English. A young Nanzatico man named Quasko Hewks witnessed the killing of the Rowley family in 1704, [145] and when he asked one of the killers why he had done it, the killer chased him "wth his Tomahawk talking Indian wch he [Quasko Hewks] did not understand." [146]

As the eighteenth century wore on, the need for official interpreters diminished. The reservation Nansemonds went to live with the Iroquoian-speaking Nottoways (see below), and they needed no Algonquian-speaking interpreter. From 1703 onward, one James Adams served as interpreter to the surviving Powhatan reservation communities, [147] but in 1727 his office was terminated, "seeing the tributary Indians understand and can speak the English language very well." [148]

Detribalized Indians had long had English first names and surnames. [149]

Some prominent core people began adopting English surnames as early as 1676—for example, "Captain John West," son of the queen of Pamunkey.[150] Commoners in the reservation cores began appearing with one English name in the 1690s[151] and with two English names in the first decade of the eighteenth century.[152] By 1750 everyone appearing in the records had English first names and surnames. It is likely that for a time the English names were merely "public" names, with Indian names used at home. Unfortunately, since the only eighteenth and nineteenth century documents containing Powhatan personal names are public records, there is no way to determine when Indian-language names in private life became completely obsolete.

Relations between the Powhatan core people and both the fringe people and the English were tense in the early eighteenth century. The core-fringe tension sprang from the fact that many ambitious Indian people wanted to leave the reservations and find a place in English society, even if that place was in the lower levels reserved for non-whites, while the core people feared the loss of the fringe people's manpower. In 1706 the English Council ordered that before any more licenses were issued for employing Indians, the governor must first ascertain that the Indians' rulers were willing to let them go. The order specifically stated that Indian men hired as hunters "obstruct[ed] their Contributing to the Support of their own Government & from the Necessary defence of their towns and habitations."[153]

Sometimes, fringe people left despite their ruler's protests. In 1709 Robin, a Pamunkey trained as a shoemaker, petitioned the governor for permission to stay in the English settlements, where he could follow his trade; permission was granted.[154] And while some Indians hired themselves out with permission from home,[155] others left to work for English employers against the will of their sovereigns.[156]

The tension between the Powhatan cores and the non-Indians surrounding them arose from the cultural and physical differences that still persisted. The only record of early-eighteenth-century Indian opinion of Africans was provided by Hugh Jones, who wrote that Indians "hate, and despise the very sight of a Negroe; but they seem to like an East-Indian,[157] and fear and revere the whites."[158] The "despising" of Negroes may have been behavior shown publicly toward slaves, or it may have been the revulsion that many people feel against those whose physiognomy and cultural background different from their own.

Revulsion was certainly what the core Indians felt against the English and their alien culture, which had been forcibly imposed upon the Virginia natives for a century. Their behavior when they were drunk has already been described. When sober, the Powhatans cloaked their hostility with reticence, which, when added to the traditional Indian's reluctance to commit himself in strange situations,[159] must have amounted at times to a stony silence. Thus, to John Clayton the Virginia Indians appeared to be "of a Dull melancholy temper, rarely affected with pleasure, or transported with passion . . . most irreconsilably, revengfull, sullen, close, & reservd."[160] Jones called Indians in general "treacherous, suspicious and jealous, difficult to be persuaded or imposed upon, and very sharp, hard in dealing, and ingenious in their way, and in things that they naturally know or have been taught; though at the first they are very obstinate, and unwilling to apprehend or learn novelties, and seem stupid and silly to strangers."[161]

Some Englishmen called the Powhatans "stupid" out loud, and the Powhatans resented it. One man in Williamsburg, probably a Powhatan, gave Francis Louis Michel a tart answer when Michel expressed surprise at the man's ability to speak English: he asked Michel "whether we thought that if they had been taught like we, they could not learn a thing just as well as we. I asked him, where he had learned to speak English, he answered, they were not so stupid."[162]

A continual sore spot with the Powhatans was English people's steadfast refusal to consider Indians as marriage partners. The English who wrote on this subject[163] were probably right in surmising that the Powhatans would have been more receptive to English culture had English people given this evidence of considering Indians as fellow human beings. As it was, not even well-meaning English missionaries were going out to the Powhatan reservations to assure the people of English esteem while trying to convert them (see below). There were only the Indians' English neighbors, most of whom were from the poorer strata of English society and were apt, in their struggle for prosperity, to maltreat Indians.[164] The "Christian" example set for the Powhatans was not a good one.[165]

Meanwhile, the English who took the trouble to inquire into Powhatan feelings discovered a few—and only a few—specific English practices that the Indians (males) were willing to admit they found peculiar. Powhatan men thought Englishmen were fools for being the entire support of their wives[166] and for not always going out armed with weapons.[167] They laughed at the small size of English spoons, which necessitated much arm work; their own spoons "generally [held] half a pint."[168] They also thought the English extravagant for buying wine, when rum brought intoxication more quickly.[169] There were probably many other items, such as the English reluctance to bathe and the English eagerness to give advice, but it would have been dangerous, as well as impolite, to mention them to inquiring Englishmen. Instead the Powhatan core people preferred to live quietly in themselves, on their small islands of tribal territory, preserving their traditional way of life as best they could.

Military and Land Affairs

In the early eighteenth century the Powhatans were so low on manpower that they had to appeal to Anglo-Virginians for help when they were harassed by outsiders. Some of these encroaching outsiders were whites from North Carolina, who took advantage of the lack of a properly surveyed boundary between that colony and Virginia by seating themselves on the land occupied by the Nansemonds. The reservation Nansemonds[170] were by that time closely allied with the Nottoways and Meherrins; all three tribes complained repeatedly to the Virginia governor while keeping up friendly relations with the still-strong Tuscaroras to the south.[171] The Pamunkeys also tried to be friends with all the Iroquoians during that time by visiting them,[172] though in 1713 they acted for the English in capturing a Tuscarora in their neighborhood.[173]

Since white Virginians accurately perceived the Tuscaroras as a threat, they sometimes complained that the Nottoways and Meherrins, and occasionally the Nansemonds, were insolent or seditious.[174] Investigation of Indian landmarks and a survey of a boundary between North Carolina and Virginia in 1710[175] did little to quiet the situation. When the Tuscaroras went to war with white Carolinians in 1711, communication with them was forbidden to all tribute-paying Virginia tribes. The Virginia government offered the Tuscaroras reservation land, to be surveyed between the upper James and Rappahannock,[176] in an effort to draw them out of conflict with other Englishmen, but the Tuscaroras remained in North Carolina as a reservation tribe. During the eighteenth century many of them moved north to join other Iroquoians. Bereft of strong allies among their relatives, some Nottoways and Meherrins went north with the Tuscaroras,[177] while the rest remained behind and entered a period of land loss, pressure for culture change, and alcoholism.[178] The reservation Nansemonds, who by then spoke Nottoway,[179] may also have split into those who left and those who stayed.

The Siouan speakers of piedmont Virginia, North Carolina, and South Carolina (Saponis, Enos, Occoneechees, Stukanoxes, and Tutelos) were also on the move during the early eighteenth century. Many of them came temporarily to rest within the Virginia colony, which tried to draw them in as tributaries and settle them peacefully around a combined fort and mission named Fort Christanna. Both before and after the fort was established, the Siouans residing there were attacked by the Nottaways and Tuscaroras.[180] Eventually the Siouans drifted away again; the mission at the fort was discontinued in 1718.[181]

The English and Powhatans in Virginia continued to be threatened by Iroquoians from the north. The tributary Powhatan communities realized their own uselessness as buffers for anyone when they were prevented from making peace with the Five Nations in 1684 and 1704.[182] In the end it was the English who succeeded in making a workable peace with the Iroquois in 1722.[183] The tributary Powhatans were safe from Iroquois attack thereafter. When hostility broke out between the English and the French with Iroquois allies later in the century, the Powhatans remained uninvolved.

The worst threat to the Powhatans for the rest of the eighteenth century came from their English neighbors. The remaining reservations continued to lose land (see map 6), while all Indian people, whether core or fringe, remained heavily pressured by the colonial laws that lumped them together with other non-whites into a disadvantaged class. Those people who wanted to remain "Indians" were finally forced to abandon the language and life-ways that were meaningful to them and to take up new symbols of what they were. That was especially true of the groups which lost their reservations altogether.

The Appamattucks survived as a landless traditional group until at least 1705. They appear in no records thereafter, but the copper badge with their name on it[184] may date from the 1711 order that tributary Indians wear copper badges when hunting,[185] thus indicating some kind of governmental recognition. The Indians from the Portobacco area may also have survived as a traditional group without land, but they are not even indirectly mentioned in the surviving records after 1705. However, individual Indians do appear in the Essex County and Richmond County records,[186] which are intact for the period, so that the group should not automatically be regarded as extinct.

The Occohannocks, consisting of the Metomkins, Kegotanks, Machipongos, Occohannocks, Pungoteagues, Onancocks, Chesconnessexes, and Nanduas, according to Beverley's reckoning,[187] were probably victims of a smallpox epidemic that raged on the Eastern Shore in 1709.[188] Their residence and that of their northern relatives in their traditional territories had been intermittent for some time. In 1697 the Maryland governor had noted that they moved frequently throughout Virginia, Maryland, and Pennsylvania, and that their numbers were decreasing. After Beverley's inventory of tribes, nothing further appears about the Occohannocks in the Virginia records, probably indicating that they had moved north permanently.

The Wiccocomico remnant, which according to Beverley consisted of three old men living the traditional life,[189] continued to live on land that by 1705 may not have been a true reservation: a man named Smith had claimed it since 1683, when he paid the tribe's annual tribute for them.[190] The tribe paid its own tribute in 1710,[191] but the matter was probably academic by then because the Wiccocomico "king," a man named Taptico, had sold the land in 1696, retaining rights of use for an indefinite time.[192] Lieutenant Governor Spotswood did not include the Wiccocomicos with the other tributaries in his list of 1712.[193] However, the Virginia government felt obliged to defend the tribe's interest in 1713 when it complained of an English neighbor who sued the mother of a runaway Indian servant and threatened to sue the rest of the tribe as well.[194] Relations with the nearby Jones family also continued to be strained: in 1716 one Indian John was charged with burning two of Maurice Jones's houses.[195]

In December 1718, William Taptico, son of Taptico and himself the last Wiccocomico "king," gave up his family's (and therefore his tribe's) right to occupy the land "owned" by the son of John Smith.[196] Thus, the Wiccocomicos became landless in every sense of the word. William Taptico also died at about that time; his wife, Elizabeth "Tapp" (origins unknown) qualified as one of his executors in June 1719.[197] The inventory of his estate[198] shows that he was a tribal leader who was both prosperous and able to function in an English-ruled world: he had varied livestock, "Boat Rigging & Oars," carpenter's tools, plenty of yard goods, several changes of English clothing, a well-appointed house by English standards, and several books, and he was owed money by both Indians and Englishmen. He was obviously less traditional in his lifestyle than Beverley realized.

The Chickahominies, who probably included remnants of the Mattaponis and Rappahannocks (see chapter 5), retained their reservation on the upper Mattaponi River for about two decades in the eighteenth century. The tribe apparently continued its connection with the Pamunkeys; just as the "James Mush" of 1704 could have been either Chickahominy or Pamunkey, so also could the "Tra Macco" (Drammaco?) who signed a Pamunkey petition as a Great Man in 1710.[199] In any case, the Chickahominy Drammaco continued to have his differences with Tom Perry, another councillor, over the reservation between the two Herring creeks that had been granted them in 1701. Drammaco's faction wanted to deed the reservation to Roger Mallory, who had bought other lands from them in 1695; Perry's faction wanted to keep the land. In 1704 violence had broken out. But Drammaco went through with the deed: in exchange for a smaller tract on the Mattaponi River, the Chickahominies let Mallory have their three-thousand-acre reservation.[200] Yet Perry's faction would not abandon the land, and in 1711 they complained to Lieutenant Governor Spotswood that Mallory was trying to dispossess them.[201] Omitting comment on the illegality of selling the reservation without the permission of the General Assembly, Spotswood ordered Mallory to answer the complaint "with all Speed," which Mallory apparently did to his satisfaction. The tribe had to settle on the smaller tract.

In 1718 the Chickahominies went to Spotswood again.[202] Roger Mallory had died, and his sons had sold away not only their father's tract between the two Herring creeks but also the small tract that he had deeded to the Chickahominies. Both the sons and the new "purchaser" were now trying to make the tribe give up the land. Spotswood referred the matter to the King William County court, whose records were burned in 1885; the outcome is therefore uncertain. Either during or after 1718, the Chickahominies sold out or agreed to leave their tract—again without consulting the General Assembly—and sometime after 1718 they became totally landless. James Adams continued to be paid as the interpreter to "the *Pamunkey* and

Chickahominy Indians" until his office was discontinued in 1727.[203] But Governor Gooch's list of tributary Indian tribes in 1730 did not include the Chickahominies by name.[204]

Lacking the records of King William County, we cannot be sure that either a landless Chickahominy group or individual Indian families continued to live in the vicinity of the old reservation. However, it appears that a group persisted, even if there are no documents surviving to prove it. Nonreservation "Indians" show up in the oldest surviving King William County records (from 1885). They were named "Adams," like the tribe's last interpreter, they lived in a settlement called "Adamstown" not far from where the last reservation tract was, and they married other "Indians." Their descendants incorporated in the 1920s as the Upper Mattaponi Tribe.

Like all other ethnic groups, the eighteenth and early nineteenth century Adamstown group had its core and fringe people, and one of their fringe people has become a staple in the interracial relations literature from Virginia.[205] One Upper Mattaponi fringe name was Dungee;[206] people of that name married both Indians and free Negroes in the nineteenth and twentieth centuries. An Indian-descended Captain John Dungee petitioned the Virginia Assembly in 1825 to let his wife, born of a liaison between a prominent white planter and his Negro slave and freed by her father's will, remain in Virginia. John Dungee's marriage has been cited as proof that the Pamunkeys of his time and earlier married Negroes.[207] But Dungee had no connection with the Pamunkeys,[208] and since he merely claimed some Indian ancestry rather than an Indian identity, there is no evidence to indicate that he fully "belonged" to the lesser-known ancestral Upper Mattaponis, either.

Some Chickahominy descendants may have left King William County and migrated southwest through New Kent County to Charles City County. The records of all three counties were burned in the nineteenth century, and the surviving property tax records from 1782 show no people with Chickahominy surnames.[209] Thus, neither a migration nor its date, if it occurred, can be traced. However, a largely endogamous non-white, non-Negro people appear from the mid-nineteenth century onward in the Charles City and New Kent county records. They share the core name of Holmes with the Upper Mattaponis, although the most common name among them is not Adams but Adkins, and they still have an oral tradition of a migration from King William County. Perhaps more significantly, these people were recommended to anthropologists in the 1890s as the "Chickahominy Indians" by the Pamunkeys (see chapter 8).

The Nansemonds had already split into two parts in the mid-seventeenth century. The nonreservation Christianized Nansemonds continued to live on the Nansemond River until either the late seventeenth or early eighteenth century, probably the latter. Then, family by family, they withdrew southeast into the back country of Norfolk County, on the northern edge of the Great Dismal Swamp. There they went on living quietly throughout the eighteenth century, keeping a Nansemond identity and living by hunting and farming on a small scale. However, the Indian identity of these people and, later, their distant Indian ancestry made some of their English neighbors unwilling to respect their citizenship. The matter was complicated by the marriage sometime in the early eighteenth century of one man to a manumitted mulatto slave;[210] in the eyes of the white community, that one marriage of a couple who may not have been ancestral at all "tainted" the reputation of the rest of the group for years to come. Therefore, sometime between 1722 and 1727 the children of Richard Bass in Norfolk County had the clerk of court write a certificate for them, reciting their ancestry and stating that "these are Peaceful Subjects of His Maitie George I . . . numbered among ye Nansiemum People, ffreeborn, & worthie of ye Respectfull Consideracon of Christians in ye Church in Carolina as in Virginia."[211] In 1727, William Bass, Sr., one of Richard's sons, had to have an inquest held by the county court to prove that he and his kinsmen were of English and Nansemond descent only and that by the Treaty of Middle Plantation in 1677 they were entitled to bear arms and to use the "cleared Lands & Swamps" that their ancestors had used "since & before English governance in Virginia."[212] The county government was plainly willing to accord the Basses privileges that ceased for other, more "Indian" groups when they lost their reservations.

The Nansemond-descended Basses continued to have problems with racist English neighbors, so in 1742 a younger William Bass went back to the county court and got a certificate stating that he was "of English & Indian descent with no admixture of negro blood" and was "numbered as a Nansemun by his own Choosing."[213] This certificate, which describes Bass as "tall, swarthy, dark eyes," is a forerunner in form to the certificates of free birth which became required for free non-whites after the turn of the nineteenth century. In 1797 another William Bass had to get yet another certificate from the county court, reciting his ancestry and stating plainly that he was "of English and Indian descent and [was] not a Negroe nor a Mulattoe as by some falsely and malitiously stated."[214] The genealogies recited in the certificates show at least two ties to the traditional Nansemond tribe; one was the Bass marriage of 1638 (see chapter 5) and the second linked the William Bass of 1797 to Great Peter, Nansemond headman on the reservation in Isle of Wight (now Southampton) County in 1710. The Christianized Nansemonds had clearly kept up ties with their reservation kinsmen for a long time, and in the long run they were the group that survived.

The reservation Nansemonds had trouble with squatters from North Carolina on their land throughout the 1720s,[215] their land being located near the state border in what is now Southampton County. They remained in possession and were living near the Meherrins in 1730.[216] But by 1744 their population had dwindled—probably by spin-off—to a few people who seven years before had gone to live with the Nottoways, also in Southampton County. These Nansemonds therefore asked the Virginia Assembly for permission to sell their old reservation and buy new lands closer to their present abode.[217] Permission was given, and the transactions were carried out in 1746.[218]

Reservation Nansemond identity became more thoroughly bound up with the Nottoways thereafter; in 1748 and 1763 the Nottoways and Nansemonds together asked permission to sell Nottoway land.[219] Finally, in 1786 the Nansemonds petitioned the Assembly to let them sell their reservation, since they now numbered only five people, all of whom were old and infirm.[220] Permission was granted,[221] but the enabling law specified a buyer who died before the transaction took place. In 1791 another enabling law was passed,[222] and the sale took place the following year.[223] Only three reservation Nansemonds survived by then; the last of them died in 1806.[224] Connections with the Christianized Nansemonds of Norfolk County had apparently ceased.

Both the Pamunkey reservation in King William County and the Gingaskin reservation on the lower Eastern Shore survived throughout the eighteenth century. The Gingaskin lands remained constant at about 650 acres and the Virginia government seems to have considered them to be the wards of Northampton County, more or less by default. Luckily for us, the Northampton County records survive intact. They show little business transacted on behalf of the tribe and many individual Indians appearing in court, most of them suing either non-Indians or other Indians for trespass and assault and battery;[225] debt[226] and other unspecified grievances[227] occur less often. It is significant that several of the free Negroes appearing in the court records had surnames that later occur among the tribesmen;[228] in time the Gingaskins were to have more documented associations with free Negroes than did any other Powahatan group. As the century wore on, an increasing number of Indian children were bound out as indigents, to earn their keep instead of being supported by the parish.[229] And Indian people were still making traditional items such as mats and baskets for sale to non-Indians.[230]

The Eastern Shore was not a hospitable abode for free non-whites by the early eighteenth century. In 1722 the white citizens' fears of the growing free Negro population had reached such proportions that they were being expressed in grievances to the county court.[231] Attitudes toward Indians were no more kindly. In 1728 the county court ruled that an Indian slave was to be sold even when he was specifically—and legally—freed by his late master's will; that ruling was made at the request of the parish churchwardens.[232] It was to these same churchwardens that Gingaskin Indian affairs were eventually to be handed.

The Gingaskins remained unenthusiastic husbandmen, preferring to hunt and fish and grow kitchen gardens for their living, as their ancestors had. They did not prosper in these traditional occupations. In 1769, after receiving a petition either from the Gingaskins or from the parish church-wardens, the Virginia Assembly passed a law allowing the churchwardens to lease out two hundred acres of the reservation, with the proceeds going to help support the Indians.[233] The churchwardens did, in fact, lease out only one hundred acres, thinking that sufficient,[234] and by 1771 they were using lease money to pay for the Indians' living expenses.[235] They also paid an Englishman in 1775 for boarding an Indian.[236]

By 1773 the Gingaskins were having trouble with neighbors laying waste to their lands, and they petitioned the Assembly for proper trustees to over-see their affairs, a petition which was granted.[237] The Gingaskins' reluc-tance to change their lifeways, the closeness of English neighbors to them, and their intermarriage with free Negroes,[238] together with the Eastern Shore whites' strong and early demonstrated fears of free non-whites, all combined in 1813 to make the Gingaskins the first Indian tribe to be allot-ted and terminated in the United States. Since their fate influenced the at-tempts made later on the other reservations, we will return to the re-mainder of their history at the end of this chapter.

The Pamunkeys were better off than the Gingaskins in several respects. They owned more land at the beginning of the period, though it was whit-tled down considerably during the century. They had their primary settle-ment on a peninsula that is almost an island in the Pamunkey River—in-deed, it was occasionally called an island in travelers' accounts—and it gave them an isolation that partially protected them. They also did less in-termarrying with non-Indians than did the Gingaskins, according to Thomas Jefferson, who was governor of Virginia in the 1780s. At that time they were still "tolerably pure from mixture with other colours . . . ,"[239] which may mean exactly that or that their out-marriages had been mainly with whites. Jefferson was less sanguine about the people on what is now the Mattaponi reservation, whose men, he said, had "more negro than Indian blood in them." However, since that reservation was then part of the Pam-unkey one and would not have paid a separate tribute to the governor, Jefferson may merely have been reporting hearsay. There is no way to prove or disprove his statement in the near-absence of tribal and county records for that period.

Pamunkey landholdings were still considerable in 1706, though not all English claims had been cleared as yet.[240] English claimants kept appearing, and in spite of Pamunkey protests about encroachments, many of the claims exhibited in Williamsburg were often found to be good, since they dated from 1702–1704,[241] a period in which many legal land transfers were made in Pamunkey Neck. Perhaps it is no coincidence that in 1706, Queen Ann of Pamunkey petitioned the Virginia governor to stop the sale of liquor to her people.[242] Though some Englishmen were indeed trespassers, it seems that the Pamunkeys' complaint stemmed as much from their own frustration as from English actions. The group's situation was certainly not a happy one: they felt hemmed in, unable to exercise their hunting rights, and they hated watching their young men leaving and being "detained" by the English.[243] For these reasons, in 1710 Queen Ann of Pamunkey asked the governor to remit the tribe's tribute, since the old men who were left were unable to hunt.[244]

By 1715, when Queen Ann complained of English buyers not notifying the tribe of surveys to be made, and of surveying more land than they had bought, the tribe had made up its collective mind to sell no more land to anyone; it would only make leases.[245] But problems continued with Englishmen claiming land and clearing too much.[246] In 1718 the matter was finally turned over to the King William County court, whose records are no longer extant. In 1723 one last purchase of land, originally made in 1687, was ratified by the Assembly at the Pamunkeys' request.[247] Meanwhile, the Pamunkeys had more trouble with an English neighbor who hindered their hunting; in 1717, the colonial council ordered him to desist.[248]

In 1748 the Pamunkeys began to divest themselves of more land. They held, at that time, at least three tracts:[249] the peninsula on which they lived (containing about 1,100 acres),[250] a contiguous tract on the mainland of about 2,000 acres, and another tract of about 88 acres four miles away. There were apparently other tracts as well (see below). The small tract of about 125 acres on the Mattaponi River, ten miles away, was also administered under the heading of "Pamunkey" by the colony and later by the state. Never sold away, it was occasionally inhabited in those days by "Mattaponi Indians"[251] who may have been Chickahominy and Mattaponi remnants from upriver, or Pamunkeys, or a combination of all three, taking their name from the river on which they resided. Only the Pamunkeys dealt with the colonial and state government in the eighteenth century, probably because they controlled enough land to sell some of it away.

The Pamunkeys were not prospering in the mid-eighteenth century. In 1730, Lieutenant Governor Gooch had estimated the entire "Pamunkey" population "in York River" at "not above tenn familys."[252] No hereditary ruler of the tribe appears in 1730 or later. The Indians' request for permission to sell land in 1748[253] was signed by seven men,[254] who were "the only surviving Men" of the tribe and who claimed that because of "long and grevous [sic] Sickness" afflicting many of them, the tribe had contracted debts for "Medicines, Doctors attendance, Corn, Clothing, and other Necessarys." The Pamunkeys had never used their eighty-eight-acre tract, so neighboring non-Indians were cutting timber on it for rails and firewood. The tribe therefore got the Assembly to allow them to sell the land and use the proceeds to pay their debts. The Assembly appointed three white trustees to oversee the sale, receive the money, and pay the debts. These three were the first of a long line of trustees for the tribe.

In 1759 the Pamunkeys obtained permission for their trustees to lease more of their land.[255] The tract in question was separate from the peninsula where the Indians lived; the text of the law says only that it was "small," "separate" from the Indians settlement, used by the Indians for logging, and "greatly wasted" by non-Indian neighbors. The leases were therefore to specify that no more trees be cut, "in order to preserve the same for the use of the said Indians." Because the Pamunkeys were prohibited by law from testifying in court against white lessees who defaulted on payments, white trustees were to do it for the Indians henceforward; they were also enabled by the Assembly to replace their own members when needed.

Not all the tribe wanted that tract leased out. In 1760 several Pamunkeys claimed that the majority of the tribe did not favor the lease and asked that the 1759 law be repealed.[256] The colonial council referred the matter to the Assembly, which in early 1761 rejected this petition.[257]

In 1769 the Pamunkeys informed the governor that all the trustees were dead and that they needed new trustees to prosecute lessees who refused to pay.[258] A new set of six trustees (one having the same name as one appointed in 1759) was therefore appointed, and they were given expanded powers: they were now able to settle disputes among the Indians concerning "their respective boundaries and titles" to any reservation lands they used.[259]

The American Revolution, in which Robert Mush and several Pamunkeys served,[260] cut off the Pamunkeys and other reservation tribes[261] from the English colonial government with which they had treaty relations, and the new Commonwealth of Virginia moved in to fill the gap. In June 1776, when the interregnum constitution of Virginia was made, Indian lands were declared inalienable except through the Virginia General Assembly.[262] A law of 1779 asserted that only the Assembly had the right to purchase Indian land and that former purchases for the crown were now to be for the benefit of the commonwealth.[263] In 1792 yet another law was passed, stating that the land of tributary Indians was inalienable, as it had been under treaties with the crown, and that Indians and their property were now to be protected by the commonwealth.[264] The amount of land involved for the Powhatans was small by that time; the laws were aimed primarily at the Indians west of the Blue Ridge Mountains, with whom the Virginia government was negotiating.[265] However, the laws had the effect of keeping the Powhatan reservations as state reservations, not federal ones. The federal Indian Non-Intercourse Law of 1790 was not construed by anyone at the time as making the new federal government responsible for the Indian remnants in coastal Virginia, a failure of interpretation which was to have detrimental consequences for the Powhatans in the nineteenth and twentieth centuries.

The Pamunkey trustees once again did not keep up their numbers by making new appointments. In 1786 the tribe had to ask for more trustees to be appointed, and this time they suggested the names of people they wanted.[266]

The Pamunkeys continued to dispose of land after 1800. In 1812 they asked the Assembly for permission to lease out a three-hundred-acre tract about two miles from their settlement, and a law was duly passed.[267] In 1828 they got permission to sell either that tract or one of similar size;[268] the actual sale cannot be confirmed because of the burning of the county records in 1885.[269] The reason for selling was to raise funds to support the indigent, who, the Pamunkeys claimed, were "many, who by reason of age, infirmity and infancy, are unprovided for" while the robust members of the tribe used the reservation "as a common property, to the entire exclusion" of orphans and those who were infirm. Some of these assertions were probably rhetoric intended to persuade the legislators. There is no evidence that the Pamunkeys of any period ever used the reservation for farming a common crop; they merely owned it in common and had life interests in certain arable portions of it. Not only that, but a document of 1842[270] asserts that the Indians were all "as one family" so that no one should suffer need. At any rate, the tribe was enabled to sell a tract that they had not occupied for "about thirty years."

The "Mattaponi" Indians may have lost an acre or so of their already small reservation in 1812. On June 23 the King William County court issued a writ to investigate the proposed condemnation of an acre of the reservation so that one John Hill could rebuild a grist mill on what is now Indian Town Creek, the reservation's northern boundary.[271] One week later a court order was issued to impanel a jury to investigate the mill site. The jury reported back on July 23 that it approved of the mill and that one acre of high ground and one-third acre of low ground should be purchased from the "Mattaponi Indians." Hill then bought materials and applied to the county court to issue a summons to the Indians to show cause why he should not rebuild the mill. The Indians apparently informed the court that they were under the jurisdiction of the state, not the county,[272] for the court ruled that Hill had to petition the General Assembly before proceeding further. Hill did so,[273] asking that a law be passed allowing him "to abut his dam to [the Indians'] land + acquire 1 A. as well"; dirt for the former mill dam had been taken from there earlier. The Assembly deemed Hill's petition "reasonable," but the bill drawn from it did not pass.[274] The reservation boundary is still Indian Town Creek.

Culture Change

Documentation for eighteenth-century Powhatan culture change is regrettably sparse. People who lost their reservations ceased to be of concern to the colonial (and later the state) government, whose records are reasonably well preserved for the eighteenth century. Even those Indians who kept their reservations appear infrequently in governmental records: they were, on the whole, law-abiding and therefore obscure, except when they sold off land. The same is true in the county records, those not destroyed by local negligence or during the Civil War: Indians—and blacks and lower-stratum whites—rarely appear, since they uually owned no land as individuals, contracted no "legal" marriages in English terms, made no wills, and broke no laws. Thus we shall have to trace Powhatan culture change as far as the records permit and then try to fill the gaps with analogies from other eastern Indians' history.

Change became a little easier for the Indians because some of the extreme harshness of the 1705 code for non-whites was ameliorated during the century. Non-whites were permitted to testify in court against slaves in capital cases in 1723,[275] but they remained unable to testify against whites until after the Civil War. In 1732 non-whites convicted of offenses within benefit of clergy were no longer to be put to death, but were to be branded in the hand and given corporal punishment instead.[276] Two years later Indians were permitted to testify in criminal cases with Indian defendants,[277] a law which sprang from the recent murder of an Englishman by a tributary Indian (tribe not recorded), when Indian evidence had been needed in court.[278] In 1744 that "concession" to Indians was given to all non-whites, who were now allowed to testify in all court cases against any other non-whites, slave or free.[279] The legislators' assumption was that "negroes, mulattoes, and Indians" all associated freely with one another, which may or may not have been true of the Indians. In 1762 the law making non-white slaves "real estate" was repealed.[280] Finally, in 1785 the definition of "mulatto" was liberalized: instead of one-eighth or more African ancestry making one a mulatto and therefore subject to the 1705 code, it now took one-quarter or more,[281] a definition which remained law until 1910. None of the surviving documents indicate that this racial definition was applied to any Indians other than the Gingaskins in the eighteenth century.

None of the Powhatan remnants, with or without reservations, was ever exposed to New England–style missionizing. No "praying towns" were ever founded in Virginia,[282] nor is there evidence of a missionary going to live in any Powhatan community and helping the Indians form their own kind of Christianity and gradual culture change.[283] The only near-exception was one Reverend Charles Jeffrey Smith, formerly a missionary in New England, who in 1770 announced plans for an academy in New Kent County that would take in both Indian and English students.[284] Nothing more is known of his venture. Instead, the major agents of culture change among the Powhatans remained primarily the near-neighbors of whose character Lieutenant Governor Spotswood so heartily disapproved. The groups without reservations withdrew to the ridges, away from the rivers, judging by where the modern "citizen" Indian groups first appeared in the mid-nineteenth century. There they probably had to shift to more intensive farming, since the edible swamp plants traditionally used to see families through the spring would have been farther away. For the reservation remnants, the trustees overseeing their affairs and the education of their boys at the College of William and Mary had a major impact. Apart from the Gingaskins, already described, we have records only about the Pamunkeys.

Sometime between the queen of Pamunkey's last appearance in 1718 and the petition signed by all the adult men in 1748, the group's political system became less formal, more democratic, and decidedly patriarchal. By mid-century the Pamunkeys had a sort of council composed of the adult men in the group. The trustees appointed to oversee their land affairs began to serve some governmental functions, through which they gradually became agents of culture change. That change was far enough advanced, and the 1677 treaty seemed "outdated" enough, that by the 1780s King William County was taxing individual Pamunkeys on their personal property, which included horses or mules (a single category) and a few slaves.[285]

The trustees' powers were limited at first to being legal go-betweens for the tribe. But their role as advisors expanded, apparently with the Pamunkeys' cooperation. In 1769 they were legally empowered to settle disputes among the tribesmen (see above). In October 1798 the men of the tribe and trustees all agreed that "the government" of the Indians had unspecified "defects" which no one had the power to remedy. The Pamunkeys were apparently not ready to attempt to make bylaws for themselves. So they and the trustees together asked the Assembly to empower the trustees "to manage + transact all affairs relative to said Indians."[286] Accordingly, a law was passed permitting the trustees to make a set of bylaws (no copies of which survive) for the tribe to approve and stating that dead trustees were in future to be replaced by a majority vote of the "Indians" of twenty-one years and over.[287] Since female suffrage was not a feature of Anglo-Virginian society at the time, and since the Pamunkeys had long since ceased to have "queens" or "kings," both the trustees and the Indians assumed that all voters would be male, an assumption that still obtains on the Pamunkey and Mattaponi reservations today.

The Indian school at the College of William and Mary[288] was founded through a bequest left in 1691 by the noted chemist Robert Boyle. Boyle's money was invested in an English farm named Brafferton, and the profits from the venture, known as the Brafferton Fund, were used for the education of Indian boys in Virginia as directed in Boyle's will.[289] The logical place to use it, in the Virginia government's opinion, was as an appendage of the only college in the colony, the College of William and Mary. However, the Indian school at the college was slow getting started, in part because of the reluctance of Powhatan parents to send their children away. When pressured, the parents cited "the breach of a former Compact made long ago by this Government, when instead of their Children receiving the promised education they were transported (as they say) to other Countrys and sold as Slaves."[290] The surviving colonial records do not corroborate that story, although it could well have happened.

Failing to get Powhatan students for their school, the English resorted to buying young Indian servants imported into the colony, until in 1711, Lieu-tenant Governor Spotswood hit upon a plan. He offered to remit the tribute of the poverty-stricken tribes if they would send some of their male children to the college.[291] The plan worked. Soon the Indian scholars included the reservation Nansemond "king's" son and cousin, two sons each from the Nottoway and Meherrin councillors, the son of the "queen of Pamunkey," with a boy to serve him, and two other Pamunkey boys to be educated. The Chickahominies also apparently sent a child.[292] By the summer of 1712 there were twenty Indian boys at William and Mary. They had "a Master to teach them and are decently clothed and maintained, so that they seem very well pleased with the change of their condition as indeed their par-ents and others of their Nations who come frequently to see them, express much satisfaction with the care that is taken of them."[293] The next year, when Spotswood made treaties with the Iroquoians of southern Virginia, the Nottoway, Meherrin, and Nansemond children were removed to Fort Christanna.[294]

By 1715 some of the Indian children at William and Mary could "read and write tolerably well, [could] repeat the Church Chatechism, and [knew] how to make their responses in ye Church, [and] both the parents and the boys themselves, have shewn a great desire they should be admitted to Bap-tizm." However, the majority of Virginia clergymen opposed baptism so soon, claiming that since the boys were born in non-Christian families they should be "capable of giving an Acc't of their Faith" first.[295] A document from within the college the next year accords with that less rosy picture. A new teacher had been installed and the former one reimbursed for the books, paper, pens, and ink he had bought for the boys. Few Indians were at the school now, and the new teacher wanted to admit English boys as well, with a partition erected in the classroom "to separate the s^d English children from the Indians."[296] The standard curriculum was entirely Euro-pean: reading, writing, "vulgar Arithmetick," and catechism.[297]

Hugh Jones, who taught English students at the college from 1717 to 1721, painted a more dismal picture yet. At first, he said, the Indian boys had not been housed in the college, but had been boarded in the town of Williamsburg—"where abundance of them used to die, either through sickness, change of provision, and way of life; or as some will have it, often for want of proper necessaries and due care taken with them."[298] When Brafferton House was built, the boys had sleeping accommodations there as well as a classroom, and in Jones's time the survival rate was apparently higher. He noted also that the boys showed a "natural" and "excellent ge-nius for drawing."[299] However, the boys who finished their education usu-ally went back to the ways of their people when they returned home,[300] "chiefly because they can live with less labour, and more pleasure and plenty, as Indians, than they can with us." Jones proposed instead that the graduates not be sent directly home, but be sent to sea or apprenticed to trades first so they would have a chance to see more of the English world and become accustomed to it. As it was, "they are rather taught to become worse than better by falling into the worst practices of vile nominal Christians, which they add to their own Indian manners and notions." William Byrd expressed similar sentiments in 1728, saying that the relapsed scholars "are apt to be more vicious and disorderly than the rest of their countrymen," for their education "had no other Effect but to make them something cleanlier than other Indians are."[301]

In the 1720s the boys who left the school after several years probably found themselves caught between two opposing ways of life, fitting into neither. Their religious learning profited them little, since their own people did not adopt Christianity until late in the century and the surrounding English were often not religious.[302] Their time away from their families retarded them in learning the skills expected of Indian men, and the skills and habits they had learned in Williamsburg were of little use as yet among their people. However, the Pamunkey boys seem to have considered literacy worth having, and in turn they sent their sons to William and Mary.

In the mid-eighteenth century the Indian boys received the same grammar school education that their predecessors had—and so did their white contemporaries. John Whiting of Newport, Rhode Island, visited the college in 1762 and told his friend Ezra Stiles that the seventy-five students were "chiefly boys & few about 15 AEt. [years of age], + that they [the President and the six teachers on the faculty] seldom Conferred Degrees."[303]

There were eight Indian students at William and Mary in 1754, five of them with Pamunkey surnames.[304] In the 1760s and 1770s the number shrank to two Pamunkeys.[305] One of them, Robert Mush (later Mursh and still later Marsh), was a student in 1769; a sample of his handwriting in later life survives (see fig. 6).[306] In 1773 there were still Indian boys at the college who were clothed in the English style with money from the Brafferton Fund.[307] The Indian school at the college closed only after the Brafferton Fund, English in origin, was diverted to the West Indies during the American Revolution; white Virginians, as usual, were not interested in perpetuating an Indian mission school. However, the boys who had attended the school must have been a constant source of English influence on Powhatan culture, even if in earlier days they did "apostasize."

Another probable source of change in Powhatan culture was the non-Indian spouses taken by Indian people who feared marrying close kinsmen. Spouses might conform to Indian custom to a considerable extent, but they would nearly always pass on some elements of their own ethnic heritage. That would be especially true of in-marrying males—whom the Pamunkeys in recent decades have tried to exclude for just that reason. In records of marriage, as for other aspects of eighteenth-century Indian life, the only surviving evidence comes from the reservations. The Gingaskin marriages among free Negroes have already been cited. Evidence for out-marriage

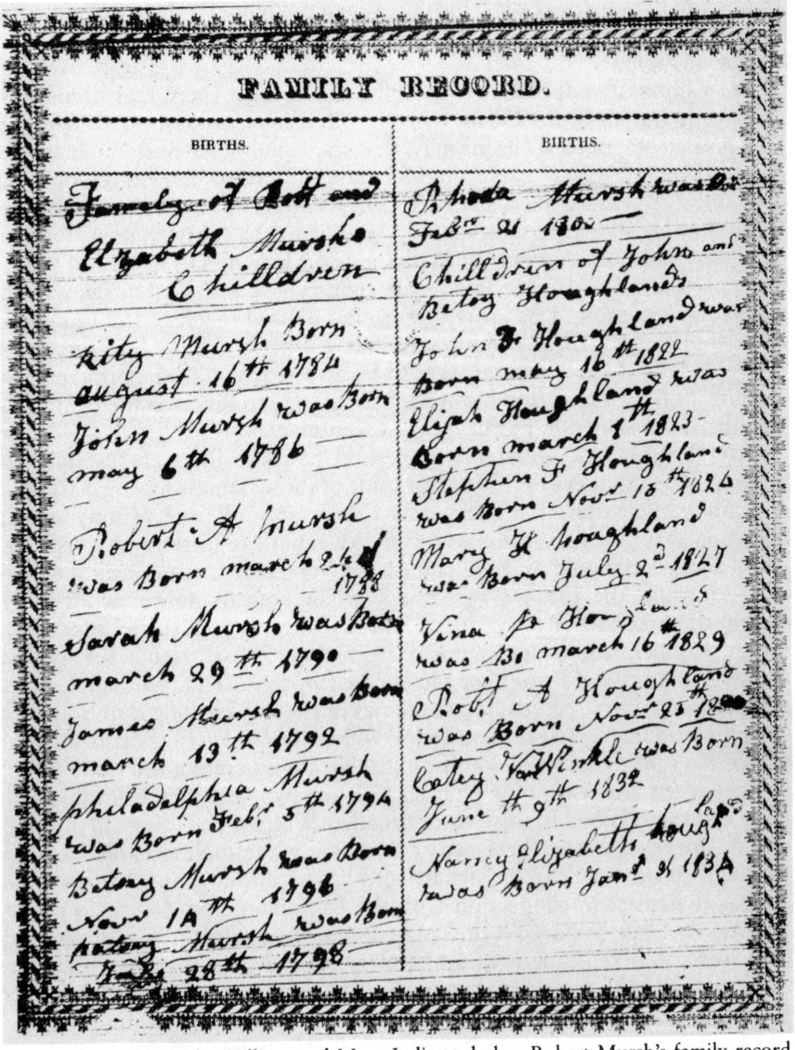
FAMILY RECORD.

BIRTHS.

Family of Robt and
Elizabeth Murshs
Childdren
Kity Mursh Born
august 16th 1784
John Mursh was Born
may 6th 1786
Robert A Mursh
was Born march 24th
1788
Sarah Mursh was Born
march 29th 1790
James Mursh was Born
march 13th 1792
philadelphia Mursh
was Born Feb.r 5th 1794
Betsey Mursh was Born
Nov 14th 1796
Patsey Mursh was Born
28th 1798

BIRTHS.

Rhoda Mursh was Born
Feb.y 21 180
Childdren of John and
Betsy Houghlands
John F Houghland was
Born may 16th 1822
Elijah Houghland was
Born march 8th 1823
Stephen F Houghland
was Born Nov.r 13th 1824
Mary H Houghland
was Born July 2d 1827
Vina F Houghlands
was Bo march 16th 1829
Robt A Houghland
was Born Nov.r 25th 18
Catey VanWinkle was Born
June th 9th 1832
Nancy Elizabeth Houghlands
was Born Jan.y 31 1834

Fig. 6. The writing of a William and Mary Indian scholar: Robert Mursh's family record. (Courtesy National Archives.)

among the Pamunkeys exists, but it is sparse; judging by that evidence and by Jefferson's observations, partners in the eighteenth century were either whites or Indians.

The Pamunkey population was still a small one. There had been "not above tenn families" in 1730 and seven adult men in 1748; in 1787 Thomas Jefferson wrote, possibly accurately, that the Pamunkeys were "reduced to about 10 or 12 men," while the "Mattaponi" group had "three or four men only." [308] Eleven men signed the legislative petition of 1798. [309] The Pamunkey legislative petition of 1812 was signed by fourteen men, [310] three of whom had been students at William and Mary in 1754. Several white men married into the tribe late in the century (see below). On the whole, the Pamunkey group was growing through natural increase and immigration. Nonetheless, the Assembly wrote an extinction clause into the 1828 land-sale law: the sale monies were to be invested, and all the principal remaining "on the extinction of the said tribe" was to revert to the commonwealth. That extinction has never yet taken place.

Several surnames, apparently inherited patrilineally, were established among the Pamunkeys by 1748, and some of those names show remarkable continuity thereafter; Langston and Cooke are still reservation names; Sampson was another until early in the twentieth century; and Mush appears at the beginning and the end of the eighteenth century and then remains through the 1830s. The name Tawhaw appears in the records only during the first half of the century, and Williams only in the 1790s, while Gunn, Cooper, and Gurley appear from the 1790s through the 1830s. Thus the majority of Pamunkey men appearing in the eighteenth and early-nineteenth-century records had surnames of reasonably long duration.

In the late eighteenth century, several white men (and perhaps also women) joined Pamunkey society, establishing their names among the population. (Evidence for women is much harder to come by.) One James Bradby, perhaps the same James Bradby who attended William and Mary in 1754[311] while Pamunkeys were there, was taxed as a white male tithable by King William County in 1787.[312] Richard and Patrick Bradby, possibly his sons, appear thereafter in connection with the Pamunkeys, labeled variously as "white" or "free coloured"; the confusion in the records may indicate that they were of mixed Indian-white ancestry or that their marriage to an Indian had changed their social status in the county. They both lived on the Pamunkey Reservation in 1798, where they were taxed as white tithables, but Richard was taxed as an Indian in 1807. Both were charter members, with their wives and with Pamunkey Indians, of Lower College Baptist Church in 1791, being enrolled in that church's separate "free coloured" list.[313] Neither man signed the Pamunkey tribe's legislative petition of 1798, mentioned above. Both therefore appear to be fringe men, and they or their close relatives were the ancestors of the modern Pamunkey Bradbys.

Edward Brisbon (or Brisby) lived on the Reservation in 1799 and thereafter, and was always taxed as a "white" man. He, too, appears with his wife in the "free coloured" charter roll of Lower College Baptist Church. His son, however, was not a fringe person, for he signed Pamunkey documents in the nineteenth century. Richard Holt was always taxed as a "white" man but lived on the reservation in 1798; he was probably the ancestor of Pamunkey Holts of the nineteenth century and the husband of Molly Holt, one of the last Pamunkeys who could speak even a little of the language (see chapter 8). William Sweat was always taxed as a "white" man, even when he lived on the reservation in 1795 and 1797. Yet he appears as a single man in the "free coloured" charter roll of Lower College Baptist Church. His descendants did not remain core Pamunkeys for long, for by the late nineteenth century they had joined the New Kent fringe (see chapter 8).

There were Pamunkey connections with non-whites as well, but only three instances are documentable, one a marriage with an Indian and the other two a marriage and a liaison with Negroes. The best-known connection, commonly and inaccurately used to "prove" that the Pamunkeys were intermarrying freely with Negroes, comes from the years 1770–1772, when several advertisements were run in the *Virginia Gazette* concerning one runaway Negro slave named Frank.[314] Frank escaped from his master several times, each time seeking refuge among the Pamunkeys, "as in one of his former Trips he got himself a Wife amongst them."[315] The identity of the wife and the likelihood of her having children by Frank is impossible to ascertain. Since Frank is the only runaway slave—out of many—who is known to have fled to Pamunkey rather than to the Indian country farther west, it does not seem likely that the Pamunkeys had a habit of taking in Negro refugees. One marriage does not make a pattern.

The second instance of a non-white spouse also involves a Pamunkey woman.[316] One Susanna (surname unrecorded) married Lewis Denry, a Canadian Indian (tribal affiliation unspecified), and the pair settled on the Pamunkey reservation with the tribe's blessing. Within a year, though, the tribe's attitude toward Denry changed for reasons unknown, and the couple was banished. They went to live in Hanover County, where Susanna soon became blind. When Denry applied for assistance from the county, he was told that Susanna did not qualify because she was a Pamunkey. The husband therefore had a choice between keeping his wife in poverty in Hanover County or sending her back alone to the reservation. Therefore, with the endorsement of two tribal trustees, he petitioned the General Assembly in 1795 to make the Pamunkeys let them both live on the reservation. The Assembly referred the matter to the county court, whose records were destroyed ninety years later.

The third instance was a liaison whose descendants included a prominent "colored" scholar and politician in the late nineteenth century. John Mercer Langston was the co-organizer of the Law Department at Howard University, president of Virginia Normal and Collegiate Institute in Peters-

burg, minister-resident and consul-general to Haiti, and a member of the
U.S. House of Representatives during his long and busy career. He was also
the son, born in 1829, of a white plantation owner named Quarles and
Quarles' mulatto mistress, a manumitted slave named Lucy Langston. Lucy
was the daughter of a slave woman named Langston who "came out of" an
Indian tribe, according to her grandson.[317] Because Lucy's name was Langston and she named two of her sons John and Gideon, both of them names
found among late-eighteenth-century Pamunkey Langstons, the tribe in
question must have been the Pamunkeys. In 1787 a Pamunkey named John
Langston owned and paid taxes on an adult slave (sex unrecorded) and
three slave children, who disappear from his household thereafter. Lucy
Langston's mother may have been one of these children. John Langston
may not have been the children's father, though. Fathers often loved their
slave children and freed them rather than selling them away, but Lucy
Langston's mother was sold. She remained a slave all her life and passed the
condition on to her daughter, who was manumitted by her white lover before son John's birth. John Langston's treatment of his slave's children was
certainly not affectionate.

The King William Personal Property Tax Books show several Pamunkeys, both men and women, as slaveowners in the late eighteenth and early
nineteenth centuries. These people owned only one slave, the exception
being John Langston (in 1787 only). The slaves' sex is not recorded. At
least two of the Pamunkey male slaveowners also had Indian or Indian-
white wives who were freeborn.[318] Yet married men having children by
slaves was not uncommon elsewhere in Virginia.[319] Such cases may have
occurred at Pamunkey, and the children may have been allowed to remain
on the reservation for a time as fringe people, until such toleration became
too dangerous (see chapter 8).

On the whole, then, the evidence for out-marriage among the Pamunkeys in the eighteenth and early nineteenth centuries is limited, although
some out-marriages to whites or other Indians occurred and assisted the
process of culture change in the group. More important for the group's
subsequent history in a very racist state, the eighteenth-century record is
too inconclusive, given the complete lack of records about the wives of
Pamunkey men, to be useful in establishing the entire racial background of
the reservation people in later periods.

It is impossible to determine from the scanty evidence whether the Pamunkeys had a definite policy on out-marriage in the eighteenth century.
Modern Pamunkey oral tradition asserts emphatically that they did, and
that the policy admitted some whites but no Negroes.[320] The first bylaws
made for the tribe in 1798 have not been preserved, but the tribe certainly
seems to have been willing in those days to oust any people who were not
congenial. The Denry case also foreshadows a Pamunkey practice of the
twentieth century, allowing Pamunkey men to marry Indians or whites

without losing their rights of residence, but forbidding Pamunkey women who married non-Pamunkey men to live on the reservation while the marriage existed.[321] That practice, whenever its inception, reinforced the patriarchal political organization the tribe had developed.

Other elements of Powhatan culture changed as well. There is but scanty direct evidence to show which traits became changed at what time, and yet again that evidence comes from the reservations. Andrew Burnaby visited the Pamunkey Reservation in 1759 and found the Indians living in traditional *yi·hakan*s while wearing English clothes; the men's chief occupations were still hunting and fishing,[322] which continued to be the case until well into the twentieth century. In 1765 Governor Francis Fauquier also wrote that some of the tributary Indians were wearing English clothing.[323]

The evidence for literacy among the Pamunkeys is mixed. The petition of 1798 was written by Robert Mursh, yet all but two of the signers of the 1812 petition (including some whose names appear among the school children of 1754) signed with their "marks." By then, family names had become patrilineal and so probably had kinship in general. Some families owned horses or mules, and a few owned slaves. Everyone spoke fluent English; most people were probably monolingual English speakers, judging by how few words were remembered later by two women born in the 1770s (see chapter 8).

By the 1780s at the latest, the way in which the Pamunkeys married one another had become semi-civil, semi-ecclesiastical. Robert Mush married a Pamunkey named Elizabeth (surname unknown) in 1783.[324] Once the match had been agreed upon by Elizabeth, "her husband Robert Mursh [*sic*] and her parents," the couple had their "marriage bonds" published three different times in "their Church or Missionary Station," whenever a Baptist preacher came to visit. The parallel with the Episcopal church's reading of the marriage banns is obvious. After the third announcement, however, there was no further ceremony. The couple simply began living together as man and wife, in keeping with traditional Powhatan marriage. The Mushes and their tribe thenceforth considered the union to be permanent.[325]

The Pamunkeys apparently converted late to Christianity, after a period (of uncertain length)[326] of religious "limbo" in which most traditional rituals and many beliefs had disappeared without being replaced by another creed. Oral tradition among the modern Chickahominies states that they were the first to convert: a missionary named James Bradby joined their group in 1793 and married an Indian woman,[327] after which Bradby's descendants are said to have married into the Pamunkeys. However, documentary evidence does not corroborate the tradition. The evidence has already been described; from it we may infer that the Bradbys and their Christianity spread from the Pamunkeys to other Indians.

Some Pamunkeys had already been baptized by 1791, when Lower College Baptist Church was organized in King William County with a charter roll that included thirteen core or fringe Pamunkey men, thirteen core or fringe Pamunkey women, and a man from the New Kent Fringe (see chapter 8).[328] These people had probably been baptized by itinerant Baptist preachers, whose activities among the Pamunkeys we know from the Mush marriage, described above. Robert Mush moved his family to the Catawba Reservation in South Carolina shortly after 1800, and in February 1806 he, his wife, and his son joined the Flint Hill Baptist Church in York District, bringing with them their letters from the Church of Christ in King William County.[329]

Thus, according to the limited evidence, the traditional Powhatan way of life changed slowly on the relatively isolated Pamunkey Reservation. The groups that had lost their reservations and become squatters on the less desirable lands away from the rivers may have changed more rapidly. No additional direct evidence can be gleaned from the surviving Virginia records, so for corroboration of and more details on Powhatan culture change, we must turn to ethnographic analogy among the coastal Algonquians north of Virginia.

The New England Algonquians made a wide variety of accommodations to the English presence, yet they show the same broad culture-change patterns as the Powhatans. The groups vary from the Mohegans of Connecticut, who remained very traditional through the mid-eighteenth century,[330] through the Stockbridge-Munsees, who after a long period of contact with whites deliberately settled themselves at a Presbyterian mission along with white families in 1734,[331] through the Narragansetts of Rhode Island, who retained a reservation government until 1880, through the Shinnecocks of Long Island, who still retain a reservation but no formal government.

The New England Algonquians were all very conservative economically. That is, they retained their traditional division of labor and continued to live by hunting, fishing, foraging, and limited horticulture until the mid-eighteenth century and beyond. Thus, we find the belief that hunting was for men and farming for women among the Stockbridge-Munsees in 1739, five years after they settled in an Indian-white mission with the idea of adapting to white ways. Not only that, but traditional emphasis on generosity to kinsmen and on harmony with nature, which had an economic leveling effect among the people, persists to the present.[332] The Shinnecocks were nearly landless by 1703, but they could not conceive of a way of life that did not involve migration from field to fishing station to hunting camp. They were therefore allowed to lease a large wooded tract in the center of Long Island on which to continue hunting. From 1792 onward they leased that land to non-Indians, but women went on gardening while the men concentrated on fishing and whaling. Seasonal employment in rich households in nearby Southampton was added in the nineteenth century, and the pattern continues to the present.[333] The Mashpees of Massachusetts and the Poospatucks of Long Island also followed a practice of women farming and men whaling in the eighteenth century.[334]

The making and selling of Anglicized traditional crafts produced income for Indians other than the Powhatans: in Pennsylvania and elsewhere the United Brethren missions staff saw Indians eking out a living selling "baskets, brooms, wooden spoons, dishes, &c."[335] Mainland Wampanoag women in Massachusetts continued making baskets and brooms.[336] In the late eighteenth century the last Indians at Paugasuck, or Chusetown, in Connecticut sold "parti-colored baskets" to supplement the living they made by hunting;[337] the Pequots in the same state did the same.[338]

Housing remained traditional for a long time; clothing changed more rapidly. In 1765 some Narragansetts still lived in wigwams, while others had frame houses and the sachem's family had "eighteenth-century English-style farmhouses."[339] On Martha's Vineyard, where Indians began converting to Christianity in the 1640s and many wore English clothing by 1700, even most converts still lived in wigwams in the early eighteenth century.[340] The nearby mainland Wampanoags lived mainly in wigwams as late as 1767, though some of these dwellings had brick fireplaces; a decade later there were forty-two shingled houses and twenty-six wigwams in the community.[341] The data are uneven for the Stockbridge-Munsees: in 1749 three-fifths of them still lived in wigwams, in 1762 they had sixty wigwams and six houses,[342] and by 1796 all the people wore European clothing.[343] A Mohegan town in 1761 consisted entirely of wigwams, and a wigwam there that Ezra Stiles sketched contained a "dresser." Stiles also sketched that year a Niantic wigwam which had a "tea table," a shelf with plates on it, chests, a table, a dresser, a chair, and platform beds covered with mats.[344] All we know about the Shinnecocks is that most of them had adopted frame houses by 1830,[345] though a few kept their wigwams as late as 1850.[346]

The sachems and the clans, matrilineal or otherwise, which had done much of the governmental work in the New England Algonquian groups, faded from the scene in the second half of the eighteenth century. Communities that were under close white supervision tended to replace them with English-style Indian political officials assisted by whites. Others, like the Shinnecocks, were under less supervision and seem to have had less formal internal government, still assisted by whites (three elected trustees, in the Shinnecock case),[347] which is the pattern that the Powhatans apparently developed.

The surviving mid-eighteenth-century reservations in Massachusetts had their own officials, approved by the Commonwealth of Massachusetts, assisted by three white "guardians"; there was also a superintendent of Indian affairs for Massachusetts after 1656.[348] Late in the century the supervision of the Wampanoags became much more paternalistic and that, coupled with a powerful but neglectful missionary, caused an outbreak of protest in 1835.[349] The Stockbridges, whose matriclans had seriously broken down before they settled at the mission,[350] and the Mashpees had more autonomy. The Indian landholders and three guardians ran Stockbridge, while the Indian and white landholders of Mashpee elected a moderator, five overseers (two of them white), a white town clerk, a white treasurer, and one or more constables.[351] Indians committing offenses away from their reservations in Massachusetts were tried in courts of oyer and terminer.[352] In the seventeenth century the Narragansetts had had a strong chief,[353] a younger chief who was his relative, and a council of minor chiefs; by 1768 there was still a hereditary chief and a five-man council. But the last hereditary chief died in the 1770s, and thereafter a leader called the "president" was elected, with bylaws being regulated by the State of Rhode Island beginning in 1792.[354] The Shinnecocks, once under strong sachems based on the Connecticut mainland,[355] had no formal governmental structure at all by the early eighteenth century, their traditional hereditary leaders having disappeared.[356] In 1792 the state of New York legislated that three white trustees were to oversee the Indians' land leases and "internal land affairs." All other governmental services for the reservation people were (and still are) handled by the town of Southampton, as for other citizens.[357]

The Indian people of Martha's Vineyard and of the "praying towns" were encouraged to become literate as an integral part of practicing Christianity. Some of them became literate in both English and Algonquian.[358] A mission school was founded for the Narragansetts by 1750.[359] The Stockbridge mission automatically included a school for Indian and white children.[360] The Shinnecocks, on the other hand, had no school and still remained illiterate in the 1790s.[361]

Some of the New England Algonquians experienced a religious "limbo," while others did not. The people of Martha's Vineyard had a mixed experience. Some converted to Christianity after epidemics in the 1640s killed traditionalists but bypassed many converts, thus showing the "powerlessness" of the traditional religion. Others, however, either converted late in life or did not convert at all during the first century or so of contact with missionaries.[362] Many coastal Indian groups, such as the Long Island Montauks[363] and Unkechaugs,[364] met few missionaries until the "Great Awakening" of the 1750s.[365] The mission that was set up among the Narragansetts around 1750 eventually converted the people;[366] until then more or less traditional weddings were the rule.[367] The success of the "praying towns" on the Massachusetts mainland was always mixed while it lasted.[368] Even among the Stockbridge-Munsees, who deliberately settled at a mission to change their way of life, only 10 percent of their numbers were active church members in 1796.[369] The others do not seem to have practiced any religion actively. Conversion of some people but not others in a tribe could cause trouble, as was the case at Potatuck in 1742 when a convert complained that tribesmen told him "if I am a Christian, then I shall not have my [share of tribal] land."[370]

The New England Algonquian remnants that survived through the eighteenth and early nineteenth century[371] were generally small enough that they needed to marry non-Indians in order to prevent inbreeding. The exceptions were the Montauks and, to a lesser extent, the Shinnecocks, to whom marriage with outsiders—especially to members of other Indian groups—was actually forbidden by white overlords who feared an uprising. The result was a "predominantly endogamous population on the reservations, with many mixed breed families in the nearby vicinity."[372] Other Indian groups, not especially racist themselves and not hindered by racist white policy, married "out." The non-Indians they took into their communities were both white and black, according to the local traditions prevalent today. Actual documentary proof is usually lacking,[373] but many outsiders claim to see both Caucasian and Negroid, as well as Indian, types among tribal members.[374] The Narragansetts are believed to have mated extensively with white and black servants during the servitude forced upon them after King Philip's War.[375] By 1792 they had learned to discriminate against people who married blacks and put the tribal reputation in danger: the new bylaws of that year stated that voting members of the tribe were to be males who were the children either of Indian women or of Indian men by non-Negro women.[376]

The eighteenth-century Powhatans, then, appear to have experienced slow culture change along the same lines as many other coastal Algonquians, particularly those who lived under the same relative neglect. People in such a position could adapt to new conditions at their own pace and therefore with less pain—although there was still some pain involved, as accounts of heavy drinking among both the Powhatans and the people of Martha's Vineyard show. Culture change outside Virginia did not automatically mean disappearance, either. Many Algonquian reservation groups faded away or were legislated away, but others hung onto their land and their Indian identity.

The Termination of the Gingaskins

English people were generally too busy with other interests in the eighteenth century to pay much attention to the Indians still among them. They were engaged in land speculation in the west, wars with the French, and later a war of independence with the English. There would be further hostilities with the English in 1812–1814. They preferred, of course, to keep their slaves working for them, even when those slaves were descended from Indians who had been illegally enslaved decades before.[377] Their laws for non-whites were repressive by today's standards, but much worse was to come in the nineteenth century.

Many whites believed in the "one-drop rule" (i.e., one "drop" of African "blood" made one black) for determining "pure" whiteness in their own marriage partners, but they still did not dream of putting that rule into force with a law. Too much mixing of white and black had already gone on, and too many respectable people would be injured by a tightening of racial definitions.[378] If anything, the decades following the American Revolution were a time of relative liberalism: it was, after all, in 1785 that Virginia changed her definition of mulattoes from one-eighth or more African ancestry to one-quarter or more (see above). People of all colors in Virginia and elsewhere mixed to some extent, never dreaming that the political and social climate would change drastically in the future and put those mixed-blood descendants—and even the prominent "white" descendants of Pocahontas—into serious jeopardy. The Powhatans and other coastal Algonquians may have gone that route, too, but the obscurity in which they lived kept records about them to a minimum so that we cannot ever be sure.

In the 1820s, after the Missouri Compromise, white attitudes in the South became more actively pro-slavery and ever harsher toward non-whites in general. The Powhatans entered a period in which being a "person of color" because one was Indian rather than Negro was no protection against a further loss of civil rights (see chapter 8). By that time, though, the Gingaskins on the lower Eastern Shore had already lost their reservation and were being pressured to leave the state. The Gingaskin case was a harbinger of what the other reservation Indians in Virginia could expect, even as they repeated the history of Powhatan groups that had become landless before them (see map 7).

The Gingaskins' white neighbors had long been more sensitive than had mainland whites to possible menaces from free Negroes. The Eastern Shore's distance from other parts of Virginia, whence help would come, made landowners feel more vulnerable in case of an uprising. The Gingaskins were contracting marriages with free Negroes by the late eighteenth century,[379] and their reputation was also poor because they were non-intensive farmers (still female horticulturists and male hunters and fishers) whose children were sometimes cared for by "concerned" non-Indians. If the 1780s were a time of relative liberalism on the mainland, they were also a time when the white citizens of Northampton County wanted the Gingaskin reservation done away with.

In January 1784 some white people petitioned the General Assembly, asking that some of the reservation land be leased out and the rest be set aside for the Indians but made "subject to taxation as other Lands."[380] The reasons given are most informative: there were supposedly only "five or six" Indians left and these did not use the land due to a "fondness for fishing, fowling + hunting, the natural insolence [read "pride"] of their disposition, + their natural disinclination to Agriculture." Otherwise, the reservation was "an Asylum for free Negroes + other disorderly persons, Who build Hutts thereon + pillage + destroy the Timber without controul [sic]; to the great Inconvenience of the honest Inhabitants of the Vicinity, who have ever considered it a Den of Thieves + Nuisance to the Neighborhood." Some pillaging may have gone on, though Gingaskin trespass suits in the county court all date to an earlier time. However, the white peti-

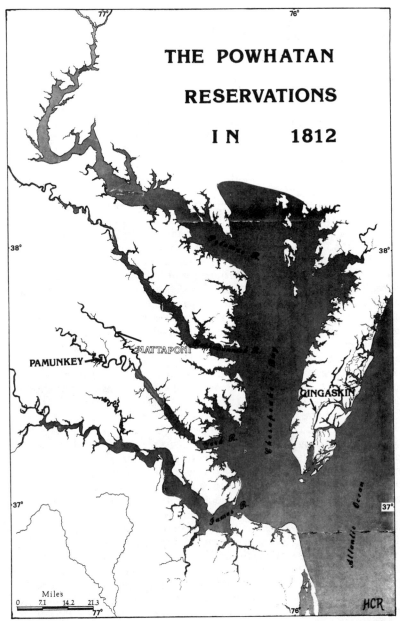

Map 7. The Powhatan Reservations in 1812. Base map adapted from *Bathymetry of Chesapeake Bay* (Virginia Institute of Marine Science, 1977).

tioners apparently assumed that Gingaskins with Negro or mulatto spouses, and their Indian-descended offspring, were not entitled to have living quarters on the reservation. They also assumed, as did mainland whites of a later time, that the vast majority of free Negroes were worthless vagrants, an assumption which is contradicted by a large body of contemporary documents.[381]

The Assembly apparently agreed with the petition.[382] In December the Northampton court, seemingly at the behest of the Assembly, appointed commissioners to report on people living illegally on the reservation. Once their report was in, a new set of commissioners was appointed to "rent & dispose" of the reservation land "as they conceive will be most to [the Indians'] advantage."[383] The reservation continued to exist, however.

In October 1787 some white citizens petitioned the General Assembly again.[384] The Gingaskins, they said, were "nearly extinct, there being at this time not more than three or four of the genuine [i.e., full-blooded] Indians at most." The "real" Indians did little farming, and instead they rented out their land for a pittance[385] while they—the men, that is—"abandon themselves almost solely to the employments of fishing and fowling, from which they chiefly derive a Maintenance." Most of the reservation had allegedly never been cultivated or used in any way to support the Indians (a questionable assertion). Meanwhile, the "adjacent Neighbourhood" had "wantonly pillaged" the timber that used to cover the reservation: the land ought to be in the hands of people who could protect it (i.e., whites). Further, the land ought to be taxed, and the "idle set of free negroes who have of late years connected themselves with the Indians and occupy the greatest part of their Lands" ought to be expelled. The petitioners therefore wanted the reservation sold and the money used to maintain "such of the said Indians as appear to be genuine descendants of the Tribe." The petition was rejected.

The Gingaskins continued on their way as before, and their white neighbors remained disgruntled. In 1792 the General Assembly had to deal with problems arising from the leasing of reservation land.[386] The county was now required to appoint trustees who would lease out land, distribute the money, and settle any disputes between themselves and the Indians.[387] The trustees were duly appointed[388] and a letter from one of them to the governor reveals that a survey of the reservation was also made.[389] The letter indicates little real understanding of the kind of people the Gingaskins were. The leasing rather than selling of the land grated upon the writer, for he had to continue to work with people whose "known habits of Indolence and aversion from every kind of profitable labour [i.e., intensive farming or trades]" indicated "the true characteristics of the tribe of Gingasking [sic] Indians, who seem to have inherited the native indolence of all that class of people." However, the trustees went on managing Gingaskin land for another twenty years, during which one trustee died and was replaced by an order of the county court.[390]

By December 1812 the Gingaskins had somehow been persuaded by their reluctant trustees to give up their reservation. The trustees therefore petitioned the Assembly for permission to divide the land among the Indians, who had "greatly increased within these twenty years" and who had, it was alleged, finally turned to farming so that they were "desirous" of receiving shares of land. Whether the Indians were actually "desirous" becomes questionable in light of the trustees' simultaneous assertion that they wanted to be "relieved from the further performance of their Duty." [391] The petition was signed by the trustees and by eleven Gingaskin Indians (with their marks). It was accompanied by a lengthy letter[392] from one trustee who described the trustees' past refusal to allow money to build more houses for the Indians (and their non-Indian spouses and, perhaps, relatives) for fear of increasing the number of "free Negroes" on the reservation. The "real" Indians were not suspected of criminal activities, but the free Negroes were, as usual. There had also been "a recent accusation brought against some of the Inhabitants of this Town, respecting a contemplated Insurrection by them + the Slaves," which was probably the event which triggered this latest pressure on the Gingaskins to disband. The Indians had refused the idea of selling any reservation land and dividing the money; but they were now willing that the land should be divided among them, to be held henceforth in fee simple.

Thus began the first "termination," or legal allotment of reservation land and detribalization of its new owners, in U.S. history. The idea was a natural culmination of English attitudes toward land and Indian people. It would be put into practice many times by various governments, state and federal, always with the same expectations of making Indians pseudo-whites or making them leave, and nearly always with the same results: some Indians gave up their plots but then took shelter with those who held onto their shares.[393]

The Virginia Assembly passed the Gingaskin termination law early in 1813.[394] The Indians were completely free to sell their plots, but as long as they kept them, they were to pay no taxes on them. The latter apparently liberal clause had the opposite effect: the whites of the county had long been bitter about the Indians' tax exemptions. One Indian man, who soon sold out, played it safe and obtained tax-exempt status by the county court on the basis of his "Indian extraction." [395] Commissioners surveyed the reservation in 1814 and allotted plots of equal size to the twenty-seven adults entitled to share in the tribal estate.[396]

The subsequent fate of the reservation land, which totaled about 692 acres, is easily summarized:

Before 1816, six plots were sold,[397] two with life interest being retained, and parts of two more[398] were sold; total: 187.5 acres. In 1819–1830, two plots[399] and one acre of one more[400] were sold; total: 59 acres. Thus in the first sixteen years after termination, only a little over one-third of the reservation acreage was alienated.

Then in November 1831, three months after the Nat Turner Insurrection

Fig. 7. Indiantown Creek, Northampton County; formerly the northern boundary of the Gingaskin Indian Reservation. (Photo by the author.)

in Southampton County and while white paranoia was running high, thirteen plots were suddenly sold,[401] one with life interest retained, and the remainder of three more partially sold-off plots were also alienated; total: 370 acres.

In the three decades after 1831, three whole plots[402] and the remaining interest in two others were sold, usually by allottees' heirs, and in one case after a civil suit to determine ownership—the suit originating in November 1831.

The evidence is overwhelming: the Gingaskins wanted to remain on their land. Two-thirds of them held on until they were forced out in 1831; of those who sold out before that time, being either irresponsible or, more likely, poor, a quarter kept a life interest in the land they sold. Allotment of the reservation and termination of the tribe did not mean a rapid disappearance of the Indians. Even after 1831 some Indian descendants continued to live nearby. A map of 1855 shows seven houses called "Indian Town" clustered on both sides of the marshy creek (see fig. 7) which was the northern boundary of the old reservation (see map 8).[403] The Gingaskin descendants had moved only a short distance from their homeland, where they lived as squatters on land the whites did not want. Eventually they merged with the local black population, in which they had already found sympathy.[404]

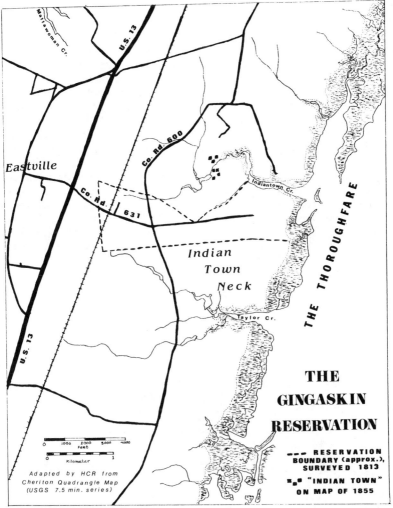

The following labels appear within the map:

Mariawoman Cr.

U.S. 13

Co. Rd. 600

Eastville

Co. Rd. 631

Indiantown Cr.

Indian
Town
Neck

THE THOROUGHFARE

Taylor Cr.

U.S. 13

THE
GINGASKIN
RESERVATION

--- RESERVATION
BOUNDARY (approx.),
SURVEYED 1813

■■ "INDIAN TOWN"
ON MAP OF 1855

0 1000 2000 3000 4000
Feet

0   1
Kilometer

Adapted by HCR from
Cheriton Quadrangle Map
(USGS 7.5 min. series)

Map 8. The Gingaskin Reservation. The author's rough synthesis of a modern map (Cheriton Quadrangle Map, U.S. Geological Survey, 7.5 min. series) with the plat map of 1813, many features of which are no longer in existence; boundaries may therefore not be precisely accurate.

Gingaskin identity did not die any more quickly than the community did. A story from about 1862, recorded in 1901, concerned Molly Stevens, daughter and one of the heirs of a Gingaskin allottee who had held onto her land even through the pressure of November 1831.[405] Molly was given to drink, and when under the influence she would cry out, "I'm the Ingin Queen!"—which, in a sense, she may have been. One day Molly "came dancing, as usual" into the lobby of the hotel in the county seat, already begrimed with previous falls. Losing her balance, she fell once more, this time into the lap of a local lawyer who was unfortunately clad in white trousers. Everyone thought the incident funny except the lawyer, who had Molly jailed for a time.[406] The story was recounted in 1901 as a humorous anecdote about an already vanished people. As many western Native Americans can attest, Indians often become comic figures to white people once they have ceased to be threatening. And the whites see the drunkenness, which for some (but by no means all) Indian people followed upon conquest and enforced culture change, as either a source of humorous stories or a cause for nostalgia for the "heyday" of the very tribes that their ancestors did so much to eliminate. The Gingaskins are an early example of the process. The Pamunkeys and "Mattaponis," on the other hand, were determined not to let it happen.

CHAPTER 8

People Who Refused to Vanish

BY 1830 THE CORE people among the Powhatans had Anglicized so much that they were no longer easily recognizable to outsiders as "real"—that is, pre-Contact—aborigines. Ironically, this cultural convergence was not appreciated by the whites whose ancestors had desired it for so long. Now they also wanted the Indians to "assimilate," that is, to disappear. Anglo-Virginians seem never to have considered removing the Powhatans to Indian Territory, probably because the Powhatan groups' credibility as "real Indians" was too slight for an expensive removal to be considered worthwhile. Instead, Anglo-Virginians wanted the Powhatans to merge with the bottom, non-white social strata in Virginia, collectively called "persons of color." (The term "colored people" came into being later in the century and had a somewhat more restricted meaning than "persons of color.")

Thus, the stage was set for conflict from 1830 onward: while Virginia whites emphatically wanted the Powhatans to assimilate with "other" persons of color, the Powhatans became even more anxious to separate themselves from "any" persons of color. Only thus could they escape the whites' increasing intolerance toward all people with real or presumed African ancestry. (In this the Powhatans resembled many Indians living in the Southeast.)[1] "Racial purity" was becoming a crucial issue to Virginians of all colors. In this chapter I examine first the status of the Powhatan groups in the 1830s and then the history of their struggle to remain unique. Throughout the chapter, I enclose in quotation marks the names of tribes not yet formally reorganized.

The "Nansemonds" in this period had a fully Anglo-American lifestyle, since they had been Christianized and had lived as private citizens for nearly two centuries. Some of them had also achieved prosperity, as is shown in a deed of trust made by Joshua Bass in 1834.[2] Bass used all his household goods as collateral on the loan, and he listed them scrupulously.[3] The list included such amenities as fourteen wooden chairs, a wide variety of tableware, a loom, and two pine tables, as well as assorted farm gear and livestock.

There is also good evidence of an Anglo-American lifestyle among the Pamunkeys, since some of them made deeds of trust which were charred but not burned in the courthouse fire of 1885. There are seven such deeds between 1835 and 1851.[4] None of them lists as many items as Joshua Bass did, either because the owners had fewer worldly goods or because they were not as deeply in debt. The Pamunkeys then owned horses, oxen, cattle, and pigs, as well as ploughs and tumbrel carts. Hunting and fishing gear is less often mentioned, but the lists included guns, a haul seine, a "muskrat spear," and two canoes. Household furnishings included "beds and furniture" (i.e., bedsteads, mattresses, and covers), iron pots, clocks, mirrors, a pine table and a walnut table, ten Windsor chairs, a spinning wheel, an oven, a bureau, and a clothespress. One man also owned two hundred acres off the reservation. All the Pamunkeys lived in log cabins and dressed like their neighbors during this period.[5]

The Pamunkeys' internal government is known to have continued to be an informal council, but documentation is lacking on tribal bylaws. The patriarchy and patrilineality of the whites had apparently been incorporated into Pamunkey culture: the tribal council consisted of all the adult men on the reservation until 1842 (see below), and surnames were passed from fathers to offspring.[6] King William County taxed them on personal property, such as mules, in spite of their treaty status.[7]

Some, if not all, of the Pamunkeys attended Baptist services at Colosse Baptist Church, which had Indians, whites, and blacks in its congregation until the Civil War ended. All the Pamunkeys spoke English, and the Indian language was dead among them. In the early 1840s, the Reverend E. A. Dalrymple was able to collect only seventeen words from the two oldest women on the reservation,[8] of which one word is Powhatan, five more may be approximations, and the rest are not Powhatan at all.[9] However, in many subtle ways, such as a non-European handling of space and time, the Pamunkeys probably remained more Indian than non-Indian. We may also infer that the men still preferred the traditional occupations of hunting and fishing, given their reluctance to use hunting and fishing gear as collateral on loans.

The Powhatans and the white Virginians probably meant widely divergent things when they spoke of "Indians" in 1830. The Anglo-Virginian definition of ethnic groups was genetically based, and rather vague about Indians.[10] There was no legal definition of "Indian" in Virginia until 1866;[11] before that time there were merely Indian-descended people who were not mulattoes, that is, who had less than one-quarter African ancestry, if they had any at all. Rightly or wrongly, many whites of that time believed that some Powhatans had some African ancestry; they felt uncertain only about the quantity and were willing, for the time being, to leave the Powhatans alone.[12] But real danger was building up for the Indians because before long many whites would believe in the "one-drop rule" (see below). Eventually the Indians and other non-whites would come to believe in it, too, though for them the learning process was an unpleasant one.

Among the Powhatans themselves, the term "Indian" appears, in the 1830s through at least the 1860s, to have meant both descent from the aborigines and kinship and social congeniality with those so descended.[13] In other words, people who fitted in comfortably were accepted as at least fringe members. Most such people were probably other Indians.[14] Thus, the Pamunkeys had had contacts with the Catawbas of South Carolina since the late eighteenth century,[15] and they were to increase these contacts in the 1830s. Other congenial people were non-Indians who were allowed to marry in and become fringe members of the group. Through fringe children brought up as Indians, new surnames appeared among the core people. The surname Collins entered the Pamunkey reservation population in that way in the late eighteenth or early nineteenth century.[16]

Meanwhile, the plot of land now called the Mattaponi Reservation became permanently occupied by Pamunkey Indians and fringe men and their Indian wives.[17] The fringe men's residence there is logical, given the Pamunkeys' traditional reluctance to allow to men marrying into their tribe any political power on their main reservation. Eventually this population at Mattaponi became a secondary core for the Pamunkeys through further marriages with reservation people, until the two groups formally split apart in 1894.

Reservation Indians continued to label themselves "Indians" after 1830, whether or not their white neighbors accepted that identity. The possession of reservations remained the cornerstone of their view of themselves; their Indian descent, with its tradition of formerly having owned all of Virginia, and their men's preference for and pride in living mainly by hunting and fishing, must have added heavily to their sense of ethnic uniqueness. The anthropologist James Mooney also recorded in 1899 that the Pamunkeys had an oral tradition of the men having worn their straight hair down to their shoulders or longer in pre-Civil War times.[18] It is impossible to establish whether that style was a carryover from longer eighteenth-century hairstyles or whether it was the men's response to the whites' growing skepticism about their Indian ancestry in the 1830s.

The feelings of the nonreservation, or "citizen," Indian groups are harder to reconstruct. The groups with which we are concerned here, the more durable groups which were ancestral to the modern citizen Indian tribes, often lived in counties which lost their records: the "Chickahominies"[19] of New Kent County (courthouse burned, 1798 and 1865) and Charles City County (some records [importantly, the Order Books] burned, 1865); the "Upper Mattaponis" of King William County (courthouse burned, 1885); the "Rappahannocks" of King and Queen County (courthouse burned, 1864), Essex County (records intact), and Caroline County (many records lost); and the "Nansemonds" of Norfolk County (records intact) and Nansemond County ([prior home] records burned, 1865). The U.S. Censuses are not much more helpful, because the "citizen" Indians lived scattered among non-Indians, and were occasionally overlooked by enumerators (or they avoided the enumerators). Additionally, the censuses before 1850 listed by name only heads of families. All the Powhatan descendants received racial designations at the discretion, and based upon the personal opinions, of the enumerators and county clerks, a practice that resulted in a wide variety of labels.[20] If the descendants told the enumerators they were "Indians," the enumerators did not necessarily write it down for posterity.

However, among the nonreservation Powhatan groups of 1830, there apparently remained a tradition of Indian ancestry, though it seems to have been coupled with a reluctance to make a public claim to being Indians. Unsatisfactory as they are, the surviving pre–Civil War records give no instance of any ancestor of the modern citizen Powhatan groups either claiming to be or being labeled Indian or of Indian ancestry—with three exceptions. The "Nansemonds" made use of a law passed in 1833 (see below) to register as persons "of mixed blood, not being negro or mulatto," which the county clerk recorded as "of Indian descent." And a "Rappahannock" ancestress was designated "of Indian extraction" when her son by her white husband got married.[21] Additionally, one "Chickahominy" ancestress[22] and the sisters of another ancestor[23] are described on their certificates of free birth (see below) as though they had an Indian appearance. Most of the descendants of these ancestors were part of the core people who eventually reorganized the citizen tribes in the early twentieth century.

Typical of ethnic groups everywhere, each core group, "reservated" or citizen, had its fringe families who married both into the group and outside it. The Indian-white Sweat family has already been mentioned. Another such family in King William County was the Wynns. One or more of the white children of Gloucester and Sarah Wynn married Pamunkeys in the early nineteenth century,[24] and by midcentury the last male of the name, Ferdinand Wynn (Sr.), had moved to New Kent County and joined the intertribal fringe there. Some of his descendants are Chickahominies today.

The New Kent County fringe is the most easily documentable one because at times it was almost an ethnic group in its own right. Records on it are available beginning with the 1840 U.S. Census. However, it may have gone back much farther: when the anthropologist Albert Gatschet visited the Pamunkey Reservation in the 1890s, he was told about some "Cumberland" Indians who had lived across the river (i.e., in New Kent County) and had occasionally been hostile "about 100 yr. ago or more."[25] The Pamunkeys of 1890 said the group was gone. However, the surviving records of Charles City, New Kent, and King William Counties show that in the second half (and, therefore, presumably also in the first half) of the nineteenth century there were fringe people in New Kent who married both Chickahominies and Pamunkeys.

Some of the New Kent fringe people were Pamunkeys who had left the reservation either temporarily or permanently: Sweats, Langstons, Sampsons, and Wynns, the last-named of whom kept a Pamunkey identity into the second generation before becoming "Chickahominy."[26] Others appear to have been Charles City people who went to Pamunkey and then moved back to New Kent: Mileses and Collinses/Howells. Still others were Holmeses, who may have been one family and who in those days appeared among the "Upper Mattaponis," the Pamunkeys, and the "Chickahominies." Yet others were of uncertain background, like Jones Pearman, whose (probable) ancestor appears as a non-white New Kent County member of Lower College Baptist Church in 1791,[27] whose neighbor in 1889 identified him as "Indian" in answer to James Mooney's questionnaire of 1889[28] and whose daughters married other fringe people in New Kent County around 1900. After the Civil War, any fringe people in New Kent who married non-Indians usually married colored people, and their descendants remained outside the Indian communities thereafter.

By 1830, the attitude of whites toward non-whites in general was hardening. Indians were perceived by whites as blocking the way of progress, even when the Indians concerned had Anglicized their culture, as the Cherokees did. Whites also perceived Indians, rightly or wrongly, as being in sympathy with free Negroes and as often intermarrying with them. Even the children of Indian-white unions were now felt to be naturally inferior to "pure" whites.[29] Therefore, because of these white beliefs the Indians continued to be affected by what was happening to their Negro and mulatto neighbors. And just as new pressures from the whites caused the "ethnogenesis" of a black American identity,[30] that pressure caused the Powhatans to tighten their groups (a sort of ethno-regenesis) in an effort to survive.

In states that declared themselves to be pro-slavery, as Virginia did in 1830, free Negroes came to be detested and feared by whites because they represented the possibility of freedom for all Negroes, an idea distinctly threatening to a white power structure whose economy was based upon slave labor. The activities of abolitionists in the North made the situation worse by increasing the possibility of slave rebellions. Whites' fears of losing their income and privileged status caused them to heighten the barriers between themselves and all non-whites.

The "one-drop rule" now made its first public appearance. Under this "rule," any white or Indian person who had—or was *believed* to have— one "drop" or more of Negro "blood" was in fact a Negro, "blood" being not a body fluid but a symbol of a person's whole ancestry, cultural background, and potential capabilities. Biological determinism of this kind developed among whites in America after 1820 (and spread rapidly after 1850) for essentially economic reasons.[31] Anglo-Virginians now valued "pure white" ancestry more highly than ever, although they made no changes in the racial definition laws as yet. But their fear of what they commonly and vulgarly called "nigger blood" grew to paranoiac proportions;[32]

such ancestry was considered to be automatically polluting, both genetically and socially. Even a distant Indian ancestress became a cause of unease for some white people. For instance, a Pocahontas descendant named Powhatan Weisiger was once told—jokingly—by a fellow soldier during the Civil War, "Powhatan, of course it makes no difference to us boys who have known and liked you all of our lives, but, if I were you, I would never say among strangers, that I was not pure white." Weisiger missed the joke and tried to assault his friend.[33] Some of the idealization of Pocahontas that began in the nineteenth century probably stemmed from a reaction to this sort of teasing.

At the same time that southern whites became more insistent on their "pure whiteness," they passed laws aimed at lowering the status of free Negroes and Indians almost to that of slaves. Virginia was only one of several states to act thus.[34] In April 1831, Virginia passed a law stating that free Negroes and mulattoes who remained illegally in the state (i.e., after being freed by their masters) were to be sold; it was also made illegal to teach slaves or free Negroes or mulattoes to read.[35] The Nat Turner Slave Insurrection occurred the following August, after which the General Assembly hastened to pass more repressive legislation. Some counties, such as Northampton on the Eastern Shore,[36] petitioned for and got permission to raise county levies to send free Negro residents out of Virginia. In the spring of 1832 it became illegal for any non-white to preach at a meeting, even if he were an ordained minister.[37] Non-whites could attend meetings only if those meetings were conducted by whites. No free non-whites were to buy slaves unless the slaves were either their spouses or their children. No non-whites were to have firearms or ammunition, and they were not to distribute liquor within one mile of any public assembly. Assaulting a white person with intent to kill became a capital offense for a non-white. Any person, white or otherwise, responsible for writing or printing a call for insurrection by non-whites was to be prosecuted. Any riots, "routs," unlawful assemblies, "trespasses and seditions" by non-whites were to be punished as though the perpetrators were slaves. Any person receiving stolen goods from a non-white was to be prosecuted as though he were the thief himself. And free non-whites were now denied jury trials: they were to be tried by justices of oyer and terminer, as slaves were.[38]

Since 1802, free non-whites had been required to carry certificates of free birth or manumission, issued by their counties.[39] Without the proof of freedom they could be jailed and, if no one came forward to testify for them, sold into slavery. But now, more than ever, free non-whites needed to carry their certificates with them, especially if they went to another county where they were not well known, for the whites' condescension had changed to active hostility. The matter was especially pressing in counties which contained no market town, such as Charles City County, whose market town was Richmond in Henrico County.

The Powhatans, who as persons of Indian ancestry were obviously not "pure white," were subjected to these laws everywhere except within the boundaries of the reservations. Under the circumstances, they had to defend themselves as best they could. Thus the ancestors of the "Chickahominies" appear in the Charles City County Order and Minute Books, receiving certificates of free birth.[40] The "Nansemonds," on the other hand, objected successfully to being added to the Free Negro Register. Probably at their instigation, the delegate from Norfolk County[41] introduced a bill which was passed in early 1833,[42] whereby people with English and Indian ancestry could be certified as "persons of mixed blood, not being free negroes or mulattoes." Many "Nansemonds" got certificates over the next two decades.[43] Members of other enclaves registered merely as freeborn people and lay low.[44]

If it was difficult to be a nonreservation Powhatan in those times, it was also a bad time to be a reservation Indian. Some reservation people began carrying certificates of freedom. One such certificate survives; it was issued by the tribal trustees and stated that the bearer was born free and was a Pamunkey Indian.[45] The bearer, Cooper Langston, later lived among the New Kent fringe,[46] so he may have wanted a certificate in order safely to transact business that he already had there. But above all, the Pamunkeys and "Mattaponis" were in an exposed position on their reservations, and the direct threats that Anglo-Virginians made specifically to "Indians" were all aimed at them.

The whites who wanted to abrogate Indian treaty rights were mainly rural people who knew few Indians (see below). The state government was perfectly willing to honor the 1677 treaty as long as there were "genuine" Indians who wanted to remain tribal—though it may not have looked that way to the beleaguered reservation people. The extent of that sympathy was unknown to them for some time because the first real test case involved a Nottoway, not a Powhatan, descendant. In 1837 Parsons Turner had received and already sold part of his share of Nottoway tribal land in Southampton County[47] when he was tried in a court of oyer and terminer for felonious cutting. He was convicted[48] and sent to prison. The next year he wrote to the governor, asking for a pardon on the grounds that his tribal rights had been violated in the way he had been tried.[49] As an Indian under treaty status, he should have received justice as though he were white, that is, a jury trial. The governor granted him a pardon, and Turner returned to his people, got the rest of his land, immediately sold it,[50] and disappeared from the records. Now, if the governor of pro-slavery Virginia was willing to uphold the Indian rights of an apparent wastrel like Turner, then it was unlikely that he would allow the Pamunkeys to be deprived of their treaty status. However, the Pamunkeys did not know that in 1836, when the first overt threat to them was made.

In that year the Pamunkeys heard a rumor that local whites would petition the General Assembly to sell the reservation, the cause being white re-sentment of non-Pamunkeys living on land set aside for Indians. The Pamunkeys promptly wrote the governor and asked for his advice.[51] There were indeed several kinds of non-Pamunkeys on the reservation: there were probably whites like the Sweats, there were "mulattoes,"[52] and by 1839, if not earlier, there were also Catawbas from South Carolina (see below). The letter was signed by all the adult men in residence on the reservation at the time,[53] and some new surnames appear in the list, indicating males marrying in.[54] The Pamunkeys asked the governor in their letter if it were "not good, nor cumley" to befriend outsiders; they began to realize the dangers of association with them. They also emphasized that they were law-abiding, patriotic people who deserved to remain where they were. However, the governor did not write back to them,[55] either out of disbelief about the threat of a petition, or from indifference,[56] or because he saw that the tribe was recognizing its endangered position without his aid.

The Pamunkeys had indeed already taken steps to remedy their problems with out-marriage and inbreeding. They had maintained contacts with the Catawbas since the late eighteenth century, and by 1839—and possibly before 1836—they invited some of them to move in.[57] The tribe planned to "intrench their Indian blood, and at the same time to annul the evils of close intermarriage within their own tribe."[58] Some marriages took place, but soon the Pamunkey partners left with their spouses for South Carolina, so that the net effect for the Pamunkeys was loss of population. It is ironic that in 1840 the Catawbas themselves fell prey to a removal act, improperly carried out, which deprived them of their land and impoverished them.[59] However, the Pamunkey spouses apparently stayed on in South Carolina. The descendants of Robert Mush were also still there; these were said to have a rather "sullen disposition" in Catawba eyes. They eventually converted to Mormonism and left for Utah in 1887.[60]

In 1842 the Pamunkeys had to defend their reservation in earnest. A petition was circulated by one Thomas W. S. Gregory and finally sent to the General Assembly in January 1843,[61] by which time the outraged Pamunkeys had sent two counterpetitions of their own to the legislature.[62]

The Gregory petition of 1843 actually has little to say about the Pamunkeys, though that little is negative: it alleges that they allowed free Negroes to live on the reservation and marry their people "until their Indian character has vanished,"[63] and therefore their two reservations[64] should be sold and the people dispersed. No evidence is presented and no details are provided to prove these allegations. Instead, most of the petition is about the white signers' belief about free non-whites in general: the supposedly bad character of all such people (the "badness" being described at length), the threat they presented to a slave-owning community, and the "necessity" of removing all of them from Virginia. The petition is expressly aimed at removing from the state the "anomalous institution" of a legally constituted free non-white cómmunity. Calling the Pamunkeys "Mulattoes" and asserting that they were no longer the kind of Indians for whom the colonial government had established the reservations was a way of doing it legally.

The plan for the reservation's termination is well buried in generalized rhetoric about non-whites. It therefore seems likely that most of the signers (and there were many) added their names because they agreed with the rhetoric; if they understood the threat to the Pamunkeys, they left their signatures on the petition because they neither knew nor cared much about the tribe. The proof of this assertion comes from a passage in one of the Indians' counterpetitions: no near neighbors of the Pamunkeys signed the petition. Even more significantly, some more distant neighbors initially signed and then, "after they found out [Gregory's] design, had there [sic] names taken of[f]." Gregory and his white neighbors wanted to see all free nonwhites expelled from Virginia, and in hitting out at the Pamunkeys they were, in effect, swatting at one of several flies in the kitchen.

The Pamunkey view of the Gregory petition was totally different. They did not realize how little personal interest the white majority actually took in them; instead they saw any move against Indians as being consciously and primarily motivated by a desire to get rid of Indians *per se*. To the Indians, in effect, there was only one fly, and it was buzzing in a different kitchen from the one the whites were thinking about. The Indians therefore took all the accusations about non-whites personally and denied them emphatically. The reservation was not a resort for vagrants, they insisted; its residents were hard-working, honest people. Though there were "some here who are not of our Tribe," most of the people on the reservation were Indians and many were more than half Indian in ancestry. The tribe was like one big family, caring for its sick and elderly without help from outside, and it would be a shame to disperse such a family. They therefore asked the legislature to consider the Indian side of the matter when the Gregory petition arrived. The tribe's trustees added their weight to the Indians' request, endorsing the first letter and stating flatly, "We are opposed to the sale of their land." Gregory's petition was, of course, rejected by the General Assembly.

The crisis, as the Indians perceived it, left a permanent mark upon Pamunkey political structure but had little effect upon Anglo-Virginian opinions of the tribe. That is to be expected in the oppositional process that makes ethnic minority groups persist. As frequently happens in majority-minority relations, the majority acts for its own nearsighted motives and in its own interests, and sometimes it knows so little about its neighboring minorities and their needs that it slights them through indifference rather than through active animosity.[65] The minorities see it differently; to them the slights are deliberate and personal, and the experience galvanizes their determination to survive. Indeed, their reaction is often so angry that the

majority is bewildered. The personal viewpoint and the hot defense serve a
real function in getting the majority to pay some attention to what it is
doing, though it never learns the lesson as thoroughly as the minority
would like. But the cost for individual members of the minority is high and
sometimes results in accelerated spin-off, at the same time that the bitterness generated serves to keep the remaining members of the ethnic group
unified and determined to remain separate from the "oppressive" majority.
That is certainly what happened with the Pamunkeys.

The Pamunkey letter of 1836 and counterpetitions of 1842–1843 show
plainly that danger from without led to more organization within: the political structure of the Pamunkeys became more formalized. In 1836 there
were three "headmen" but all the other men still signed official documents
as well. In 1842 the signatures of the headmen alone were sufficient to represent the tribe. At least two of the three headmen—James Langston, who
wrote the 1836 letter, and Tazewell Langston, who wrote the 1842–1843
counterpetitions—were literate men who could write flowing rhetoric of
their own. It is safe to say that the literacy of these tribal leaders was primarily responsible for awakening the General Assembly to the Indian view
of Gregory's petition, so that the reservations were saved.

Even though Gregory's effort had been beaten down, most Anglo-
Virginians went on thinking of the Pamunkeys as "persons of color," when
they thought about them at all. Few whites other than their trustees (who
did not write books) took enough interest to get to know them in any
depth. Henry Howe, for instance, described the Pamunkeys in his *Historical Collections of Virginia* (1845) without, apparently, having gone to the
trouble of visiting them. Thus he was able to write, "Their Indian character
is nearly extinct."[66] And the writer who used the pseudonym "Father
William" recorded after a visit of only one afternoon that the people were
"hospitable and social"—and, paradoxically, that they were "vicious" and
drunken and prone to keep fierce dogs.[67] Evidently some of the tribesmen
had learned to fear outside visitors, and with good reason. In the future,
there would be a major difference of opinion within the tribe as to the attitude to take toward working with outsiders, including other Indians.[68]

Another adjective that fit the Pamunkeys before the Civil War was "powerless." In 1855 the Richmond and York River Railroad ran a track through
the northern part of the reservation, taking about twenty-two acres of land
without compensation. Not until 1971 did the tribe believe that times had
changed enough that it could try to seek recompense, and then nine years
were required to get it.[69]

Conditions for all non-whites worsened as the Civil War drew closer and
white fears for their own social system escalated. As far as the surviving
records show, the Powhatan descendants merely lay low during this time
and stayed out of trouble. Records about their members are therefore
scarce. The "Chickahominies" continued to marry mainly within their own

Fig. 8. Thomas S. and Keziah Dennis (Pamunkeys), about the time of their marriage (1855). (Courtesy National Anthropological Archives, Smithsonian Institution, negative no. 889.)

group and to get certificates of free birth.[70] The Nansemonds had enough sympathy with their neighbors that the Methodist Church founded a mission for them in 1850.[71]

However, the Pamunkeys, with their Indian privilege of bearing arms, found themselves under suspicion no matter how they behaved. In 1857 local whites disarmed the tribe, which sent several men straight to the governor with a protest. The governor sent these men back with a letter to the trustees[72] in which he said that he himself had "no power to interpose," but that the state laws clearly gave Indians the right to bear arms. "They tell me their mode of living is by hunting, and to deprive them of their fire arms is in effect to drive them away from their lands which the laws most emphatically forbid." The trustees should therefore have the laws enforced through "the usual . . . process of redress." The governor also added that an annual census should be taken and "kept of their numbers, names, marriages, births and deaths, in order first to identify the persons entitled to be deemed + treated as Tributary Indians; and to ascertain their blood in the second place, for if any become one fourth mixed with the Negro race then they may be treated as free negroes or mulattoes." The advice about keeping a tribal roll was sensible. The advice about determining tribal membership by "blood" was typical of white views of the time and was the answer to the question the Pamunkeys had asked back in 1836. Thanks to the crisis of 1842–1843, that advice was unnecessary by 1857: the Pamunkeys were fully aware of the importance of "blood" in proving their Indianness to outsiders.

Most Pamunkeys and "Mattaponis" were neutral during the Civil War, since they refused to enlist with the Confederacy[73] and were not likely to endanger their position by acting pro-Union. A few men quietly joined the Union Army in 1863 and were expelled from Colosse Baptist Church for it.[74] The Pamunkeys sustained some damage from Union troops during a skirmish in 1864,[75] for which they were recompensed later.[76] The Mattaponis preserve today an oral tradition of gunboats going past their reservation and of a ship containing slaves being sunk nearby.[77] James Mooney wrote in 1907 that some Virginia Indians had served with Union forces, while others had fled to Canada to avoid conscription by the Confederates;[78] however, he must have meant the "Chickahominies," who preserved an oral tradition to that effect in 1941.[79] The "Rappahannocks," whom Mooney did not visit, also had a tradition of flight to Canada when Frank Speck worked with them in 1920.[80]

Several "Chickahominy" families took refuge with an Ojibwa band, with whom some intermarriage took place.[81] Some of these families were slow to return to the United States, for the U.S. Census of 1900 shows several "Chickahominies" as having been born in Canada in 1870 and 1871 and naturalized as U.S. citizens thereafter. But these Canadian-born people should be considered fringe people: they are on James Mooney's Chickahominy census of 1899, but none of them joined the tribe when it organized formally in 1907 or claimed an Indian identity in the U.S. Census of 1910.[82] Those who left their people during the war also left them when the tribe "went public."

Reconstruction both gave the Powhatan groups more freedom to breathe and placed more burdens upon them. Some energetic Indians became public officials, now that it was temporarily possible for non-whites to do so. In 1870 "Chickahominy" ancestor Harris Miles was elected overseer of the poor on June 16 and clerk of court for four years on December 15.[83] Ferdinand Wynn, the Pamunkey who became part of the New Kent fringe, became the overseer of the roads in Tyler Township, Charles City County, for a few months in 1872.[84] The Pamunkeys also produced their first Christian

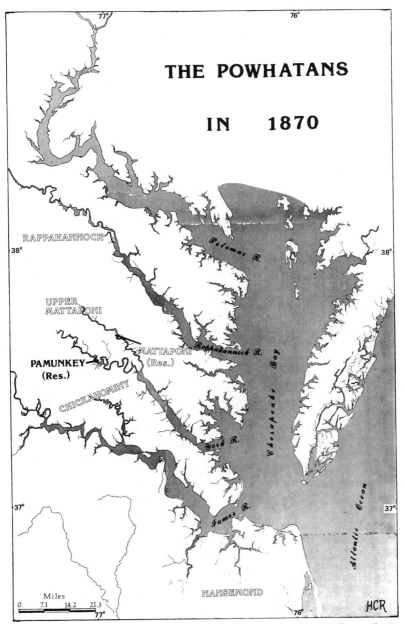

THE POWHATANS

IN 1870

RAPPAHANNOCK

UPPER
MATTAPONI

PAMUNKEY
(Res.)

MATTAPONI
(Res.)

CHICKAHOMINY

Potomac R.

Rappahannock R.

Chesapeake Bay

York R.

James R.

Atlantic Ocean

NANSEMOND

Miles
0   7.1   14.2   21.3

HCR

Map 9. The Powhatans in 1870. Base map adapted from *Bathymetry of Chesapeake Bay* (Virginia Institute of Marine Science, 1977).

minister, William P. Miles, who subsequently also joined the New Kent fringe and was licensed to perform marriages by the King William County court in 1870.[85]

However, a power struggle was already taking shape between Virginia blacks, now enfranchised, and Virginia whites, who were disenfranchised if they had fought with the Confederacy. The Indians, as usual, were in danger of being caught in the middle. Now that slavery was illegal, the whites were denied their former means of keeping social distance from non-whites, that is, by legal superiority coupled with frequent and intimate social contacts. So instead they erected new social barriers through segregation, later solidified into Jim Crow laws.[86] The result was to unify the previously disparate interests of negroes and mulattoes in new opposition to the whites.[87] In 1866 the laws of Virginia first defined Indians, and at the same time the term "colored person" made its debut: "Every person having one-fourth or more of negro blood shall be deemed a colored person, and every person not a colored person having one-fourth or more of Indian blood shall be deemed an Indian."[88] Thus the Indians had a legal as well as traditional basis for refusing to join forces with the large but still minority "colored" population (a refusal which earned them great resentment). Henceforth "racial purity" would be a major public issue in defining Indians; it would be a veritable cornerstone of the Indians' self-identity.

Churches were the first institution in Virginia to be segregated by race. For example, where Colosse Baptist Church had been attended by whites, blacks, and Indians before the war, in 1865 it became a white church and the blacks and Indians formed their own separate congregations. Thus, Pamunkey Indian Baptist Church, founded in 1865, is the oldest Indian church in Virginia. As the other tribes took formal shape—the Mattaponis by law and the citizen Indians by charter of incorporation—a tribal church would become their first group institution. Churches, after all, were safe places for public gatherings, thanks to American freedom of religion.

Education also became a segregation issue in Reconstruction Virginia, but schools were an institution that Indians had to fight harder to get. Although publicly funded education was mandatory under the new regime, white parents saw to it that their children had separate schools from non-white children. Indian children were welcome only in the black schools. Therefore, to preserve their "Indianness" in their own and in outsiders' eyes, the Indians had to refuse to allow their children to enter those black schools. This situation worked a double hardship on Indian communities. First, they had to find ways to educate their children separately—an expensive proposition because county school boards, composed of people who thought of "real" Indians as full-blooded "savages," were unwilling to create a third set of schools for "Indians" who did not appear sufficiently "different" from other citizens. Second, the Indians had to raise even higher

Fig. 9. Pamunkey Indian Baptist Church, 1970. (Photo by the author.)

the barriers between themselves and their black neighbors, which naturally caused resentment on the part of the blacks, who regarded the Indians as fellow oppressed people. It was during the Reconstruction period that the Powhatan groups truly came to be actively in opposition to some of the aims of both whites and blacks—a lonely position that has done much to help the groups maintain a unique, Indian identity.

The Pamunkeys were probably the least threatened of the Powhatan descendants in the 1870s. They had a reservation, state recognition, and a church. They also had a school, which consisted of a log building, like all the other houses on the reservation.[89] It is uncertain whether the state supplied a teacher for the children at that time. The "Mattaponis," being technically part of the Pamunkeys, were welcome at the Pamunkey church and school, but their location ten miles away must have made it difficult for them to take advantage of these privileges.

Some, at least, of the "Upper Mattaponis" attended church on the Pamunkey Reservation and were even permitted to live on the reservation in the late nineteenth century;[90] however, most of them had more contact with the "Mattaponis" than with the Pamunkeys.[91] The "Rappahannocks" appear to have done without a church or school in these years. Norfolk County built a small school for the "Nansemonds" next door to the Methodist mission church in 1889,[92] and it functioned off and on with approximately fifteen students until 1928.[93]

The "Chickahominies" were the most energetic of the nonreservation Indian groups. Their initial move toward tribal organization took the public form of creating their own Baptist congregation, rather than treading the harder path of establishing a separate but publicly funded school. For many years they had attended Cedar Grove Baptist Church, which before the Civil War was probably a church for all races but with tacitly agreed-upon separate seating inside. After the war, the congregation emerged as a "colored" one; according to Chickahominy oral tradition,[94] the blacks had been absent before but now began "infiltrating" and gradually took over the congregation. Resentments built up and violence occurred in the neighborhood until the "Chickahominies" abandoned Cedar Grove in favor of Samaria Baptist Church, which had a white congregation. The move to a new church preceded a move toward formal organization of a tribe in the 1890s: some families who later declined to join the tribe continued to go to Cedar Grove and are buried in its cemetery.[95] When the congregation at Samaria disbanded in 1888,[96] the Indian members continued to use the building for services of their own. Their formal organization as Samaria Indian Baptist Church coincided with their formal organization as a tribe in 1901.[97] In that year they began serious work on their own public school.

In 1889 the Smithsonian Institution began to take an interest in the Indians of Virginia, possibly a result of the activities of a Pamunkey group which reenacted the Pocahontas "rescue" at public events (such as the Yorktown Centennial) after 1880.[98] The initiative was taken by James Mooney of the Bureau of American Ethnology, who sent out a questionnaire to more than a thousand prominent citizens in Virginia, Maryland, Delaware, and North Carolina.[99] In it he asked for information on Indian-descended people, local Indian place names, and archaeological sites. The replies he got from Virginia are interesting in that they show little interest in or sentimentality about the Powhatans among Virginia's white population. The Pamunkeys were the most widely known group; people living in all the neighboring counties and in York County mentioned them. One former legislator, living south of the James River, remembered the Gregory petition of 1843 and wrote confidently that the tribe had been terminated.[100] The Pamunkey chief, who was also an addressee, furnished information on his tribe and on the "Mattaponis," who had their own chief, he said. The "Mattaponis" were less well known: people in their own county and the county across the Mattaponi River mentioned them, but no one else did. No one mentioned the "Chickahominies," either; Mooney was to hear about them only when he went to visit the Pamunkey Reservation. However, two second-generation Pamunkey Wynns in the New Kent fringe group were mentioned; there were also some supposedly Pamunkey "mixed

bloods" in Henrico County, one of whom was fringe person Jones Pearman. No one mentioned the "Upper Mattaponis" or the "Rappahannocks"
or the "Nansemonds." Of the Gingaskins on the Eastern Shore, several descendants remained; the one cited by name in the questionnaire was Edmund Press, who was genuinely descended from a Gingaskin allottee.

In the 1890s three men visited the Pamunkeys and wrote accounts about
them: Albert Gatschet,[101] John Garland Pollard,[102] and James Mooney.[103]
There are additionally several short descriptions of the Pamunkeys by other
writers between 1893 and 1908.[104] From the Pamunkeys, Gatschet and
Mooney both heard of the Mattaponis, "Chickahominies" and "Nansemonds," and Mooney also heard of the "Upper Mattaponis," the "Rappahannocks," and several other remnants. The status and living conditions
of the Pamunkeys and the other groups around 1890 can therefore be
reconstructed.

The Pamunkeys had a population in 1889 of about 100 in residence,[105]
living in twenty-seven wooden houses,[106] and 20 more lived away. In 1899
Mooney found 152 people in thirty-nine households, with 14 of these
people living away.[107] The houses were not clustered, but were scattered
about the fields,[108] just as the houses had been in most Powhatan towns in
1607. The house in which Gatschet stayed was heated by an open fireplace;
the housewife had "been trained to cook in some good hotel," probably
during a period of working off the reservation "in service in the city [Rich-
mond] or on some of the steamers which ply the Virginia waters."[109] Gat-
shcet felt that his accommodations were plain but very good. The women
made some pottery still, although the availability of mass-produced earth-
enware discouraged many women, and the art of potting was in decline.[110]
There was a general store on the reservation, "conducted . . . by a joint
stock company, composed of members of the tribe."[111] This was probably
the "small store" the tribe started in 1874–1875 with their Civil War compensation money; they sold "ardent spirits" at the store, "for which privilege they pay the retail liquor dealer's tax."[112] By 1919, when Frank Speck
arrived, the store was gone.

The men were professional hunters, fishers, trappers, and guides for
white visitors who came to the reservation to hunt. The Indian men still
preferred log canoes to "modern boats."[113] Each family had about ten acres
to farm, but the Pamunkeys were not avid cultivators or orchard keepers:
"They plant chiefly corn, and some of the land is not tilled at all."[114] Much
of the farm labor was done by hired Negro laborers.[115] The wooded land,
which made up a large part of the reservation, was not divided up, but was
kept as a communal game preserve.[116] The tribe paid no taxes to the state;
instead, an annual tribute was taken to the governor.[117]

The Pamunkeys had had chiefs for many years: Gatschet collected a list
of chiefs that went back to the man who preceded the headman who wrote
the letter to the governor in 1836.[118] Although chiefs had once been elected

Fig. 10. The Simeon Collins family (Pamunkey, with "New Kent fringe" wife), 1899. (Courtesy National Anthropological Archives, Smithsonian Institution, negative no. 884.)

for life,[119] by 1894 the chief and four councilmen[120] were elected every four years, using corn kernels and beans for the balloting. According to Pollard, if two candidates were running against each other, voters who placed a corn kernel in the ballot box voted for the first candidate, and those placing a bean in it voted for the second.[121] There were also five white trustees, appointed by the state rather than by the Indians,[122] who had the power to approve or oppose new tribal laws. The chief and council had the power to deal with ordinary civil offenses on the reservation, although more serious cases such as homicide would go to the county court or, as the Indians claimed, to the commonwealth courts.[123] Off-reservation cases were extremely rare,[124] although later a divorce case did go to the county court.[125]

The Pamunkey Reservation's laws as of 1887 are quoted *in toto* by Pollard.[126] At the top of the list are laws affecting the preservation of an Indian population on the reservation. The first law bars marriages with any people other than Indians and whites, on pain of expulsion from the tribe. The second governs the conditions under which nonresidents could live on the reservation for limited periods of time, and reads as follows: "No nonresident shall be allowed to be hired or sheltered more than 3 months—and if anny [*sic*] person are [*sic*] known to hire or shelter anny sutch persons shall pay 50c pr. day for every day over the above mentioned time. Amendment. Should sutch person [or] persons be quiet and agreeable they may be hire[d] 30 or 60 day[s] under good behavior." In recent decades the Pamunkeys have claimed always to have had another preventative law[127] which prohibits their women (but not their men) from bringing white spouses to live on the reservation.[128] No such construction could be based upon the code of 1887 or upon the current tribal bylaws.[129] The modern custom is just that, a custom.[130]

The other tribal laws of 1887 concern penalties for civil offenses such as trespass or non-attendance at tribal meetings. The roads on the reservation were to be kept up by all "[male] citizens age 16 to 60," and the roadways were thirty feet wide.[131] Much of that width consisted of grass which served as common pasture.[132] One of the landings, called the "Hall Sain [haul seine] Shore of Indian Town," was to be rented out annually for the benefit of the tribal treasury. People, such as newlyweds, who wanted to build houses on the reservation had to claim and receive a plot of land and then build on it within eighteen months, and male claimants of age eighteen and over were to get no land unless their annual "dues" to the tribe were paid up.

The Pamunkeys had a law and some very strong feelings about association with blacks, reinforced by possession of their own Baptist church and a state-supported school on the reservation.[133] Pollard phrased it this way: "No one who visits the Pamunkey could fail to notice their race pride. Though they would probably acknowledge the whites as their equals, they consider the blacks far beneath their social level." Their feelings were shown publicly when a "colored" teacher was sent to teach in their school by the state; they refused to accept her, and sent her back to Richmond.[134] Since most of the people on the reservation were closely related, the tribe had recently been attempting to induce some North Carolina Cherokees to settle among them.[135] However, even without the Cherokees, the Pamunkeys still looked very Indian: Gatschet, Pollard, and Mooney all agreed upon that point. Gatschet felt that the women looked more Indian than the men,[136] Pollard estimated the Indian blood quantum to be "from one-fifth [sic] to three-fourths,"[137] and Mooney wrote, "I was surprised to find them so *Indian,* the Indian blood being probably nearly 3/4, the rest white, with a strain of negro."[138] (Whoever was meant by that "strain of negro" is gone today.)

The Indian language was long since dead; Gatschet heard that Rhody Arnold (Dalrymple's informant) and Cooper Langston had been the last speakers. From what we have seen of Dalrymple's word list, the language was actually dead even before their time. Some "Indian" dances[139] and a "old P[amunkey] dance song"[140] were still performed, but Gatschet's and Mooney's descriptions of them are so poor as to be meaningless.

The Mattaponis in the 1890s had a population of thirty-five to forty-seven,[141] who were governed by a chief even before official separation from the Pamunkeys (see below). They were "in constant communication" with

Fig. 11. The Lee Major family (Mattaponi), 1900. (Courtesy National Anthropological Archives, Smithsonian Institution, negative no. 851-a.).

the Pamunkeys, with whom they shared a church and school, but little else was recorded about them. Their small reservation also had wide, grassy roadways which were used as common pasture; in at least two places there were gates across the roads which controlled the cattle and horses using the pasture.[142]

Both Gatschet and Mooney heard about the "Chickahominies" from the Pamunkeys. Gatschet's notes are especially interesting: "Chickahominies are not 'enchieved' [i.e., formally organized] but show better blood (better old Indian blood) than *we*, the Pamunkeys. And they *stick* together." [143] He heard that the group had "only about six families, scattered widely around Providence Forge Station." Mooney visited the group in 1899 and took a census of them, finding 197 people living in thirty-nine households. [144] No proper ethnographic fieldwork was done among the Chickahominies until Theodore Stern lived among them in the early 1940s.

Gatschet and Mooney also heard of the Nansemonds from the Pamunkeys, who said that there were Indians "around Norfolk, Va." [145] Mooney wrote to the Norfolk County clerk, obtained Augustus A. Bass's address, and wrote to him. [146] He got an enthusiastic reply, [147] stating that there were about 180 Indians in the group, [148] which had its own church and school. Bass delightedly asked for copies of anything Mooney wrote and also for the addresses of the other tribes he had visited. Thus encouraged, Mooney visited the group, took a census of them, and included them in his *American Anthropologist* article. The "Nansemonds" preserved their tribal name but not their language. They made their living primarily as truck farmers, secondarily as "sailors on coasting vessels," and the large number of family names among them [149] indicated much intermarriage with whites. There was also much spin-off into the white community. [150]

Mooney did not visit the "Upper Mattaponis," but he heard from the Pamunkeys that they had about forty people. They were far from prosperous. They had occasional contacts with the Mattaponis and rarer ones with the Pamunkeys. [151] No fieldwork was carried out with them until Frank Speck arrived, and unfortunately his work was not extensive.

Mooney heard of the "Rappahannocks," presumably from the Pamunkeys, and noted that "they are said to show as much of Indian blood as the Pamunkey . . . and are represented as fairly prosperous and intelligent. They are probably the descendants of the old Nandtanghtacund tribe, known later, with others, under the name Portobacco." [152] Frank Speck was the first to do real fieldwork among that group, and he found them to be at least as poor as the "Upper Mattaponis" and far more fearful of their neighbors (see below).

Mooney heard of several other groups from the Pamunkeys, groups which I have been unable to locate in the 1970s and 1980s. There were supposed to be "Accomacs" at "Drummondtown on the eastern shore of Virginia," and a family of Pamunkey Sampsons was reputed to live near Gloucester Point. Another group with the surname Wise was said to live at the head of the Poquoson River in York County. In the 1920s Frank Speck wrote of some of these, as well as other groups (see below), but apparently he did not try to visit them.

The interest taken by the Smithsonian Institution in the early 1890s ap-

Fig. 12. Nansemond Indians, 1900. The oldest man is probably William W. Weaver; man behind him is Augustus Bass. (Courtesy National Anthropological Archives, Smithsonian Institution, negative no. 869.)

pears to have created a spirit of optimism and some real activism in some Pamunkeys. The activism took the form of putting on commemorative pageants at even more public events[153] and by seeking representation at major exhibitions.

The Pamunkeys saw to it that they were represented at the Chicago

Fig. 13. William Terrill Bradby (Pamunkey) in his regalia, 1899. (Courtesy National Anthropological Archives, Smithsonian Institution, negative no. 893.)

World's Fair of 1893. The man they sent was William Terrill Bradby (fig. 13), who was later to serve as James Mooney's primary informant. On June 26, 1893, the chief and council on the reservation wrote a letter of introduction for Bradby, who was "to visit the Indian Bureau in Washington and in all other Departments and Indian tribes, and also to visit the Columbian Exposition in Chicago."[154] Bradby acquired a letter of introduction to the "World's Fair Tribal authority" from the governor of Virginia on July 6[155] and proceeded to Washington. There he met Otis Tufton Mason of the U.S. National Museum and presented him with several Pamunkey artifacts for the Museum's collection.[156] On July 14, the day he made the gift, Bradby received from Mason a letter of introduction to the commissioner of Indian affairs that read, in part, "He is well known to us here and has been very serviceable in preserving for our use the history of the tribe." Bradby used the letter the next day, and as a result of his visit, Assistant Commissioner Frank Armstrong wrote to F. W. Putnam, chief of the Ethnographical Department at the World's Fair, that Bradby was "one of the very few remaining descendants of the Pamunkey Indians of Virginia" and had therefore been given a ticket to Chicago. Putnam appointed Bradby "Honorary Assistant in the Department of Ethnology of the World's Columbian Exposition," and as such Bradby represented his people at the Fair.

Terrill Bradby's later efforts to represent his people were less successful. In 1898, he wrote to the commissioner of Indian affairs, asking for help in attending the Omaha Exposition as a Pamunkey delegate; his request apparently reached the office after the Exposition had closed.[157] In July 1899 he wrote to the governor of Virginia asking that the Pamunkeys be represented at the Paris Exhibition; the governor replied that Virginia had no authority to send a delegation to that Exhibition,[158] and the plan came to naught.

The Pamunkeys also sought publicity for their reservation in the 1890s by embarking upon a road their descendants have trodden ever since: they chose certain occasions on which to dress in "Indian" style in public. A photograph survives of the Pamunkey participants on such an occasion.[159] The "Indian" style the group chose was not the aboriginal Powhatan one: had they dressed authentically in the Victorian late nineteenth century, they would have been arrested for indecent exposure. Instead, they wore more modest trousers, shirts and dresses, made of buckskin with fringes and adorned with beads. The headdresses worn by most of the men were fabric coronets with wild turkey feathers sticking straight up; the one exception is a headdress that seems to be a stuffed turkey, and the wearer holds a "shield" made of wild turkey feathers. The people in the picture were dressed for a performance for which an advertisement still exists; in 1898 the Pamunkeys had a travelling troupe[160] which put on a "Green Corn Dance, Pamunkey Indian Marriage, Snake Dance . . . War Dance, [and the] Capture of Capt. John Smith and the saving of his life by Pocahontas."

The Pamunkeys and the "Mattaponis" remained officially a single tribe until 1894.[161] However, the "Mattaponis" were growing apart from the Pamunkeys, small group though they were. They had had a somewhat different population from the Pamunkeys for many years, although the people were probably just as "Indian." The "Mattaponis" had apparently had informal leaders long before the official split from Pamunkeys in 1894. When Gatschet visited the Pamunkeys in 1889, he heard that the "Mattaponi" headman was John B. Allmond.[162] Mattaponi oral tradition names All- mond's mother, Eliza Mobley Major Allmond, as an earlier "queen" of the group.[163]

Ten miles on bad roads is a long distance, and the Indians of King William County had only one school and one church, at Pamunkey. It would be natural for the people on the Mattaponi Reservation to want to direct their own affairs, particularly if they did not agree with the activism that the Pamunkeys began to show in the 1890s. There also may have been some hard feelings over the fact that neither Gatschet nor Pollard visited the Mattaponi Reservation; if a dispute already existed between the two reservations, it is possible that the Pamunkeys discouraged their visitors from proceeding to Mattaponi, causing further enmity. In any case the sep- aration of Mattaponi political affairs from those of the Pamunkeys seems to have been triggered by a dispute of some sort, judging by the text of the law that created the Mattaponi Tribe.

In March 1894 the General Assembly of Virginia passed a law[164] ap- pointing (white) trustees for the Mattaponi Indian Tribe, "formerly known as a branch of the Pamunkey Indian tribe." These trustees were to function for the Mattaponis in the same way that trustees did for the Pamunkeys. However, a significant proportion of the law is devoted to dealings with unwanted people: "upon a vote of the majority of the trustees, Chief and members of the tribe above twenty-one years of age, to expel from their reservation any person who has no right upon said reservation or any mem- ber of the tribe who shall be guilty of any unlawful offence," the offender having the right of appeal to the county court. Two years later this law was amended[165] slightly: there had specifically to be a majority of the tribe, as well as a majority of the trustees. Thus the Mattaponis and the Pamunkeys separated. The Mattaponis apparently created bylaws for themselves based upon the ones at Pamunkey;[166] since those at Pamunkey were, in turn, based upon usages in Anglo-Virginian society, and since in Anglo-Virginian society of the time women did not have the vote, then the women of both Pamunkey and Mattaponi also lacked the vote.

As the whites regained political power in Virginia in the late nineteenth century, they drew still farther apart from the black community and took steps to ensure that that population did not threaten their privileged status again. At the turn of the century they began putting their opinions into law in the form of "Jim Crow" legislation. All public facilities and public rec- ords were to be separated into two categories: "white" and "colored" (which meant "black" in the minds of whites).[167] In 1910 the first step was taken to tighten up the definition of the "white race": anyone with one- sixteenth or more African ancestry was a "colored person," and could not be either a white person or an Indian.[168]

The Powhatan descendants were caught in the middle once more. By pushing the blacks farther away from themselves, the whites had also made it much more difficult for Indians to prove their "Indianness." Now there were several steps that had to be followed to gain credibility: the Powhatans had to protest loudly that they had no Negro ancestry at all, win authoritative rulings that they could use non-Negro facilities (difficult, because those facilities were specifically for "whites"), and then—and only then—assert that they were biologically descended from the Virginia aborigines. In the absence of sufficient documents, thanks to limited record keeping and then the destruction of many of those records in the nineteenth century, both the Indians and the white supremacists who opposed them relied upon the same evidence: oral tradition and hearsay.

Even the reservation Indians had difficulty in fighting through. A good example is the railroad case of 1900. In July 1900 the "Jim Crow coach" law went into effect in Virginia.[169] It provided for separate coaches for "white people" and "colored people," with power vested in the train conductors to determine which coach any given passenger was to occupy. Originally, occupancy in the "white" coach was to be only for those of "pure" white ancestry. An anecdote current in the 1920s said that an exception had soon to be made for people of distant Indian ancestry when "it was found that the exclusion [of non pure types] would have to begin with the governor of the State," who traced his ancestry back to Pocahontas.[170] In actual fact, the railroad conductors immediately began running afoul of the Pamunkeys, who used the railroad as their transportation to Richmond.

In a very short time the Pamunkeys took the railroad to the King William County court, which ruled on July 28, 1900, that the Pamunkeys had to ride in the "colored" coach.[171] The Pamunkeys did not let it rest there, nor did others inconvenienced by the law, such as the white prison guard escorting a black prisoner manacled to him.[172] By mid-August the tribe was soliciting help among Richmond lawyers, most of whom favored a strict interpretation of the law, for they wanted a ruling from the railroad commissioner.[173] The Richmond press was sympathetic, on the whole: a sensible solution would be to let the Pamunkeys ride the "white" coach, raising the question of whether that made them "white."[174] On August 21, the superintendent of the Richmond Division of the Southern Railroad ruled that the Pamunkeys were not "colored" and could ride in the "white" coaches.[175] Later in the year all races except the "black" one were permitted to ride with whites.[176]

Under conditions such as these, Indians who needed to use public transportation found it advisable to carry certificates of identification with them. The Pamunkeys and the "Chickahominies" both began issuing tribal identification cards,[177] and one "Nansemond" family got a Portsmouth lawyer to certify them as Indians who associated and married exclusively with whites.[178] The "Chickahominies" then went one step farther and organized formally in 1901.

For some time, the Pamunkeys' Terrill Bradby and anthropologist James Mooney had encouraged the "Chickahominies" to organize. The modern Chickahominies remember Terrill Bradby's encouragement better,[179] but it was Mooney who more strongly urged the group to make out a tribal roll that stated the amount of Indian ancestry for each person,[180] in the same fashion that tribal rolls on federal reservations do. The group thereupon made up a list of members[181] and began holding "reunions" annually. At the reunion of July 15, 1900, the group elected officers, announced their existence as an Indian group, and set the date for a September meeting.[182] One of their white mentors, Judge I. H. Christian, helped them with publicity and encouraged them in their attempts to get some of their young people admitted to Hampton Normal School (now Hampton University),[183] which many Indians from western, "federal" tribes then attended.

Chief W. H. Adkins (fig. 14) presided over the September meeting, which was also attended by the Pamunkey assistant chief.[184] In May 1901 the Chickahominy tribal church was organized as Samaria Indian Baptist Church; it called as its pastor the Pamunkey church's minister, P. E Throckmorton, who accepted the post after verifying that the group was really considered Indian by local people.[185] There were, of course, some fringe people, cousins of the core people, who declined to join the tribe; they remained part of the "colored" community and for the most part are disavowed even as relatives by some modern Chickahominies.[186]

Several matters came to a head for the reservation people in 1916–1918. First of all, in 1916 the Pamunkeys and Mattaponis raised a serious question as to whether or not their treaty status exempted them from buying hunting licenses. The state's attorney general ruled that since the licensing law did not exempt Indians, the reservation people had to buy licenses.[187] This did not sit well with the Indians, who raised the question with game wardens thereafter and usually had their way. In 1960 another attorney general was impelled to advise the Indians to have a law passed specifically exempting them from needing hunting and fishing licenses,[188] and that law was passed in 1962.[189]

When the United States entered World War I, the nonreservation Powhatan men were drafted. The Chickahominies, at least, were inducted as Indians.[190] The Pamunkeys and Mattaponis, as wards of the state, were not draftable; when called up, they refused to go until the state's attorney general ruled on their nondraftability,[191] after which they volunteered. One Pamunkey was killed in action.[192]

The Mattaponis also had trouble about that time with the Chesapeake Corporation's agents invading the reservation, over the chief's protests, to load cordwood on the Indians' wharf, whence corporation boats would take it downstream. The attorney general ruled that the tribe's trustees had full power to go to court on the tribe' behalf,[193] but the trustees apparently held back and the attorney general had to reaffirm that opinion the next year.[194]

Fig. 14. William H. Adkins (Chickahominy), 1905. (Courtesy National Anthropological Archives, Smithsonian Institution, negative no. 852.)

Meanwhile, King William County had been assessing the reservation people not only for the land which some of them owned off the reservation, but also for personal property held on the reservation. The Indians and their trustees had not protested before. But given the climate of the time, the county's efforts to tax the revenues from a general store on the Mattaponi Reservation ignited resentment. The attorney general was appealed to again in 1917, and he ruled that since reservation people paid no taxes to the state while domiciled on the reservations, they should not be required to pay taxes to the county.[195] Not long afterward a Mattaponi trustee helped them get a school on their own reservation.[196]

In 1919 Frank Speck, began visiting Virginia looking for Indian remnants whose history and "Indian trait" survivals he could record. Speck and his work were to have a lasting impact upon the Powhatan groups, but his fieldnotes show that his visits were short and rather spotty.[197] He came to Virginia with the intention already formed of organizing into tribes any "Indian" groups he found, rather than observing them at length and collecting documents about them before acting. Perhaps he felt that the people were under such pressure from non-Indians that immediate organization was necessary for their survival, and real fieldwork could come later if he found time for it.[198] He concentrated both his interest and his writings on Virginia Indian technology, although he was perfectly capable of observing and analyzing other aspects of Indian life.[199] It is probable that technology was the least controversial aspect of life among the early-twentieth-century Powhatans, and therefore the one about which they would most readily talk to him.[200]

Speck found about ninety people living on the Pamunkey Reservation and another thirty living away; he recorded much about the tribe's methods of hunting and fishing. He also heard that Opechancanough was buried in a mound of earth near the railroad track.[201] (Today Pamunkey oral tradition says that the burial was Powhatan's.) The Mattaponis had sixty-seven people in residence, with half a dozen more living away, and Speck got the impression that they were descended from a "bunch of Pam[unkey] who came over for hunting and fishing." He visited the Chickahominies and got from them a short Indian word list which he later identified as Ojibwa.

Speck found the "Upper Mattaponis" living in poverty in log cabins and in ignorance about their tribal antecedents. They thought they might be the "offspring of the Pamunkey Tribe."[202] They had had their own school only sporadically. They had supplied land and a building for a school in the late 1800s, and King William County had grudgingly hired a teacher. But the minimum of ten students was not met and the school was closed, after which children either went to Pamunkey or did without schooling. In 1917 a second tiny school, Sharon School, was built, and it continued until integration closed it in the 1960s. The group had no church of its own before 1942.[203]

The "Rappahannocks" likewise were poor and uncertain of their tribal antecedents. However, they had an origin story that was definitely romantic: an aristocratic Revolutionary War officer named Carey Nelson saved three Indian girls during a raid; he later married one, a man named Johnson married the second, and a man named Spurlock married the third. Nelson and Johnson were still family names in the group,[204] and mention has already been made of the historically documented "Rappahannock" ancestress "of Indian extraction," Susan Spurlock. The group had no church of its own. It also lived in three different counties, which prevented any one county being willing to establish a school for Indians. Informal classes were held in homes until the 1950s, when a small school was established and a teacher hired.[205]

The "Nansemonds" were truck farmers, shipyard workers, and hunting guides in the Great Dismal Swamp. Indiana United Methodist Church, no longer a mission and having a white and "Nansemond" congregation, was still theirs in a sense. However, they had lost their separate school after about 1900 and were being pressured by their neighbors to send their children to the "colored" schools. This they refused to do. When entrance was denied them to the "white" schools, they had a white friend appeal to the attorney general, who ruled in 1922 that the county school board was to determine the genuineness of their "Indian" claims and, if they were Indian, set up a separate school for them.[206] They got their school.[207] A precedent in Virginia Indian affairs was set thereby: buck passing. Neither the attorney general nor anyone else wanted the responsibility of defining what "Indians" were.

Speck also made contact with other groups. He found an Indian-descended group in Stafford County whose primary surname was Newton and whom he called "Potomac,"[208] based on his belief that Indian remnants always remained in their homeland through the centuries. (The data presented in this volume should show that belief to be oversimplified.) My own field visit to that group disclosed a tradition of Indian descent coupled with a complete lack of tradition about a specific tribal name.[209] Speck also heard about a group at "Allmondsville" on the York River which he labeled "Werowocomoco," and "Wicomico" descendants on the Northern Neck. However, my inquiries in those districts in 1973 and 1974 failed to turn up any Indian descendants. There are Allmonds at Allmond's Wharf[210] on the York River, but they are white and have no tradition of Indian ancestry.[211] Speck also heard about a group in York County, in what is now the town of Poquoson. Yet Calvin Beale's visit to them in the 1960s[212] showed them to be triracial (Indian affiliation unknown) in origin but "black" in identity, and one of their number who is a high school history teacher has since talked publicly about their position in the black community.[213]

Speck gave the Powhatan groups an even greater pride in their Indian ancestry. He also gave the as yet unorganized groups needed symbols of identity, namely tribal names and tribal organizations. Together with Chief George Major Cook and Paul Miles from Pamunkey, he encouraged several of the nonreservation groups to organize into tribes. Thus the Rappahannocks and the Upper Mattaponis both chose tribal names and organized formally in 1921[214] and 1923[215] respectively. The Upper Mattaponi reorganization was officially presided over by the Pamunkey chief, who also gave

Fig. 15. Paying "tribute" to the governor, 1920s. Tribute is still paid in this way. However, these Indians are Chickahominies, who voluntarily paid tribute at the time they were working to get a reservation. (Courtesy National Anthropological Archives, Smithsonian Institution, negative no. 57,032.)

the tribe its bylaws.[216] A great deal of encouragement from Speck and the Pamunkeys was needed in the Rappahannock case, because the group was genuinely afraid of retaliation by neighboring whites if they organized.[217] Once they were publicly visible, however, the Rappahannocks played their part well. Their first chief, George Nelson, actually wrote and sent a proclamation in flowing oratory for the president of the United States to issue: its gist was that all Indians in the county should form tribal governments with federal recognition and receive legal redress for grievances of long standing.[218] Nelson, like many other Indian leaders in the country's history, was ahead of his time.

The Chickahominies were already organized, and they now decided, with Speck's blessing, to press for another symbol of Indianness: state recognition. Accordingly, in 1920 they began collecting affidavits from white neighbors testifying to their "Indian" status in the community, and the chief secured formal letters of introduction from the governor of Virginia in 1920 and 1923.[219] In 1922 the Charles City school board and the Commonwealth of Virginia finally agreed to help the Chickahominies pay the teachers in the school they had built themselves, an arrangement which lasted until 1925 and resumed in 1930.[220] Some tribal members even wanted the group to buy a tract of land and get the state to recognize it as a reservation; unfortunately, these people also disagreed with their fellows about the retention of the pastor at Samaria Indian Baptist Church. The coinciding of these two basic factional differences split the tribe apart. Those who favored a reservation and a new pastor founded their own church, named Tsena Comocko Indian Baptist Church, in September 1922,[221] and they organized themselves as the Chickahominy Indians, Eastern Division, in 1925.[222] Both Chickahominy groups lost some of their momentum thereafter.

Two other organizations that emerged in 1923 did not survive for long. One was the "Nansemonds," who selected Jesse Bass as their chief and attended pan-Indian gatherings for some years. But Bass was not an energetic organizer of people,[223] and energetic, not to say charismatic, people are necessary to the formation of any newly organized group if it is to last. The "Nansemonds" never took out a charter of incorporation; instead the "tribe" faded away after a few years, its members continuing to disperse themselves over southeastern Virginia with only family memories to hold them in contact.

The other entity which did not last was a new "Powhatan Confederacy," apparently formed under Speck's guidance.[224] Many older people among all the modern Powhatan tribes have fond memories of intertribal gatherings that took place in the early 1920s; some remember going to similar gatherings held by Indian descendants in Maryland and Delaware. Contact with other eastern Indian people was a powerful force in boosting the pride of each Powhatan group. However, no formal pan-tribal organization seems to have resulted from these activities, nor did one forceful and long-lived Indian leader emerge to hold them together. (Frank Speck, an Anglo, was not so presumptuous as to try to lead them.) Thus, when outside pressure against Indians increased after 1923, the gatherings gradually ceased as the tribes returned to fighting for their own survival.

CHAPTER 9

The Racial Integrity Fight

AT THE SAME TIME that the nonreservation Powhatan groups were organizing their tribes, churches, and schools and were trying to establish a public identity as "citizen Indians," white Virginia was becoming even harsher toward people who were not "pure" white. "Racial purity" became an issue over which the Indians were attacked in the public media and over which they themselves became more adamant about their Indian-and-white ancestry. Now, as never before, people's genetic makeup—and beliefs about it, in the absence of adequate documents—became a prime determinant of "Indianness" in Virginia.

The "one-drop rule" became a matter of law in Virginia in 1924, and with the passage of that law[1] the primary watchdog for "racial purity" in the state became the Bureau of Vital Statistics. Because of his lobbying for and enthusiastic enforcement of "racial integrity" policies, the head of that bureau became a symbol to the Indians of all the enmity that white society seemed to feel toward them. Registrar Walter Ashby Plecker personally made many Virginia Indians' lives miserable for twenty-two years. If any one person can be said to be responsible for the enduring strength of the Indian identity among Powhatan core people in those years, Plecker, ironically, is the man.

Plecker was born in 1861 in Augusta County, Virginia, and graduated from the University of Maryland Medical School in 1885.[2] After doing postgraduate work in obstetrics at New York Polyclinic, he practiced medicine in several southern localities: Rockbridge County, Virginia (1886), Birmingham, Alabama (1887–1890), and Hampton, Virginia (1890–1910). He also claimed later that he had observed American Indians "in the west,"[3] but he never mentioned where. In 1912 he was appointed registrar of the Virginia Bureau of Vital Statistics, and because he was an energetic and capable organizer, he rebuilt the bureau into what is essentially its modern form.[4] From 1912 onward, all babies born in Virginia received birth certificates from the bureau—with the racial designations the midwives sent in, for the first twelve years, though some of those designations were to be questioned later—and all midwives were under close supervision to make sure their procedures were sanitary.

While Plecker's early work at the bureau was laudable, his personality was a difficult one. Even white people with whom he had few quarrels found him to be a "martinet," "tough as pig-iron," and, at best, "a pistol."[5] Opposition merely made him more determined to have his way. He was a Presbyterian[6] and "a strict Calvinist,"[7] and in his later years he readily aired his beliefs about preordained categories for people. Once he became involved in the eugenics movement in the 1920s, the human categories in which he was most interested were racial ones. For the rest of his life—and he retired only a few months before he died in 1946 at the age of eighty-five—Plecker saw only two "races" to be dealt with in Virginia: Caucasian and non-Caucasian. And these, he felt, could be and should be strictly segregated in all areas of life.[8]

The eugenics movement in the United States[9] was reaching its peak when Registrar Plecker became involved in it. The movement had begun as an optimistic semiscientific effort to better the entire human species. However, by 1920 the science of human genetics had proved far more complex than its early students had expected, and most of the people still interested in eugenics were laymen whose "knowledge" of genetics came from the early state of the science. These laymen were also more pessimistic about mankind by then: many of them aimed merely at neutralizing "inferior types" so that the species would not be "dragged downward." Under pressure from such "eugenicists," for instance, many states passed laws allowing for the sterilization of certain mental patients and some criminal offenders.[10]

The eugenics movement of the 1910s and 1920s was fertile ground for racists, whose numbers greatly enlarged the membership. The term "eugenics" began to take on a new meaning: it stood for the protection of and continued political control by a "superior type" (i.e., Caucasians of the middle and upper classes) and the segregation and neutralization, if not elimination,[11] of all others, who were deemed "inferior." The "inferiority" of these other people was "proved" by social scientists who pointed out that non-white and mixed-blood people had more crime, more illegitimacy, and lower scores on intelligence tests than did whites.[12] The social causes of these conditions, such as poverty due to economic discrimination, were given short shrift;[13] only heredity was described at length in the studies. Eugenicists reasoned that if non-Caucasians were "inferior," then anyone with a non-Caucasian ancestor anywhere in his lineage was "inferior" to a "pure" Caucasian (a phenomenon whose existence modern anthropologists have been unable to prove). The "one-drop rule" now had a pseudoscientific basis and was ready to be passed into law. And in Virginia Registrar Plecker stood ready to enforce the law.

Therefore the Powhatan groups now found that they had to oppose a state law, an influential bureau in the state government, and among whites a widespread grassroots sentiment that backed both the law and the bureau.

In 1924, Virginia's Racial Integrity Law was passed.[14] Ostensibly it provided for the issuance of certificates by the Vital Statistics Bureau for those born before 1912, who otherwise would have had no official birth certificates of any kind; "registration" to receive a certificate from the bureau was voluntary. However, these certificates required the recording of the race of all known ancestors, and they justified the now required presentation of a certificate of birth when enrolling in a school, registering for the draft, and so forth. Thus, in a real sense, "registration" was not voluntary. Further, the law made it a felony to falsify one's race on a certificate. In time, "falsification" came to mean disagreement with the classification made by the Vital Statistics Bureau.

The Racial Integrity Law also defined the term "white person" with the idea that everyone in the state could then be classified once and for all. "The term 'white person' shall apply only to such person as has no trace whatever of any blood other than Caucasian; but persons who have one-sixteenth or less of the blood of the American Indian and have no other non-Caucasic blood shall be deemed white persons." That exception was made for a peculiarly Virginian reason: there were still prominent whites in the state who traced their ancestry back to Pocahontas, who was not Caucasian. In 1930 the definitions of non-whites were brought into line with the Racial Integrity Law:

> Every person in whom there is ascertainable any Negro blood shall be deemed and taken to be a colored person, and every person not a colored person having one-fourth or more of American Indian blood shall be deemed an American Indian; except that the members of Indian tribes living on reservations allotted them by the Commonwealth having one-fourth or more of Indian blood and less than one-sixteenth of Negro blood shall be deemed tribal Indians so long as they are domiciled on such reservations.[15]

Enforced separation of "white persons" and "colored persons" was supposed to preserve "the purity of both the white and the black races,"[16] but the definitions themselves show that the legislators were actually concerned with protection of the whites.

It was now very difficult to be "white" in Virginia and very easy to be "colored," but "on account of the Pocahontas descendants,"[17] Virginia had to leave a loophole in her race law through which many people were tempted to jump. The public facilities set aside for "colored" people were usually far inferior to those for "whites." Whites controlled the public moneys, and they often allocated significantly fewer funds for the establishment and upkeep for "colored" institutions. Non-whites were allotted menial jobs that made them rarely able to save enough money to improve their own institutions by cash donations. Therefore, many people of mixed African and European ancestry sought to improve their own and their children's lives by the time-honored method of "passing" as white.[18] Some of these people, whose looks were not quite "white" enough, claimed some Indian

ancestry—which they may well have had—and "passed" anyway. Therefore Plecker and his bureau were determined to obliterate this "way-station
to whiteness."[19] And the Powhatan groups, who merely wanted to be "Indian" rather than "colored"[20] and retain access to the better "white" facilities, immediately got in Plecker's way.

The Powhatans, being people of their time, believed in not one but two
"one-drop" rules. They, like the whites, said that "one drop" of Negro
"blood" made one black, and they emphatically denied that they had any
Negro ancestry at all.[21] But they also believed that if an Indian married a
white person, the children were Indians. They did not expect miscegenation
with whites to produce white children; the children were to remain within
the Indian community and be brought up as Indians, a cultural definition of
"Indians" that social scientists agree with today. Thus, when Registrar
Plecker charged that the Indians wanted above all else to "pass" as white[22]
in order to be able to marry whites, he misunderstood them altogether.
They wanted access to the better facilities open to whites and also the freedom to marry congenial whites in order to prevent close inbreeding, but
they did not necessarily want to be "white." Conflict therefore arose between Plecker and his followers, who saw the Indians as recalcitrant "colored" people who were a threat to the white community, and the Indians
and their supporters, who insisted that they were "Indian" and had no idea
of threatening anybody. It was this conflict that had the ultimate effect of
trimming away the less stalwart fringe people and leaving a much tougher
and more determined core of Indians in the Powhatan tribes.

Plecker was methodical: he began collecting old county and federal records on the Indians, many of which listed them as "persons of color." But
Plecker was a doctor, not a historian: he took no interest in the conditions
under which the records had been made about illiterate people or in the
changes that had occurred in the meanings of words. To him, "color" in
1830 meant the same thing that "color" did in 1930, and if the term appeared in an old document, the negritude of the person so designated was
"proved." Even the admonitions of a "neutral" agent like the U.S. commissioner of Indian affairs could not change Plecker's mind, as we shall see. He
and his colleagues therefore set about compiling a "Racial Integrity File,"[23]
consisting of surviving county and U.S. census documents and also "testimony" from "respected" local people about other people's ancestry.[24] The
contents of the file became "proof" of Negro ancestry for a wide variety of
Virginians, including the Powhatan tribes.

Plecker also expected all county records, past and future, to be made to
conform with his Bureau records in Richmond; no "Indian classification
was to be tolerated. To this end, he instructed county clerks that the new
records they made about Indians should read "colored" and the old records
that said "Indian" should be changed or marked in some way. The Indians
naturally protested, putting the county clerks in the middle.

Thus, the records of counties in which Indian people lived show divergent listings.[25] The King William County clerk continued to list the Pamunkeys, Mattaponis, and Upper Mattaponis as "Indian," as they had been earlier. The clerks of Charles City and New Kent counties knuckled under, for new records said "colored," while older records reading "Indian" after the Chickahominy organization were either marked (Charles City) or left alone (New Kent). Because of the new policy in those two counties, not a single Chickahominy got a marriage license—the only public records over which they had any geographical control short of moving away—in his or her home county from 1924 through 1945. The Essex, King and Queen, and Caroline county clerks had never used the term "Indian" for anyone, and they did not begin now. The Norfolk County clerk continued to label the Nansemonds as either "Indian" or "white."

The birth certificates issued for Indians from 1912 through 1924 read "Indian," and Plecker left them alone for the time being. However, after 1924, the certificates for Indian babies read "colored," and there was nothing that the parents or the midwives could do about it. Since Indian parents were adamant about sending their children to Indian schools or to none at all, the birth certificate issue was not a pressing one; but when America prepared to enter World War II and Indian men faced being inducted into the armed services, birth certificates became a real bone of contention.

The Powhatan groups had more than just county clerks to contend with in the 1920s. Registrar Plecker worked actively to give them a reputation in the public mind as a "colored" group that was trying illegally to become "white." To this end, he gave public lectures on the "danger." He also wrote a pamphlet in 1924, entitled "Eugenics in Relation to the New Family,"[26] and sent a copy of it out with each birth certificate his bureau issued. In the pamphlet he exhorted all adults to marry within their own race and only with "healthy stock." Racial mixtures, he proclaimed, made for degraded stock which endangered society; that was why Virginia had "wisely" passed a law against whites marrying anyone "containing a trace of any other than white blood."[27] Plecker went on to give examples of "degraded" mixed-blood groups, with information drawn largely from the as yet unpublished work of Estabrook and McDougle. Only at the end of the pamphlet did he get around to the Powhatan groups. First he cited nineteenth- and early-twentieth-century scholars[28] who had said at best that the Powhatan groups were very much reduced and at worst that they had mixed with Negroes and were no longer very Indian. Plecker then described a meeting he had had with the Chickahominies in December 1924[29] at which he got them to "accept" the status of "mixed Indians." On the whole, he concluded there were no Indians in Virginia unmixed with Negro "blood," and therefore there were no "true" Indians left in the state. Thousands of families received this pamphlet over the next few years.

The reaction of the tribes to this kind of publicity can be imagined. They promptly told Frank Speck, who advised them to collect and send him affidavits from their white friends, testifying to their Indian status in the community, so that he could present their case with the weight of his scholarly reputation behind it.[30] He had already urged tribal leaders to go to a conference of eastern Indian tribes at Nanticoke in November 1924, where the people would "have to adopt some definite policy on the status of race question."[31] Most of the Powhatan tribes began collecting affidavits. The Pamunkeys, however, planned a different tack: they had their lawyer take their tribal censuses of 1852 and 1861 to the county court and file a decree establishing these as a tribal roll,[32] so that descendants of the people listed could prove they were entitled to Indian status. Unfortunately, they seem never to have followed through, for no decree was ever issued.[33]

Thus, the lines of battle were drawn in the 1920s, and both sides insisted upon the correctness of their claims thereafter. Speck did not remain active for long: he had commitments with other eastern Indians. He published a book on the Rappahannocks in 1925, they being the tribe which probably needed the most bolstering at the time, and his book on all the Powhatan tribes came out in 1928. Powhatan people still cherish their copies. But Plecker attempted to have Speck's books banned from public libraries in Virginia, which embarrassed Speck considerably.[34] After 1925 he appears to have concentrated his fieldwork elsewhere for a time.

Plecker then continued actively and more or less successfully to place Indian people where he thought they belonged. County clerks had the right, according to the Racial Integrity Law, to deny marriage licenses to couples who could not prove upon demand that they were of the same race. By his own account, Plecker also "furnished information upon which to base annulments of interracial marriages, and . . . perhaps prevented other similar marriages by giving out the facts to inquiring young people whose suspicions were aroused."[35]

In at least one case in the late 1920s, the registrar moved to have the children of an Indian family removed from a white school they attended and informed the authorities that they belonged in the "colored" school. The family lived in Hampton, where the father was the railroad ticket agent for the town and had made enough white friends that he had been invited to join the Elks Club, an invitation that he declined for fear that his ancestry might be held against him by some members.[36] Plecker's subsequent "exposure" of the family was embarrassment enough: the children were expelled from the white school, and rather than go to the "colored" school, they obtained admission to the Catholic parochial school and finished their education there.[37]

Plecker also attempted to remove Indian patients from "white" hospital and sanitorium facilities to "colored" ones, but here he was less successful. In one case, which occurred in 1937, reservation Indians were involved and their protest went all the way to the state's attorney general. That official ruled that since the committal had been done in proper form, it should stand; and furthermore, reservation Indians, whose treaty established their rights to "white" privileges, did not lose their "domicile" on the reservation when they went to the hospital.[38] Most of Richmond's hospitals placed reservation and "citizen" Indian patients in "white" wards, ignoring Plecker's admonitions.[39]

There were also attempts by other people at an erosion of the reservations' treaty rights after the Racial Integrity Law went into effect. In 1924 yet another effort was made to tax the revenues of the general store on the Mattaponi Reservation, and the state's attorney general had to rule that reservation businesses, like reservation property, could not be taxed.[40] There were also recurrent problems with game wardens arresting Indian men who were fishing without licenses. In 1933 the state attorney general had to notify the commonwealth's attorney in West Point that no more arrests were to be made, pending an inquiry,[41] in which the Indians' rights to fish in public waters were upheld. Boundary difficulties also continued to plague the reservation people from time to time: neither reservation had ever been surveyed since the opening of Pamunkey Neck in 1699. Even the plat of that original survey has been lost. In 1937 a sympathetic member of the State Board of Education wrote to the U.S. ambassador in London, asking his help in searching the British archives for the survey. An embassy secretary replied that a preliminary search of the British Public Records Office had found nothing, but that a longer and more extensive search was possible.[42]

Some Powhatan people continued to appear publicly and proudly as Indians, as the reservation people did when paying their annual tribute in the fall.[43] They wore the "Indian" regalia which readily identified them in the public mind. They also followed the lead of their white friends, most of whom believed in the "noble savage" stereotype, in reminding the public that they were descended from such people, more sinned against than sinning. Many Powhatans endorsed the stereotype on a deep emotional level; in the hardest times, it was the main thing that would keep them going.[44]

Other Powhatans, mainly Indians who were not tribal officials, either lay low or left Virginia in an attempt either to escape the pressure or to make a better living in urban areas of the North. The exodus, of course, was nothing new: spin-off had been occurring among the Virginia tribes for three centuries. Many of those who left went to Pennsylvania and New Jersey, where they could be mistaken for Italians or other non-Nordic "whites" and allowed to live quietly.[45] Some of these people remained away permanently except for occasional visits, while others moved back to Virginia either during the civil rights era or when they retired.

The Powhatan groups did not lose consistently; they had some staunch supporters among state officials in their struggle against Plecker and his followers in the late 1920s. The governors remained willing to write letters of

introduction for "citizen" Indian tribal chiefs.[46] In addition, the higher officials who worked with Indians in both the Game and Inland Fisheries
Commission and the Board of Education seem generally to have become
sympathetic because of that contact. Some of these officials then tangled
with Plecker publicly. An example of this strife occurred in 1929.

M. D. Hart of the Game and Inland Fisheries Commission attended an
annual powwow of the "Powhatan Confederacy" which was held among
the Eastern Chickahominies in mid-May. Speaking at that powwow,[47] Hart
decried the "almost-constant harrassment" of Indians and the repeated
efforts by racial purists to tighten the racial laws further to eliminate any
possibility of there being Indians in the state.[48] He urged that Indian people
be given the chance to define their own groups, send the names to the Vital
Statistics Bureau, and then be left alone to marry strictly within their own
"Indian" communities. "There are only a few of them left," Hart said, "and
I plead in the name of humanity, give them what the white man would desire were the conditions reversed." Far from being sympathetic to Hart's
statement, Registrar Plecker was incensed. He attempted to have Hart's superiors in the commission censure him, which they refused to do on the
ground that Hart had spoken as a private citizen. The press took up the
story,[49] siding with Hart and adding an editorial which depicted the Indians
as poor, bewildered innocents and condemned "the continual nagging at
an inoffensive people."[50] That was one of the few rounds that Plecker lost
completely.

A much more acrimonious conflict arose over the U.S. Census of 1930.
The tribes were determined to be listed as Indians; Plecker was equally determined that they be listed with the "colored" population. The Census Bureau, caught in the middle, either could not see or would not admit that it
was being used as a pawn in one state's "racial integrity" battle. The Census Bureau was, it claimed, merely gathering statistics: it declined to notice
that older U.S. Census records were already being used as historical evidence in a political conflict.

Registrar Plecker began his campaign early. In January 1925 he wrote to
William M. Steuart, director of the census, that after making "some inves-
tigations" he had found that Howe, in his *Historical Collections of Virginia*
(1845), was correct "and that we have no Indians in Virginia that are not
heavily mixed with negro as well as white blood." He therefore asked that
the Census Bureau cooperate with his Vital Statistics Bureau in making racial classifications of people claiming to be Indian in 1930.[51] In November
1926 Plecker renewed the matter with Leon E. Truesdell, chief statistician
for population in the Census Bureau.[52] He said that the Indians' claims
were false, and he cited names and genealogies for the Chickahominies,
some of which were incorrect.[53] Though he grudgingly admitted that the
reservation people might have to be recorded as Indians, he felt that the Rappahannocks should not be, for "we have their pedigree back." Plecker closed

the letter by saying that he was sending separately an old petition of 1843 "to abolish the reservations on the ground that the occupants are simply 'Free Mulattoes.'"

Thus, by 1926 Plecker's researches had taken him, or a colleague, through the legislative petitions in the State Library. The 1843 Gregory petition was wonderful grist for his mill, and he had it copied, with some copyist's errors left in it.[54] At the bottom of the copy he included a brief but deliberately erroneous summary of the two long Indian counterpetitions: "In a counter petition, B 1208, they beg for pity and *admit the truth of the claims made by the white petitioners.*[55] They say: 'There are many here who are more than one half blooded Indian, tho we regret to say that there are some here that are not of our tribe.'" Aside from the lie about the Pamunkeys' "admission," the very emphasis that this summary put on the alleged racial makeup of the Gregory petition is a diatribe about free non-whites in general. Be that as it may, Plecker had this "document" mimeographed and began sending it to anyone interested in the "true background" of the Indians of Virginia. And since he was considered an official authority on minority races in Virginia, many people, including professional scholars, sent him inquiries.[56]

In spite of this careful "preparation" by Plecker, the Census Bureau went ahead with plans to record people as accurately as possible through first-hand observation and conversation with those being enumerated. In September 1929 the bureau began to hear again from both sides. In particular, the bureau began to hear from friends of the Indians such as Hart of the Game Commission and Mrs. Fred Pfaus of the Women's Missionary Union.[57] The director of the census wrote back politely each time, saying blandly that "the census data are collected for statistical purposes only." In his letter to Hart, he added, "I do not see how the Indians lose or gain anything by the manner in which they are reported on the census schedules. . . ."[58]

In January 1930, Otho Nelson, now the Rappahannock chief, wrote to Chief Statistician Truesdell that his group had 218 people and they wished to appear as Indians in the census of that year.[59] Truesdell replied that enumerators were being given special instructions about Indians; he did not say what the instructions were.[60] Two and a half months later, Chief Nelson wrote again, this time to both Steuart and Truesdell, complaining that the enumerators either classified people "as they see fit" or they omitted the "race" question and then wrote what they liked later on.[61] Similar problems were complained of by Indian-descended people in Amherst County.[62] Frank Speck added his weight by writing to the Census Bureau to affirm that the people in question really were Indians.[63]

The Census Bureau assured the Rappahannocks that the enumerators, not the bureau, were responsible for classifying people, and in any case, one's status in the U.S. Census did not establish legal racial status.[64] Perhaps that did not happen in the District of Columbia, but status in the census mattered very much in Virginia at the time. In fact, Steuart's answer to Speck unconsciously shows why it mattered: the Census Bureau had told its enumerators that "a person of mixed Indian and Negro blood should be returned a Negro, unless the Indian blood predominates and the status as an Indian is generally accepted in the community."[65] In other words, enumerators were being asked to determine whether or not people's claims to being "Indians" were valid, based upon what the local communities believed about them. They were therefore told to use the very same sources that the pro-Indian and anti-Indian forces did—limited county records, old census schedules, and oral tradition—and then they were to express an opinion which one side would inevitably use against the other. It is no wonder that the enumerators felt caught in a vise and that one of them, in Amherst County, refused to record anyone's "race."[66] Getting no satisfaction from Washington, the Rappahannocks took action by visiting the Fredericksburg office of John W. Green, supervisor of the Fifth Census District of Virginia, presenting him with "their papers," presumably meaning their charter of incorporation, and getting him to enter them on the spot as Indians.[67]

While the census schedules were tabulated during the remainder of that year, the conflict continued. Registrar Plecker sent the Census Bureau information on people who were "passing" as Indians, which prompted Chief Statistician Steuart to send a list to Supervisor Green. The list contained the names of all the heads of household in the Powhatan groups except the Nansemonds, and Green was told to change their racial designation or not at his own discretion.[68] Green decided to back his enumerators and change nothing: the Indians were to remain "Indian."[69]

Plecker then took another tack. He sent an inquiry to county officials in Essex, King and Queen, and Caroline counties as to whether they knew of any Indians within their counties.[70] The treasurer and clerk of Caroline County responded promptly that they knew of no Indians, and Plecker forwarded their letters to the Census Bureau as evidence that the Rappahannocks, at least, should not appear as "Indians" in the census schedules.[71] Census Director Steuart then offered a compromise: the people in question would appear as Indians in the schedules, but there would also be an asterisk by that classification and a footnote to the effect that their status as Indians was questioned. Plecker refused the offer.[72] However, the Census Bureau declined to go further than that,[73] and the footnote duly appeared in the published census schedules. Plecker and the Indians had both won— or lost—that round.

The world looked no brighter for the Powhatans after the census skirmish than it had before. The tribes continued to exist in a desperately uncomfortable limbo, neither "white" nor "colored," never knowing what fresh public embarrassments they might meet. The conditions under which they lived in the 1920s through 1950s have been vividly described for them and for other eastern nonreservation people in Brewton Berry's *Almost White* (1961).

During these decades some Virginia tribes tried to induce the federal government to come to their aid, only to be turned down. The first attempt came in 1934, when the Wheeler-Howard or Indian Reorganization, Act was passed by Congress. On behalf of the Virginia tribes, John Crosby of the State Board of Education wrote to Commissioner of Indian Affairs John Collier, asking if Virginia truly had jurisdiction over the two reservations. Collier replied that the Virginia reservations were not a federal responsibility, and that since western states had "sovereignty" over federal reservations, then logically Virginia had sovereignty over the Pamunkey and Mattaponi reservations. He also admonished Crosby that a federal law of 1924 made Indians citizens: Crosby had written that the Virginia reservation people "do not vote." [74] The political climate in Virginia continued to keep Indians from voting for two more decades.

Undaunted by the reply to Crosby, Western Chickahominy Chief O. W. Adkins wrote to Collier on behalf of his tribe and the Rappahannocks: they wanted help, through Wheeler-Howard funds, in buying land, getting libraries and schools and clinics, and acquiring tractors and one year's seed. Collier replied politely that though the act had been passed, no funds had been appropriated yet,[75] and the project quietly died.

In 1939, Frank Speck reentered the Virginia Indian scene, and this time he brought graduate students with him. Their arrival was timely: at the same time that they did more fieldwork and produced a welter of anthropological publications on the Virginia tribes,[76] a new conflict was appearing on the horizon as Europe entered World War II, and America began bracing herself for involvement.

Like Adkins before him, Speck hoped to gain some federal interest in the Virginia tribes, and one project he involved himself in was the effort to obtain limited federal recognition for the Eastern Chickahominies. The choice of that tribe was logical: it was a tightly organized group under an energetic chief who still dreamed of a reservation.[77] The Western Chickahominies had just lost their chief and had to elect another;[78] the reservations were not interested; and the Upper Mattaponis, Nansemonds, and Rappahannocks were no longer securely enough organized to try for such a thing.[79]

Speck began the campaign by sending a memorandum to Washington, saying that the Eastern Chickahominies wished to petition for "indorsement [*sic*] by the Dep't of Indian Affairs, of recognition on the lists of the Dep't as an Indian tribe not under Federal jurisdiction, not desiring direct Federal support in any other form, in their endeavor to develop along social and cultural lines as an Indian minority group." He included some information about the tribe, such as the year of their incorporation and the fact that they claimed "between 3/8 and 5/8 Indian blood for the group as a whole, a tribe with accredited Indian ancestry. . . ."[80] In early 1940,

Chief E. P. Bradby sent copies of tribal documents as well.[81] Nothing happened in Washington, and the effort died.

Speck also wanted the Powhatan tribes to form a cooperative pressure group, but cooperation was foiled by tribal distrust and apathy. In particular, the reservations remained aloof from "citizen" Indian affairs for fear of losing some of their own limited credibility,[82] although the chief at Pamunkey in 1940 was personally interested in helping.[83] The pressure group remained only an idea.

Speck further wanted the tribes to revitalize their crafts, preferably under Indian teachers, but again his plan was foiled. The younger Eastern Chickahominies of that time had tried and given up beadwork and pottery,[84] although Chief E. P. Bradby and some others were making wooden artifacts and sending them to Speck.[85] Pamunkey pottery had been revived in the early 1930s through the offices of B. H. Van Oot, state supervisor of Trade and Industrial Education. But Van Oot wrote regretfully to Speck that he had found the Pamunkeys badly enough factionalized that an Indian teacher would probably not be practicable.[86] Indian crafts were being taught in the Mattaponi school at the time, but by white teachers.[87] Simultaneously, the Women's Missionary Union was pressuring the Indian Baptist churches to let their white ministers go and let the union call Indian pastors from out West; only the Eastern Chickahominies appear to have been amenable to that idea.[88]

Speck's activities coincided with the U.S. Census of 1940. In this census, the Indians were less successful in getting their status upheld than they had been in 1930. U.S. Census Bureau staff spent several days going through Registrar Plecker's Racial Integrity File, after which, as Plecker himself put it, "The census enumerators were furnished lists of these families and instructed to list them as they had been classified in the early days when their origin was well known."[89] The result was that most of the enumerators did as Plecker told them. The U.S. Census for 1940 shows many fewer Indians in all the relevant Virginia counties than did the census of 1930. Only in King William County were there enough Indians listed to make a single tribe; that was probably the tribe whose "chief found out what was going on, caught up with the census takers, who were local men, on the road, and persuaded them to change all the forms for his tribe from negro to Indian on the spot."[90]

By early 1941, America's eventual entry into World War II was certain, and the Indians of Virginia began to brace themselves for conflicts over their draft status.[91] They began volunteering for service and being inducted with whites, but they understood that future inductions might be with blacks and they became worried. Consequently, the Virginia state superintendent of public instruction asked the U.S. War Department for a ruling, in order "to protect [the Indian status of] our schools on the reservations and to pacify the Indians."[92] The War Department forwarded the letter to the Selective Service, which answered that the induction of all Indians was being held up pending an inquiry.[93] The outcome was of interest to all Virginia Indians, since the reservation Indians were U.S. citizens (since 1924) and were subject to the draft just as "citizen" Indians were.

The Selective Service eventually ruled that people classified as "Negroes" by their local draft boards could appeal the classification within sixty days; the criteria for classification as Indians were that the people had "not lived in association with negroes and . . . that they were considered Indians by their neighbors."[94] It was the 1930 census battle all over again.

The Powhatans and their friends began gathering testimony with which to counter the assertions made by the Bureau of Vital Statistics, so that both sides would be clearly heard in any controversy over an Indian's draft status. First, Speck wrote to Commissioner of Indian Affairs John Collier to the effect that the Virginia tribes were certainly "Indian" and should be so regarded by federal agencies.[95] Then one of Speck's graduate students, Robert Solenberger, wrote to a Richmond judge, assuring him of the Indians' separateness from the black community and telling him that Speck "believes that the Indian component in the ancestry of the Powhatan tribes varies, in general, from about 2/5 to 3/5 [sic], either of which proportion would be more than enough to entitle them to free schooling in Oklahoma." He therefore urged the judge to send a copy of the letter to Douglas Southall Freeman, editor of the News-Leader in the same city.[96] A lawyer for the Pamunkey tribe, consulted by an Army colonel who was apparently involved in the case, wrote to the colonel that in 1926 he had prepared the decree establishing a tribal roll and confirming their reservation land.[97] Another friend of the Indians, James R. Coates of Norfolk, became active in encouraging the Indians to collect tribal rolls and affidavits concerning their status. One resulting affidavit established the Indian-white ancestry of the Upper Mattaponi chief's wife.[98]

For his part, Registrar Plecker continued to show people what the old records said and to resist issuing for Indian people birth certificates that read "Indian." In January 1942, for instance, he sent a crushing letter to a Chickahominy midwife, informing her that she had violated a state law by "falsifying" a baby's race, thus making her liable to criminal prosecution. He went on at some length, knowing that the woman would take the letter to her chief:

> This 'Indian' stuff has gone far enough, but I am not prepared just at present to say what will be done to make examples of some people. . . . [Three Rappahannock men had been sentenced to prison the day before for refusing to serve in the Army with blacks (see below)] It did not take the Judge long to decide what they were. . . . We expect a correct copy of this [birth] certificate to come in at once. . . . [Other "Indian" certificates would be returned to her, and] Each case is a separate offense should it come into court.[99]

The woman did indeed take Plecker's letter to her chief, O. Oliver Adkins, son of O. W. Adkins. He promptly sent copies of it to friends, at least one of whom made further copies and distributed it to other friends.

The sympathy aroused for the Indians grew considerably when people read Plecker's own words.

Plecker also took steps in the late 1930s and early 1940s to negate the "Indian" label on birth certificates issued before 1924 by the Vital Statistics Bureau. Initially, he merely wrote on the backs of certificates in his files and issued copies of both the front and the back of certificates when they were requested.[100] The owner of the certificate discovered Plecker's writing only when he or she requested a copy, perhaps years later. A Chickahominy woman therefore received a copy of her certificate on the back of which Plecker had written a statement about the racial label of her grandparents in the county marriage registers. She told me in 1976, "You have no idea how embarrassing that is!" Virginia law never empowered anyone to add anything to a certificate after it reached the central bureau in Richmond,[101] but through regular usage by Plecker and his colleagues, the back as well as the front of a Virginia birth certificate became "legally" part of the document—and remained that way until the Indians got a law to the contrary passed in 1972 (see chapter 10).

As time went on, Plecker's writings on the backs of birth certificates became longer and more formalized. In 1942 a man in another Indian-descended group (not Powhatan) received a typed note on the back of his certificate, the note being obviously a form which the bureau had begun using:

> The early records of this State show this group of people are descendants of free negroes.
>
> Under the law of Virginia, [person's name] is, therefore, classified as a colored person.
>
> W. A. Plecker, M.D.
State Registrar of Vital Statistics
Feb. 27, 1942.[102]

When the recipients of another such certificate protested, Plecker wrote them a curt note, saying, "We are returning the photostat copies and decline to make any change in the racial classification[,] which is in accordance with the one accepted in our office as correct. If you do not desire the certificates, destroy them; it is useless to send them back."[103]

Soon thereafter Plecker began mass-producing his "corrections" to "Indian" birth certificates by attaching a printed "warning" document[104] to the backs of certificates he sent out. The "warning" is as big a piece of paper as the certificates to which it was attached; it is 728 words long, in fine print, and bears the stamp of Plecker's writing style. It cites references in the eleventh edition of the *Encyclopaedia Britannica* to eastern tribal Indians,[105] as well as to various mixed-blood groups such as the Melungeons, and it includes quotations from the 1843 Gregory petition, as well as "results" from the Estabrook and McDougle book, *Mongrel Virginians*. After these citations, it concludes that all people claiming to be "Indian, Mixed Indian, . . . or other similar non-white terms" have Negro ancestry and should be classed as "colored." The "warning" ends as follows: "The above statement of information now available is given for the guidance of those to follow us in this work, and is intended to apply to the individual whose birth is reported on the certificate Vol. __ No. __ to which this is attached." This long-winded document also became "legally" part of official copies of certain non-white people's birth certificates in Virginia.

Meanwhile, the drafting and induction of Indian men began. The Nansemond men were inducted with whites. The reservation men were inducted on a special "Indian day" and served with whites, and after some initial difficulty the Upper Mattaponi men were allowed to do the same.[106] Fourteen Pamunkeys, ten Mattaponis, and ten Upper Mattaponis fought in the war.[107] The Western Chickahominy men were inducted with blacks, after their papers had been debated and Plecker's evidence heard.[108] They therefore refused to leave their barracks. Their chief wrote to the president of the United States in protest, and through his efforts and those of an influential Army friend, he got the men reclassified; the ten men who fought in the war served with whites.[109] The Eastern Chickahominies went through a similar process. One of their members, who lived in Hampton and had been one of the schoolchildren Plecker had removed from the "white" public school system, had his own struggle with the Draft Board there: the board classified him as "colored," and the violence of his protests practically caused the board to go into hiding. Eventually a compromise was reached, in which he agreed not to shoot anyone and the board agreed to classify him as "nationality unknown." He served with whites.[110]

The Rappahannocks, scattered over three counties, fared less well than any other tribe. Twenty-three of them fought in the war. However, four of their men from Caroline County refused induction with blacks and were prosecuted for it. One young man, Oliver Fortune,[111] was especially adamant about not serving except with whites, and his lawyer's defense of him in the trial was not at all satisfactory to the tribe.[112] While the case was continued, Speck pressured the governor of Virginia, who in turn sent Speck's letter to the state director of Selective Service. The director answered Speck directly: he, too, was anxious to see justice done, but the young man's family appeared as "colored" in the Caroline County records for two generations back and he himself had "attended colored schools and churches."[113] Seeing little hope in that direction, Speck turned to urging the other tribes to sign petitions on the youth's behalf. But the tribes were slow in responding and in the meantime no other lawyer would take the case.[114] Ultimately, Fortune and two others were convicted and sentenced to two years in the federal prison at Richmond.

The Rappahannocks and Speck then set about trying to get the conviction reversed and the pressure on Indians generally lessened in the state.

They appealed first to federal agencies to help the Virginia tribes.[115] However, all the Bureau of American Ethnology and the commissioner of Indian affairs felt capable of doing was to write letters of support to Speck and the Indians and letters of admonition to Plecker. Neither did much good, especially the latter.

An excellent indication of what the Indians and Speck had to contend with in this period is provided in an exchange of letters between Registrar Plecker and Commissioner John Collier. Collier wrote to Plecker suggesting that his policy toward Indians was overly strict. Plecker answered that the policy was justified, remarking upon the "racial genealogical expert never equaled" who was on his staff, adding that, "Your staff member is probably correct in his surmise that Hitler's genealogical study of the Jews is not more complete."[116] Collier wrote back to suggest that genealogies and censuses are "known to be susceptible to a high degree of error," that older works in history and anthropology are dated, that anthropometric studies might be useful, and that Virginia's strict definition of "Indians" was "unrealistic."[117] Plecker replied that anthropometry did not interest him, Howe's 1845 history "recorded facts as they existed at his time,"[118] "The truth never gets out of date," and meanwhile "several thousand mulattoes [are] striving to pass over into the white race by the Indian route."[119] Neither side had any impact upon the other.

However, one of Speck's correspondents in Virginia was a Petersburg lawyer and amateur linguist, who was soon able to help. When Speck appealed to Charles Edgar Gilliam on behalf of Oliver Fortune, Gilliam readily agreed to investigate what could be done.[120] Proceeding cautiously so as not to seem interfering, and asking for further data on Fortune's background, Gilliam found that there were several routes to take, the most promising being another hearing at which Fortune could establish himself as a conscientious objector—"he objecting solely upon his conscientious belief that he is an Indian."[121] This route proved successful, and Fortune and the other Rappahannock men then spent the war years working in hospitals with other conscientious objectors.

Late in 1943 the Powhatan tribes discovered that Plecker had employed a new maneuver since January of that year: he had compiled a circular that listed, county by county, the surnames of all families attempting to escape designation as "colored" who were suspected of having African ancestry. Most of the names on the list are non-Indian; however, all the Indian surnames mentioned in Mooney's and Speck's works, plus names from the New Kent fringe, are there. Plecker sent the circular to all public health and county officials in the state as well as to the U.S. Census Bureau, together with a long covering letter which called such people "mongrels" and alleged that they were "now making a rush to register as white." The recipients of the circular were now to join him, he said, in preventing "a break in the dike" by "pseudo-Indian[s]," whom "One hundred and fifty thousand other mulattoes in Virginia . . . [were] ready to follow in a rush."[122]

The Indians found out about the circular from a sympathetic intern at a Richmond hospital, and naturally they were outraged. Speck heard simultaneously from the Eastern Chickahominy chief and from James Coates,[123] who in turn had heard from the Pamunkey chief.[124] Speck advised that all the tribes be notified and helped to unite their efforts, as he had long wanted them to do: as long as they could not cooperate together, they would remain powerless.[125] He then wrote a lengthy testimonial for the Virginia Indians,[126] while Coates set about talking cooperation to the various tribes, writing to federal officials, and attacking Plecker in public speeches.[127]

Coates' efforts had mixed success. The Pamunkeys declined to work with other tribes, feeling that "it is best to fight for [the] Pamunkey Tribe exclusively, and let the other tribes fight for themselves." [128] They feared that too close an association with nonreservation tribes would endanger their own state recognition as Indians.[129] The Mattaponis seem likewise to have remained aloof. The "citizen" tribes, on the other hand, cooperated in helping Coates to collect old birth certificates that read "Indian" and affidavits and petitions from their neighbors about their "Indian" status in the community.[130] In May 1945, Coates began to pressure the tribes to make up official rolls of their membership on forms he had prepared and return them to him.[131] The two Chickahominy tribes and the Upper Mattaponis complied,[132] but after an initially enthusiastic response,[133] the reservations declined and the Rappahannocks and the Nansemonds proved to be too much "in a state of unpreparedness." [134] The collecting of documents went slowly.

The campaign to enlist officials on the Indians' side also had mixed success. Early in 1945, Dr. W. T. Sanger of the Medical College of Virginia went on record saying that Indians would be admitted to his institution as "whites." [135] But the response from federal officials to the Powhatan tribes' plight during the 1940s was sympathetic but distant. The answer made by John Collier to Douglas Southall Freeman in 1943 was typical: the federal government had no treaty with any Indians in Virginia, and therefore "as a matter of largely historical accident" it had no responsibility toward such Indians.[136] The term "Indian country" in the federal Indian Non-Intercourse Act of 1790 was still being interpreted to mean Indian land concerned in treaties with the federal government. No change of interpretation would occur until the 1970s. However, as the pressure on Indian people continued from the state Bureau of Vital Statistics, and as James Coates and others continued to request help from Washington, the attitude of the Office of Indian Affairs did change somewhat as the war ended. The change concerned Indian education in Virginia.

The reservations, the Upper Mattaponis, and the two Chickahominy tribes continued to have their own separate schools, while the Nansemonds attended white schools and the Rappahannocks struggled to get any school at all. However, such tribal schools as existed offered no high school courses, in spite of repeated requests from the tribes. The few Indian children able to get such courses had had to go to church-run colleges such as Bacone College in Oklahoma. Speck, Belle Boone Beard, and at least one county superintendent of Public Welfare[137] tried to obtain federal help for the tribes, but to little avail. After Coates became active in the affairs of the tribes in 1942, he put some serious pressure on the federal Office of Indian Affairs to admit at least the reservation youth in Virginia to federal Indian boarding schools. The office's initial response was the usual one: the federal government had no responsibility for the Virginia reservations, and "the situation seems to be one which requires the cooperation of state and local authorities."[138] However, D'Arcy McNickle, one of the staff of the office and himself a Flathead Indian, visited the Indian-descended people of Amherst County in January 1945, after which he began to pressure his superiors to admit that group's children to the school at Cherokee, North Carolina.[139] At that point the door opened a little, and the Virginia Indians and their friends hastened to push it farther open.

Letters began to flow: Coates told Wiliam Brophy of the Indian Affairs Office that the lack of high school courses for Indian children within Virginia was appalling;[140] Mrs. Hallie Baldridge, the social worker in King William County, persuaded Willard Beatty to visit the two reservations;[141] and the Rappahannock tribal secretary wrote a letter which eventually reached the federal area superintendent and the Cherokee agent, asking help in getting a Rappahannock girl into Haskell Institute.[142] The Office of Indian Affairs began to take notice. It queried Speck and received a strong letter on the genuineness of their Indian descent,[143] and then firsthand reports came in that said that the people looked Indian and not negroid.[144] For the first time, in late 1945, the office seriously considered doing something about the plight of Virginia Algonquian people by admitting their children to federal Indian schools. Meanwhile, the Cherokee agency began marketing Pamunkey pottery.[145]

With Speck's recommendation in mind, Director of Education Beatty decided that the children of the Virginia reservation tribes could enroll in high school courses at Cherokee, with alternative placements at Haskell in Kansas or Flandreau in South Dakota, if necessary.[146] Beatty therefore notified Speck that the reservation children would be accepted at Cherokee and Haskell,[147] and Speck followed up the victory by writing back that he hoped "that in the near future there will be admissions from the Adamstown band, the Rappahannocks and Chickahominy."[148] That suggestion did some good. Five weeks later Beatty wrote the Upper Mattaponi chief that a youngster from his group could go to Cherokee the next fall if the King William County social worker approved.[149] At that point the Western Chickahominy chief and a Bacone-educated member of his tribe promptly asked if the same privilege could be extended to their group; Beatty said he would have the Cherokee agent visit the tribe.[150] Thus, over the summer of 1946 agent Joseph Jennings visited the Chickahominies and the Mattaponi

Reservation, with the result that their children were also accepted.[151] For the next several years, Virginia Indian children received their high school education at either federal or church-run high schools out of state.

Another epoch came to an end for the Powhatan tribes in 1946: Walter Ashby Plecker finally retired from the Bureau of Vital Statistics. He left with one last salvo aimed at the Indians, namely, that he intended to spend his retirement studying them,[152] but his retirement was soon cut short. His death was in character: he crossed the street without looking and was hit by a truck.[153] His successor carried on his policies at the Bureau, but with much less vigor as the civil rights era dawned. She retired in 1959, and the new registrar had the Racial Integrity File destroyed.[154] A still later registrar would allow the Indians' birth certificates to be changed to read "Indian" (see chapter 10).

In 1950 substantial portions of all Powhatan tribes were still living away from the home area, often outside Virginia. Those who remained outwardly resembled their non-Indian neighbors in that they tended either to be farmers or rural blue-collar workers. By now, it was mainly in their knowledge of their own history and ancestry and in their attitudes toward the rest of society, based upon searing firsthand experience, that made them unique as communities. That uniqueness was reinforced by tribal governments and by churches which belonged to them but were run on Anglo-Virginian lines.

G. W. J. Blume of the State Board of Education published a "time-capsule" on the tribes in 1950[155] which shows their status to be as follows. The Pamunkeys had a population of fifty-five on the reservation (twenty-five men, twenty-two women, eight children), nineteen elsewhere in Virginia, and forty-five outside the state. Fifteen men farmed, twenty fished in season, and other held positions as painters, a mechanic, a caretaker of an estate, and "other phases of public work." The women apparently all worked at home, with the exception of the potters, who worked at the craft part-time. Livestock on the reservation consisted primarily of hogs. For the twenty farmers, there were two tractors, and for the nineteen households there were eight cars and seven trucks. Several of the young members of the tribe, who generally left the reservation in search of better opportunities, had been to high school out of state, at Cherokee (one) Haskell (three), and Bacone (two); two of these had gone on to college at other schools.

The Mattaponis had sixty people in residence: seventeen men, eleven women, and thirty-two children. There were thirteen more off the reservation in Virginia and ninety out of state. The occupations followed by the men were wood cutting (twelve), fishing in season (all men), farming (three), mechanics, carpentry, merchandising (there was still a store on the reservation), sales, and the ministry. No women were listed as working outside their homes. As at Pamunkey, most of the livestock consisted of hogs.

The people had among them six tractors, ten cars and seven trucks, nine electric washing machines, and eight electric refrigerators. Seven young people were taking high school courses at Bacone College, while the reservation's school had recently been increased by the addition of the few Pamunkey pupils.

The Upper Mattaponis had 175 people, including 20 living out of the state, with 55 men, 50 women, and 70 children. Most of the people rented rather than owned their homes, and the men's occupations tended to be lumbering, carpentry, or construction work. The only women employed outside their homes were four who did "industrial work" and the woman who ran the cafeteria at the tribal school. The tribe's school was grossly inadequate for the number of children needing it: only 31 could be packed into the one classroom and the other children went without schooling. Eight young people were taking high school courses elsewhere, five of them in Michigan. The tribal members among them owned three tractors, ten cars, three trucks, and various electrical home appliances.

The Rappahannock population numbered 225, of whom 160 lived in the home area; there were 85 men, 70 women, and 90 children (Blume's figures do not add up). The group, whose members were predominantly renters of land, had no church and no school at the time. In spite of the lack of opportunities locally, eighteen young people were in school elsewhere and two were in college. Men's occupations included farming (thirteen), carpentry (four), "government work" (three), sawmilling and auto mechanics; one person was qualified as a teacher but not working. No women are listed as working outside the home. The group as a whole owned five tractors, sixteen cars, and six trucks. No household electrical appliances were listed for them.

The Eastern Chickahominies had 86 people on their rolls, of whom 17 lived outside Virginia and 69—12 men, 14 women and 43 children—lived in the home area. The tribe's school had just been closed and the twenty children from it were sent to the Western Chickahominy school. Two more young people were at Bacone College for their high school work, and one tribal member was in college. The men worked "in railroad or other public works" (thirteen), or as carpenters (four), mechanics (three), farming, or the ministry; one woman worked outside her home by running the Chesapeake and Ohio Railroad flagstop at Windsor Shades. The people as a whole owned nine cars, three trucks, and various electric home appliances.

Last but not least, the Western Chickahominies had the biggest population of all: 392 members, including 109 men, 88 women and 195 children, with 41 of these people living outside Virginia. The tribe had a school with five teachers, two of them Indian (one Chickahominy, one Seneca); the tribe also had its own all-Indian chapter of the Woodmen of the World, a fraternal-cum-insurance lodge. The men worked as farmers (eleven), loggers and lumbermen (eight), carpenters (eight), merchants (four), haulers (six), painters, and laborers. The women listed as working outside the home included the Chickahominy teacher mentioned above, two "industrial workers," one domestic worker, and a saleswoman. There were 120 children in the tribal school, which had the elementary and junior high grades, plus 23 in high school and three students at Bacone College. The livestock owned by the Chickahominies consisted of 38 horses, 20 cows, and 150 hogs. The group also owned five tractors, thirty-five cars and twenty-four trucks, as well as many household electrical appliances.

The remainder of the 1940s, the decade of the 1950s, and the 1960s (before the integration of the schools) saw a gradual improvement in most aspects of the Indians' lives. In 1948 the federal Office of Indian Affairs issued an edict that all Indians in the country were legally entitled to vote in the presidential election of that year. Virginia Indians then began slowly to use the franchise. In 1954 the Virginia General Assembly amended the racial definition of Indians so that more people could qualify in the eyes of the law: "members of Indian tribes existing in this Commonwealth having one-fourth or more of Indian blood and less than one-sixteenth of Negro blood shall be deemed tribal Indians." [156] The "citizen" Indians now had partial recognition by the state. The poll tax law was also amended in that year so that people's wishes to be designated as tribal Indians in the poll tax books could be granted if they presented an affidavit "made by the Chief of any Indian tribe existing in this State, that such person is a member of such tribe and . . . to the best knowledge and belief of the Chief is a tribal Indian as defined" in the Code of Virginia. [157] In 1957 the reservation people got a ruling from the attorney general that they were exempt from buying county license tags for their cars; [158] they have had "Pamunkey Indian Reservation" or "Mattaponi Indian Reservation" tags alongside their state license plates ever since.

Some of the tribes made themselves more publicly and proudly visible than ever before. In 1951 the Western Chickahominies began holding an annual fall festival, at which there were speeches and dancing by a tribal dance team. The event has been a time for intertribal visiting ever since. Oliver Adkins, the tribe's chief, continued to be active in Virginia Indian affairs and in pan-Indian activities such as the Chicago Conference of 1961. [159] The Mattaponis got a new and more publicity-minded chief in 1949. O. T. Custalow was a true showman who made an indelible impression on all who knew him, Indian and non-Indian alike. At his first public appearance, the funeral of his father and predecessor, he conducted the "Indian part" of the funeral in "the Indian language" before turning the ceremony over to the Baptist minister. [160] In subsequent years Custalow was ordained as a Baptist minister and traveled long distances to lead services and conduct revivals, dressed in Indian costume. [161] In 1956 his tribe agreed to lease the road on their reservation to the state, which then paved it with macadam. The reservation was now truly open to the public, and Custalow

Fig. 16. Samaria School, formerly the Chickahominy Tribes' School, 1976. (Photo by the author.)

extended the welcome by erecting a museum, filling it with mementoes and curios, and directing the public to it by means of highway signs. In a very popularized way, O. T. Custalow literally put his people on the map, thereby paving the way for his successor to be a pan-tribal leader in the 1970s (see chapter 10).

The tribal schools also improved. In 1950 the two Chickahominy schools merged and some high school work began to be offered; however, the state ceased paying for advanced students to finish high school elsewhere, and the Charles City County School Board agreed to assume the costs of tuition and one-way fare to Bacone College in Oklahoma. The tribe then purchased land for a new Indian elementary and secondary school, the new building (fig. 16) being completed in 1951. Reservation youngsters were offered high school education there, and the Mattaponis accepted.[162] The teachers were primarily Chickahominies who had graduated from the high school and college departments of Bacone College, where several of them had been outstanding students.[163] Eleventh-grade work was added in about 1954 with the hiring of a non-Indian teacher, who was generally welcomed by the Indians and snubbed by the white community in Charles City County.[164] As high school courses were added to the school, the need for admission to Cherokee High School and Bacone College diminished.

In 1951 the school on the Pamunkey Reservation closed and the four or five remaining students were bused to Mattaponi's school.[165] High school courses were added to the Mattaponi school in 1958 with the hiring of another white teacher.[166] Meanwhile, one ambitious Mattaponi student who had finished his high school work at Cherokee and Bacone went on to graduate from Bluefield College, a Baptist institution in West Virginia, and later from the Medical College of Virginia as well. He is now a practicing physician in Newport News and his tribe's favorite success story.[167]

The Upper Mattaponis still retained their small school, Sharon School, which King William County funded stingily.[168] Like so many Indian schools in Virginia, it was next door to the tribal church. The children's parents were still poor and unable to supply them with much more than encouragement.[169] The school had only one room, and when the tribe wanted to add a lunchroom and kitchen, the lumber had to be donated by James Coates and the labor of building, and then of providing and cooking the food, had to be supplied by the tribe's adults.[170] Dental and visual examinations for the children were arranged only when a local white woman aggressively pursued the matter with an optometrist in West Point; she and the school's one teacher supplied the transportation.[171] It was only in the late 1950s that a larger (eight-room) building was provided by the county.

The Rappahannocks finally established a private school in 1962 by donating a building in Essex County with some land around it. The county rented the building and hired a teacher. This school was closed in 1964 and the children bused to the new Sharon School for three years, until that school also was closed as a result of integration.[172]

The Powhatan tribes watched the gains won by blacks in the civil rights era, and they themselves benefited greatly by those gains in the long run. However, no Indians joined the civil rights movement in Virginia. The reason is obvious: their memories of Plecker enforcing the Racial Integrity Law were too fresh, and their realization that many whites still thought about them as Plecker had was too keen to permit them to do anything that would associate them in anyone's mind with the black community. All of the tribes, the reservation people included, still felt far too insecure about their public recognition as Indians to endanger it by seeking immediate gains through cooperation with black activists. They were sympathetic with an oppressed people fighting back, but they had no wish to join them.[173] For that reason, the enforcement of integration in the public schools, which caused the closing of the Indian schools, was downright repugnant to Indian parents. They foresaw correctly that many white families would send their children to private academies and that the public schools would be predominantly black for many years to come. To Indian parents, integration meant first being pushed into black schools and only secondarily equal opportunity in education.

The reservation school at Mattaponi was closed in 1966,[174] after the parents negotiated a deal whereby the state would pay for the children's tuition,[175] cafeteria meals, and textbooks at public schools. In 1970, there were four Pamunkey and twelve Mattaponi children in the King William County schools.[176] They were doing well there, and parental participation in the Parent-Teacher Association and other programs was moderate.[177] In 1972 the county high school's valedictorian was Mattaponi, the salutatorian was half Mattaponi and half Eastern Chickahominy, and the principal speaker at commencement was the Mattaponi physician—who had not been permitted to attend that school in his youth.[178]

The Chickahominies lost formal control of their school in 1967, but Samaria School remained predominantly Indian and available for Chickahominy civic affairs for four more years. Then, in 1971, the federal judge in Richmond readjusted the proportions of school children in the county: Samaria School became predominantly black, as is Charles City County's population. The tribe considered setting up its own academy and applying for funds under federal legislation for Indian education in order to get another school,[179] but nothing was done in the end.

Instead of setting up an Indian academy, the Chickahominies went the same route that the other Virginia tribes had: they gave up on schools as a basis for a separate Indian identity and turned their attention to pan-Indian affairs and to getting grants of federal "Indian" monies for their people. They became activists in a larger arena.

CHAPTER 10

The Further Rise of Powhatan Activism

THE POWHATAN TRIBES entered upon several pan-tribal activities around 1970, sometimes with prompting from outsiders, more usually without. Regardless of its origin, their interest in Indian affairs outside their tribes and even outside their state soon made them more sophisticated about dealing with public agencies, including federal ones. And that sophistication, coupled with some genuinely successful efforts in fund raising, gave them a renewed visibility as Indians and pride in their heritage.[1]

The earliest pan-tribal organization was not successful in the long run. Beginning in 1969, Dr. Jack Forbes, an anthropologist then with the University of California at Davis, tried to organize yet another "Powhatan Confederacy." He himself publicly claimed "Powhatan" descent, and by 1973 he was accepted into the Rappahannock Tribal Association as a member.[2] By September 1970 four tribes had joined: the Rapphannocks, the Upper Mattaponis, and both the Chickahominy tribes. Western Chickahominy Chief Oliver Adkins was named the first head of the new "confederacy" and he and Forbes then carried on the organizational work together. But the reservations held off joining, and the then-dispersed Nansemonds were not contacted; the Haliwas and Lumbees of North Carolina and the Catawbas of South Carolina were invited to join, but nothing came of it.[3] Forbes remained active, mainly from California, by making Powhatan "language" tapes to teach with and by publishing a newspaper laced with historical research and activist rhetoric.[4] However, Forbes was never able to persuade some groups, especially the conservative reservations, to cooperate with his aims,[5] and by 1980 he faded from the Virginia scene and shifted his operations to expatriate Powhatans living in New Jersey.[6] The "confederacy" died once more.

In 1971 the Coalition of Eastern Native Americans (CENA) was inaugurated, with Mattaponi Chief Curtis L. Custalow, Sr. (see fig. 17), on the steering committee[7] and Chief Oliver Adkins also active.[8] The organization's purpose was to provide information and moral support among Indian groups which were not federally recognized as Indians, as well as the pressuring of the federal government to assume some responsibility for these groups. As luck would have it, the organization of CENA coincided

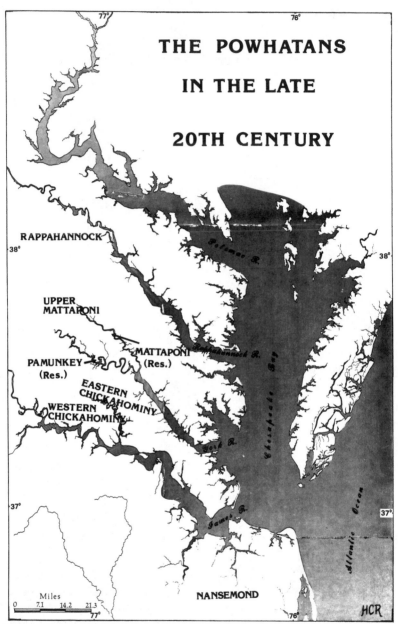

THE POWHATANS
IN THE LATE
20TH CENTURY

RAPPAHANNOCK

UPPER
MATTAPONI

MATTAPONI
(Res.)

PAMUNKEY
(Res.)

EASTERN
CHICKAHOMINY

WESTERN
CHICKAHOMINY

Potomac R.

Rappahannock R.

Chesapeake Bay

York R.

James R.

Atlantic Ocean

NANSEMOND

Miles
0   7.1   14.2   21.3

HCR

Map 10. The Powhatans in the Late Twentieth Century. Base map adapted from *Bathymetry of Chesapeake Bay* (Virginia Institute of Marine Science, 1977)

with the American Indian Movement's takeover of the Bureau of Indian Affairs offices in Washington. Although members of the CENA steering committee actually tried to help negotiate a peaceful outcome of the takeover, non-Indians were distinctly nervous about CENA and the presence of Indian organizations in general. As Gertrude Custalow, the Mattaponi chief's wife, put it when speaking about King William County, "What did they think, we were going to come down and take West Point [Virginia] away from them?"[9] Nevertheless, CENA more than lived up to its goals while it existed, and the sophistication of the Virginia tribes about eastern Indian groups and the federal government increased dramatically.[10] The Mattaponis, the Pamunkeys, the Rappahannocks, and both the Chickahominy tribes all benefited, although the Rappahannocks dropped out of the organization in 1976 because they balked at CENA's advice that the tribes should keep all their records and tribal rolls up to date.[11]

Fig. 17. Chief and Mrs. Curtis L. Custalow, Sr. (Mattaponi), 1970. Custalow was newly elected at the time this photograph was taken, and was still collecting regalia. (Photo by the author.)

Fig. 18. Chief Tecumseh Deerfoot Cooke (Pamunkey), 1970. Cooke wears a necklace of eagle feet and carries a drum he made himself. (Photo by the author.)

The Virginia tribes also became involved in the activities of the Native American Rights Fund (NARF) in the early 1970s. Mattaponi Chief Curtis Custalow was a member of NARF's steering committee in 1972[12] and remained a member of their board for several years. Three years later the Pamunkey Reservation people invited NARF to take over their case against the Southern Railroad (see below). Meanwhile, the Mattaponi physician, Dr. Linwood Custalow (see fig. 24), helped to found the Association of American Indian Physicians, becoming their treasurer in 1972[13] and rising to the presidency in 1977–1979.

The Virginia tribes took an interest in the activities of the radical American Indian Movement, particularly the occupation of Wounded Knee in 1972–1973, though the statements the press heard from them depended upon who was being interviewed. Conservative Pamunkey Chief Tecumseh Deerfoot Cooke (fig. 18) called the occupation "un-Christian" and said there was "no sense in the uprisings."[14] Mattaponi Chief Custalow and Western Chickahominy Chief Adkins both backed all Indian efforts to uphold treaties, though they deplored the violence.[15] The young assistant chief of the Western Chickahominies, Clifton Holmes, expressed sympathy with people who could not get attention in any other way,[16] and two Rappahannocks who lived in New Jersey went out to Wounded Knee and joined the occupying force.[17]

In the early 1970s, the Powhatan tribes had a lifestyle that was in many ways outwardly Anglo-Virginian and inwardly Indian: from the mid-1970s onward, the Indian elements became more publicly visible.

The vast majority of Indian adults had places in the work force if they wanted them,[18] but they continued to feel the effects of job discrimination. Some employers regarded these people who "falsely" claimed an Indian identity as potential troublemakers. Thus, in 1970 a Rappahannock woman was turned down for a job in Tappahannock for which she was fully qualified and had a teacher's recommendation, after she answered the employer's question about "race."[19] Most of the reservation men still of working age in the early 1970s continued to prefer to work as wood procurers under contract to the Chesapeake Corporation, an occupation in which they were technically self-employed. Independence on the job meant a great deal to them because of their Indian-hunter heritage,[20] but it also shielded them from humiliations that they might still have encountered in other jobs.

Discrimination in educational opportunities also continued in the early 1970s, before federal educational funds became available to nonfederal eastern Indians. For example, the valedictorian and salutatorian of King William High School in June 1972 were both Indians, and both came from families which could not afford to pay for their college education. They were obvious candidates for the limited number of locally awarded scholarships. However, one such scholarship which had annually been given to the best students in the high school went that year to white students in the middle of their graduating class. The Mattaponi chief's wife, Gertrude Custalow, queried the West Point ladies' organization which gave the scholarship, and she was told that the group had decided that year to give "an opportunity" to an "average" student for a change. She was also told that the scholarship was for Americans, and "you're not part of American society." Clenching her teeth, Mrs. Custalow asked, "If we're not part of American society, then what *are* we part of?" There was no reply.[21] The student who was valedictorian managed to get a church-supported scholarship a year later; he has since done graduate work. The student who was salutatorian did not pursue further education and is now married to a Chickahominy man.

On the other hand, the overall job and educational situation did improve in the late 1960s and early 1970s, and consequently there were signs of a higher standard of living in the Indian communities. More new houses appeared among the "citizen" Indians; among the reservation people, who could sell houses only to other reservation people, new mobile homes began to be bought. State Highway Department signs for both the reservations were put up in 1971 on the state and county roads that led to them. On the Mattaponi Reservation, where electricity had come only in about 1950 and the first telephone in 1967,[22] street lights were installed in 1972.[23] Also in 1972, Chief Curtis Custalow of Mattaponi and Chief Oliver Adkins of Western Chickahominy were appointed to the eighteen-member Governor's Minority Economic Development Advisory Commission.[24] Federal funding from the Department of Labor began to be available to reservation people, at least, in 1972, but neither tribal council was much interested in applying for it as yet.[25] However, in 1973 the Mattaponis applied for and received a grant from the Department of Health, Education and Welfare, aimed at supplementing county expenditures for the tribe's school children, while the Pamunkeys obtained CETA money (see below) through CENA for environmental protection measures.[26]

The scene began to change even more rapidly in 1975. By this time the Eastern Chickahominies, if not others, were receiving the *Federal Register,*[27] and the Western Chickahominies were compiling a community planning profile for use in applying for federal funds.[28] The Mattaponis, meanwhile, received a large grant for improvement of housing, in preparation for which they had to draw up a housing code.[29] They were also invited in that year to send a representative to a meeting of the Ad Hoc Committee of the National Advisory Council on Indian Education.[30]

There were still some local difficulties in using the federal funds that began to come in during that year. The Western Chickahominies got money from the Department of Health, Education and Welfare for a remedial summer program in reading and mathematics for Indian children in the Charles City County schools. Regrettably, this aroused jealousy among their black neighbors, who had to be pacified by having it pointed out to them that the books used in the program would go to the schools' libraries afterward, where everyone could use them.[31] However, the next year the program was canceled because the county treasurer said that no matching funds were available.[32]

It was in 1975 that Comprehensive Employment Training Act (CETA) Title III funds began to flow into Virginia Indian communities. In that first year, the United Southeastern Tribal Association, based in Nashville, got a grant under the act for job placement among Southeastern Indians. Some of the grant money went to Charles City and New Kent counties, where the Community Action Agency placed twenty Indian people in one-year positions as aides, cafeteria helpers, and mechanic's helpers, while other funds went to the two reservations in King William County for similar purposes.[33] Over the next several years, CETA funds were acquired for the Powhatan tribes and administered through county community action agencies.

In 1977 some CETA funds were directed towards craft classes which were open to all the Powhatan tribes and held in the Western Chickahominy tribe's new tribal center.[34] In 1979 $126,500 in CETA funds was awarded for tribal crafts alone in Virginia,[35] and a Chickahominy man, Michael Holmes, resigned his position as county administrator to become a subcontractor for the Governor's Employment and Training Council, which was administering the funds.[36] Another Indian, Warren Cook of Pamunkey, supervised all CETA monies in the state[37] and also began serving as the governor's advisor on Indian affairs.[38] When CETA came to an end in 1981, by which time sixty to seventy Indian people were being served[39] and the funds were being administered entirely by Indians, the intertribal administrative organization continued its work of applying for and overseeing the expenditure of funds under a new name: Mattaponi-Pamunkey-Monacan Job Training Partnership Act Consortium.[40]

With successes like these, it is little wonder that the Powhatan tribes gradually substituted a new basis of Indian identity for the schools they had lost in the 1960s. Now they were pulling in federal funds for various community projects—including schools—not in order to *be* Indians but because they *were* Indians. And because they were Indians, they were applying for federal funds available to them either specifically as Indians or as a people with an identifiably unique heritage.[41] For once, they were involved in a beneficial cycle, not a vicious one.

Legal changes in Virginia in the 1970s also made the Powhatans less subject to public humiliation than they had been in the past. In 1972 a law was passed to the effect that any writing on the backs of birth certificates was not to be copied and included with certified copies of birth certificates issued before July 1, 1960.[42] The lateness of the date is explained by the fact that W. A. Plecker's successor continued writing on birth certificates until she retired in 1959.[43] As discussed in chapter 9, that writing had never been legal in the first place.

In 1975, Virginia repealed its segregation and racial definition laws altogether.[44] People could be whatever they claimed to be; however, in practice they could be tribal Indians only if a tribe admitted them as members. The Powhatan tribes themselves were still formally recognized in two different ways: the reservations remained under the Treaty of 1677, while the "citizen" tribes kept their charters of incorporation. Formal recognition of the "citizen" tribes as specifically *Indian* tribes would come later.

The federal Department of Justice was responsible for some of these legal changes in Indians' and other non-whites' status. However, in 1975 it went a bit too far in the case of the Chickahominies when it ruled that in Charles City County the ballots in the 1976 presidential election should be in both English and Chickahominy. The reasoning behind the ruling was that the Chickahominies made up more than 5 percent of the county population. The Virginia attorney general sent a strong letter back, informing the department that the Chickahominy language was long extinct and that all the Indians were monolingual English-speakers.[45] The department initially heeded the advice and backed down,[46] but the next spring it reversed itself again and demanded that the ballots in the county be bilingual.[47] Not knowing the internal politics involved, many of us outsiders were amused: here was a huge bureaucracy making an inconvenient but harmless mistake because it did not know the grassroots very well.[48] The Chickahominies, however, viewed the matter differently. They saw it as an attack on the Indianness, for they felt that the anti-Indian chairman of the County Board of Supervisors had prodded the Justice Department in order to expose the Chickahominies as having lost their Indian language. That chairman was so abrupt when Indians approached him on the subject that the tribe decided merely to lie low and let the bureaucrats fight it out.[49] In the end, the ballot was in English only.

Two Powhatan tribes had let their organizations and their charters of incorporation lapse by 1970: the Rappahannocks and the Upper Mattaponis. Both groups had chiefs whose elections dated back to the 1920s and who died at an advanced age in about 1970.[50] Both groups also experienced problems of a geographical nature: the Rappahannocks remained scattered across three counties, while many of the younger Upper Mattaponis had moved to nearby Richmond in search of job opportunities. Now the sons of both chiefs (see figs. 19 and 20), elected as chiefs in their own right, began to try to reorganize their tribes, with the result that both tribes had charters again by 1976.[51]

The land case successfully brought by the Penobscot, Passamaquoddy, and Malecite Indians, with federal assistance, against the State of Maine in the late 1970s has had a number of repercussions in Virginia, although activism among the Powhatans had already begun before that time. In particular, the reinterpretation of the federal Indian Non-Intercourse Act of 1790 which makes the federal government responsible—retroactively—for the welfare of "state" reservations such as Mattaponi and Pamunkey has triggered one land case (so far) in Virginia. The concomitant establishment of the Recognition Sector of the Bureau of Indian Affairs has inspired the nonreservation Powhatan tribes to work for and achieve state recognition, and at this writing some of the groups dream of federal recognition as well. Meanwhile, the Virginia attorney general's office has been inspired to investigate the legal boundaries of both reservations as well as the location of the reservation formerly owned by the Chickahominies.[52]

The Pamunkey land case arose because in 1855, when the predecessor of the Southern Railway Company took about twenty-two acres of the Pamunkey Reservation in order to run a track between Richmond and West Point, no compensation was made to the tribe. In 1971 the Pamunkeys began attempts to gain redress with local legal help, to no avail, so in 1975 they asked the Native American Rights Fund to take their case. In 1979 the railroad finally settled out of court: reparations of $100,000 were to be paid, which included rent on the twenty-two acres for the next decade; the

Fig. 19. Chief Captain Nelson (Rappahannock) and his family, 1976. (Photo by the author.)

Fig. 20. Chief Andrew Adams (Upper Mattaponi), 1976. *Left,* the chief's wife, Ocie Allmond Adams (Pamunkey); *right,* the chief's sister, Elizabeth Adams. (Photo by the author.)

railroad was to have perpetual right of way along its track, but it was to pay rent for the land, the amount of rent being reset every ten years. Seven unused acres were also to be returned to the Pamunkeys, and if the track were ever abandoned, the entire acreage would revert to the tribe.[53] The success of this land case, long as it was in coming, has encouraged the Pamunkeys and the Mattaponis to look into other possibilities, such as the land sale of 1828 and the condemnation of 1812. There were also twelve acres of marshland which the Pamunkeys believed were illegally sold to the hunt club next door; the club was willing to return the land, except for one member, who was sued.[54]

Both Virginia reservations, with their uninterrupted occupancy from colonial times, were eligible for federal recognition under the criteria set up by the Recognition Sector of the Bureau of Indian Affairs. That bureau has put out several "feelers" to both groups since 1969,[55] but neither tribe's council was interested in assuming "a lot of red tape" which would go with the recognition.[56]

The 1982 project for state recognition of the nonreservation Powhatan tribes involved the two Chickahominies, the Upper Mattaponis, and the Rappahannocks, and the impetus came entirely from within those groups. They initially approached the Native American Rights Fund; then they decided to work instead with the Indian Information Project of United Indians of America, Inc., a Lumbee-sponsored organization. The first step was taken by the Western Chickahominies, who pressured the General Assembly—even to the extent of hiring a lobbyist to make their pressure more acutely felt[57]—to form a committee to investigate the situation of the "citizen" Indians. Accordingly, House Joint Resolution 97 was passed in early 1982,[58] creating the Joint Subcommittee to Study the Historical Dealings and Relationships Between the Commonwealth of Virginia and Virginia Indian Tribes.

With a governor-appointed membership consisting of five "citizen" Indians[59] and five non-Indians, the subcommittee began working with the four "citizen" tribes to collect documents on their history.[60] The results were presented formally to the subcommittee in November 1982,[61] with the result that House Joint Resolution 54 was drawn, voted upon, and passed by the General Assembly in January 1983.[62] Thus state recognition came at last to the Chickahominy Tribe, to the Chickahominy Tribe-Eastern Division, to the Upper Mattaponi Tribal Association, and to the United Rappahannock Tribe. Ironically, shortly before the bill was signed into law, the Rappahannock tribe fissioned and the offshoot group found itself in the position of having to apply separately for state recognition.[63] The Nansemonds reorganized and gained recognition the next year (see below).

A "Commission on Indians" (now titled the Council on Indians) was set up,[64] with five "citizen" Indians and five non-Indians (expanded in 1989 to eight tribal positions, two "at-large" Indian positions, and three non-

Fig. 21. Signing the Recognition Resolution, 1983. Left to right: Robert Adams (Upper Mattaponi), Gerald Stewart (Eastern Chickahominy), Stephen R. Adkins (Chickahominy), Eunice Adams (Upper Mattaponi), Hardaway Marks (Virginia House of Delegates), Norman Hogge (Eastern Chickahominy), Moses Adams (Upper Mattaponi), Michael Holmes (Chickahominy), Dorothy Richardson (Rappahannock), Virginia Governor Charles Robb, Paul Richmond (pastor, Tsenna Commocko Indian Baptist Church), Captain Nelson (Rappahannock), O. Oliver Adkins (Chickahominy), Malcolm Tupponce (Upper Mattaponi), Llewellyn Richardson (Rappahannock), Kathy McKee (Indian Information Project), W. J. Strickland (Indian Information Project), Martha Adkins (Chickahominy), Thomasina Jordan (Indian Information Project), and Nokomias Fortune Lemons (Rappahannock). (Courtesy Virginia Department of Highways and Transportation, Richmond.)

Indian positions). The two reservation tribes remained upset at not having been consulted until the last minute in any of these proceedings; in fact, they requested the Native American Rights Fund to learn whether or not the "new" recognitions could harm their treaty status (the answer was "no"). In a belated attempt to encourage cooperation among "reservated" and "citizen" Indians, the governor of Virginia asked Warren Cook, the Pamunkey advisor to the governor on Indian affairs, to join as an *ex officio* member. Cook remained the reservation people's direct link with the Governor, however.[65] Meanwhile, in 1988–1989, all the Powhatan tribes, including both reservations, moved to start yet another intertribal organization, United Indians of Virginia. Unified action, for the modern Powhatans, comes hard.[66]

Most of the Powhatan tribes' activist efforts after 1975 were directed at improving the lives of their own people, but the remainder were aimed at educating the public to the fact that "real" Indians still live in Virginia. Tribal officials, both while in office and after retirement, spent increasing time serving as intermediaries between their people and the public. In that capacity, they often felt obliged to wear "Indian" dress, consisting minimally of beadwork jewelry and maximally of Plains-inspired buckskin clothing and feather headdresses.[67] Among the Mattaponis, tribal bylaws specify that a chief representing the tribe must wear ceremonial garb. The reason, of course, is so that an ignorant public will recognize them readily.

Often these tribal leaders have encountered the same difficulties that Indian leaders do elsewhere in the country. They perforce become experts on tribal welfare, and then they feel that their people are either opposing them or leaning too much on them. Both these feelings are justified at times. Tribal leaders also grow to feel that other tribal leaders both compete with them and offer them moral support. The end result is eventually an emotional bleeding-dry of a leader, followed by replacement by someone else—who then goes through the same enervating experience.[68] This process has long existed among Virginia Indian leaders and is now accelerating.[69] Some elderly leaders have also felt conflict with younger tribal members simply because of the age difference, which makes the elders remember the "bad old days" and the youth eager to reach out toward new opportunities. Considering what the Powhatans have lived through in this century, the "generation gap" for them is a tremendous one.

In the 1980s more Virginia Indians than ever before were employed doing "Indian things." Indian people were called upon frequently with requests for speaking engagements and for their participation in crafts fairs. A few people were already making such affairs their full-time occupation. The museum at Jamestown Festival Park had hired Indian "interpreters" of Indian exhibits for many years; by 1980 there were both museums and trading posts with Indian personnel on each reservation as well.[70]

The Pamunkey Reservation, covering about 1,200 acres,[71] has been a Virginia Historical Landmark since 1979; National Historical Landmark status is pending in the late 1980s. When I first worked on the reservation in 1970, its population of about sixty persons consisted mainly of older families whose breadwinners were retired. Jobs were scarce in the county, except as hunting and fishing guides or wood procurers. In the 1980s the population of about fifty[72] (rising to eighty during school vacations) includes several young families, whose breadwinners live either by producing Indian crafts or by commuting to jobs in Richmond. Mobile homes now slightly outnumber frame houses on the reservation, and dwellings are still scattered over the cleared land rather than clustered together. Electricity and indoor plumbing are the rule. Few yards are fenced anymore, since almost no livestock is kept. The roads on the reservation used to be main-

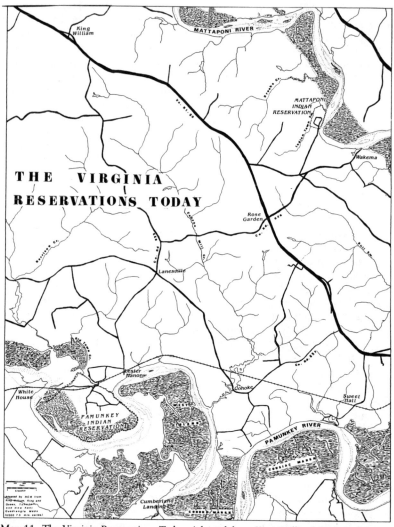

Map 11. The Virginia Reservations Today. Adapted from King William, King and Queen, Tunstall, and New Kent quadrangle maps (U.S. Geological Survey, 7.5 min. series).

tained by a tribal member on a piecework basis, but the state paved them and took over their maintenance in the winter of 1982–1983.

The tribal government[73] consists of a chief and seven councilmen, who are nominated by a three-man committee and elected every four years. In order to vote in an election, one must be a Pamunkey, i.e., descended from

Pamunkeys on one or both sides of the family and recognized as such by the residents of the reservation; a male age eighteen or over; and a resident of the reservation for at least six months of each year. Candidates are voted upon by placing either a corn kernel (yea) or a pea (nay) in a pot or hat that is passed around, and the majority rule is used. Meetings are held quarterly and attendance is required for all voters; outsiders may attend by invitation only. The tribal council votes on issues, with the chief acting as tie breaker if necessary, and the other men either give or withhold ratification.

There are still seven trustees from the local white community, and though they are rarely consulted anymore because of the great increase in sophistication among the Indians, they are still invited annually to a men-only fish fry in April, just to keep up contacts. Tribute in game or fish is paid to the governor of Virginia annually around Thanksgiving. The Indian presenters dress in "Indian" garb for the occasion, the costume being heavily influenced by the pan-Indian styles derived from Plains Indian culture. Sometimes the former chief also did a war dance around the governor while the press snapped pictures; an ignorant public expects it.[74] The meaning of the tribute paying is still deadly serious, however: in the absence of a general Office of Indian Affairs in Richmond, the reservation tribes still deal directly with the governor, whom they see face-to-face at least once a year.

Pamunkey-descended people recognized by the tribe as eligible for tribal membership—through genealogical connections and the possession of Indian and white but no other ancestry—may claim land on the reservation. This rule does not extend to Pamunkey-descended women who are currently married to white husbands.[75] Claimants apply to the tribal council during a meeting, and if their request is approved, they must begin building upon their plot within two years. The widows of landholders may live on their husbands' plots for the rest of their lives, but any children of landholders must apply for plots separately. Unclaimed farmland may be rented to an Indian for money or to a non-Indian for a share in the crop. The wooded and marshy areas of the reservation are divided into hunting territories[76] which are reallocated every fall through a bidding system; successful bidders may then hunt the land or sublet it to non-Indians for the winter season. Shad fishing still goes on in the spring, and the small houses for fishing gear at the river's edge are still there. However, several of these have been converted into cottages in recent years.

The two truly public buildings on the reservation are the church and the museum. The church building dates to 1865 but has been renovated regularly since. The museum is the descendant of the old trading post, which used to be housed in the late-nineteenth-century one-room school house next door. That building is used for storage today. The museum was erected as part of a project to use grants totaling $310,000 from the Housing and Urban Development Administration and the Economic Development Administration received by the tribe after 1977. Originally, there was to be a museum, a craft center, and a reconstructed aboriginal village,[77] and fur-

Fig. 22. Chief William H. Miles (Pamunkey), 1984. (Courtesy *Newport News Daily Press.*)

ther funding from the Governor's Employment Training Council and CETA was to be used to train Indian personnel to build and run the museum and to encourage more Indians to make pottery for the craft shop.[78] The museum and craft shop, together with a large community meeting room with kitchen, were built, dedicated on October 11, 1980,[79] and successfully put into operation. However, the aboriginal village, which had begun in 1975 as a summer field school led by Dr. Errett Callahan, was seriously underfunded from the beginning and depended heavily upon volunteer laborers who did not appear in large enough numbers.[80] After 1980 the village project had to be abandoned.

Only two resident Pamunkeys have held positions in the public eye in recent years. Assistant Chief Warren Cook, as already mentioned, is advisor to the governor on Indian affairs and an ex-officio member of the Council on Indians. He has also served as representative to the National Governors' Association, the Governors' Interstate Indian Council, and the board of directors of the United Indian Planners' Association. The present chief, William H. Miles (fig. 22), lived for many years in Colts Neck, New Jersey, where he served as mayor, town councilman, postmaster, fire chief, and president of the fire company; he was also a co-founder of the local Lions Club and the Colts Neck Historical Society, as well as being very active in the local [Dutch] Reformed Church (his wife, a trained genealogist, is of Dutch colonial descent).

The Mattaponi Reservation covers about 125 acres.[81] About sixty people live on it,[82] and today many of them are in young families whose breadwinners commute to jobs in the county or in Richmond. The reservation is so crowded that there is limited room for kitchen gardens and almost no pasturage; many men own (and pay taxes on) nonreservation land nearby for timbering and hunting purposes. The dwellings, about evenly divided today between mobile homes and improved frame houses, are necessarily clustered, but they do not face one another across the road in the regimented fashion of Anglo-Virginian housing developments. Electricity and indoor plumbing are the rule, and there is now a reservation housing code.

Law on the reservation consists of a constitution, bylaws, and a body of unwritten customary law.[83] Mattaponi chiefs are elected for two or four years, the choice being theirs upon election. An assistant chief and a minimum of three councilmen are also elected by voters who are Mattaponi, male, age eighteen or over, and in residence on the reservation for at least six months of the year. Meetings are open to all voters and to others when invited; the proceedings are secret, but the women can eavesdrop and the

Fig. 23. The Mattaponi Reservation, 1970. The two-story building once housed the general store, which was exempted from county taxes in 1917. (Photo by the author.)

Fig. 24. Father and son, both chiefs: Webster Custalow (Mattaponi) and Linwood Custalow, M.D. (Upper Mattaponi), 1985. The son, a Newport News physician, was barred by his reservation's six-month residence rule from participating politically; yet his Upper Mattaponi membership through his mother enabled him to become chief of that tribe. (Photo by the author.)

men can discuss specific issues with any outsiders involved. There are four white trustees, but they, like the Pamunkey trustees, are seldom consulted because they are seldom needed today. The Mattaponis also pay tribute to the governor in game or fish around Thanksgiving; their representatives wear at least one item of "Indian" regalia for the occasion, in accordance with the tribe's bylaws.

Limited land is the biggest problem for the Mattaponis. Everyone who works must do so off the reservation, except in the shad-fishing season. Mattaponi-descended people who are recognized by the tribe as eligible for membership—by genealogical connections and by possession of Indian and white and no other ancestry—can claim plots of land, but in practice there is a lengthy waiting list today. Indian people can bring white spouses to live on the reservation, but in the case of a white husband, he is on "probation" for good behavior for six months before he is permitted to establish residence,[84] and then his residence does not carry voting privileges.

There are three public buildings on the reservation today. The church was established and built in 1932 and has been steadily improved since. Today, like the other tribal churches, it has year-round climate control. The museum founded by the late Chief O. T. Custalow is still very much as he left it and is run by his children, who take turns staffing it. One of his daughters, Gertrude Minnie-Ha-Ha Custalow, and her husband, retired Chief Curtis L. Custalow, Sr., also run the Minnie-Ha-Ha Educational Trading Post nearby, where lessons on Indian history, crafts, and dancing are taught. Both institutions were built with family funds and are privately owned. The former schoolhouse has been refurbished as a tribal center with classrooms, meeting hall, and kitchen.

The Mattaponi who has been most in the public eye for the last few years is former Chief Curtis Custalow, who while he was chief served on the board of the Native American Rights Fund (1971–1983), the board of the short-lived Powhatan Confederacy, the steering committee (1971– 1972) and then the executive board of CENA (1972–1973), the Governor's Minority Economic Development Advisory Committee (before 1975), and several other organizations. His nephew Kenneth Custalow, an accountant in Richmond, was elected to the board of the Native American Rights Fund in 1983.

The Eastern Chickahominies in 1985 had a population of forty-two adults and twenty-nine children in residence, with others living away. Most of the local members live in an enclave of adjacent dwelling sites near Windsor Shades, and the frame houses and mobile homes are fully modernized. The men work either in the county or in Richmond. The tribe has a chief and assistant chief and a council of five people, elected by secret ballot every year in April by all adults in the tribe age sixteen and over. Tribal council meetings are held quarterly; they are open to tribal members but closed to outsiders except by invitation. There are also two general tribal meetings annually, on the second Saturday of April and of October.

The tribe's church, which had been lovingly kept up since 1925, was replaced in 1983–1984 with the help of individual donations and a grant from the Virginia Baptist General Board's State Mission Offering.[85]

Several of the tribe's people have been active in New Kent County in recent years. The chief, Marvin D. Bradby (fig. 25), has been a member of the Planning Commission since 1974 and chairman of it since 1982; he is also job steward for Local 2390 of the Communication Workers of America in the Richmond area. In 1989 he was elected chairman of the newly formed United Indians of Virginia. Councilman William A. Stewart was a member of the state's Council on Indians in 1983–1986.

The Western Chickahominies are the largest tribe in Virginia today, with a population of about 550 persons, who live interspersed with non-Indians along a few county roads in Charles City County. Perhaps another five hundred relatives live away. The majority of people in the tribe live in well-kept frame houses with all the modern conveniences. Several tribesmen

Fig. 25. Chief Marvin D. Bradby (Eastern Chickahominy) and his daughters, 1985. (Photo by the author.)

own their own businesses in Charles City County, others have college and graduate degrees and teach in the county school system, while yet others work in Richmond. A few still farm locally. Those living away include a lawyer in Richmond and a veterinarian in Hampton.

The chief and a council of nine are elected every year for staggered three-year terms by adults age sixteen or over. Meetings for the whole tribe are held in June, while the tribal council (titled the board of directors) meets on the second Monday of February, April, June, August, October, and December. Council meetings are open to any tribal member; both general and council meetings are closed to outsiders except by invitation.

Today meetings are held in the tribal center, a big building with a meeting hall, kitchen, and several large classrooms for which the tribe raised the money (about $100,000) without outside assistance in 1976–1978. Since then the tribe has purchased a 275–acre farm; they intend to use it at least in part for building sites, to encourage more young people to stay in the county, where residential land to buy is becoming scarce.

There are several intratribal organizations which are active publicly. The tribe has its own chapter of the fraternal organization Woodmen of the World; there are several groups within the tribe's Samaria Indian Baptist

Fig. 26. Samaria Indian Baptist Church, 1976. This is the largest of the Indian churches in Virginia. (Photo by the author.)

Church (fig. 26), including the gospel singers "The Samaria Messengers"; and the Chickahominy Redmen Dancers (fig. 27), with about thirty participants, travel widely to powwows, school assemblies, and the like. Their dances, with the exception of the Eagle Dance, which was borrowed recently, and the Nanticoke Dance, which dates from pan-Indian gatherings of the 1920s, have remained unique to the tribe.[86] Their costumes, on the other hand, have become increasingly pan-Indian for the men and traditional Powhatan for the women—that is, the clothes of the "better sort" of people, which covered more of the body.

The Chickahominies have produced a number of public leaders in recent years. Their assistant chief, Steven Adkins (fig. 28), is a member of the Council on Indians and a former chairman of the county school board; Michael Holmes is a former county administrator and administrator in the Community Action Agency. O. Oliver Adkins retired in 1986 as chief and died in 1987. His successor, Leonard Adkins, has a master's degree in education and is retired from teaching in the county high school.

The Upper Mattaponis have an enrollment of about seventy-five people, most of whom live and work in the Richmond metropolitan area; about three hundred more are eligible to enroll.[87] Monthly tribal meetings and seasonal parties are held in the home territory in King William County. The

Fig. 27. Two of the Chickahominy Redmen Dancers. (Photo by the author.)

Fig. 28. Assistant Chief Stephen R. Adkins (Chickahominy), 1985. (Photo by the author.)

chief, up to three Assistant chiefs, secretary, treasurer, and seven council-men are elected every four years by adults age eighteen and over. Dual membership in two Virginia tribes is explicitly recognized by the Upper Mattaponis: a former chief is the Mattaponi physician mentioned earlier; his mother is Upper Mattaponi. There is minimal tribal conflict of interest involved here, because he lives in Newport News and does not vote at Mattaponi. Provision has also been made for associate members (long-time reservation Indian spouses of members) who may vote but not hold office.[88]

The tribal center for many years was the tribe's Indianview Baptist Church; larger meetings and parties are held in the cafeteria of King William High School. Gala installations of officers were held there late in 1983 and 1987, with the installing being done by the Western Chickahominy chief (Oliver Adkins in 1983, Leonard Adkins in 1987).[89] The Sharon School building was won back from the county in 1987 and has become a tribal center.

Several Upper Mattaponis have been active in their communities in recent years. The current chief, Raymond S. Adams, is an up-and-coming businessman in Newport News. Former Chief Linwood Custalow, M.D., has represented the Association of American Indian Physicians at the National Congress of American Indians and in 1968 was elected to appear in

Outstanding Personalities of the South. He is a member of several medical associations, and before he became so active in church affairs he was an enthusiastic Kiwanian. His sister, Shirley Custalow McGowan, and a relative, Ronald Adams, are both on the staff of the Mattaponi-Pamunkey-Monacan Job Training Partnership Act Consortium. Malcolm Tupponce has served as tribal chief and a member of the General Assembly's subcommittee of 1982 and its successor, the Council on Indians. In 1989, Eunice Adams, the tribe's treasurer, was chosen Woman of the Year by the City of Chesapeake Chamber of Commerce.[90]

The United Rappahannock Tribe has about 150 members living scattered through Essex, Caroline, and King and Queen counties, with another 70 or so living away.[91] A few of the men are self-employed, while the rest work at various salaried occupations. The people live in frame houses of various ages, and the degree of modernization of the houses accords with the economic standing of the families living in them.

The chief, assistant chief, and either eight or ten councilmen are elected (and usually reelected) every three years by adults age eighteen and over. Tribal council meetings occur quarterly and are closed to non-councilmen unless they have business to transact. General tribal meetings are called irregularly and when necessary. Membership in the tribe is by genealogy first and congeniality second; a tribal roll was finally completed in 1981.

There is a tribal center consisting of a house donated by a member of the tribe; a larger one is planned. The tribal church, Rappahannock Indian Baptist Chruch, has never been attended by all tribal members.[92] In 1983 a splinter group fissioned off, took the name Tri-County Rappahannock Tribe, and began the hard process of organization, incorporation, and recognition. At this writing (1989), their coalescence is uncertain and they have not applied for state recognition. Meanwhile, Nokomis Fortune Lemons has represented her people first on the General Assembly's subcommittee of 1982 and then on its successor, the Council on Indians, in Richmond.

The Nansemond tribe fell apart again after the 1920s, and many of its members dispersed into the cities of southeastern Virginia and kept up only minimal ties with their kin. Several children of Chief Jesse Bass remained on or near the old family property, however, and they and some relatives continued attending Indiana United Methodist Church. The *de facto* chief after Jesse Bass's death was his son Earl, an avid hunter and non-scholar who in many ways personified the Anglicized Indians of olden times.[93] Earl Bass was acknowledged by many Indians and non-Indians as the Nansemond patriarch by the time the "citizen" Indians moved toward state recognition, but he was not the man to reorganize his people in the bureaucratic 1980s.[94]

In December 1982, when the newspapers began carrying stories about Indians seeking recognition, another Nansemond descendant, Oliver Perry,

Fig. 29. Nansemonds in 1985. *Center,* Chief Earl L. Bass; *right,* Assistant Chief Oliver L. Perry; *left,* Honorary Member James R. Coates. (Photo by the author.)

caught fire from it and began researching his own genealogy. Perry is a retired civil servant, and research and bureaucratic red tape did not daunt him. The project grew into a Nansemond genealogy and then, by August 1984, into Nansemond reorganization.[95]

The Nansemond descendants elected Earl Bass their chief and Oliver Perry their assistant chief (see fig. 29), along with a secretary, treasurer, and five councilmen the following November.[96] They became chartered as the Nansemond Indian Tribal Association in December, sought the cooperation of the Commission on Indians for state recognition in late December, and received their recognition by a resolution of the General Assembly in February 1985. The month before they had held a large "powwow-and-pig-pickin'" at which Western Chickahominy Chief Oliver Adkins installed the officers and his tribe's Redmen Dancers performed, while people from most of the Virginia tribes as well as several state legislators looked on.[97] Oliver Perry became a member of the Council on Indians in 1986 and since then has annually represented Virginia Indians at the Governor's Interstate Conferences on Indians.

The tribe has about one hundred enrolled and an estimated three hundred more are eligible. Membership is genealogically determined. Because of their newness and the (favorable) media attention surrounding their reorganization, the Nansemonds soon had to deal with a problem that other Virginia groups may face in the future: applications for membership by relatives so distant as to be known to no one in the tribe. Luckily, the Nansemonds and I had already compiled a genealogy that goes back to the early seventeenth century (for Nansemond ancestors; English ones go back to the sixteenth century). Such applicants—some of them members of the Daughters of the American Revolution these days!—can therefore be dealt with and are usually accepted.

General tribal meetings are held at the former mission church in Chesapeake on the fourth Sunday of each month and are closed to non-members except by invitation. Tribal council meetings are usually held monthly in a member's home. The tribe now hosts a powwow once a year and, like the other Virginia groups, actively represents Indians today through crafts displays and speaking engagements.

In 1987 several Virginia tribes approached the Bureau of Vital Statistics, now headed by Russell Booker (my former informant), about getting the racial designation changed from "white" or "colored" to "Indian" on birth certificates, death certificates, and so forth. Booker was amenable, providing the people showed documentary evidence that they were descendants of Indians of earlier times (James Mooney's time was sufficiently far back).[98] Since then, many Powhatans who were born in Virginia have now changed their certificates and those of their immediate ancestors.

Now the Bureau of Vital Statistics records agree with what the Powhatans have been telling the U.S. Census Bureau for so long. Now the Commonwealth of Virginia recognizes the organized tribes of Powhatan descendants, whether they retain their reservations or not. Only federal recognition is lacking. And there have been rumbles in Virginia's "Indian country" that they might even try for that.[99]

Ethnic Identity Among the Powhatan Indians of Virginia

POWHATAN INDIAN ETHNIC identity has existed without a break for four centuries and more. English historical records tell us (indirectly) about the nature of that identity, because since 1607 many aspects of Powhatan ethnicity have been a reaction to the interests and activities of Englishmen in Virginia.

The ethnic identity of all people is a contrast conception (i.e., "we" versus "they"). While nearly all definitions of "ethnic group" depend upon factors such as common descent, language, beliefs, and cultural practices,[1] in fact much of an ethnic group's *consciousness* of "peoplehood" stems from their perceiving differences between their descent, language, and so forth, and those of other people.[2] Thus, it is a truism that before the invasion by Europeans and Africans, there was no "American Indian" identity, only "tribal" identities. As discussed in chapters 1 and 2, the Powhatans initially perceived the Spanish and English as just two more "tribes." Only later did they realize that these "Europeans" lumped them linguistically with the Monacans, Susquehannocks, and others into a category called "Indians."

Ethnic groups that persist for long periods often do so because of, not in spite of, opposition from neighboring groups attempting to take them over.[3] Pressure from outside binds people together in resistance; periods of such stress are often periods of a great sense of unity among those who stay within the group.[4] The Powhatans have had several such periods since Jamestown was founded, and opposition from the English, in the form of pressure to disappear, was without letup.

Two or more ethnic groups living in contact with one another will both change over time, and the change will be "a dialectical one."[5] When "they" attempt something new, "we" react to it, and "they" react to that in turn, and so on. Thus all ethnic groups are deeply affected by the other groups with which they are in contact, and in the course of history, interacting ethnic groups can cause great changes in one another's behavior. When one ethnic group becomes clearly dominant over another, as the English did over the Powhatans during the seventeenth century, the dominant group tends to do the "acting" and the subordinate group the "reacting."[6] The latter may choose to assimilate, accommodate in public while remaining "unique" in private, or emphasize their uniqueness in all areas of life.[7] Some individual Powhatans have chosen the first reaction over the centuries; the surviving tribes, though, have variously practiced the second and third, depending upon the dominant group's attitudes toward them. In all of their adaptations to changing circumstances, the Powhatans, like other ethnic groups, have selected varying symbols of their differentness, symbols both meaningful to themselves and recognizable by "outsiders."

Any ethnic group has at any one time a set of traits that it considers to be symbols of its differentness from the other people with whom it is in contact. Where everything about its physique, language, and culture is different, as with the early-seventeenth-century Powhatans in comparison to the English, then the symbols are many and each is only moderately significant in signaling a group's uniqueness. On the other hand, where only a few differences are left, those traits become charged with great symbolic meaning in the people's minds. A lost homeland can be especially effective as a symbol of ethnic differentness; it has served that purpose for American Indians for four centuries and for Jews for two millennia.[8] Other ethnic symbols may come and go as relations between a group and its neighbors change. The symbols of Powhatan identity will be discussed below, period by period.

Most scholars write of ethnic groups having "boundaries" that are more or less "permeable." The implication of a definite line of demarcation between "insiders" and "outsiders" is unfortunate. As I stated in the Prologue, I prefer as more realistic the concept of an ethnic "fringe" which surrounds a "core" group. Ethnic groups are sociating groups, that is, they are made up of human beings who interact with each other. The nature of these interactions can vary widely. The idea of a long continuum of behavior, from "core" through "fringe" to "outsider," is a realistic one. Core people are those whose most frequent and most intimate interactions are with one another and for whom the ethnic symbols current at the time are a pervasive force in life. Fringe people are those whose interactions with members of the ethnic group are in varying degrees less frequent and less intimate and for whom the ethnic symbols are less meaningful. Thus fringe people use the symbols of ethnic uniqueness selectively: they may choose a few limited symbols and draw the rest of their repertoire from other ethnic groups (of which they are also fringe members), or they may use all the symbols but only use them some of the time.

In the early seventeenth century the interests of the English centered around settling in Virginia and conquering, "civilizing," and incorporating the aborigines into English society. However, the Powhatans were still strong enough, numerically and politically, to resist these English aims with occasional violence. They also retained enough of their aboriginal territory that they could pursue their traditional way of life, which featured slash-

and-burn horticulture coupled with hunting and fishing—traditions which required large tracts of land.

Therefore, early-seventeenth-century Powhatan ethnic identity centered around an entire culture—economy, law, polity, religion, language—which differed greatly from that of the English. The major symbols of Powhatan ethnicity, in Indian minds, appear to have been the land on which the people lived and the political leaders, especially the paramount chiefs, who governed them. Those symbols would have been the logical ones to expect, given the obvious English aims of taking Indian land and transferring to themselves Indian allegiance.

Fringe people in the early seventeenth century were those who were less than fully loyal to the paramount chief and his *weroances*. For many years such fringe people were to be found among the tribes at the geographical peripheries of Powhatan's and (later) Opechancanough's "empire": the Eastern Shore, the south bank of the Potomac River, and possibly the north bank of the Rappahannock River. Being a fringe person in the early seventeenth century did not usually mean adopting English religion and culture, although after about 1614 a few Powhatan Indians began working for English settlers and learning the rudiments of the English lifestyle.

Once the Powhatans had been militarily defeated in 1646, the intertribal polity broke up once and for all, in spite of its attempted revival in 1677. The Powhatan tribes were now on their own in dealing with the English, a situation that has prevailed ever since. The English now insisted upon the sovereignty of their king over each and every tribe, regardless of its location in eastern Virginia, a claim that the shrinking Powhatan populations were not able to refute. The Powhatans remained extremely conservative in economic matters, insisting upon following their traditional economy, which required large tracts of territory. However, English settlers moved in massive numbers to take up lands that were either deserted or abandoned under duress by the decimated Powhatans. Indian poverty and further loss of prestige in English eyes were the result.

Powhatan core people continued to follow their traditional ways in the second half of the seventeenth century and the first half of the eighteenth; thus, their culture and language must have remained an important point of contrast with the English. Indian people also remembered that their ancestors had been the original owners of the lands which the English newcomers now held. This near-vanished "homeland" made the remaining islands of Indian territory doubly precious in Indian minds, at the same time that it bolstered Indian pride in having "been there first."

Each island of Indian territory had, of course, a core population living on it and a fringe population consisting of people whose way of life was Anglicized in varying degrees. This culturally based fringe, which replaced the earlier, politically based one, had more frequent contacts with English people than core people did, usually in the role of employees. The traditional Powhatan way of life was appealing to Indian people, but in the late seventeenth century it was no longer fully viable; many Indians therefore moved toward fringe status, at least part-time. The Indian core people eventually learned that they had to struggle to keep some of their relatives at home; after 1700 the leader of the core among the Pamunkeys began formally protesting against English encouragement of Indians to become fringe people.

Most fringe people moved back and forth between Indian and English territory, so that an exact census of Indian populations at any given time was difficult. (This is still true today.) Fringe people at the "English" extreme included expatriate Indians like Edward Gunstocker, who left his tribe altogether to become an English-style landowner; the slightly insecure status of his ownership and his leaving of his land to relatives who were still members of a tribe were described in chapter 6.

Some pressure on Indian land continued. By the second third of the eighteenth century, most of the Powhatan groups had lost their tribal land altogether and become squatters on the poorer lands the English did not want. The remaining reservations were minuscule in size; they could not support their Indian populations, who still remained economically conservative, without the addition of off-reservation hunting and fishing rights specified in the treaties with the English government. Thus even Indian core people now came into fairly frequent contact with English Virginians, though the only missionizing of Powhatan Indians took place at the College of William and Mary, where a few reservation boys went to school. The gradual Anglicization of the core people was the result, especially since the Indians were left alone to do it on their own terms. Regrettably, this change in Indian lifeways was almost unremarked by the Anglo-Virginians of the mid-eighteenth to early nineteenth centuries, who were more interested in wresting political control of Virginia from their English overlords.

The Powhatan core people on the reservations chose in the middle and late eighteenth century to change many of their ways of life but remain "Indian" somehow. Accordingly, they began to do some intensive farming and animal husbandry, while the men continued to hunt and fish frequently. They adopted English dress and, eventually, housing and furniture. They all learned to speak English, while the Powhatan language faded away. At last they became Baptist Christians and went to church with Baptists of other colors, by which time Powhatan culture as a whole had converged closely with Anglo-Virginian culture. However, the core people retained their memories of their aboriginal ancestry, their once larger homeland, and their current lack of civil rights in spite of the Treaty of 1677; these three important symbols apparently kept them feeling different from other Virginians of their time.

Fringe people in the mid-eighteenth to early nineteenth centuries continued to be those who moved back and forth between reservation and English territory and who therefore associated more with Anglo-Virginians than core people did. Their numbers were greatly swelled, however, by the Indian groups who had lost their reservations. The latter had perforce to change their ways considerably, unless they could retreat to a swampy area, for when they lost their land they lost their treaty rights for hunting and fishing on many English-owned lands. Without the limited treaty protection offered by the Virginia government, a traditional lifestyle was extremely difficult to maintain, and many of these landless people probably "spun off" into other populations The nature of social relations among those who remained in these groups is uncertain. Anglo-Virginians recorded practically nothing about former reservation Indians: they were peaceful and they were poor, so they were ignored. Fringe status seems appropriate for them. Only later in the nineteenth century do more tightly integrated cores appear in the records again. It is not unusual for an ethnic group to fade partially away and then regenerate itself later, especially "in the sphere of political participation."[9] It is also not uncommon for ethnic minorities to exist successfully for long periods without a formal organization to tie them together politically, especially when they resemble their neighbors in many ways and many of the services they need are performed by those neighbors.[10] Therefore, these fringe people without reservations or tribal councils should not be considered as anything other than "Indian Virginians."

Once the Anglo-Virginians had helped their fellow "Americans" quell British ambitions regarding the United States, they turned their attention to consolidating their control over non-whites in their territory. Between 1830 and 1850 many Southern states whose economy was agricultural and heavily based upon slave labor came to favor a two-caste system: white masters and non-white servants. Those who did not fit in, (for example, free Negroes and mulattoes) were to be harassed into leaving. Southern whites further refined their definitions of non-whites. Legal definitions of the "races" had been in Virginia's law books since 1705; these were not changed officially until 1910, but unofficially the "one-drop" rule became popular. With or without good reason, the Powhatans were believed by their neighbors to be "tainted" and therefore not "Indians."

It is not unusual for "insiders" and "outsiders" to disagree about who belongs to an ethnic group and who does not.[11] The hard fact for the Powhatans has long been that, living in a state of "internal colonialism,"[12] they have been subject to laws made by the majority. And the majority in Virginia could pass laws, realistic or not, defining "Indians." Those definitions specified "blood quantum," but "blood" in fact meant social and linguistic, as well as genetic, background.[13] Indians who had Anglicized their language and culture were not seen by the majority as "real" Indians, even if they looked Indian. Local beliefs about African ancestry were trotted out when it was useful. So these people who supposedly were not "real" Indians were considered merely "colored," and therefore a threat to slave-owning society. The fact that they had ancestors who once owned all of Virginia and, for the reservation people, that they still owned remnants of that homeland—immensely important ethnic symbols to the Indians—were brushed aside by the majority as irrelevant.

The Powhatan core people on the reservations found themselves considered a threat simply because they existed as a free non-white community responsible only to the governor of Virginia. The efforts made to "terminate" them centered on allegations of their having "Negro" ancestry; the real complaints were probably their independence and their having Anglicized their culture so that they no longer seemed "aborigines" needing the governor's protection. Pressure from white Virginians in this period galvanized the Indians into resistance. The reservation people fought off the threats, but thereafter they formalized their government and tightened restrictions concerning outside associations. The major symbols of their Indianness remained the land they owned, the land they had once owned, their descent from the aborigines of Virginia (increasingly emphasized), and now their tribal government, which served for them the functions that county governments did for non-Indians.

Powhatan fringe people continued to be those whose contacts with outsiders were more frequent and intimate than those of core people. The fringe also included descendants of former reservation groups such as the Chickahominies, Nansemonds, and Rappahannocks. These descendants, as far as can be determined from the scanty surviving records, began to draw more tightly together after 1830 in an attempt to separate themselves from other free non-whites and escape some of the pressure. For them, descent from the aborigines of Virginia and memories of the lost "homeland" served as symbols of ethnic identity. The former was seldom admitted by the whites with whom they dealt (the law passed for the "Nansemonds" in 1833 is an exception), although a few records show that some of the people in these regenerating cores still looked distinctly Indian.

After the Civil War, while Virginia's whites struggled to get their political power back, Virginia law provided for definitions of whites, "colored" people, and—grudgingly—Indians. Once the whites were back in power, they moved to stay there, first through *de facto* segregation and then, around the turn of the century, through Jim Crow legislation (*de jure* segregation) coupled with a law that allowed a smaller amount of African ancestry to determine "colored" status. Then in the 1920s white Virginia was seized by a veritable mania for "racial purity" and the "one-drop rule" became a matter of law. All people classified as "colored" were relegated to inferior jobs, schools, residential areas, and so on.

Pressure on them to disappear made the existing Powhatan cores "go public" instead, although they needed the encouragement of anthropologists such as James Mooney and Frank Speck to do it. When the whites segregated themselves from non-whites, the Indians responded by segregating themselves from blacks and trying to establish a third "race" in Virginia. They founded "Indian" churches[14] and got the state (for the reservations) and some counties to set up "Indian" schools. Several nonreservation groups organized "tribal" governments (actually corporations, the legality of which could not be questioned) to represent them formally in their communities. These institutions soon became major symbols of Indian identity in the tribes.

Since tribes with Christian churches, Anglicized schools, and (nonreservation) corporations still were not accepted as Indians by "outsiders," the Powhatan groups also became adept at manipulating those outsiders' stereotypes of Indians in their public behavior. Some people grew their hair long; many wore "Indian" regalia on occasion; and the Pamunkeys of the 1890s mounted plays that reminded the public of the friend the early colonists had had in Pocahontas.[15] These ethnic "cues" (physiognomic aspects) and "clues" (consciously presented reminders)[16] helped somewhat in the tribes' struggle to get others to recognize them as Indians. Ironically, in the process, many Powhatans came to believe even more fervently in the "noble savage" stereotype than non-Indians did.

As "racial purity" became paramount to the whites, it also became paramount to the Indians, and not just because they wanted to escape the political, social, and economic disadvantages of being "colored." Indians who wanted to be accepted as "Indian"—as descendants of their own ancestors—now had scrupulously to avoid associations, much less marriages, with Afro-American people; they had to assert publicly that they had no African ancestry whatever; and they had to cultivate sympathetic whites who would say the same thing, for many whites discounted non-white testimony. For Powhatan core people after 1900, the memories of a lost homeland and descent from Virginia's aboriginal owners became secondary (in public, at least) to the insistence that they had always eschewed contacts with Afro-Americans. Thus arose another major symbol of "Indianness."

The Powhatan fringe area changed somewhat during these years. As times became harder socially and later, with the Great Depression, economically, many Powhatan families moved to northern cities in search of better opportunities and perforce became fringe people. Thus, it is fair to say that a truly geographically based fringe formed once more. For those who remained behind, the fringe area contracted: associations with whites were more limited because of whites' preferences, and associations with blacks were more limited because of Indians' preferences. Indians who "married wrong" were disowned altogether as a danger to their people.

The civil rights era of the mid-twentieth century annulled the *de jure* segregation and discrimination imposed on non-whites in Virginia, although informally many former practices continued. With their recent adoption of segregation from blacks as a symbol of Indian identity, the Powhatan groups were understandably reluctant to throw in their lot with the black Americans who were winning opportunities for all. Desegregation of the schools was especially traumatic for the tribes: their hard-won separate schools (another important symbol of their identity) were closed—or, in the case of the Chickahominies, taken over—and their children went to public schools with blacks, while white parents often set up private "academies" for their offspring. But the new opportunities elsewhere soon had their effect. Indians could get better jobs and send more of their children to college, so that an upward spiral was soon established. They were also encouraged by black successes to organize intertribally for their own purposes (e.g., the Coalition of Eastern Native Americans in 1971), which in turn helped to make federal grants available to Indian communities.

Today the Powhatan core people remain proudly Indian. Their identity is based upon descent from the aborigines who once owned all of Virginia ("racial purity" is still an important issue), official recognition as Indians by the Commonwealth of Virginia, possession of reservations (in the case of the Pamunkeys and Mattaponis), formally organized tribal governments (with the reservation ones still replacing the county government for people in residence there), tribal churches, participation in some intertribal events (e.g., the Virginia Council on Indians), and the winning of federal grant funds for specifically "Indian" purposes (e.g., crafts education) and for community improvement in general.

Fringe people are still those who have fewer associations with core people than do core people. Today many fringe people live away from the reservations or areas inhabited by core people, usually for economic reasons. Associations with blacks are still severely limited by those who wish to remain within the tribes; associations with whites, in today's climate, are more frequent and more intimate than they have ever been before, even for core people. Remaining in a Powhatan core group means an existence which is rural at least part of the time. The attractions of the cities and the possibility of being accepted there as "Indian" make many core members decide to move away and become fringe people.

There are also formalized fringe statuses in some of the "citizen" Powhatan tribes today. These statuses are associate membership, which is for spouses of Indians, and honorary membership, which is for friends, pastors, and anthropologists who have proved themselves firm allies of various tribes.[17]

Some core people among the Powhatans currently see the increasing associations and marriages with whites as threats to the continued existence of "Indian" communities. Still firm believers in the social qualities of "blood," they look back to what they believe is a recent past of Indian full-bloodedness and see any dilution of the "blood" as a dilution of the Indian culture and identity. I have failed in my attempts to tell them that their outlook is dated. Their recent ancestors were not "fossils" any more than they themselves are now, and for most of Powhatan-English history, "purity" of ancestry has not been the major criterion of Indianness in anyone's mind. Instead it is possible, in spite of the myth of the "melting pot," for Powhatan culture to continue to converge with Anglo-Virginian culture without ever entirely disappearing, and for Indian communities to go on surviving in Virginia.

The Powhatan Indian identity has already survived nearly four centuries of culture change, spin off to and from the English population, and times of repressive laws alternating with times of lenience. If the Powhatans did not completely disappear in the century and more between 1725 and 1830, when a quiet exit would have been easy, they are not likely to disappear in the next generation or two because of a further increase in associations with whites. The appearance of the present Indians' grandchildren may be "whitened," and they will not be so isolationist as their immediate ancestors have had to be. But a tradition of descent from the "original owners of Virginia" will probably remain strong enough to make people keep up family—and therefore tribal—connections. I suspect that this will be true whether the pendulum of American governmental policies swings into a liberal phase, in which organized ethnic communities can gain a great many tangible benefits, or swings back toward more repression of non-Anglo-Americans, an opposition that will be sure to keep ethnic groups organized. Whatever happens, the Powhatans are likely to be around for a long time to come.

Powhatan survival also gives us an indication of what may happen among Native American tribes in the rest of the United States. Those people will probably not vanish, either. They may well continue to "whiten" physically and Anglicize culturally, as the Powhatans have done. But even if they lose their native languages and the rest of their ancient traditions—an eventuality that is by no means certain—their collective memories of descent from aborigines who once owned all of North America will give them a different enough view of American history to keep a unique ethnic identity alive. The Powhatans are ample proof that the "vanishing Indian" is indeed a myth.

Notes

Prologue. The Powhatan Indian Way of Life in 1607

1. Not all the Virginia Algonquians were under the sway of the man Powhatan; see below.

2. For a discussion of these writers and the conditions under which they made their observations, see Rountree 1989, Prologue.

3. Rountree 1989.

4. Turner 1973; Feest 1973.

5. Wright (1981, p. 24) postulates a proto-historic Powhatan population of "170,000 and perhaps considerably more." See also Jennings 1975, chap. 2, and Dobyns 1983. The effects of epidemics on the sixteenth-century mid-Atlantic Coast are impossible to assess at present. They did occur in North Carolina (Hariot 1972 [1590], p. 28) and very probably occurred in Virginia, whose people were friendly with the Carolina natives. But no specific Virginia Indian reference to them is found in any English records, and archaeology has as yet turned up no tangible evidence.

6. Binford (1964), followed by Fausz (1977), believes that the Nansemonds were not part of Powhatan's organization. John Smith and William Strachey give no evidence that the Nansemonds were independent, as I have argued (Rountree, 1989, pp. 14–15). The Chesapeakes, on the other hand, were definitely independent and were wiped out by Powhatan around 1607–1608.

7. The Powhatans were riverine people, as will be shown, and the James River runs northwest-southeast, while the Virginia–North Carolina boundary runs due east-west. The two Iroquoian peoples lived on the rivers bearing their name.

8. Feest (1978, p. 255) places the boundary south of the Rappahannock River; Fausz (1985, p. 238) places it down the center of the Rappahannock. Both placements are a response to the fact that the northern area of Powhatan's claimed "empire" was probably not fully loyal to him. I label that area and the Eastern Shore as "fringe" areas adjacent to an ethnic "core" and include them in the "empire." Turner (1982, p. 49, and 1985, p. 214) places the northern boundary where I do.

9. Smith 1986b [1612], p. 150 (almost exactly copied in Smith 1986c [1624], p. 107; Strachey 1953 [1612], p. 49.

10. For a detailed description of the plain and its rivers, plants, and animals, see Rountree 1989, pp. 17–29, and Rountree Forthcoming.

11. Thus the two channels traversed by the Chesapeake Bay bridge tunnel. The Ice Age Susquehanna continued eastward and made the Baltimore Canyon at the edge of the continental shelf, while the James diverged to the southeast and made the Norfolk Canyon. See McIntyre 1976.

12. Lippson and Lippson 1984, p. 6.

13. Rountree, n.d., Fieldnotes (interviews with Indians and non-Indians); most of the county roads were paved in the 1930s during the New Deal.

14. Some of these show up later in the century as landmarks in the land patents (Nugent 1934 and 1977).

15. Personal observation; I have lived most of my life in the Hampton Roads area. See also Rountree Forthcoming.

16. Plant resources in the region: Harshberger 1958 [1911], pp. 427–443 (Latin names used); Harvill 1970 (common names). See also Rountree Forthcoming.

17. Smith 1986b [1612], pp. 164–65 (copied in Smith 1986c [1624], p. 118); closely copied, with minor additions and deletions, by Strachey 1953 [1612], p. 83; Spelman 1910 [1613?], p. cvii.

18. Winne 1969 [1608], p. 246; Smith 1986b [1612], p. 155 (copied in Smith 1986c [1624], p. 111).

19. Strachey 1953 [1612], p. 80; copied with additions from Smith 1986b [1612], pp. 162–163 (copied in Smith 1986c [1624], pp. 116–117). For a detailed list of available fish and edible plants, ecozone by ecozone, and an analysis of corresponding richness or poorness of tribal territories, see Rountree Forthcoming.

20. Strachey 1953 [1612], p. 114.

21. Spelman 1910 [1613?], p. cxi; Percy 1969a [1608?], p. 134; Smith 1986b [1612], p. 157 (copied in Smith 1986c [1624], p. 112), and closely paraphrased by Strachey 1953 [1612], p. 118.

22. They varied between one hundred and two hundred feet square (Strachey 1953 [1612], p. 79; Spelman 1910 [1613?], p. cvi). John Smith's 1612 account agrees, though his 1624 version inserts the word "acres," giving an impression of very large fields (1986b [1612], p. 162; 1986c [1624], p. 116).

23. Smith 1986b [1612], pp. 157–158 (copied in Smith 1986c [1624], pp. 112–113); Strachey 1953 [1612], pp. 79, 118–119; Spelman 1910 [1613?], pp. cxi–cxii; Beverley 1947 [1705], pp. 143–144 (copied, with additions, from Banister, 1970, p. 357).

24. Smith 1986b [1612], p. 157 (copied in Smith 1986c [1624], p. 112); copied, with additions, in Strachey 1953 [1612], pp. 79, 119.

25. English accounts of Indian farming are detailed, but mention no fertilizer of any kind. Ceci (1975) has shown that the New England Algonquians did not use fertilizer, either.

26. Smith 1986b [1612], p. 174 (copied in Smith 1986c [1624], 127); paraphrased by Strachey 1953 [1612], p. 87.

27. Strachey 1953 [1612], p. 78.

28. Reconstructed from scanty evidence in Rountree, 1989, pp. 46, 61–62; corroborated by other Woodland peoples, cited there.

29. Thus the sudden appearance of "new" groups of Indians within established tribal territories in the seventeenth-century Indian records. Examples are Old and New Nimcock within Opiscatumek territory, Machodoc within Sekakawon territory, Warrany within Chickahominy territory, Totuskey within Rappahannock territory, and Manskin with Pamunkey territory (see chap. 5).

30. Smith's description of trying to reach Powhatan's house in February 1608 places the town at Purtan Bay.

31. Reconstructed from English descriptions of "Nansemonds" and "Pamunkeys" from either side of the river in 1608 and 1614, respectively (Smith n.d. [1608]; Smith 1986a [1608], p. 81; Smith 1986c [1624], pp. 178–179, 205).

32. Smith n.d. [1608], Tindall n.d. [1608], and Nugent 1934, pp. 98, 198 for Weyanock; Smith n.d. [1608], Smith 1986a [1608], pp. 52–53, and Anonymous 1969 [1608] for Rappahannock.

33. For the benefit of inlanders, a "point" is land that is bounded on two or three sides by water.

34. Smith 1986b [1612], p. 161 (copied in Smith 1986c [1624], p. 116); paraphrased, with additions, in Strachey 1953 [1612], p. 77.

35. For example, the Chickahominy town of 1677 (McIlwaine 1915, 3:349).

36. Smith 1986b [1612], p. 161 (copied in Smith 1986c [1624], p. 116); Strachey 1953 [1612], p. 78; Spelman 1910 [1613?], p. cvi.

37. Smith 1986b [1612], pp. 169, 173 (copied in Smith 1986c [1624], pp. 122, 126); Strachey 1953 [1612], pp. 78, 88–89, 95; Spelman 1910 [1613?], pp. cv, cvi.

38. Smith 1986b [1612], p. 162 (copied in Smith 1986c [1624], p. 116). Morgan (1975, p. 55) exaggerates in describing all the Virginia forest as a "veritable park."

39. The evidence is negative: John Smith's map (Smith n.d.) names a great many towns but makes no attempt at setting tribal boundaries. Thomas (1985, p. 135) has corroborated these kinds of demarcations in the upper Connecticut River valley, where Indian deeds for village lands are available. In those deeds, the boundaries near the river were given precisely, while boundaries back in the forest were vague.

40. The Appamattucks were observed to have "iron" at the first arrival of the English (see chap. 2). The French had been trading iron tools to the north for some time, and some of these had reached Virginia through Indian intermediaries.

41. Soils are thin and bedrock outcrops not uncommon from the fall line west; east of the fall line, the land surface slopes downward 200 feet to ocean level and the bedrock surface beneath it slopes even more rapidly, from the surface at Richmond to 2,250 or more feet down at Norfolk (Cedarstrom 1945). River floods over the ages have deposited cobbles from upstream in the sediments, to be exposed by water action or by more recent plowing.

42. The evidence for these and the knives and arrowheads is archaeological; the English say nothing about them.

43. Smith 1986b [1612], p. 163 *et passim* (copied in Smith 1986c [1624], p. 117 *et passim*); Strachey 1953 [1612], pp. 81–82 *et passim*.

44. Strachey 1953 [1612], p. 109.

45. Smith *passim*; Strachey *passim*; Spelman 1910 [1613?], p. cxi; Potter 1989.

46. See below; see also Fausz 1979.

47. Smith 1986b [1612], pp. 161, 245 (copied in Smith 1986c [1624], pp. 116, 194; Strachey 1953 [1612], p. 78.

48. Smith 1986b [1612], pp. 160–161 (almost exactly copied in Smith 1986c [1624], p. 115); copied by Strachey 1953 [1612], pp. 71–72. Feather mantles are recorded only for the "better sort" (Strachey 1953 [1612], pp. 65, 71–72; Smith 1986b [1612], p. 161 [copied in Smith 1986c [1624], p. 115]) and priests (Strachey 1953 [1612], p. 95). Common people may not have been permitted to wear them.

49. Archer 1969a [1607], p. 93; Strachey 1953 [1612], p. 132; Banister 1970, p. 321. The mussels were of the *Anodonta* genus (Lippson and Lippson 1984, p. 39).

50. Strachey 1953 [1612], pp. 65, 75; Banister 1970, pp. 322–323, 373 (copied, with additions, by Beverley 1947 [1705], pp. 227–228). Another type of shell jewelry, *runtees*, consisted of pipe beads or fat, round beads or coin-shaped pendants, made from the central column and adjacent area of conch shells (Banister 1970, p. 373; Beverley 1947 [1705], pp. 168–169, 227–228).

51. Banister 1970, p. 373. The famous "Powhatan mantle" is embroidered with *Marginella roscida* shells (Feest 1983).

52. Smith 1986c [1624], p. 167; Percy 1969a [1608?], p. 137. The Patawomecks called it *matchqueon*.

53. Strachey 1953 [1612], pp. 70–71; copied, with additions, from Smith 1986b [1612], p. 161 (copied in Smith 1986c [1624], p. 115). The plant was *Lithospermum caroliniense*, which is very rare in Virginia.

54. Smith 1986a [1608], p. 69.

55. Strachey 1953 [1612], pp. 65, 74.

56. Ibid., pp. 68, 107.

57. Smith 1986c [1624], p. 151.

58. Smith 1986b [1612], p. 162 (copied in Smith 1986c [1624], p. 116); Strachey 1953 [1612], pp. 81, 114.

59. Loincloths: Smith 1986b [1612], p. 160 (copied in Smith 1986c [1624], p. 115); copied by Strachey 1953 [1612], p. 71]. Leggings (both sexes): Archer 1969c [1607], p. 102;

Strachey 1953 [1612], p. 73. Moccasins (both sexes): Archer 1969c [1607], p. 102; Strachey 1953 [1612], p. 108; Smith 1986b [1612], p. 163 (copied in Smith 1986c [1624], p. 116).

60. Purchas 1617, p. 954; Smith 1986b [1612], p. 169 (copied in Smith 1986c [1624], p. 122, and by Strachey 1953 [1612], p. 88).

61. Percy 1969a [1608?], p. 136; Smith 1986b [1622], p. 160 (almost exactly copied in Smith 1986c [1624], p. 114); Strachey 1953 [1622], p. 73; Spelman 1910 [1613?], p. cxiii.

62. Smith 1986b [1612], p. 162 (copied in Smith 1986c [1624], p. 116); Strachey 1953 [1612], pp. 114–115; Spelman 1910 [1613?], pp. cxii–cxiii.

63. Strachey 1953 [1612], p. 72.

64. Ibid., p. 72.

65. Percy 1969a [1608?], p. 142; Strachey 1953 [1612], p. 114.

66. The original Powhatan word was *meskote·* (Siebert 1975, p. 325).

67. Archer 1969c [1607], p. 102; Smith 1986b [1612], pp. 160–161 (copied in Smith 1986c [1624], p. 115; Strachey 1953 [1612], p. 71.

68. Archer 1969c [1607], p. 103; Smith 1986b [1612], p. 162 (copied in Smith 1986c [1624], p. 116); Strachey 1953 [1612], p. 81.

69. Strachey 1953 [1612], pp. 112–113.

70. Ibid., p. 84.

71. Ibid., pp. 112–113.

72. It is not possible to posit actual "classes" for the Powhatans. English observers speaking of the "better sort" do not indicate clearly whether they mean chiefly families or a larger, more inclusive group of people corresponding to the English nobility.

73. Only the "Powhatan mantle," probably from early-seventeenth-century Virginia, survives (Feest 1983); it is made of four deer hides and is embroidered with thousands of *Marginella* shells. Its cost in human labor, both for hunting and for embroidering, is very high. For an illustration of a fringed buckskin mantle, see the painting of Eiakintomino (Feest 1978, p. 260) and the engraving derived from it (Rountree 1989, fig. 10).

74. Spelman (1910 [1613?], p. cviii) disobeyed an order from a minor chief's wife and earned himself a beating from her and her co-wife.

75. Spelman (1910 [1613?], p. cxiii) speaks of female servants bringing dishes to both men and women of the "better sort" in a meal.

76. Strachey 1953 [1612], p. 65.

77. Smith 1986b [1612], p. 173 (elaborated in Smith 1986c [1624], p. 126); almost exactly copied by Strachey 1953 [1612], pp. 59–60.

78. The quantities of food offered to important guests were enormous, since it was assumed that the guests would eat and then pass the rest along to their retinue (Smith 1986a [1608], pp. 65–69; Smith 1986c [1624], pp. 148, 150).

79. Percy 1969a [1607], p. 135; Archer 1969a [1607], p. 84; Smith 1969a [1608], p. 65; Smith 1986b [1622], pp. 167–168 (copied in Smith 1986c [1624], pp. 120–121); almost exactly copied in Strachey 1953 [1612], pp. 84–85. The English never thought to ask whether a corresponding courtesy was extended to visiting female chiefs.

80. Smith 1986b [1612], pp. 174–175 (copied in Smith 1986c [1624], p. 127; Strachey 1953 [1612], p. 60). See also the case of Amarice, who overstayed his leave from Powhatan (Strachey 1953 [1612], p. 62), and the man who was tomahawked for interrupting his *weroance* at a meeting in 1676 (Beverley 1947 [1705], pp. 225–226).

81. Spelman 1910 [1613?], pp. cx–cxi.

82. Archer 1969c [1607], p. 103; Strachey 1953 [1612], p. 75.

83. Hamor 1957 [1615], pp. 38–45.

84. Spelman 1910 [1613?], p. cxii.

85. Powhatan's paramount chiefdom was not a redistributive chiefdom, as far as the evidence shows. For a full discussion of the amount of tribute collected and what was done with it, see Rountree 1989, pp. 109–111.

86. Smith 1986b [1612], pp. 169–170 (copied in Smith 1986c [1624], p. 122); copied by Strachey 1953 [1612], p. 95.

87. Smith 1986b [1612], p. 169 (copied in Smith 1986c [1624], p. 122); Strachey 1953 [1612], p. 94; Spelman 1910 [1613?], p. cx.

88. Smith 1986b [1612], p. 172 (copied with additions in Smith 1986c [1624], p. 125); Strachey 1953 [1612], p. 100.

89. Strachey 1953 [1612], pp. 61–62.

90. Spelman 1910 [1613?], cviii.

91. Smith 1986b [1612], pp. 174, 247 (copied in Smith 1986c [1624], pp. 127, 196).

92. Strachey 1953 [1612], pp. 63, 65, 67.

93. Purchas 1617, pp. 956–957; he describes Opitchapam as "decripit and lame."

94. Strachey 1953 [1612], 69.

95. Ibid., p. 64.

96. Ibid., p. 46; Argall 1904–1906 [1613], p. 93.

97. I use the term in Service's sense (1971, chap. 5).

98. For the benefit of non-anthropologists, "protohistoric" refers to the period immediately before permanent contact with Europeans was established. It is a period of scattered visits and equally sparse documents.

99. Strachey 1953 [1612], p. 68. Archaeological verification of the presence of chiefdoms is very difficult; see Turner 1986.

100. Strachey 1953 [1612], pp. 68–69. See also Rountree 1989, chap. 7.

101. Turner 1976, 1985 pp. 209–211; Potter 1982.

102. Service 1971, pp. 135–139.

103. With four major estuaries traversing a region only 80 miles wide from north to south, all ethnic groups had access to a large variety of econiches; see Rountree 1989, chaps. 1 and 2, and Rountree Forthcoming.

104. Smith 1986b [1612], p. 148 (almost exactly copied in Smith 1986c [1624], pp. 103–105, 107); Strachey 1953 [1612], p. 49.

105. Smith 1986b [1612], p. 173 (copied in Smith 1986c [1624], p. 126); Strachey 1953 [1612], pp. 44, 56.

106. Strachey 1953 [1612], pp. 68–69.

107. The traditional term "confederacy" is a complete misnomer. See Rountree 1989, chap. 7.

108. The Patawomecks led Powhatan to think they were part of his "empire"; see various references to them in succeeding chapters.

109. Strachey 1953 [1612], pp. 63–69.

110. See Rountree 1989, Epilogue.

111. Strachey 1953 [1612], p. 44.

112. Varying creation stories: Strachey 1953 [1612], pp. 89, 102; Purchas 1617, pp. 954–955. Varying afterlife beliefs: Strachey 1953 [1612], p. 100; Archer 1969c [1607], p. 104; Purchas 1617, p. 955.

113. Smith 1986b [1612], p. 169 (copied in Smith 1986c [1624], pp. 121–122); closely paraphrased by Strachey 1953 [1612], pp. 88–89; Purchas 1617, pp. 954–955; Beverley 1947 [1705], pp. 200–201.

114. Smith 1986b [1612], p. 170 (copied in Smith 1986c [1624] pp. 122–123); paraphrased by Strachey 1953 [1612], pp. 95–96; Spelman 1910 [1613?], p. cxiii.

115. Purchas 1617, p. 955. This contradicts Alexander Whitaker's assertion (1936 [1613], p. 26) that they lived like celibate hermits.

116. Smith 1986a [1608], p. 59; Smith 1986b [1612], p. 171 (copied in Smith 1986c [1624], p. 124); Strachey 1953 [1612], p. 98; Spelman 1910 [1613?], pp. cix–cx; Percy 1921–1922 [1612], p. 277; Whitaker 1964 [1611], p. 498.

117. Smith 1986b [1612], p. 160 (copied in Smith 1986c [1624], p. 115); copied by Strachey 1953 [1612], p. 76.

118. Smith 1986a [1608], p. 59; Smith 1986b [1612], pp. 170–171; Strachey 1953 [1612], pp. 96–97; Smith 1986c [1624], pp. 149–150.

119. Strachey 1953 [1612], p. 104; copied with additions from Smith 1986b [1612], p. 165 (copied in Smith 1986c [1624], p. 119).

120. Clayton 1968 [1687], p. 435.

121. The Siouan Monacans and Mannahoacks, and the Iroquoian Massawomecks and Pocoughtraonacks; see Rountree 1989, p. 120.

122. Smith 1986b [1612], p. 255 (a "half moon" formation to surround enemies); Smith 1986c [1624], p. 144 (a "square order").

123. Archer 1969a [1607], p. 96; Archer 1969c [1607], p. 103; Spelman 1910 [1613?], pp. cxiii–cxiv.

124. Wingfield 1969 [1608], p. 216; Archer 1969c [1607], p. 104; Percy 1969a [1608?], p. 145; Smith 1986b [1612], p. 162 (copied in Smith 1986c [1624], p. 116); Strachey 1953 [1612], p. 113. Smith wrote of men going about nearly naked in weather so cold that "a dogge would scarse have indured it" (1986a [1608], p. 73).

125. Strachey 1953 [1612], p. 113.

126. Ibid., pp. 56, 113–114.

127. Smith 1986b [1612], p. 166 (copied in Smith 1986c [1624], p. 119); copied by Strachey 1953 [1612], p. 109. This practice was followed in the obliteration of the Piankatanks (Strachey 1953 [1612], p. 44) and was cited as "the law of nations" by Opechancanough in 1619 (Kingsbury 1906–1935, 3:228). However, Strachey says plainly (1953 [1612], pp. 104–105) that the Chesapeakes were all exterminated, women and children too, so the "law" was not always obeyed.

128. White 1969 [1608?], p. 150; Smith 1986b [1612], p. 175 (copied in Smith 1986c [1624], p. 127); almost exactly copied by Strachey 1953 [1612], p. 60; Percy 1921–1922 [1612], p. 263.

129. White 1969 [1608?], pp. 147–149; Smith 1986b [1612], pp. 171–172 (copied in Smith 1986c [1624], pp. 124–125); Strachey 1953 [1612], pp. 89, 96, 98–99; Spelman 1910 [1613?], pp. cv–cvi; Banister 1970, pp. 380–381; Beverley 1947 [1705], pp. 207–210.

130. Strachey 1953 [1612], p. 104; his wording is: men warred "principally for revendge, so vindicatiue and ielous they be, to be made a dirision of, and to be insulted vpon by an enemy." I apply their "vindictiveness" to intratribal insults as well, based upon John Smith's general description of Indians as "soone moved to anger, and so malitious, that they seldome forget an injury" (1986b [1612], p. 160 [copied in Smith 1986c (1624), p. 115], copied by Strachey 1953 [1612], p. 75). Observers' accounts from other Woodland peoples indicate a similar pride and touchiness, though often any malice toward fellow tribesmen was released only in covert ways.

131. I have written briefly about this process elsewhere (see Rountree 1975).

132. They were closely similar, that is, as far as the archaeological record and the limited cultural data from the fringe areas show. They were not identical; the Patawomecks' afterlife beliefs differed from those in the James River valley, and the Eastern Shore people lacked the *huskanaw*.

133. Singer (1962, p. 423) writes of "ethnogenesis" as happening to a "portion" of a population that becomes distinct, but he also says (n. 12) that that is only one of "several kinds of 'group forming' processes." An example is the Hutterites in their early history in Europe. I would add that "ethnogenesis" can be applied to portions or wholes of several ethnic groups which coalesce into one new group, e.g., the Seminole Indians.

134. Strachey 1953 [1612], p. 37; also spelled Tsenacommacah (ibid., p. 56).

135. My evidence for this is not ideal: it consists of English writers' describing so much autonomy in Indian tribes' dealing with them that they (the writers) felt it necessary to specify on most occasions which segments of the paramount chiefdom they were talking about. The polity that was forming the new ethnic group was only moderately strong.

136. I saw this process at firsthand in 1983, during a six-week tour of Ivory Coast and

Tanzania sponsored by the U.S. Department of Education's Group Study Abroad Program. We met and interviewed many bureaucrats and were fortunate enough to have a session with President Julius Nyerere. The consensus among all those people was that a major part of nation building is the construction of a new, supratribal identity. I suggest here that the build-ing of a paramount chiefdom is similar. The process is often begun by ambitious politi-cians—for the Ivorians and Tanzanians, first by Europeans who colonized those areas and then by astute native politicians; so it was with many European polities through time. Ini-tially the supratribal group is a political entity, but if it lasts long enough and gives enough benefits to its constituents, its members become an *ethnic* as well as a political group. The length of time required is measured in decades, not merely years.

137. Since their "Indian" identity was specifically Virginia Algonquian Indian, I continue to use the ethnologists' collective term "Powhatan" for them after 1646.

138. I derived my "core-and-fringe" model from an early reading of Harte 1959 (which speaks of "core" and "marginal" families) and from my later extensive research on modern Indian genealogies, which show groups of intermarrying families comprising "fringes" (my own term).

139. Spicer 1971. A good long-term study demonstrating this process is Spicer 1980.

Chapter One. Before the English Came

1. For a good, though somewhat dated, summary of eastern North American prehistory, see Dragoo 1976. For a more recent summary of the Southeast, see Steponaitis 1986.

2. Strachey 1953 [1612], p. 40.

3. A recent synthesis by Turner (n.d.) shows that the nucleus of the chiefdom is repre-sented by two ceramic wares in Late Woodland times: the Townsend (York River basin and areas northeast and east) and the Gaston (upper James River basin and areas south and southwest). However, both wares, as well as the others of the Virginia coastal plain, go back several hundred years to a single, "circum-Chesapeake" Middle Woodland ware (the Mock-ley), which argues for *in situ* diversification rather than migrations.

4. Wroth 1970, pp. 82–83, 90. Paul Hoffman (in press) believes that Verrazzano missed both Chesapeake Bay and Delaware Bay and visited New York harbor instead.

5. Lewis and Loomie 1953, p. 13; see also Quinn 1974, p. 190.

6. Spanish sources do not agree on Don Luis' age or how he was picked up (Lewis and Loomie 1953, pp. 15–17); and they say nothing at all about his physical appearance.

7. Lewis and Loomie 1953, p. 16.

8. Ibid., p. 131.

9. Ibid., pp. 18, 24.

10. Major published sources on the mission are Lewis and Loomie 1953 and Gradie 1988.

11. Gradie n.d.

12. Lewis and Loomie 1953, pp. 36–42. There may also have been high mortality from disease, part of a pandemic that spread from Spanish contacts with Indians far to the south; see Dobyns 1983. The Spanish sources say nothing specific about disease in the Chesapeake region.

14. Lewis and Loomie 1953, p. 44.

15. Ibid., p. 44.

16. In his choice he may have been influenced by priests among his own people (Quinn 1985, p. 209), though a later Powhatan priest (Uttamatomakkin) showed great toleration for the alien religion until repeatedly badgered at first hand by English clergymen (Purchas 1617, p. 955). Quinn also suggests (ibid.) that the Powhatans knew from Indians to the south that Spanish missionaries were a prelude to Spanish military takeovers, and therefore mission-aries were a threat. That is entirely possible.

17. Lewis and Loomie, 1953, p. 45.

18. Ibid., p. 52.

19. Ibid., p. 54; Alonso was said to have forgotten much of his Spanish while among the Indians.

20. Ibid., pp. 67–68.

21. Nancy O. Lurie (1959) was the first scholar to treat this matter in any depth; more recent scholars assume it as a given, along with the concept of a sophisticated Indian culture.

22. In 1614; Hamor 1957 [1615], p. 13.

23. Ibid., p. 13.

24. Powhatan was variously said in 1608 to be about sixty (Smith 1986b [1612], p. 173 [copied in Smith 1986c (1624), p. 126]) or eighty (Strachey 1953 [1612], p. 57), though John Rolfe later heard that each of these years should be a half-year, given Powhatan reckoning (Purchas 1617, p. 957). Only if Powhatan was much less than sixty in 1607 and Don Luis a mature man in 1559–1561 could they be father and son.

25. Beverley 1947 [1705], p. 61.

26. C. Robinson 1905–1906, pp. 394, 395.

27. Bridenbaugh 1980, chap. 2, and 1981, chap. 1. I find several points in Bridenbaugh's writing about Opechancanough to be disturbingly ethnocentric; see below. He is also careless in portraying Opechancanough as being of near-gigantic stature, when no English writer describes him at all, and the engraving on the Smith map (Smith n.d.)—although Smith consulted with the engraver—is somewhat polemical in showing a conflict scene (so that a giant Indian seems more threatening).

28. Lewis and Loomie 1953, pp. 60–61.

29. Kingsbury 1906–1935, 3:584. The Big Dipper is part of the constellation called *Ursa Major*, the Great Bear, by Europeans.

30. Bridenbaugh, 1981, pp. 34–35.

31. The latter syllables are uncertain in meaning, but *mangoi* is the Powhatan word for "great" or "large" (Strachey 1953 [1612], pp. 175, 188, 192.

32. Kingsbury, 1906–1935, 3:552; Anonymous 1900–1901, p. 210.

33. See chap. 4 of this volume.

34. Smith 1986c [1624], p. 308. Bridenbaugh (1980, p. 31, and 1981, p. 42) reads Opechancanough's boast in the same way.

35. Quinn 1974, p. 255, and 1985, p. 42.

36. Lewis and Loomie 1953, p. 56.

37. Quinn 1955, p. 246.

38. Ibid., pp. 244–246.

39. Ibid., pp. 257–258.

40. Hulton, 1984, p. 86.

41. Quinn 1955, pp. 106, 110.

42. Smith n.d. [1608].

43. Quinn 1955, pp. 247.

44. Ibid., p. 854. Old Point Comfort was an island until well into the colonial period; together with Buckroe Beach and Grand View it forms a modified barrier-island-salt-ponds complex.

45. Archer 1969a [1607], p. 85.

46. Quinn 1955, p. 494, and 1985, pp. 248ff.

47. Quinn 1984, 1974, chap. 17, and 1985, pp. 345ff.; and personal communications 1983. See also Kupperman 1984, pp. 137–140; however, Kupperman errs in saying (p. 138) that Strachey wrote that colonists refugeed to the Chesapeake area (see below).

48. Quinn 1985, pp. 345–353.

49. Personal communications, 1983; Quinn 1985, pp. 362ff.

50. Strachey 1953 [1612], p. 91.

51. Ibid., p. 34; brackets mine.

52. Purchas 1904–1906 [1625], 19:228.

53. Other scholars besides myself have found them so: Fausz (1985, p. 241) writing of Strachey's accusation and Jennings (1975, pp. 78–82) writing of "Virginia's Verger."

54. Barbour 1969, p. 265; brackets mine.

55. See Wax and Thomas 1961 (even though I admit that it is risky to assume that twentieth-century traditional Indian etiquette is closely similar to that of sixteenth-century Indians). The "good manners" described by Wax and Thomas are so widespread over North America that one may argue for a great time depth.

56. Analogy with the Powhatan practice; data about Chesapeake culture are almost nonexistent.

57. Inference from what is known of Powhatan propensity to adopt and resocialize foreign captives.

58. Percy 1969a [1608?], p. 140. Mosco, John Smith's guide in 1608 (see chap. 2) was a grown man, not even a youth, in 1608; Smith took him for a Frenchman's son, but he may rather have been half Spanish, a product of contacts with Spanish visitors in the 1580s.

59. Quinn (1985, p. 375) also finds this puzzling.

60. Smith 1986a [1608], p. 49.

61. Quinn 1955, pp. 258–259.

62. Smith 1986a [1608], p. 63.

63. Strachey 1953 [1612], p. 34. Strachey's spelling of the first two towns' names is "Peccarecanick" and "Ochanahoen."

64. Smith 1986b [1612], p. 244, 265–266 (almost exactly copied in Smith 1986c [1624], pp. 193, 215).

65. Canner 1904–1906 [1603]; the account is not precise as to geography; Quinn 1985, pp. 355–356.

66. The place, described as "exceeding pleasant and full of goodly Trees, and with some shew of the entrance of a River," could have been either the mouth of Lynnhaven River or, more likely, the mouth of one of the creeks on the lower Eastern Shore. The former is in the Dune Forest zone, while the latter is Pine Barrens with Mixed Forest close behind.

67. Smith 1986a [1608], p. 51.

68. Wingfield 1969 [1608], p. 227.

69. Quinn 1974, pp. 428–429. See also Quinn 1970 for data on Mace's voyage, without mention of a landing in Powhatan territory.

70. Quinn 1974, chap. 16; Quinn 1979, 5:166.

71. Smith 1986 [1608], p. 51.

72. Knowles 1940, p. 219.

73. Smith 1986b [1612], p. 229 (copied almost exactly in Smith 1986c [1624], p. 169).

74. B. Hoffman 1964, pp. 195–206; Brasser 1971, p. 68; Dobyns 1983, essays 1, 2, 6, 7.

75. Ashburn 1947; A. Crosby 1972, chap. 2; Dobyns 1983; Jennings 1975, chap. 2; Ramenofsky 1982. However, evidence from the southeastern U.S. (excluding Florida) is ambiguous before the 1670s; see M. Smith 1987.

76. Hariot 1972 [1590], p. 28.

77. Smith 1986b [1612], p. 247 (almost exactly copied in Smith 1986c [1624], p. 196); brackets mine. E. Randolph Turner (personal communication, 1984) feels that the statement merely reflects Powhatan's being an old man who had outlived his contemporaries, and he points out that though Virginia archaeology is in its infancy, no mass burials like those necessary in an epidemic have been found on the Virginia coastal plain.

78. Smith 1986b [1612], p. 225 (copied almost exactly in Smith 1986c [1624], p. 163).

79. Multiple burials in graves are unusual in eastern Virginia, so far. An ossuary, or collection of human bones gathered up after exposure of the bodies, is obviously not proof of an epidemic in any case. Ossuary burials are normally bundles of unarticulated bones, often with the smaller bones (of fingers and toes) missing. In a mass grave in an epidemic, all the bodies are buried immediately after death (i.e., all are complete, articulated skeletons).

80. E.g., the social disruption caused by the first major outbreak of bubonic plague in Europe: see Gottfried 1983, chap. 5 (especially pp. 97–103), and Deaux 1969, chap. 7.

81. Turner (1985, p. 212) believes that if such a depopulation had happened and resulted in such a political development, the English would have recorded it. Yet the English colonists were not attuned to looking for social causes of historical events, in their own or in other societies; most scholars of that time did not do so, either. They looked instead for prominent persons as the causes.

82. No English document mentions his parents, even indirectly. Only the list of his heirs shows his position to have been passed on matrilineally. Fausz (1977, p. 65) suggests that a "marriage alliance" between Powhatan's two parents united the two river valleys for him to inherit, an interesting idea that is impossible to prove.

83. Smith 1986b [1612], p. 173 (copied in Smith 1986c [1624], p. 126); Strachey 1953 [1612], p. 57.

84. Strachey 1953 [1612], p. 57; copied in part from Smith 1986b [1612], p. 173 (copied in Smith 1986c [1624], p. 126).

85. For a listing of Algonquian-speaking ethnic groups of the Virginia coastal plain, see Rountree 1989, pp. 9, 11–12.

86. Strachey 1953 [1612], p. 68.

87. Ibid., pp. 104–105.

88. Smith 1986a [1608], p. 79; brackets Barbour's.

89. The 1612 account was written by others and approved by Smith; the 1624 account was the 1612 one, copied and added to by Smith. Smith was ultimately responsible for both versions.

90. Strachey 1953 [1612], p. 108. He does not name a ruler for that group in his list of *weroances* (pp. 63–69), yet he and Smith both call the new inhabitants "Chesapeake" in a presumably current list of tribes and manpower (Smith 1986b [1612], pp. 146–148 (almost exactly copied in Smith 1986c [1624], pp. 103–105, 107); Strachey 1953 [1612], pp. 43–46.

91. Smith 1986b [1612], p. 175 (copied in Smith 1986c [1624], p. 128); Strachey 1953 [1612], p. 44. Strachey copies Smith here without comment ("the cause was to vs vnknowne"), but there are cases of inconsistency in his work and this may be another.

92. If, by chance, there were full-blooded English people left, then Powhatan stood to lose, no matter what he did. If they survived and made contact with the Jamestown English, the English-Chesapeake alliance would be a certainty. If Powhatan killed them, he had to prevent the Jamestown people from finding out about it so that he could make them allies. But there seems to have been no cover-up, as shown already. So it seems likely that no dilemma existed for Powhatan because no full-blooded English refugees survived among the Chesapeakes.

93. Smith 1986a [1608], p. 27.

Chapter Two. Watching a Struggling Colony

1. For a non-heroic view of the colony (he calls its early years a "fiasco"), see Morgan 1975, chap. 3. Jennings (1975, p. 33) describes the poor or nonexistent support of colonists abroad in that period as "what we like to call an oriental disregard for human life. Adventurers abroad paid their own way or were abandoned."

2. Obviously, American Indians were neither, but the English never really saw beyond the stereotypes, which they applied alternately and with disastrous results for the Indians. For a full discussion, see Sheehan 1980; for an anthropologist's view of Puritans doing the same, see Simmons 1981. For an alternate view of English appreciating some "human" qualities among the Indians of the Atlantic coast until 1622, see Kupperman 1980; I feel that those English she refers to were few in number but very visible, for they included major writers like Smith and Strachey.

3. I pass over the fact that the clean-shaven, lightly clad Powhatans bathed daily and the

bearded, woolen-wrapped English hardly at all. One could speculate that Englishmen's body odor served the Powhatans as an early-warning system when the wind was right!

4. Smith 1986a [1608], p. 27. The men on the ship who "seconded" their landing party by "making a shot" at attackers must have been using muskets, at least, in order to fire safely over the landing party's heads.

5. Percy 1969a [1608?], pp. 134; the explorations of April 26 and 27 appear to have been in the vicinity of Seashore State Park; that of April 28 was west of Lynnhaven Bay.

6. Ibid., pp. 135–136. The Indians there showed only initial wariness; apparently they realized at once that the strangers were not Spaniards.

7. Their dealings with the Powhatans from the beginning indicate such a list, which could have come from Thomas Hariot, a man known to have helped an expedition of 1602 in this way (Quinn 1974, pp. 410–412). The other source would be the Algonquian-speaking Indians who were in England in 1603 (see chap. 1).

8. Percy 1969a [1608?], p. 136.

9. Strachey 1953 [1612], p. 66.

10. His presence there misled the English into calling that territory "Tappahanna" (Strachey 1953 [1612], p. 64), and the place-name remained attached to a nearby marsh for the next two hundred years.

11. Percy, our source for the incident, wrote that "he seemed to take displeasure of our being with the Paspihes"; that "displeasure" may instead have been an emphatic reminding of the Paspahegh of the "injury" done the Rappahannock.

12. Percy 1969a [1608?], p. 137.

13. Ibid., pp. 137–138.

14. Ibid., p. 138.

15. Lippson 1973, p. 7.

16. Percy (1969a [1608?], p. 141) put words to that effect into the mouth of the *weroance* of Powhatan town.

17. The age in which they lived had no ethnographic fieldworkers. Those of us who are fieldworkers become acutely aware of how we may appear to the locals and sensitive to what we hear they are saying about us. We also know that if those impressions are too negative, we will suffer for it sooner or later. Any newcomers to a society encounter the same thing, be they anthropologists or immigrants.

18. Percy 1969a [1608?], p. 142; Smith 1986a [1608], p. 33.

19. Percy 1969a [1608], p. 138.

20. Ibid., p. 139.

21. Newport and his crew left behind 105 colonists that summer (Smith 1986b [1612], p. 209 [100 in Smith 1986c (1624), p. 142]); Percy, who does not name names, says 104 (1969a [1608?], p. 143). The Paspahegh chiefdom had about 40 warriors.

22. Percy 1969a [1608?], pp. 139–40. It was probably a satellite town, to be reachable on foot. Smith's map (n.d. [1608]) shows the Paspahegh capital town across the Chickahominy River's mouth.

23. Percy 1969a [1608?], p. 140.

24. Archer 1969a [1607], pp. 82–95; Percy 1969a [1608?], pp. 140–141; Smith 1969a [1608], pp. 29–33.

25. The cross, with its inscription "Jacobus Rex 1607," and the cheer the English gave as it was raised were explained as two crosspieces representing Christopher Newport and Powhatan, a junction symbolizing their alliance, and a shout of "reverence [that] he [Newport] dyd to Pawatah" (Archer 1969a [1607], p. 88; brackets mine).

26. The Arrohateck *weroance* "stopt his eares, and exprest much feare, so likewise all about him; some of his people being in our boate leapt over boorde at the wonder hereof . . ." (Archer 1969a [1607], p. 91).

27. The Pamunkey "king" of May 1607 "set his Countenance stryving to be stately, as to our seeming he became foole." I disagree with Bridenbaugh (1980, p. 20, and 1981, p. 17)

who says it was Opechancanough playing the clown. A meeting like that one was a time to be genuinely impressive if possible; later documents indicate, by never saying anything to the contrary (even after 1622), that Opechancanough was fully capable of appearing formidable. Of the two remaining brothers, Opitchapam was lame, a trait that Archer would have remarked upon if he had seen it. That leaves Kekataugh.

28. Archer 1969a [1607], pp. 97–98.

29. Ibid., pp. 95–98.

30. Smith 1986a [1608], p. 33.

31. Earle (1979, pp. 97–103) believes that the death toll in that first summer was primarily due to typhoid and amoebic dysentery, picked up from drinking the stagnant, brackish James River water at that season, while salt poisoning caused a great deal of the apathy and factionalism among the colonists. At Jamestown Island, tidal salt water meets currents of fresh water with about equal force in the summer and also during dry, cold winters. The result was that human wastes from the English fort drained slowly from that section of the river. Earle feels that the colonists did not in fact face starvation since they were still able to go fishing for sturgeon, a big fish that would have supplied them with plenty of protein and vitamins. However, I would point out that the colonists' accounts indicate that they were too weak to do much fishing.

32. The first year of a colonist's exposure to Virginia's "bugs" came to be known as the "seasoning," during which a person either survived or (frequently) perished; see Rutman and Rutman 1976. However, Earle (1979, p. 113) argues against the maladies that made up the "seasoning" (malaria, bacillary dysentery, and paratyphoid) being a major cause of high mortality in the Virginia colony and suggests typhoid, amoebic dysentery, and salt poisoning instead (p. 110).

33. That is my guess; no English writer attempts to account for the sniping in terms other than the hostility that "civilized" people can expect from ignoble "savages" (see Sheehan 1980, chap. 3).

34. Wingfield 1969 [1608], pp. 214–215.

35. Ibid., p. 215; Smith 1986b [1612], p. 213.

36. Wingfield 1969 [1608], p. 215.

37. It is likely that the Rappahannock *weroance* had gone home. The identity of this *weroance* of Quiyoughcohannock is uncertain. Pepiscunimah was deposed for wife-stealing sometime before 1610 (Strachey 1953 [1612], pp. 64–65) and he had good reason to favor the English while opposing Powhatan. In 1607, however, he may still have ruled the Quiyoughcohannock and been loyal to Powhatan.

38. Wingfield 1969 [1608], pp. 215–216; Percy (1969a [1608?], p. 143) places the date as July 27.

39. Wingfield 1969 [1608], p. 216.

40. Date inferred from Smith's juxtaposition of Indians bringing corn "ere it was halfe ripe, to refresh vs" with "about the tenth of September there was about 46. of our men dead" (1986a [1608], p. 35); also Wingfield's placing the September seventh return of a boy (William White) before the "relief" by the Indians in his text (1969 [1608], pp. 216, 218). A first harvest in September means that a significant part of the Indians' crops had failed; see the Prologue. If the English had asked for or been offered help in the form of (low-prestige) wild plant foods, their hunger would have been alleviated long before September.

41. Percy 1969a [1608?], p. 145; Smith 1986a [1608], p. 35.

42. For evaluations of Smith's career and character, see Barbour 1964, Vaughan 1975, Glenn 1944, Randel 1939, Raup 1953, Rozwenc 1959, Goodman 1981, and Rountree MS. D.

43. Fausz 1985, p. 239. Fausz has elsewhere called him a "contact specialist" (1977, p. 251).

44. Smith 1986b [1612], p. 211 (exact wording except "famished" for "starved" in Smith 1986c [1624], p. 144). In the 1624 account he has the English—six or seven of them—at-

tacking the Kecoughtans with muskets and the latter fleeing and then attacking with their god's image in the forefront, only to be repulsed by more gunfire.

45. Smith 1986a [1608], pp. 35–37.

46. Ibid., pp. 37–39.

47. It was encounters of this kind that made Gabriel Archer write of the Powhatans that they were brazen thieves in dealing with foreigners.

48. Smith 1986a [1608], pp. 39–41.

49. Ibid., pp. 41–45.

50. Wingfield 1969 [1608], p. 226.

51. Smith 1986a [1608], p. 91.

52. Smith's calling the town Orapax in his account of 1624 (1986c [1624], p. 147) is probably inaccurate.

53. It is true, on the other hand, that Smith's 1608 account was edited, without his knowledge, and published. Some threatening or violent episodes may have been deleted.

54. Smith 1986a [1608], pp. 49–51; Smith 1986b [1612], p. 213 (slightly elaborated in Smith 1986c [1624], p. 147, where he describes awing the Indians with his "round Ivory double compass Dyall").

55. Smith 1986a [1608], p. 59; brackets mine.

56. Fausz (1977, p. 237) says that the ritual was "to purify him for having shed Pamunkey blood." Aside from the fact that the tribal identity of Smith's victim is unknown, Smith himself wrote plainly that the ritual was for divination. No purification ritual after shedding blood was ever recorded or even hinted at in any English account of the Powhatans.

57. Smith 1986b [1612], p. 213; written by Thomas Studley and approved by Smith.

58. Smith 1986a [1608], pp. 49–53. In his 1624 account (1986c [1624], pp. 149–150), Smith places the divination after this tour instead of before it.

59. Behind Lee Marsh, inside a bend of Pamunkey River in King William Co. (Rountree MS. A, place-name section).

60. Smith said Opitchapam in 1624 (1986c [1624], p. 150).

61. Located on Purtan Bay in Gloucester County (Rountree MS. A, place-name section, and McCary 1981.

62. Smith 1986a [1608], pp. 53–57; Smith 1986b [1612], p. 213 (elaborated in Smith 1986c [1624], pp. 150–151).

63. That was the opinion of an anonymous early-seventeenth-century annotator of Smith's 1608 work (Smith 1986a [1608], p. 59n).

64. Between Timberneck and Cedarbush creeks in Gloucester County. (Rountree MS. A, place-name section); a farm there still bears the name.

65. Smith 1986a [1608], p. 57.

66. Smith 1986c [1624], p. 151.

67. Barbour 1964; Mossiker 1976; Fausz 1977, p. 236.

68. E.g., Vaughan (1975, p. 37) purposely leaves the matter hanging: "The truth lies buried with the captain of his Indian captors."

69. Rozwenc 1959, p. 30.

70. Some scholars point out that the 1608 and the 1612 accounts both may have had the violence edited out, since the colony was then recruiting people to come and settle. But the same and more could be said in 1624: the Virginia colony was trying to get people to come and settle *and expel the Indians*.

71. For example, in the case of the young women's warlike dance at Werowocomoco in 1608, Smith's 1612 account says that the Indian onlookers in general calmed the fears of the English (1986b [1612], pp. 235–236), while in 1624 Smith adds that Pocahontas dramatically "will[ed] him to kill her if any hurt were intended" (1986c [1624], pp. 182–183). I would suggest that introducing her into the story was not necessary to convince a 1612 audience that the dance was purely entertainment.

72. Purchas 1904–1906 [1625], 18:471–472.

73. Kingsbury 1906–1935, 3:556.

74. Smith 1986a [1608], p. 65.

75. The letter he quoted in 1624 was probably written while he composed the *Generall Historie*. In 1617 Pocahontas had friends in London in very high places, and any recommendation from the adventurer John Smith would have been unnecessary; see chap. 3.

76. Smith 1986c [1624], p. 151.

77. Barbour (1964, p. 438) suggests it for the "rescue" alone; Fausz (1977, p. 236) says it was "almost assuredly" so for the "rescue" and the sequel both.

78. See Rountree 1989, p. 122.

79. Date of Smith's arrival: Smith 1986a [1608], p. 61; date of Newport's arrival: Perkins 1969 [1608], p. 159. A companion ship, under Captain Nelson, was blown off course and damaged so that it did not reach Virginia until April 20.

80. In 1624 Smith wrote (1986c [1624], p. 152) that Pocahontas personally sent him food every four or five days. In 1612, however, his followers wrote (with his approval; Smith 1986b [1612], p. 215) that "the Salvages" brought presents to him "every other day"; and in 1608 Smith wrote (1986a [1608], p. 61) that "The Empereur Powhatan each weeke once or twice sent" him food, while Francis Perkins wrote that spring (1969 [1608], p. 160) that the Indians were willing to trade and Powhatan had sent people to teach the English "how to plant the native wheat, and to make some gear such as they use to go fishing. . . ." Pocahontas does not even appear in contemporary accounts until later that spring.

81. Smith 1986a [1608], p. 61.

82. Ibid., pp. 63–79; Smith 1986b [1612], pp. 215–217 (elaborated in Smith 1986c [1624], pp. 154–157; e.g., crossing Indian bridge [similar to 1608 account]).

83. John Smith's followers, who wrote the account, do not say it specifically on this occasion; they wrote only of inconvenience.

84. The Indian town of Werowocomoco probably covered both points between the three creeks (hence the bridge, for constant coming and going), but the exact location of the paramount chief's house is unknown.

85. Smith described it as "hung round with bowes and arrowes" (1986a [1608], p. 67).

86. According to the 1608 version; Smith's 1612 version says the boys were exchanged on the spot.

87. Smith remarked in 1624 (1986c [1624], p. 156) that it would have been cheaper to buy corn from the Spanish.

88. In 1624 Smith added (1986c [1624], p. 156) that he told Powhatan that blue beads were made of rare material and therefore worn only by royalty in Europe.

89. Smith 1986b [1612], p. 217 (copied in Smith 1986c [1624], p. 156).

90. They were traditional enemies of the Algonquians of the coastal plain; see Rountree 1989, p. 120.

91. Smith 1986a [1608], p. 79; actual date calculated by me.

92. Ibid., pp. 79–81. The purpose was apparently exploration only; there is no mention of seeking information on the Lost Colonists or of visiting the Elizabeth River on the same trip.

93. If the Chesapeake group had been exterminated before April 1607 and if the attackers at Cape Henry were Nansemonds as Smith suspected (ibid., p. 79), then Christopher Newport would have had good reason to suspect a trap. Smith's later works do not mention a trip to Nansemond River at all.

94. Ibid.

95. Zuniga 1969 [1608].

96. Ibid., footnote.

97. Smith 1986a [1608], pp. 81–95.

98. Englishmen were extremely slow to learn the dangers of walking outside the fort; Smith wrote that "no punishment will prevent [it] but hanging" (ibid., p. 89).

99. In late spring corn was a commodity that only the richest Indians could have (see the Prologue). It is doubtful that the English realized the value of this gift.

100. English witnesses vary: she was ten years old in spring 1608 (Smith 1986a [1608], p. 93), less than thirteen or fourteen in spring 1609 (Smith 1986b [1612], p. 274), eleven, twelve or less in 1609 and pubescent in 1610 (Strachey 1953 [1612], p. 72); and twenty-one in spring 1617 (caption on portrait engraving made that spring, illustrated in Barbour 1969).

101. Times of Pocahontas's visits to the fort: May 1608 as first and only time mentioned (Smith 1986a [1608], pp. 93–95); first visit to fort in May 1608, after which she came "very oft" to the fort (Smith 1986b [1612], p. 274); "sometimes resorting to our Fort" (Strachey 1953 [1612], p. 72); several encounters with Pocahontas mentioned in retrospect (Smith 1986c [1624]): January 1608 at Werowocomoco (p. 151), bringing food to Jamestown in January–February 1608 (p. 152), May 1608 at Jamestown (p. 160), and visits to Jamestown having ceased (p. 243).

102. Strachey 1953 [1612], p. 72. This is the only detailed description we have of her activities in the fort; we have only indirect evidence that she cast admiring glances at John Smith (see below).

103. Ibid., p. 113.

104. Inference from Smith's followers writing in 1612 (Smith 1986b [1612], p. 274) "... her especially he ever much respected: and she so well requited it, that when her father intended to haue surprized him [probably in the mutual ambush of January 1609], shee by stealth in the darke night came through the wild woods and told him of it."

105. Smith 1986a [1608], p. 93; brackets mine. The actual writers of the passage are followers of Smith's.

106. The same followers wrote (Smith 1986b [1612], p. 274; brackets mine) that "it [was never] suspected hee had ever such a thought [of gaining power by marrying her], or more regarded her, or any of them, then in honest reason, and discreation he might." Smith himself recorded sentences in the Powhatan language, one of which reads, "Bid Pokahontas bring hither two little Baskets, and I wil give her white beads to make her a chaine" (ibid., p. 139 [copied in Smith 1986c (1624), p. 132]); the tone is of an adult dealing with a child.

107. Smith considered him ugly but "of a subtill wit, and crafty understanding" (1986a [1608], p. 93).

108. A later account (Smith 1986b [1612], p. 220) adds that he had the prisoners "corrected" first and also hunted other Indians "vp and downe the Ile" to terrify them; this is probably not true.

109. Ibid., pp. 224–229; embellished in Smith 1986c [1624], pp. 162–169.

110. Smith 1986b [1612], p. 227; the ore proved merely to have valueless silvery glitter in it. This was the antimony that was widely traded for use in body paint.

111. Mosco, whose heavy black beard led Smith to deem him "some French mans sonne" (Smith 1986c [1624], p. 173), appears only in the *Generall Historie*.

112. Smith 1986b [1612], p. 227 (paraphrased in Smith 1986c [1624], p. 167).

113. Timing: Smith 1986c [1624], p. 167.

114. Slater 1984, p. 34.

115. Smith 1986b [1612], pp. 230–233; embellished in Smith 1986c [1624], pp. 170–180.

116. Massawomeck canoes being made of birchbark: Smith 1986b [1612], p. 166; copied in Smith 1986c [1624], p. 119.

117. "... anthropometric reconstruction of a few skeletal remains computes to an average male height of 5 feet 3.7 inches" (Jennings 1978, p. 363; see references he gives).

118. Smith 1986b [1612], p. 232 (almost exactly copied in Smith, 1986c [1624], p. 172); possession of metal tools may explain some of the fear in which the late protohistoric Powhatans held the Massawomecks.

119. Details of English dealings with Mannahoacs all come from Smith's 1624 account.

120. This part of the voyage appears only in his 1624 account.

121. Smith 1986b [1612], p. 234 (almost exactly copied in Smith 1986c [1624], p. 181).

122. Smith 1986b [1612]. p. 239 (copied in Smith 1986c [1624], p. 186); the speakers were Chickahominies, who in their hostility to the English may have exaggerated.

123. Smith 1986b [1612], pp. 235–237 (closely paraphrased in Smith 1986c [1624], pp. 182–184).

124. Implied in the way Powhatan greeted guests, seated on a "bed," while his wives and councillors sat on the floor; see Rountree 1989, p. 106 and fig. 24.

125. Anonymous 1947 [1610], p. 6.

126. Smith 1986b [1612], p. 237 (copied in Smith 1986c [1624], p. 184). The mantle may be the same as the embroidered deerhide artifact in the Ashmolean Museum (Feest 1983; see also Rountree 1989, pp. 105–106), although that piece is not documented before 1638.

127. Smith 1986b [1612], p. 238 (copied in Smith 1986c [1624], p. 184, with names of two Monacan towns visited, namely, Massinacak and Mowhemenchouch, added).

128. Strachey 1953 [1612], p. 106.

129. Smith 1986b [1612], pp. 239, 240, 242 (see also Smith 1986c [1624], pp. 186 [exact copy], 187 [almost exact copy], 191–192 [elaborated]). The fall communal hunt was on at the time, but the completeness of the desertion indicates avoidance of the English.

130. Smith 1986b [1612], p. 239–240 (copied in Smith 1986c [1624], pp. 186–187).

131. Smith 1986b [1612], p. 129 (copied in Smith 1986c [1624], p. 186).

132. Smith 1986b [1612], p. 242 (copied in Smith 1986c [1624], p. 192).

133. For European notions of their "rights" vis-à-vis natives, based upon "natural law," see Washburn 1971, pt. 1 (for "right to trade," see p. 11).

134. Smith was taken to view it on his second day at Werowocomoco (1986b [1612], p. 246 [copied in Smith 1986c (1624), p. 195]); the house was not then finished, nor was it ever finished, because Powhatan abandoned Werowocomoco a few days later.

135. Smith 1986b [1612], pp. 244–245 (copied in Smith 1986c [1624], p. 193).

136. Smith 1986b [1612], p. 245 (embellished in Smith 1986c [1624], p. 194); the source for the rest of the expedition's history comes from pp. 245–256 (and 1986c, pp. 194–206).

137. The Indians would not have had to withdraw very far to be "out of reach" of Englishmen who still did not know the terrain well. Planting fields away from the rivers, on "the ridge," would have been enough; it almost was in 1623.

138. In his 1624 account (1986c [1624], pp. 198–199), Smith wrote that Pocahontas warned him "with the teares runninge downe her cheekes" that if they disarmed during the meal they would be ambushed again. That statement is corroborated in Smith 1986b [1612], p. 274; her warning seems to have been the only time at which she did in fact act as a "savior" to the colony, and ironically, at that point in time, no warning was needed.

139. Strachey 1953 [1612], p. 57.

140. Smith 1986b [1612], p. 252 (copied almost exactly in Smith, 1986c [1624], p. 202).

141. This incident, plus a fear of losing his inheritance, would have been enough to make Opechancanough an inveterate enemy of the English nation for ever after. Bridenbaugh (1980, pp. 20, 28, and 1981, p. 19) believes likewise. For detailed cultural background, see Rountree 1989, chap. 4, on manly pride and vengefulness and chap. 6 on royal dignity.

142. Smith 1986b [1612], p. 253 (copied almost exactly in Smith, 1986c [1624], pp. 202–203).

143. The identity of the poison is not known; it merely made the English sick (Smith 1986b [1612], p. 255 [copied in Smith 1986c (1624), p. 205]).

144. Smith 1986b [1612], p. 256 (copied in Smith 1986c [1624], p. 205).

145. Smith 1986b [1612], p. 256 (copied in Smith 1986c [1624], p. 206; brackets mine.

146. Smith 1986b [1612], p. 260; later (1986c [1624], p. 209) Smith omitted mention of help from the Poles.

147. Smith 1986b [1612], p. 261 (copied in Smith 1986c [1624], p. 210).

148. Smith 1986b [1612], p. 262 (copied almost exactly in Smith 1986c [1624], p. 211).

149. These habitations were houses dispersed among fields; firing one could fire the other.

150. Kingsbury 1906–1935, 4:37.

151. Smith 1986b [1612], p. 265 (elaborated in Smith 1986c [1624], p. 214: Smith adds that the knowledge gave the English power enough over the Indians that the latter dared not steal anything further from the former).

152. The *weroance* who was the friend is never specified in Smith's accounts; it was probably Pepiscunimah (also called Pipsco), by then a lesser *weroance* with a grudge against Powhatan. For his background, see Rountree 1989, chap. 6.

153. Smith 1986b [1612], p. 266 (copied in Smith 1986c [1624], p. 215).

154. Smith 1986b [1612], pp. 267, 268 (paraphrased in Smith 1986c [1624], pp. 216–217, 218).

155. Smith 1986b [1612], pp. 268–269 (paraphrased in Smith 1986c [1624], p. 219); the captains were Ratliffe (Sicklemore), Martin and Archer.

156. Earle (1979, pp. 107–108 sees Smith's move as a canny recognition that he could lessen the summer death toll by moving his people out of the middle (and more polluted) reaches of the James River. That may have been one motive, but his choice of upriver and downriver settlement sites—namely, the two places where the English could expect the maximum opposition from the Indians (see the text)—indicates to me that politico-military motives were uppermost in Smith's mind.

157. Percy 1921–1922 [post-1612], pp. 262–265; Smith 1986b [1612], pp. 269–270 (copied almost exactly in Smith 1986c [1624], p. 221).

158. Percy 1921–1922 [post-1612], pp. 263–265; Smith 1986b [1612], pp. 270–272 (copied almost exactly in Smith 1986c [1624], pp. 221–222); Spelman 1910 [1613?], p. cii.

159. Spelman was not consulted, according to his own account. He soon went to visit his fellow settlers and in returning missed connections with Parahunt, who probably thought the English had taken the boy back.

160. Strachey's wording (1953 [1612], p. 72) implies that he saw her there, after his arrival in Virginia in May 1610; Smith, on the other hand, claimed later that she had ceased visiting the fort after he left Virginia (1986c [1624], p. 243).

161. Strachey 1953 [1612], p. 62; for what this marriage tells us about Pocahontas's real status among her people, see Rountree 1989, pp. 112–113.

162. Smith 1986b [1612], p. 275: "neere halfe their men" out of 120 at the falls and nearly that at Nansemond.

163. Percy 1921–1922 [post-1612], pp. 265–266; Anonymous 1947 [1610], p. 17; Spelman 1910 [1613?], p. ciii.

164. Percy 1921–1922 [post-1612], p. 264; Smith 1986b [1612], p. 275.

165. Smith 1986c [1624], p. 248.

166. Spelman 1910 [1613?], p. ciii. He lived with Iopassus until Samuel Argall found and retrieved him in September 1610. John Smith wrote in 1624 (1986c [1624], p. 232) that Pocahontas saved his life in helping him escape, but Spelman's own account mentions no one's help except Iopassus's.

167. Percy 1921–1922 [post-1612], p. 266.

168. Smith's followers in the colony do not sound particularly judgmental (Smith 1986b [1612], p. 275). In English culture at that time, much more selfish behavior was tolerated from the nobility (West was a baron's brother) than from the lower orders (Stone 1965, pp. 31–32). Percy adds in extenuation that West's crew pressured him into the act (1921–1922 [post-1612], p. 266).

169. Exceptions were the men at Fort Algernon, who survived handsomely on hoarded food (Percy 1921–1922 [post-1612], p. 268).

170. Ibid., p. 267; the dead were exhumed, and one man murdered and ate part of his wife, for which he was executed. Earle (1979, p. 110) notes that dry, very cold winters, of which the winter of 1609–1610 was one, can reduce precipitation and therefore freshwater flushing of rivers, and the "salt plug" that came inland and collected pollution in late summer

at Jamestown Island could have returned upriver in the winter. That hypothesis accords with the high death rate on the island that winter.

171. Ibid., pp. 108−109. The commonly cited number of five hundred English before the winter set in is probably exaggerated.

172. Barbour 1969, pp. 262−268; also printed in Kingsbury 1906−1935, 3:14−21.

173. Percy 1921−1922 [post-1612], p. 269; the date was June 7, 1610.

174. One was Humphrey Blunt, ambushed while retrieving a longboat near Nansemond River (Strachey 1964 [1610], p. 88).

175. From this incident the city of Hampton traces its history as the oldest continuous English-speaking settlement in North America.

176. Strachey 1964 [1610], pp. 91−92.

177. Percy 1921−1922 [post-1612], p. 271.

178. Strachey 1964 [1610], p. 92.

179. Percy 1921−1922 [post-1612], p. 271.

180. Thomas West, third Lord de la Warr and son of Anne Knollys West (Burke 1967, p. 711), making him a first cousin, twice removed, of Queen Elizabeth I.

181. This was Kemps, made a prisoner in spring 1608, who liked his kind treatment by the English and remained with them, for the most part, until he died of scurvy at Jamestown in 1611 (Rountree MS. A, personal name section).

182. Percy 1921−1922 [post-1612], p. 271.

183. Smith 1986c [1624], p. 236.

184. Percy 1921−1922 [post-1612], pp. 271−272. Fausz (1977, p. 275) points out, I think correctly, that the greater cruelty shown to Indians here was due to English frustration after the "starving time," combined with Lord de la Warr's greater discipline. The result was more aggressiveness which focused on Indians.

185. It was overgrown when Sir Thomas Dale visited it on May 21, 1611 (Dale 1964 [1611], p. 493).

186. Strachey, 1953 [1612], pp. 66−67.

187. Only two sources talk of even intermittent "war" in this period: Hamor (1957 [1615], p. 2) and John Clark (reported in de Molina et al. 1964 [1611], p. 520).

188. The term is Fausz's (1977, p. 267), although he places the war's beginning in 1609, when Indians sniped at the English during their "starving time." My emphasis on diplomatic relations leads me to place it in 1610. I disagree with Fausz, however, when he calls this war a "holy war" (ibid., pp. 272−273) because the English desecrated the Nansemonds' temple in 1609. There is no evidence (that survives) to indicate that the victims then fought back for religious reasons.

Chapter Three. Powhatan's Last, Ineffectual Years

1. Jennings 1975, p. 131.

2. Strachey 1953 [1612], p. 58.

3. The English considered these groups "friendly," but the groups did not in fact go out of their way to help the English or adopt many English cultural practices in this period.

4. Strachey 1953 [1612], p. 106. This is the only English reference to an alliance between the Monacans and the Powhatans. The duration of the formal alliance is unknown, but the Monacans remained friendly with the Powhatans long after the Powhatan paramount chiefdom crumbled.

5. Spelman 1910 [1613?], p. civ; Smith 1986c [1624], p. 236.

6. This instance of Powhatan priests' conjurations was described by Alexander Whitaker (in Brown 1964 [1890], p. 498); it is discussed in its cultural context in Rountree 1989, p. 133.

7. Strachey 1953 [1612], p. 64; Percy 1921−1922 [1612], pp. 273−274. The lone survivor was the same "taborer" who had enticed the Kecoughtan Indians from their town earlier.

8. Strachey 1953 [1612], pp. 66–67; Percy 1921–1922 [1612], pp. 274–275.

9. Percy 1921–1922 [1612], pp. 275–276.

10. Smith 1986c [1624], p. 239.

11. Dale 1964 [1611], p. 492.

12. Anonymous 1947 [1612], p. 27.

13. This was the skirmish in which the Nansemonds tried to make rain to dampen English powder; the incident is described in full by Percy (1921–1922 [1612], p. 277) and, in its cultural context, in Rountree 1989, pp. 132–133.

14. Hamor 1957 [1615], pp. 27, 29–31 (no mention of Nemattanew); Percy 1921–1922 [Percy 1921–1922 [1612], p. 280. For an evaluation of his career and power, which Fausz (1977, 1981) says was charismatic and religious in nature, see Rountree 1989, pp. 77–78.

15. Percy 1921–1922 [1612], p. 280.

16. Ibid., pp. 280–281.

17. Strachey 1953 [1612], p. 61.

18. Hamor 1957 [1615], p. 31; Smith 1986c [1624], p. 242. Opossunoquonuske herself was wounded (Strachey 1953 [1612], p. 64).

19. Smith 1986c [1624], p. 242.

20. These were Pepiscunimah and Chopoke.

21. Whitaker 1936 [1613], p. 40; Purchas 1904–1906 [1625], 19:91–94. Samuel Argall wrote (in Purchas, cited above) that the Eastern Shore groups formed their good opinion of the English after talking with the Indians of "Pembrooke" River, as he calls the Potomac (for corroboration, Strachey [1953 (1612), p. 57] calls the north bank of the York "Pembrook-syde").

22. Hamor 1957 [1615], p. 10.

23. Japazaws is the most common spelling of his name today, but Strachey's spelling, Iopassous (1612, p. 46) or Iopassus (1612, p. 101), is probably closer to the Algonquian original.

24. Argall 1904–1906 [1613], p. 92.

25. Hamor 1957 [1615], p. 4. The identity of these friends is unknown.

26. Argall 1904–1906 [1613], p. 92.

27. Ibid., p. 93. Details of the betrayal come from Hamor 1957 [1615], pp. 5–6.

28. Smith (1986c [1624], p. 244) implies that with howling and crying she put one on anyway, which is doubtful.

29. Hamor 1957 [1615], p. 6.

30. Argall 1904–1906 [1613], p. 93; Hamor and Smith both wrote, probably inaccurately, that Powhatan delayed a considerable time before answering at all.

31. Ibid., pp. 93–94.

32. Hamor 1957 [1615], p. 7.

33. Ibid., pp. 7–11; Smith 1986c [1624], p. 245.

34. The name of the Indian town involved in the skirmish was not recorded.

35. ". . . the chiefest residencie Powhatan had" (Hamor 1957 [1615], p. 9); judging by Smith's map (Smith n.d. [1608]) it was located on the eastern bank of Pamunkey River behind Eltham Marsh, probably near the modern settlement of Eltham (Rountree MS. A, place-name section).

36. Quoted in full in Hamor 1957 [1615], pp. 61–68.

37. Possibly Opitchapam; Hamor (1957 [1615], p. 10) spells Opechancanough's name fairly accurately as "Apachamo." Bridenbaugh, however, believes the uncle to have been Opechancanough (1980, p. 23; 1981, p. 23). Feest suggests (personal communication 1986) that the uncle may have been her mother's brother, never mentioned in any other English record.

38. Wording in Hamor (1957 [1615]) is unclear; possibly Opitchapam's sons.

39. Hamor 1957 [1615], p. 11; brackets mine.

40. Letter of Sir Thomas Dale, quoted in Hamor 1957 [1615], p. 55.

41. Smith 1986c [1624], pp. 258, 262; also caption on her engraved portrait, made from life in 1617, illustrated in Barbour 1969.

42. See Smits 1987 for the early seventeenth century, and chap. 6 for the late seventeenth century.

43. Fausz (1977, p. 284) says the Indians were beaten down militarily and psychologically, but I doubt that. The Indians had not made their best efforts, and they (especially Opechancanough) knew it. And in 1615 the English settlements were not so extensive, nor the capture-conversion of Pocahontas so disastrous, that a peace would seem a permanent defeat.

44. The date on which Dale wrote about it to a friend; letter quoted in full in Hamor 1957 [1615], pp. 51–59. Hamor's own account of the matter is on pp. 11–12. Bridenbaugh sees Opechancanough as the instigator of the Chickahominies' suing for peace (1980, pp. 23–24; 1981, pp. 24–25). But no contemporary writer even hinted at such a thing, and the Chickahominies were astute enough themselves to see that they needed a truce.

45. Hamor 1957 [1615], pp. 11–12.

46. Ibid., pp. 13–14; brackets mine.

47. For details of the visit during which this proposition was made, see Hamor 1957 [1615], pp. 37–46.

48. See his biography in Brown 1964 [1890], pp. 869–874, especially p. 873.

49. Hamor 1957 [1615], pp. 41–42. She had recently been married off for a handsome amount of bridewealth. For details on Powhatan marriage practices, see Rountree 1989, p. 90.

50. He had annulled Pocahontas' first marriage by consenting to her union with John Rolfe.

51. Hamor's wording is clear: "himselfe resolued vpon no termes whatsoeuer to put himselfe in our hands, or come amongst vs. . . ."

52. The bottle held "three quarts or better," but by 1614 "not much aboue a pint" had been drunk yet. Hamor and interpreter Thomas Savage were served "some three spoonefuls" in large oyster shells. Powhatan plainly considered the sack to be a status symbol, available only to guests.

53. William Parker, kidnapped from Fort Henrico in 1611, according to Hamor.

54. The things were probably sent, though no record mentions it.

55. McIlwaine 1979 [1924], p. 28.

56. Kingsbury 1906–1935, 4:61. The writer of this document, Richard Fretthorne, tells of a kinsman of his master finding an Indian could hit a mark the first time that he himself could not hit at all. Fretthorne, writing in 1623, gives no date for the incident, so that it may have happened as early as 1616.

57. McIlwaine 1979 [1924], p. 28.

58. Wise (1911, p. 27) wrote that when the English sent settlers to the Eastern Shore during this period, they found some Englishmen already settled there since 1610, married into the Nassawaddox chiefdom, and living a partially native life; however, he gave no source for the statement except "tradition," and no contemporary records support it.

59. Rolfe 1848 [1616], p. 106.

60. Kingsbury 1906–1935, 4:93; brackets mine.

61. Smith 1986c [1624], pp. 256–257.

62. Also called Ozinies. Near the mouth of Diascund Creek; Anglicized to Warrany in the 1640s, the name survives today as Wahrani in a swamp tributary to Diascund Creek (Rountree, MS. A, place-name section).

63. This places the events in midsummer 1616 or later.

64. Kingsbury 1906–1935, 4:117–118.

65. Purchas 1617, p. 956; closely paraphrased in Purchas 1904–1906 [1625], 19:118.

66. Fausz (1977, p. 322, and 1985, p. 243) has written that Powhatan abdicated in 1617, citing his visit that year to Mayumps; there is no direct evidence of such a formal stepping-

down. Bridenbaugh has written (1980, p. 25, and 1981, p. 25) that Powhatan altered the succession to place Opitchapam before Opechancanough. That idea is negated by John Smith, whose friends wrote in 1612 (1986b [1612], p. 247) that Opitchapam came before Opechancanough in order of birth, so that Powhatan always expected Opitchapam to succeed first.

67. Thomas Rolfe was born sometime before his parents left for England; the precise date and place of his birth were not recorded.

68. McClure 1939, 2:12; also quoted in Sainsbury 1860, 1:17.

69. Anglicized to Tomocomo (Purchas 1617, pp. 954–955; Purchas 1904–1906, 19: 117–119) or Tomakin (Kingsbury 1906–1935, 3:73–74. Only Smith (1986c [1624], p. 261) gives his full name, "Uttamatomakkin."

70. Purchas 1617, p. 954.

71. For a personal description of James I in 1616, see Willson 1956, pp. 378–380. James was a sick man at that time, which may partially account for his behavior; but at no time had he ever had polished manners (see Willson 1956).

72. Smith 1986c [1624], p. 261.

73. Purchas records Uttamatomakkin's exasperation in his 1617 account, but in his 1625 version he makes the Indian priest sound like a violent heretic from the beginning.

74. Beverley 1947 [1705], p. 43.

75. Smith 1986c [1624], p. 258, 260; Purchas 1904–1906 [1625], 19:118; her allowance was "fower pound a weeke" (McClure 1939, 2:66).

76. Purchas 1904–1906 [1625], 19:118.

77. McClure 1939, 2:50; also quoted in Sainsbury 1860, 1:18. This hospitality of James's appears to have spawned a legend. Robert Beverley wrote in 1705 (1947 [1705], p. 44; brackets mine) that someone suggested to James that John Rolfe had taken advantage of the royal Pocahontas while she was a prisoner and "forc'd her to marry him. But upon a more perfect Representation of the Matter [by someone else], his Majesty was pleased at last to declare himself satisfied." In 1747, William Stith (1969 [1747], p. 142; brackets mine) wrote further that James had been angry specifically because Pocahontas' marriage to a commoner violated the semi-divinity of royalty. "However, [his anger] passed off, without any farther bad Consequences, than a little Displeasure and Murmuring."

78. McClure 1939, 2:50, 66.

79. Ibid., 66.

80. Ibid., 50.

81. Stith 1969 [1747], p. 143.

82. Smith 1986c [1624], pp. 261–262. He claims to have been very busy preparing to go to New England, a trip he did, in fact, make; however, while Pocahontas was being feted in London, it is doubtful that the company members who exhibited her would have encouraged any attentions from Smith, who came of the yeoman class. Smith may have held off visiting her precisely because her friends in England outranked him.

83. Mossiker (1976, pp. 275–286) reconstructs a highly speculative death scenario, with the sister Matachanna in attendance (p. 279) at the deathbed. There is no record of Matachanna's having gone to England with her husband Uttamatomakkin; had she done so, Purchas might well have mentioned it when speaking of their marriage (1617, p. 955).

84. Smith 1986c [1624], p. 262.

85. As Mossiker (1976, pp. 283–286) points out after summarizing previous searches for the grave, Pocahontas's bones cannot be brought home because they cannot be found.

86. Again, no contemporary source identifies his malady.

87. Kingsbury 1906–1935, 3:70–71. Some of the young people in Pocahontas's retinue voluntarily remained behind in England. One "some times dwelt a servant wth a mercer in Cheapside" and later became a lodger "at Mr Gough^e in the Black Friers"; at the latter place she became ill of a respiratory ailment and in May 1620 had to have the Virginia Company pay for her medicines (Kingsbury 1906–1935, 1:338). In the summer of 1621 two Indian

women who had been living on an allowance from the company were sent to Bermuda "wth one servante apeec towards their preferm^t in marriage wth such as shall accept of them wth that means—wth especiall dyreccon to the Gou^{9}nor & Counsell there for the careful bestowing of them" (ibid., 485, 496). John Smith heard that the women were eventually supposed to return to Virginia to "civilize" their people (1986c [1624], p. 384); in early 1622 one of the women married "a husband fit for her, attended with more then one hundred guests, and all the dainties for their dinner [that] could be provided" (ibid., p. 386; brackets mine). Nothing further is known of these women.

88. Carson 1950.
89. Nugent 1934, p. 29.
90. McIlwaine 1979 [1924], p. 28.
91. Smith 1986c [1624], p. 262.
92. Ibid.
93. C. Robinson 1905−1906, p. 395.
94. Powhatan was said to be visiting "ye K. of May—umps," possibly Miompse on Potomac River in Doeg (Tauxenent) territory (Kingsbury 1906−1935, 3:73).
95. Ibid. It is doubtful that they succeeded, though Opechancanough let Dale think they had.
96. Ibid., 92; brackets mine.
97. Ibid.; brackets mine.
98. Smith 1986c [1624], p. 263.
99. Kingsbury 1906−1935, 3:92.
100. Young Rolfe got permission, at least, to visit his uncle in 1642; see chap. 4.

Chapter Four. Opechancanough's Regime

1. Purchas 1617, pp. 956−957.
2. Nugent 1934, maps facing pp. 96 and 224.
3. Fausz 1977, p. 311.
4. Like Fausz, I do not call it a "massacre," which it was, because the word is too commonly used for Indian killings and too seldom for European killings. I also do not use Fausz's term "uprising" because that word implies attacking people who are in control. The English of 1622 did not rule the Powhatans by any means.
5. Explicitly stated in Fausz 1984, p. 97; explained at length in Fausz 1977.
6. Wallace 1956; Wallace 1966, pp. 30−39, 157−166.
7. Wallace 1966, p. 159. An exception to the rule is the movement led by Tecumseh (Joel W. Martin, personal communication, 1989). Revitalization movements may, on occasion, be more a means to organize resistance than a concomitant cause (with social breakdown) of such resistance (Nicholas Honerkamp, in discussion with the author, 1989).
9. Nash 1974, p. 65 (Virginia); Hudson 1981, pp. 162−163, 165−171 (Southeast); Merrell 1984, pp. 552−553 (South Carolina); Thomas 1985 (Connecticut). Thomas has also written at more length (1976) about the nature of the competition for land in the Connecticut River Valley, pointing out (p. 14) that English and Indian families used "nearly identical amounts of farm land" per family, while other zones were used for differing but often competing purposes.
10. See, for instance, Kingsbury 1906−1935, 3:79, 93.
11. Smith 1986c [1624], pp. 264−265. The traders were acting without licenses, on the sly. The Chickahominies involved, said Smith, killed them partly for their goods and partly in revenge for friends they said Yeardley had killed (in 1616?).
12. Smith 1986c [1624], p. 291. The connection between the two is mine, not Smith's, and it is speculation. The Eastern Shore was a semi-loyal fringe area, and renegade Chickahominies—or others unnamed—may have considered it ripe for the taking, without interference from Opitchapam.

13. McIlwaine 1979 [1924], p. 28.

14. Thomas Rolfe later said that the Smith's Fort tract in Surry County had been given him by Opechancanough (Surry Co., Deeds, Wills, and Orders 1671–1684, p. 54 [about a deed of 1654]). I am indebted to Martha McCartney for this reference.

15. Kingsbury 1906–1935, 2:52–53.

16. Ibid. 1:307–308, 586–589, 3:102, 117; for an overview, see W. Robinson 1952. Some of the money bought ten thousand acres at Henrico, with half of the profits from farming to be used for an Indian school; this formed the antecedents of the College of William and Mary, a project that did not come to fruition until 1693, after the last major Indian territories in eastern Virginia were opened.

17. With the dispersed settlement pattern of the Virginia English, no "praying towns" were ever contemplated in the colony. For those towns and similar ventures in New England and the factors accounting for their success or failure, see Salisbury 1974 and Ronda 1981.

18. This was a practice common in England since at least as early as the fifteenth century, when a Venetian ambassador was horrified by it; see Sneyd 1847, pp. 24–25. In the seventeenth and other centuries, economic and political advantage was often the motive: children were "fostered out" to people who offered them a home and then asked their parents for favors, or just as often they were sent to live with someone who could teach them skills and provide them with connections additional to those of their parents (Slater 1984, pp. 126–138). The early Jacobean English further had a policy of rearing and "civilizing" the sons of Scottish chieftains, who were in reality hostages for their fathers' cooperation (MacLeod 1928, chap. 12).

19. Kingsbury 1906–1935, 1:588.

20. Morgan 1971, pp. 195–198.

21. Kingsbury 1906–1935, 3:100–101.

22. Ibid. 1:320; 3:220. Recipients were those who "adventured" to Virginia; land grants given for paying others' passage came later.

23. Morgan 1975, pp. 158–164.

24. Kingsbury 1906–1935, 1:350.

25. Morgan 1975, p. 101.

26. Morgan 1971, and Morgan 1975, chap. 6.

27. McIlwaine 1915, 1:10.

28. Kingsbury 1906–1935, 3:128–129.

29. The captain was John Martin, who was convicted and fined and who lost a later appeal to the Virginia Company; Kingsbury 1906–1935, 3:157, 4:515.

30. For a review of Spelman's career, along with that of Thomas Savage and Robert Poole, see Fausz 1987.

31. Kingsbury 1906–1935, 3:242.

32. Colonial Council of Virginia 1907 [1619], pp. 274–275; brackets mine.

33. Kingsbury 1906–1935, 3:244, 247.

34. It was not for several years yet that the English appeared as strong and powerful to the Indians as they thought they did.

35. Kingsbury 1906–1935, 3:244–245.

36. Ibid., 220, 244–245. Because of the description of Rolfe's "ailment" (see below), the fevers may have been malarial.

37. They were probably Siouan speakers.

38. Kingsbury 1906–1935, 3:228. "Law of nations" is an English phrasing; Nemattanew probably indicated that killing of women and children was contrary to common Powhatan usage.

39. The incentive was real, since Indian parents had been "in noe sort willinge to sell [apprentice] or by fayer meanes to part with their Children" (ibid.; brackets mine).

40. Ibid., 4:10. For the custom of secondary burial for Indian "royalty," see Rountree 1989, p. 113.

41. Anonymous 1900−1901, p. 213. The species cannot be positively identified. However, there is a strong likelihood that it was *Cicuta maculata* (L.), variously known as cow bane, poison hemlock, water hemlock or beaver poison. This plant grows throughout eastern Virginia in small quantities but occurs abundantly on the Eastern Shore; all parts of the plant are poisonous, but a walnut-sized piece of the tuber-like root can kill a cow (Thomas Wieboldt and Donna Ware, via Martha McCartney, personal communication, 1985).

42. Sources are vague about his identity; it may have been the "Laughing King of Accomac." He in turn may have been the Esmy Shichans who ruled Accomac in 1635 (see below).

43. Kingsbury 1906−1935, 4:10.

44. Smith 1986c [1624], p. 293; Anonymous 1900−1901, p. 213. Only Smith gives a rough date of the killing (Purchas paraphrases him [1904−1906 (1625), 19:168−169]); other contemporary accounts of the period before the attack of 1622 (Anonymous 1900−1901, p. 213; Waterhouse, in Kingsbury 1906−1935, 3:541ff.; George Wyatt, in Fausz and Kukla 1977, p. 117; and Council in Virginia, in Kingsbury 1906−1935, 4:10−11) either do not mention precisely when Nemattanew was killed or indicate a short lapse of time between his death and the attack.

45. Kingsbury 1906−1935, 4:11. I think that John Smith erred when he said the killing occurred only two weeks before the attack of 1622, for he was looking for an easy way to make sense of an attack that was otherwise incomprehensible to him and his contemporaries. Other modern historians follow Smith. But in polishing this part of my text, I must have reread the Council of Virginia's original at least a dozen times, and I still read it as placing Nemattanew's death before Wyatt's arrival and therefore five months before the attack. Perhaps that is because, as a social scientist, I look first for social processes in the causation of events such as wars, where historians are prone to focus upon personalities. Here, for those who wish to decide for themselves, is the text:

> Neither was it to be imagined yᵗ vppon yᵉ death of *Nenemachanew,* a man soe farr owt of the favor of Apochancono yᵗ he sent worde to Sr. George Yardley beinge then Gouʳnor by his interpreter, yᵗ for his p̱te he could be contented his throte were Cutt, there w[ould] falle owte a generall breach, wee beinge in treatie wᵗʰ him and offeringe to doe him Justice Accordinge to the Articles of the peace, yf vppon the takinge vpp of the dead bodies yt might apere yᵗ *Nenemachanew* had noe hande in there deaths wᶜʰ was all yᵗ Apochancon[o] requred [*sic*] and ther vppon sent oute as he fainde to search for yᵉ bodies, and in the mean tyme sent woorde yᵗ the death of *Nenemachanew* beinge but one man should be noe occasione of the breach of yᵉ peace, and yᵗ the Skye should sooner fall then [yᵉ] Peace be broken, one his p̱te . . . Notwᵗʰstandinge order was taken generally through owt yᵉ whole Colony to stande vppon theire guards, vntill further tryall, but yᵉ Indyans Cominge daylie amongst us and puttinge them selves into ouʳ powers, bread in our People a securitie . . . [brackets Kingsbury's, except *sic,* which is mine]

46. The other source, Anthony Chester's passenger, writing at a time much closer to the events, merely states that Nemattanew tried to escape and was shot dead.

47. Smith 1986c [1624], p. 293; George Wyatt, father of Governor Francis Wyatt, conjectured that the immunity was conferred by an "ointment," and also wrote as though he understood the planning of the great attack of 1622 to be a joint project of Nemattanew and Opechancanough (Fausz and Kukla 1977, p. 117).

48. John Smith wrote of Opechancanough's being infuriated and the English having to intimidate him to remain peaceful. I see that as another instance of Smith's trying to explain an attack in 1622 that was otherwise "inexplicable" to him and other Englishmen. Nemattanew may have been temporarily out of favor with Opechancanough, but his death was a severe blow to the latter's plans nonetheless. Bridenbaugh, on the other hand, believes that

Nemattanew was not only out of favor but also uninvolved in any plans for an attack, due to his brashness (1981, pp. 39–40).

49. Kingsbury 1906–1935, 4:11.

50. Ibid. 3:550; 1:504.

51. Thorpe was not specifically a missionary; as Jennings points out (1975, p. 55), he was not sent to Virginia as a missionary to the Indians.

52. Kingsbury 1906–1935, 3:446.

53. Virginia Company documents of the period commonly say little or nothing about Indians; Virginia was regarded as practically "empty" territory to be occupied.

54. Kingsbury 1906–1935, 3:584. He was said to have acknowledged that the English God "loved us better than them, and that he thought the Cause of his Anger againste them, was theire Coustome of makinge their Children black boyes," i.e., putting them through the *huskanaw.* The accuracy of Thorpe's understanding of Opechancanough's sincerity in saying such a thing (if he did say it) is questionable.

55. Purchas 1904–1906 [1625], 19:153.

56. Kingsbury 1906–1935, 3:552.

57. Quoted in Smith 1986c [1624], p. 286.

58. Kingsbury 1906–1935, 3:495.

59. Ibid. 2:94 (decision rendered in London, July 17, 1622).

60. Ibid. 3:584. Bridenbaugh (1981, p. 38) quotes Opechancanough's new name as "Massatamohtnock," which he has apparently misread for the tribal group "Massituppamohtnock," mentioned in 1619. It is interesting—and probably significant—that the lackluster Opitchapam appears in the English records by each of his new names in succession, while the charismatic Opechancanough is always called by the name he used when the English first met him.

61. See the Prologue, and also Rountree 1989, pp. 79–80.

62. The name change could also have derived from some unrecorded procedure for validating the position of new *mamanatowick* and his successor, at or near the time of transference of his predecessor's bones to their final resting place.

63. Fausz 1977, pp. 359–360, and 1985, p. 245; Sheehan 1980, p. 171.

64. Kingsbury 1906–1935, 3:550.

65. Ibid., 673; the wording is "those Indians whom God vsed as instruments . . . ." John Smith (and Edward Waterhouse before him) are overly dramatic when they say of "Pace's Indian" that "thus them that escaped was saved by this one converted Infidell" (Smith 1986c [1624], pp. 297–298; Waterhouse in Kingsbury 1906–1935, 3:555). However, most historians have followed them.

66. Writers in Virginia describing this Indian's warning: unnamed correspondent of Mead (1963 [1622–1623], p. 408) and Anonymous 1900–1901, pp. 212–213; writers in England on same subject: Mead 1963 [1622–1623], pp. 408–409; Waterhouse in Kingsbury 1906–1935, 3:555; and Smith 1986c [1624], pp. 297–298. Location of Pace's plantation: Nugent 1934, p. 10. No writer gives a name for the boy; he is referred to either as "an Indian" or "a youth."

67. Kingsbury 1906–1935, 2:538.

68. Ibid. 4:98; the script on the original document, which I have seen on microfilm in the Library of Congress, and in which "n's" are distinguishable from "u's," says plainly "Chauco," not Chanco.

69. Sainsbury (1860, 2:41), summarizing the same letter, calls him "He who had saved many lived on the day of the massacre." The original, printed in Kingsbury (cited above), reads "one [of the two messengers sent by Opechancanough] who had lived much amost [*sic*] the English, and by revealinge yt [that] pl[ot] To divers vppon the day of Massacre, saued theire lives . . ." (Kingsbury's brackets for "plot"; others mine). Many historians feel that Chauco and Pace's employee were the same person. I disagree: I think it possible but very

doubtful that a youth living among the English south of the James right up until the uprising would then leave the employer he had warned (in a fit of conscience about his own people), go to the Pamunkey, and be taken into Opechancanough's staff in a trusted position within a year. I have no difficulty in seeing several Indian people "caught in the middle" in 1622. Ethnic politics are never simple, especially for fringe people; and the Indians who voluntarily lived among the English for long periods were definitely fringe people. Christian Feest, on the other hand, has suggested (personal communication, 1986) that "Chanco" was actually the "Chacrow" or "Shacrow" who was reported to have been taught by Englishmen to use firearms around 1616 (McIlwaine 1979 [1924], p. 28). This, I think, is entirely possible, but it then makes him too old to be a "youth" living south of the James. "Pace's Indian" and Chauco must have been two different people.

70. For a detailed account of the massacre, with accompanying map, see Fausz 1977.

71. Kingsbury 1906–1935, 3:551, 555.

72. Smith 1986c [1624], p. 296.

73. For a report on excavations there, see Noel Hume 1982.

74. Kingsbury 1906–1935, 1:587. See also Noel Hume 1982.

75. Ibid. 3:612.

76. For evidence of scalping found on remains of victims, see Noel Hume 1982, pp. 242–244, 287–288.

77. Kingsbury 1906–1935, 3:553.

78. E.g., two captives escaped from the Nansemonds later that summer (Smith 1986c [1624], pp. 308–309).

79. Kingsbury 1906–1935, 4:238.

80. Ibid. 2:115.

81. Smith 1986c [1624], p. 312.

82. Ibid., p. 308.

83. Kingsbury 1906–1935, 3:556; Mead 1963 [1622–1623], p. 409. Martha McCartney (personal communication, 1985) believes that the story is apocryphal, the invention of a racist English writer eager to make Indians look like fools. She may be right. In that case, John Smith, who used the story in another context, was equally racist, as he wrote his *Generall Historie* in 1624. By 1622 the Powhatans had probably learned that gunpowder was not the seeds of a plant.

84. Officially there were 347 dead out of a colony of about 4,000, according to Waterhouse (Kingsbury 1906–1935, 3:554, 571). However, since there were in reality only about 1,240 colonists in Virginia at the time (Morgan 1975, p. 101) and about 330 people were in fact killed (Fausz's calculations; see Fausz 1977, pp. 394–399), the fraction is about one-fourth. A good summary of the overall damage to the colony is in Fausz 1977, pp. 370–399.

85. Kingsbury 1906–1935, 3:671–673.

86. Thus John Smith's inaccurate placing of Nemattanew's death just before the uprising; he felt that some single dramatic incident had to be the cause of the violence.

87. Situations like this still occur in Indian-Anglo dealings; an example from New Mexico in the 1950s: "While the Zunis and Navahos perceive the conflicting attitudes and aims of the Mormons in their relationships with them, the Mormons do not perceive this conflict at all realistically and are often surprised by the negative responses they receive to their missionary efforts. The Mormon bishop expressed astonishment when we asked how he expected to convert the Navahos when he and his kinsmen had taken their lands in the past and were currently treating them as dependent laborers and customers in the Mormon economic system" (Vogt 1966, p. 70).

88. Morgan 1975, p. 404.

89. Smith 1986c [1624], pp. 304–305, 308–310.

90. Since he described Opitchapam as "his brother" (possibly a parallel cousin), family feeling may have been involved. See Rountree 1989, p. 117n. The name of this primary

weroance of Potomac was never recorded; for all we know, Iopassus's elder brother may have died and he himself was this *weroance* in the early 1620s.

91. Smith 1986c [1624], p. 309; the only tribe mentioned by name is the Nacotchtank.

92. Ibid., p. 309.

93. Kingsbury 1906–1935, 3:654–655; brackets mine.

94. Smith 1986c [1624], p. 309.

95. Details differ according to the source; Smith 1986c [1624], pp. 309–310; Kingsbury 1906–1935, 4:450–451.

96. The source is Smith (1986c [1624], pp. 312–314), who may have been biased against Madison.

97. The source was a neighboring *weroance* who had been driven out of his territory by the Iroquoian-speaking Anacostians, and whom the Patawomeck *weroance* had refused to help recover his birthright. At his refuge at "Nazatica," this *weroance* spoke well of the Patawomecks as a people but slandered their *weroance* to interpreter Poole; he subsequently told Poole that the Patawomeck *weroance* had renewed his alliance with Opechancanough (Smith 1986c [1624], pp. 312–313).

98. Smith writes of a massacre of "thirty or forty [Patawomeck] men, women and children."

99. Kingsbury 1906–1935, 3:697.

100. Smith 1986c [1624], p. 314.

101. Kingsbury 1906–1935, 4:9.

102. Ibid. 2:115.

103. Sir Edwin Sandys wrote that as many more people had died of hunger as in the uprising itself (ibid. 4:71).

104. Ibid. 3:614. Some settlements were harried by warriors who killed people when they could (ibid. 3:652–653). Altogether, about twenty more English people were shot by mid-April (ibid. 4:234); thirteen people, listed by name, had been killed by Indians by January 1624 (Jester and Hiden 1956, pp. 14, 19, 41, 48). Only at Elizabeth City (formerly Kecoughtan) did any Englishmen risk a spring planting (Smith 1986c [1624], p. 304).

105. There is evidence that word of the massacre of the English did not even reach London until July 13 (Mead 1963 [1622], p. 408).

106. McIlwaine 1979 [1924], p. 11. Hunger and disease killed nearly twice as many people as the Indian attacks had (Fausz 1977, pp. 464–476).

107. Smith 1986c [1624], pp. 310, 314–315. The Nansemonds fired their own houses and escaped with their newly gathered corn as the English arrived.

108. Smith 1986c [1624], p. 315. English greed kept the damage from being worse. Sir George Yeardley was accused of taking corn but leaving too many Indians alive (Kingsbury 1906–1935, 4:37); these Indians would then raise corn another year for Yeardley to "harvest." Yeardley's trafficking in corn became "a scandal" (Fausz 1977, 476).

109. Ibid., pp. 246–247. I think, however, that Fausz overdoes his description of English kindness to the Patawomecks; see the events of 1622, above.

110. Kingsbury 1906–1935, 4:9–10; the document is a summary of activities against Indians in 1622, and I presume the attacks on the Chickahominies et al. were those of the summer.

111. Fifteen as of March 5, 1623, according to two captured Indians (ibid., pp. 41, 238); "aboute twenty" as of April 4, 1623 (ibid., p. 98; nineteen plus Mrs. Boyce as of April 2, 1623 (Smith 1986c [1624], p. 309).

112. Kingsbury 1906–1935, 4:37.

113. Ibid., pp. 98–99, 102.

114. Ibid., pp. 83, 108–109; Mead 1963 [1622–1623], p. 410; Smith 1986c [1624], pp. 320–321. Spelman foolishly visited an Indian town unarmed, after the town's ruler had smoothed over Spelman's suspicions; the English later attacked the Piscataways, having decided that they were the killers (Kingsbury 1906–1935, 4:450).

115. Ibid.; Sainsbury 1860, 3:56.

116. Kingsbury 1906–1935, 2:483.

117. Ibid. 4:232, which names him; however, the English writer could have used "Opechancanough" to represent the Indians in general.

118. Ibid., 102; more details come from Robert Bennett, who placed the meeting at Patawomeck and wrote of the entire day with pride (ibid., 221–222). Anthony Chester's passenger (Anonymous 1900–1901, p. 214) places the meeting at Pamunkey.

119. One of them, Jane Dickenson, later complained that the man, Dr. John Pott, who paid her ransom of two pounds of beads, kept her in strict servitude after her return to the English settlements, claiming that her husband's indenture (which was to another Englishman) entitled him to the widow's services (Kingsbury 1906–1935, 4:473). She also claimed that the drudgery he had her perform was much like the life she had been forced to live among the Indians while she was a captive.

120. The Virginia Company later censured him as "the poisoner of the savages" (Sainsbury 1860, 3:69). (Fausz [1977, p. 498n.] finds this document "dubious.") Pott was not a very savory character, as his actions in 1623 show. In 1628 he became interim governor of the colony (McIlwaine 1979 [1924], p. 190; Sainsbury 1860, 5:116), but in 1630 he was confined on charges that included murder (ibid.) and was subsequently found guilty of cattle stealing (McIlwaine 1924, p. 479).

121. The Virginia Company heard variously that the death toll was 150 (Kingsbury 1906–1935, 2:478) or 40 (Sainsbury 1860, 2:48). William Tucker lived at Basse's Choice, where there was a baptized Indian in his household named "William Crashaw" (Jester and Hiden 1956, p. 49). He cannot be said to have hated all Indians.

122. Kingsbury 1906–1935, 4:250–251.

123. Ibid., 450.

124. Ibid., 451.

125. Ibid., 292, 399–400, 450–451.

126. Ibid., 476.

127. At least five such orders were given between 1624 and 1629; see McCartney 1984b.

128. Kingsbury 1906–1935, 4:583; Hening 1809–1823, 1:126–128.

129. Kingsbury 1906–1935, 4:447–448, 470.

130. McIlwaine 1979 [1924], pp. 29–30.

131. Kingsbury 1906–1935, 4:507–508; Sainsbury 1860, 3:70.

132. The Indian figure seems too high compared to the low English figure; some bragging after a victory may be involved.

133. For overviews of the period from the English point of view, see Vaughan 1978; Powell 1958; Fausz 1977; Sheehan 1980, pp. 175ff.; Nash 1974, pp. 67ff.; and Morgan 1975, chaps. 7, 8.

134. Morgan 1975, p. 404.

135. It is an axiom that Indian people most often appeared in English records when they were in trouble: either military (a threatened uprising) or economic (having to sell land or become indentured servants to Englishmen). This gives an unavoidably negative bias to any history written about them. Barbara Tuchman (1978, p. xviii) summed it up beautifully in what she called Tuchman's Law: "The fact of being reported multiplies the apparent extent of any deplorable development by five- to tenfold (or any figure the reader would care to supply)."

136. McIlwaine 1979 [1924], p. 48.

137. Kingsbury 1906–1935, 4:566.

138. Ibid., 528.

139. Powell 1958, pp. 68–69.

140. McIlwaine 1979 [1924], p. 128.

141. Ibid., p. 129; the killers were presumably from Powhatan town a few miles upriver.

142. Ibid., p. 116.

143. Ibid., p. 111.
144. Kingsbury 1906–1935, 3:451.
145. McIlwaine 1979 [1924], p. 136; England's war with Spain made attacks from Spanish colonials likely.
146. Kingsbury 1906–1935, 4:37.
147. Hening 1809–1823, 1:141.
148. Nugent 1934, p. 44.
149. McIlwaine 1979 [1924], p. 151.
150. Nothing more is heard of the Arrohatecks or Quiyoughcohannocks after 1612, and the Weyanocks lived only on the south side of the James at that time. The Kecoughtans and Paspaheghs had been dispersed since 1610.
151. McIlwaine 1979 [1924], p. 483.
152. Ibid., p. 153.
153. Ibid.
154. Ibid.
155. Ibid., p. 172.
156. Ibid., p. 165. Projectile points made of glass have been found by archaeologists in several locations in Virginia.
157. Three unidentified Indians lived on public funds at Jamestown in October 1629 (Hening 1809–1823, 1:143). About that time a man and his wife and four children came in, wishing to "become English both in affection and religion," and in the campaigns of 1629 he acted as a guide for the English (letter of January 23, 1630, of Joseph Mead, quoted in Powell 1958, p. 74).
158. The report of William Pierce, dated August 1629, says, "as for the natives Sasapen is the chief, over all those people inhabiting the rivers next unto us, who hath been the prime movver of all them, that since the massacre have made war upon us" (quoted in Neill 1866, p. 60; abstracted by Sainsbury [1860, 1:100] without mentioning Sawsapen; original document is B.P.R.O., C.O. 1/5, pt. 1, fol. 69). This is the last mention of him by name after 1624. There is no indication that Pierce or any other Englishman had as yet realized that Opechancanough was still alive.
159. McIlwaine 1979 [1924], p. 198; the treaty is merely mentioned in passing in this document. No full copy of the treaty survives.
160. Ibid., p. 484.
161. Ibid., p. 174.
162. Ibid., pp. 184–185.
163. Ibid., pp. 189–190.
164. Ibid., p. 198.
165. Ibid., p. 482; Hening 1809–1823, 1:140–141.
166. Letter of January 23, 1630, of Joseph Mead, quoted in Powell 1958, p. 74.
167. Smith n.d. [1608].
168. McIlwaine 1979 [1924], p. 482; C. Robinson 1905–1906, p. 400.
169. These consist mainly of orders for projected campaigns (Hening 1809–1823, 1:153, 173).
170. Hening 1809–1823, 1:167; brackets mine.
171. Ibid., 176; brackets mine.
172. McIlwaine 1979 [1924], p. 480.
173. Ibid., p. 484.
174. Hening 1809–1823, 1:193.
175. McIlwaine 1979 [1924], p. 480; this part of McIlwaine consists of the terse excerpts made by Conway Robinson before most of the Minutes of Council were destroyed in the Civil War, so the precise circumstances of the peace and the articles of the treaty have been lost.

176. Laws of August 1632 forbade selling either to Indian people (Hening 1809–1823, 1:219).

177. Northampton County, Orders 9:49; Nugent 1934, p. 30. The ruler was Esmy Shichans, perhaps the same as the man known earlier as the Laughing King of Accomac. Destruction of county records elsewhere precludes our knowing how much land, if any, was given or sold by Indian leaders to Englishmen.

178. Sainsbury 1860, 9:250; in this remonstrance of King Charles I, the trade with the Dutch appears an especially sore point with him.

179. Ibid., 268. Matters were not helped by hostilities with Indians of the Maryland Eastern Shore. In July 1639 men were levied from Lower Norfolk and perhaps other counties to "march against" the Nanticokes (Lower Norfolk Co., Minute Book 1637–1646, p. 10 vol. p. 19, in repagination).

180. Patents for Nansemond River towns in 1638 (Nugent 1934, p. 105) and 1643 (ibid., pp. 153–154); patents for last remaining Nansemond towns on northwest branch in 1648 and on southern branch in 1653 (ibid., pp. 173, 244).

181. Ibid., p. 138. The town tract was patented in the 1630s (Charles City County, Orders 1661–1664, p. 35), but the patentee may not have settled on it immediately.

182. Still inhabited in 1638 (Nugent 1934, p. 98).

183. Ibid., p. 136.

184. Name applied to creek in 1638 (ibid., p. 83; "Diascund" came later); town mentioned only after its desertion in 1646 (ibid., p. 162).

185. Ibid., p. 120.

186. The order is now lost, but is mentioned in the first northern patent (previous note). A precedent exists in the February 1633 Order of Assembly which also allowed fifty acres to settlers taking up land in the vicinity of modern Williamsburg (Hening 1809–1823, 1:208–209).

187. MacLeod 1928, chap. 12; Jennings 1975, pp. 106–107. The incentive operated also in the claiming of lands along the James earlier in the 1630s.

188. Re-granting escheated land became a big business later on in Virginia; the escheator general in the 1660s was colonial councilman Miles Cary, my one and only prominent ancestor.

189. I.e., the "massacres" of 1622 and 1644 and the wars that followed them.

190. Nugent 1934, p. 132.

191. Ibid., p. 149.

192. Hening 1809–1823, 1:329; this law of 1646 cites a time limit that was stated in the text of the original grants of the early 1640s.

193. McIlwaine 1979 [1924], p. 500; orders like this one were, of course, difficult to enforce among the scattered English settlements.

194. Nugent 1934, p. 150. Northampton County, Deeds, Wills, Etc. 2:28v.

195. McIlwaine 1979 [1924], p. 478.

196. Northampton County, Deeds, Wills and Orders, 2:156r.

197. McIlwaine 1979 [1924], p. 478; that order of June 1640 intended the captive to be kept as a hostage, pending the delivering of the actual thief into English hands. The order is the ancestor of the law made the next year (see below).

198. Ibid.

199. Literally, "man-money"; a fine as punishment for murder. See Rountree 1989, p. 115.

200. McIlwaine 1979 [1924], pp. 478, 483. This is the first reappearance of Opechancanough by name in the English records since 1624.

201. Anonymous 1901, pp. 53–54; this law is ancestral in turn to the laws of 1663 (Hening 1809–1823, 2:193–194) and 1665 ibid., 218–219) holding the next town of Indians answerable "with their liues and liberties" until they find Indian murderers of Englishmen; these laws in turn formed the basis for the captivity and forced dispersal of the entire

Nanzatico tribe in 1705 (see chaps. 5 and 6 of this volume). We have this 1641 link in the chain of orders and laws only because an officer in McClellan's army happened to save some old manuscript pages from his men, who were burning colonial court records from Charles City Court House to heat their coffee. The officer's son later gave the pages to the Virginia Historical Society.

202. Entry in a sermon book dated 1675, in possession of modern Nansemond descendants, photographs of all pages of which are in my possession. Also quoted (with apparent mixing with other Bass documents) in Bell 1961, section on Indian-descended Basses, p. 12.

203. I.e., the fund provided by the will of Nicholas Farrar (Kingsbury 1906–1935, 3:576).

204. McIlwaine 1979 [1924], pp. 477–478; the philanthropy was Nicholas Farrar's, established in 1619. Before coming to Menifye, the boy had lived with Capt. William Perry, deceased husband of Menify's wife (he married her in 1638; Jester and Hiden 1956, pp. 267–268). If the Indian was in fact a young man, not a "boy," as in the racial slur, then he would not have been the same person as the "boy" that Perry took to England in 1624 (see above). The Weyanocks lived somewhat closer to Perry's plantation than the Nansemonds did, so he may have been Weyanock.

205. C. Robinson 1905–1906, pp. 394, 395; this terse excerpt was made by Robinson before 1861.

206. Mossiker (1976, p. 312–313) is speculating when she says the two were the same and that a touching reunion took place between an aunt and nephew who had been separated since 1617.

207. Nugent 1934, p. 29; Rolfe is shown as one of the transportees for whom Captain William Pierce collected headrights in land. His father had been remarried ca. 1619 to Jane Pierce, daughter of William Pierce (Jester and Hiden 1956, p. 281; Stanard 1913).

208. Nugent 1934, p. 121; his land was in Surry County, south of the James.

209. We know the date, for instance, only because April 18 was set aside as an annual day of remembrance the next year (Hening 1809–1823, 1:290).

210. McIlwaine 1979 [1924], pp. 501, 502 (Northern Neck and Rappahannock Indians to be attacked, June and September 1644 respectively); Hening 1809–1823, 1:293 (Occohannock and Rappahannock Indians to be conferred with, February 1645). Beverley (1947 [1705], p. 61) corroborates the list, saying that the Indians involved came from south of the James River and the heads of the James and York rivers.

211. Frank 1957, p. 85.

212. McIlwaine 1979 [1924], p. 501.

213. Anonymous 1947 [1649], p. 11.

214. Hening 1809–1823, 1:287.

215. It was taken over as part of Fort James in 1645 (ibid., 293) and was patented in 1648 (Nugent 1934, p. 175).

216. Inferred from the 1646 patent of land by Richard Lee on south side of Pamunkey River, six or seven miles up the river, where "the foot Company met with the Boats" (Nugent 1934, p. 162).

217. A site on Tanx Matadequin Creek (ibid., p. 244); Herrick Creek was then called Tanx Matadequin (Rountree MS. A, place-name section).

218. The precise location of the town at that time, shown as "Menmend, an ancient seat of Opachancone ye late Emperour" on the Anthony Langston map of ca. 1662 (fig. 4 of this volume; British Public Record Office, Maps and Plans General, item 311; for details, see McCartney, 1984a, pp. 100, 103, 106–107), was on an island east of Manquin Creek, some twelve miles upriver from the modern Pamunkey Indian Reservation.

219. Hening 1809–1823, 1:287–288; counties not involved in Indian raids provided funds to reimburse the expenses of the counties that were. The counties not assessed were Upper Norfolk (later Nansemond County), Charles City, and Henrico, and the Indians living near them are therefore probably the ones attacked.

220. Inference from five Indians being sold in 1646 as part of the estate of an Englishman who had served at Fort Royal (York County, Records 2:130—131). It is possible, though, that the five were people traded to the English by other tribes and not prisoners of war at all (Martha McCartney, personal communication, 1985).

221. Anonymous 1900, pp. 349—350; brackets mine.

222. See chap. 5 of this volume.

223. Hening 1809—1823, 1:289—293; McIlwaine 1979 [1924], p. 563.

224. Deposition of the surgeon on that trip ([Lower] Norfolk County, Minute Book 1637—1646, p. 294).

225. McIlwaine 1979 [1924], p. 564. Martha McCartney identifies Western Island as Tangier Island in Chesapeake Bay (McCartney 1989, p. 174n.).

226. Shown on the Anthony Langston map of circa 1662 as "The Indian Fort" (McCartney 1984a, pp. 102—104).

227. Hening 1809—1823, 1:293, 315. Proprietorships were granted in early October 1646, after hostilities ceased: Nugent 1934, p. 187 (600 A. and houses "upon Condition that he . . . should maynetayne ten men upon the Same dureing the tyme of three years"), 234, 255.

228. Nugent 1934, p. 234.

229. Hening 1809—1823, 1:317—319.

230. Anonymous 1947 [1649], p. 7. This is the only nearly contemporary source that mentions the party's leader or the result of the mission.

231. Beverley 1947 [1705], pp. 61—62. The law authorizing the march was not specific about how a peace "honourable" to the English was to be obtained.

232. Anonymous 1947 [1649], p. 7; brackets mine.

233. Beverley (1947 [1705], p. 62); Beverley embroiders this outline by adding Opechancanough's physical condition and death with details of the old man's heavy eyelids having to be lifted so that he could see (a medically verified condition: Nancy O. Lurie, personal communication, 1985); Berkeley's planning to take to England an enemy who had "ten times more Indians" than Berkeley had men in his whole colony (not true); and the old man's protesting to Berkeley when a crowd of visitors was let in to see him, saying that he would not have done the same to Berkeley had Berkeley been the prisoner (not likely, remembering Opechancanough's showing off of the captured John Smith in 1607).

234. Inferred from the location of Necotowance Creek adjacent to the present Pamunkey Reservation (Nugent 1979, p. 56 *et passim*).

235. Hening 1809—1823, 1:323—326; brackets mine.

236. Few did. See the next chapter of this volume.

237. Hening 1809—1823, 1:328—329; brackets mine. Since the treaty itself was ratified by being passed as an Act of Assembly, the burgesses may have felt free to pass another act subsequently that amended it. However, legally the conflicting part of the earlier act should have been repealed, and both morally and legally the assent of the Indians to a change in the treaty should have been obtained. No repeal is contained in the later act (in fact, there is not even any recognition of a conflict), and no record survives of Indians having been consulted.

Chapter Five. A Declining Minority

1. Morgan 1975, p. 9.

2. Jennings 1975, pp. 56—57.

3. Other discussions of their status are W. Robinson 1953 and 1959.

4. Anonymous 1908—1916 (vol. 19) p. 6.

5. Anonymous 1947 [1649], p. 13.

6. Hening 1809—1823, 1:349.

7. Billings 1975, pp. 65—66. Ossakican was probably Chiskiack, for he is mentioned as that group's deceased *weroance* in a Chiskiack document of 1655 (Mason 1946, frontispiece).

8. Billings 1975, p. 68; repassed in 1658 (see below).

9. Ibid., pp. 63–65. For details on shell money values, see below.

10. Bland 1911 [1651], p. 18.

11. Northumberland County, Deeds and Wills 1650–1652, p. 59r.

12. Northampton County, Deeds, Wills, and Orders 3:175, 217v–217r, 219v, 219r; Deeds, Wills, Etc. 4:40r–40v, 36v, 37v.

13. Billings 1975, pp. 39–40; Hening 1809–1823, 1:382.

14. Hening 1809–1823, 1:396. Without its being stated anywhere, the 1654 law enabling Eastern Shore Indians to sell land to individuals remained in force (see below).

15. Ibid., 391.

16. Lancaster County, Orders, Etc. 3:125–126.

17. Hening 1809–1823, 1:389–390.

18. Lancaster County, Deeds, Etc. 1:95; the *weroance's* death occurred before December 1655.

19. Old Rappahannock County, Records 1 (transcr. version; Deeds 2 in original):12–13. I use this nineteenth-century transcription of already damaged records because the originals have suffered further destruction since.

20. Old Rappahannock County, Records 1:28 (transcribed version) (printed in *Virginia Magazine of History and Biography* 38:391–392). The date has long been eaten away by worms.

21. John Lederer, writing thirteen years later, called them "*Mahocks* and *Nahyssans*" (1958 [1672], p. 16); the General Assembly that dealt with their settlement gave them the name of Richahecrian only after the fight. Hoffman (1964, p. 221) suggests instead that they may have been Eries, an idea that White (1978, p. 412) finds unlikely.

22. Hening 1809–1823, 1:402–403.

23. Charles City County, Records 1655–1665, p. 61.

24. Lederer 1958 [1672], p. 16; Mathew 1947 [1705], p. 14. Lionel Gatford ("Public Good Without Private Interest," p. 8, quoted in Neill 1866, pp. 246–247) added that "the King's" wife and children were with him at the time—which is unlikely—and that he commended them to the care of the English, who failed thereafter to honor his wishes. Neither Lederer nor Gatford gives the Pamunkey *weroance's* name.

25. Hening 1809–1823, 1:422–423.

26. McIlwaine 1979 [1924], p. 505.

27. Hening 1809–1823, 1:467–468.

28. Ibid. 2:138–143, 149–156.

29. Four such badges have come to light in the last two centuries. The silver ones from Machodoc ("ye Kingge of Matchotick") and Patawomeck ("ye King of Patomeck") were found on a farm far up the Rappahannock River. Both badges are owned today by the Virginia Historical Society. The silver badge from Pamunkey ("ye King of Panunkie [*sic*]") is shown in fig. 2; it is owned by Anthony M. Phillips and it went on display for the first time at the DeWitt Wallace Museum in Colonial Williamsburg in 1985. And the copper badge from Appamattuck ("Appamattock"), which could date to either 1662 or 1711 (McIlwaine 1925, 2:286), was found on a farm in Dinwiddie County early in this century; it is privately owned today. For further details, see McCary 1983.

30. B.P.R.O., C.O. 1/20 f llro. For a sample of the rumors, and a report of militia activity not corroborated in other records, see Charles City County, Records 1655–1666; pp. 513, 614.

31. Anonymous 1897, p. 49.

32. Ibid., pp. 47–48; Anonymous 1900, pp. 350, 2, 4, 5.

33. Hening 1809–1823, 2:237–238.

34. Old Rappahannock County, Deeds 2:201–202 (printed in *William and Mary Quarterly*, 2d ser., 18:297–298); Stafford County, Records 1664–1668, 1689–1693, p. 18 (printed in *Virginia Magazine of History and Biography* 44:192).

35. Old Rappahannock County, Deeds 3:257–258 (printed in *William and Mary Quarterly*, 2d ser., 16:590).

36. Old Rappahannock County, Deeds 3:57–58 (printed in *William and Mary Quarterly*, 1st ser., 8:165); McIlwaine 1979 [1924], pp. 488–489 (contains enumeration of tribes). The latter document says the war had been coming for four years.

37. Lancaster County, Orders, Etc. 3:95, 116, 127, 164.

38. Northampton County, Orders 8:117v.

39. Accomac County, Deeds and Wills 1663–1666, pp. 42v–44r.

40. Ibid., p. 44v.

41. Accomac County, Orders 1666–1670, pp. 47r–47v.

42. Morgan 1975, p. 404; Craven (1949, p. 269) says about 40,000. Morgan also estimates the English population in 1662 to be about 25,600, and in 1674 to be about 31,900.

43. Hening 1809–1823, 2:274–275.

44. John Smith mentions an "Appamatuck" on the upper Rappahannock River in the area of Pissaseck (1986a [1608], p. 53), but those were probably Pissasecks living on Mattox Creek, a tributary of the Potomac River, only five miles away.

45. B.P.R.O., C.O. 1/4 f 131.

46. McIlwaine 1979 [1924], pp. 361, 515.

47. Hening 1809–1823, 2:289.

48. See, among other sources, Washburn 1957, Billings 1970 and 1974, and Morgan 1975, chaps. 9–10.

49. In succeeding paragraphs, I base my account on Washburn 1957.

50. Westmoreland County, Deeds and Wills 1653–1659, p. 110.

51. Nugent 1977, p. 74.

52. Henrico County, Deeds and Wills 1677–1692, p. 33.

53. Longleat Papers, Vol. 77, fol. 101, cited in Washburn 1957, pp. 37–38.

54. Hening 1809–1823, 2:341–348, 350–351, 351–352.

55. Northumberland County, Orders 1666–1678, p. 138r.

56. Mathew 1947 [1705], pp. 14–15.

57. Berry and Moryson 1896 [1677], pp. 137–138.

58. Surry County, Deeds and Wills 2:141v.

59. Richmond County, Orders 2:15. She petitioned two years later and got her freedom (ibid., p. 184).

60. Berry and Moryson 1896 [1677], pp. 140–141.

61. Neville 1976, p. 274. Chronology in the records is not exact. Martha McCartney believes that the frightening away of the Pamunkeys occurred earlier and the despoiling of their town happened after they returned (personal communication, 1985).

62. Old Rappahannock County, Deeds (Will section) 6:76 (printed in *William & Mary Quarterly*, 2d ser., 16:593). Gunstocker's career as a detribalized Indian is traced in chapter 6.

63. Letter of January 30, 1678, to Sec. Coventry, Longleat Papers LXXVIII, fol. 204, cited in Washburn 1957, p. 160.

64. Commissioners' "Exact Reportory of the General and Personal Grievances Presented to us," B.P.R.O. C.O. 5/1371, ff 305–306, cited in Washburn 1957, p. 123.

65. Hening 1809–1823, 2:404; McIlwaine 1915, 2:69.

66. Earlier version: B.P.R.O., C.O. 1/40 ff 202–203, published in Neville 1976, pp. 287–290. Later version: Commissioners Appointed Under the Great Seale of England for the Virginia Affairs 1906 [1677]. For a good background and more details than I can provide here, see McCartney 1989.

67. For details, see Herbert Jeffreys, letter of November 6, 1677, in Coventry Papers, vol. 73, Bath 65, ff 64–65.

68. B.P.R.O., C.O. 1/40 ff 202–203.

69. Nicholas Spencer, letter of June 22, 1677, in B.P.R.O., C.O. 1/40. ff 249–250.

70. McCartney 1989.

71. These people were Shurenough from Manakin; Mastegonoe, a "young King" from Saponi; Tachapoake, a "Chiefe man" from Saponi; and Vnuntsquero from Meherrin; the name of the Nottoway leader was not recorded.

72. Anonymous 1914, p. 141. Jewel House Warrants show expenditures for purple "cloth" robes lined with scarlet shalloone and white sarcenet, crimson velvet caps trimmed with ermine, and silver "crowns" with false stones (Neville 1976, pp. 182–184).

73. These presents for Cockacoeske included a necklace and pair of bracelets "of false stones," a robe of silver and gold brocade lined with cherry sarcenet, and a scarlet robe lined (probably) with purple manto. Her son was to have "a pair of pistols richly inlaid with silver," a lined coat and breeches with gold and silver buttons, scarlet worsted stockings "with large tops" and stitched "all down the leg in black silk," a "white beaver hat with a gold and silver band," a sword with a gold and silver hilt and "a false scabbard," a belt embroidered with gold and silver, and 67 1/2 ounces of gold and silver lace. Cockacoeske's "councellor" and interpreter each were to get a coat and breeches, and the interpreter was additionally to have scarlet worsted stockings (Neville 1976, pp. 182–185).

74. McCartney 1989, p. 184n.

75. Martha McCartney (1989, p. 182) feels that it is part of the "necklace" mentioned in the Jewel House warrants. Tradition has it that the "frontlet" remained in Pamunkey possession for about 175 years before being given to an Anglo-Virginian (Hudson 1960, p. 22). The genealogist and historian George H. S. King disagreed: the piece passed into the hands of a man from Stafford County in the late eighteenth century, and it is mentioned in his son's will dated 1817. King further believed that it was a decoration for a "velvet Crown," the cloth portion of which eventually disintegrated (King letter of February 6, 1961, to J. Paul Hudson, copy in Virginia Research Center for Archeology).

76. McIlwaine 1915, 2:89.

77. Longleat vol. 73, Bath 65 ff 202–203.

78. C. Robinson 1901–1902, pp. 48, 188; Middlesex County, Deeds 1673–1680, p. 190v (1679 March to head of Rappahannock River); Hening 1809–1823, 2:440.

79. Hening 1809–1823, 3:82–85.

80. McIlwaine 1925, 1:13.

81. Ibid., 53.

82. Ibid., 54.

83. Old Rappahannock County, Orders 1:19–23, 24–25.

84. McIlwaine 1925, 1:70–71; McIlwaine 1918, p. 88.

85. McIlwaine 1918, p. 169.

86. Stafford County, Records 1664–1668; 1689–1693, pp. 199, 200–201, 231 (printed in *Virginia Magazine of History and Biography* 46:26), 240–243, 281, 296; McIlwaine 1925, 1:216.

87. McIlwaine 1925, 1:367, 368, 369, 375. McIlwaine 1915, 3:105, 111, 158. McIlwaine 1918, p. 248, 272. Sainsbury 1860, 15:579, 634, 641, 673; ibid. 16:8–9. Essex County, Deeds 9:323. Henrico County, Orders 1694–1702, p. 228. Virginia Colonial Papers, Folder 12, Document 17.

88. Sainsbury 1860, 15:456. The tribes are not named.

89. B.P.R.O., C.O. 5/1310, no. 26, ff 243–246; cited in W. Robinson 1959, pp. 58–59.

90. B.P.R.O., C.O. 5/1312, pt. 2, ff 221–222 (printed in *Virginia Magazine of History and Biography* 1:363). Specific tribal populations in this list will be given in the discussion of tribes, below.

91. That term, in days when water transport was the major link between English settlements, probably meant not only large rivers but also some estuaries today called "creeks."

92. Merrell 1984, pp. 542–549; Merrell 1989, chaps. 1–3.

93. Nugent 1934, p. 244.

94. McIlwaine 1979 [1924], p. 508. Nonetheless, there is one Indian in the records spe-

cifically described as Christian: Kitt, who left a noncupative (verbal) will in 1697 (Richmond County, Orders 2:300).

95. A record was made of their movements during the Boundary Line Proceedings between Virginia and North Carolina in the early 1700s; Anonymous 1896−1897, Anonymous 1900.

96. Billings 1975, pp. 65−66. The land was probably located far up in the headwaters of Powell's Creek (my own and Martha McCartney's independent conclusions).

97. Nugent 1934, pp. 188, 198, 202. The land was located far up in the headwaters of Powell's Creek.

98. Surry County, Orders, Deeds, and Wills 1645−1672 (transcr. version), pp. 142−143 (printed in *William and Mary Quarterly*, 1st ser., 6:214−215).

99. Hening 1809−1823, 2:155.

100. Anonymous 1897, pp. 47−48; Anonymous 1900, 7:350, 8:2, 4.

101. Anonymous 1897, p. 48; Anonymous 1900, pp. 4, 5−6.

102. Anonymous 1897, p. 48; Anonymous 1900, p. 5.

103. Anonymous 1897, p. 48; Anonymous 1900, pp. 350, 6.

104. B.P.R.O., C.O. 5/1355 ff 326−356. I am indebted to Martha McCartney for showing me this reference.

105. Anonymous 1897, p. 49.

106. Anonymous 1900, p. 350.

107. McIlwaine 1918, pp. 80−81.

108. B.P.R.O., C.O. 5/1312, pt. 2, ff 221−222.

109. Beverley 1947 [1705], p. 232.

110. Isle of Wight County, Deeds 5, 6, 7, 8, 10 *passim.* "Cockarouse" was a Powhatan word for "councillor" or "great man." Alternate spellings of "Wineoak" in Nottoway deeds: Wainoake, Wanoak, Waynoak, Waynoke, Wine Oak, Winoake, Wynoak.

111. Southampton County, Deeds 8: *passim;* Commonwealth of Virginia, Executive Papers, July 18, 1808. See also Rountree 1987.

112. Nugent 1934, pp. 238−239.

113. Nugent 1977, p. 92.

114. Ibid., pp. 89, 92, 135, 137; the last two patents refer to "the old town," suggesting the Indians had moved.

115. Lederer 1958, p. 33.

116. Nugent 1977, p. 269.

117. McIlwaine 1915, 2:343.

118. Beverley 1947 [1705], p. 232.

119. Byrd et al. 1637−1743, pp. 46, 85. Martha McCartney (personal communication, 1984) identifies the place as the modern site of the Maury Cemetery in Richmond.

120. Herrman 1673.

121. McIlwaine 1915, 2:89.

122. Nugent 1977, p. 335.

123. Byrd et al. 1637−1743, item no. 103. Martha McCartney (personal communication, 1984) places this site near the northern end of modern Mayo's Bridge in Richmond.

124. Virginia Colonial Papers, Folder 22, Document 18 (printed in Palmer 1875, 1: 127−128).

125. McCartney 1984a, pp. 106−107.

126. Billings 1975, pp. 65−66.

127. Nugent 1934, p. 194.

128. B.P.R.O., Maps and Plans General, item 311; for details and background information, see McCartney 1984a.

129. Nugent 1934, p. 235.

130. Hening 1809−1823, 1:380.

131. Mathew 1947 [1705], p. 14. Her personal name appears as Cocka Coeske or Cock-

acoekoe in the land patents (Nugent 1934, pp. 533–534) and in her correspondence with the English governor (B.P.R.O., C.O. 1/42 ff 177 [abstract printed (with "r" for "k" in her name) in *Virginia Magazine of History and Biography* 23:402]). Since nine of the twelve names listed by Strachey for Powhatan's wives end with an "SKE" sound (1953 [1612], p. 61), I have chosen to use the former version.

132. John Gibbon, who stayed in Virginia from November 1659 to January 1661, met her husband sometime during that period (Hiden and Dargan 1966, p. 11).

133. Hening 1809–1823, 1:467–468.

134. McIlwaine 1979 [1924], pp. 508, 509.

135. Ibid., p. 510.

136. Nugent 1934, pp. 533–534.

137. It also appears on John Lederer's map (Lederer 1958 [1672], facing p. 1) as slightly upriver from "Shikoham" (Chickahominy), while "Tottopotama" (Pamunkey) is considerably farther upriver. The identity of the "Manskins" is uncertain. That name appears only on Herrman's map (which does not show a Chickahominy town as such), on Lederer's map, and as the name of a "fort" in a land patent of 1664 (Nugent 1934, p. 514).

138. McIlwaine 1979 [1924], pp. 370–371 (printed in *William and Mary Quarterly*, 2d ser., 20:103).

139. Ibid., p. 384.

140. Mathew 1947 [1705], p. 14. Mathew is specific about his age: "a stripling twenty years of age."

141. George H. S. King letter of February 6, 1961, to J. Paul Hudson, copy on file at Virginia Research Center for Archeology.

142. McIlwaine 1915, 2:89.

143. Ibid., 115.

144. McIlwaine 1979 [1924], p. 519.

145. McIlwaine 1925, 1:79.

146. MacDonald Papers 7:157–158, cited in Bruce 1935, p. 499.

147. McIlwaine 1925, 1:94, 523.

148. McIlwaine 1925, 1:281, 284, 304, 311, 337, 338, 343, 351, 363, 373, 411, 456; McIlwaine 1918, pp. 260, 261.

149. des Cognets 1958, pp. 57–63; Nugent 1979, pp. 56, 57, 60, 61, 63, 65, 68, 72, 80, 86, 102.

150. Totaled from patents in Nugent 1979 (see n. 148, above).

151. Beverley 1947 [1705], p. 232.

152. B.P.R.O., C.O. 5/1312, pt. 2, ff 221–222 (printed in *Virginia Magazine of History and Biography* 1:363).

153. B.P.R.O., C.O. 5/1312, pt. 1, f 318 (printed in Beverley Fleet's *Virginial Colonial Abstracts*, vol. 14, King & Queen County, 5th collection, p. 4, and abstracted in Sainsbury 1860, 19:654). This document is the only one in which "Mrs. Betty" appears. The other signatories to the land cession were Mr. Namotte, Mr. George, Mr. Marshall, and Mr. Bones; only Mr. Marshall appears as a councillor in any other Pamunkey document.

154. An unnamed Pamunkey "queen" appears in two petitions, those of April 24, 1705 (McIlwaine 1915, 4:92) and April 20, 1706 (McIlwaine 1925, 3:81). Then the Pamunkey petition of August 1706 (Palmer 1875, 1:105) is signed by "Queen Pamamuck, Ann." Her relationship to her successor, and the date of her accession, is unknown.

155. McIlwaine 1925, 2:455.

156. Ibid.

157. McIlwaine 1915, 4:98.

158. Nugent 1977, p. 116. Piscataway Creek is a tributary of the Rappahannock.

159. Old Rappahannock County, Records 1 (transcribed version): 28 (printed in *Virginia Magazine of History and Biography* 38:391–392). The signers of the treaty were Tupeisens (the *weroance*), Owmohowtne, Mennenhcom, Eriopochke, and Peponngeis; spelling here is

copied from original version of Deed Book 1; spelling in *Virginia Magazine* is copied from transcribed version of Deed Book 1.

160. Old Rappahannock County, Records 1 (transcribed version): 142.

161. Hening 1809–1823, 2:155; since Goodrich was summoned to "answer the [*weroance's*] complaint," he may have been the one who did the burning, or he may have been negligent in letting others do it.

162. Old Rappahannock County, Records 1 (transcribed version): 249–250 (printed in *William and Mary Quarterly*, 2d ser., 18:298).

163. Old Rappahannock County, Deeds 3:381, 425–426 (printed in *William and Mary Quarterly*, 2d ser., 16:592).

164. Nugent 1977, pp. 27, 40, 56.

165. Ibid., p. 87.

166. McIlwaine 1925, 1:53.

167. Nugent 1977, p. 287.

168. Ibid., pp. 299, 369; Nugent 1979, pp. 68–69.

169. Cockacoeske's son, Captain John West, married a woman from Chickahominy whose mother had been reared there but born of Pamunkey parents. When the Pamunkeys and Chickahominies fell out over Cockacoeske's sovereignty in 1677–1678, West's wife left him; two Chickahominy councillors subsequently tried to make the wife's mother leave and go back to "her people," but she refused to leave her daughter (B.P.R.O., C.O. 1/42 f 177).

170. Hening 1809–1823, 1:380.

171. Ibid., 467–468.

172. Ibid., 2:34, 35, 39.

173. Lederer 1958, p. 15.

174. B.P.R.O., C.O. 1/42 ff 177, 276; Longleat vol. 73, 5V51.

175. B.P.R.O., C.O. 1/42 ff 277.

176. Nugent 1979, p. 50. The patent says "leased of the Pamunkey Indians," but the location is plainly near the Chickahominies and far beyond the three-mile limit for the Pamunkeys.

177. Longleat vol. 73, fol. 281.

178. McIlwaine 1979 [1924], pp. 370–371.

179. McIlwaine 1925, 1:135–136 (printed in *William and Mary Quarterly*, 2d ser., 20:105–106).

180. Nugent 1977, p. 287.

181. Palmer 1875, 1:22 (this is an abstract; original is Virginia Colonial Papers, Folder 6, Document 24).

182. This is probably the same place as Quackcohowan on John Smith's map (Smith n.d. [1608]) and Quaconamaock on the "Zuniga" map (Zuniga 1969 [1608]).

183. McIlwaine 1925, 1:320.

184. Confirmed in 1701: McIlwaine 1915, 3:286.

185. des Cognets 1958, pp. 57–63. The modern creek names are Ayletts and Dorrell/Herring.

186. McIlwaine 1915, 3:349.

187. B.P.R.O., C.O. 5/1312, pt. 2, ff 221–222 (printed in *Virginia Magazine of History and Biography* 1:363).

188. Sainsbury 1860, 20:557–558.

189. McIlwaine 1925, 2:271.

190. Beverley 1947 [1705], pp. 196–198. See also Rountree 1989, pp. 134–135.

191. Beverley 1947 [1705], p. 195.

192. McIlwaine 1925, 2:364.

193. Ibid., 359.

194. Ibid., 367.

195. Ibid., 380.

196. Beverley 1947 [1705], p. 233.
197. Mason 1946, frontispiece.
198. Billings 1975, pp. 65–66.
199. Nugent 1934, p. 180. The patent does not even mention Indians.
200. Ibid., pp. 210, 239.
201. Hening 1809–1823, 1:382.
202. Folio 1, Brock Box 256, Huntington Library (printed in Mason 1946, frontispiece); I am indebted to Martha McCartney for the Huntington Library reference. Pindavako's name has been rendered since as Pindeabank (*Virginia Magazine of History and Biography* 1:423n).
203. McIlwaine 1979 [1924], p. 506.
204. Hening 1809–1823, 2:39.
205. Ibid., 153; McIlwaine 1915, 2:13.
206. Hiden and Dargan 1966, p. 11.
207. Anonymous 1908–1916, 17:347.
208. Nugent 1977, p. 121.
209. McIlwaine 1979 [1924], p. 401.
210. Hening 1809–1823, 2:411–412.
211. Nugent 1977, p. 316. The Gloucester County records were destroyed in the Civil War.
212. Nugent 1934, p. 272; Lancaster County records are complete from 1653.
213. Evidence: Rappahannock deed of 1651 (see below) and 1667 deposition of English buyer of Totuskey Town that he had paid the "Morattico and Totuskey" Indians in full (Old Rappahannock County, Deeds 3:356).
214. Old Rappahannock County, Deeds 2:146.
215. Nugent 1934, pp. 251, 505.
216. Old Rappahannock County, Deeds 2:250–252 (printed in *William and Mary Quarterly*, 2d ser., 18:299). For details of the Rappahannocks' troubles, which were settled by the Assembly, see first section of this chapter.
217. Old Rappahannock County, Deeds 3:356.
218. Nugent 1977, p. 91.
219. Nugent 1934, p. 259.
220. The original document is now lost, and our only source is fallible: Meade 1857, pp. 478–479. The Rappahannock councillors appear as Wionance, Toskicough, Coharneittary, Pacauta, Mamogueitan, Opathittara, Cakarell James, Minniaconaugh, and Kintassahaer.
221. Codicil to above document in Meade. It is possible that Meade's copy is inaccurate and that Taweeren may not have claimed to rule "Moratoerin."
222. Hening 1809–1823, 1:382.
223. Lancaster County, Orders, Etc. 3:125–126.
224. Hening 1809–1823, 1:389–390.
225. Lancaster County, Orders, Etc. 3:95.
226. Hening 1809–1823, 1:456–457.
227. Old Rappahannock County, Deeds 2:146.
228. Old Rappahannock County, Records 1 (transcribed version) 1:39–40. Councillors mentioned in the deed are Masco (probably not Mosco of Captain John Smith's time, who came from Wiccocomico), Wharoy, and Caskameno.
229. Hening 1809–1823, 2:14–15; McIlwaine 1915, 2:9.
230. Hening 1809–1823, 2:36; McIlwaine 1915, 2:12.
231. Hening 1809–1823, 2:152–153; McIlwaine 1915, 2:16.
232. Old Rappahannock County, Deeds 2:252 (printed in *William and Mary Quarterly*, 2d ser., 18:299–300).
233. B.P.R.O., C.L. 1/42 ff 276.

234. McIlwaine 1925, 1:54.
235. Old Rappahannock County, Orders 1:19–23, 24–25.
236. Old Rappahannock County, Orders 2:230.
237. Sainsbury 1860, 17:576.
238. Beverley 1947 [1705], p. 233. Rappahannock County split in 1692, becoming Essex County (south of the river) and Richmond County (north of the river).
239. Smith n.d. [1608].
240. Nugent 1934, p. 324.
241. Ibid., p. 200.
242. Nugent 1977, pp. 18 *et passim.*
243. McIlwaine 1915, 2:41. The wording is a little unclear. In 1666 an Englishman patented land on the south side of Rappahannock River "about two Miles above *Portobacco* Town which is now included within the bounds allotted . . . to the *Nanzatico* Indians."
244. McIlwaine 1979 [1924], p. 227.
245. Old Rappahannock County, Orders 1:20 says plainly that the Rappahannocks were taken to "the Portobagoe fort."
246. B.P.R.O., C.O. 5/1312, pt. 2, ff 221–222 (printed in *Virginia Magazine of History and Biography* 1:363).
247. Beverley 1947 [1705], p. 233.
248. Feest 1978, p. 255, and personal communications.
249. Nugent 1934, pp. 324, 457. Feest (personal communication, 1986) holds that they should all be subsumed under "Nansatequond."
250. Nugent 1934, pp. 291, 292.
251. McIlwaine 1915, II:41, IV:74.
252. Nugent 1934, p. 334 (town not named); Nugent 1977, p. 209 (patent reviewed for land formerly an Indian habitation called "Nanzatico").
253. Old Rappahannock County, Deeds 7:31–34.
254. McIlwaine 1979 [1924], pp. 493, 507.
255. Old Rappahannock County, Deeds 7:31.
256. McIlwaine 1979 [1924], p. 400; Nugent 1977, p. 209.
257. B.P.R.O., C.O. 5/1312, pt. 2, ff 221–222 (printed in *Virginia Magazine of History and Biography* 1:363). Thirty bowmen for the two tribes may be excessive. In 1705 the Portobaccos had only five (Beverley) and the Nanzaticos had only about 15 (Richmond Co. records), so either the 1702 figure is exaggerated or there were other Indian remnants included in the 1702 figure.
258. McIlwaine 1925, 2:359; McIlwaine 1918, p. 391.
259. McIlwaine 1918, pp. 391, 403; McIlwaine 1915, 4:74; McIlwaine 1925, 2:369.
260. Richmond County, Miscellaneous Papers, pp. 30–33.
261. Richmond County, Orders 3:361–364, 373–384; McIlwaine 1925, 2:389–390. The guilty parties' names were Old Master Thomas, Bearded Jack, Jack the Fidler, Tom Anthony, and George.
262. McIlwaine 1925, 2:395, 396, 397, 400, 456; McIlwaine 1918, pp. 413–414; McIlwaine 1915, 4:97–98.
263. Hening 1809–1823, 2:218–220.
264. McIlwaine 1915, 4:97–98; McIlwaine 1918, pp. 417, 419, 421–422, 425–426; McIlwaine 1925, 3:5–6. The adults were transported to Antigua, where they disappeared without a trace (Patrick Lewis, historian from Antigua, personal communication, 1983). Thirteen children between the ages of nine months and ten years were bound out, mainly to members of the colonial council.
265. Westmoreland County, Deeds and Wills 1:75 (printed in *William and Mary Quarterly,* 1st ser., 8:23–24 and 15:178–179).
266. Hening 1809–1823, 2:149–152; McIlwaine 1915, 2:14–15.
267. McIlwaine 1979 [1924], p. 508; the nature of the present was not recorded.

268. Nugent 1934, p. 434.

269. Pronounced "ma-CHO-doc" today; original pronunciation uncertain.

270. Fausz (1985, pp. 225–226) notes the peaceful sale of town lands to Englishmen by the Yeocomicos but does not mention that some, at least, of the Indians abandoned the area soon thereafter. Yeocomico move: Anonymous 1910 [1635], pp. 73–74; evidence for movement to Virginia: presence of "Yeocomico River" tributary to Potomac, where none was in earlier maps, and (less convincingly) John Smyth's 1683 request for permission to survey "Yeocomico" Indians' lands which he bought from the Wiccocomicos (Palmer 1875, 1:14).

271. Nugent 1934, pp. 198ff., 223; sale on Yeocomico River by the "king" of "Muchchotas": Northumberland County, Deeds and Wills 1650–1651, p. 50r.

272. Northumberland County, Orders 1652–1665, p. 54r. Councilmen who also signed: Wonussaromen, Terossamoh, and Tahorts.

273. Northumberland County, Orders 1652–1665, pp. 110r–110v (printed in *William and Mary Quarterly*, 1st ser., 6:118–119). The Indians are referred to as "the Indians of Machoatick and Nomeny."

274. Northumberland County, Orders 1652–1665, p. 122.

275. Westmoreland County, Deeds and Wills 1:9 for original patent; renewal: Nugent 1934, p. 421.

276. Nugent 1934, p. 373.

277. Similar names indicating varied tribal origins in a later Indian group have been recorded in the Carolina piedmont; see Merrell 1984, p. 548; Merrell 1989, p. 43.

278. Nugent 1934, p. 343.

279. McIlwaine 1979 [1924], p. 505; this is merely an abstract of a record burned in the Civil War, so no details are available.

280. Lancaster County, Deeds and Wills 2:191 ("Wiccocomico" town had appeared on Corrotoman Creek). This and all subsequent records of the town call it "Wiccocomico."

281. Northumberland County, Orders 1652–1665, p. 39v.

282. Ibid., p. 35r.

283. Ibid., p. 54r.

284. Ibid., p. 54r.

285. Hiden and Dargan 1966, p. 11.

286. Northumberland County, Records 1666–1672, p. 47v; Records 1658–1666, p. 142; the report and the governor's confirmation of it were recorded in 1664.

287. McIlwaine 1924, p. 506; Hening 1809–1823, 1:515. This is a good example of men in high places using the "inside" information available to them to get their land claims in first. It was expected in those times that political office brought one profits, either directly or indirectly.

288. Hiden and Dargan 1966, p. 11.

289. Northumberland County, Orders 1652–1665, pp. 121v–122r.

290. Ibid., pp. 121v, 122r, 125r, 126r.

291. Ibid., p. 126r; Records 1658–1666, p. 85v; Hening 1809–1823, 2:14; McIlwaine 1915, 2:8–9.

292. Northumberland County, Records 1658–1666, p. 85v.

293. Northumberland County, Orders 1666–1678, p. 31r.

294. Ibid., pp. 35v, 37v; Records 1666–1672, p. 65r.

295. Northumberland County, Orders 1666–1678, p. 50r.

296. Ibid., 83r, 86r.

297. Ibid., p. 83r.

298. Palmer 1875, 2:14.

299. McIlwaine 1925, 2:284.

300. Beverley 1947 [1705], p. 233.

301. Kingsbury 1906–1935, 4:551.

302. Nugent 1934, p. 77.

303. The initial "g" is soft; location of the accent is uncertain.

304. Mentioned in Nugent 1977, p. 241.

305. Northampton County, Deeds, Wills, and Orders 3:207r (printed in *William and Mary Quarterly,* 1st ser., 5:82–83).

306. Hening 1809–1823, 1:391, 470.

307. Ibid. 2:13–14.

308. Northampton County, Deeds and Wills 7/8 [2d half]:19v.

309. Northampton County, Orders 9:48v.

310. Ibid., 111v.

311. McIlwaine 1979 [1924], p. 353. If more volumes of the *Minutes of Council* had survived the Civil War, we would know much more about this case and similar ones.

312. Ibid., p. 369; C. Robinson 1901–1902, p. 46.

313. McIlwaine 1979 [1924], p. 381.

314. Nugent 1977, pp. 211–212; reaffirmed in 1712 (Northampton County, Deeds and Wills 1711–1718, pp. 33–34).

315. Northampton County, Orders 11:57, 63–64, 69, 97, 108.

316. Northampton County, Deeds, Wills, and Orders 2:156r.

317. Northampton County, Deeds, Wills, and Orders 3:226r; Deeds, Wills, Etc. 4:35v.

318. Northampton County, Deeds, Wills, Etc. 7/8:51r.

319. Northampton County, Deeds, Wills, Etc. (1657–1666) 9:51v (printed in *William and Mary Quarterly,* 2d ser., 16:589).

320. Northampton County, Deeds, Wills, and Orders 3:135a-v, 166v, 223v; Deeds, Wills, Etc. 4:125v, 174v.

321. Northampton County, Deeds, Wills, Etc. 4:90r (printed in *Virginia Magazine of History and Biography* 5:35–36), 225r; Deeds, Wills, Etc. 7/8:10v.

322. Northampton County, Deeds, Wills, and Orders 3:135a-v, 166v, 223v; Deeds, Wills, Etc. 4:174v; Deeds and Wills 7/8:13r, 14r, 51r; Deeds and Wills 1657–1666, p. 6r, 44v, 73r, 74r, 78r; Orders 8:88v, 88r. Accomac County, (which budded off from Northampton County in 1663), Deeds and Wills 1663–1666, pp. 22r, 39v, 40v, 45r, 53r, 57v, 64v, 74r.

323. Northampton County, Deeds, Wills, Etc. 4:225r; Deeds, Wills, Etc. 7/8:10v, 13r.

324. Accomac County, Orders and Wills Etc. 1671–1673, pp. 143, 150; Wills 1673–1676, p. 33.

325. des Cognets 1958, p. 66.

326. Beverley 1947 [1705], p. 232.

327. Sainsbury 1860, 15:425.

Chapter Six. The Powhatans as Minority Persons

1. Example of damage by cattle: Northampton County, Orders 8:72r.

2. Northampton County, Deeds, Wills, Etc. 4:141r, 170r; Orders, Deeds, and Wills 5:18r, 55v, 151v; Orders, 8:93v. Surry County, Orders 1671–1691, pp. 2, 55, 90. Accomac County, Orders, Wills, Etc. 1671–1673, pp. 146–147; Orders 1676–1678, p. 80. McIlwaine 1979 [1924], p. 521.

3. Hening 1809–1823, 2:316–317; repassed 1694: Anonymous 1902–1903, p. 59.

4. Hening 1809–1823, 3:109; Surry County, Orders 1691–1713, pp. 75, 83.

5. One case that got to court: Accomac County, Wills, Deeds, and Orders 1678–1682, pp. 278–279.

6. Hening 1809–1823, 1:410.

7. Ibid., 415–416. This law also specified that it was legal for Indians to hunt on English lands once they had "checked in," so to speak, with "some person to be nominated on the head of each river." That idea was elaborated in later laws.

8. Northampton County, Deeds, Wills, and Orders 3:203v, 212v (printed in *Virginia*

Magazine of History and Biography 10:68); Orders 8:55v. Charles City County, Records 1655–1665, p. 495.

9. Hening 1809–1823, 1:415 (1656); C. Robinson 1900–1901, p. 164 (1656); Hening 1809–1823, 2:350 (1676); McIlwaine 1915, 2:89 (1677); Commissioners Appointed Under the Great Seale of England for the Virginia Affairs 1906 [1677], p. 292 (1677); and Hening 1809–1823, 3:467 (1705).

10. Hening 1809–1823, 1:416 (1656: open trade); ibid., 525 (1659: open); ibid., 2:124 (1662: open except fur trade); ibid., 336 (March 1676: closed except by license); ibid., 350 (June 1676: closed except for traditional Indian goods such as corn and baskets). Ibid., 410–412, Accomac County, Orders 1678–1682, p. 13, and Henrico County, Deeds and Wills 1677–1692, p. 35 (1677–1678: closed except at stated locations). Hening 1809–1823, 2:480 (1680: open); ibid., 3:69 (1691: open); ibid., 468–469 (1705: open except for liquor trade).

11. Most of the land sales cited in the foregoing paragraphs specified payment in either matchcoats or arms' length of roanoke. For valuation of roanoke, see below. Note also the goods looted from the Pamunkey *weroansqua*'s house in 1676, described above.

12. Hening 1809–1823, 2:20 (1661); ibid., 124 (1662: licensing fur traders); ibid., 337 (March 1676: for "matchcoates, hoes and axes" that Indians needed to live). Indian people were trading with—and thereby threatening—the English again as early as 1648 (York County, Records 2:389).

13. This was usually accomplished by licensing done through the county courts; Hening 1809–1823, 1:470 (1658); Anonymous 1902–1903, p. 58. For laws relating to Indian indentured employees, see below.

14. Billings 1975, pp. 39–40 (1651); Hening 1809–1823, 1:393–394 (1656), 457 (1658); Accomac County, Orders 1666–1670, pp. 142–143 (1669).

15. Lancaster County, Orders, Etc. 3:253. Stafford County, Records 1664–1668, 1689–1693, p. 18. Surry County, Orders 1671–1691, pp. 33, 79, 105. Henrico County, Deeds and Wills 1688–1697, p. 249. Essex County, Orders 2:86, 139; Deeds 10 (Orders section):73, 137; Orders 3:34. Northampton County, Wills, Etc. 14:214. Charles City County, Records 1655–1665, p. 142.

16. Hening 1809–1823, 2:236, 282.

17. Ibid., 274–276 (1669, being passed); ibid., 282 (1670, being repealed).

18. Accomac County, Orders 1676–1678, p. 76, in which the bounty was reduced to 150 pounds of tobacco (1677). The going rate elsewhere was 100 pounds at that time. In 1696 the bounty was standardized at 100 pounds (Hening 1809–1823, 3:141–142).

19. Hening 1809–1823, 3:282. Englishmen got two hundred or three hundred pounds of tobacco, depending upon the means used to kill the wolf; Indians got one hundred pounds regardless of means used.

20. Bland 1911 [1651]; Lederer 1958 [1672]; Sainsbury 1860, 7:270 ff.

21. Accomac County, Deeds and Wills 1663–1666, p. 92v; Wills 1673–1676, p. 296; Wills, Deeds, and Orders 1678–1682, p. 309. Northampton County, Orders and Wills 12:185 (Indian and Englishman in this case received unequal pay: Englishman got two hundred pounds of tobacco, Indians got thirty). Henrico County, Orders 1678–1693, p. 413; Orders 1694–1701, p. 124.

22. Surry County, Orders 1671–1691, p. 269 (1679); Hening 1809–1823, 3:82–84 (1691), 98–101, 116–117; Henrico County, Deeds and Wills 1688–1697, pp. 250, 355, 448, 608; McIlwaine 1925, 1:333.

23. Northumberland County, Orders 1666–1678, p. 138r. Old Rappahannock County, Deeds (will section) 6:76 (Gunstocker's will; printed in *William and Mary Quarterly*, 2d ser., 16:593). Henrico County, Deeds and Wills 1677–1692, p. 22; Orders 1678–1693, p. 197 (Indian war veteran being exempted from taxes).

24. [Lower] Norfolk County, Minutes 1637–1646, p. 6.

25. Northampton County, Orders 11:29 (1679).

26. Accomac County, Orders 1666–1670, p. 27v; brackets mine.

27. Accomac County, Wills, Deeds, and Orders 1678–1682, p. 284. The Indian's name was Robert Atkinson; at that date his possession of an English name probably indicates that he was detribalized.

28. Hening 1809–1823, 1:391; repassed in 1658 (ibid., 470) and in 1694 (Anonymous 1902–1903, p. 58). Also ordered on the county level: Accomac County, Orders 1666–1670, p. 27v; Charles City County, Records 1655–1665, p. 295.

29. Henrico County, Deeds and Wills 1677–1692, pp. 314, 327.

30. McIlwaine 1979 [1924], pp. 505, 511. Stafford County, Records 1664–1668, 1689–1693, p. 84. Northumberland County, Orders 1666–1678, pp. 40r, 40v, 83v, 85v, 93v, 103v. Northampton County, Orders 8:101v; Orders and Wills, etc. 10:73, 75, 138, 191. Lancaster County, Orders, Etc. 3A:210, 220, 239, 251. Accomac County, Orders 1666–1670, pp. 27r–27v; Wills 1673–1676, p. 196. Henrico County, Deeds and Wills 1677–1692, p. 102; Orders 1678–1693, pp. 319, 320, 348, 358, 376. Charles City County, Records 1655–1665; p. 14, 69, 72, 154, 295.

31. Northampton County, Orders 8:28v.

32. Ibid., 183r, 186r. Mongram pleaded ignorance of the law, apologized, and was freed after giving bond for his future behavior. As a landowner and tithe payer, Mongram was legally an English subject like any other in those days, though he was less well behaved generally than his non-white compatriots (Breen and Innes 1980, especially pp. 106–107).

33. McIlwaine 1915, 2:89.

34. McIlwaine 1925, 1:202.

35. Ibid. 2:14, 28. Resulting licenses: Henrico County, Orders 1694–1701, pp. 252–253, 259, 267, 277. None were recorded in Northumberland County (where the Wiccocomicos lived) or Surry County (where the Weyanocks and part of the Nansemonds lived); other counties containing Indian populations at the time lost their records in the nineteenth century.

36. Northampton County, Deeds, Wills, and Orders 3:78v, 151v; Accomac County, Orders, Wills, Etc. 1671–1673, p. 70.

37. Farrar 1905, p. 45; Isle of Wight County, Records of Wills, Deeds, Etc. 2:117.

38. Northampton County, Orders 11:13 ("Indian Trayes").

39. Isle of Wight County, Records of Wills and Deeds, Etc. 2:117.

40. Northampton County, Orders 9:25, 99; Accomac County, Orders 1676–1678, p. 49; Henrico County, Deeds and Wills 1688–1697, p. 116.

41. Accomac County, Orders, Wills, Etc. 1671–1673, p. 41.

42. Farrar 1905, p. 45; Northampton County, Orders 9:33v.

43. Noel Hume 1962; Noel Hume 1963, pp. 149, 283. The Indians themselves also began to use it: Stern 1951, pp. 44–46.

44. Martha McCartney, personal communication, 1985.

45. Henrico County, Deeds and Wills 1688–1697, p. 235.

46. For a description of Virginia Indian shell money and its manufacture, see Rountree 1989, pp. 71, 73, illus. p. 74.

47. Billings 1975, p. 63.

48. Ibid., p. 67.

49. Accomac County, Wills, Etc. Orders 1682–1697, p. 215r.

50. Northampton County, Orders 8:93v.

51. Accomac County, Orders 1666–1670, p. 27v; brackets mine.

52. Hening 1809–1823, 2:337.

53. Coarse woolen cloth.

54. Henrico County, Deeds and Wills 1688–1697, p. 511.

55. Northampton County, Orders, Wills, Etc. 10:203.

56. Northampton County, Deeds, Wills, and Orders 3:148v–148r. This document is

concerned with the adultery case and makes very racy reading. The sleeping place of the Indians probably reflects their custom at home of sleeping near the central fire.

57. Lederer 1958 [1672], p. 42.

58. Hening 1809–1823, 3:468.

59. Morgan 1975, chap. 11.

60. Hening 1809–1823, 2:350.

61. Lancaster County, Orders, Etc. 3:2. Northampton County, Orders 8:55v; Orders, Wills, Etc. 10:203. Accomac County, Deeds and Wills 1663–1666, pp. 79r, 94r; Orders 1676–1678, p. 133. Northumberland County, Orders 1678–1698, p. 23.

62. Kukla 1975, p. 84.

63. Hening 1809–1823, 3:82–85.

64. Ibid., 467.

65. See chap. 7 of this volume.

66. Cases where injury is not specified: McIlwaine 1979 [1924], p. 518. C. Robinson 1901–1902, p. 47. Accomac County, Deeds and Wills 1663–1666, p. 38v; Orders, Wills, Etc. 1671–1673, p. 117. Northumberland County, Orders 1666–1678, p. 31r. Old Rappahannock County, Orders 2:91.

67. Cases where injury is not specified: Northampton County, Deeds, Wills, and Orders 3:61a-r. Accomac County, Orders 1676–1678, p. 96; Wills, Deeds, and Orders 1678–1682, p. 323. Lancaster County, Deeds, Etc. 1:198. Surry County, Orders 1671–1691, p. 489.

68. Accomac County, Orders 1666–1670, p. 194; Orders and Wills 1671–1673, p. 41. Northampton County, Wills, Etc. 14:102.

69. Northampton County, Orders and Wills 13:352; Accomac County, Orders, Wills, Etc. 1671–1673, p. 117. Wills 1673–1676, p. 314.

70. McIlwaine 1979 [1924], pp. 503, 520. Lancaster County, Deeds, Etc. 1:43; Orders, Etc. 3:98. Northampton County, Orders 9:40. Accomac County, Wills, Deeds, and Orders 1678–1682, pp. 53, 217.

71. Accomac County, Deeds and Wills 1663–1666, pp. 55r–55v; Wills, Deeds, and Orders 1678–1682, pp. 181–182 (the victim in this case was an Englishman's Indian employee, so the killer's animus may not have been against Englishmen). McIlwaine 1979 [1924], p. 380.

72. Old Rappahannock County, Deeds 2:176–177.

73. Accomac County, Orders 1676–1678, pp. 80, 85. The treaty, interestingly enough, was the 1677 one, which no Eastern Shore Indian leader had signed. The court assumed that the Eastern Shore Indian people were covered, while Virginia's governors generally ignored them.

74. Accomac County, Deeds and Wills 1664–1671, p. 166.

75. McIlwaine 1924, pp. 230, 238.

76. Accomac County, Orders 1666–1670, p. 53r. Other cases of Indian thieves: Northampton County, Orders, Deeds, and Wills 5:151v; Orders and Wills 13:510–511 (a 1697 case of a Gingaskin accused by that town's neighbor, Harmanson).

77. Hening 1809–1823, 2:316–317.

78. McIlwaine 1979 [1924], pp. 230, 238.

79. Hening 1809–1823, 1:541, 547. The county court willingly referred the *weroance*'s case to the governor (Charles City County; Records 1655–1665; p. 251).

80. Accomac County, Orders 1682–1697, p. 75.

81. Nugent 1934, p. 566; C. Robinson 1900–1901, p. 237.

82. Old Rappahannock County, Deeds 6:76 (printed in *William and Mary Quarterly*, 2d ser., 16:593).

83. Old Rappahannock County, Deeds 7:22.

84. Old Rappahannock County, Orders 1:100, 244.

85. Old Rappahannock County, Orders 2:63.

86. Interestingly, there were two Nanzatico people, named Betty and Mattox Will (already mentioned in connection with the Machodoc), who almost got their freedom when the adult Nanzaticos were ordered to be transported from Virginia (McIlwaine 1918, p. 414). Although there is no evidence to support it, Betty could have been the Betty who sold Gunstocker's land, someone who would therefore be known to be friendly to the English. However, the Assembly decided to transport Betty and Mattox Will with the others.

87. Richmond County, Deeds 3:1–2.

88. Richmond County, Orders 2:336–337, 373–377.

89. Sainsbury 1860, 15:456; brackets mine. He conveniently forgot the captive Pocahontas. For a good overview of efforts to convert and educate Indians in colonial Virginia, see W. Robinson 1952.

90. Hening 1809–1823, 1:395–396.

91. Ibid., 396 (1656); ibid., 471 (1658); county treaties of 1656 and 1657 and colonial treaty of 1677 (see above).

92. The word "servant" did not take on its present degraded meaning in English society until after World War I. Before that, the word meant "employee for farm or household work."

93. Old Rappahannock County, Orders 2:151.

94. For an overview that compares policies in all the colonies, see Lauber 1913.

95. Northampton County, Deeds, Wills, Etc. 4:34r.

96. Charles City County, Records 1655–1665, p. 374.

97. York County, Records 2:99, 130–131.

98. York County, Records 2:329.

99. Northampton County, Deeds, Wills, and Orders 3:183r.

100. Lancaster County, Deeds, Etc. 1:9, 10.

101. Billings 1975, pp. 64–65.

102. Hening 1809–1823, 1:410.

103. Ibid., 455:456, 481–482.

104. Accomac County, Orders 1666–1670, p. 196.

105. Charles City County, Records 1655–1665, pp. 390, 398.

106. Hening 1809–1823, 1:546.

107. Accomac County, Orders 1666–1670, p. 62v.

108. Hening 1809–1823, 2:280–281, 283.

109. B.P.R.O., C.O. 1/29 f 72–75.

110. Accomac County, Orders 1666–1670, pp. 33v, 35r (Kegotank boys, bound out by town's councillors), 40v–41r (Onancock boys and Metomkin boy and girl, bound out by towns' councillors), 43r, 44r–44v, 159, 181, 194.

111. Accomac County, Orders 1666–1670, p. 40v.

112. Accomac County, Wills, Deeds, and Orders 1678–1682, pp. 266, 271, 281, 289, 291.

113. Ibid., pp. 295–296.

114. Accomac County, Orders 1666–1670, p. 35.

115. Accomac County, Orders, Wills, Etc. 1671–1673, p. 119.

116. Accomac County, Wills 1673–1676, p. 249.

117. Ibid., pp. 264, 296.

118. Had the problem been specifically with his master, it is probable that that fact would have come out in court and been recorded.

119. Accomac County, Orders 1676–1678, pp. 54–55.

120. Hening 1809–1823, 2:341–348. Flight is specifically stated as evidence of hostility. For an overview of Indian slavery in Virginia, see Lauber 1913.

121. Hening 1809–1823, 2:404, 440.

122. Ibid., 490–492.

123. Henrico County, Orders 1678–1693, pp. 135, 136, 138, 139, 140–141, 146, 161, 163, 211, 213, 282, 351, 354; Surry County, Orders 1671–1691, p. 419 (in which owners

were told they had three months to have the ages of new purchases' judged), 444, 450, 489; Norfolk County, Orders 1675–1686, p. 216; Accomac County, Wills, Etc. Orders 1682–1697, pp. 28v, 47r, 51r, 61v, 86r, 86v, 102v; Northampton County, Orders and Wills 12:176, 217, 356. In the 1710s there was a brisk trade in importing Indian slaves from the Carolinas by boat (B.P.R.O., C.O. 5/1320, ff 5–6, 8, 10 [reference from Martha McCartney]); that trade may have flourished considerably earlier as well.

124. Henrico County, Deeds and Wills 1677–1692, p. 282.

125. Ibid., pp. 359, 388.

126. Hening 1809–1823, 2:492. The text reads that Indian women are "tithables" "in like manner as negroe women."

127. Henrico County, Orders 1678–1693, pp. 195, 197.

128. McIlwaine 1925, 1:157.

129. Henrico County, Deeds and Wills 1677–1692, p. 371.

130. Old Rappahannock County, Orders 2:230.

131. Henrico County, Orders 1678–1693, p. 280.

132. Henrico County, Orders 1694–1701, p. 77.

133. Henrico County, Deeds and Wills 1688–1697, p. 645. Hagar received two worn blankets and a broken gun, and she and her mother together got 146 pounds of salt pork.

134. Henrico County, Orders 1694–1701, p. 191.

135. Hening 1809–1823, 3:69n. See also Ballagh 1902, pp. 50–51; freedom did not come easily, however, for those enslaved between 1691 and 1705.

136. Henrico County, Orders 1678–1693, pp. 394, 430; Deeds and Wills 1677–1692, p. 479; Orders 1694–1701, pp. 40, 65, 71, 80, 112, 117, 149, 169, 194, 200, 210, 213, 218, 229, 230, 231, 235, 237, 263, 285; Deeds and Wills 1688–1697, p. 639. Isle of Wight County, Deeds 1 (Orders section):25. Scurry County, Orders 1691–1713, p. 170. Richmond County, Orders 2:405. Northumberland County, Orders 1699–1713, p. 360.

137. Henrico County, Orders 1678–1693, p. 413; Orders 1694–1701, pp. 51, 82, 105, 116, 124, 204, 225, 234, 236, 239, 292. Surry County, Orders 1691–1713, p. 86 (this runaway was a woman). One runaway in 1699 was an "East Indian slave" (Essex County, Orders 2:146–147); he may have been the Occanough from Madras who sued successfully for his freedom in 1701 (Essex County, Orders 3:319).

138. McIlwaine 1925, 2:41; B.P.R.O., C.O. 5/1311, ff 702–703, cited in W. Robinson 1953, p. 252. There is no record of the case in the Surry County court records.

139. Essex County, Orders 1:33.

140. See Morgan 1975, pp. 329ff.

141. Henrico County, Deeds and Wills 1688–1697, pp. 557–558.

142. Accomac County, Orders 1682–1697, p. 75r; documentary evidence of his parentage is lacking.

143. Northampton County, Orders 8:183r.

144. Northampton County, Deeds and Wills 7/8:11; Orders, Deeds, and Wills 5:135.

145. Morgan (1975, p. 336) points out that an imbalanced sex ratio (many more men than women) may have made white men more jealous of their women and therefore more punitive toward Indian men who slept with them.

146. Northampton County, Deeds, Wills, and Orders 3:48r, 64v–64r.

147. Old Rappahannock County, Orders 1:32.

148. Northumberland County, Orders 1699–1713, p. 233.

149. Accomac County, Wills, Deeds, and Orders 1678–1682, p. 276; regrettably, details of the production of that bastard are lacking.

150. Henrico County, Orders 1678–1693, p. 277.

151. Hening 1809–1823, 3:86–87.

152. See Williamson 1980, chap. 1.

153. Hening 1809–1823, 3:252. This was the first legal attempt to define "races" in Virginia.

154. McIlwaine 1918, p. 262.

155. Ballagh 1902, p. 50. Even then, the idea was not acceptable to some whites for another ninety years (cases of 1792 and 1793, cited in Ballagh 1902, p. 51).

156. Hening 1809–1823, 3:251; Indians are specifically mentioned, along with other non-whites.

157. Ibid., 298; brackets mine.

158. Ibid., 449–450.

159. Ibid., 452–453; Indians are not mentioned specifically.

160. Ibid., 453–454; Indians are not mentioned specifically.

161. Ibid., 459; brackets mine.

162. Ibid., 448–449.

Chapter Seven. A Century of Culture Change

1. Merrell 1979; when he wrote, it was usual for scholars to assume that "cultural disintegration followed on the heels of political subordination" (p. 549), and he cites my work as an exception to the trend. Another exception is Brasser (1971, pp. 75–76).

2. The clergymen included: John Clayton (1657–1725), resident in Virginia 1684–1686 as minister at Jamestown; traveled up and down James River and was close friend of William Byrd II, who knew the Appomattuck Indians. John Banister (1650–1692), resident in Virginia from 1678 onward, minister in Bristol Parish on Appomattox River after 1680, and friend of William Byrd I; saw Appamattucks and Monacans, and may have visited the Pamunkeys. Anonymous minister whose account of 1689 (edited by Pargellis) shows knowledge of Powhatans, Tuscaroras, and possibly others. Thomas Glover, physician and possibly clergyman, who resided in Virginia several years before 1676 and whose movements are uncertain. Hugh Jones (1692–1760), resident in Virginia 1717–1721 as teacher of natural philosophy and mathematics at the College of William and Mary; knew Indian students at the college, visited Fort Christanna (inhabited by non-Powhatan Indians), and traveled to Maryland at least once before writing his book. It was not unusual in Britain of those days for men interested in natural history to be ordained and make their living as clergymen.

The travelers included: John Lederer (ca. 1644–?), German scholar and explorer who in 1670 made three expeditions to the Virginia Appalachians using Powhatan Indian guides. Durand de Dauphine, French Huguenot who visited the Indians in the Nanzatico-Portobacco area in 1687. Thomas Story, who saw Indians on the Blackwater River in 1698 and proselytized at the Chickahominy town on Mattaponi River in 1699. Francis Louis Michel, Swiss traveler who visited Monacan town and witnessed tributary Indian participation in Williamsburg's celebration of accession of Queen Anne of Great Britain in 1702. John Fontaine, French Huguenot who visited Indian house on Pamunkey Neck in 1716 before passing on to Fort Christanna.

The Virginia landowners included: Robert Beverley (ca. 1673–1722), who inherited thousands of acres in King and Queen County and knew the Chickahominies and others on Mattaponi River as neighbors; he represented the Indians' land claims in the survey of Pamunkey Neck in the 1690s (Sainsbury 1860, 20:547) and later wrote about the Indians at length, borrowing some passages from Banister in the process. Thomas Mathew, planter on the Northern Neck who was a member of the colonial Council in 1676 when the Council interviewed the Queen of Pamunkey; however, he did not write about her or the events of Bacon's Rebellion until twenty-nine years later.

3. For a detailed description of this way of life, see Rountree 1989.

4. Beverley's somewhat vague estimate of bowmen (1947 [1705], pp. 232–233) multiplied by four. Contrast that with Morgan's estimate (1975, p. 404) of 62,800 non-Indians in the Virginia colony.

5. Banister said they lived "within the English pale" in 1690 (1970, p. 381), while Beverley wrote in 1705 (1947 [1705], p. 232) that they lived "in Collonel *Byrd's* Pasture. . . ."

6. Banister 1970, p. 382.

7. Ibid., p. 383.

8. Beverley 1947 [1705], pp. 181–182.

9. Story 1847 [1698] (this account is unpaginated).

10. Clayton 1965 [1687], p. 39; Clayton 1968 [1687], p. 434.

11. Jones 1956 [1724], p. 55.

12. Burnaby 1812 [1760], p. 718; brackets mine. Traveler Burnaby's late account shows continuity in an Indian male occupation established in the 1610s.

13. Pargellis 1959, p. 243; Banister 1970, p. 385; Beverley 1947 [1705], pp. 154–155.

14. Glover 1904 [1676], pp. 23–24; Beverley 1947 [1705], p. 149; Clayton 1968 [1687], p. 418.

15. Burnaby 1812 [1760], p. 718.

16. See Hudson 1981.

17. Beverley 1947 [1705], p. 155.

18. Glover 1904 [1676], pp. 25–26.

19. Banister 1970, p. 386. There were still some beaver in the coastal plain, judging by the references to "beaver dams" as landmarks in the land patents (Nugent 1977 and 1979).

20. Banister 1970, p. 385; brackets and assignment of sex to items made are mine.

21. Implied in Stern 1951, pp. 44–46.

22. Durand de Dauphine 1934 [1687], p. 153.

23. Beverley 1947 [1705], p. 230.

24. Durand de Dauphine 1934 [1687], p. 153.

25. Clayton 1965 [1687], p. 39; Clayton 1968 [1687], p. 434; Pargellis 1959, p. 232; Banister 1970, p. 382.

26. See chap. 6.

27. Banister 1970, p. 376.

28. Anonymous 1900, p. 3.

29. McIlwaine 1925, 2:364.

30. Clayton 1965 [1687], p. 37; Clayton 1968 [1687], p. 434; Banister 1970, p. 377; Beverley 1947 [1705], p. 181.

31. Banister 1970, p. 377; Beverley 1947 [1705], p. 181; Jones 1956 [1724], p. 55.

32. Beverley 1947 [1705], p. 178.

33. Clayton 1968 [1687], pp. 434–435. Beverley (1947 [1705], p. 177) speaks of trebling the pale for extra security.

34. Beverley 1947 [1705], p. 177; Jones 1956 [1724], p. 55.

35. Beverley 1947 [1705], p. 177.

36. Clayton 1968 [1687], p. 435.

37. Jones 1956 [1724], p. 55.

38. McIlwaine 1915, 3:349; Story 1847 [1698].

39. Jones 1956 [1724], p. 55.

40. Beverley (1947 [1705], p. 174) misspells it "wigwangs," and borrows the term from New England.

41. Glover 1904 [1676], p. 23; Clayton 1968 [1687], p. 435; Pargellis 1959, p. 231; Durand de Dauphine 1934 [1687], p. 152; Banister 1970, p. 383; Story 1847 [1698]; Beverley 1947 [1705], p. 174, 176. Fontaine (1853 [1715], entry for June 12, 1715) differs: "an Indian cabin, which was built with posts put into the ground, the one by the other as close as they could stand, and about seven feet high, all of an equal length. It was built four-square, and a sort of roof upon it, covered with the bark of trees."

42. Glover 1904 [1676], p. 23; Clayton 1968 [1687], p. 435; Pargellis 1959, p. 231; Banister 1970, p. 383; Story 1847 [1698]; Beverley 1947 [1705], p. 174.

43. Beverley 1947 [1705], p. 174.

44. Ibid., p. 174, illus. p. 175.

45. Archaeological evidence of Indian housing in the protohistorical and early contact

periods is very limited at present (Clarence Geier and E. Randolph Turner, personal communications).

46. For evidence for extended families living in houses, see Rountree 1989, pp. 90–91.

47. Banister 1970, p. 373; Pargellis 1959, p. 230; Jones 1956 [1724], p. 56. Fontaine (1853 [1715], entry for June 12, 1715) describes breechclouts for women, which Beverley echoes by saying that breechclouts were worn by "the common sort" (1947 [1705], p. 162). Editors Joseph and Nesta Ewan describe duffields as "three-quarter-width blankets of a coarse wool mixture designed especially for the Indian trade"; it was dyed with cheap pigments and sent over in 30-yard by 1 3/4-yard pieces (p. 373 n. 9).

48. Beverley 1947 [1705], p. 162.

49. Pargellis 1959, p. 230; passage was added to the manuscript by a second anonymous writer.

50. Banister 1970, pp. 373–374. Editors' note on colors: "Off-white, red, and blue." This account is seconded by Jones (1956 [1724], p. 56), who wrote that Indians "think themselves very fine in such coats as our common soldiers wear, or of any taudry colours."

51. Durand de Dauphine 1934 [1687], p. 157.

52. Ibid., p. 153; this may be true only of the Rappahannocks/Portobaccos.

53. Pargellis 1959, p. 230.

54. Leggings of cloth: Jones 1956 [1724], p. 56; moccasins of "cotton or leather": Banister 1970, p. 374. Illus. of both: Beverley 1947 [1705], p. 172.

55. Beverley 1947 [1705], p. 159.

56. Banister 1970, p. 373; Glover 1904 [1676], pp. 21–22 (writing of both sexes); Michel 1918 [1702], p. 130; Beverley 1947 [1705], pp. 159, 162.

57. Beverley 1947 [1705], p. 159.

58. Banister 1970, p. 373.

59. Jones 1956 [1724], p. 57.

60. Durand de Dauphine 1934 [1687], p. 152.

61. Mathew 1947 [1705], p. 14.

62. Banister 1970, p. 378.

63. Berry and Moryson 1896 [1677], pp. 140–141.

64. Beverley 1947 [1705], p. 162.

65. For a detailed description of that currency, see Beverley 1947 [1705], pp. 227–228; see also Rountree 1989, pp. 72–73, illus. p. 74.

66. Pargellis 1959, p. 230.

67. Banister 1970, p. 373; Beverley 1947 [1705], p. 162; Michel 1918 [1702], p. 130 (illustration following that page shows a coronet with a checkerboard design; the Gribelin engraving in Beverley [1947 (1705), p. 163] shows a similar design with a suggestion of scrolling in purple beads).

68. Beverley 1947 [1705], p. 166; brackets mine.

69. Banister 1970, p. 373.

70. Beverley 1947 [1705], p. 162.

71. Since it was the Chickahominy town, it is probable that this man was only one of several councillors, not a ruler.

72. Story 1847 [1698]; brackets mine.

73. Banister 1970, p. 380; repeated by Beverley 1947 [1705], p. 207, who adds "or oftener."

74. Beverley 1947 [1705], p. 208.

75. Ibid., p. 232.

76. Though one "King Tom" was sentenced to a whipping in 1697 for receiving stolen goods (Northampton County, Orders and Wills 13:510–511). There is no indication in the document that the "King" in his name referred to any office he held among his people.

77. Beverley 1947 [1705], p. 233.

78. See the reference to a "secret medicine" owned by the elders and used in trapping beaver, above.

79. Glover (1904 [1676], p. 22) and Jones (1956 [1724], p. 54) wrote forty-eight years apart that every Indian town had a "king," a statement that was never true for the Chickahominies and that was less true for other Powhatan groups as time went on.

80. The identity of this man is not certain. He may have been a husband of the niece of Cockacoeske who inherited from her aunt in 1686, or he may have been a successor to this niece.

81. Clayton 1965 [1694], pp. 105–106. One "Captain Pipsco" is also recorded as having a horse in 1670 (McIlwaine 1979 [1924], p. 230); his tribal identity is unknown, but his title, "captain," indicates fairly high status.

82. Beverley 1947 [1705], p. 226.

83. Clayton 1965 [1687], p. 22; Clayton 1968 [1687], p. 435; Beverley 1947 [1705], pp. 174, 225; Jones 1956 [1724], p. 54.

84. Michel 1918 [1702], p. 131.

85. Beverley 1947 [1705], p. 226. The term "black boys" may refer to boys newly initiated into manhood; see Rountree 1989, pp. 80–82.

86. Beverley 1947 [1705], pp. 186–189; part of Beverley's description is from Hennepin and does not concern the Powhatans.

87. Clayton 1965 [1687], p. 22.

88. Glover 1904 [1676], p. 26; Pargellis 1959, p. 243; Beverley 1947 [1705], p. 226; Jones 1956 [1724], pp. 57–58.

89. Clayton 1968 [1687], p. 435; Jones 1956 [1724], pp. 54, 57.

90. Pargellis 1959, p. 235. We cannot even be certain that this statement refers to Powhatan towns. The number seven was important in kinship and politics in the traditional Cherokees.

91. Pargellis 1959, p. 232; brackets mine.

92. Beverley 1947 [1705], pp. 170–171.

93. Pargellis 1959, p. 233.

94. Beverley 1947 [1705], pp. 170–171. He went on to say that "the *Indians* themselves disown any such custom" as having children before marriage.

95. Ibid., p. 189.

96. Pargellis 1959, p. 233; Jones 1956 [1724], p. 60.

97. Durand de Dauphine 1934 [1687], pp. 153–154; Pargellis 1959, pp. 233–234.

98. Pargellis 1959, p. 234; Banister 1970, p. 381.

99. Jones 1956 [1724], p. 60.

100. Clayton 1965 [1687], p. 38; Beverley 1947 [1705], pp. 177, 221, 224.

101. Clayton 1965 [1687], pp. 38–39; Beverley 1947 [1705], p. 221.

102. Pargellis 1959, p. 232.

103. Clayton 1965 [1687], p. 38; Durand de Dauphine 1934 [1687], p. 153.

104. Durand de Dauphine 1934 [1687], p. 153; Beverley 1947 [1705], p. 145.

105. Clayton 1965 [1687], p. 38.

106. Mary Ellen Hodges Norrissey, personal communication, 1985.

107. See Lurie 1974, for an overview of Native American drinking patterns.

108. Michel 1918 [1702], p. 132.

109. Clayton 1965 [1687], p. 37; Michel 1918 [1702], p. 132; Beverley 1947 [1705], p. 182; Jones 1956 [1724], p. 56.

110. Beverley 1947 [1705], p. 182. He was more accurate than he knew in drawing a parallel between inebriation by alcohol and trance inducement through smoking native tobacco in a religious context. Perhaps significantly, seventeenth-century English colonists often used the term "drinking" tobacco for "smoking" it.

111. Pargellis 1959, p. 231; since we do not know the movements of this anonymous writer within Virginia, we cannot be sure he was speaking of Powhatan people.

112. Clayton 1968 [1687], p. 436; Pargellis 1959, p. 230; Banister 1970, p. 377.

113. For a detailed discussion of these functions, see Rountree 1989, pp. 130–133.

114. Pargellis 1959, p. 232.

115. My evidence, in the absence of detailed skeletal studies from Virginia, is the Narragansett cemetery of 1650–1670 reported on by Robinson, Kelley, and Rubertone (1985). Tuberculosis and dental caries were rife in that population, and the vast majority of the people did not reach the age of fifty—in contrast to an earlier Contact Period Narragansett population (cemetery excavated by Simmons [1970]).

116. Clayton 1968 [1687], p. 435.

117. Clayton 1965 [1687], p. 21.

118. Clayton 1968 [1687], p. 435—in which he says that he was not able to substantiate any of the stories because the Indians would not talk; Pargellis 1959, pp. 232–233; Beverley 1947 [1705], pp. 201–202.

119. Beverley 1947 [1705], pp. 204–205.

120. This New England Algonquian word has been borrowed into English as "powwow." As late as the 1880s it was used by Anglo-Americans such as Mark Twain to mean a noisy confabulation or uproar.

121. Clayton 1965 [1687], p. 22. Beverley himself did not connect the Byrd anecdote and his own observations on Indian taciturnity; he simply retails the anecdote in a neutral way.

122. Ibid., pp. 24–25. A Hanover County man was also sent once to the Pamunkey weroansqua's town for a cure (Chamberlayne 1940, p. 18).

123. John Clayton and Robert Beverley were unusual for their time. So was Nicholas Moreau, who wrote in 1697 that "our Indians . . . have the best secrets of any Physician in Europe might have" (Chamberlayne 1937, Appendix). Yet Moreau wrote down practically nothing of what he learned about those "secrets," saying it was "too tedious."

124. Wounds: Clayton 1965 [1687], p. 23; both maladies: Glover 1904 [1676], p. 27.

125. Glover 1904 [1676], p. 27; his claim for recovery in all cases where the Indian cure was used may be exaggerated.

126. Clayton 1965 [1694], p. 112. Since Claiborne died in 1677, the incident dates to that year or before.

127. Beverley 1947 [1705], p. 195.

128. Ibid., p. 200.

129. For a detailed discussion of Powhatan religious beliefs in the early seventeenth century, see Rountree 1989, chap. 8.

130. Banister 1970, p. 378.

131. Beverley 1947 [1705], p. 198: "a several name in every Nation, as Okee, Quioccos, Kiwasa." From these variants I conclude that the Powhatan word was kwiokos (pl., kwiokosuk).

132. Clayton 1968 [1687], p. 435. According to Feest (personal communication, 1986), the word means "evil spirit."

133. Glover 1904 [1676], p. 25; Clayton 1968 [1687], p. 435; Durand de Dauphine 1934 [1687], p. 153; Michel 1918 [1702], p. 131. Beverley 1947 [1705], pp. 198, 200–201.

134. Beverley 1947 [1705], p. 196.

135. The only writer to mention the sun says specifically, "None of them worship the sun or moon" (Pargellis 1959, p. 236).

136. Ibid., p. 236 (no further details given); because the writer is anonymous, his movements in Virginia and the Indians he met are unknown.

137. Clayton 1968 [1687], p. 436; Pargellis 1959, p. 236; Michel 1918 [1702], pp. 131–132—couched in terms of warm climate to the east and cold climate to the north; Beverley 1947 [1705], p. 202. The quotations are from Beverley.

138. The anonymous writer of 1689 expresses it differently (Pargellis 1959, p. 236): souls "wander up and down about their marishes and feed on coarse herbs. They say that this horrible wild place . . . is within sight of the other [i.e., heaven], but they can never come at it, for the bushes and briars, and swamps and marshes that are between them and it." The food in hell is raw, "as frogs, flies etc., there being nothing there to dress their victuals withall."

139. Beverley 1947 [1705], p. 201.
140. Pargellis 1959, pp. 231–232; Beverley 1947 [1705], pp. 214, 216.
141. Implied in Glover 1904 [1676], pp. 24–25; the Indian communities described are uncertain.
142. Pargellis 1959, p. 234; again, communities described are uncertain.
143. Clayton 1968 [1687], p. 434; Durand de Dauphine 1934 [1687], p. 154.
144. Story 1847 [1698].
145. The crime for which the tribe was dispersed by the English; see chap. 5.
146. Richmond County, Orders 3:362; brackets mine. Note the similarity between the Nanzatico "Quasko Hewks" and the Pamunkey (or possibly Chickahominy) "Coscohunk." The meaning of this personal name is uncertain.
147. McIlwaine 1918, p. 368 *et passim*.
148. McIlwaine 1915, 6:30; Hening 1809–1823, 4:461.
149. E.g., James Revell and Edward Gunstocker; see chap. 6.
150. Mathew 1947 [1705], p. 14.
151. The Pamunkey called "Mr. Marshall" appears in 1699 (McIlwaine 1925, 2:22).
152. E.g., John Mush of Pamunkey or Chickahominy in 1704 (see chap. 5); John West, an Indian on the Eastern Shore who collected a bounty on a wolf's head in 1707 (Northampton County, Wills Etc. 14:379) may have been a "core" member of the Gingaskins, since the surname West appears in the tribe through the 1810s.
153. McIlwaine 1925, 3:81.
154. Palmer 1875, 1:133–134; McIlwaine 1925, 3:226.
155. E.g., Pamunkeys hired by Richard Littlepage in 1710 (Palmer 1875, 1:150–151).
156. The Pamunkeys complained in 1711 of people "kept" by the English against the queen's will (McIlwaine 1925, 3:288). The queen blamed the employers, but the employees were also at fault.
157. The Powhatans could have met some people from India, for east Indians were occasionally brought to Virginia as slaves. One named Occanough, born in Madras, hired himself out to an unscrupulous English ship's captain, who sold him as a slave upon their arrival in England; brought by his "master" to Virginia in 1694, Occanough sued successfully for his freedom in 1707 (Essex County, Orders 3:370, 376, 379). An East Indian was also implicated, along with a black slave, in a robbery at Gloucester in 1737 (*Virginia Gazette* [Claiborne] April 22, 1737 [reference from Martha McCartney]).
158. 1956 [1724], p. 50. It is uncertain whether Jones was writing of the Powhatan boys he knew at William and Mary or of the non-Powhatan people settled at Fort Christanna.
159. I inferred that the Powhatans had that trait in Rountree 1989, p. 96.
160. Clayton 1968 [1687], p. 434.
161. Jones 1956 [1724], p. 57.
162. Michel 1918 [1702], p. 134.
163. Beverley 1947 [1705], pp. 38–39; Spotswood 1882, 2:227 (also printed in Sainsbury 1860, 29:281–282); Byrd 1966, p. 160.
164. Spotswood 1882, 2:227 (also printed in Sainsbury 1860, 29:281–282).
165. Clayton (1968 [1687], p. 436) says the Indians learned their worst vices from the English and quotes one drunken Indian telling another, "Swear, you be Englishman swear, wth that he made a horrid yelling, imperfectly vomited up oaths, whereupon the other cryd, of! now your [*sic*] be Englishman." Story (1847 [1698]) also records that when an Indian became drunk, "then, swearing, ranting, and blaspheming, he'll cry aloud, I am now all one Englishman."
166. Pargellis 1959, p. 232; Banister 1970, p. 382.
167. Banister 1970, p. 382.
168. Beverley 1947 [1705], p. 182; brackets mine; based upon Banister 1970, p. 377.
169. Clayton 1965 [1687], pp. 37–38.

170. Distinguished from the Christianized, nonreservation Nansemonds living in Nansemond and Norfolk counties.

171. McIlwaine 1925, 2:315–316, 331, 405, 410, 453; ibid. 3:12–13, 45, 49, 83, 98, 101, 143, 152, 172, 200, 204–205, 214, 220, 240, 287, 296–297, 303–304, 306; McIlwaine 1915, 4:91, 92–93, 98; Sainsbury 1860, 26:278.

172. McIlwaine 1925, 3:198, 220.

173. Ibid., 352.

174. Ibid. 101, 223–224, 265, 296–297, 306.

175. Anonymous 1896–1897; Anonymous 1900; Byrd 1966.

176. In 1713; terms of treaty; Sainsbury 1860, 27:307–310.

177. Boyce 1978, pp. 286–287.

178. For a detailed history of the Nottoways, see Rountree 1987.

179. A single interpreter was employed to deal with the Nottoways, Meherrins, and Nansemonds (McIlwaine 1915, 5:180, 222); these Nansemonds lived on the Nottoway Reservation by 1744 (see below). The Christianized Nansemonds, on the other hand, may have spoken only English by 1700; no document survives to indicate their language.

180. McIlwaine 1925, 3:510 *et passim;* another, unpublished, document that is relevant is Virginia Colonial Papers, Folder 20, No. 22.

181. Spotswood 1882, 2:282.

182. See chap. 5.

183. McIlwaine 1925, 4:8 *et passim;* Hening 1809–1823, 4:103–106.

184. McCary 1983.

185. McIlwaine 1925, 3:286.

186. Essex County, Orders 4:51; Orders 10:259; Orders 16:292; Orders 17:75; Wills 9:84 (also printed in *William and Mary Quarterly,* 2d ser., 16:599); Orders 23:145; Richmond County, Orders 7:53.

187. Beverley 1947 [1705], p. 232; I am using modern spellings of the names, which survive in the creeks of the area.

188. Sainsbury 1860, 24:481.

189. Beverley 1947 [1705], p. 233.

190. See chap. 5.

191. McIlwaine 1925, 3:237.

192. Cited in deed of 1718, Northumberland County, Record Book 1718–1726, pp. 95–96.

193. Sainsbury 1860, 27:15. Spotswood enumerates Pamunkeys, Chickahominies, Nansemonds, Nottoways, Meherrins, Saponis, Stukanoxes, Occoneechees, and Tutelos, estimating their total population at 700. The size of the Powhatan component was probably small.

194. McIlwaine 1925, 3:356.

195. Northumberland County, Orders 1713–1719, p. 173.

196. Northumberland County, Record Book 1718–1726, pp. 95–96.

197. Northumberland County, Orders 1713–1719, p. 321, and Record Book 1718–1726, pp. 61–62.

198. Northumberland County, Record Book 1718–1726, pp. 79–80. The name of the decedent in this document is "William Tapp," but the names of the other executors and the date of their qualification match those of the June 1719 document.

199. Virginia Colonial Papers, Folder 22, No. 18; printed with errors (as being written 1708 and signer as "Fra. Maoco") in Palmer 1875, 1:127–128.

200. Done by Drammaco: McIlwaine 1925, 3:272; terms of "exchange": ibid., 487.

201. Ibid., 272.

202. Ibid., 487.

203. McIlwaine 1918, pp. 666, 689, 707; McIlwaine 1915, 5:224; ibid. 6:15. All of these referenes mention both tribes.

204. Sainsbury 1860, 37:217–218.

205. Commonwealth of Virginia, Legislative Petitions, King William County, December 19, 1825.

206. A name totally discounted by Upper Mattaponis today (Rountree, Fieldnotes and Correspondence), although I have met a current member of the tribe with that name. Some Dungees appear in turn-of-the-century county records as "Indians" and in one U.S. Census (1910) as living on the Mattaponi Reservation. One "Indian" Dungee family, who cannot be traced to Adamstown people, went "colored" in the early twentieth century; a granddaughter, who was a "black" student of mine in the mid-1970s at Old Dominion University, told me one of her cousins had lived variously as black, white, or Indian when it suited him.

207. Not the least erudite scholar to make this mistake has been Johnston (1970, pp. 277–279).

208. An exhaustive search of federal, state, and county records has shown me no Dungees among them at any time.

209. These names are Adkins and Bradby. The origin of "Adkins" is uncertain. The ancestor of the Chickahominy Bradbys was John Bradby, born ca. 1780. He probably came from the Pamunkey Bradbys, though connections are vague and there was already a white man named Edward Bradby (usually "Bradley") in Charles City County from 1787 to 1802.

210. One of several William Basses alive at the time sold land in 1737 (Norfolk County, Deeds 12:188) that his wife, the former Sarah Lovina, had inherited from Lt. Col. John Nichols in 1697. Nichols left nothing to his wife's children by a former marriage, and instead he divided his estate between the son and daughter of "my negro woman Named Joan Lovina" and freed them both (Norfolk County, Record Books 5:95). Historians usually read such generosity as a sign of paternity (see Johnston 1970, pp. 218–226). I have been unable to place this William Bass positively anywhere in the Nansemond genealogy I have compiled. In that genealogy, I used the Norfolk County records, U.S. Censuses, Bell 1961, the family Bible and Sermon Book, and one of the certificates Bell cites (all still in Nansemond hands), Wingo 1961, 1963, and 1981, and interviews with modern Nansemonds, especially old-timers.

211. Certificate in possession of Bass descendants; printed in Bell 1961, section on Indian-descended Basses, p. 15.

212. Certificate in possession of Bass descendants; printed in Bell 1961, section on Indian-descended Basses, p. 16.

213. Certificate in possession of Bass descendants; printed in Bell 1961, section on Indian-descended Basses, p. 15.

214. Certificate in possession of Bass descendants; photographed copy in my possession.

215. McIlwaine 1925, 4:2 et passim; Sainsbury 1860, 33:299; Virginia Colonial Papers, Folder 31, No. 20.

216. Sainsbury 1860, 37:217–218.

217. Hening 1809–1823, 5:269–273.

218. Isle of Wight County, Deeds 7:267–269; McIlwaine 1925, 5:211–212.

219. McIlwaine 1915, 7:293; ibid. 10:181–182.

220. Legislative Petitions, Southampton County, October 30, 1786.

221. Hening 1809–1823, 12:386–387.

222. Ibid. 13:288–289.

223. Southampton County, Deeds 7:714–716.

224. Rountree 1987.

225. Indians complaining: Northampton County, Orders 20:26, 35; Orders 22:109, 112, 297, 312–313, 331, 354; Orders 24:400, 406; Minute Book 1761–1765, p. 35.

226. Indians suing: Northampton County, Orders 18:186; Indians suing each other: Northampton County, Orders 22:127–128, 145, 175, 196–197.

227. Indians being sued: Northampton County, Orders 19:51, 77; Minute Book 1777–1783, p. 186, 252.

228. Northampton County, Orders 20:26, 142; Orders 22:243; Minute Book 1765–1771, p. 382 (in which "Nathan Drighouse Negro" was bound out at age three; he may have

been the Nathan Drighouse [descended from a seventeenth-century Rodriguez] who received a share of the Gingaskin land in 1813); Minute Book 1771–1777, p. 225, 240; Orders 30:51.

229. Northampton County, Orders 24:355; Minute Book 1754–1761, p. 230; Minute Book 1761–1765, p. 4; Minute Book 1765–1771, p. 64; Minute Book 1777–1783, p. 278.

230. Northampton County, Deeds and Wills 19:300, 303; Wills, Etc. 15:14, 101, 151, 156, 204, 213 (1720s).

231. Northampton County, Orders 17:192.

232. Northampton County, Wills 26:110; Orders 18:326. Another case, in 1752, involved two Indian slaves who had sued for their freedom: the court ruled that they had "no right to their Freedom" and no leave to prosecute for it (Orders 23:171, 186–187).

233. Hening 1809–1823, 8:414–415.

234. Hungars Parish Vestry Book, pp. 33, 34.

235. Hungars Parish Vestry Book, p. 41.

236. Hungars Parish Vestry Book, p. 54.

237. McIlwaine 1915, 13:14; Hening 1809–1823, 8:661.

238. They were accused of it in the petitions sent to the Assembly later (see below); I have been able to document it in the county records of the late eighteenth and early nineteenth centuries.

239. Jefferson 1954 [1787], p. 96. Jefferson does not mention Indians paying tribute, but that is probably the occasion on which he saw them.

240. Palmer 1875, 1:105 (a petition whose signatories were Queen Ann, Mᵣ John Mᵣ Peck, Mᵣ Rogers, Mᵣ Bacon, Mᵣ Leason, and Mᵣ Myunk); McIlwaine 1925, 3:133. The petition is the first English document in which Queen Ann of Pamunkey appears by name.

241. McIlwaine 1925, 3:272, 355–356, 359–360.

242. Ibid., 81.

243. For example, their 1708 complaint that their young men Robin, George Tawhaw, Tom Rosen, and Parrahoa had been "invigled away" (ibid., 198).

244. Virginia Colonial Papers, Folder 22, No. 18; printed (with errors, including date of 1708) in Palmer 1875, 1:127–128. The signatories to this petition were "Queen Pamamuck, Ann," Mᵣ Younks, Mᵣ John, Mᵣ Powhite, Thos. Beck, Tra-Macco, Sham-Mearen, Henry Marshall, James Corran, Thos Rogers, Charles, Thos. Secawean, and John Hicks.

245. Ibid., 184–185. This is the last of the three English documents in which Queen Ann appears by name.

246. McIlwaine 1925, 3:466, 487 (1718). An unnamed Pamunkey queen, probably Ann, is named in this document, the last clear, contemporary reference to a Pamunkey ruler.

247. Winfree 1971, pp. 263–265. An unnamed Pamunkey queen consented to the sale; however the wording of the document is not clear as to whether her consent was given in 1723 or at an earlier time.

248. McIlwaine 1925, 3:444.

249. So stated in the preamble to the 1748 law (Winfree 1971, pp. 416–418).

250. As far as I know, the Pamunkey Reservation has never been formally surveyed.

251. The only references for this name before 1894 are Thomas Jefferson (1787) and a legislative petition of 1812 (see below). The King William Land (and Personal Property Tax) Books speak of only one "Indian Town," the one at Pamunkey. Henceforth, until that reservation formally split apart from the Pamunkeys in 1894, I will call it "Mattaponi," with quotation marks because I am not positive about the tribal origins of all of the people.

252. Sainsbury 1860, 37:218.

253. Winfree 1971, pp. 416–418, brackets mine; the original petition has been lost, but the law's lengthy preamble probably gives much of the text of it.

254. George Langston, John Langston, William Langston, George Tawhaw, John Sampson, Thomas Cook, and Thomas Sampson.

255. Hening 1809–1823, 7:298–299.

256. McIlwaine 1915, 9:166–167.

257. Ibid., 206, 222.

258. Ibid. 11:239–240.

259. Hening 1809–1823, 8:433–434.

260. Mush's service was for seven years, as a private: 1776–1779 in 15th Virginia Regiment, then 11th Virginia Regiment, then 1st Virginia Regiment; he fought at Brandywine and Germantown and after the American surrender at Charlestown, he was a prisoner of war fourteen months until exchanged; he received and promptly sold a bounty of land after the war ended (National Archives, Revolutionary War Pensions and Bounty Land Warrant Application Files, microcopy M-804, reel 1797). Other Pamunkeys' service: Legislative Petitions, King William County, November 6, 1779, paying reimbursement of moneys paid to soldier's wives and children; probable Indian wives include Nancy Cooke [sic], Lucy Langton (sic), Sarah Mush, Nancy Sampson, Nancy Major and Sarah Major (a fringe name). Various Cooks, Langstons, Sampsons, Gunns and Majorses show up in Virginia regiments, with only William Langston and John, Richard, and George Sampson being combinations that actually appear on Pamunkey documents; Robert Mursh is listed in the Virginia Battalion (National Archives, Revolutionary War Rosters).

261. Gingaskins, "Mattaponis," and Nansemonds among Algonquian speakers; the Iroquoian Nottoways remained in possession of a reservation as well.

262. Hening 1809–1823, 9:119.

263. Ibid. 10:97–98.

264. Shepherd 1835, 1:166–167.

265. Executive Papers, *passim*. At this writing the Virginia Executive Papers have never been fully inventoried. However, in 1983 I made an inventory of all Indian-related documents through 1857 in that collection (copy on file at Virginia State Library).

266. Legislative Petitions, King William County, December 7, 1786.

267. Legislative Petitions, King William County, December 4, 1812; Acts of Assembly 1812–1813, p. 116.

268. The original petition has been lost, though the resulting law's lengthy preamble probably quotes much of it; Acts of Assembly 1827–1828, pp. 109–110.

269. Charred deeds survive for most years—except for 1823–1834.

270. See chap. 8.

271. This and the other county court documents were copied to accompany Hill's petition to the Assembly, and they comprise the papers filed with the legislative petition of December 1, 1812.

272. No document from the Indians is preserved in the case.

273. Legislative Petitions, King William County, December 1, 1812; brackets mine.

274. No Act of Assembly was passed for Hill at any time, and the King William County Land Books show John Hill paying taxes on the same acreage (1266 A.) in 1811, 1812, and 1813.

275. Hening 1809–1823, 4:126–128.

276. Ibid., 326.

277. Ibid., 405–406.

278. B.P.R.O., C.O. 5/1323, f 306.

279. Hening 1809–1823, 5:244–245.

280. McIlwaine 1915, 10:84.

281. Hening 1809–1823, 12:184.

282. Fort Christanna comes the closest, but it always retained its military character.

283. Hugh Jones wrote that "the missionaries that are now sent, generally keep among the English, and rarely see an Indian, or when they do, know but little how to manage them" (1956 [1724], p. 62). For an excellent example of the process of gradual and successful mixing of Christianity and Indian culture, see Ronda 1981, about Martha's Vineyard.

284. *Virginia Gazette* (Rind edition), March 15, 1770, supplement p. 1.

285. King William County, Land (and Personal Property Tax) Books, 1782–1850.

286. Legislative Petitions, King William County, December 27, 1798.

287. Shepherd 1835, 2:162.

288. For a good summary of its history, see Stuart 1984.

289. W. Robinson 1952, p. 162.

290. Spotswood 1882, 1:125.

291. Ibid., 122 (also printed in Sainsbury 1860, 26:158).

292. Ibid., 122, 134; McIlwaine 1925, 3:290 291. Wiccocomicos and Gingaskins are not mentioned, although Spotswood wrote that "there are now Hostages from all the Towns of our Tributary Indians."

293. Spotswood 1882, 1:174 (also printed in Sainsbury 1860, 17:171).

294. Spotswood 1882, 2:88.

295. Ibid., 91.

296. Anonymous 1896, pp. 165, 172.

297. College statutes, quoted in Stuart 1984, p. 31.

298. Jones 1956 [1724], p. 114.

299. Ibid., p. 60.

300. Ibid., pp. 62, 114.

301. Byrd 1966, pp. 220, 221.

302. Spotswood 1882, 2:227 (also printed in Sainsbury 1860, 29:281–282).

303. Stiles 1916, p. 158.

304. William and Mary College, Bursar's Book 1754–1770, p. 1 (list also printed in *William and Mary Quarterly*, 1st ser., 6:188). The boys were John Sampson, Charles Murphey, Gideon Langston, William Cooke [*sic*], John Langston, Thomas Sampson, William Squirrell, John Montour. Squirrell was a Nansemond name (Isle of Wight County, Deeds 7:267–269). John Montour was the son of Andrew Montour, an interpreter of mixed Indian and French-Canadian ancestry; he went on to command a company of Delaware Indians on the American side in 1782 (Stuart 1984, p. 58). Murphey may have been a misspelling of Mursh or Mush, a Pamunkey name. All the others are Pamunkeys.

305. William and Mary College, Catalogue 1859. The list includes John Sampson in 1764 and John Tawhaw in 1765 (p. 37); Robert Mush and George Sampson in 1769 (p. 38); George Sampson and Reuben Sampson in 1775 (p. 41); and James Gunn and Edmund Sampson in 1776 (p. 42). All were Pamunkeys.

306. Submitted by his wife in her application for a pension as widow of a Revolutionary War veteran (National Archives, Revolutionary War Pensions and Bounty Land Warrant Application Files, Microcopy M-804, Reel 1797).

307. Tyler 1907–1908, pp. 172–173.

308. Jefferson 1954 [1787], p. 96.

309. Robert Mursh, Francis Sampson, John Sampson, Sr., Lewis Gunn, Willis Langston, William Cooper, Thomas Gurley, John Langston, Sr., John Langston, Jr., Armistead Sampson, and James Williams. The text of the petition is unclear as to whether these were all the adult males of the tribe. James Williams appears in no other contemporary document, Pamunkey or white.

310. Willis Langston, William Cooper, James Langston, John Langston, Thomas Cooke [*sic*], Archibald Langston, Louis Gunn, William Gunn, Gideon Langston, John Sampson, William Sampson, John Mursh, Louis Langston, and Henry Sampson.

311. William and Mary College, Bursar's Book 1754–1770, pp. 1, 8; William and Mary College, Catalogue 1859, p. 32. The same Bursar's Book shows a James Whittall Bradby attending in 1763–64 (p. 46); the 1859 Catalogue's entry lists James Whittall Bradby from Surry County attending in 1754, so the compiler of the catalogue may have confused the two Bursar's Book entries.

312. King William County, Land [and Personal Property Tax] Books.

313. Colosse Baptist Church, Minute Book 1814–1834.

314. *Virginia Gazette* (Purdie and Dixon edition), November 29, 1770, p. 3; September 12, 1771. The Pamunkeys are known to have harbored one mulatto man in ca. 1770 (*Virginia Gazette* [Purdie and Dixon edition], March 5, 1772, p. 2; *Virginia Gazette* [Rind edition], March 12, 1772), but no marriage is mentioned for him. Three other runaway slaves with Indian connections appear in the *Virginia Gazette*, but the tribal affiliation of the Indian Father (Purdie and Dixon edition, November 26, 1772, p. 2, and December 3, 1772, p. 3) or wives (Dixon and Hunter edition, March 11, 1775, p. 3, and August 3, 1776) cannot be ascertained.

315. Only one of the advertisements specifies this much: Purdie & Dixon edition, September 12, 1771.

316. Legislative Petitions, King William County, November 25, 1795.

317. Langston 1969 [1894], p. 13. Stuart (1984, p. 59) identifies the tribe as Pamunkey and the Indian grandfather as either Gideon Langston or John Langston. I partially agree.

318. Gideon Langston's wife was Judy Sweat, probably a daughter of the fringe man William Sweat. Robert Mush's wife was a Pamunkey (surname unrecorded) by her own account and was treated as a white woman after the family moved to South Carolina.

319. Johnston 1970; Williamson 1980.

320. Rountree, Fieldnotes.

321. Ibid. The custom was invoked in the case of a woman with a white husband in 1984 (*Richmond Times-Dispatch,* January 20, 1985, pp. C–1, C–4), and several such women challenged it in 1989. The tribal laws printed in Pollard 1894 include no such law.

322. Burnaby 1812 [1760], p. 718.

323. B.P.R.O., C.O. 323, vol. 20; cited in W. Robinson 1959, p. 63.

324. National Archives, Revolutionary War Pensions and Bounty Land Warrant Application Files, Microcopy M–804, Reel 1797; this marriage and Elizabeth Mursh's attempts to get widow's pensions are recorded here.

325. The Murshes were remarried in the Baptist Church in 1797, after their conversion to Christianity and Robert's decision to become a preacher himself. Ironically, it was because of the lateness of this second, supposedly "real" marriage that the federal government denied Elizabeth her widow's pension after Robert's death in 1837. It took her twelve years to establish the legality of her pre-Christian tribal marriage. For the career among the Catawbas of Robert Mursh (later called Marsh), see Merrell 1989, pp. 242–243. Merrell says Robert married a Catawba woman whom he was unable to convert to Christianity; either Elizabeth later left the church, or the wife was a Catawba wife of Robert and Elizabeth's son John. Elizabeth was Pamunkey, as implied in the records of her pension application.

326. There is no eighteenth-century document after Robert Beverley that mentions the presence or absence of traditional priests among the Pamunkeys or other Powhatan remnants, so the date of death of the last traditional priest is unknown.

327. Eastern Chickahominy Chief E. P. Bradby, quoted in Stern 1952, p. 192.

328. Colosse Baptist Church, Minute Book 1814–1834. That church, the first organized in the county, was subsequently renamed Colosse. The New Kent man was "William Pearman N. K."

329. Flint Hill Baptist Church, York District, Records 1792–1899, p. 29; cited in D. Brown 1966, p. 272.

330. Autobiography of Samson Occom, manuscript quoted in Love 1899, p. 23.

331. Not all of the Algonquian tribes (mainly the Mahican) ancestral to the Stockbridge-Munsees settled at the mission; instead, those families who wished to adapt under white supervision became the Stockbridge-Munsees, while other families went elsewhere and kept other names (Mochon 1968, pp. 191–192).

332. Ibid., pp. 194, 208.

333. Hayes 1976, pp. 4, 6–8.

334. Implied in Weinstein 1986, p. 91, and Gonzalez 1986, pp. 120–121.

335. Loskiel 1794, p. 130. F. Porter (1980, p. 46) uses this passage as an analogue of eastern Indian behavior in general in the eighteenth century.

336. Weinstein 1986, p. 91.

337. Orcutt 1972 [1882], p. 67.

338. Apes 1829, p. 10.

339. Simmons and Simmons 1982, p. xxx.

340. Ronda 1981, p. 386n.

341. Weinstein 1986, pp. 91–92.

342. Stiles 1916, p. 167.

343. Mochon 1968, pp. 193, 195.

344. Stiles 1916, pp. 117, 131, 155.

345. Hayes 1976, p. 6.

346. Brasser 1966, p. 22.

347. Brasser 1966, p. 22.

348. Kawashima 1969, p. 49.

349. Apes 1835; Massachusetts 1861, pp. 29–46.

350. Mochon 1968, p. 190; the causes of the breakdown were the shift to individual trapping for the fur trade, permanent land sales to Europeans by some clans, European insistence on using their own courts for settling disputes, and loss of population due to disease. Strong leaders emerged among the Mahicans after the matriclans faded, and one of these leaders took his people to the Stockbridge mission.

351. Kawashima 1969, pp. 52–53; Weinstein 1986, p. 90.

352. Kawashima 1969, p. 48.

353. Salwen (1978, p. 168) indicates that strong sachems among the peoples of southern New England may have developed after a series of epidemics decimated the population in 1616–1619.

354. Boissevain 1963, pp. 495–496. For references to a chiefly stratum in Narragansett society, see Stiles 1916, p. 27 *et passim*.

355. Salwen 1978, p. 168.

356. Brasser 1966, p. 22.

357. Hayes 1976, pp. 5, 9.

358. Ronda 1981, 375 *et passim*; Weinstein 1986, p. 92.

359. Boissevain 1963, p. 495.

360. Mochon 1968, p. 192.

361. Hayes 1976, p. 4.

362. Ronda 1981.

363. Brasser 1966, p. 22.

364. Gonzalez n.d., p. 7; a Methodist church was established on their reservation in 1812 (Gonzalez 1986, p. 125).

365. For further data on Indians and the "Great Awakening," see Love 1899 and Simmons and Simmons 1982.

366. Boissevain 1963, p. 495.

367. Described in Stiles 1916, p. 142.

368. Salisbury 1974.

369. Mochon 1968, p. 195.

370. Orcutt 1972 [1882], pp. 51–52.

371. As in Virginia, most of the groups did not survive due to the loss of population and, finally, of reservations. For a summary, see Conkey, Boissevain, and Goddard 1978.

372. Brasser 1966, p. 22.

373. For an exception, see Gonzalez 1986, p. 124.

374. The issue is a sensitive one in New England, as it is in Virginia. George Hicks felt compelled to adopt the pseudonym "Monhegan" for a group with which he worked, whose

members clearly included persons of African as well as European ancestry. See Hicks 1975 and 1977, and Hicks and Kertzer 1972.

375. Contemporary evidence comes from Stiles (1916, pp. 114–115), showing a couple of mulattoes married in but otherwise apparently endogamous marriages. Stiles also mentioned marriages to Negroes among the much diminished Hassanimisco (ibid., p. 203).

376. Boissevain 1963, pp. 494, 496.

377. Hening and Munford Reports, cited in Ballagh 1902, pp. 50–51; in these two cases of 1792 and 1793, the plaintiffs, descendants of such Indians, were freed, although the white defendants appealed.

378. For lengthy accounts of the mixing and of white reluctance to legislate fine distinctions of race, see Johnson 1970 and Williamson 1980.

379. Northampton County, Marriage Register No. 1 (1706–1852), *passim*.

380. Legislative Petitions, Northampton County, January 26, 1784; brackets mine.

381. See Jackson 1971 [1942].

382. The law following from the petition has been lost.

383. Northampton County, Orders 30:210, 246–247; no copy of the commissioners' report has survived.

384. Legislative Petitions, Northampton County after October 10, 1787.

385. One wonders, then, what the appointed commissioners were doing about Gingaskin lands.

386. Northampton County, Orders 32:193.

387. Hening 1809–1823, 13:551.

388. Northampton County, Orders 32:283.

389. Palmer 1875, 6:649.

390. Northampton County, Orders 32:447.

391. Legislative Petitions, Northampton County, December 2, 1812.

392. Filed with the petition in the Virginia State Library.

393. For a list of cases nationwide, see Rountree 1973, chap. 4.

394. Acts of Assembly 1812–1813, pp. 117–118.

395. Northampton County, Orders 35:358–359.

396. Northampton County, Orders 35:395, 412, 416–417; Plat Book, Plat Map 37.

397. Following plot numbers on the plat map: #2: William West: sold whole plot 1816 (Deeds 26:315–316). #3: James West: got tax exemption in 1813; sold whole plot 1814 (Deeds 26:212, 248, Orders 35:518). #5: Molly West: sold whole plot 1814 (Deeds 26:77–78, Orders 35:409). #6: Rachel West: sold whole plot 1814 (Deeds 26:76–77, Orders 35:409). #23: Solomon Jeffery: sold whole plot but kept life interest in 5 A., 1815 (Deeds 26:142–143, Orders 35:444). #25: Edmund Press: sold plot but kept life interest 1816 (Deeds 26:238, Orders 36:27).

398. #8: Sophia Jeffery Carter: sold half plot 1816 (Deeds 26:278–279) and rest in 1831 (Deeds 29:228). #11: William House sold most of plot 1814 (Deeds 26:165–166) and rest in 1831 (Deeds 29:191).

399. #10: John Carter, son of Nanny (allottee #7): dead by 1819; father James Carter sold part of plot in 1819 (Deeds 27:8) and the rest in 1826 (Deeds 28:300). #24: Tabby Francis: dead by 1828 and heirs were husband, Thomas Francis, and daughters; husband sold his interest in plot in 1828 (Deeds 29:8), one daughter sold hers in 1829 (Deeds 29:27–28), and other daughter sold hers in 1857 (Deeds 35:191–192).

400. #9: Susan Beavans: left land to free Negro husband John Beavans, who sold 1 A. in 1821 (Deeds 27:130); his heirs sold the rest in 1831 (Deeds 29:494).

401. #1: Betsey Bingham Baker: died 1816 and left land to her Gingaskin husband Thomas Baker (owner of #27). #7: Nanny Carter: dead by 1826; plot sold by free Negro husband James Carter in 1831 (Deeds 29:217). #13: Betsy Shepherd Collins (sister of allottee #26): used plot as security on loan 1824 (Deeds 28:18–19) and redeemed it; sold plot but kept life interest in house and 2 acres in 1831 (Deeds 30:427). #14: Thomas Jeffery:

dead by 1828 and plot divided among heirs (Plat 94); all four sections sold in 1831 (Deeds 29:223, 230, 232). #15: Betsy Collins Powell: used plot as security on loan in 1822 (Deeds 27:275) and redeemed it in 1831 (Deeds 29:231) just in time to sell it (Deeds 29:235–236). #16: Ann Drighouse (Mrs. Charles Pool as of 1820): used plot as security on loan 1829 (Deeds 29:35) and redeemed it; sold plot in 1831 (Deeds 29:222). #17: Betty Drighouse (Mrs. Ben Carter as of 1823 and Mrs. Isaiah Carter as of 1831): used plot as security in 1814 (Deeds 26:80–81; Orders 35:414) and redeemed it (Deeds 29:220–221); sold plot in 1831 (Deeds 29:281). #18: Nathan (or William) Drighouse: sold plot in 1831 (Deeds 29:282). #19: Sam Beavens, husband of Molly Press (she appears as the allottee in Commissioners' Report): sold plot in 1831 (Deeds 29:285). #21: John Bingham: heirs sold plot in 1831 (Deeds 29:239, 282). #22: Molly Fisherman Press (wife of Littleton Press): dead by 1831, and heirs sold plot in 1831 (Deeds 29:218–219, 341). #27: Thomas Baker (husband of allottee #1): his heirs sold his and his wife's plot in 1831 (Deeds 29:233, 374).

402. #12: Peggy Bingham (Mrs. William Francis as of 1829): used plot as security on loan in 1822 (Deeds 27:273) and redeemed it; sold plot in 1835 (Deeds 30:151–152). #20: Littleton Jeffery: heirs sold plot 1832 after suit originating in 1831 (Deeds 29:339–340). #26: Ibby Shepherd Francis (sister of allottee #13): died in early 1835, heirs sold plot to a daughter's husband 1835 (Deeds 30:307–308), and husband and wife sold plot in 1838 (Deeds 30:558). Daughter in question was Mary or Molly, who was Mrs. George Stevens; she was the "Injin Queen" of 1862 (see below). I have not been able to account for allottee #4, Stephen Jeffery.

403. Marzone 1855.

404. Northampton County, Marriage Registers. In 1970, I was assured by a member of the white gentry that the Indians had died off quietly from broken hearts (Rountree, Fieldnotes)!

405. Ibby Francis, allottee #26. Molly's husband bought out the other heirs, but the couple sold the land in 1838 (see note 402, above).

406. Upshur 1901–1902, p. 92.

Chapter Eight. People Who Refused to Vanish

1. See the various chapters in Williams 1979, as well as F. Porter, 1980 and 1986.

2. Norfolk County, Deeds 59:418.

3. The full list of items is: 8 windsor chairs, 6 flag chairs, a buffet, 3 sets of cups and saucers, 4 pitchers, 2 decanters, 4 cup plates, a butter plate, a cream pot and vinegar cruets, 2 sugar dishes, 5 bowls, 16 plates, 3 basins, 1 bread basket, 2 pewter dishes, an earthen dish, 3 candle sticks, 4 tea spoons, a mug, a salt stand, 3 flasks, a knife box and contents, 2 sugar boxes, 13 spoons, 2 coffee pots, a looking glass, 2 candle molds, 3 flat irons, a gun, 4 jugs, 7 fat pots, 3 beds and "furniture," 1 loom and gear, 2 loom wheels, 2 cotton wheels, 1 trunk, 2 pine tables, 1 chest of drawers, 1 small trunk and chest, 3 meal tubs, 4 weeding hoes, 2 ploughs, 2 grubbing hoes, 1 grind stone, 3 axes, 1 hand mill, 2 saddles, 1 horse cart and wheels, 2 sets of plough gear, 2 curry combs, 4 baskets, a lot of "wooden ware," 2 spiders (or skillets), 3 pots and hooks, 1 griddle, 2 pot hangers, 1 "oven" (covered iron pot for hearthside cooking), 1 set of measures, on 1 1/2-peck measure, 5 wedges, 1 lot of "adz &c.," several barrels, 2 sets of cart gear, a pair of steelyards, a mortar and pestle, 2 jugs, 7 stacks of fodder, 56 barrels of corn, a mare and colt, a bay mare, 11 hogs, a red cow, a brindle heiffer, a pied steer, a slate, a chair, a basket, 32 "fowls," 2 1/2 bushels of green-eyed peas, one half-bushel of cow peas, and 25 pounds of cotton.

4. Core people only: King William County, Records 9:97 (1835); 11:40, 137 (1841); 13:162 (1847); 14:332, 340, 423 (1851). Though more Pamunkeys had to make deeds of trust as time went on, the amount and nature of the collateral remained relatively constant.

5. "Father William" 1854, pp. 129–130.

6. King William County, Marriage Register 1853–1935, which lists parents of bride and

groom; most Pamunkeys of the 1850s took their father's name and appear to have been children of legal marriages.

7. King William County, Personal Property Tax Books. This practice, now considered illegal, went on until the Civil War.

8. Dalrymple 1840–1843, p. 2; printed in *Historical Magazine and Notes and Queries concerning the Antiquities, History and Biography of America* 2 (1858):182. The two women were Molly Holt (aged eighty-plus) and Rhoda Arnold (aged seventy-plus). Dalrymple was cited as making "an exhaustive study of the Pamunkey and Mattapony Indians" (O. Mason 1877), but nothing about the Indians other than the word list survives among his papers at the Maryland Historical Society.

9. Author's comparison of the list with her own MS. A. Frank Speck analyzed the list for John Swanton in 1940 and pronounced the numerals to be "a counting-out rhyme used in a game. How funny to find this worked into an actual vocabulary" (MS. 4069, National Anthropological Archives).

10. Indians appear under various labels (Indian, free colored, mulatto, white) in contemporary documents, including U.S. Censuses; this is true elsewhere in the United States as well (see Beale 1958).

11. Acts of Assembly 1865–1866, p. 84.

12. Other people were left alone, too: before 1850 there was a real reluctance in some southern states to make a strict definition of "mulatto," for fear of causing embarrassment to prominent "white" families. See Johnston 1970, pp. 193–194, and Williamson 1980, pp. 13–14, 18–20.

13. Modern Powhatan oral tradition, both on and off the reservations, insists that the one-drop rule was held strictly by the Indians of this period. (Many white Virginians today say the same thing about their ancestors.) However, the presence of fringe and "outside" names among the groups suggests that if this rule was held, it was not considered a hard-and-fast legal matter. Thus more stringent rules about selection of members had to be made later when pressure from whites increased and/or some non-reservation groups organized formally (see below).

14. Documentation of connections between Virginia groups is poor before ca. 1880, due to loss of county records. Early surviving marriage records usually indicate a high degree of endogamy already in progress.

15. The Mursh family settled among that tribe in the late eighteenth century (see chap. 7) and their descendants married Catawbas; contacts were probably retained with relatives in Virginia thereafter.

16. The Collinses apparently come from a man named William Collins, who was taxed as a white man by King William County in 1794 (King William Land [and Personal Property Tax] Books) yet became a charter member of Lower College Baptist Church, with wife Jane, on the "free coloured" roll (Colosse Baptist Church, Minute Book 1814–1834). Jane may have been an Indian. Two generations later, in 1836, a Richard Collins, "a descendant of the Indian Tribe," enrolled at the same church (Colosse Baptist Church, Minute Book 1814–1870, p. 20).

17. Older Mattaponi names include Major, Allmond, and Custalow. The earliest Major on record was William Major, who lived on the Pamunkey Reservation in 1799, apparently as an Indian (he is merely recorded as non-white; King William Land [and Personal Property Tax] Books). His descendants lived at Mattaponi from at least 1860 through the 1920s; one lived on the Pamunkey Reservation in 1850 (U.S. Censuses).

The Allmonds descend from a "man of colour" named Thornton Almond; he is supposed to have come from an Indian settlement in Gloucester County (Speck 1928, p. 263), but this claim is unverifiable thanks to the destruction of that county's records in the Civil War. Thornton Allmond lived on the Pamunkey Reservation in 1840 and 1850 and at Mattaponi after 1860 (U.S. Censuses). His children married Pamunkey Langstons, Bradbys, and Sampsons, as well as fringe (or "Mattaponi") Tuppences and Custalows.

There have been Custalows in King William County since 1791, when Agnes Custalow became a charter member of Lower College Baptist Church on the "free coloured" roll (she may or may not have been Indian connected; Colosse Baptist Church, Minute Book 1813–1834). Her children probably included the Jack Custalow who lived all his life as a "person of colour" away from any reservation and whose son Norman married first a daughter of Thornton Allmond (King William County, Ended Chancery Cases, File 32) and second a Pamunkey Langston (living in New Kent County; New Kent County, Marriage Registers). Norman Custalow moved with his Allmond wife to the Mattaponi tract before 1870 (U.S. Censuses) and his descendants married other "Mattaponi" people as well as Pamunkey Langstons, Mileses, and Sweats.

18. Fieldnotes, File 2218, National Anthropological Archives.

19. For the enclaves, as for the Mattaponi reservation, I will use quotation marks to indicate that no formal political organization had yet taken place in these groups.

20. E.g., "free person of color," "person of color," no designation (i.e., white), or, most commonly, "mullato," a term apparently applied by clerks and enumerators to anyone whose looks varied from "almost pure white" to "almost pure Negro" (my terms). The U.S. Censuses show tremendous variation in the way the reservation people as a group were handled: "free colored" in 1830 and 1840, "mulatto" in 1850, "black," "mulatto," and no designation (i.e., white) in 1860, "Indian" in 1870, "mulatto" in 1880 (though few reservation people appear in that census), "Indian" in 1890 (population schedules were burned; see U.S. Bureau of the Census 1894); and "Indian" thereafter.

21. Essex County, Marriage Register 1 (1854–1921), p. 8, line 22 (repeated on p. 9, line 8); the woman was Susan "Sullens alias Spurlock," wife of William Saunders (marginal note says "the parents never married") and mother of John Saunders.

22. Mrs. Daniel Adkins (maiden name unknown but began with "A"): "a woman of very bright complexion straight hair high cheek bones" (Charles City County, Minute Books 4:508 [1858]). Significantly, she and her husband and children are not labelled "Mulattoes," the label commonly given to other "persons of color" including "Chickahominy" ancestors on certificates of freedom.

23. Rebecca Frances Bradby ("a woman of very bright complexion . . . strait black hair and gray eyes"), Christianna Bradby ("very bright complexion . . large full face dark grey eyes straight hair"), and Sally Margaret Bradby ("very bright complexion . . . large full face straight dark hair") (Charles City County, Orders 1860–1872, pp. 93–94 [1861]). Sally and her brother, Alexander Bradby, were Chickahominy ancestors; the brother, three sisters already mentioned, and one more sister got certificates of free birth which described them all as having a "very bright complexion" and which did not call them "Mulatto."

24. Gloucester Wynn (d. 1802) and his wife and children appear as white landowners being taxed in the county Land Books. Two daughters had names (Nancy and Oney) which appear later as Wynn wives of Pamunkey men (marriage records of their children, in turn, which list parents' names). From the estimated ages of Gloucester's daughters, I infer that it was a brother of theirs who married a Pamunkey, siring daughters given family names, and also a son, Ferdinand Wynn, Sr., who in turn named one of his sons "Gloster" (U.S. Censuses); these family connections are, however, conjectural in the absence of concrete evidence.

25. Gatschet post-1893. Frank Speck also heard about the hostile "Tribe from Cumberland neck, . . . 3 mils [sic] below Res." (Speck Papers, IV-F-1-f).

26. Mooney's 1899 census of the "Chickahominies": MS. 1299, National Anthropological Archives.

27. Colosse Baptist Church, Minute Book 1814–1870.

28. MS. 2199, National Anthropological Archives, in which his name is given as "J. T. Pearman." His parentage cannot be traced because of the destruction of New Kent County's records in the Civil War.

29. For a discussion of Anglo-Americans' change from enthusiastic acceptance of Indian-white unions as a means of assimilation to revulsion at the mixing of two supposedly different "species," see Bieder 1980. A study of European history and migrations for the past three thousand years or so will also show that there is probably no such thing as a "pure white" person.

30. Singer 1962.

31. Williamson 1980, pp. 2, 71–75. Williamson puts it succinctly: "They had already opted for slavery over freedom, and they had committed themselves to a racial defense of the slave system. A slave was a slave because he was black. Slaves, by definition, could not be white. The fact that slavery was getting whiter [through miscegenation], that in reality many slaves were more white than black, was a fact with which the proslavery argument could not cope. Either it could ignore the problem, which it did explicitly [i.e., legally], or it could brusquely dismiss it by applying the one-drop rule to persons in slavery, which it did implicitly [i.e., socially]" (p. 73, brackets mine).

32. Because of widespread white-Negro miscegenation, many "whites" were either Negro-descended people "passing" for white, or the descendants of such people; the existence of these people within their group made many nineteenth-century whites literally "paranoid" on the subject of racial "purity" (ibid., pp. 100–106).

33. Stanard 1929, p. 204.

34. For a good overview of Southern legislation in the period, see Wilson 1965, pp. 32–41. Jackson 1971 [1942], chap. 1, reviews the situation in Virginia.

35. Acts of Assembly 1830–1831, pp. 107–108.

36. Legislative Petitions, Northampton County, December 6, 1831; Acts of Assembly 1831–1832, p. 23.

37. In this law, the General Assembly tacitly recognized the power of Negro ministers as leaders of their people.

38. Acts of Assembly 1831–1832, pp. 20–22. Wilson (1965, p. 30) has pointed out that "perhaps the worst feature of all such laws was that they commonly provided for immediate punishment—usually whipping—without trial."

39. Code of Virginia 1819, 1:438–439; Matthews 1856–1857, 1:207–208. Certificates of this sort began being issued in Northampton County, at least, in 1794 (Northampton County, Orders 32:354, 358, 364), no testimony of white persons yet required.

40. The relevant courthouses for the New Kent fringe, the "Upper Mattaponis," and part of the "Rappahannocks" were burned during the Civil War.

41. Journal of the House of Delegates of the Commonwealth of Virginia . . . 1832–1833, p. 131.

42. Acts of Assembly 1832–1833, p. 51.

43. Norfolk County, Minute Books 23:180; 24:27, 43, 44, 67; 26:436; 29:122; 30:216, 226, 250, 341, 346; 32:198; 33:241, 457; 35:2. Norfolk County, Register of Free Negroes and Mulattoes, 1809–1852 (entries say "Indian descent" instead of "born free").

44. I am uncertain why the "Chickahominies" of Charles City County and the "Rappahannocks" of Essex and Caroline counties—whose records are preserved—did not get certified as "persons of mixed blood." They did not know of the law, or they could not get any whites to testify for them, or they did not qualify for certification.

45. Photostat of original in Coates Papers; original belonged to Mrs. Mary Langston in the 1940s.

46. However, his daughter married the Custalow ancestor and the pair lived on the Mattaponi Reservation, eventually becoming ancestors of nearly everyone there.

47. Southampton County, Order Book of County Court 18:333; Deeds 24:175.

48. Southampton County, Order Book Law and Chancery 1831–1841, p. 231; Order Book County Court 18:328, 329.

49. Executive Papers, November 29, 1838.

50. Southampton County, Order Book Law and Chancery 1831–1841, pp. 320, 344, Deeds 24:520.

51. Executive Papers, letter of February 18, 1836.

52. So stated in the letter of February 18, 1836.

53. These were: James Langston, Tazewell H. Langston, and Isaac Miles, Jr., as "headmen"; John Langston, Willis Langston, Robert Arnold, Joseph Arnold, William Sampson, Cooper Sampson, Tazewell Gurley, Anderson Holt, William Holt, Ben Holt, Jesse Bradby, Archia Miles, [Syl]vanus Miles, Pleasant Miles, Edward Brisbon [Brisby], William Sweat, Abram Sweat, Cooper Langston, Lewis Sampson, Hartwell Gurley, Allen Sweat, Francis Sampson, Beverley Bradby, William Langston, and Elzey Brisbon [Brisby].

54. I.e., Miles (Chickahominy?) and Arnold (unknown; n.b.: Rhoda Arnold, aged seventy-plus, was a linguistic informant for E. A. Dalrymple in 1840–1843 [see above]).

55. I have thoroughly searched the Executive Letter Books, all of which are extant for that period.

56. It is entirely possible that the governor saw in the letter promise that the Pumunkeys would marry enough outsiders that they would eventually disappear on their own momentum, without force being applied from outside. This is the sort of passive hostility that will uphold tribal rights while doing nothing to keep the Indians from eventually disqualifying themselves as "genuine" Indians.

57. Report of commissioners to legislature of South Carolina, 1839, cited in H. L. Scaife, *History and Condition of the Catawba Indians of South Carolina* (Philadelphia: Indian Rights Assn., 1896), p. 9, cited in turn in Stern 1951, pp. 50–51.

58. Speck 1939, p. 416 (his source was oral tradition recited by both Pamunkey and Catawba informants); see also D. Brown 1966, pp. 272n., 314. The "Pamunkey" surnames then transferred to the Catawbas were Mush (Marsh) and Gunn (both genuinely Pamunkey) and also Kegg (probably Catawba): Brown 1966, p. 272, (and my own conclusion).

59. See Brown 1966 and C. Hudson 1970.

60. Letter of September 20, in Gatschet Letters Received, MS. 4047, National Anthropological Archives. The people referred to were all "descendants of a single man named John Mush, who came to the Catawbas . . . in the early part of this century, + died among them about 1860." Merrell (1989, p. 264) suggests that the Catawbas' prolonged reluctance to accept non-Catawbas living among them may account for the sullenness.

61. Legislative Petitions, King William County, January 20, 1843.

62. Legislative Petitions, King William County, November 26, 1842, and January 12, 1843.

63. This assertion is refuted by the firsthand observations of Gatschet, Mooney, and Pollard in the late nineteenth century (see below).

64. The "Pamunkeys" in the petition are actually the Pamunkeys and the "Mattaponis," since both reservation tracts are mentioned. Apparently the counterpetitions were written on behalf of the residents of both reservation tracts, whose administrative title was "Pamunkey."

65. This is obviously not the case in legislation of the 1830s, which was deliberately repressive toward non-whites. But much legislation that affects Indians and other non-Negro minorities—and women—fits this description.

66. Howe 1969 [1845], pp. 349–350; he did at least mention that whites had married in as well as Negroes.

67. Father William 1854, p. 130.

68. See below, for possible reasons for Pamunkey-Mattaponi reservation split in 1894; see also chap. 9.

69. By that time, the railroad involved was the Southern Railroad; see chap. 10.

70. Charles City County, Marriage Registers, and Order and Minute Books, *passim*.

71. Indiana United Methodist Church [no longer a mission] Pastor William E. Kube, personal communication, 1984.

72. Executive Letter Book 1856–1860, pp. 47–49.

73. Letter of April 30, 1883, by J. G. Shea, in Gatschet n.d., p. 46.

74. Terrill Bradby and his brother Sterling were two (King William County, Ended Chancery Cases, File 32). There were also several others who were "excluded" from Colosse Baptist Church at the January 1864 meeting because of joining "the enemy" (Colosse Baptist Church, Minute Book 1814–1870; rule about enemy activities made in May 1862).

75. Gatschet post-1893.

76. Palmer 1875, 1:li; based on Gregory 1875.

77. Rountree, Fieldnotes 1970.

78. 1907, p. 145.

79. Stern 1952, p. 206.

80. Speck Papers IV-F-1-f.

81. Stern 1952, p. 206.

82. One of these people was the woman who married Robert Cotman, described to Mooney as being from "some 'foreign' Va. tribe, grandfather white" (Chickahominy census of 1899, MS. 2214, National Anthropological Archives), and identified as "colored" in the U.S. Censuses of 1900 and 1910; the pair were divorced in 1919 after she left him (Charles City County, Chancery Orders 3:448). The Chickahominies today disavow the name Cotman as ever being "Indian" (Rountree, Correspondence 1976).

83. Charles City County, Orders 1860–1872, pp. 441, 494.

84. Charles City County, Orders 1860–1872, p. 593, Chancery Law Orders 2:282.

85. King William County, Records 17:223.

86. For details of the two models of race relations used here, i.e., legal superiority/intimacy versus legal near-equality/distance, see van den Berghe 1966.

87. Williamson 1980, pp. 62, 78ff.

88. Acts of Assembly 1865–1866, pp. 84–85, a law which also abolished the courts of oyer and terminer for non-whites. These racial definitions held until they were changed in 1910.

89. Childhood memory of Mrs. Theodora O. Cook, born in 1863, recorded in Speck Papers IV-F-2-p.

90. Rountree, Fieldnotes.

91. Mooney 1907, p. 151.

92. Norfolk County, Minute Books 45:444–445.

93. Rountree, Fieldnotes 1985; minutes of Nansemond Indian Tribal Association, April 1985.

94. Stern 1952, p. 208; essentially continued in modern oral tradition.

95. Rountree, Fieldnotes.

96. Stern 1952, p. 208.

97. See below.

98. Feest 1987, p. 8.

99. List of addressees and their replies: MS. 2190, National Anthropological Archives. One addressee was the chief at Pamunkey.

100. And in 1974 when I met his granddaughter and casually mentioned his mistake, she became angry and insisted that he could not have been wrong. My having visited and even lived on the Pamunkey Reservation did not convince her!

101. Gatschet n.d. and post-1893. Gatschet was a Smithsonian anthropologist.

102. Pollard 1894. Pollard was a politician who subsequently became governor of Virginia.

103. Fieldnotes, File 2497, National Anthropological Archives; W. Terrill Bradby Papers [abstracted], File 2218, National Anthropological Archives; Correspondence, National Anthropological Archives; Mooney 1907. Mooney was a Smithsonian anthropologist.

104. Clarke 1897, pp. 1–2 (mainly quotes Pollard 1894); Sams 1916, pp. 326–336; letter of Col. William R. Aylett in U.S. Bureau of the Census 1894, p. 602.

105. Gatschet post-1893 (no pagination); Pollard (1894, p. 10) took a census in 1893 and arrived at ninety resident and twenty nonresident Indians.

106. Gatschet post-1893. Sams (1916, pp. 329–330) found twenty houses (and five more unoccupied) and described them thus: "All are of frame, and most below the general average of size and appointment found among the smaller of the white farmers, although all are framed according to our general plans for such structures. Two were of two stories, and pretty good houses, but most are very small."

107. Mooney 1907, pp. 147–148. His 1899 census is not extant. The fourteen off-reservation people lived in eight households located variously in Newport News and Petersburg, Va., Philadelphia, and New York. (In 1908 Sams met a New York-based Pamunkey family [the mother being Chickahominy] which spent the summer school vacation on the reservation [1916, p. 332].) One resident family was technically in the New Kent fringe. The tribe's surnames were Allmond, Bradby, Collins, Cook, Dennis, Hawkes, Holmes, Langston, Miles, Page, Sampson, and Swett.

108. Sams 1916, p. 329. The same holds true today.

109. Pollard (1894, p. 10) says that some of these were the normal occupations of Pamunkeys who lived away. The term "service" probably means employment in a hotel or large, wealthy household.

110. Ibid., p. 18; potting and making dugout canoes were listed as the only surviving arts.

111. Ibid., p. 15.

112. Gregory 1875. County taxes on retail sales on reservations were legally struck down forty years later (see below).

113. Aylett letter in U.S. Bureau of the Census 1894.

114. Gatschet post-1893 (no pagination).

115. Pollard 1894, p. 15.

116. Gatschet post-1893.

117. Writers vary on the time of year this was done: the Aylett letter (U.S. Bureau of the Census 1894, p. 602) says "about Christmas," and Sams says New Year's Day (1916, p. 334). No one mentions whether or not the Indians dressed up in "Indian" style for the occasion.

118. They were: William Sampson, James Langston (writer of 1836 letter), Tazewell Langston (writer of 1842–1843 counterpetitions), Joseph Arnold (d. long before Civil War), Thomas Cook (d. 1882), Thomas Langston (d. ca. 1886), William A. Bradby (chief in 1889). Mooney's list (1889–1907, MS. File 2218) adds Thomas Cook as chief in 1861 and inserts Sterling Bradby between him and Joseph Arnold, in 1858. Speck's list (Speck Papers IV-F-1-5) omits Joseph Arnold and Sterling Bradby. The next chief after Gatschet's visit was Charles S. Bradby (Pollard 1894, p. 11), followed by Theophilus T. Dennis (chief in 1899 when Delancey Gill photographs were taken), and by 1908 the chief was George Major Cook (Sams 1916; p. 327; corroborated in Speck's list).

119. Pollard 1894, p. 16.

120. The Aylett letter says five (U.S. Bureau of the Census 1894) and Gregory 1875 says three, but all the other sources agree on four.

121. Pollard 1894, p. 16. The present usage, with corn and peas, differs; see chap. 10.

122. Ibid., p. 15; Gregory 1875 says three trustees chosen by the Indians.

123. Pollard 1894, p. 16.

124. Mooney, Fieldnotes, File 2218. He had visited the county courthouse, burned fourteen years earlier, and had found "no record of prosecutions [of Indians] there."

125. King William County, Ended File No. 16. In 1904 a Pamunkey man had been ordered by the tribal council to marry a Pamunkey woman who claimed he had made her pregnant, or else be turned over to the county court. Certain that he was not the father, he had nonetheless married the woman as the councilmen demanded; but he refused to live with her afterward and he got a divorce in 1907, when he was able to prove that the woman had lived rather loosely among white people in Richmond. The coercive power of the council was considerable, since disobedience could bring expulsion from the reservation and into a hostile non-Indian world.

126. 1894, pp. 16–17; brackets mine.

127. Rountree, Fieldnotes 1970, 1976, 1981. The tribal laws are almost never made available to non-Indians.

128. See chap. 10.

129. Rountree, Fieldnotes.

130. There has been at least one marriage that contravened this custom. In 1900 a Pamunkey woman named Minerva Cook married a New York Tuscarora Indian "doctor" named John Ioma (King William Marriage Registers). The couple were still living on the Pamunkey Reservation in 1910 (U.S. Census, 1910), and he (or they) moved later and apparently voluntarily to Oklahoma (Speck Papers IV-F-2-r).

131. Pollard 1894, pp. 16—17.

132. Sams (1916, p. 329) observed on a visit he made in 1908 that "our road was always down some green lawn, about thirty feet wide, bordered by cornfields, and enclosed by fences. These roadways were kept as a common of pasture by the tribe. The ruts cut by the carriages did not much disfigure them, and the general appearance of the whole place was made picturesque by these long stretches of green grass."

133. The precise date at which the state began to support a reservation school is uncertain. The school is mentioned for the first time by an outsider in a newspaper article written "from correspondence sent by Albert S. Gatschet in November 1890" (Gatschet post-1893).

134. Pollard 1894, pp. 10—11.

135. Ibid., p. 11.

136. Gatschet post-1893.

137. Pollard 1894, p. 11. By "one-fifth" he probably meant three-eighths.

138. Correspondence, letter of October 22, 1899. The Aylett letter (U.S. Bureau of the Census 1894) says the people look Indian, "though there has been a considerable mixture of white and black blood, principally the former."

139. Gatschet (post-1893) mentions "war dances" in passing.

140. Mooney, W. Terrill Bradby Papers: gives the words (nonsense syllables) but only describes the music as either "plaintive + slow" or "with vigor." Bradby said he had learned the song from his mother. Brackets are mine.

141. Gatschet post-1893 and Clarke 1897, p. 2 (thirty-five); Mooney Correspondence (forty-seven). The Aylett letter (in U.S. Bureau of the Census 1894) gives a figure of "about 50." Mooney's 1899 census, which is not extant, showed nine households with thirty-eight people, with one two-person household living in Philadelphia; two more women were married to Pamunkey men [I did not include them in the thirty-eight, since they appear in the Pamunkey count]. Their surnames were Allmond, "Costello" (Custalow), Major, Reid, and "Tuppins" (Tuppence) (Mooney 1907, p. 148).

142. Rountree, Fieldnotes.

143. Gatschet post-1893; brackets mine.

144. This census is still extant: MS. 2199, National Anthropological Archives. The surnames are Adkins, Bradby, Cotman [fringe family], Holmes, Jefferson, Jones, Miles, "Stuart" (Stewart), "Swett" (Sweat, fringe family), Thompson (fringe person), and Wynn. The average of five persons per household is misleading: several households consisted of one person, while many large households had eight or more children. As in the other tribes, some families on the census lived away from the home territory, in Isle of Wight County, James City County, and Newsport News, but they kept up their ties. My figure of 197 includes a few non-Indian spouses.

145. Gatschet post-1893.

146. MS. 2190, National Anthropological Archives, Mooney letter of October 25, 1899. Mooney's letter to Bass is not extant.

147. MS. 2190, National Anthropological Archives, A. A. Bass letter of December 5, 1899.

148. Bass's estimate; Mooney's 1899 census, no longer extant, shows about 213 people, including non-Indian spouses, living in 61 households, some of them living out-of-state (in sporadic contact, so that their children are not known) (Mooney 1907, pp. 150—151).

149. These were Bass, Bateman, Bissell, Bond, Bright, Brady, Caple, Collins, Craigins,

Gaylord, Gray, Green, Harmon, Holloway, Howard, Jones, Okay, Osborn, Porter, Price, Rowland, Sawyer, Scott, Sebastian, Simcoe, Weaver, White, Wilkins, and Williams.

150. Amply documented in the Norfolk County and other local records.

151. Mooney 1907, p. 151.

152. Ibid., p. 151. Mooney's fieldnotes (File 2497, National Anthropological Archives) make only one reference to the group: "Thomas Nelson—carpenter . . . (Essex co., Va.?) White & indian."

153. They advertised their Pocahontas "rescue" play in a printed handbill in 1898 (MS. 4969, National Anthropological Archives). Feest (1987, p. 10) says that by 1915 the play had become an annual spring "Forefathers' Festival" on the reservation, citing an article in an Iowa newspaper as evidence. I have not found any other documents mentioning such a festival.

154. Pollard 1894, p. 11. This letter was endorsed by the Clerk of Court of King William County (File 2218, National Anthropological Archives).

155. This and all other 1893 papers, unless otherwise cited, were abstracted by James Mooney and form the "W. Terrill Bradby Papers" (page 10 of File 2218, National Anthropological Archives).

156. Receipt in Terrill Bradby Papers (cited above) for six pieces of pottery, two hammers, a tomahawk, an axe, a pestle, and three spearheads. The Pamunkey clay sora horse, five-holed "pipe-for-joy," and dugout canoe mentioned in the U.S. National Museum Annual Reports (1893, p. 224, and 1894, p. 112) were collected by J. G. Pollard in 1891, displayed at the World's Fair in 1893, and then given to the museum.

157. Abstract in "W. Terrill Bradby Papers," p. 10 of File 2218, National Anthropological Archives.

158. Request: announced in the *Times* (Washington, S.C.), July 6, 1899, clipping in Gatschet post-1893; reply: abstracted in "W. Terrill Bradby Papers," p. 10 of File 2218, National Anthropological Archives. See also Feest 1987, pp. 9–10.

159. Photographic taken in October 1899, National Anthropological Archives; reproduced in Feest 1978, p. 264.

160. The advertisement (MS. 4969, National Anthropological Archives) is printed with blank spaces for the place and the month and day of the performance.

161. I have been told by some people (not by tribal officials; Fieldnotes, 1970) that the Mattaponis were always a separate tribe from the Pamunkeys. The statements show that oral tradition says as much about people's present feelings about themselves as it does about their historical past.

162. Gatschet post-1893.

163. Rountree, Fieldnotes 1981. She was Eliza Major (also called Mollie), and she married the Allmond ancestor who came from Gloucester County. The succession from mother to son in this case was probably an isolated case, since the tribe shows no trace otherwise of matrilineality in the nineteenth and twentieth centuries; instead the tribe has shown a preference for sons to succeed fathers (either directly or eventually).

164. Acts of Assembly 1893–1894, pp. 973–974.

165. Acts of Assembly 1895–1896, pp. 922–923.

166. The laws they inform outsiders about are very similar today (Rountree, Fieldnotes), except that Mattaponi women marrying whites can bring their husbands to live on the reservation (see chap. 10).

167. For the scope of this legislation, consult the Code of Virginia 1919: sections 2279 (land books); 2300 (personal property books); 3716 (waiting rooms); 3962, 3965, 3967, 3968, and 3983 (railroad cars); 3979, 3980, 3981, and 3983 (street cars); 4022, 4024, and 4026 (steamboats); 3042–3053 (city and town districts).

168. Acts of Assembly 1910, p. 581.

169. Acts of Assembly 1899–1900, pp. 236–237.

170. Stanard 1929, pp. 203–204.

171. *Richmond Dispatch,* July 28, 1900, p. 1; *Richmond Times,* July 29, 1900, p. 5.

172. *Richmond Dispatch,* August 4, 1900, p. 6.

173. *Richmond Times,* August 18, 1900, p. 2; *Richmond Dispatch,* August 18, 1900, p. 6.

174. *Richmond Dispatch,* August 19, 1900, p. 4.

175. *Richmond Times,* August 21, 1900, p. 7; *Richmond Dispatch,* August 21, 1900, p. 8.

176. *Richmond Dispatch,* November 11, 1900, p. 5.

177. There are Chickahominy examples from 1904 in the Coates Papers.

178. Coates Papers.

179. Chickahominy Chief O. Oliver Adkins, personal communication, 1976.

180. W. F. Jones letter of March 1, 1940, to Frank Speck, in Speck Papers IV-F-2-s.

181. Adkins Papers; copy in author's possession, courtesy of O. Oliver Adkins.

182. *Richmond Times,* July 15, 1900, p. 2; *Richmond Dispatch,* August 12, 1900, p. 8 (written by speaker at that reunion). Stern (1952, p. 215) says this happened in 1908; his source of information is obscure.

183. *Richmond Dispatch,* August 12, 1900, p. 8.

184. Notebook in Adkins Papers. I give this much detail because an enemy of the Indians' later claimed that the group's organization occurred much more informally and with less good reason than it actually did.

185. Throckmorton affidavit of 1920, in both Coates Papers and MS. 112, National Anthropological Archives.

186. These fringe people are identifiable because some people or children of people appearing in James Mooney's census of 1899 told the enumerators of the 1910 U.S. Census—who were willing to write "Indian" for the tribal members—that they themselves were "colored." There was also one core family whose father either did not sense an enumerator's sympathy or who felt reluctant to claim an "Indian" identity publicly in 1910. The modern black community has an oral tradition to the effect that membership in the tribe in 1900 was determined by whether or not people's hair would go through a fine comb; however, the authenticity of this tradition is impossible to verify (Puglisi 1989, p. 103).

187. Opinions of the Attorney General 1916, pp. 111–112.

188. Opinions of the Attorney General 1960–1961, pp. 141–142.

189. Acts of Assembly 1962, p. 847.

190. Copy of honorable discharge certificate, Coates Papers.

191. Opinions of the Attorney General 1917, pp. 163–164 (Pamunkey) and 1918, p. 86 (Mattaponi).

192. Listed on Roll of Honor, *Virginia Magazine of History and Biography* 27:212.

193. Opinions of the Attorney General 1917, pp. 161–163.

194. Opinions of the Attorney General 1918, pp. 86–87.

195. Opinions of the Attorney General 1917, p. 160. In practice, the Indians continued to pay taxes on land they owned out in the county.

196. Letter of Everett Edwards to John Crosby, in Crosby Papers.

197. Speck Papers IV-F-1-f. The fieldnotes *per se* are not extensive, often being cryptic jottings on whatever paper was at hand; Speck's papers were organized only after his death, by Anthony F. C. Wallace. Speck had been trained in anthropology by Franz Boas and for many years was on the faculty of the University of Pennsylvania.

198. I may be too generous here. Speck kept few records indicating his own state of mind and knowledge about the tribes; his correspondence (Speck Papers IV-F-1-g, i; IV-F-2-s; IV-F-5-c) consists almost entirely of others' letters to him, with rare carbon copies of his own letters. I have failed to find many of his letters kept by their recipients. Speck's papers are an object lesson in how *not* to keep an archive on one's fieldwork.

199. Royal B. Hassrick (student of Speck), personal communication, 1971; the range of culture covered in Speck 1950 corroborates this.

200. Many Pamunkeys still felt this way in 1984 (Warren Cook, personal communication, 1984).

201. Since the "mound" has never been excavated, it is impossible to prove or disprove that it is in fact a prehistoric mound. Mounds are certainly rare, if not nonexistent, on the Virginia coastal plain. This one also has an unusual shape: triangular. It is therefore more likely that the "mound" resulted from the building of the railroad track in 1855, when the tribe "had trouble in preventing two burial grounds being cut away for this work. They were saved, however, and stand out like little hills, on the green sward which now covers the part dug away" (Sams 1916, p. 327).

202. Speck Papers. One tradition on the Mattaponi Reservation has long held that these "Adamstown" people were Mattaponis who moved from an overcrowded reservation to "upper" King William County, hence the appropriateness of their current name, Upper Mattaponi (Rountree, Fieldnotes). The probability of their having Chickahominy descent has already been discussed in chap. 7.

203. All the above information: Rountree, Fieldnotes, 1970.

204. Speck 1925, *passim.*

205. Rountree, Fieldnotes 1970 (I was told that one county began to help after the group bought an abandoned Negro school, hired a teacher, and provided her with transportation) and Fieldnotes 1971 (I was told that the county finally rented a house from a group member and paid an Indian teacher [salary: $40/mo. in 1960]).

206. Opinions of the Attorney General 1922–1923, pp. 301–302.

207. Rountree, Fieldnotes: interviews with former students in that school, 1985.

208. Speck 1928, pp. 282–284.

209. Rountree, Fieldnotes 1973: interview with Luther Newton's daughter and others. Interestingly, a map of 1862–1863 shows a place called "Indian Town" a few miles away, at or near modern Cash Corner in King George County (Hotchkiss n.d., map 2).

210. Maps issued by the U.S. Geological Service, the Virginia Department of Highways, and other sources call the place "Allmondsville." Nevertheless, the county road signs and the residents themselves call the place "Allmonds Wharf" (Rountree, Fieldnotes).

211. Rountree, Fieldnotes 1973 and 1974. Nearly all the Gloucester County records were destroyed in the Civil War, but the Land Tax Books are extant, and they show no people named Allmond living continuously in that district. There may, however, have been a tenant population there which does not show up in the records.

212. Copy of Beale MS. fieldnotes in my possession.

213. *Newport News Time-Herald,* July 10, 1978, p. 16.

214. Corporation Commission Charter Book 111:85–86.

215. Speck 1928, p. 266n.; testimony, state recognition hearing of November 5, 1982, in Virginia State Library's Indian File. I wrote in 1982–1984 (Rountree 1986, p. 195) that the Nansemonds had also organized; recent research by their tribal officers and myself shows that they never reached the point of getting a charter of incorporation.

216. Rountree, Fieldnotes 1970.

217. Speck Papers, Field Notebook No. 1: "Some even asked if they were in danger of being killed by white people . . . Already 76 enrolled & more promised."

218. Copy attached to testimony in state recognition hearing of November 5, 1982, in Virginia State Library's Indian File.

219. Rountree, Fieldnotes 1976; Coates Papers; MS. 112, National Anthropological Archives; Virginia State Library's Indian File.

220. Testimony, state recognition hearing of November 5, 1982, in Virginia State Library's Indian File.

221. Testimony, state recognition hearing of November 5, 1982, in Virginia State Library's Indian File.

222. State Corporation Commission Charter Book 132:567–568; Speck letter of May 16, 1925, to George Nelson in Speck Papers IV-F-5-c (Speck was informed after the fact).

223. Rountree, Fieldnotes 1984.

224. Rountree, Fieldnotes 1970. Speck himself makes no mention of such a group.

Chapter Nine. The Racial Integrity Fight

1. For a good overview of the formulation and passing of that law, see Sherman 1988.
2. This and the other biographical data come from American Historical Society 1924.
3. Plecker letter of October 26, 1943, in Federal Archives.
4. Russell Booker, of Vital Statistics Bureau, personal communication, 1973.
5. Rountree, Fieldnotes 1973.
6. American Historical Society 1924.
7. Rountree, Fieldnotes 1973.
8. ". . . there is danger of the ultimate disappearance of the white race in Virginia, and the country, and the substitution therefor of another of brown skin, as has occurred in every other country when the two races have lived together. In every instance this mongrelization has meant the permanent ruin of often splendid civilizations" (Plecker 1926, p. 10). Writers with similar points of view held that the Egyptians, among others, were once "white," an opinion that has been disproved by studies of hundreds of mummies.
9. For an overview of the movement, see Haller 1963 and Ludmerer 1972.
10. The first "legal" sterilization in Virginia occurred in 1924 and resulted in a case that went all the way to the U.S. Supreme Court (*Buck vs. Bell*); that Court "held that sterilization fell within the police power of the state" (Haller 1963, pp. 138–139).
11. The movement was also strong in Germany, where Hitler took it to its logical extreme in the 1930s and 1940s.
12. A classic example from Virginia is Estabrook and McDougle 1926.
13. Estabrook and McDougle were refuted only two years later by a graduate student at the University of Virginia who worked with the same people (Wailes 1928), but that thesis has never been published. The cultural bias in intelligence tests has been shown repeatedly since those days.
14. Acts of Assembly 1924, pp. 534–535.
15. Acts of Assembly 1929–1930, pp. 96–97. The assumption that the Pamunkeys and Mattaponis had Negro blood that had to be allowed for is plain; whether or not they needed that allowance remains uncertain.
16. Plecker 1927, p. 7.
17. Plecker's words, in his letter of November 15, 1926, in Beale's Papers.
18. For nineteenth-century examples of it, see Williamson 1980, pp. 100–106.
19. Plecker 1926, p. 10; the wording is mine.
20. Their oral tradition and personal reminiscences state this emphatically (Rountree, Fieldnotes). I believe that the statement is true. It is significant that the survivors of those times as well as their descendants are still publicly "Indian" today, even though few outsiders would challenge a claim from one of them being "white." They *could* "pass," but they *don't* "pass."
21. Rountree, Fieldnotes.
22. Plecker 1928, p. 11.
23. Plecker 1924b, p. 9: "We are . . . filing away all information reaching us. . . ." He also referred to the file and to the women whose full-time job it was to add to it in correspondence of 1930 (see below).
24. In 1973 I interviewed a bureau employee who had seen that file before it was destroyed; he said it was full of "unsubstantiated letters" from people, "petty things," and he, with legal training behind him, had been "horrified" (Rountree, Fieldnotes 1973).
25. Note: the marriage records, which were the most logical place for racial designations to appear, often did not have such designations until later in the nineteenth century: King William County in 1884 (earliest marriage record dates to 1853), Charles City County in 1875 (earliest record dates to 1789), New Kent County in 1879 (earliest record dates to 1865), Essex County in 1842 (earliest record dates to 1804), King and Queen County in 1900 (earliest record dates to 1865), and Caroline County in 1893 (earliest record dates to 1787).

26. Plecker 1924a.

27. Ibid., p. 7; one wonders what non-white parents thought who read that paragraph.

28. Howe 1969 [1845]; A. F. Chamberlain, anthropologist, who wrote the article "Indian, North American," for the 11th ed. of *Encyclopaedia Britannica* and who cited in turn Pollard 1894 and *Science* 17:85—89 (1891). Plecker also cited Philip A. Bruce's "new history of Virginia" (Bruce 1924); but in fact, that book does not deal with modern Indians at all, and its only reference to Indians after the seventeenth century (p. 334) merely mentions the small populations of the mid-eighteenth century.

29. Corroborated by Plecker letter of January 28, 1925, in Beale Papers. In that letter he says he allowed the compromise because "many of them have so much white blood that they may easily be classified as white. When we get them registered as Indians we know that they are *not* white" (emphasis his).

30. Speck's letters to chiefs have not been preserved, as far as I know (most of the chiefs' personal papers have not been made available to me); their replies to him (Speck Papers IV-F-2-s) indicate what he had said.

31. Speck letter of October 24, 1924, to Rappahannock chief, in Speck Papers IV-F-5-c.

32. Copy of Chief G. M. Cook letter of April 20, 1925, to Speck, in possession of author and of Nansemond Chief Emeritus Oliver Perry; copy of letter of October 1926 from legal firm of Montague and Montague, in Virginia State Library's Indian File.

33. No such decree is on record in the King William County courthouse, and the present Pamunkey chief has no papers concerning it (Rountree, Fieldnotes 1985).

34. James R. Coates, personal communication, 1985.

35. Plecker 1926, p. 7. I know of one Indian-white marriage thus broken up; the Indian man involved killed himself in despair as a result (Rountree, Fieldnotes 1970).

36. One of his friends giving that invitation was my great-grandfather, Robert L. Tennis; H. A. Rountree, Jr. (my father), personal communications.

37. H. A. Rountree, Jr. (schoolmate), personal communication; William A. Stewart (one of the children so removed), personal communication.

38. Attorney General's letter of February 19, 1937, to state commissioner of public welfare, in Crosby Papers.

39. The Eastern Chickahominies benefited from this policy in 1940: Chief E. P. Bradby letter of July 8, 1940, to Frank Speck, in Speck Papers IV-F-5-c.

40. Report of Attorney General 1924, p. 224.

41. Letter of March 9, 1933, in Crosby Papers.

42. John Crosby letter of November 20, 1937, to Ambassador Bingham, and secretary's letter of December 23, 1937, to Crosby, in Crosby Papers.

43. As far as the surviving records show, the Pamunkeys and (since 1894) the Mattaponis have assiduously paid their annual tribute to the governor since 1677, when the treaty went into effect.

44. Rountree, Fieldnotes. The "noble savage" stereotype is still going strong among the Powhatans as the twentieth century ends; I can make myself very unpopular among the tribes by writing even in passing that Powhatan men ever scalped anybody. However, the Indians seem largely unconscious that they are idealizing their ancestors for any reason. The idea that the stereotype keeps them going in hard times is my own.

45. Rountree, Fieldnotes.

46. Letters of introduction for Western Chickhominy Chief O. W. Adkins, dated 1928 and 1930, in Coates Papers.

47. *Richmond News-Leader* May 15, 1929.

48. Corroborated in Plecker 1925, p. 10: legislation was proposed annually to eliminate the racial definition for "Indians" in the Code of Virginia.

49. *Richmond News-Leader,* September 21, 1929, p. 8.

50. Undated clipping from unnamed paper, in Coates Papers.

51. Letter of January 14, 1925, in Beale Papers.

52. Letter of November 15, 1926, in Beale Papers.

53. That is my evaluation after researching the subject myself: Margaret Stewart's children were not, as Plecker claimed, "the progenitors of practically all of these people in that county now calling themselves Indians." Plecker does not mention any Adkinses at all, and the vast majority of the Chickahominies are named—and descended from—Adkinses.

54. These were simply copying errors.

55. Emphasis mine.

56. I have found copies in several places while doing my research. Plecker's willingness to share his "find" probably accounts as well for the mention given the Gregory petition by several writers on Indian-Negro relations in the South: Porter, 1932, p. 314; Johnston 1929, pp. 28–30; Frazier 1939, pp. 215–216; Johnston 1970, pp. 275–277. When these writers mention the Pamunkey counterpetitions at all, they speak of only one such counterpetition—which is the way Plecker phrased it; if they had read the original documents in the State Library, they would know about there being two counterpetitions. The Gregory petition was also known to students of Indian history as early as 1913: Russell either found it himself or was told of it by the same "prominent citizen of Richmond" who stated authoritatively that some Pamunkeys looked Negroid (Russell 1913, p. 129). None of the writers appear to have visited the reservation or looked at the photographs made by Delancey Gill and Frank Speck, which would have shown them how Indian and Caucasian the people actually looked.

57. Eastern Chickahominy Chief E. P. Bradby letter of September 9, 1929, to Hart; Hart letter of September 9, 1929, to Steuart; Pfaus letter of September 22, 1929, to Steuart—all in Beale Papers.

58. Steuart's two letters of October 25, 1929, in Beale Papers.

59. Otho Nelson letter of January 10, 1930, in Beale Papers.

60. Letter of February 8, 1930, in Beale Papers.

61. Letter of April 26, 1930, in Beale Papers.

62. Several letters in Beale Papers.

63. Letter of April 30, 1930, to Steuart, in Beale Papers.

64. Truesdell letter of May 3, 1930, to Nelson, in Beale Papers.

65. Letter of June 13, 1930, in Beale Papers.

66. Letters in Beale Papers; one letter is from Plecker, who said that reminiscences of elderly people in the community give "absolute and positive facts."

67. Green's letter of February 16, 1931, in Beale Papers.

68. Letter of January 28, 1931, with enclosed list, in Beale Papers. The list, compiled by the Census Bureau, contains people reported as "Indian" by various enumerators. Yet all are Powhatans—there are no Amherst Indians, or any of the other people Plecker claimed were trying to "pass" as Indians—so that one suspects that the list was made with the help of a detailed list of Powhatan households supplied by Plecker.

69. Green letter of February 16, 1931, in Beale Papers.

70. The letter to Caroline County is preserved in the Beale Papers.

71. Letters of June 27, 1931, and June 29, 1931, in Beale Papers. The sheriff of Caroline County made a similar response on July 6, 1931, and on July 22, 1931, the clerk of Essex County wrote the same thing directly to Steuart at the Census Bureau (Beale Papers).

72. Letter of July 17, 1931, in Beale Papers; in the absence of Steuart's letter offering the compromise, Plecker's answer remains our evidence that a compromise was offered.

73. Steuart letter July 21, 1931, in Beale Papers.

74. Letters of February 22, 1934, and March 9, 1934, in Crosby Papers.

75. Letters of April 14, 1934, and August 3, 1934, documents presented in recognition hearing of November 5, 1982, in Virginia State Library's Indian File.

76. Hassrick and Carpenter 1944; Mook 1943a, 1943b, 1943c, 1944; Rowell 1943; Speck 1941; Speck and Schaeffer 1950; Speck, Hassrick and Carpenter 1942; Stern 1951 and 1952.

77. E. P. Bradby letter of July 18, 1940, in Speck Papers IV-F-5-c.

78. Chief O. W. Adkins died on December 3, 1939, (*Richmond News-Leader,* December 4, 1939). The tribe eventually settled upon his son, Oliver Adkins.

79. Both the Upper Mattaponis and the Rappahannocks had to renew their charters of incorporation in the 1970s, while the Nansemonds never got a charter at all until 1984; see chap. 10.

80. Note made in 1939, in Speck Papers IV-F-5-a; brackets mine.

81. Bradby letters of May 24, June 19, and July 18, 1940, in Speck Papers IV-F-5-c.

82. James R. Coates, personal communications.

83. Chief Walter Bradby letter of November 19, 1940, and Eastern Chickahominy Chief E. P. Bradby letter of June 19, 1940, in Speck Papers IV-F-2r and IV-F-5-c, respectively. A new and more isolationist chief, Tecumseh Deerfoot Cook, was elected at Pamunkey in 1942 and remained chief until 1984.

84. W. F. Jones letter of March 1, 1940, in Speck Papers IV-F-2-s.

85. E. P. Bradby letters in Speck Papers IV-F-5-c. Paul Miles of Pamunkey was doing the same (Speck Papers IV-F-2-s).

86. Letter of December 14, 1939, in Speck Papers IV-F-2-s; there were "controversies" both between political factions (the issue was probably isolationism) and "between the men-folk and the women-folk."

87. Rountree, Fieldnotes.

88. E. P. Bradby letter of July 8, 1940, in Speck Papers IV-F-5-c.

89. Plecker letter of April 6, 1943, to John Collier, in Federal Archives.

90. Robert Solenberger (graduate student of Speck's) letter of February 28, 1942, in Speck Papers IV-F-1-g.

91. For a more detailed survey of Virginia Indians' draft problems, particularly from the Selective Service's side, see Murray 1987.

92. Letter of March 21, 1941, in Crosby Papers.

93. Letters of March 24, 1941, and March 31, 1941, from War Department and Selective Service, respectively, in Crosby Papers.

94. Summary of newspaper article of January 1942 by Robert Solenberger, in his letter of February 28, 1942, in Speck Papers IV-F-1-g.

95. Letter of February 13, 1942, attached to testimony in recognition hearing of November 5, 1982, in Virginia State Library's Indian File.

96. Letter of February 28, 1942, in Speck Papers IV-F-1-g.

97. Letter of Hill Montague of March 28, 1942, to Col. Bryan Conrad, in Virginia State Library's Indian File.

98. Coates Papers.

99. Plecker letter of January 13, 1942, copies in Beard Papers and in Federal Archives.

100. James R. Coates, personal communications; examples of such birth certificates in Coates Papers.

101. My search of the Acts of Assembly from 1924 through 1946 showed no law affecting the Vital Statistics Bureau that even mentioned altering birth certificates after their arrival in Richmond.

102. Coates Papers.

103. Plecker letter of March 3, 1942, in Coates Papers; brackets mine.

104. I have seen copies of this document in several collections of papers; the title "Warning" is significant.

105. The ones mentioned are Pamunkey, Chickahominy, Nansemond, Mashpee, Narragansett, and Gay Head.

106. Rountree, Fieldnotes 1975 and 1976: interviews with then-Chiefs Curtis L. Custalow, Sr. (Mattaponi), and Andrew Adams (Upper Mattaponi).

107. Blume 1950. Blume is my source for subsequent numbers of War veterans.

108. Strongly implied in Oliver Adkins letter of February 15, 1943 to Speck, in Beard Papers.

109. Rountree, Fieldnotes: interviews in 1975 and 1976 with Chief O. Oliver Adkins; Anthony S. Casale [husband of Chickahominy wife] letter of January 13, 1946, to commis-

sioner of Indian Affairs (protesting persecution of tribe and citing its recent history), in Federal Archives.

110. Rountree, Fieldnotes 1976: interviews with William A. Stewart, the man involved; corroborated by Henning A. Rountree, Jr., whose father, Henning Sr., was on that Draft Board. Stewart told me he finally offered to shoot the entire board; my father merely told me that the board feared to meet for some weeks. At my first meeting with Stewart in 1976, his reaction, upon hearing my last name and whose granddaughter I was, was explosive, and he had to leave the room and calm down. We subsequently made friends.

111. The following account is based both on contemporary documents and on my interviews with Oliver Fortune himself in 1976, when he was assistant chief of the Rappahannocks. I am also indebted to him for reviewing these pages in 1985.

112. Chief Otho Nelson's letter of October 31, 1942, to Speck, in Speck Papers IV-F-1-g. According to the letter, the lawyer had told the youth to give in, and the youth had not been summoned to testify in his own defense.

113. Letter of November 2, 1942, in Speck Papers IV-F-1-g. In the absence of a tribal church before 1964, some Caroline County Rappahannocks attended St. Stephen's Baptist Church, which had a multiracial congregation (whites, blacks, and Indians). The absence of a tribal school for the Rappahannocks in any of the three counties left Indian parents with only two choices for their children, if they could not teach them themselves: illiteracy or "colored" schools. The family of one man of my acquaintance chose the latter course; he is a college graduate in a white-collar job today, but he is no longer—and does not claim to be—a Rappahannock. Oliver Fortune has remained firmly within the Indian community, in spite of the outside schooling which made him one of the more literate members of his generation.

114. Chief Nelson letter of December 2, 1942, to Speck, in Speck Papers IV-F-1-g.

115. Speck letters of February 3 and March 4, 1943, to Bureau of American Ethnology, in MS. 112, National Anthropological Archives; letters of April 6 and April 10, 1943, and copies of Chickahominy documents sent to Bureau of American Ethnology by Chief O. Oliver Adkins, and letters to Adkins of April 16, 1943, by Frank H. H. Roberts, Jr., and D'Arcy McNickle, respectively, in MS. 112, National Anthropological Archives.

116. Plecker letter of April 6, 1943, in Federal Archives.

117. Collier letter of May 1, 1943, in Federal Archives.

118. The reader will recall that Howe wrote about the Pamunkeys without, apparently, ever visiting them; see chap. 7.

119. Plecker letter of October 26, 1943, in Federal Archives.

120. Gilliam letter of July 19, 1943, in Speck Papers IV-F-1-i.

121. Letters of July 21 and July 24, 1943 (quotation from the latter), in Speck Papers IV-F-1-i.

122. As with the "warning," I have found copies of both circular and letter in several places: Coates Papers, Beale Papers. The brackets are mine.

123. Coates letter of December 2, 1944, and Speck's reply of December 7, 1944, mentioning E. P. Bradby's letter, in Speck Papers IV-F-1-g.

124. Tecumseh D. Cook letter of November 23, 1944, to Coates, copy in Speck Papers IV-F-1-g. Characteristically, the Cook letter mentions only the threat to the reservations.

125. Speck letter of December 7, 1944, to Coates, in Speck Papers IV-F-1-g; Speck cites aloofness on the part of some Pamunkeys as a major obstacle to cooperation.

126. Letter of December 8, 1944, in Coates Papers.

127. Coates letter of December 14, 1944, to Speck, in Speck Papers IV-F-1-g; Frank H. H. Roberts letter of December 15, 1944, to Coates, in Coates Papers; *Richmond Times-Dispatch*, January 5, 1945, and January 6, 1945.

128. Chief Cook letter of December 18, 1944, to Coates, in Speck Papers IV-F-1-g.

129. James R. Coates, personal communications.

130. Coates letters to Speck of January 17, March 3, March 31, April 30, and May 7, 1945, in Speck Papers IV-F-1-g (Coates did not keep Speck's letters to him, and Speck made

no carbons); copy of Beard letter of January 29, 1945, to Coates, in Speck Papers IV-F-1-g.

131. Coates letters of May 7 and May 17, 1945, to Speck, in Speck Papers IV-F-1-g, and Coates letters to chiefs of ca. May 10, 1945, in Coates Papers.

132. Tribal rolls in Coates Papers.

133. Coates letter of May 17, 1945, to Speck, in Speck Papers IV-F-1-g.

134. Coates' note, attached to copy of letter to chiefs, in Coates Papers. A Coates letter of July 23, 1945, to Speck (in Speck Papers IV-F-1-g) says that he had finally persuaded the Pamunkeys to make up a roll for him, but that roll was either lost or never delivered.

135. Copy of Sanger letter of February 5, 1945, to Pamunkey Chief Cook, in Coates Papers. There was an unforseen hitch, however: Indian babies born in the "white" wards of M.C.V. thenceforward received birth certificates as "whites." Thus the elder children in some Indian families have "Indian" certificates and the younger children have "white" ones (Gertrude Custalow [mother of such a family], personal communication, 1985).

136. Collier letter of May 3, 1943; in November 1982 recognition hearing documents, Virginia State Library Indian File. Freeman, editor of a major Richmond newspaper, had written Collier at the urging of Western Chickahominy Chief Oliver Adkins.

137. Miss Richardson of New Kent County joined Speck and Beard in pressuring for more educational opportunities for Indians in 1940: E. P. Bradby letter of June 19, 1940, to Speck, in Speck Papers IV-F-5-c.

138. W. Zimmerman, assistant commissioner of Indian Affairs, letter of November 25, 1944, to Rep. Dave E. Satterfield, Jr., in Speck Papers IV-F-1-g.

139. Letter of March 25, 1947, of Willard W. Beatty, director of education in the Office of Indian Affairs, to agent Joseph Jennings at Cherokee, in Federal Archives.

140. Letter of July 27, 1945, in Federal Archives.

141. Beatty letter of December 26, 1945, to Jennings, in Federal Archives.

142. Susan Nelson letter of July 30, 1945, in Federal Archives.

143. Speck letter of December 9, 1945, to Willard W. Beatty, in Speck Papers IV-F-1-g.

144. Beatty letter of December 26, 1945, to Jennings, in Federal Archives; Beatty had visited Pamunkey and Mattaponi a week after Jennings had been there. The Indian Office was concerned that no Negroid-looking non-Cherokee be admitted to the school at Qalla.

145. Mary Bradley letter of December 3, 1945, and Mrs. James Miles letter of January 30, 1946, to Jennings, and Jennings letter of December 17, 1945, to Bradley, in Federal Archives.

146. Beatty letters of December 26, 1945, and January 16, 1946, to Jennings, and Jennings letter of January 9, 1946, to Beatty, in Federal Archives. The second Beatty letter mentions that Pamunkey men have "fairly good jobs" and are not interested in potting.

147. Letter of January 21, 1946, in Speck Papers IV-F-1-g.

148. Letter of March 6, 1946, in Speck Papers IV-F-1-g.

149. Letter of March 6, 1946, to Jasper Adams, in Coates Papers and Speck Papers; Coates letter of April 29, 1946, conveys to Speck the chief's and his own delight at the breakthrough (Speck Papers IV-F-1-g).

150. Beatty letters of June 5 and June 14, 1946, to Chief Oliver Adkins and Miss Lula Whitehead, respectively, the former forwarded to Jennings with request that he visit the group; in Federal Archives.

151. Jennings' memorandum of July 29, 1946, on visit of June 14 to the latter group (the reservation; the Upper Mattaponis are not mentioned), in Federal Archives.

152. *Norfolk Ledger-Dispatch* and *Norfolk Virginian Pilot,* May 16, 1946. James Coates wrote a rebuttal for the next day's editorial page. Any lingering doubts the reader may have about Plecker's being motivated over the years largely by personal animosity toward the Indians should be dispelled by that statement of his upon his retirement. He had not been merely a civil servant doing his job, as he had claimed in earlier years.

153. Rountree, Fieldnotes; the detail of the truck and the feeling of his death being in character come from interviews not only with Indians but also with a white staff member of the Bureau of Vital Statistics, 1973.

154. Rountree, Fieldnotes, 1973: Russell Booker, who already worked at the bureau in

1959, told me that "few racial files that I saw were better destroyed." I contacted Plecker's (retired) successor as registrar through the bureau in 1973, but she declined to be interviewed. Her successor in turn has retired, and Booker himself is now registrar.

155. Blume 1950. The article is unpaginated.

156. Acts of Assembly 1954, p. 905.

157. Acts of Assembly 1954, p. 703.

158. *Richmond News-Leader,* July 14, 1957.

159. Rountree, Fieldnotes; for many years, until I caught up with him, he knew more anthropologists than I did.

160. *Richmond News-Leader,* March 24, 1949; the words he used were not understood by anyone present (Rountree, Fieldnotes 1970).

161. In photographs, the costume appears to be pan-Indian, and derived from Plains Indian styles. Traditional Powhatan male dress was so skimpy and the hairstyle so different from that of modern Virginia (i.e., half the head shaved) that looking truly authentic was out of the question for a man who was also a Baptist minister.

162. Chickahominy testimony in state recognition hearing of November 5, 1982, in Virginia State Library's Indian File.

163. *Richmond Times-Dispatch,* June 11, 1951.

164. Ida Himes (the teacher), personal communications, 1973 through 1988. She retired to my hometown and joined the church of which I was a member.

165. *Richmond Times-Dispatch,* May 25, 1969, p. 3–B; Rountree, Fieldnotes 1971. The school still functioned in 1950 (Blume 1950).

166. Dr. Daniel Slabey (the teacher), personal communication, 1970.

167. Rountree, Fieldnotes, including interviews with Linwood Custalow, M.D. He is also active in tribal and intertribal affairs; see chap. 10.

168. Rountree, Fieldnotes.

169. Helen Hill (the school's teacher), personal communications.

170. Rountree, Fieldnotes: communications from Coates and from the Upper Mattaponis; corroborated by Blume 1950.

171. Olive Cosby Mason (the woman), personal communications.

172. Testimony in state recognition hearing of November 5, 1982, in Virginia State Library's Indian File; Nokomis Lemons, personal communication.

173. Rountree, Fieldnotes. This attitude is found also among other Indians in the United States, and ironically it has disillusioned many non-Indian "liberals" who would otherwise have espoused the cause of this "oppressed people" (Nancy O. Lurie, personal communication, 1985). Expecting downtrodden minority people to be innocent angels is unrealistic.

174. State Board of Education Papers.

175. That is, tuition to schools within King William County, or an equal amount toward tuition at another school outside the county, the difference to be made up by the parents (State Board of Education Papers).

176. Virginia Board of Education Papers.

177. Rountree, Fieldnotes 1970: interview with Indian parents and school principals.

178. Rountree, Fieldnotes 1973.

179. Rountree, Fieldnotes 1971.

Chapter Ten. The Further Rise of Powhatan Activism

1. For the last time capsule written before the tribes' involvement in pan-Indian affairs, see Rountree 1972. There is enough overlap, especially in family, religious and political matters, with my mid-1980s time capsule below, that I have not gone into detail here.

2. Rountree, Fieldnotes 1971, 1973, and 1983. I have heard of no evidence of any documentation he submitted on his ancestry before enrollment by the Rappahannocks.

3. Rountree, Fieldnotes 1970 and 1971.

4. *Attan Akamik,* six issues from 1969 to 1975.

5. Rountree, Fieldnotes 1976.

6. Rountree, Fieldnotes 1986.

7. Curtis L. Custalow, Sr., personal communications, 1972, and 1973.

8. *Richmond Times-Dispatch*, October 12, 1977.

9. Gertrude C. Custalow, personal communication, 1973.

10. Rountree, Fieldnotes. I played no part in the process, because I was never asked to. The Indians did it themselves.

11. Rountree, Fieldnotes 1976; Jack Forbes had found CENA not "activist" enough in 1971, when he attended the organizational meeting (Rountree, Fieldnotes), and he may have influenced the Rappahannocks in that decision. In that same year they declined to cooperate with the Doris Duke Foundation's Oral History Program, which invited them to record their oral history (Rountree, Fieldnotes 1976; I was to be the recorder).

12. *Newport News Daily Press*, December 7, 1972, p. 22; Rountree, Fieldnotes.

13. *Newport News Daily Press*, May 16, 1972.

14. *Newport News Daily Press*, March 10, 1973, p. 21.

15. Curtis L. Custalow, Sr., personal communication, 1973; *Norfolk Virginian Pilot*, September 23, 1973.

16. *Newport News Daily Press*, March 30, 1973, p. 40.

17. Rountree, Fieldnotes 1973.

18. Most married women remained housewives, although the proportion of working wives has steadily increased.

19. Rountree, Fieldnotes 1970. The atmosphere in the office changed when she answered that question, giving her the impression that "race" was the problem.

20. Rountree, Fieldnotes 1970, 1971; the men felt very strongly about this.

21. Rountree, Fieldnotes 1973, 1974.

22. Rountree, Fieldnotes 1981.

23. Rountree, Fieldnotes 1973.

24. *Newport News Daily Press*, June 6, 1972, p. 2.

25. Curtis L. Custalow, Sr., personal communication, 1983.

26. Rountree, Fieldnotes 1974 and 1985.

27. Rountree, correspondence 1976.

28. Copy of profile, given me by then assistant chief Clifton W. Holmes.

29. Rountree, Fieldnotes 1981.

30. Copy of letter, given me by then chief Curtis L. Custalow, Sr.

31. Rountree, Fieldnotes 1976.

32. *Newport News Daily Press*, July 11, 1976, p. F–4. The treasurer was black.

33. *Newport News Daily Press*, November 22, 1975, p. 23.

34. *Newport News Daily Press*, March 26, 1978, p. F–1. That tribal center was built by the Indians without federal aid; see below.

35. *Newport News Daily Press*, September 28, 1978, p. 72.

36. *Newport News Daily Press*, October 20, 1978, p. 45.

37. *Newport News Daily Press*, November 23, 1979, p. 17.

38. Rountree, Fieldnotes.

39. *Richmond Times-Dispatch*, December 6, 1981, p. C–8.

40. "Monacan" today refers to the Indian-descended people of Amherst County described in Wailes 1928. In 1989 they received state recognition as an Indian group.

41. "Heritage" funding included oral history projects, buying books on a group's heritage for school libraries, etc., and was available to many ethnic groups in the United States.

42. Acts of Assembly 1972, p. 582.

43. Rountree, Fieldnotes 1971. In the 1950s, a Chickahominy child could still receive a birth certificate that read "white" on the front and had a notation on the back about her grandparents' having been married as "colored."

44. Acts of Assembly 1975, pp. 1172–1774.

45. *Newport News Daily Press*, September 13, 1975, p. 21.

46. *Newport News Times-Herald,* December 18, 1975, p. 26.

47. Ibid., April 22, 1976.

48. I myself almost wrote to Washington to offer to translate the ballot into the poorly recorded Powhatan language; the result would have been gibberish to everyone concerned, including me.

49. Rountree, Fieldnotes, summer 1976; the chairman was black. The old resentments between Indians and blacks in the county continue to fester.

50. Rappahannock Chief Otho Nelson died in 1970, and Upper Mattaponi Chief Jasper Adams died in 1971 at the age of 91.

51. The Rappahannocks got their new charter in 1974, the Upper Mattaponis in 1976.

52. Correspondence between that office and the Virginia State Library, in the Virginia State Library's Indian File.

53. Ratified (in detail) in Acts of Assembly 1980, pp. 139–140; see also *Newport News Daily Press,* November 6, 1979, p. 9; *Newport News Times-Herald,* November 7, 1979, p. 10. Neighbors of the reservation also have to ratify the agreement, stating that they are in fact neighbors of the reservation. Ironically, the one neighbor who refused to cooperate, and who had to be sued as a result, was a trustee of the tribe!

54. Rountree, Fieldnotes 1983.

55. Rountree, Fieldnotes; Warren Cook, personal communication, 1985.

56. Rountree, Fieldnotes 1983; quote by Curtis L. Custalow, Sr., of Mattaponi. I have also been repeatedly pressured by a friend in the BIA Tribal Affairs Office to "push" the reservations toward federal recognition. He cannot believe my policy of not interfering unless the people ask me to do so.

57. *Norfolk Virginian Pilot,* January 27, 1982.

58. Acts of Assembly 1982, p. 1641.

59. None of these ranked above the level of assistant chief.

60. One of the white subcommittee members was the state librarian. However, no other professional historian or ethnohistorian was consulted until the last minute, at the preference of most of the Virginia Indian people involved (Rountree, Fieldnotes 1987). Though I had always sent preview copies of my writings to tribal chiefs, most of these assistant chiefs and grassroots people had not had access to my published work, to learn to trust me, and some of them did not even know I existed (Rountree, Fieldnotes 1985). Communications between chiefs and other tribal members are often imperfect among the Virginia groups.

61. As an ethnohistorian and cultural anthropologist I testified on the nature of ethnic groups and demonstrated how the "citizen" Indian tribes fitted the criteria for unique ethnic groups.

62. Acts of Assembly 1983, pp. 1270–1271. The resolution included the two reservations, who subsequently asked that their names be stricken because they already had formal recognition (Warren Cook, personal communication, 1985).

63. Rountree, Fieldnotes 1983, 1984.

64. Acts of Assembly 1983, pp. 31–32; this law established or ratified several bodies, including the commission.

65. Warren Cook, personal communications, 1984 and 1985.

66. That is a perennial condition among Indian people all over the country; see Lurie 1979.

67. Most of the headdresses were bought commercially until recently. The Upper Mattaponi chief's headdress, however, was made of wild turkey feathers by his wife; his daughter remade it for her brother, her father's successor (Margaret Adams Allmond, personal communication, 1987). Since 1984, Pamunkey and Nansemond tribal officials have purchased similar headdresses from her.

68. Nancy O. Lurie, personal communication, 1973; Rick Hohman (Cheyenne; Native American Studies Department, University of Montana), personal communication, 1983.

69. Rountree, Fieldnotes 1981, 1983, 1985 onward.

70. The trading post at Pamunkey and the museum at Mattaponi both have long histories; it is the museum at Pamunkey and the trading post at Mattaponi that are fairly new.

71. A recent estimate, after an aerial projection was made in connection with the case against the railroad; the reservation has still never been surveyed (Chief William Miles, personal communication, 1985).

72. In September 1986 there were twenty-nine households with forty-six persons who were either permanently or occasionally resident on the reservation (Rountree, fieldnotes made with assistance of Chief William H. Miles and his wife).

73. The following account is based upon interviews with Chief Tecumseh Deerfoot Cook in the summer of 1970 and Chief William Miles in July 1985.

74. Chief Tecumseh Deerfoot Cook, retired in 1984, also enjoyed demonstrating how spry he was in his eighties. He is a past master at jocularly "playing Indian" to protect the privacy of his people.

75. The antiquity of this rule is open to question; see previous chapters. In the 1970s this rule was attempted to be applied even to the Pamunkey widow of a white man. In 1989 several more Pamunkey women married to whites unsuccessfully challenged the custom; their case drew national press attention (Rountree, Fieldnotes).

76. Mapped by Frank Speck, in Speck Papers.

77. *Norfolk Virginian Pilot,* November 25, 1977, p. B–3.

78. *Historic Preservation,* fall 1979.

79. *West Point Tidewater Review* (Va.), September 24, 1980, p. 1; *Newport News Daily Press,* October 11, 1980, p. 12.

80. Summer field school brochures, sent me by Callahan, plus Callahan, personal communications. Funding: $10,000 HUD grant in 1977, no funding in 1978 (*Newport News Daily Press,* March 26, 1978, p. F–1; *Richmond Times-Dispatch,* November 10, 1978, p. C–1).

81. The information for this account has been gathered during many visits and other communications since the fall of 1969. I am particularly indebted to retired Chief Curtis L. Custalow for the data on tribal government, which he furnished me in 1970.

82. In 1970 there were forty people in thirteen households; in October 1981 there were sixty people in twenty-one households; in August 1985 there were fifty-seven people in twenty-one households—all figures changeable due to an influx during school vacation times (Rountree, Fieldnotes).

83. Former Chief Curtis L. Custalow, Sr., personal communication, 1985.

84. He would have to obey tribal laws while on probation; if his behavior was unsatisfactory, he would remain indefinitely on probation as long as his wife wanted to remain on the reservation.

85. Rountree, Fieldnotes 1983 and 1985.

86. Unfortunately I have found no documents to verify the dancers' claim, made to the general public, that their dances have been handed down from aboriginal times. On the other hand, the Chickahominies have not followed the North Carolina Haliwa example of going completely Plains-inspired pan-Indian in their dances or the song that accompanies them. The Chickahominies also do no "Forty-Nining."

87. That number includes seventy-five children of present enrollees (Eunice Adams [tribal treasurer], personal communication, 1985) plus other adults who have factional differences with the present tribal government (Ronald Adams, personal communication, 1985).

88. At this writing there are two such members, a Mattaponi and a Pamunkey who have been married to Upper Mattaponi husbands for at least forty years and who have identified themselves during all that time with the tribe.

89. James Coates was still active in encouraging that tribe until his death in May 1987; he and I attended Upper Mattaponi functions together in 1983–1986. In August 1985 we were both elected honorary members of the tribe, along with several white spouses of Upper Mattaponis.

90. Linwood Custalow, personal communication, 1985.

91. Data from this section are from interviews with Chief Captain Nelson in 1974, former Assistant Chief Oliver Fortune in 1974, 1976, and 1985, and Council on Indians Representative Nokomis Fortune Lemons in 1986.

92. Rountree, Fieldnotes 1974.

93. Rountree, Fieldnotes 1971, 1972, 1973.

94. Rountree, Fieldnotes 1985.

95. Rountree, Fieldnotes 1983, 1984; he contacted James R. Coates and me in January 1983, and the sharing of documents has been continuous ever since. Coates and I also attended the meetings first by invitation and later as honorary members. I have functioned there from the beginning in August 1984 as "anthropologist and note taker" (now as "acting recording secretary"), occasionally adding historical comments to my minutes, which are then checked by Perry and his successor as assistant chief and mailed to all members by the secretary, as an aid to keeping up organizational momentum. The monthly minutes serve the purpose of a newsletter.

96. Earl Bass was naturally the chief; Oliver Perry as assistant chief took on most of the bureaucratic and public-speaking work.

97. Rountree, Fieldnotes 1985.

98. Rountree, Fieldnotes 1987; correspondence with Booker after he attended a Nansemond meeting to tell them how to get the changes made.

99. The two reservations would have no trouble, of course, but they say they are not interested.

Epilogue. Ethnic Identity Among the Powhatan Indians

1. Isajiw 1974; Schermerhorn 1974.

2. Barth (1969, p. 10) is one of the few scholars to state this specifically: an ethnic group is "a category distinguishable from others of the same order."

3. Spicer 1971, pp. 797–798.

4. Coser 1964 [1956], p. 207.

5. Keyes 1981, p. 15.

6. Spicer 1971, p. 798. See also Castile and Kushner 1981.

7. Barth 1969, p. 33.

8. Spicer 1971, p. 798.

9. Ibid., p. 799.

10. See, for instance, Breton 1964, pp. 194, 204.

11. Isajiw 1974, p. 122.

12. Blauner 1969.

13. Shibutani and Kwan 1965, p. 39.

14. Wallace (1966, p. 26) notes that "religion is frequently a way of asserting an ethnic or class or racial identity in a situation of intergroup conflict."

15. Lyman and Douglass (1973, pp. 347) discuss ethnic groups' "impression management" and the power games that result from it, while Newman (1976) reviews the difficulties that minorities face in handling varying interpretations of "what they are."

16. Lyman and Douglass 1973, p. 361.

17. As stated in chap. 10, the Upper Mattaponis and the Nansemonds manipulate these statuses somewhat differently. The Upper Mattaponis reserve associate memberships for long-married spouses, who today are reservation Indian women. The Nansemonds, who have no spouses from other Virginia Indian tribes, allow white spouses to become associate members.

Bibliography

Accomac County, Virginia
  1663 to present. County Records. Accomac, Virginia (copy in Virginia State
      Library, Richmond).
Adkins, O. Oliver
  n.d.   Papers, personal and tribal.
American Historical Society, comp.
  1924   *Virginia Biography.* Vol. 5 of *History of Virginia.* New York: American
      Historical Society.
Anonymous
  1896   Proceedings of the Visitors of William and Mary College, 1716. *Vir-
      ginia Magazine of History and Biography* 4:161–175.
Anonymous
  1896–1897 The Boundary Line Proceedings, 1710. *Virginia Magazine of His-
      tory and Biography* 4:30–42, 5:1–12.
Anonymous
  1897   Colonial Letters, &c. (Ludwell Papers). *Virginia Magazine of History
      and Biography* 5:42–53.
Anonymous
  1900   Indians of Southern Virginia, 1650–1711: Depositions in the Virginia
      and North Carolina Boundary Case. *Virginia Magazine of History and
      Biography* 7:337–352, 8:1–11.
Anonymous
  1900–1901 Two Tragicall Events: The Voyage of Anthony Chester, Made in
      the Year 1620 . . . . *William and Mary Quarterly,* 1st ser., 9:203–214.
Anonymous
  1901   The Virginia Assembly of 1641. A List of Members and Some of the
      Acts. *Virginia Magazine of History and Biography* 9:50–59.
Anonymous
  1902–1903 An Abridgement of the Laws of Virginia, compiled in 1694. *Vir-
      ginia Magazine of History and Biography* 9:273–288, 369–384;
      10:49–64, 145–160, 241–254.
Anonymous
  1908–1916 The Randolph Manuscript. *Virginia Magazine of History and Bi-
      ography* 15:390–405; 16:1–15, 113–131; 17:1–13, 113–132,
      225–248, 337–351; 18:1–24, 129–139, 241–255, 353–373; 19:
      1–12, 149–156, 240–247, 337–347; 20:1–13, 113–126, 225–235,
      337–346; 21:1–8, 113–121, 225–233, 337–358; 22:14–21, 113–
      121, 225–231, 337–347.

Anonymous
  1910 [1635]   A Relation of Maryland, 1635. In *Narratives of Early Maryland,*
          1633–1684, ed. Clayton Colman Hall, 70–112. New York: Charles
          Scribner's Sons.
Anonymous
  1914   Virginia in 1677–78. *Virginia Magazine of History and Biography* 22:
          140–149, 297–302, 395–403.
Anonymous
  1947 [1610]   A True Declaration of the Estate of the Colonie in Virginia . . . .
          In *Tracts and Other Papers,* vol. 3, no. 1, ed. Peter Force. New York:
          Peter Smith.
Anonymous
  1947 [1612]   For the Colony in Virginia Britania. Lavves Divine, Morall, and
          Martiall, & c. In *Tracts and Other Papers,* vol. 3, no. 2, ed. Peter Force.
          New York: Peter Smith.
Anonymous
  1947 [1649]   A Perfect Description of Virginia . . . . In *Tracts and Other Papers,*
          vol. 2, no. 8, ed. Peter Force. New York: Peter Smith.
Anonymous
  1969 [1608]   Map of Virginia [the so-called Zuniga map]. In *The Jamestown*
          Voyages Under the First Charter, 2d ser., vol. 137, ed. Philip L. Bar-
          bour, facing 239. Cambridge: The Hakluyt Society.
Apes, William
  1829   *A Son of the Forest. The Experience of William Apes, a Native of the*
          Forest, Comprising a Notice of the Pequod Tribe of Indians. New
          York: Privately printed.
  1835   *Indian Nullification of the Unconstitutional Laws of the Massachu-*
          setts, Relative to the Mashpee Tribe: or, The Pretended Riot Explained.
          Boston: Jonathan Howe.
Archer, Gabriel
  1969a [1607]   Relatyon of the Discovery of Our River. In *The Jamestown Voy-*
          ages Under the First Charter, 2d ser., vol. 136, ed. Philip L. Barbour,
          80–98. Cambridge: The Hakluyt Society.
  1969b [1607]   Description of the River and Country. In *The Jamestown Voy-*
          ages Under the First Charter, 2d ser., vol. 136, ed. Philip L. Barbour,
          98–102. Cambridge: The Hakluyt Society. Also (with entry below) in
          Quinn 1979 (q.v.), vol. 5, 274–276.
  1969c [1607]   Description of the People [authorship uncertain]. In *The James-*
          town Voyages Under the First Charter, 2d ser., vol. 136, ed. Philip L.
          Barbour, 102–104. Cambridge: The Hakluyt Society.
Argall, Samuel
  1904–1906 [1613]   A Letter of Sir Samuel Argall touching his Voyage to
          Virginia, and Actions there: Written to Master Nicholas Hawes. In
          Hakluytus Posthumus or Purchas His Pilgrimes, vol. 19, ed. Samuel
          Purchas, 90–95. Glasgow: James MacLehose and Sons.
Ashburn, Percy M.
  1947   *The Ranks of Death: A Medical History of the Conquest of America.*
          New York: Coward-McCann.
Attan Akamik [newspaper]
  1969–1975 (6 annual issues).   Davis, California.

B.P.R.O., C.O. = British Public Record Office, Colonial Office.

Ballagh, James Curtis
1902   A History of Slavery in Virginia. Johns Hopkins Studies in Historical and Political Science, extra vol. 14. Baltimore: Johns Hopkins University Press.

Banister, John
1970   John Banister and His Natural History of Virginia, 1678–1692. Eds. Joseph Ewan and Nesta Ewan. Urbana: University of Illinois Press.

Barbour, Philip L.
1964   The Three Worlds of Captain John Smith. Boston: Houghton Mifflin.
———, ed.
1969   The Jamestown Voyages Under the First Charter. 1st ser., vols. 136–137. Cambridge: The Hakluyt Society.

Barth, Frederick.
1969   Ethnic Groups and Boundaries. London: Allen and Unwin.

Beale, Calvin L.
n.d.   Papers. In Mr. Beale's possession; Xeroxed copy of Virginia-related papers in author's possession.
1958   Census Problems of Racial Enumeration. In Race, Individual and Collective Behavior, ed. Edgar T. Thompson, 537–543. Glencoe, Illinois: The Free Press.

Beard, Belle Boone
n.d. [1943] Papers. Incomplete collection [many thrown away by Beard], given by her to author in 1973.

Bell, Albert D.
1961   Bass Families of the South. Rocky Mount, North Carolina: Privately printed.

Berry, Brewton
1963   Almost White. New York: Macmillan.

Berry, John, and Francis Moryson
1896 [1677] A True Narrative of the Rise, Progresse, and Cesation of the Late Rebellion in Virginia, Most Humbly and Impartially Reported by his Majestyes Commissioners Appointed to Enquire into the Affaires of the Said Colony. Virginia Magazine of History and Biography 4:117–154.

Beverley, Robert
1947 [1705] The History and Present State of Virginia. Ed. Louis B. Wright. Chapel Hill: University of North Carolina Press.

Bieder, Robert E.
1980   Scientific Attitudes Toward Indian Mixed-Bloods in Early Nineteenth Century America. Journal of Ethnic Studies 8(2):17–30.

Billings, Warren M.
1970   The Causes of Bacon's Rebellion: Some Suggestions. Virginia Magazine of History and Biography 78:409–435.
1974   The Growth of Political Institutions in Virginia, 1634 to 1676. William and Mary Quarterly, 3d ser., 31:225–242.
1975   Some Acts Not in Hening's Statutes: The Acts of Assembly, April 1652, November 1652, and July 1653. Virginia Magazine of History and Biography 83:22–76.

Binford, Lewis R.
1964   Archaeological and Ethnohistorical Investigation of Cultural Diversity

and Progressive Development Among Aboriginal Cultures of Coastal Virginia and North Carolina. Ph.D. diss., University of Michigan.

Bland, Edward, et al.
1911 [1651]   The Discovery of New Brittaine . . . . In *Narratives of Early Carolina, 1650–1708*, ed. Alexander S. Salley, pp. 1–19. New York: Barnes and Noble.

Blauner, Robert
1969   Internal Colonialism and Ghetto Revolt. *Social Problems* 16:393–408.

Blume, G. W. J.
1950   Present Day Indians of Tidewater Virginia. *Quarterly Bulletin of the Archeological Society of Virginia* 6 (2):1–8.

Boissevain, Ethel
1963   Detribalization and Group Identity: The Narragansett Indian Case. *Transactions of the New York Academy of Sciences*, 2d ser., 25:493–502.

Boyce, Douglas W.
1978   Iroquoian Tribes of the Virginia-North Carolina Coastal Plain. In *Handbook of North American Indians*, Vol. 15, *Northeast*, ed. Bruce G. Trigger, 282–289. Washington, D.C.: Smithsonian Institution.

Bradby, William Terrill
1893–1989   Papers, abstracted by James Mooney. File 2218, National Anthropological Archives, Smithsonian Institution, Washington, D.C.

Brasser, T. J.
1966   *Indians of Long Island, 1600–1964*. Monographs on the American Indian. Publication no. 1. Colorado Springs: Wanblee Supply Co.
1971   The Coastal Algonquians: People of the First Frontiers. In *North American Indians in Historical Perspective*, ed. Eleanor Burke Leacock and Nancy Oestreich Lurie, 64–91. New York: Random House.

Breen, T. H., and Stephen Innes
1980   *"Myne Owne Ground": Race and Freedom on Virginia's Eastern Shore, 1640–1676*. New York: Oxford University Press.

Breton, Raymond
1964   Institutional Completeness of Ethnic Communities and the Personal Relations of Immigrants. *American Journal of Sociology* 70:193–205.

Bridenbaugh, Carl
1980   *Early Americans*. New York: Oxford University Press.
1981   *Jamestown 1544–1699*. New York: Oxford University Press.

Brown, Alexander
1964 [1890]   *The Genesis of the United States*. 2 vols. New York: Russell and Russell.

Brown, Douglas Summers
1966   *The Catawba Indians: People of the River*. Columbia: University of South Carolina Press.

Bruce, Philip Alexander
1924   *History of Virginia*. Vol. 1, *Colonial Period 1607–1763*. Chicago: American Historical Society.
1935   *Economic History of Virginia in the Seventeenth Century*. 2 vols. New York: Peter Smith.

Burke, John
1967   *Burke's Genealogical and Heraldic History of the Peerage, Baronetage and Knightage*. 104th ed., ed. Peter Townend. London: Burke's Peerage.

Burnaby, Andrew
  1812 [1760]   Travels Through the Middle Settlements in North America, in the
                Years 1759 and 1760 . . . . In *Voyages and Travels,* vol. 13, ed. John
                Pinkerton, 701–752. London: Longman, Hurst, Rees and Orme.
Byrd, William
  1966   *The Prose Works of William Byrd of Westover.* Ed. Louis B. Wright.
                Cambridge: Harvard University Press.
Byrd, William, et al.
  1637–1743   William Byrd's Title Book. MS., Virginia Historical Society,
                Richmond.
Canner, Thomas
  1904–1906 [1603]   A Relation of the Voyage Made to Virginia in the Elizabeth
                of London . . . in the Yeere 1603. In *Hakluytus Posthumus or Purchas
                His Pilgrimes,* vol. 18, ed. Samuel Purchas, 329–335. Glasgow: James
                MacLehose and Sons.
Caroline County, Virginia
  1727 to present (fragmentary).   County Records. Bowling Green, Virginia
                (copy in Virginia State Library, Richmond).
Carson, Jane
  1950   The Will of John Rolfe. *Virginia Magazine of History and Biography*
                58:58–65.
Castile, George Pierre, and Gilbert Kushner, eds.
  1981   *Persistent Peoples: Cultural Enclaves in Perspective.* Tucson: Univer-
                sity of Arizona Press.
Ceci, Lynn
  1975   Fish Fertilizer: A Native North American Practice? *Science* 188(4183):
                26–30.
Cedarstrom, D. J.
  1945   Structural Geology of Southeastern Virginia. *Bulletin of American As-
                sociation of Petroleum Geologists* 19:71–95.
Chamberlayne, C. G., transcr.
  1937   *Vestry Book and Register of St. Peter's Parish, 1684–1786: New Kent
                and James City Counties, Virginia.* Richmond: The Library Board.
  1940   *The Vestry Book of St. Paul's Parish, Hanover County, Virginia, 1706–
                1786.* Richmond: The Library Board.
Charles City County, Virginia
  1655–1665, 1769 to present. County Records.   Charles City, Virginia (copy in
                Virginia State Library, Richmond).
Clarke, Peyton Neale
  1897   *Old King William Homes and Families.* Louisville, Kentucky: John P.
                Morton.
Clayton, John
  1965 [1687]   "The Aborigines of the Country": Letter to Dr. Nehemiah Grew.
                In *The Reverend John Clayton,* eds. Edmund Berkeley and Dorothy S.
                Berkeley, 21–39. Charlottesville: University of Virginia Press.
  1965 [1694]   Seven Severall Sorts of Snakes—and Vipers Most Deadly. In *The
                Reverend John Clayton,* eds. Edmund Berkeley and Dorothy S. Berke-
                ley, 105–121. Charlottesville: University of Virginia Press.
  1968 [1687]   Another Account of Virginia. Ed. Edmund Berkeley and Dorothy
                S. Berkeley. *Virginia Magazine of History and Biography* 76:415–436.

Coates, James R.
  n.d.   Papers. In Mrs. Eunice Adams' possession; Xeroxed duplicate in au-
              thor's possession.
des Cognets, Louis, comp.
  1958   *English Duplicates of Lost Virginia Records*. Princeton, New Jersey:
              Privately printed.
Colonial Council of Virginia
  1907 [1619]   A Report of the Manner of Proceeding the Virginia Assembly
              Convened at James City in Virginia, July 29, 1619. In *Narratives of
              Early Virginia, 1606–1625*, ed. Lyon G. Tyler, 249–278. New York:
              Barnes & Noble.
Commissioners Appointed Under the Great Seale of England for the Virginia
Affairs
  1906 [1677]   Articles of Peace between the most Mighty Prince . . . Charles the
              II . . . And the severall Indian Kings and Queens &c . . . the 29th day
              of May: 1677. . . . *Virginia Magazine of History and Biography* 14:
              289–296.
Conkey, Laura E., Ethel Boissevain, and Ives Goddard
  1978   Indians of Southern New England and Long Island: Late Period. In
              Handbook of North American Indians, Vol. 15, *Northeast*, ed. Bruce C.
              Trigger, 177–189. Washington, D.C.: Smithsonian Institution.
Coser, Lewis A.
  1964 [1956]   [Excerpt from] The Social Functions of Conflict. In *Sociological
              Theory: A Book of Readings*, 2d ed., ed. Lewis A. Coser and Bernard
              Rosenberg, 205–209. New York: Macmillan.
Craven, Wesley Frank
  1949   *The Southern Colonies in the Seventeenth Century*. Baton Rouge: Loui-
              siana State University Press.
Crosby, Alfred
  1972   *The Columbian Exchange*. Westport, Connecticut: Greenwood Press.
Crosby, John
  n.d.   Papers. Part of Commonwealth of Virginia, Board of Education, Rec-
              ords and Papers.
Dale, Thomas
  1964 [1611]   Dale to the Council. In *The Genesis of the United States*, ed. Al-
              exander Brown, 488–494. New York: Russell and Russell.
Dalrymple, E. A.
  1840–1843 [Actually to 1844 or later.]   Common Place Book. MS. 275–77.
              Maryland Historical Society Library, Baltimore. (Printed in *Historical
              Magazine and Notes and Queries Concerning the Antiquities, History
              and Biography of America* 2 [1858]:182.)
Deaux, George
  1969   *The Black Death, 1347*. New York: Waybright and Talley.
Dobyns, Henry F.
  1983   *Their Number Become Thinned: Native American Population Dynam-
              ics in Eastern North America*. Knoxville: University of Tennessee Press.
Dragoo, Don W.
  1976   Some Aspects of Eastern North American Prehistory: A Review 1975.
              American Antiquity 41:3–27.

Durand de Dauphine
1934   *A Huguenot Exile in Virginia . . . from the Hague Edition of 1687.*
        New York: Press of the Pioneers.
Earle, Carville V.
1979   Environment, Disease, and Mortality in Early Virginia. In *The Chesa-
        peake in the Seventeenth Century: Essays on Anglo-American Society,*
        eds. Thad W. Tate and David L. Ammerman, 96–125. Chapel Hill:
        University of North Carolina Press.
Emerson, Everett H.
1967   Captain John Smith as Editor: The Generall Historie. *Virginia Maga-
        zine of History and Biography* 75:143–156.
Essex County, Virginia
1656–1692. Records of Old Rappahannock County. Tappahannock, Virginia
        (copy in Virginia State Library, Richmond).
1692 to present. County Records. Tappahannock, Virginia (copy in Virginia
        State Library, Richmond).
Estabrook, Arthur H., and Ivan E. McDougle
1926   *Mongrel Virginians: The WIN Tribe.* Baltimore: Williams and Wilkins.
Farrar, Michael Lloyd, contrib.
1905   The Farrar Papers at Magalene College, Cambridge. *Virginia Magazine
        of History and Biography* 11:41–46.
Father William [pseud.]
1854   *Recollections of Rambles at the South.* New York: Carlton and Phillips.
Fausz, J. Frederick
1977   The Powhatan Uprising of 1622: A Historical Study of Ethnocentrism
        and Cultural Conflict. Ph.D. diss., College of William and Mary.
1979   Fighting "Fire" With Firearms: The Anglo-Powhatan Arms Race in
        Early Virginia. *American Indian Culture and Research Journal* 3(4):
        33–50.
1981   Opechancanough: Indian Resistance Leader. In *Struggle and Survival
        in Colonial America,* eds. David G. Sweet and Gary B. Nash, 21–37.
        Berkeley: University of California Press.
1984   Anglo-Indian Relations in Colonial North America. In *Scholars and
        the Indian Experience: Critical Reviews of Recent Writing in the Social
        Sciences,* ed. W. R. Swagerty, 79–105. Bloomington: University of In-
        diana Press.
1985   Patterns of Anglo-Indian Aggression and Accommodation Along the
        Mid-Atlantic Coast, 1584–1634. In *Cultures in Contact: The Euro-
        pean Impact on Native Institutions in Eastern North America, A.D.
        1000–1800,* ed. William W. Fitzhugh, 225–268. Washington, D.C.:
        Smithsonian Institution Press.
1987   Middlemen in Peace and War: Virginia's Earliest Indian Interpreters,
        1608–1632. *Virginia Magazine of History and Biography* 95:41–64.
Fausz, J. Frederick, and Jon Kukla
1977   A Letter of Advice to the Governor of Virginia, 1624. *William and
        Mary Quarterly,* 3d ser., 34:104–129.
Feest, Christian F.
1973   Seventeenth Century Virginia Algonquian Population Estimates. *Quar-
        terly Bulletin of the Archeological Society of Virginia* 28:66–79.
1978   Virginia Algonquians. In *Handbook of North American Indians,* Vol.

15, *Northeast,* ed. Bruce G. Trigger, 253–270. Washington, D.C.: Smithsonian Institution.

1983　　"Powhatan's Mantle" and "Skin Pouch" [the "Virginia Purse"]. In *Tradescant's Rarities,* ed. Arthur MacGregor, 130–137. Oxford: Clarendon Press.

1987　　Pride and Prejudice: The Pocahontas Myth and the Pamunkey. *European Review of Native American Studies* 1(1):5–12.

Fleet, Beverley
1942　　*Virginia Colonial Abstracts,* 6th Collection, Vol. 15. Richmond: privately published.

Fontaine, John
1853 [1715]　Journal of John Fontaine. In *Memoirs of a Huguenot Family,* comp. and trans. Ann Maury. New York: George P. Putnam.

Frank, Joseph, ed.
1957　　News from Virginny, 1644. *Virginia Magazine of History and Biography* 65:84–87.

Frazier, E. Franklin
1939　　*The Negro Family in the United States.* Chicago: University of Chicago Press.

Gatschet, Albert S.
n.d.　　Notebook. MS. 1449, National Anthropological Archives, Smithsonian Institution, Washington, D.C.

post-1893　*Pamunkey Notebook.* MS. 2197. National Anthropological Archives, Smithsonian Institution, Washington, D.C.

Glenn, Keith
1944　　Captain John Smith and the Indians. *Virginia Magazine of History and Biography* 52:228–248.

Gloucester County, Virginia
1862 to present.　County Records. Gloucester, Virginia (copy in Virginia State Library, Richmond).

Glover, Thomas
1904 [1676]　*An Account of Virginia, Its Scituation, Temperature, Inhabitants and Their Manner of Planting and Ordering Tobacco, etc.* [Originally published in *Philosophical Transactions of the Royal Society.*] Oxford: B. H. Blackwell.

Gonzalez, Ellice B.
1986　　Tri-Racial Isolates in a Bi-Racial Society: Poospatuck Ambiguity and Conflict. In *Strategies For Survival: American Indians in the Eastern United States,* ed. Frank W. Porter III, 113–137. New York: Greenwood Press.

n.d.　　From Unkechaug to Poosepatuck. MS. (written in 1983). Copies in possession of National Park Service and the author.

Goodman, Jennifer Robin
1981　　The Captain's Self-Portrait: John Smith as Chivalric Biographer. *Virginia Magazine of History and Biography* 89:27–38.

Gottfried, Robert S.
1982　　*The Black Death: Natural and Human Disaster in Medieval Europe.* New York: The Free Press.

Gradie, Charlotte M.
1988　　Spanish Jesuits in Virginia: The Mission That Failed. *Virginia Magazine of History and Biography* 96:131–156.

n.d. The Divided Nature of Spanish Policy Toward the Powhatans in the Late Sixteenth Century. In *Powhatan Foreign Policy, 1500–1722*, ed. Helen C. Rountree. In progress.

Gregory, Roger
1875 Letter of August 24, 1875, to W. R. Palmer. Archives of Virginia Historical Society, Richmond, Virginia.

Haller, Mark H.
1963 *Eugenics: Hereditarian Attitudes in American Thought.* New Brunswick, New Jersey: Rutgers University Press.

Hamor, Ralph
1957 [1615] *A True Discourse of the Present State of Virginia.* Richmond: Virginia State Library.

Hariot, Thomas
1972 [1590] *A Briefe and True Report of the New Found Land of Virginia.* New York: Dover.

Harshberger, John W.
1958 [1911] *Phytogeographic Survey of North America.* New York: Hafner Publishing Co.

Harte, Thomas J.
1959 Trends in Mate Selection in a Tri-Racial Isolate. *Social Forces* 37: 215–221.

Harvill, A. M., Jr.
1970 *Spring Flora of Virginia.* Parsons, West Virginia: Privately printed.

Hassrick, Royal B., and Edmund Carpenter.
1944 Rappahannock Games and Amusements. *Primitive Man* 17:29–39.

Hayes, Rose Oldfield
1976 Shinnecock Land Ownership and Use: Prehistoric and Colonial Influence on Modern Adaptive Modes. Paper read at American Anthropological Association meetings, November 1976, Washington, D.C.

Hening, William Waller, comp.
1809–1823 *The Statutes at Large, Being a Collection of all the Laws of Virginia from the First Session of the Legislature.* 13 vols. New York: R. & W. & G. Bartow.

Henrico County, Virginia
1677 to present (fragmentary). County Records. Richmond, Virginia (copy in Virginia State Library, Richmond).

Herrman, Augustin
1673 Virginia and Maryland as it is Planted and Inhabited this Present Year 1670, Surveyed and Exactly Drawne by the Only Labour & Endeavour of Augustin Herrman Bohemiensis. London. (Copy in Virginia State Library, Richmond.)

Hicks, George L.
1975 The Same North and South: Ethnicity and Change in Two American Indian Groups. In *The New Ethnicity: Perspectives From Ethnology,* ed. John Bennett, 75–94. Saint Paul: West Publishing.

1977 Separate but Similar: Adaptation by Two American Indian Groups. In *Ethnic Encounters,* eds. George L. Hicks and P. Leis, 63–83. North Scituate, Massachusetts: Duxbury Press.

Hicks, George L., and David I. Kertzer
1972 Making a Middle Way: Problems of Monhegan Identity. *Southwestern Journal of Anthropology* 28:1–24.

Hiden, Martha W., and Henry M. Dargan
  1966   John Gibbon's Manuscript Notes Concerning Virginia. *Virginia Maga-
            zine of History and Biography* 74:3–22.
Hoffman, Bernard G.
  1964   Observations on Certain Ancient Tribes of the Northern Appalachian
            Province. *Bulletin of the Bureau of American Ethnology* 191:195–206.
Hoffman, Paul
  In press A New Andalucia and a Way to the Orient: A History of the Southeast
            During the Sixteenth Century. Baton Rouge: Louisiana State University
            Press.
Hotchkiss, Jed
  n.d.   The Battlefields of Virginia. Collection. Map no. 2: Map of a Portion of
            the Rappahannock River and Vicinity, Virginia. . . . [1862]. Library of
            Congress, Washington, D.C.
Howe, Henry
  1969 [1845]   *Historical Collections of Virginia.* Baltimore: Regional Publishing.
Hudson, Charles M.
  1970   *The Catawba Nation.* Athens: University of Georgia Press.
  1981   Why the Southeastern Indians Slaughtered Deer. In *Indians, Animals,
            and the Fur Trade: A Critique of Keepers of the Game,* ed. Shepard
            Krech III, 155–176. Athens: University of Georgia Press.
Hudson, J. Paul
  1960   A Silver Badge for a Virginia Queen. *Virginia Cavalcade* 10(2):19–22.
Hulton, Paul
  1984   *America 1585: The Complete Drawings of John White.* Chapel Hill:
            University of North Carolina Press.
Hungars Parish [Northampton County] Vestry Book.
  1753–1782   In Virginia State Library, Richmond.
Isajiw, Wsevolod
  1974   Definitions of Ethnicity. *Ethnicity* 1:111–124.
Isle of Wight County, Virginia
  1650s (fragmentary), 1661 to present.   County Records. Isle of Wight, Virginia
            (copy in Virginia State Library, Richmond).
Jackson, Luther Porter
  1971 [1942]   *Free Negro Land and Property Holding in Virginia, 1830–1860.*
            New York: Russell and Russell.
Jefferson, Thomas
  1954 [1787]   *Notes on the State of Virginia, 1787.* Ed. William Peden. Chapel
            Hill: University of North Carolina Press.
Jennings, Francis
  1975   *The Invasion of America: Indians, Colonialism, and the Cant of Con-
            quest.* Chapel Hill: University of North Carolina Press.
  1978   Susquehannock. In *Handbook of North American Indians,* Vol. 15,
            Northeast, ed. Bruce G. Trigger, 362–367. Washington, D.C.: Smith-
            sonian Institution.
Jester, Annie Lash, and Martha Woodroof Hiden
  1956   *Adventures of Purse and Person: Virginia 1607–1625.* Princeton:
            Princeton University Press.
Johnston, James Hugo
  1929   Documentary Evidence of the Relations of Negroes and Indians. *Jour-
            nal of Negro History* 14:21–43.

1970   Race Relations in Virginia & Miscegenation in the South, 1776–1860. Amherst: University of Massachusetts Press.

Jones, Hugh
1956 [1724]   The Present State of Virginia. Ed. Richard L. Morton. Chapel Hill: University of North Carolina Press.

Kawashima, Yasu
1969   Legal Origins of the Indian Reservation in Colonial Massachusetts. American Journal of Legal History 13:42–56.

Keyes, Charles F.
1981   The Dialectics of Ethnic Change. In Ethnic Change, ed. Charles F. Keyes, 4–30. Seattle: University of Washington Press.

King and Queen County, Virginia
1864 to present.   County Records. King and Queen, Virginia (copy in Virginia State Library, Richmond).

King William County, Virginia
1702 to present (fragmentary before 1885)   County Records. King William, Virginia (copy in Virginia State Library, Richmond).

Kingsbury, Susan Myra, comp.
1906–1935   Records of the Virginia Company of London. 4 vols. Washington, D.C.: Library of Congress.

Knowles, Nathaniel
1940   The Torture of Captives by the Indians of Eastern North America. Proceedings of the American Philosophical Society 82:151–225.

Kukla, Jon, ed.
1975   Some Acts Not in Hening's Statutes: The Acts of Assembly, October 1660. Virginia Magazine of History and Biography 83:77–97.

Kupperman, Karen Ordahl
1980   Settling With The Indians: The Meeting of English and Indian Cultures in America, 1580–1640. Totowa, New Jersey: Rowman and Littlefield.
1984   Roanoke: The Abandoned Colony. Totowa, New Jersey: Rowman and Allanheld.

Lancaster County, Virginia
1651 to present.   County Records. Lancaster, Virginia (copy in Virginia State Library, Richmond).

Langston, John Mercer
1969 [1894]   From the Virginia Plantation to the National Capitol. New York: Arno Press.

Lauber, Almon Wheeler
1913   Indian Slavery in Colonial Times Within the Present Limits of the United States. Columbia University Studies in History, Economics and Public Law 54(3). New York: Columbia University Press. Reprint. Williamsburg, Mass.: Cornerhouse, 1970.

Lederer, John
1958 [1672]   The Discoveries of John Lederer. Ed. William P. Cumming. Charlottesville: University of Virginia Press.

Lewis, Clifford M., and Albert J. Loomie
1953   The Spanish Jesuit Mission in Virginia, 1570–1572. Chapel Hill: University of North Carolina Press.

Lippson, Alice Jane, ed.
1973   The Chesapeake Bay in Maryland: An Atlas of Natural Resources. Baltimore: Johns Hopkins University Press.

Lippson, Alice Jane, and Robert L. Lippson
  1984   *Life in the Chesapeake Bay.* Baltimore: Johns Hopkins University Press.
Longleat Papers.
  Collection of colonial papers in Longleat House, Wiltshire, England.
Loskiel, George H.
  1794   *The History of the Mission of the United Brethren Among the Indians in North America.* London: n.p.
Love, W. DeLoss
  1899   *Samson Occom and the Christian Indians of New England.* Boston: The Pilgrim Press.
Lower Norfolk County *see* Norfolk County, Virginia
Ludmerer, Kenneth M.
  1972   *Genetics and American Society: A Historical Appraisal.* Baltimore: Johns Hopkins University Press.
Lurie, Nancy Oestreich
  1959   Indian Cultural Adjustment to European Civilization. In *Seventeenth Century America: Essays in Colonial History,* ed. James Morton Smith, 33–60. Chapel Hill: University of North Carolina Press.
  1974   The World's Oldest On-Going Protest Demonstration: North American Indian Drinking Patterns. In *The American Indian,* ed. Norris Hundley, Jr., 55–76. Santa Barbara: Clio Press.
  1979   The Will-o'-the-Wisp of Indian Unity. *Currents in Anthropology: Essays in Honor of Sol Tax,* ed. Robert Hinshaw, 325–335. The Hague: Mouton.
Lyman, Stanford M., and William A. Douglass
  1973   Ethnicity: Strategies of Collective and Individual Impression Management. *Social Research* 40:340–365.
MacLeod, William Christie
  1928   *The American Indian Frontier.* London: Routledge and Kegan Paul. Chapter 12, pp. 152–171, Reprinted as Celt and Indian: Britain's Old World Frontier in Relation to the New. In *Beyond the Frontier,* eds. Paul Bohannan and Fred Plog, 25–41. New York: Natural History Press, 1967.
Marzone, William
  1855   *Map & Profile—An Experimental Survey—New York & Norfolk Railway.* Copy on file in Virginia Research Center for Archaeology, Richmond, Virginia.
Mason, Otis Tufton
  1877   Anthropological News. *American Naturalist* 11:627.
Mason, Polly Cary, ed. and comp.
  1946   *Records of Colonial Gloucester County, Virginia,* vol. 1. Newport News, Va.: Privately printed.
Massachusetts, Commonwealth of
  1861   Report to the Governor and Council, Concerning the Indians of the Comonwealth, under the Act of April 6, 1859. John Milton Earle, Commissioner. Boston: William White.
Mathew, Thomas
  1947 [1705]   The Beginning, Progress and Conclusion of Bacon's Rebellion in Virginia in the Years 1675 & 1676. In *Tracts and Other Papers,* vol. 1(8), ed. Peter Force. New York: Peter Smith.

Matthews, James M.
  1857–1858   *Digest of the Laws of Virginia of a Civil and Permanent Character
              and General Operation.* 2 vols. Richmond.
McCartney, Martha W.
  1984a   The Draft of York River in Virginia: An Artifact of the 17th Century.
          Southeastern Archaeological Conference Journal 3(2):97–110.
  1984b   Seventeenth Century Apartheid: The Suppression and Containment of
          Indians in Tidewater, Virginia. Occasional Papers of the Mid-Atlantic
          Archaeological Conference. Ms.
  1989   Cockacoeske, Queen of Pamunkey: Diplomat and Suzeraine. In *Pow-
          hatan's Mantle: Indians in the Colonial Southeast,* eds. Peter Wood,
          Gregory Wasilkov, and Thomas Hatley, 173–195. Lincoln: University
          of Nebraska Press.
McCary, Ben C.
  1981   The Location of Werowocomoco. *Quarterly Bulletin of the Arch-
          eological Society of Virginia* 36:77–93.
  1983   The Virginia Tributary Indians and Their Metal Badges of 1661/62.
          Quarterly Bulletin of the Archeological Society of Virginia 38:182–
          196.
McClure, N. E., ed.
  1939   *Letters of John Chamberlain.* American Philosophical Society, Memoir
          12, pts. 1 and 2. Philadelphia.
McIlwaine, H. R., comp.
  1915   *Journal of the House of Burgesses.* 13 vols. Richmond: Virginia State
          Library.
  1918   *Legislative Journals of the Council of Colonial Virginia.* 3 vols. Rich-
          mond: Virginia State Library.
  1925   *Executive Journals of the Council of Colonial Virginia.* 5 vols. Rich-
          mond: Virginia State Library.
  1979 [1924]   *Minutes of the Council and General Court of Virginia, 1622–
          1632, 1670–1676.* 2d ed. Richmond: Virginia State Library.
McIntyre, Andrew, et al.
  1976   The Glacial North Atlantic 18,000 Years Ago; A CLIMAP Reconstruc-
          tion. In *Investigation of Late Quaternary Paleoceanography and Pa-
          leoclimatology,* eds. R. M. Cline and J. D. Hays, pp. 43–76. Geological
          Society of America Memoir 145. Boulder, Colorado.
Mead, Joseph
  1963 [1622–1623]   The Indian Massacre of 1622: Some Correspondence of
          the Reverend Joseph Mead. Ed. Robert C. Johnston. *Virginia Magazine
          of History and Biography* 71:408–410.
Meade, William
  1857   *Old Churches, Ministers and Families of Virginia.* 2 vols. Philadelphia:
          J. B. Lippincott.
Merrell, James H.
  1979   Cultural Continuity among the Piscataway Indians of Colonial Mary-
          land. *William and Mary Quarterly,* 3d ser., 36:548–570.
  1984   The Indians' New World: The Catawba Experience. *William and Mary
          Quarterly,* 3rd ser., 41:537–565.
  1989   *The Indians' New World: Catawbas and Their Neighbors from Euro-
          pean Contact Through the Era of Removal.* Chapel Hill: University of
          North Carolina Press.

Michel, Francis Louis
  1918 [1702] Report on the Journey of Francis Louis Michel from Berne, Swit-
      zerland, to Virginia, October 2, 1701–December 1, 1702. Ed. and
      transl. William J. Hinke. *Virginia Magazine of History and Biography*
      24:1–43, 113–141, 275–303.
Mochon, Marion Johnson
  1968 Stockbridge-Munsee Cultural Adaptations: "Assimilated Indians." *Pro-
      ceedings of the American Philosophical Society* 112(3):182–219.
de Molina, Diego, et al.
  1964 [1611] Report of the Voyage to Virginia. In *Genesis of the United States*,
      vol. 1, ed. Alexander Brown, 511–523. New York: Russell and Russell.
Mook, Maurice
  1943a The Anthropological Position of the Indian Tribes of Tidewater Vir-
      ginia. *William and Mary Quarterly*, 2d ser., 23:27–40.
  1943b Virginia Ethnology from an Early Relation. *William and Mary Quar-
      terly*, 2d ser., 23:101–129.
  1943c The Ethnological Significance of Tindall's Map of Virginia, 1608.
      William and Mary Quarterly, 2d ser., 23:371–408.
  1944 The Aboriginal Population of Tidewater Virginia. *American Anthro-
      pologist* 46:193–208.
Mooney, James
  1889–1907 Papers [concerning Indians of Virginia]. National Anthropologi-
      cal Archives, Smithsonian Institution, Washington, D.C.
  1889 Indian Tribes of the District of Columbia. *American Anthropologist*,
      o.s., 2:259–266.
  1970 [1894] *Siouan Tribes of the East.* New York: Johnson Reprints. (Origi-
      nally Bulletin 22 of Bureau of American Ethnology.)
  1907 The Powhatan Confederacy, Past and Present. *American Anthropolo-
      gist*, n.s., 9:129–152.
Moreau, Nicholas
  1937 [1697] Letter of April 12, 1697, to Rt. Hon. Lord Bishop of Lichfield &
      Coventry. In *Vestry Book and Register of St. Peter's Parish, 1684–1786,
      New Kent and James City Counties, Virginia*, ed. and transcr. C. G.
      Chamberlayne, appendix. Richmond, Virginia: The Library Board.
Morgan, Edmund S.
  1971 The First American Boom: Virginia 1618 to 1630. *William and Mary
      Quarterly*, 3d ser., 28:169–198.
  1975 *American Slavery, American Freedom.* New York: W. W. Norton.
Mossiker, Frances
  1976 *Pocahontas: The Life and Legend.* New York: Knopf.
Murray, Paul T.
  1987 Who is an Indian? Who is a Negro? Virginia Indians in the World War
      II Draft. *Virginia Magazine of History and Biography* 95:215–231.
Nash, Gary B.
  1974 *Red, White, and Black: The Peoples of Early America.* Englewood
      Cliffs, N.J.: Prentice-Hall.
Neill, Edward D.
  1866 *Virginia Carolorum.* Albany, N.Y.: John Munsell's Sons.
Neville, John Davenport, comp.
  1976 *Bacon's Rebellion: Abstracts of Materials in the Colonial Records
      Project.* N.p.: Jamestown Foundation.

New Kent County, Virginia
   1865 to present.   County Records. New Kent, Virginia (copy in Virginia State
      Library, Richmond).
Newman, William M.
   1976   Multiple Realities: The Effects of Social Pluralism on Identity. In *Ethnic Identity in Society,* ed. Arnold Dashevsky, 39–48. Chicago: Rand
      McNally.
Newport News Daily Press
Newport News Times-Herald
Noel Hume, Ivor
   1962   An Indian Ware of the Colonial Period. *Quarterly Bulletin of the
      Archeological Society of Virginia,* 17(1).
   1963   *Here Lies Virginia: An Archaeologist's View of Colonial Life and History.* New York: Knopf.
   1982   *Martin's Hundred.* New York: Knopf.
Norfolk County, Virginia [now cities of Chesapeake, Portsmouth, and Norfolk]
   1637 to present.   County Records. Chesapeake, Virginia (copy in Virginia State
      Library, Richmond).
Norfolk Ledger-Dispatch
Norfolk Virginian Pilot
Northampton County, Virginia
   1632 to present.   County Records. Eastville, Virginia (copy in Virginia State Library, Richmond).
Northumberland County, Virginia
   1652 to present.   County Records. Heathsville, Virginia (copy in Virginia State
      Library, Richmond).
Nugent, Nell Marion, comp.
   1934   *Cavaliers and Pioneers: Abstracts of Virginia Land Patents and Grants,
      1623–1800.* Vol. 1. Richmond: Dietz Press.
   1977   *Cavaliers and Pioneers: Abstracts of Virginia Land Patents and Grants,
      1623–1800.* Vol. 2. Richmond: Virginia State Library.
   1979   *Cavaliers and Pioneers: Abstracts of Virginia Land Patents and Grants,
      1623–1800.* Vol. 3. Richmond: Virginia State Library.
Old Rappahannock County, Virginia *See* Essex County, Virginia
Orcutt, Samuel
   1972 [1882]   *The Indians of the Housatonic and Naugatuck Valleys.* Hartford,
      Connecticut: Case, Lockwood & Brainard.
Palmer, William P., ed.
   1875   *Calendar of Virginia State Papers, and Other Manuscripts, 1652–1781.*
      11 vols. Richmond, Virginia.
Pargellis, Stanley, ed.
   1959   The Indians of Virginia. [1688; author possibly John Clayton.] *William
      and Mary Quarterly,* 3d ser., 16:228–253.
Percy, George
   1969a [1608?]   Observations Gathered out of a Discourse of the Plantation of
      the Southern Colonie in Virginia by the English 1606. In *The Jamestown Voyages Under the First Charter,* 2d ser., vol. 136, ed. Philip L.
      Barbour, 129–146. Cambridge: The Hakluyt Society. Also in Quinn
      1979 (q.v.), vol. 5, 266–274.
   1921–22 [1612]   A Trewe Relacyon. *Tyler's Quarterly* 3:259–282.
Perkins, Francis
   1969 [1608]   Letter of March 18, 1608. In *The Jamestown Voyages Under the*

First Charter, 2d ser., vol. 136, ed. Philip L. Barbour, 158–162. Cambridge: The Hakluyt Society.

Plecker, Walter Ashby
1924a   *Eugenics in Relation to the New Family and the Law on Racial Integrity, Including a Paper Read Before the American Public Health Association.* Richmond: Superintendent of Public Printing.
1924b   *Report of the Bureau of Vital Statistics.* Richmond.
1925   *Report of the Bureau of Vital Statistics.* Richmond.
1926   *Report of the Bureau of Vital Statistics.* Richmond.
1927   *Report of the Bureau of Vital Statistics.* Richmond.
1928   *Report of the Bureau of Vital Statistics.* Richmond.

Pollard, John Garland
1894   *The Pamunkey Indians of Virginia.* Bureau of American Ethnology Bulletin 17. Washington, D.C.: U.S. Government Printing Office.

Porter, Frank W., III
1980   Behind the Frontier: Indian Survivals in Maryland. *Maryland Historical Magazine* 75:42–54.
1986   The Nanticoke Indians in a Hostile World. In *Strategies for Survival: American Indians in the Eastern United States,* ed. Frank W. Porter III, 139–171. New York: Greenwood Press.

Porter, Kenneth W.
1932   Relations Between Negroes and Indians Within the Present Limits of the United States. *Journal of Negro History* 17:287–367.

Potter, Stephen R.
1982   An Analysis of Chicacoan Settlement Patterns. Ph.D. diss., University of North Carolina.
1989   European Effects on Virginia Algonquian Exchange and Tribute Systems in the Seventeenth Century: An Example from the Tidewater Potomac. In *Powhatan's Mantle: Indians in the Colonial Southeast,* eds. Peter Wood, Gregory Waselkov, and Thomas Hatley, pp. 151–172. Lincoln: University of Nebraska Press.

Powell, William S.
1958   The Aftermath of the Massacre. *Virginia Magazine of History and Biography* 66:44–75.

Puglisi, Michael J.
1989   Controversy and Revival: The Chickahominy Indians Since 1850. In *Charles City County, Virginia: An Official History,* eds. James Wittenberg and John Coski, pp. 97–104. Salem, West Virginia: Don Mills.

Purchas, Samuel, comp. and ed.
1614   *Purchas His Pilgrimes.* 2d ed. London.
1617   *Purchas His Pilgrimes.* 3d ed. London.
1904–1906 [1625]   *Hakluytus Posthumus or Purchas His Pilgrimes.* 20 vols. Glasgow: James MacLehose and Sons.

Quinn, David Beers
1970   Thomas Hariot and the Virginia Voyages of 1602. *William and Mary Quarterly,* 3d ser., 27:268–281.
1974   *England and the Discovery of America, 1481–1620.* New York: Knopf.
1984   *The Lost Colonists and Their Probable Fate.* Raleigh: North Carolina Department of Cultural Resources.
1985   *Set Fair for Roanoke: Voyages and Colonies, 1584–1606.* Chapel Hill: University of North Carolina Press.

————, ed.
1955   *The Roanoke Voyages, 1585–1590.* 2d ser., vol. 104. Cambridge: The
        Hakluyt Society. Series 2, Vol. 104.
1979   *New American World: A Documentary History of North America to
        1612.* New York: Arno Press.
Ramenofsky, Ann F.
1982   The Archaeology of Population Collapse: Native American Response
        to the Introduction of Infectious Disease. Ph.D. diss., University of
        Washington.
Randel, William
1939   Captain John Smith's Attitudes Toward the Indians. *Virginia Magazine
        of History and Biography* 47:218–229.
Raup, George B.
1953   Captain John Smith, Adventurer Extraordinary. *Virginia Magazine of
        History and Biography* 61:186–192.
Richmond County, Virginia (formerly part of Old Rappahannock County, whose
        records are in Essex County Courthouse)
1692 to present.   County Records. Warsaw, Virginia (copy in Virginia State Li-
        brary, Richmond).
Richmond Dispatch
Richmond Times
Richmond Times-Dispatch
Robinson, Conway
1900–1901   Notes from the Council and General Court Records 1641–1682.
        Virginia Magazine of History and Biography 8:64–73, 162–170,
        236–244, 407–412.
1901–1902   Notes from the Council and General Court Records of Virginia,
        1641–1682. *Virginia Magazine of History and Biography* 9:44–49,
        186–188, 306–309.
1905–1906   Notes from the Council and General Court Records, 1641–1659.
        Virginia Magazine of History and Biography 13:389–401.
Robinson, Paul A., Marc A. Kelley, and Patricia E. Rubertone
1985   Preliminary Biocultural Interpretations from a Seventeenth-Century
        Narragansett Indian Cemetery in Rhode Island. In *Cultures in Con-
        tact: The Impact of European Contacts on Native American Cultural
        Institutions, A.D. 1000–1800,* ed. William W. Fitzhugh, 107–130.
        Washington: Smithsonian Institution Press.
Robinson, W. Stitt
1952   Indian Education and Missions in Colonial Virginia. *Journal of South-
        ern History* 18:152–168.
1953   The Legal Status of the Indian in Colonial Virginia. *Virginia Magazine
        of History and Biography* 61:247–259.
1959   Tributary Indians in Colonial Virginia. *Virginia Magazine of History
        and Biography* 67:49–64.
Rolfe, John
1848 [1616]   Virginia in 1616. Vol. 1, no. 3 of *Virginia Historical Register.*
        Richmond: MacFarlane & Ferguson.
Ronda, James P.
1981   Generations of Faith: The Christian Indians of Martha's Vineyard.
        William and Mary Quarterly, 3d ser., 38:369–394.

Rountree, Helen C.
  n.d. [1969 to present.]   Fieldnotes on Powhatan and other Virginia Indians.
  n.d. [1970 to present.]   Correspondence about Powhatan and other Virginia
        Indians.
  1972   Powhatan's Descendants in the Modern World: Community Studies
        of the Two Virginia Indian Reservations, with Notes on Five Non-
        Reservation Enclaves. *The Chesopiean* 10(3):62–96.
  1973   Indian Land Loss in Virginia: A Prototype of Federal Indian Policy.
        Ph.D. diss. University of Wisconsin, Milwaukee.
  1975   Change Came Slowly: The Case of the Powhatan Indians of Virginia.
        Journal of Ethnic Studies 3(3):1–20.
  1979   The Indians of Virginia: A Third Race in a Biracial State. In *South-
        eastern Indians Since the Removal Era*, ed. Walter L. Williams, 27–48.
        Athens: University of Georgia Press.
  1986   Ethnicity Among the "Citizen" Indians of Virginia, 1800–1930. In
        Strategies For Survival: American Indians in the Eastern United States,
        ed. Frank W. Porter III, 173–209. New York: Greenwood Press.
  1987   The Termination and Dispersal of the Nottoway Indians of Virginia.
        Virginia Magazine of History and Biography 95:193–214.
  1989   *The Powhatan Indians of Virginia: Their Traditional Culture.* Nor-
        man: University of Oklahoma Press.
  Forthcoming   "A Guide to the Late Woodland Indians' Use of Ecological Zones
        in the Chesapeake Region." In (tentatively titled) *The Archaeology
        of Eastern North America: Essays in Honor of the William Henry
        Holmes Centenary*, ed. R. Joseph Dent and Stephen R. Potter. Wash-
        ington: Smithsonian Institution Press. Forthcoming.
  MS. A   (with Martha McCartney) Powhatan Words and Names.
  MS. B   On the Nature of Ethnicity.
  MS. C   The Historic Indians of Coastal Virginia: A Sourcebook.
  MS. D   The Early Ethnographers of Virginia: An Evaluation of John Smith,
        William Strachey, and Henry Spelman.
Rowell, Mary K.
  1943   Pamunkey Indian Games and Amusements. *Journal of American Folk-
        lore* 56:203–207.
Rozwenc, Edwin C.
  1959   Captain John Smith's Image of America. *William and Mary Quarterly*,
        3d ser., 16:27–36.
Russell, John H.
  1913   *The Free Negro in Virginia—1619–1865.* Johns Hopkins University
        Studies in Historical and Political Science, series 31, no. 3. Baltimore:
        Johns Hopkins University Press.
Rutman, Darret B., and Anita H. Rutman
  1976   Of Agues and Fevers: Malaria in the Early Chesapeake. *William and
        Mary Quarterly*, 3d ser., 33:31–60.
Sainsbury, W. Noel, comp.
  1860   *Calendar of State Papers, Colonial Series.* 60 vols. London: Longman,
        Green and Roberts.
Salisbury, Neal
  1974   Red Puritans: The "Praying Indians" of Massachusetts Bay and John
        Eliot. *William and Mary Quarterly*, 3d ser., 31:27–54.

Salwen, Bert
1978   Indians of Southern New England and Long Island: Early Period. In *Handbook of North American Indians*, Vol. 15, *Northeast*, ed. Bruce G. Trigger, 160–176. Washington, D.C.: Smithsonian Institution.
Sams, Conway Whittle
1916   *The Conquest of Virginia: The Forest Primeval*. New York: G. P. Putnam's Sons.
Schermerhorn, R. A.
1974   Ethnicity in the Perspective of the Sociology of Knowledge. *Ethnicity* 1:1–14.
Service, Elman R.
1971   *Primitive Social Organization: An Evolutionary Perspective*. 2d ed. New York: Random House.
Sheehan, Bernard W.
1980   *Savagism and Civility: Indians and Englishmen in Colonial Virginia*. New York: Cambridge University Press.
Shepherd, Samuel, comp.
1835   *The Statutes at Large of Virginia . . . Being a Continuation of Hening*. 3 vols. Richmond, Virginia: Privately printed.
Sherman, Richard B.
1988   "The Last Stand": The Fight for Racial Integrity in Virginia in the 1920s. *Journal of Southern History* 54:69–92.
Shibutani, Tamotsu, and Kian M. Kwan
1965   *Ethnic Stratification*. New York: Macmillan.
Siebert, Frank T., Jr.
1975   Resurrecting Virginia Algonquian from the Dead: The Reconstituted and Historical Phonology of Powhatan. In *Studies in Southeastern Indian Languages*, ed. James M. Crawford, 285–453. Athens: University of Georgia Press.
Simmons, William S.
1970   *Cautantowwit's House: An Indian Burial Ground on the Island of Conanicut in Narragansett Bay*. Providence: Brown University Press.
1981   Cultural Bias in the New England Puritans' Perception of Indians. *William and Mary Quarterly*, 3d ser., 38: 56–72.
Simmons, William S., and Cheryl L. Simmons, eds.
1982   *Old Light on Separate Ways: The Narragansett Diary of Joseph Fish, 1765–1776*. Hanover, New Hampshire: University Press of New England.
Singer, L.
1962   Ethnogenesis and Negro Americans Today. *Social Research* 29: 419–432.
Slater, Miriam
1984   *Family Life in the Seventeenth Century: The Verneys of Claydon House*. London: Routledge & Kegan Paul.
Smith, John
n.d. [1608]   Virginia Discouered and Described by Captayn John Smith, 1606. Map, in various editions. Richmond: Virginia State Library.
1986a [1608]   A True Relation. In *The Complete Works of Captain John Smith (1580–1631)*, vol. 1, ed. Philip L. Barbour, 3–118. Chapel Hill: University of North Carolina Press.

1986b [1612] A Map of Virginia. [Historical section compiled from various texts by William Simmond.] In *The Complete Works of Captain John Smith (1580–1631*, vol. 1, ed. Philip L. Barbour, 119–190. Chapel Hill: University of North Carolina Press.

1986c [1624] *The Generall Historie of Virginia, New England, and the Summer Isles, 1624.* In *The Complete Works of Captain John Smith (1580–1631)*, vol. 2, ed. Philip Barbour, 25–488. Chapel Hill: University of North Carolina Press.

Smith, Marvin T.
1987 *Archaeology of Aboriginal Culture Change in the Interior Southeast: Depopulation During the Early Historic Period.* Gainesville: University of Florida Press.

Smithsonian Institution
1893 U.S. National Museum Annual Report. Washington, D.C.
1894 U.S. National Museum Annual Report. Washington, D.C.

Smits, David D.
1987 "Abominable Mixture": Toward the Repudiation of Anglo-Indian Intermarriage in Seventeenth Century Virginia. *Virginia Magazine of History and Biography* 95:157–192.

Sneyd, Charlotte Augusta, transl.
1847 *A Relation, or Rather a True Account, of the Island of England, with Sundry Particulars of the Customs of these People, and of the Royal Revenues under King Henry the Seventh, About the Year 1500.* London: Printed for the Camden Society by John Bowyer Nichols & Son.

Southampton County, Virginia (formerly part of Isle of Wight County)
1749 to present. County Records. Courtland, Virginia (copy in Virginia State Library, Richmond).

Speck, Frank G.
1916 Remnants of the Machapunga Indians of North Carolina. *American Anthropologist* (n.s.) 18:271–276.
n.d. Papers, 1919–1950. Library of American Philosophical Society, Philadelphia.
1924 The Ethnic Position of the Southeastern Algonkian. *American Anthropologist* 26:184–200.
1925 *The Rappahannock Indians of Virginia.* Indian Notes and Monographs, vol. 5, no. 3. New York: Heye Foundation.
1928 *Chapters on the Ethnology of the Powhatan Tribes of Virginia.* Indian Notes and Monographs, vol. 1, no. 5. New York: Heye Foundation.
1939 The Catawba Nation and Its Neighbors. *North Carolina Historical Review* 16:404–417.
1941 The Gourd Lamp Among the Virginia Indians. *American Anthropologist* 43:676–678.
1950 *Penobscot Man.* New York: Octagon Press.

Speck, Frank G., Royal B. Hassrick, and Edmund S. Carpenter.
1942 Rappahannock Herbals, Folk-lore and Science of Cures. *Proceedings of the Delaware County Institute of Science* 10:7–55.

Speck, Frank G., and Claude E. Schaeffer
1950 The Deer and the Rabbit Hunting Drive in Virginia and the Southeast. *Southern Indian Studies*, vol. 2, no. 1.

Spelman, Henry
   1910 [1613?] Relation of Virginea. In *The Travels and Works of Captain John Smith*, eds. Edward Arber and A. G. Bradley, ci–cxiv. New York.
Spicer, Edward
   1971   Persistent Identity Systems. *Science* 174:795–800.
   1980   *The Yaquis: A Cultural History.* Tucson: University of Arizona Press.
Spotswood, Alexander
   1882   *The Official Letters of Alexander Spotswood, Lieutenant-Governor of the Colony of Virginia, 1710–1722*, vol. 1. 2 vols. Collections of the Virginia Historical Society. Richmond: Virginia Historical Society.
Stafford County, Virginia
   1664 to present (fragmentary).   County Records. Stafford, Virginia (copy in Virginia State Library, Richmond).
Stanard, W. G.
   1913   The Ancestry and Descent of John Rolfe with Notices of Some Connected Families. *Virginia Magazine of History and Biography* 21:209–211.
   1929   An Exhibition of Contemporary Portraits of Personages Associated with the Colony and Commonwealth of Virginia Between the Years 1585 and 1830. *Virginia Magazine of History and Biography* 37:193–216.
Steponaitis, Vincas P.
   1986   Prehistoric Archaeology in the Southeastern United States, 1970–1985. *Annual Review of Anthropology* 15:363–404.
Stern, Theodore
   1951   Pamunkey Pottery Making. *Southern Indian Studies,* vol. 3.
   1952   Chickahominy: The Changing Culture of a Virginia Indian Community. *Proceedings of the American Philosophical Society* 96:157–225.
Stiles, Ezra
   1916   *Extracts from the Itineraries and Other Miscellanies of Ezra Stiles, D.D., LL.D., 1765–1794, With a Selection from his Correspondence,* ed. Franklin Bowditch Dexter. New Haven: Yale University Press.
Stith, William
   1969 [1747] *The History of the First Discovery and Settlement of Virginia.* New York: Johnson Reprints.
Stone, Lawrence
   1965   *The Crisis of the Aristocracy, 1558–1641.* Oxford and New York: Oxford University Press.
Story, Thomas
   1847 [1698] *Extracts from a Journal of the Life of Thomas Story.* N.p.: Isaac Thompson.
Strachey, William
   1953 [1612] *The Historie of Travell into Virginia Britania*, 2d ser., vol. 103, ed. Louis B. Wright and Virginia Freund. Cambridge: The Hakluyt Society.
   1964 [1610] A True Reportory of the Wreck and Redemption of Sir Thomas Gates . . . . In *A Voyage to Virginia in 1609, Two Narratives,* ed. Louis B. Wright. Charlottesville: University of Virginia Press. Also in Quinn 1979 (q.v.), vol. 5, 288–301.

Stuart, Karen A.
  1984   "So Good a Work": The Brafferton School, 1691–1777. Master's the-
           sis, College of William and Mary.
Surry County, Virginia
  1652 to present (fragmentary before 1671).   County Records. Surry, Virginia
           (copy in Virginia State Library, Richmond).
Thomas, Peter A.
  1976   Contrastive Subsistence Strategies and Land Use as Factors for Under-
           standing Indian-White Relations in New England. *Ethnohistory* 23:
           1–18.
  1985   Cultural Change on the Southern New England Frontier, 1630–1665.
           In *Cultures in Contact: The Impact of European Contacts on Native
           American Cultural Institutions, A.D. 1000–1800,* ed. William W.
           Fitzhugh, 131–161. Washington: Smithsonian Institution Press.
Tindall, Robert
  n.d. [1608]   Robert Tyndall's Draughte of Virginia 1608. Copy in Virginia State
           Library, Richmond.
Treaty of 1677   *See* Commissioners for the Virginia Affairs
Tuchman, Barbara W.
  1978   *A Distant Mirror: The Calamitous Fourteenth Century.* New York:
           Knopf.
Turner, E. Randolph
  1973   A New Population Estimate for the Powhatan Chiefdom of the Coastal
           Plain of Virginia. *Quarterly Bulletin of the Archeological Society of
           Virginia* 28:57–65.
  1976   An Archaeological and Ethnohistorical Study on the Evolution of Rank
           Societies in the Virginia Coastal Plain. Ph.D. diss., Pennsylvania State
           University.
  1982   A Reexamination of Powhatan Territorial Boundaries and Population,
           ca. A.D. 1607. *Quarterly Bulletin of the Archeological Society of Vir-
           ginia* 37:45–64.
  1985   Socio-Political Organization Within the Powhatan Chiefdom and the
           Effects of European Contact, A.D. 1607–1646. In *Cultures in Con-
           tact: The European Impact on Native Cultural Institutions in Eastern
           North America, A.D. 1000–1800,* ed. William W. Fitzhugh, 193–224.
           Washington: Smithsonian Institution Press.
  1986   Difficulties in the Archaeological Identification of Chiefdoms as Seen in
           the Virginia Coastal Plain During the Late Woodland and Early His-
           toric Periods. In *Late Woodland Cultures of the Middle Atlantic Re-
           gion,* ed. Jay F. Custer, 19–28. Newark: University of Delaware Press.
  n.d.   Protohistorical Native American Interactions in the Virginia Coastal
           Plain. In *Powhatan Foreign Relations, 1500–1722,* ed. Helen C. Roun-
           tree. In progress.
Tyler, Lyon G., comp.
  1907–1908   Papers Relating to the College. *William and Mary Quarterly,* 1st
           ser., 16:162–173.
U.S. Bureau of the Census (formerly the Census Office)
  1820   Fourth Census. *Population Schedules.*
  1830   Fifth Census. *Population Schedules.*

1840   Sixth Census. *Population Schedules.*
1850   Seventh Census. *Population Schedules.*
1860   Eighth Census. *Population Schedules.*
1870   Ninth Census. *Population Schedules.*
1880   Tenth Census. *Population Schedules.*
[1890, Eleventh Census   *Population Schedules* for Virginia burned.]
1894   *Report on Indians Not Taxed in the United States (Except Alaska) at
        the Eleventh Census: 1890.* Washington, D.C.: U.S. Government Print-
        ing Office.
1900   Twelfth Census. *Population Schedules.*
1910   Thirteenth Census. *Population Schedules.*
1915   *Indian Population in the United States and Alaska, 1910.* Washington,
        D.C.: U.S. Government Printing Office.
1940   Sixteenth Census. *Population,* vol. 2, pt. 7.
U.S. Government
    Federal Records Center, East Point, Georgia.
    National Anthropological Archives, Smithsonian Institution
    U.S. National Museum, Annual Reports.
Upshur, Thomas T.
1901–1902   Eastern Shore History, an Address Delivered at Accomack Court-
        house on June 9, 1900, Being the Occasion of the Dedication of the
        New Courthouse at that Place. *Virginia Magazine of History and Biog-
        raphy* 9:89–99.
van den Berghe, Pierre L.
1966   Paternalistic Versus Competitive Race Relations: An Ideal-Type Ap-
        proach. In *Racial and Ethnic Relations: Selected Readings,* eds. Ber-
        nard E. Segal, 53–69. New York: Thomas Y. Crowell.
Vaughan, Alden T.
1975   *American Genesis: Captain John Smith and the Founding of Virginia.*
        Boston: Little, Brown.
1978   "Expulsion of the Salvages": English Policy and the Virginia Massacre
        of 1622. *William and Mary Quarterly,* 3d ser., 35:57–84.
Virginia, Commonwealth of
    Acts of Assembly.
    Attorney Generals' Reports.
    Board of Education, Records and Papers (includes papers of John Crosby).
    Bureau of Vital Statistics, Annual Reports.
    Code of Virginia.
    Colonial Papers (loose documents in folders; some published in Palmer 1875).
    Corporation Commission, Charter Books.
    Executive Letter Books.
    Executive Papers.
    House [of Delegates] Journal and Documents.
    Legislative Petitions.
    Opinions of the Attorney General (now part of Annual Report of Attorney
        General).
Virginia Gazette. Williamsburg, Virginia: Rind edition and Purdie & Dixon
    edition.

Vogt, Evon Z.
    1966   Intercultural Relations. In *People of Rimrock: A Study of Values in Five Cultures*, eds. Evon Z. Vogt and Ethel M. Albert, 46–82. Cambridge: Harvard University Press.
Wailes, Bertha Pfister
    1928   Backward Virginians: A Further Study of the WIN Tribe. Master's thesis, University of Virginia.
Wallace, Anthony F. C.
    1956   Revitalization Movements. *American Anthropologist* 58:264–281.
    1966   *Religion: An Anthropological View.* New York: Random House.
Washburn, Wilcomb Edward
    1957   *The Governor and the Rebel: A History of Bacon's Rebellion in Virginia.* Chapel Hill: University of North Carolina Press.
    1959   The Moral and Legal Justifications for Dispossessing the Indians. In *Seventeenth Century America: Essays in Colonial History*, ed. James Morton Smith, 15–32. Chapel Hill: University of North Carolina Press.
    1971   *Red Man's Land/White Man's Law.* New York: Charles Scribner's Sons.
Wax, Rosalie, and Robert K. Thomas
    1961   American Indians and White People. *Phylon* 22:305–317.
Weinstein, Laurie Lee
    1986   "We're Still Living on Our Traditional Homeland": The Wampanoag Legacy in New England. In *Strategies For Survival: American Indians in the Eastern United States*, ed. Frank W. Porter III, 85–112. New York: Greenwood Press.
Westmoreland County, Virginia
    1653 to present.   County Records. Montross, Virginia (copy in Virginia State Library, Richmond).
West Point Tidewater Review (Virginia)
Whitaker, Alexander
    1936 [1613]   *Good Newes from Virginia.* New York: Scholars' Facsimiles & Reprints.
    1964 [1611]   Letter to Releigh Croshaw. In *The Genesis of the United States*, ed. Alexander Brown, 497–500. New York: Russell and Russell.
White, Marian E.
    1978   Erie. In *Handbook of North American Indians.*Vol. 15, *Northeast*, ed. Bruce C. Trigger, 412–417. Washington, D.C.: Smithsonian Institution.
White, William
    1969 [1608?]   Fragments Published Before 1614. In *The Jamestown Voyages Under the First Charter*, 2d ser., vol. 136, ed. Philip L. Barbour, 147–150. Cambridge: The Hakluyt Society.
William and Mary, College of
    1754–1770   Bursar's Book (MS.)
    1763–1770   Bursar's Book (MS.)
    1770–1777   Bursar's Book (MS.)
    1859   *A Catalogue of the College of William and Mary in Virginia, from its Foundation to the Present Time.* Williamsburg, Virginia.
Williams, Walter L., ed.
    1979   *Southeastern Indians Since the Removal Era.* Athens: University of Georgia Press.

Williamson, Joel
 1980 *New People: Miscegenation and Mulattoes in the United States.* New York: The Free Press.
Willson, D. Harris
 1956 *King James VI and I.* New York: Henry Holt.
Wilson, Theodore Brantner
 1965 *The Black Codes of the South.* Southern Historical Publications, no. 6. Tuscaloosa: University of Alabama Press.
Winfree, Waverly K., comp.
 1971 *The Laws of Virginia, Being a Supplement to Hening's Statutes at Large, 1700–1750.* Richmond: Virginia State Library.
Wingfield, Edward Maria
 1969 [1608] Discourse. In *The Jamestown Voyages Under the First Charter,* 2d ser., vol. 136, ed. Philip L. Barbour, 213–234. Cambridge: The Hakluyt Society. Also in Quinn 1979 (q.v.), vol. 5, 276–285.
Wingo, Elizabeth B.
 1961 *Marriages of Norfolk County, Virginia 1706–1792.* Norfolk, Virginia: Privately published.
 1963 *Marriages of Norfolk County, Virginia 1788, 1793–1817.* Norfolk, Virginia: Privately published.
 1981 *Norfolk County, Virginia, Tithables 1751–1765.* Norfolk, Virginia: Privately published.
Winne, Peter
 1969 [1609] Letter to Sir John Egerton. In *The Jamestown Voyages Under the First Charter,* 1st ser., vol. 136, ed. Philip L. Barbour, 245–246. Cambridge: The Hakluyt Society.
Wise, Jennings Cropper
 1911 *Ye Kingdome of Accawmacke, or The Eastern Shore of Virginia in the Seventeenth Century.* Richmond, Virginia: Bell Book and Stationery.
Wright, J. Leitch, Jr.
 1981 *The Only Land They Knew: The Tragic Story of the American Indians of the Old South.* New York: The Free Press.
Wroth, Lawrence C.
 1970 *The Voyages of Giovanni da Verrazzano, 1524–1528.* New Haven: Yale University Press.
York County, Virginia
 1633 to present (fragmentary). County Records. Yorktown, Virginia (copy in Virginia State Library, Richmond).
Zuniga, Pedro de
 1969 [1608] Letter to Philip III. In *The Jamestown Voyages Under the First Charter.* 2d ser., vol. 136, ed. Philip L. Barbour, 163. Cambridge: The Hakluyt Society.

Index